This is the first major archivally based study of the political career of Wenzel Anton Kaunitz, State Chancellor of the Habsburg Monarchy from 1753 to 1792. Author of the diplomatic revolution of 1756 and brilliant foreign minister of the Austrian Empire, Kaunitz was also the most important statesman in the development of enlightened absolutism in central Europe. Virtually the third head of state under Maria Theresia and Joseph II, he was the driving force behind the many reforms which sought to modernize the Monarchy. Using Kaunitz as a focus, the author explores the dynamic of the development of enlightened absolutism in the Habsburg Empire through its most influential proponent and spokesman. Enlightened absolutism in the Habsburg Monarchy produced some of the boldest innovations in eighteenth-century Europe, and this book analyzes the full complexity of the decision-making process.

Kaunitz and enlightened absolutism 1753–1780

Kaunitz and enlightened absolutism 1753–1780

Franz A. J. Szabo

Carleton University, Ottawa, Canada

CAMBRIDGE
UNIVERSITY PRESS

Published by the Press Syndicate of the University of Cambridge
The Pitt Building, Trumpington Street, Cambridge, CB2 1RP
40 West 20th Street, New York, NY 10011-4211, USA
10 Stamford Road, Oakleigh, Melbourne 3166, Australia

First published 1994

A catalogue record for this book is available from the British Library

Library of Congress cataloguing in publication data

Szabo, Franz A. J.
Kaunitz and enlightened absolutism, 1753–1780/by Franz A. J. Szabo.
    p. cm.
Includes bibliographical references.
ISBN 0 521 45163 9 hbk   ISBN 0521 46690 3 pbk
1. Kaunitz-Rietberg, Wenzel Anton, Fürst, 1711–1794.   2. Austria –
History – Maria Theresa, 1740–1780.   3. Austria – Politics and government –
1740–1780.   I. Title.
DB69.9.K38S96   1994
943.6′03′092 – dc20   93-5069   CIP

ISBN 0 521 45163 9 hardback
ISBN 0 521 46690 3 paperback

Transferred to digital printing 2004

TAG

For my mother
Theresia Bauer Szabo

and in memory of my father
Gottfried M. Szabo
(1921–1990)

Nous ne demandons qu'à faire voir à l'Europe
combien la vraie philosophie, c'est à dire la philosofie
bienfaisante, fait de progrès dans ce siècle. Vous
êtes Monsieur à la tête de ceux qui l'encouragent...
Voltaire to Kaunitz, 3 July 1766

Contents

x   Contents

Preface

In 1882, having recently completed his monumental ten-volume biography of the Habsburg Empress, Maria Theresia, the great nineteenth-century Austrian liberal historian, Alfred von Arneth, was commissioned to write the biographical entry for the Empress's foreign minister in the forty-volume *Allgemeine Deutsche Biographie*.[1] This brief biographical sketch of Wenzel Anton von Kaunitz-Rietberg inspired Arneth to begin research on a large-scale biography of the famous minister, but after two years the project was abandoned. A 200-page "fragment" of this projected biography was published after Arneth's death.[2] It traced Kaunitz's youth and early political career, ending in 1750, three years before Kaunitz began his forty-year tenure of the Habsburg Foreign Office. Arneth abandoned the project because he began to realize that doing Kaunitz justice would require him to repeat virtually the entire ten-volume Maria Theresia biography over again. There was no doubt in Arneth's mind that Kaunitz was "the first and greatest" of Maria Theresia's political advisers whose influence extended "to virtually all branches of the political life [of the Monarchy]," so that a biography of him "certainly required no justification."[3] The task, however, was to be left to another generation.

The century that followed, however, while producing a number of thumbnail sketches and encyclopedia entries of varying quality,[4] did not

[1] Alfred Ritter von Arneth, "Kaunitz," *ADB* XV (1882), 487–507.
[2] Alfred Ritter von Arneth, "Biographie des Fürsten Kaunitz: Ein Fragment," *AÖG* LXXXVIII (1900), 1–201.
[3] *Ibid.*, pp. 3–7.
[4] The three major contributions in this vein before Arneth's *ADB* entry were: Friedrich Schlichtegroll, "Wenzel Anton, d.h.R. R. Fürst von Kaunitz," in *Nekrolog auf das Jahr 1794* (5. Jahrgang), 2 Vols. (Gotha, 1796), I, 129–162; Joseph Freiherr von Hormayr, "Fürst Kaunitz," in *Österreichischer Plutarch*, Vol. XII (Vienna, 1807), pp. 231–283 (partially reprinted as *Lebensbilder großer Österreicher* [Vienna, 1947], on Kaunitz, I, 28–34, subsequent citations are from this edition); and Constant von Wurzbach, "Kaunitz-Rietberg" in *Biographisches Lexikon des Kaiserthums Oesterreich*, 60 Vols. (Vienna, 1856–1891), XI (1864), 70–86. In the century after Arneth, the most significant have been Alfred Dove, "Kaunitz," in *Ausgewählte Schriften* (Leipzig, 1898), pp. 94–110; Heinrich Kretschmayr, "Kaunitz," in Peter Richard Rohden, ed., *Menschen die Geschichte machten*, 2nd ed. (Vienna, 1933), II, 251–256; Friedrich Walter, "Kaunitz," in

yield the larger study which "required no justification." In the years following the First World War, the Prussian historian, Georg Küntzel, extracted a brief and often inaccurate Kaunitz biography from the then published sources in order to round out his largely mechanistic, Berlin-centered image of Austro-Prussian dualism in the eighteenth century.[5] At about the same time the University of Vienna Ph.D. candidate, Leon Posaner, completed an even briefer and sketchier dissertation on the role of Prince Kaunitz in the domestic reforms of Austria, which, while based on some archival research, barely managed to scratch the surface, and which never found its way into print.[6] After the Second World War the Austrian historian, Alexander Novotny, in an effort to resurrect a distinctive Austrian identity from the rubble of Hitler's Third Reich, also turned to a brief Kaunitz biography, this time placing the famous statesman into the cultural and intellectual context of the eighteenth century.[7] In the late 1960s and early 1970s the long-awaited project seemed on the verge of being taken up by the Austrian historian, Grete Klingenstein, with a brilliant dissertation on the family background and early life of Kaunitz which was published in 1975.[8] But Klingenstein's research interests then took her in other directions, and further work on Kaunitz was abandoned. Finally, in 1984, the journalist Tibor Simányi, apparently impatient with the apparent gap in the literature, produced another hasty and incomplete "biography" based on secondary sources, and without any scholarly apparatus or pretense.[9] The major study based on broad archival research planned by Arneth, however, remained unwritten.

This did not mean that Kaunitz was neglected. The notorious Leopold

Männer um Maria Theresia (Vienna, 1951) (revised edition issued as *Die Paladine der Kaiserin* [Vienna, 1959]); Alexander Novotny, "Staatskanzler Fürst Kaunitz (1711–1794)," in Hugo Hantsch, ed., *Gestalter der Geschicke Österreichs* (Innsbruck, Vienna and Munich, 1962), pp. 253–261; Karl Otmar Freiherr von Aretin, "Kaunitz, Wenzel Anton," *NDB* XI (1977), 363–369; Franz A. J. Szabo, "Staatskanzler Fürst Kaunitz und die Aufklärungspolitik Österreichs," in Walter Koschatzky, ed., *Maria Theresia und Ihre Zeit* (Salzburg and Vienna, 1979), pp. 40–45; and Szabo, "Wenzel Anton Kaunitz-Rietberg (1711–1794)," in John E. Findling and Frank W. Thackeray, eds., *Statesmen who Changed the World* (Westport, Conn., 1993), pp. 268–277.
[5] Georg Küntzel, *Fürst Kaunitz-Rittberg als Staatsman* (Frankfurt am Main, 1923).
[6] Leon Posaner, "Die Rolle des Staatskanzlers Fürsten Kaunitz in den Reformen der inneren Verwaltung Oesterreichs" (unpublished Ph.D. dissertation, University of Vienna, 1923).
[7] Alexander Novotny, *Staatskanzler Kaunitz als geistige Persönlichkeit* (Vienna, 1947).
[8] Grete Klingenstein, "Habsburgischer Adel im Zeitalter des Absolutismus: Herkunft und Bildung des Staatskanzlers Kaunitz" (unpublished Ph.D. dissertation, University of Vienna, 1972), published as *Der Aufstieg des Hauses Kaunitz: Studien zur Herkunft und Bildung des Staatskanzlers Wenzel Anton* (Göttingen, 1975).
[9] Tibor Simányi, *Kaunitz: Staatskanzler Maria Theresias* (Vienna and Munich, 1984).

von Sacher-Masoch even produced a novel based on his life,[10] while virtually every historical article, monograph, or source collection which addressed itself to any aspect of the age of enlightened absolutism in the Habsburg Monarchy, whether foreign or domestic, found itself obliged to allude to or focus on Kaunitz.[11] For diverse political reasons these works have seldom been very sympathetic to Kaunitz, but his central role in the development of eighteenth-century Austria was never questioned, and, indeed, continues to be stressed more and more in recent literature. It is, of course, to be expected that diplomatic historians could scarcely avoid a man who was foreign minister of one of the great powers of Europe for forty years. The significant trend amongst newer works on the Habsburg Monarchy of the eighteenth century, however, is the re-discovery of Kaunitz as the key figure in the evolution of enlightened absolutism through the reigns of the well-known Habsburg monarchs of the age to the point where he is regarded as virtually "the third head of State" in the Monarchy during the era of Joseph II and Maria Theresia.[12]

Thus, I initially came to the subject of Kaunitz through an awareness of a patent biographical lacuna in central European historiography which was well known and widely lamented. As I began to investigate the role of Kaunitz in the rise of enlightened absolutism in the Habsburg Monarchy, however, I began to see that his political role in particular was so complex that the problem of context not only required considerable attention, but the very nature of the context itself also had to be reassessed in light of his activities. The sweep and scope of conventional biography, I began to see, could not address these problems adequately. Hence, while the subject of the ensuing analysis is the political activity of a specific individual, this study is not intended to be a biography in the traditional sense of the word. Rather, I have envisioned it first and foremost as an effort to come to grips with the dynamic of the evolution of enlightened absolutism in the

---

[10] Leopold von Sacher-Masoch, *Kaunitz: Ein kulturhistorischer Roman* (Prague, 1865), reworked and reprinted by Franz Karmel (Vienna, 1945).

[11] The only attempt to produce an historiographical survey of the disparate sources pertaining to Kaunitz, Gertraud Jäger, "Die Persönlichkeit des Staatskanzlers Kaunitz in der Historiographie" (unpublished dissertation, Vienna, 1982), is weak, superficial and thin on non-German sources.

[12] P. G. M. Dickson, *Finance and Government under Maria Theresia, 1740–1780*, 2 Vols. (Oxford, 1987), I, 255. Other examples: Joseph Karniel, *Die Toleranzpolitik Kaiser Josephs II.* (Stuttgart, 1986), p. 503; Éva H. Balázs, "A felvilágosult abszolutizmus Habsburg variánsa," in Győző Ember and Gustáv Heckenast, eds., *Magyarország története, 1686–1790*, 2 Vols., Part 4 of Zsigmond Pál Pach, ed., *Magyarország története tíz kötetben* (Budapest, 1989), II, 863–872. Balázs has stressed the centricity of Kaunitz for many years, and has repeatedly emphasized this point in her works. These Kaunitz references have now been conveniently collected in her pamphlet *Kaunitz és Magyarország* (Doktori tézises összefoglaló) (Budapest, 1990). I thank the author for presenting me with a copy.

Habsburg Monarchy, using its most influential proponent and spokesman as the access point to the larger problem.

It has been argued that any fair assessment of enlightened absolutism must focus as much on its intentions as on its accomplishments, and, indeed, some of its most spectacular failures come closest to the heart of its true motivations. This, in turn, requires disentangling the politics behind the choices made, by examining the options rejected as well as those adopted, by investigating the interaction between intent and effect – in short, by laying bare in detail the often difficult and erratic course of reformist politics in the second half of the eighteenth century. In this sense a biographical focus serves as the prism through which the inner dialectic of the regime's external dynamic is refracted. If this leads to a more complex but, hopefully, more meaningful analysis of the phenomenon of enlightened absolutism, I trust it will at the same time also underscore the critical element of human agency in historical development.

The conception of the analytical problem in these terms is the principal reason why the following investigation eschews the traditional chrono-logical framework of biography and opts instead for an approach that concentrates on the constituent problems of eighteenth-century central European politics, society and culture. The nature of the problem addressed naturally also precludes any detailed analysis of the international relations of the Habsburg Monarchy, and Kaunitz's principal ministerial responsibility – that of conducting the foreign affairs of the Monarchy – is therefore adduced in the pages that follow only insofar as it is necessary for a broader understanding of the domestic problems of enlightened absolutism. For similar reasons I have excluded any substantive discussion of the unique internal developments within the two peripheral provinces of the Habsburg Monarchy, which Kaunitz administered through his foreign ministry under a completely separate rubric, Belgium and Milan.

I have conceived my analysis of enlightened absolutism in two interconnected parts. The first, presented here, deals with the emergence and development of enlightened absolutism in the reign of Maria Theresia. The second, yet to be written, will address the flowering and crisis of enlightened absolutism in the reigns of Joseph II and Leopold II. The old view which regarded the year 1780 as the great watershed between conservative traditionalism and enlightened absolutism has long been abandoned by historians; but in a more profound sense 1780 does mark a distinct hiatus. After 1780 many of the developments of the previous decades were brought to fruition, and it was only then that the full implications of the dramatic transformations of the culture and the society became apparent. This opened a whole new set of problems which were highlighted only all too dramatically by the subsequent outbreak of the

French Revolution, and by the confrontation with the revolution's ideology. The two component parts of my proposed larger study in a sense, therefore, wish to address two sets of interlinked but distinct analytical problems.

As a consequence of the multi-national character of the Habsburg Monarchy, nomenclature has always caused difficulties for even the most well-intentioned historian, and confusion for even well-informed readers. Like others before me, I have striven for some coherence and consistency without offending too many political sensitivities, and have found myself making some arbitrary decisions nonetheless. I have translated the names of all monarchs and their relatives into English, since this is how they are usually identified in the English-language historical literature. The single exception is Maria Theresia, whose name I have kept in the German, since the logical translation of "Mary Theresa" struck me as absurd, while the usual compromise of Maria Theresa did not roll easily off my central European lips. In the Christian and surnames of all other individuals mentioned, I have allowed myself to be guided by how these people chose to sign their names themselves, where this information was available, and I have generalized this as a rule throughout. In practice this means that most names are rendered in their Germanized version. For Hungarian names, on the other hand, I have adopted Hungarian spellings throughout. The same rule was applied to place names. Where commonly accepted English equivalents exist with countries, provinces or cities, they have been used. Otherwise the German names appearing in the sources are used except for the Kingdom of Hungary. In all these cases I have also listed alternate or present-day names in brackets at first mention of any locality. The currency of the realm, abbreviated as "fl." for "florins," was always called "Gulden" when spoken out, and I have preferred this latter usage. I have also translated all ministries and government offices into English and have given preference to these throughout the text, though the original is always given in brackets on first mention.

During the era of academic recession and my own frequent academic migrations in the 1970s and 1980s both the time and financial resources needed to carry on research in this country as well as in Austria and Czechoslovakia were elusive at best, so that the modest support I did receive was all the more precious. The Social Sciences and Humanities Research Council of Canada funded occasional brief visits to Vienna between 1977 and 1984, which permitted the mapping out of the relatively extensive research project whose first portion is presented here. A small research grant from Carleton University subsequently allowed some research to be continued, while a timely and generous grant from the Austrian Foreign Ministry, secured in 1990 with the indefatigable assistance of Dr. Artur Bablok, Cultural Attaché of the Austrian Embassy in Ottawa, allowed me to fill those archival gaps which had emerged in the writing over the years, and to finish the manuscript.

Even more than financial support, this study would not have been possible without the unflagging intellectual support, encouragement and stimulation offered by my colleagues both in North America and Europe. First and foremost I owe a debt of great gratitude to Grete Klingenstein of the University of Graz, whose stimulating comments and criticisms have helped this manuscript grow from the outset. In addition, Ernst Wangermann of the University of Salzburg has proved as invaluable and engaging a guide in his conversations as in his publications, and Carlo Capra of the University of Milan patiently suffered through the painfully slow growth of this manuscript with unflagging enthusiasm. At every stage of the development of my study, I also benefited from the advice of other friends and colleagues. At the early stages I was indebted to Helen Liebel-Weckowicz and George Rothrock, both of the University of Alberta, Adam Wandruszka of the University of Vienna, and William Slottmann of the University of California at Berkeley. As my manuscript developed beyond its original limited scope, I benefited from invaluable comments offered by R. J. W. Evans of Brasenose College, Oxford University, Éva Hunyady-Balázs of the University of Budapest, Gerhard Croll of the Institut für Musikwissenschaft at the University of Salzburg, Elisabeth Garms-Cornides of the Austrian Cultural Institute in Rome, and James Van Horn Melton of Emory University.

The staff of the various archives of the Austrian State Archive in Vienna and of the Austrian National Library were courteous and helpful at every turn, and I regret only that I cannot acknowledge by name the dozens of individuals who assisted me. I do want to single out the then-director of the Haus-, Hof- und Staatsarchiv, Anna Coreth, who first introduced me to the full scope of the archival material that faced me, as well as the former Archivräte Walter Pillich and Robert Strop, who handled my microfilm requests over the years with a care and attention to detail that went well beyond the call of duty. The archivist of the archive of the Akademie der Bildenden Künste, Dr. Walter Czerny, and the archivist of the Deutscher Orden Zentralarchiv, Father Bernhard Demel, O. T., also displayed unusual cooperative flexibility with my research requests. In Brno, Czechoslovakia, the courtesy and helpfulness of Dr. Milan Čoupek, of the Moravian Provincial Archive, greatly facilitated my research there. Dr. Bohumil Samek of the Czech Department of Monuments in Brno arranged a close examination of the Kaunitz chateau in Slavkov u Brna, where Ing.

Libuše Sedláčková of that department's Gardens and Grounds Section, and Ing. Jan Špatný, Head of the Historical Museum of Slavkov-Austerlitz, served as invaluable guides. No acknowledgments would be complete without also thanking my friend and colleague Walter Leitsch, head of the Institute of East European History at the University of Vienna, and his associate at the Institute, Andreas Moritsch, without whose help over the years my repeated accommodation in Vienna could hardly have been as pleasant and as smooth as it was.

Finally, I want to thank my wife, Kateryna. She not only has lived indulgently with the development of this manuscript for a decade, and has borne all the usual burdens one might expect from such a process with irrepressible humor and cheerfulness, but has patiently proofread successive drafts and offered valuable stylistic suggestions at every turn.

Abbreviations

AABK	Archiv der Akademie der bildenden Künste
ADB	*Allgemeine Deutsche Biographie*
AÖG	*Archiv für österreichische Geschichte*
AVA	Allgemeines Verwaltungsarchiv
DOZA	Deutscher Orden Zentralarchiv
HHStA	Haus-, Hof- und Staatsarchiv
HKA	Hofkammerarchiv
KA	Kriegsarchiv
MIÖG	*Mitteilungen des Instituts für österreichische Geschichtsforschung*
MÖStA	*Mitteilungen des österreichischen Staatsarchivs*
MTJC	Arneth, ed., *Maria Theresia und Joseph II.: Ihre Correspondenz*
MZA	Moravskí Zemskí Archiv
NDB	*Neue Deutsche Biographie*
ÖGL	*Österreich in Geschichte und Literatur*
ÖNB	Österreichische Nationalbibliothek
ÖStWB	Mischler and Ulbrich, eds., *Österreichisches Staatswörterbuch*
ÖZV	Heinrich Kretschmayr, *et al.*, *Die Österreichische Zentralverwaltung*
VSWG	*Vierteljahrschrift für Sozial und Wirtschaftsgeschichte*

1   Introduction

In Vienna, the capital of the sprawling Danubian Empire of the Habsburgs, the spring and summer of 1794 were not a happy time. The great revolution in France was reaching its climax. The Reign of Terror was entering its final phase and Habsburg authorities feared similar revolutionary uprisings in their own lands. A Habsburg archduchess and Queen of France had been executed the previous fall by French revolutionary authorities and, since then, the revolutionary armies were well on their way to defeating the European coalition which faced them. Again, it was Habsburg armies and Habsburg territories which were the principal victims. To many, it seemed almost inconceivable that, only a few years earlier, Austria and France had been allies; that then Vienna, not Paris, had been the locus of the most radical reforms attempted by any European government. Now all traces of that pre-revolutionary world seemed to be lost.

Yet, in the Viennese suburb of Mariahilf still lived the grizzled octogenarian architect of the erstwhile alliance with France and the driving spirit of radical reform within the monarchy: Prince Wenzel Anton von Kaunitz-Rietberg. Though still fit and alert, he was embittered, isolated and widely regarded as a living monument of bygone days. He had been principal minister of the Habsburgs for almost forty years, but in August 1792, he had submitted his resignation when he discovered that his own subordinates had deceived and betrayed him and, further, convinced a youthful new emperor to disregard his advice. Thereafter, the old minister became a sort of fossil, honoured but scarcely acknowledged. Out of respect for his services to the dynasty, he was allowed to retain his seat on the imperial advisory council after laying down his other offices. From this vantage point, he continued to offer his earnest advice, in most cases neither solicited nor heeded. In 1794 alone, he availed himself of this channel on fifty-two separate occasions. On the forty-sixth of these, only days before his death on June 27, he commented on a minor customs matter with some broad generalizations of principle. Momentary benefits ought to be sacrificed to greater, surer, long-range gain, he asserted. Government ought to concern itself, if not exclusively then at least

1

primarily, "with genuine improvements in domestic conditions". Summing up, he pointed out: "It is a matter of common knowledge that I have long been of the opinion that the Austrian Monarchy is in a position to procure such power and strength through wise domestic reforms as to make the most spectacular [foreign] conquests superfluous."[1]

These may appear to be incongruous sentiments from a man who today is chiefly remembered as one of the most deft practitioners of the notoriously Machiavellian diplomacy of the eighteenth century, as the main author of the famed "Diplomatic Revolution" of 1756, and as one of the most powerful and enduring foreign ministers of European history. Nevertheless, for Kaunitz himself this domestic premise had been the focal point of his foreign policy for decades. By all appearances the Habsburg Monarchy was one of the greatest powers on the European continent – in size second only to Russia, in population roughly equivalent to France, in resource potential as rich as any country that rivalled it. Yet the Monarchy fared poorly in the fiercely competitive world of the early and mid-eighteenth century and by 1740 was on the verge of complete collapse. Surrounded by greedy neighbours, it nearly succumbed to complete partition. For Kaunitz, however, it was not Austria's relative position on the geo-political chess board of Europe that constituted her weakness, but her relative backwardness. The Monarchy's weak showing internationally was a mere symptom of her domestic underdevelopment. Diplomacy could provide a palliative; only major social, economic and structural reform could provide the cure.

Absolutism and enlightened absolutism in the Habsburg Monarchy[2]

By the 1740s, it was not difficult to perceive the relative backwardness of the Habsburg Monarchy in the international arena. Beginning with the setbacks suffered during the War of the Polish Succession, through the humiliating reverses of the Turkish War of 1737–1739, to the near-catastrophic blows of the War of the Austrian Succession, the weakness of the Habsburg Monarchy was graphically revealed by its military defeats

---

[1] HHStA, Kabinettsarchiv: Kaunitz-Voten, Karton 6, No. 1857 of 1794, Kaunitz Staatsrat Votum, n.d. (June 1794). Cf. Franz A. J. Szabo, "Prince Kaunitz and the Balance of Power", *International History Review* I (1979), 400–401.

[2] The following section is especially indebted to Grete Klingenstein, "Riforma e crisi: la monarchia austriaca sotto Maria Teresa e Giuseppe II. Tentativo di una interpretazione," in Pierangelo Schiera, ed., *La dinamica statale austriaca nel XVIII e XIX secolo* (Bologna, 1981), pp. 93–125, and Ernst Wangermann, *The Austrian Achievement, 1700–1800* (London, 1973).

and territorial losses. However, it did not take military disasters to highlight the degree to which Habsburg resources were inadequate to deal with the crises that faced the Monarchy. Even during the preceding era of spectacular military conquests under the famous Prince Eugene of Savoy, prominent statesmen, including the prince himself, had earnestly advised that only an internal transformation could give substance to the external acquisitions. This meant, above all, attempting to bring some cohesion to what Robert Evans has aptly called "a mildly centripetal agglutination of bewilderingly heterogeneous elements",[3] and effectively mobilizing its resources in times of war. It was a task that was easier said than done.

The weaknesses of the Habsburg conglomerate were numerous, and even when this was clearly recognized, not only the diagnoses but the prescriptions differed. Essentially, the problem existed at all levels – social, economic, political and intellectual – and each level was related in such a complex fashion to the others that it became difficult to disengage and address them individually. To begin with, the Habsburg conglomerate in central Europe even lacked a political identity: it was a collection of duchies and kingdoms, each with its own historical tradition, constitutional structure, economic framework and ethnic peculiarity. The only common denominator was the dynasty itself, and the political power of the dynasty was so feeble as to render the significance of this shared identity negligible. In each province or kingdom, the ruler's role was mediated by a powerful aristocratic oligarchy, which wielded effective political power through its respective provincial Estates. These Estates needed not only to consent to taxation, but were the agents of collection as well. The seigniorial elite further enjoyed virtually unlimited power over its peasant labour force, and was the first judicial instance on the local level. What central government existed took the form of provincial chancelleries, the crown's household administration and the co-ordination of diplomatic and military decision-making. But even the "ministerial posts" which these functions provided were occupied by men whose family and property connections tended to incline them to provincial particularism and seigniorial solidarity.[4]

The emergence of the concept of the impersonal state and the concomitant rise of absolutism made little headway in this kind of environment. Despite the apparent victories of the crown in the seventeenth century, political initiative and economic power remained in the hands of a relatively limited oligarchy of some 200 prominent families within the monarchy. What is more, these social and political drawbacks were aggravated by the fact that central and east central Europe gradually fell

[3] R. J. W. Evans, *The Making of the Habsburg Monarchy, 1550–1700* (Oxford, 1979), p. 447.
[4] Jean Bérenger, *Finances et absolutisme autrichien dans la seconde moitié du XVIIe siècle* (Paris, 1975).

farther and farther behind western Europe economically throughout the seventeenth and early eighteenth centuries. The dislocations of the Thirty Years' War adversely affected population figures and agricultural production, and recovery was slow and sporadic thereafter. Agricultural production remained inefficient and resulted in relatively low yields; industrial production was stifled by guild restrictions; commerce was hampered by tariff restrictions. While signs of modest economic growth could be perceived from the late seventeenth century onwards in various areas to various degrees, this growth was always more prodigious in its promise than in its results. Intellectually, too, the Counter-Reformation mentality operated on increasingly out-dated intellectual premises; the education system focused more on spiritual than practical matters, and in its Baroque ostentation, the Church often also neglected its pastoral role and other traditional social charges, which only exacerbated social problems such as endemic poverty.

For the Habsburg Monarchy to become a competitive, great power, in short, it had to acquire a whole new identity, undertake major structural change, foster sustained economic growth, and change the assumptions and attitudes of its subjects. A beginning in this direction was made with the promulgation of the famous "Pragmatic Sanction" of 1713, which affirmed the principle of the indivisibility and inalienability of the Habsburg complex. This, at least, created a theoretical state entity, even if it remained a state without a name, which would serve as the subsequent focus of political action. However, for the moment, endorsement of this document both by foreign powers and domestic Estates had to be purchased at great political and financial cost, and represented no real guarantee. It was only the existential crisis of the War of the Austrian Succession that laid the inadequacies of the Monarchy glaringly bare, and made the kind of drastic implementation of change possible which would not even have been conceivable previously.

The task that faced Maria Theresia upon her accession to the Habsburg lands in 1740 was to make a reality out of the theoretical assertion of the Pragmatic Sanction. What this ambitious programme required was a thorough modernization of the Monarchy. Normally a complex and controversial concept, "modernization" in the case of the Habsburg Monarchy was simply a desire to be "up-to-date", and to overcome perceived relative underdevelopment.[5] The perception of relative underdevelopment, of course, came first and foremost from assessing the causes

---

[5] The Italian term *aggiornamento*, as Marc Raeff has pointed out, would be clearer and less ambiguous: "The Well-Ordered Police State and the Development of Modernity in Seventeenth and Eighteenth Century Europe: An Attempt at a Comparative Approach", *American Historical Review* LXXX (1975), 1232.

of the military defeats at the hands of Prussia during the early 1740s. But a general awareness of the inadequacy of much of the Habsburg political, economic and intellectual framework had pervaded many segments of society even before then. The Silesian debacle, however, galvanized the court and its officials into action, and the Habsburg Monarchy managed to implement major structural reforms in an astonishingly short time after the restoration of peace in 1748. There is little doubt that much of this reform was inspired by the cameralist police ordinances which had been implemented with such apparent exemplary success in the smaller German states (especially in Protestant ones) in the seventeenth and early eighteenth centuries.[6] But Habsburg reform proceeded not only much more rapidly, but also set forces into motion whose interaction constantly tended to expand the areas of human activity it saw in need of reform. In a very short period of time the reforms outpaced the traditional cameralist prescriptions, and, informed by the ideology and rhetoric of the Enlightenment, soon metamorphosed seventeenth century conceptions of absolutism into the more characteristic forms of enlightened absolutism of the second half of the eighteenth century. By the 1780s the Habsburg Monarchy had become the locus of the boldest and most ambitious innovations in Europe.

The reforms began with the military–fiscal imperative of raising and maintaining an adequate force to fend off rapacious neighbors such as Prussia and defend the integrity of the Habsburg inheritance as defined by the Pragmatic Sanction. However, this was not accomplished through the traditional intermediary groups, but by setting up a wholly new bureaucratic framework from the central government down to the local level. Once these new bureaucratic instances were set up, their scope and competences grew year by year – usually in a completely unplanned (and often unexpected) manner as a result of pragmatic responses to specific problems. The reform dynamic soon gained an impetus that was difficult to arrest. Ever more social, economic, political and cultural problems came under its purview, until reform for its own sake, and for the sake of uniformity became an adequate warrant for change. In this kind of environment, the eudemonist ideals of seventeenth century cameralists received much more humanist, autonomist focus and radical articulation. It attempted to give society a new form, to infuse its economic activity with a new spirit and to change the whole customary value system of people. The result was the liberation of individuals from traditional bonds –

---

[6] Marc Raeff, *The Well-Ordered Police State* (New Haven, Conn., and London, 1983); James Van Horn Melton in "Absolutism and 'Modernity' in Early Modern Central Europe," *German Studies Review* VIII (1985), 383–398.

whether ecclesiastical, patrimonial, communal or other – and the complete transformation of the social and political order.

But neither the rapidity of this transformation (which, in the final analysis, panicked subsequent governments into extreme reactionary positions) nor its humanitarian dimension were inevitable. Many historians have been inclined to belittle the genuineness of "enlightened absolutism" and to regard it merely as traditional society's instrument of adaptation rather than of transformation – in Perry Anderson's scathing phrase, "the new political carapace of a threatened nobility."[7] Such analyses, which stress repressive features of enlightened absolutism and try to demonstrate that it had more retarding than developing effects, however, tend to rely more heavily on Prussian rather than Austrian examples – in short, rely on what most eighteenth-century intellectuals were still wont to regard as Germany's pariah not its messiah. Absolutism and enlightened absolutism in the Habsburg monarchy were entirely different from elsewhere, particularly Prussia. Two of the most fundamental elements that made them so different were an antipathy to traditional intermediary bodies that transcended the common tension between early modern monarchs and their estates, and a willingness to embark on policies entailing fundamental social change. There is an important link between these two elements. In most central European cases, despite ruler–Estate antagonisms, princes relied on intermediary corporations to implement reform. This could work well where the goal was social peace, popular piety, economic productivity and sometimes even fiscal efficiency. It could not work where the goal or incidental by-product was major social change. Hence, the awareness of the scope of social transformation implicit in the government's actions was precisely why ruler–Estate relations were characterized with such exceptional rancor in the Habsburg Monarchy.

There are a number of factors which account for this distinct approach in the Habsburg Monarchy. The first is the personalities of the rulers involved. One need not even accept some of the surprisingly social revolutionary statements of the monarchs at face value, to perceive that the Habsburg dynasty was willing to endorse changes with more far-reaching social and intellectual consequences than their fellow monarchs elsewhere, even if the consequences were often but dimly perceived. Much more significant, but much less studied, is the role played by the Habsburg bureaucracy – and particularly at its lower levels: the county officials at the provincial level and the ministerial councillors at the level of the central government. I hope to make the former the subject of a future study, but even a cursory glance at the Habsburg bureaucracy in the second half of

---

[7] Perry Anderson, *Lineages of the Absolutist State* (London, 1974), p. 18.

the eighteenth century reveals a body whose features are quite different from those drawn by Rosenberg and Johnson of the Prussian one.[8] It clearly bred an atmosphere where lesser bureaucrats could not only survive but actually thrive and hope to win the approval of their sovereigns and superiors with strident critiques of their social betters such as: "He assumes good sense only in people of noble birth. What presumption! It would be more correct to say that it is good sense that ennobles."[9]

Finally, we must consider the role of the key individuals at the ministerial level. In the Habsburg Monarchy ministerial initiatives counted for everything. Even Joseph II, who tried in so many ways to emulate Frederick II of Prussia, never degenerated into the kind of "irresponsible central executive" for which Frederick's autocratic "cabinet" government aimed.[10] In 1760, administrative reforms created institutional safeguards which substantially widened the responsibilities of ministerial-level bureaucrats and conversely also widened the scope of their influence on the development of the Monarchy. Clearly "the men around Maria Theresia" fell into discernible political "parties" or interest groups, and their influence varied substantially from individual to individual. But no analysis of Habsburg enlightened absolutism without careful attention to the often subtle and bitter ministerial debates is conceivable. A final consequence of this reality is that quite frequently the political input of single individuals made a dramatic difference to the direction reform would take. The broad contours of the development of Habsburg central Europe may have been shaped by social, economic and intellectual forces that gripped all of Europe, but its specific features and distinct paths were shaped by particular individuals. Of these men who helped mold the unique construct of Habsburg enlightened absolutism, the most significant was Wenzel Anton Kaunitz-Rietberg.

Family background and early life of Kaunitz

The Kaunitzes (Kunici, Kounici, Kaunici) were descendants of the old Bohemian nobility, with Záviše z Újezdec a Kounic, son of the burgrave of Prague and himself Grand Chamberlain of Bohemia from 1327 to 1333, the first in the recorded family line.[11] The core of the Kaunitz estates, the

---

[8] Hans Rosenberg, *Bureaucracy, Aristocracy and Autocracy: The Prussian Experience*, 1660–1815 (Cambridge, Mass., 1958); Hubert Johnson, *Friedrich the Great and His Officials* (New Haven, Conn., 1975).

[9] Franz A. J. Szabo, "Unwanted Navy: Habsburg Naval Armaments under Maria Theresia", *Austrian History Yearbook* XVII–XVIII (1981–1982), 46.

[10] Rosenberg, *Bureaucracy*, p. 22.

[11] Wurzbach XI, 60–68; Franz Vlasák, *Der altböhmische Adel und seine Nachkommenschaft nach dem dreissigjährigen Kriege* (Prague, 1866), pp. 61–62; Roman von Procházka, *Genealogisches Handbuch erloschener böhmischer Herrenstandsfamilien* (Neustadt an der

seigneurie of Austerlitz (Nouozedeliz, Slavkov) in Moravia, was acquired by the family in 1531. During the Reformation, the Kaunitzes were swept up in the evangelical tide. They were among the prominent noble families who gave refuge to Anabaptist émigrés. Oldřich Kounic (1569–1617) himself confessed membership in the Moravian Brethren, and was one of the members of the Moravian Estates in the forefront of opposition to Habsburg Counter-Reformation policies. The two eldest of his four sons, Karel and Bedřich, participated in the Bohemian rebellion of 1618, the latter being one of the Directors of the Estates' regime. With the defeat of the Protestants, both went into exile while their property was confiscated and passed on to Habsburg loyalists. The third son, Maximilian, who declared himself converted to Catholicism and loyal to the Habsburgs, retained his estates but died of the plague without issue shortly thereafter. The fourth son, Lev Vilém Kounic (1614–1655), an orphaned minor, came under the guardianship of the provincial governor, Cardinal Franz von Dietrichstein, initiator of the re-Catholicization of Moravia.

Dietrichstein's guardianship and patronage proved of inestimable value to the rise of the Kaunitz family. Thanks to him, the Kaunitz estates were enlarged substantially between 1629 and 1634. Having showed himself a model of post-Trentine Catholic piety at the Jesuit College of Olomouc, Lev Vilém was raised to the rank of count by Emperor Ferdinand III in 1642 and in 1647 he married the grand-niece of the cardinal. With this marriage, the Kaunitzes came into the direct orbit of the immensely wealthy, powerful and influential Dietrichstein family, which also included, among others, Prince Karl Eusebius von Liechtenstein, *primus inter pares* of the Habsburg aristocracy, Count Walter Leslie, assassin of Wallenstein, field-marshall and head of the War Ministry, and Count Friedrich von Trauttmansdorf, imperial representative at the Westphalian peace conference and Grand Master of the Household under Ferdinand III. By the age of thirty-six, Lev Vilém was an imperial chamberlain and privy councillor and launched on what promised to be an illustrious career when he was named chief justice of the Margravate of Moravia. Thus, in a single lifetime, the Kaunitz family had catapulted from rebellion and disgrace to the "strategic elite"[12] – the inner circle of dynastic decision makers – of

Aisch, 1973), p. 137; Jan K. Linhart, *Kounicové* (Brno, 1982). Most references to the young Kaunitz in the secondary literature and in reference works were based on Arneth, "Biographie," which remains an important source but which contains a number of errors. The single most important work on the Kaunitz family and some of its leading members since the Reformation, and on the youth and background of Wenzel Anton, however, is the magisterial Klingenstein, *Aufstieg des Hauses Kaunitz*. The following section, unless otherwise noted, is based largely on this work.

[12] The term from Thomas H. Barker, *Army, Aristocracy, Monarchy: Essays on War, Society, and Government in Austria, 1618–1780* (New York, 1982), p. 31.

the Monarchy. Like a dozen other old Bohemian families tainted with Protestantism, the Kaunitzes survived the crisis, joined the select elite of indigenous magnates that provided the political leadership in the Kingdom, and "entrenched themselves ever more firmly with the triple guarantee of latifundium, Catholic orthodoxy and fairly unswerving dynastic loyalty."[13]

Lev Vilém did not live to enjoy the fruits of this success, dying prematurely after a lengthy illness in 1655. His only son and heir, Dominik Ondřej Kounic (1654–1705), however, fairly fulfilled the promise inherent in the family position. Only a few months old at his father's death, he too became a Dietrichstein ward which smoothed his path into the immediate entourage of Emperor Leopold I after he attained his majority. By this time, Czech had given way to German as the dominant language of administration, and Dominik Ondřej would probably be best identified by the Germanized version of his name: Dominik Andreas Kaunitz. The German dimension was, in any case, strengthened by his subsequent career. In 1682, he became Habsburg ambassador to Bavaria and succeeded in winning the Elector to the Emperor's cause. He played a key role in the negotiations that led to the conclusion of the League of Augsburg, and in 1687, as imperial returning officer, decisively influenced the election of the anti-French Wittelsbach candidate for the Electorate of Cologne. During 1694–1697, he was imperial ambassador to the Netherlands and, thereafter, imperial representative at the Peace of Rijswijk. By this time, he had already reached the pinnacle of success for in 1698, with strong support from the Electors of Bavaria, Brandenburg, and the Palatinate, he was made Vice-Chancellor of the Holy Roman Empire – a post which gave him the dominant voice in foreign policy councils within the Habsburg complex as well.[14]

This political ascent of Dominik Andreas Kaunitz found reflection in symbolic honours as well. In 1683, he was confirmed in his quest for the status of Count of the Holy Roman Empire which gave him immediate status (*Reichsunmittelbarkeit*) to the Emperor – a position he subsequently strengthened by arranging the marriage of his son with the heiress of the free County of Rietberg in North Germany.[15] In 1685, he joined an even more select group by being named to the Imperial Privy Council, and two years later, he ascended to the most exclusive fraternity of all when he was raised to the Order of the Golden Fleece. In the world of the late seventeenth-century aristocracy, however, wealth and power alone did not suffice in retaining a high profile at court. The socio-economic and political preeminence had to be visibly displayed both to gain the respect of one's

[13] Evans, *Making of the Habsburg Monarchy*, p. 205; on the general trend, pp. 200–216.
[14] See below, pp. 38–39.   [15] Arneth, "Biographie," pp. 7–9.

peers and, it was felt, as a concrete instrument of power. Illiterate subjects were felt not to be susceptible to reason and had to be constrained to accept the "rationality" of the social hierarchy by an overt and demonstrative assault on their senses. This baroque compulsion for allegorical display of power led to a conspicuous consumption manifest in such things as clothing, jewelry, collectables but, above all, sumptuous palaces on a scale thought to be appropriate to the political and social status of the individual.[16] Dominik Andreas was no exception. He increased the size of his latifundia by about a third, with purchases not only in Moravia but in the aristocratic quarter of Vienna. He undertook the expansion and rebuilding of his château at Austerlitz, collected valuables, and, of course, presented himself as a man of importance with luxurious exhibitionism. Since this was considered especially important in the diplomatic service, where envoys still covered their own expenses, Dominik Andreas soon found his expenses outpacing his revenues. Though a wealthy man with substantial assets, he was cash poor. He sought to remedy this with proto-industrial enterprise – erecting a textile manufactory on his estates – but profits proved too meager to alleviate chronic debt. Upon his death, his estate was saddled with a debt of 200,000 Gulden.

Two important aspects of Dominik Andreas' thought ought to be adduced as contributing important elements to the Kaunitz family tradition. In foreign policy, he belonged to a group led by Karl Theodore von Salm and including Prince Eugene of Savoy, which favoured a diplomatic reorientation of the Monarchy. The group recommended detente with France, deprecated the Spanish connection and focused on the territorial and political consolidation of the Austro-Bohemian core of the Monarchy, seeing Bavaria, Milan and the Balkans as preferred areas of expansion. These men were also sensitive to the inadequacy of Habsburg material resources to carry out any ambitious programmes and, therefore, lent a ready ear to cameralist prescriptions for economic development. Advocates of reform and of support for commercial and industrial enterprise, they strove to implement what the cameralist economists had preached. The War of the Spanish Succession tended to lessen the appeal of such policies and may account for the decline of Dominik Andreas' political influence during his last years – though his energies were also much depleted by illness.[17]

---

[16] On this, see Hubert Ch. Ehalt, *Ausdrucksformen absoluter Herrschaft* (Vienna, 1980), especially pp. 63–71.

[17] Max Braubach, *Versailles und Wien von Ludwig XIV. bis Kaunitz* (Bonn, 1952). On Dominik Andreas Kaunitz, see his "Graf Dominik Andreas Kaunitz (1655–1705) als Diplomat und Staatsmann," in Heinrich Fichtenau and Erich Zöllner, eds., *Beiträge zur neueren Geschichte Österreichs* (Vienna, Cologne and Graz, 1974), pp. 225–242; Klingenstein, *Aufstieg des Hauses Kaunitz*, pp. 41–74.

The impecunious legacy of Dominik Andreas left his surviving children in a difficult position. Career prospects for the two sons and marriage prospects for the three daughters were diminished by the relative poverty of the family. The elder son, Franz Karl Kaunitz (1676–1717), showed an early inclination towards an ecclesiastical career. His father was able to use his influence to secure him positions as canon at Olomouc, Salzburg and Passau as well as provost of Altötting, whose prebends produced an adequate though not opulent income. Having studied theology in Rome, he remained there for over a decade as Imperial Auditor until he finally secured the meager Bishopric of Laibach (Ljubljana) in 1711. But before he could use the influence of his new position for the benefit of his family, he died prematurely at the age of forty-one. The younger son and heir of the patrimony was Maximilian Ulrich Kaunitz (1679–1746), who devoted himself single-mindedly to rebuilding his family's political and material fortune. His own political career remained modest. It included some special diplomatic missions, but was in the main confined to the governorship of Moravia, which he held from 1720 to 1746. In this capacity, he showed himself very much a pragmatist, an acute assessor of the realities of his time, and a strong advocate of reform in the cameralist tradition of "the well-ordered police state."

Maximilian Ulrich's main ambition, however, was to secure a bright future for his large brood of children in order to re-assert the "splendor" of his family. Blessed with sixteen children, eight sons and three daughters survived infancy and, hence, careful and elaborate plans for their development preoccupied him. These included the establishment of a familial secundogenitur and an imposing foray into the politics of ecclesiastical sinecures. In the event, however, much of Maximilian Ulrich's energy was expended for naught. One son after the other died in later childhood, adolescence or early manhood, and only one survived his father. This was his sixth child and second son, Wenzel Anton, who was born in the family's Vienna residence on 2 February 1711.[18]

Young Wenzel Anton Kaunitz showed himself to be a gifted and assiduous lad. Maximilian Ulrich early appreciated these talents and approached his son's education with a strong and earnest sense of responsibility. Neo-stoic by temperament and conviction, Maximilian Ulrich's philosophy of education was influenced by Jansenist and Protestant models, which deprecated maternal and female influences and

[18] Kaunitz was baptized in the Church of Our Lady to the Scots on 3 February 1711. The baptismal register records his full name as: Wenceslaus Antonius Josephus Maria Blasius. Geburtenvermerk der Abteikirche Unsere Liebe Frau zu den Schotten, Vienna, Tom 24, Fol. 37 (3 February 1711). Cf. Novotny, *Staatskanzler Kaunitz*, pp. 200–201.

stressed hard work, self- discipline and emotional restraint. Inclination to sober and pragmatic frugality was reinforced by necessity since the fiscal flexibility of the Kaunitz family remained severely restricted by debts throughout Maximilian Ulrich's lifetime. Under the circumstances, Maximilian Ulrich was compelled to look to the Church to secure an adequate living, especially for his younger sons. For over a decade, he was deeply engaged in trying to secure suitable prebends in numerous cathedral chapters where canonicates became vacant. These included several in the region around Westphalia where his wife's Rietberg connections might prove useful as well as the more traditional Austro-Bohemian grazing grounds of Salzburg, Passau and Olomouc. Although negotiations could be lengthy and positions difficult to acquire, prebends, once awarded, became virtual family property and could be passed from brother to brother. Thus it was that Wenzel Anton, on the eve of reaching the canonic age of consent of fourteen, was awarded a prebend in the Cathedral Chapter of Münster in the fall of 1724, even if an ecclesiastical career was the farthest thing from the mind of either father or son. Wenzel, his father reported, showed no inclinations in this direction, and Maximilian Ulrich saw his son rather follow in the footsteps of his own father, Imperial Vice-Chancellor, Dominik Andreas. The position of canon at Münster, therefore, was merely being held in trust until one of the younger brothers was old enough to assume it. In the event, it proved to be superfluous to the family's plans; a formal resignation followed in 1734. In that intervening decade, young Wenzel Anton had been trained for a secular career at court.

Maximilian Ulrich was not the kind of man who doubted the social and political role he felt God entrusted to the aristocratic elite, but he was a man painfully aware of changing times and of the need to change with them. Above all, both in his capacity as governor of Moravia and as father, he was aware of the inadequacies of the educational institutions of the Monarchy, of their inability to provide the kind of practical, technical and professional skills necessary to exercise a role of political leadership successfully. Hence, rather than send his son to the local Jesuit college, Maximilian Ulrich resolved to engage a private tutor for the boy once he reached the age of fifteen. This tutor was to receive the post of major-domo (*Hofmeister*) to the young Kaunitz heir; he was first to act as instructor; then he was to supervise the young man's university studies; finally, he was to accompany him on his grand tour, which in those days represented the culmination of a noble's education. The qualifications Maximilian Ulrich sought in a major domo were imposing, but he seems to have found them to his entire satisfaction in the native Bohemian, Johann Friedrich von Schwanau.

Schwanau was a typical product of the early German Enlightenment. He had studied philosophy, law and history at Prague, Halle and Leyden, and followed in the intellectual tradition of Christian Thomasius with his tolerant pluralism and eudemonism. Schwanau was also a disciple of the mathematical deductive rationalism of Christian Wolff, which manifested itself above all in his insistence on rigorous logic. Under the stern eye of Maximilian Ulrich, an earnest taskmaster who personally administered history and geography tests to his children, Schwanau tutored Wenzel Anton for four years in a manner far more rigorous than anything his peers were experiencing. Then, in the fall of 1730, his young charge was ready for university. From February 1731 to July 1732, young Kaunitz enrolled in various courses at the University of Leipzig, one of the best institutions of its day. Schwanau laid out a carefully-prepared curriculum in public and private law, German history, German grammar, rhetoric, classics, Latin and music, all of which his pupil discharged with distinction. Kaunitz's term of study at Leipzig was longer and more intense than those of other nobles. Schwanau specifically arranged for frequent examinations, and from Moravia paternal exhortations demanded application and serious-ness and deprecated traditional youthful frivolities.

Even the subsequent grand tour, begun in July 1732, tended to stress the educational dimension rather than amusement. Maximilian Ulrich had made it clear to Schwanau in no uncertain terms that he did not send his son on tour just for amusement. The itinerary was carefully planned to avoid locations "where no profit was to be derived", focusing instead on areas where political lessons could be learned. Acquiring aristocratic polish was "praiseworthy" but the first priority had always to remain "the painstaking acquisition of knowledge."[19] Thus, in addition to learning about different political systems and social structures first hand and making the acquaintance of numerous prominent personages, the purpose of Wenzel Anton's cavalier tour was to amplify the academic dimension already so well grounded at Leipzig. The tour took him from Leipzig to Berlin, whence it proceeded through north-western Germany to the Netherlands. It then moved southward through Brussels to Cologne, Frankfurt and Munich. Crossing the Alps, the Kaunitz party spent Christmas in Venice, continuing on to Rome and Naples. After some four months in Rome, they traveled northwards via Florence, Milan, Genoa and Turin to France. Another four months were spent in Paris, before the homeward journey began by way of Lorraine, Württemberg and the Danube valley to Vienna.

Kaunitz arrived in the Habsburg capital in the carnival season on 13 February 1734. His parents, who awaited him there, used the occasion to

---

[19] Klingenstein, *Aufstieg des Hauses Kaunitz*, pp. 230–231, 244.

introduce their son to court society in a series of balls, theatrical presentations, outings and the like, both to present the young Kaunitz heir to the inner circles of political power and to find him a suitable bride. Introduced to the powerful Starhemberg family, Wenzel Anton soon found his bride in the eighteen-year-old Maria Ernestine Starhemberg (1717–1749). The two were married on 22 April 1736, and offspring followed almost immediately. Maria Ernestine bore Kaunitz seven children, six sons and a daughter, well-nigh annually between 1737 and 1745, before her own premature death in 1749. Thereafter, Kaunitz never remarried, and when his older sister, Maria Antonia (1708–1778), was widowed childless in 1752, she ran her brother's household for the subsequent quarter century.

Kaunitz's political career began slowly. He secured a titular position in the provincial government of Lower Austria in June 1734, but this never entailed any real responsibility. He also entered the Aulic Council as a councillor in January 1735. The Aulic Council acted as an imperial Court of Appeal, and though young noble councillors occasionally assessed pending cases, a position in the Aulic Council was not an end in itself, but was regarded at the time as a mere springboard for higher office at court. That the young Kaunitz in the event remained in this pool of candidates anticipating further court employ for six years was due less to his talents and more to his financial resources. These were still so strained that the expenses that a diplomatic mission entailed could not even be considered. However, with the death of Emperor Charles VI in October 1740 and the flurry of diplomatic activity surrounding the accession of his daughter, Maria Theresia, the demand for suitable noble diplomats increased dramatically. Just before Christmas 1740, Maria Ernestine's grandfather Starhemberg approached Wenzel Anton with an offer of an embassy in Copenhagen.

While there is every indication that Kaunitz was anxious for a court commission and yearned to demonstrate his capacity, family finances remained an insurmountable impediment. The Kaunitzes were still not liquid enough to cover the costs of such an embassy. Wenzel therefore prevailed on Starhemberg over the Christmas holidays, that in recommending candidates for the Copenhagen embassy to the court, he bring up Kaunitz's name in such a way that his zeal to serve would be noticed but that someone else be chosen for this specific task. Starhemberg agreed, but the stratagem obviously left Kaunitz with little choice but to accept whatever offer came next. Fortunately, it was a much less costly one. On 7 March 1741, Maria Theresia's husband, Francis of Lorraine, asked Kaunitz whether he would be prepared to undertake a journey to the Italian courts at Turin, Florence and Rome to announce the birth of an heir to the Habsburg throne which was expected within a matter of days. Secretly, he was also to sound out the diplomatic mood especially with Savoy, in the developing Austrian Succession crisis. Kaunitz agreed, and left Vienna shortly after the birth of the heir, Joseph, on 13 March. Kaunitz obviously did not fail to impress. As the diplomatic crisis deepened that summer, negotiations with prospective allies, England and Savoy, opened further opportunities. On 11 October 1741, Maria Theresia herself received Kaunitz and offered him one of these two critical embassies, only to have her request reluctantly denied: raising the necessary capital to finance such missions had proved "simply impossible" for the hard pressed Maximilian Ulrich and his ambitious son.[20]

By now, Kaunitz was fairly chafing at the bit, frustrated at the degree to which financial exigencies retarded his career. By the spring of 1742, he resolved to take on any burden necessary, even to mortgage the family entailed estates, to be able to accept any further commissions that were proffered to him. The opportunity came in June. A preliminary accord had been reached with Savoy in February, but an accredited ambassador was needed to work out a formal agreement and co-ordinate military plans between the allies. When Kaunitz was offered the opportunity to take up this challenge early in June, he accepted without hesitation – indeed, without confirming whether the family could even afford it. Royal consent was required to offer creditors an entailed estate as collateral, and it was seldom given. But in this case, Maria Theresia acceded to the request on 29 June.[21] This permitted the Kaunitz family to borrow the requisite amount of money so that Wenzel was able to depart for Turin the very next day.

The Turin embassy was a difficult one, for although the Duke of Savoy inclined to a Habsburg alliance, he was being courted by the Bourbons as well. While fear of a Bourbon preponderance on the Italian peninsula eventually confirmed the Habsburg connection, the Duke was nevertheless able to extract a sizeable territorial ransom for the compact. What is more, his military posture remained largely defensive despite Kaunitz's best effort to press him into offensive action.[22] The intensity of Kaunitz's efforts and the frustration at the lack of results had two important consequences. On the one hand, Kaunitz began to manifest symptoms of an illness which

---

[20] The canard reported by the Venetian ambassador that Kaunitz was hedging his bets until the issue of the Austrian succession had been settled (Arneth, "Biographie,", p. 33), has been effectively laid to rest by Klingenstein, *Aufstieg des Hauses Kaunitz*, pp. 278–279.

[21] Arneth, "Biographie", p. 35.

[22] For the Turin embassy, see William J. McGill, "The Roots of Policy: Kaunitz in Italy and the Netherlands, 1742–1746", *Central European History* I (1968), 131–149; his "The Political Education of Wenzel Anton von Kaunitz-Rietberg" (unpublished Ph.D. dissertation, Harvard University, 1961); Arneth, "Biographie", pp. 33–65.

was to plague him recurrently for decades. He developed headaches and
fever and complained of weakness and partial paralysis of his left arm.[23]
These outbursts of illness tended to reduce his ability to carry on his task
and often tempted him to resignation. The second important consequence
of the Turin embassy was that Kaunitz began to formulate the outlines of
what was to become his famous *renversement des alliances* of 1756. His first
grand speculative survey of Habsburg foreign policy was submitted from
Turin on 18 March 1743, and had amongst its most decisive immediate
results the complete captivation of his sovereign. The breadth of his
conception and the lucidity and inexorable logic with which it was
presented so impressed Maria Theresia, that Kaunitz soon came to be held
in highest regard. She hastened to confide him her confidence and assure
him that he would not be held responsible for any failure to prompt the
Duke of Savoy into a more energetic course.[24]

As a mark of Maria Theresia's confidence in her young ambassador, she
informed him in November 1743 that he would be withdrawn from Turin
and appointed major-domo to her sister, Maria Anna. She and her
husband had been made the governors of the Austrian Netherlands.
Kaunitz was also promoted to the rank of Actual Privy Councillor before
he finally left Turin on 20 April 1744. Though he feared he was being
"promoted" out of a position of influence to a purely ceremonial post,
these fears were groundless. In a letter to her sister, Maria Theresia waxed
lyrical over Kaunitz, making it clear that he had been appointed to help the
vice-regal couple in political decision-making, not merely in ceremonial
matters.[25] In short, the appointment confirmed that Kaunitz had become
one of the young queen's favourites amongst her diplomatic servants.

The Belgian appointment proved to be an even more thankless task than
the Turin embassy had been. When Kaunitz arrived in Brussels on 17
October 1744, he found Archduchess Maria Anna, who had just delivered
a stillborn child, stricken by what was to be a mortal illness. Feverish
efforts to enlist the best medical advice then available all went for naught,
the princess passing away on 16 December. This alone would have been
enough to leave Kaunitz distraught, but to make matters worse, he was
now forced to oversee the collapse of the Austrian Netherlands in the face
of a French invasion under Marshall Maurice of Saxony, and chary
support by the Maritime Powers. Again, the most frenetic efforts by
Kaunitz, who on 13 February 1745 had been promoted once more, to the

---

[23] For a discussion of Kaunitz's illness, see pp. 20–21.

[24] Arneth, "Biographie", pp. 55–56.

[25] *Ibid.*, pp. 66–67; cf. Alfred Ritter von Arneth, *Geschichte Maria Theresias*, 10 Vols.
(Vienna, 1863–1879), (hereafter cited as *Maria Theresia*) II, 562; Ghislaine de Boom, *Les
Ministres Plénipotentiaires dans les Pays-Bas autrichiens, principalement Cobenzl* (Brussels,
1932), pp. 45–49.

rank of Authorized Minister for the Austrian Netherlands, could not prevent disaster. The Battle of Fontenoy in May 1745 sealed the fate of Belgium. As the French moved from one triumph to another, Kaunitz was finally forced to surrender Brussels and sign a formal capitulation in February 1746.[26]

In the face of this defeat, Kaunitz's health once more began to deteriorate. From August 1745 he began to request to be relieved of his duties, and by the spring was complaining of being confined to bed for days at a time with a high fever. Finally, in June his wish was granted, allowing him to withdraw to the famous health resort at Spa. But no sooner had he arrived at Spa than he received word from Vienna that preliminary peace negotiations were about to open at Breda, and that Maria Theresia wished him to be her official envoy. While it seems that Kaunitz's plea of ill health was not taken as seriously in Vienna he might have wished, on this occasion he was able to turn down even insistent pleas by Maria Theresia herself and devote himself to what he considered his top priority – the recovery of his physical health. Then, after two weeks in Rietberg on family business, Kaunitz received word that his father had passed away on 10 September 1746. He hurried at once back home to Moravia.[27]

By the late fall, Kaunitz's health had been fully restored and he was, once again, ready and willing to serve. This becomes clear from the arrangement Kaunitz now proceeded to make with the man who, over the previous decade, had become his closest friend and associate: Baron Friedrich Binder von Kriegelstein (1708–1782). Binder was the son of an Aulic Councillor and imperial representative to the Westphalian Circle of the Holy Roman Empire. Born in Wetzlar, he had studied law at Giessen, and came in contact with Kaunitz shortly after the latter's return from his cavalier tour. Becoming Kaunitz's personal secretary, Binder was soon named Stadtholder of the Kaunitz family principality of Rietberg in 1742. During this period, a deep bond of friendship developed between the two men until Binder became an irreplaceable right-hand man. Shortly after the death of his father, Kaunitz offered Binder a new position as his own aide and political adviser, which clearly anticipated imminent appointment to a major government post.[28] For the next thirty-five years, he was to remain Kaunitz's closest friend and confidant, and his most trusted political adviser. Energetic, perspicacious, erudite, punctilious and disarm-

[26] MZA, Rodinný archiv Kounicǔ, Carton 3, Maurice of Saxony to Kaunitz, 16 March, 18 and 20 May, 5 and 17 July 1746.
[27] On the Belgian appointment, see McGill, "Kaunitz in Italy and the Netherlands", pp. 141–148; Arneth, "Biographie", pp. 65–106.
[28] Hermann Scherl, "Die Grafschaft Rietberg unter dem Geschlecht der Kaunitz" (unpublished Ph.D. dissertation, University of Vienna, 1962), pp. 95–103; *ADB* II, 648–649.

ingly frank, Binder's unwavering loyalty and devotion combined with his professionalism became a staff on which Kaunitz gladly relied.

For the moment, however, Kaunitz settled in Vienna and became part of the immediate social entourage of what was by now the imperial couple (Francis having been elected Holy Roman Emperor in 1745). He participated in the glittering social life at court and cemented his political position with Maria Theresia. In the celebrations following the birth of Archduke Leopold, for example, Kaunitz was one of the noble actors who mounted the Viennese première of Jean-François Regnard's 1705 comedy *Les Ménechmes* on 31 May 1747 in the Schönbrunn palace theater.[29] But clearly, the Empress was also anxious to employ him politically as soon as possible. On 21 July, the Privy Conference was considering candidates to replace the governor of Lombardy, Gian Luca Pallavicini, when a surprise written order arrived from Maria Theresia: only two men were to be considered, Ferdinand Bonaventura Harrach (whom the Conference in the event recommended) and Kaunitz.[30] Kaunitz, for his part, needed not to be consoled long for his loss. After the disappointing military campaign of 1747, Maria Theresia was prepared to negotiate peace. The man she selected as plenipotentiary to the peace conference which was to assemble at Aachen was the man she had already wished to undertake the task at Breda the previous year. This time Kaunitz did not refuse.

Delayed by illness once again, Kaunitz did not arrive in Aachen until mid-March 1748. The peace negotiations also proved thoroughly disappointing, confirming the disillusionment Kaunitz had already developed towards Austria's traditional allies – England and the United Netherlands – and re-affirming, in his mind, the need to re-assess Habsburg diplomatic priorities.[31] Upon his return to Vienna, Kaunitz was appointed to the top foreign policy decision-making council of the Monarchy, the Privy Conference, where Habsburg policies were now subjected to a thorough review in light of the bitter experiences of the previous decade. In a series of conferences in the spring of 1749, Kaunitz soon distinguished himself by focusing on the new Prussian threat that had emerged. Considering this the primary problem of Habsburg foreign policy, he suggested other policies had to be tailored to this reality. He underlined the weaknesses of the

---

[29] Rudolf Khevenhüller-Metsch and Hanns Schlitter, eds., *Aus der Zeit Maria Theresias: Tagebuch des Fürsten Johann Josef Khevenhüller-Metsch*, 8 Vols., (Vienna and Leipzig, 1907–1972), II, 160–161; Gustav Zechmeister, *Die Wiener Theater nächst der Burg und nächst dem Kärntnerthor von 1747 bis 1776* (Vienna, 1971), p. 436.

[30] Khevenhüller-Metsch II, 168.

[31] On Kaunitz in Aachen, see William J. McGill, "Wenzel Anton von Kaunitz-Rittberg and the Conference of Aix-la-Chapelle, 1748", *Duquesne Review* XIV (1969), 154–167; Arneth, "Biographie", pp. 112–153; Adolf Beer, "Zur Geschichte des Friedens von Aachen im Jahre 1748", *AÖG* XLVII (1871), 72–93.

traditional alliance system, stressed the importance of an alliance with Russia and suggested the old enmity with France was outdated. It followed that an effort should be made to diffuse timeworn French hostility to Austria and, optimistically, win her benevolent neutrality or even support in any future conflict.[32]

After some debates, Kaunitz's policy received official endorsement, and in the summer of 1749, he was designated as the new Habsburg ambassador to Paris, where he was to sound out French sentiments. French delays in making a reciprocal ambassadorial appointment deferred Kaunitz's actual departure from Vienna for more than a year and it was not until 27 October 1750 that he actually arrived in the French capital. During that year, Kaunitz continued his activities as a member of the Privy Conference, which completed the captivation of the Empress. More and more, Kaunitz became Maria Theresia's primary adviser in foreign affairs. Even before he left for Paris, the Empress confided to her secretary that there was no man like Kaunitz, that he was her "only help" (*seule ressource*) among her ministers, and that she could not imagine how she would be able to do without him while he was in Paris.[33] In short, Kaunitz already eclipsed the nominal foreign minister before he left on his French embassy, and it seems clear the Empress intended him for titular foreign minister at the very first opportunity.

Kaunitz spent slightly over two years in Paris, during which the impediments to a prospective Austro-French rapprochement became abundantly clear. His embassy, again interspersed with lengthy bouts of illness,[34] bore no immediate diplomatic fruits. In the face of this, Kaunitz advocated a policy of caution, flexibility and patience – a policy which sacrificed no birds in the hand in pursuit of those in the bush, but one which nonetheless kept the previously stated priorities and long-range interest of the monarchy clear. Such a comprehensive agenda, clearly, was beyond the scope of a mere ambassador; it was the domain of the minister responsible for foreign affairs. The Empress, for her part, was anxious to elevate

[32] Substantial excerpts from Kaunitz's famous memorandum for the conferences of 1749, as well as the full text of the Privy Conference minutes of 19 April 1749, were originally published in Adolf Beer, ed., *Aufzeichnungen des Grafen William Bentinck über Maria Theresia* (Vienna, 1871), pp. xxxvii–lxix, 129–142. The Kaunitz memorandum has now been published in full: Reiner Pommerin and Lothar Schilling, eds., "Denkschrift des Grafen Kaunitz zur mächtepolitischen Konstellation nach dem Aachener Frieden von 1748," in Johannes Kunisch, ed., *Expansion und Gleichgewicht* (Berlin, 1986), pp. 165–239. Cf. William J. McGill, "The Roots of Policy: Kaunitz in Vienna and Versailles, 1749–1753," *Journal of Modern History* XLIII (1971) 229–235; Arneth, "Biographie", pp. 153–185; and his *Maria Theresia* IV, 262–284.

[33] Arneth, *Maria Theresia* IV, 542.

[34] HHStA, Staatenabteilung: Frankreich Varia, Karton 22, Ludwig Zinzendorf to Uhlfeld, 31 December 1750, and 3, 7, 8 January 1751; *ibid.*, Frankreich Berichte, Karton 77, Kaunitz to Colloredo, 11 April 1751.

Kaunitz to this dignity as quickly as possible. When the opportunity arose in December 1751, she wasted no time in secretly offering Kaunitz the post. Thus, when he returned to Vienna on 19 April 1753, Kaunitz was foreign minister-designate of the Habsburg Monarchy. During the grand ceremonies surrounding Maria Theresia's thirty-sixth birthday on 13 May, the appointment was officially announced. At the age of forty-two, Wenzel Anton Kaunitz-Rietberg had become the most prominent minister at the Habsburg court.[35]

Personality and mind of Kaunitz

It is one of the ironies of history that one of the most oft-cited characterizations of Kaunitz remains the caustic *bon mot* of his notoriously derisive arch-foe, Frederick II of Prussia: "frivolous in his tastes and profound in business."[36] This kind of dualistic compartmentalization of Kaunitz's policies and character, however, seemed to strike both contemporaries and historians. The Court Chamberlain, Khevenhüller, noted that he and Maria Theresia wondered "how one can combine the qualities of a superior genius with ridiculousness bordering on extravagance itself," and historians seem to have followed suit. Hormayr's famous biographical dictionary of 1807 already described the remarkable contrast between the public and private man,[37] and this assertion went largely unchallenged in all subsequent treatments of Kaunitz. No one, it seems, would deny that Kaunitz was exceptionally gifted but all would assert that he was odd, occasionally fantastic and even ridiculous, and at all events highly eccentric.

A good many of these "peculiarities" were associated with Kaunitz's concern for his physical health – an obsession which bordered on hypochondria in his mature years. In his youth, Kaunitz seemed to be highly susceptible to respiratory infections and colds. During his bouts of illness in maturity, he complained of weakness and dizziness, fever, headaches, and a swelling of his hands and feet as well as a partial paralysis of his left arm. These outbreaks were usually aggravated by stress and could at times incapacitate him for weeks and even months.[38] Naturally, the "cures" effected by the medical experts of the day only served to exacerbate the

---

[35] On the French embassy, see McGill, "Kaunitz in Vienna and Versailles", pp. 236–242; for Kaunitz's secret reports from Paris, see Hanns Schlitter, ed., *Correspondance secrète entre le Comte A. W. Kaunitz-Rietberg, Ambassadeur impérial à Paris, et le Baron Ignaz de Koch, Secrétaire de l'Impératrice Marie-Thérèse, 1750–1752* (Paris, 1899). On Kaunitz's appointment to the foreign ministry, see below, pp. 45–47.

[36] Alexander Novotny, "Staatskanzler Fürst Kaunitz," p. 206.

[37] Khevenhüller-Metsch IV, 70–71; Hormayr, *Lebensbilder*, pp. 28–34.

[38] For Kaunitz's reports on his illness, see Arneth, "Biographie", pp. 105, 109; Schlitter, ed., *Correspondance*, pp. 157–158. Cf. Klingenstein, *Aufstieg des Hauses Kaunitz*, pp. 182–185.

symptoms. Kaunitz's father reproached him for behaving "just like your mother with indispositions of all kinds" and firmly believed it was all in his son's mind.[39] The notion that Kaunitz's illness was purely psychosomatic seemed to be shared by a number of his contemporaries and by most historians who have complacently observed how Kaunitz became "conveniently" ill whenever he found himself in a difficult situation. Of course, it is extremely difficult to make posthumous diagnoses, but a careful analysis of the symptoms and medical history of the family clearly reveals the likelihood that Kaunitz was suffering from epidemic neuromyasthenia. Stress, or more correctly, strenuous exertion would indeed cause debilitation of the kind described by Kaunitz, but its origin was physiological rather than psychological.[40]

The measures Kaunitz took to preserve his health contributed much to make him the laughing-stock of his peers. Suspicious of doctors and medicines, he instituted a personal regimen which he felt would have salutary results: he limited the intake of coffee and sugar, displayed a strong preference for chicken over other meats, tried to maintain a meticulous balance between food groups, and was enthusiastic about the medicinal effects of fresh fruit. He upheld high standards of personal hygiene and even indulged in the then very uncommon practice of brushing his teeth after meals. Afraid of infections, he avoided drafts and drastic temperature changes. He had a horror of infectious diseases and quarantined himself from all cases of such ailments, in particular, from any cases of the then still endemic smallpox. He exercised with great regularity but in moderation by riding daily whenever possible. Manège, indeed, was not only his form of exercise but also his passion. A student and devotee of the art, he considered himself an equine expert of the first rank, and even as an old man he mastered spirited stallions with joy.[41]

Above all, Kaunitz concluded, his delicate constitution compelled him to avoid overexertion. While there can be no doubt that he was diligent, his refusal to overtax himself often gave the impression of laxity. This especially became a source of irritation with the impatient young Joseph II

---

[39] Klingenstein, *Aufstieg des Hauses Kaunitz*, p. 184. Kaunitz, incidentally, also bore an uncanny physical resemblance to his mother, Ernestine Rietberg, which is clearly evident in the life-sized family portrait series displayed in the château at Austerlitz.

[40] In Europe epidemic neuromyasthenia is usually referred to as myalgic encephalomyelitis. Other chronic infectious diseases, such as tuberculosis, which might fit some of the symptoms, would have to be ruled out since these would usually call for an early death. Brucellosis, however, has always to be considered and remains a slim possibility. I am indebted to the world's foremost authority on epidemic neuromyasthenia, Dr. Byron Hyde, for his valuable comments.

[41] HHStA, Kabinettsarchiv: Nachlaß Zinzendorf, Part III: Tagebuch, Vol. 7, 16 March and 27 December 1762; Schlichtegroll I, 150–153; Wurzbach XI, 81–85; Hormayr, *Lebensbilder*, pp. 28–34; Arneth, *Maria Theresia* VII, 287–288, 547–548.

who remained ever perplexed and frustrated at Kaunitz's studied approach to life and to his work. For Kaunitz, physical necessity combined with intellectual propensity: he trained himself to be stolid and self-disciplined. Never impulsive in word or in deed, he always stressed reserve and moderation. Avoiding "enthusiasms" was thus both a medical prescription and philosophy of life.[42] There can be little doubt Kaunitz was a conscious epicurean, for he clearly believed in indulging the senses in moderation, and we can conclude from his behavior that in best epicurean fashion he defined pleasure as the absence of pain not as libertine self-indulgence. He clearly enjoyed the company of women and was seen in the company of actresses so often that Khevenhüller confidently reported some of these as his mistresses,[43] and even Maria Theresia felt compelled to ask him not to frequent these notoriously loose women.[44] Women who knew him spoke with great enthusiasm about his amiability, vivacity and humour,[45] and he was reported to have charmed a great many ladies.[46] He was certainly no ascetic or puritan: he collected erotic literature and delighted in the nudes in his art collection.[47] But he is reported to have shrunk from excessive carnal indulgence.[48] He apparently laid out a fine table, collected recipes of particularly favourite dishes, and was a connoisseur of good wines, but never held excessively lavish and boisterous dinner parties, and, as we have seen, was extremely moderate in his own consumption.[49]

This moderate and self-disciplined life-style was enhanced and buttressed by what Kaunitz himself described as his almost compulsive commitment to a "spirit of order". He was such a man of routine, a lover of neatness and exactness, that the charge of pedantry was frequently leveled at him. His work habits were meticulous, and he prized punctuality and frugality. His life, in short, followed a path of predictable regularity.[50] Love of order also characterized Kaunitz's mind. We have seen how his tutor, Schwanau, was at pains to inculcate the mathematical deductive

---

[42] Schlichtegroll I, 144; Hormayr, *Lebensbilder*, pp. 28–34; Wurzbach XI, 81–85.
[43] Khevenhüller-Metsch III, 253.
[44] HHStA, Familienarchiv: Sammelbände, Karton 70, Maria Theresia to Kaunitz, n.d.
[45] Charlotte Sophia von Aldenburg, Countess Bentick, to Voltaire: Theodore Besterman, ed., *Voltaire's Correspondence*, 75 Vols. (Geneva, 1953–1965) XXX, 166–167, No. 6334.
[46] HHStA, Kabinettsarchiv: Zinzendorf Tagebuch, Vol. 20, 7 October 1775.
[47] Franz A. J. Szabo, "Intorno alle origini del giuseppinismo: motivi economico-sociali e aspetti ideologici," *Società e storia* No. 4 (1970), 173.
[48] Hormayr, *Lebensbilder*, p. 32.
[49] MZA, Rodinný archiv Kounicŭ, Cartons 3 and 11, diverse recipes; HHStA, Staatenabteilung: Frankreich Varia, Karton 22, Kaunitz to Koch, 20 November 1741; Schlitter, ed., *Correspondance*, pp. 50–51, 64; Carl Hinrichs, ed., *Friedrich der Grosse und Maria Theresia: Diplomatische Berichte von Otto Christoph Graf von Podewils* (Berlin, 1937), pp. 146–147.
[50] Wurzbach, XI, 81–85; Hormayr, *Lebensbilder*, pp. 28–34; Arneth, "Biographie," p. 80.

reasoning of Christian Wolff in young Kaunitz, and all through his life he was to be celebrated for his inexorable logic. It was precisely this characteristic that so impressed Maria Theresia about her young ambassador's reports, and so silenced his critics that his reputation as a superior genius remained untouched. His conclusions invariably left the impression of almost Thomistic certainty, though this Cartesian "political algebra" was invariably devoid of sentiment and illusion, stressing always careful reflection and critical analysis.[51] He abhorred hastiness and superficiality and refused to be rushed. As a consequence, his reports were often delayed and, when finally presented, frequently prolix – though seldom verbose and invariably stylish and easy to read. Orally, on the other hand, Kaunitz was a man of few words. Generally taciturn, frequently quite curt, he was reluctant to press a point after rational argument had been exhausted and remained calm and patient when his point was lost – though he was not above dryly recollecting it if events proved him right in the long run.[52]

When analyzing Kaunitz's studied reserve and considered restraint, it becomes clear to what extent he was influenced by one of the main intellectual currents of his age: neo-stoicism. The enthusiasm of Thomasius and Wolff for the popular neo-stoic, Justus Lipsius, remained a hallmark of Leipzig during Kaunitz's university years, and certainly the neo-stoic legacy was evident in Kaunitz's thought: his eudemonism and stress on the common good; his self-conception as a dutiful and upright citizen who never tired of stressing civic virtues to others; his notion of the state as a rational construct buttressing an ethical social order; and his disdain for confessional intolerance. But much of the neo-stoic ideal is also evident in Kaunitz's demeanor: a confident, cultivated, courteous gentleman, he disdained false and base behaviour, strove for urbanity, and set great store by the cultivation of his aesthetic sensibilities.[53]

The cultivation of the arts, Kaunitz confessed, was his principal consolation in adversity.[54] Unlike many members of his class, however, he did not consider the arts a mere form of amusement or escapism, but a self-enriching process in which he prided himself on "very extensive theoretical and practical knowledge."[55] He had a particular enthusiasm for the visual

[51] For a discussion of Kaunitz's "political algebra" see Walter L. Dorn, *Competition for Empire*, 1740–1763 (N.Y., 1940), pp. 296–297 and Harm Klueting, *Die Lehre von der Macht der Staaten* (Berlin, 1986), pp. 171–172.
[52] Wurzbach, XI, 81–85; Hormayr, *Lebensbilder*, pp. 28–34.
[53] Fritz Arnheim, "Das Urtheil eines schwedischen Diplomaten über den Wiener Hof im Jahre 1756. Aus dem schwedischen Reichsarchiv in Stockholm," *MIÖG* X (1889), 292.
[54] HHStA, Sonstige Sammlungen: Grosse Korrespondenz, Fasz. 405, Kaunitz to the Duke of Braganza, 7 October 1781.
[55] *Ibid.*, Kaunitz to Raniero Calzabigi, 18 September 1775.

arts and prided himself on having more than doubled the painting collection accumulated by his ancestors by 1780.[56] A report from 1800 indicated that the private collection in his summer palace in Mariahilf consisted of over 2,000 pictures.[57] When one considers his passionate interest in engravings and his extensive collection of engraved reproductions of the great works of Western art, it is clear that Kaunitz had a broad knowledge of art history. In fact, he developed such an impeccable reputation as a man with wide knowledge in the arts that he was appointed to supervise the organization of the imperial gallery in the Belvedere, including every detail from cataloguing to deciding where and how the pictures were to be hung. The "tasteful manner" in which this was done earned the profuse praise of Joseph II.[58]

With respect to the art of his day, Kaunitz was in the vanguard of the neo-classical revival from its very earliest stirrings. He had a great respect for Pompeo Batoni whose elegant neo-classicism found its roots in Raphael and whose deliberate attempt to keep alive the classical values of the Renaissance pre-dated the neo-classical revival of the 1760s.[59] A similar transitional figure was Sebastiano Conca, whose work Kaunitz also sought and purchased.[60] Bernardo Bellotto, a man famous for his neo-classical *vedute*, was commissioned to paint the Kaunitz *palais* in Mariahilf in 1759,[61] and Anton Raphael Mengs, whose "Parnassus" was the first manifesto of the neo-classical movement, as well as the pellucid early Goya were also represented in Kaunitz's collection.[62] Local artists whom Kaunitz patronized, such as František Antonín Palko, Johann Nepomuk Steiner, Friedrich Heinrich Füger, and Martin Knoller, though all relatively minor figures, shared an urbane neo-classicism which Kaunitz admired.[63] Above all, it is clear he prized the intellectual contributions of the art historian Johann Joachim Winckelmann, perhaps the single most important figure in the neo-classical revival of the eighteenth century. Kaunitz arranged a

---

[56] *Ibid.*, Kaunitz to the Duke of Braganza, 7 October 1781.
[57] Novotny, *Staatskanzler Kaunitz*, p. 123.
[58] HHStA, Familienarchiv: Sammelbände, Karton 70, Joseph to Kaunitz, 22 November 1780. Cf. below, p. 204.
[59] HHStA, Staatskanzlei: Vorträge, Karton 119, Kaunitz to Maria Theresia, 5 September 1775; AABK, Verwaltungsakten, Fasz. 2, Kaunitz to Maria Theresia, 31 December 1772, 2 April 1773.
[60] HHStA, Sonstige Sammlungen: Grosse Korrespondenz, Fasz. 405, Kaunitz to Chevalier Mechel, 22 August 1783.
[61] HHStA, Kabinettsarchiv: Zinzendorf Tagebuch, 22 January 1762, 26 June 1763; Stefan Kozakiewicz, *Bernardo Bellotto*, 2 Vols. (London, 1972), I, 122–125; II, 211–212, 215.
[62] Novotny, *Staatskanzler Kaunitz*, p. 124.
[63] Jiří Kroupa, "Václav Antonín Kaunitz-Rietberg a výtvarná umění (Kulturní politika nebo umělecký mecenát?)," *Studie Comeniana et Historica* XVIII (1988), 75–78. I am indebted to R. J. W. Evans for drawing my attention to this article.

generous reception for Winckelmann in Vienna in 1768,[64] and a decade later he was flattered to have the posthumous reprint of Winckelmann's masterpiece, *Geschichte der Kunst des Altertums*, dedicated to him. He lamented Winckelmann's early death since he was anxious to bring him to the Vienna Art Academy in an official capacity.[65] Austrian art students sent to Rome on government scholarships were advised by Kaunitz that though they were naturally free to adopt any style they wished, he recommended that they take advantage of the examples of antiquity. Above all, he praised the classicism of the Roman school, which, since Raphael's time, had sought to preserve the qualities of "noble simplicity, truth, quiet grandeur, unaffected but refined expression, easy contour of figures, and particularly the precise drawing of the character of the genuinely beautiful".[66]

One such scholarship recipient was Franz Anton Zauner, who quickly became a Kaunitz favourite, and in due course one of the most famous sculptors in the Habsburg Monarchy during the Revolutionary and Napoleonic era. In connection with one of his earliest works, the serene *Clio* of 1779, Zauner asserted that he consciously strove to follow Kaunitz's guidelines, and it is hardly surprising that it was subsequently snapped up by Kaunitz for his private collection. Kaunitz was also instrumental in securing Zauner the chair of sculpture in the Vienna art academy over other more senior and well-connected candidates. Unfortunately, the three busts of Kaunitz (in plaster, marble and bronze respectively), executed by Zauner between 1782 and 1789, have since all been lost.[67] Kaunitz's personal architect of choice was the uncompromisingly neo-classical Johann Ferdinand Hetzendorf von Hohenberg. Coming to Kaunitz's attention during the 1760s, while participating in the decoration of the imperial theater at Schönbrunn, Hohenberg soon became Kaunitz's principal architectural protégé. He was commissioned to build a study for Kaunitz, and participated in the expansion and renovation of Kaunitz's *palais* in Mariahilf. Kaunitz secured him a position as professor of architecture at the Academy of Visual Arts in 1770, within two years propelled him to the post of director of the school of architecture there, and by 1776 secured him the title of Actual Court Architect. In 1783 Hohenberg

[64] DOZA, Handschriften, Vol. 64, Ludwig Zinzendorf to Karl Zinzendorf, 18 June 1768. Winckelmann was killed by his homosexual lover in Trieste. Theft of the presents Winckelmann received in Vienna was apparently the motive for the homicide. Winckelmann's last words before expiring were a request to inform Kaunitz of his fate and to thank him for his generosity.
[65] AABK, Verwaltungsakten, Fasz. 2, Kaunitz to Sperges, n.d. (1776).
[66] ÖNB, Handschriftsammlung: Autographe 195/21, "Kaunitz Ausweisung nach welcher die vier Kais. Königl. pensionirte Künstler während ihres Aufenthalts zu Rom sich zu verhalten haben," n.d. (1771). Cf. Hermann Burg, *Der Bildhauer Franz Anton Zauner und seine Zeit* (Vienna, 1915), pp. 32–34.   [67] Ibid., pp. 47–49, 51–55, 167, 169.

was made "Prince Kaunitz Architect" and commissioned to build a parish church on his patron's estate at Austerlitz, which became one of the most impressive neo-classical churches in central Europe. Finally, Hohenberg was also the expert on whom Kaunitz relied to remodel the park of the Schönbrunn palace along neo-classical lines, with sculptures supplied by the workshop of the neo-classical sculptor, Johann Christian Wilhelm Beyer, following strict guidelines drawn up by Kaunitz personally.[68]

Kaunitz was similarly in the vanguard of the neo-classical revolution in music. His own instrument was the cello, and his strong interest in music was already clear on his cavalier tour. In the list of people whom he met on his tour, there are an exceptionally large number of composers and musicians.[69] In Venice, Kaunitz sought out the famous concerts of Antonio Vivaldi at the Pio Ospedale della Pietà, and generally frequented as many operas and concerts as he could.[70] Then, in Vienna, he staged recitals and concerts at his *palais* which frequently included large orchestras and choruses.[71] But Kaunitz's musical apogee was reached when he became the political linchpin of Christoph Willibald von Gluck's opera reform. As main protector and patron of the Gluck circle – the theater manager, Giacomo Durazzo, the librettist, Raniero Calzabigi, and the amateur, Duke John Charles of Braganza (all personal friends of Kaunitz) – he was instrumental in getting Gluck's clique the upper hand in the cultural circles of the capital.[72] Gluck was a frequent dinner guest at Kaunitz's palais, and Kaunitz in turn attended house concerts at Gluck's residence.[73] Kaunitz apparently even supervised the rehearsals of Gluck's compositions for court festivals,[74] and was a generous supporter of Gluck personally. The composer thanked Kaunitz for "the high protection and especial favour" which the latter "heaped upon me [him] at all times" and acknowledged that he already had "enough evidence" of the Chancellor's generosity.[75] Kaunitz also proved to be one of the strongest patrons of the young Wolfgang Amadeus Mozart when the boy visited Vienna in 1762 and 1767–1768. He was one of the most frequent hosts of the Mozart family,

[68] Erwin Hainisch, *Der Architekt Johann Ferdinand Hetzendorf von Hohenberg* (Innsbruck & Vienna, 1949); Joseph Dernjac, *Zur Geschichte von Schönbrunn* (Vienna, 1885); Arneth, *Maria Theresia* X, 6–8, 751–752. Cf. below, pp. 199–200.
[69] Arneth, "Biographie", pp. 25–26.
[70] Klingenstein, *Aufstieg des Hauses Kaunitz*, p. 243.
[71] C. F. Pohl, *Joseph Haydn*, 3 Vols. (Leipzig, 1882–1927), II, 160, 163.
[72] Robert Haas, *Gluck und Durazzo im Burgtheater* (Zürich, Vienna and Leipzig, 1925), pp. 16, 68, 101–105; Alfred Einstein, *Gluck* (London, 1964), pp. 39–40, 64–66; Bruce Alan Brown, *Gluck and the French Theatre in Vienna* (Oxford, 1991), pp. 43–49.
[73] Theophil Antonicek, "Glucks Existenz in Wien," in Gerhard Croll and Monika Woitas, eds., *Gluck in Wien*, Vol. I of *Gluck Studien* (Kassel, Basel, London and N.Y., 1987), p. 34.
[74] Novotny, *Staatskanzler Kaunitz*, p. 108; Brown, *Gluck*, p. 46.
[75] Hedwig and E. H. Mueller von Asow, eds., *The Collected Corrrespondence and Papers of Christoph Willibald Gluck*, Stewart Thomson, trans. (N.Y., 1962), pp. 25–26.

and his Mariahilf palace became the scene of some rehearsals for Mozart's opera, *La Finta Semplice*, in September 1768.[76] During Mozart's mature years in Vienna, he gave private recitals at the Kaunitz residence, and reported that no one was more kind, courteous and appreciative of him than Kaunitz.[77]

Classicism and neo-classicism similarly dominated Kaunitz's taste in literature. Long enamored of French classical theater, and a special enthusiast for Molière and Voltaire, Kaunitz led the drive to retain an active French stage in Vienna against highly unfavourable odds. He became without question the foremost proponent of French theater in the Monarchy, and clung to this infatuation to the bitter end. Even shortly before his death in 1794, he staged a private performance of Molière at his palace.[78] This passionate commitment to French drama, however, has to be seen in its proper context. In the period between 1740 and 1780 Vienna underwent what might best be called a double theatrical revolution. At the court, where splendid but convoluted Italian baroque spectacles had been the order of the day with the generation of Charles VI, a reaction set in favouring the simpler and more compelling elegance of the French stage, with its Augustan meters and refined musical interludes, which had begun with Molière and Lully and was still at its vibrant height with Voltaire and Rameau. The younger generation of nobles, including Kaunitz, were inexorably drawn to this sublimely graceful entertainment, and the new taste of the younger generation became the dominant voice of the Court Theater in the 1750s. Gluck's opera reform, in fact, began with commissions for the musical numbers of precisely such productions.

During the same time German drama at Vienna's municipal theater was also undergoing a dramatic change of direction when popular burlesque antics began to give way to more high-minded dramas, consciously modeled on the French classical precedents by such theorists as Johann Christoph Gottsched. The attempt to displace popular burlesques with a more literate theater, however, was not as successful as the displacement of Italian baroque spectacles by French classical drama. Far too turgid for plebeian tastes accustomed to satirical slapstick, these German plays were generally also patently inferior, for more refined tastes, to the French models on which they were based. Small wonder, then, that the educated elite, and especially Kaunitz, preferred the more sophisticated theater. But

---

[76] Otto Erich Deutsch, ed., *Mozart: A Documentary Biography*, Eric Blom, Peter Branscome and Jeremy Noble, trans. (Stanford, Calif. 1966), pp. 16, 80; Emily Anderson, ed. and trans., *The Letters of Mozart and his Family*, 2nd ed., 2 Vols. (London, 1966), I, 6–7, 75, Nos. 2, 3, 50.

[77] Anderson, ed., *Letters of Mozart*, II, 889, No. 525, 814–815, No. 459; Deutsch, ed., *Mozart*, pp. 224–239.

[78] Wurzbach XI, 82; Novotny, *Staatskanzler Kaunitz*, p. 202. Cf. below, pp. 205–208.

this is far from saying that Kaunitz's literary tastes were exclusively French. In German literature he certainly had little sympathy for the *Sturm und Drang* movement, expressing, for example, some respect but no affection for Friedrich Gottlieb Klopstock. But this was not in the least unusual, for the *Sturm und Drang* movement found little resonance in Austria in general, where its excessive sentimentality could never be taken quite as seriously and unironically as it appeared to be in other German quarters.[79] On the other hand, Kaunitz was much more positively inclined to the anacreontic roots of the literary neo-classical movement, which he discovered above all through Christoph Martin Wieland.[80] Nor was he hostile to the development of German drama as such, as a superficial reading of the events of the 1770s might suggest. For example, in 1775 Kaunitz's personal friend and ambassador to Berlin, Gottfried van Swieten, persuaded Gotthold Ephraim Lessing to travel to Vienna where the latter was not only cordially received by Kaunitz, but also repeatedly urged to stay in the capital in order to undertake a reform of the German stage in the way Gluck had reformed opera.[81] Once it began to achieve the sophisticated heights of the mature classical stage with Lessing, German theater also won the support of Kaunitz. In short, not language or provenance, but quality was the deciding factor in his literary tastes.

The fact that Kaunitz often used French as his language of choice has also frequently been offered as evidence for his putative francophilia. This, too, has been much misconceived. Kaunitz acquired fluent command of the French language and used it in much diplomatic and personal conversation and correspondence. He read many French books and was familiar with virtually the entire repertoire of the seventeenth- and eighteenth-century French stage. He was fond of French fashions and imported clothing and utensils from Paris.[82] Yet Kaunitz was also entirely comfortable with Italian. He spoke and corresponded widely in it. He collected *objets d'art* from Italy, was familiar with the works of its leading intellectuals, and loved Italian-language operas. Nor had the family roots in the old Czech nobility been entirely lost. Kaunitz not only retained a command of the Czech language, but when the court visited his estate at

---

[79] HHStA, Staatskanzlei: Vorträge, Karton 104, Kaunitz to Joseph, 16 August 1769; Kaunitz to Maria Theresia, 17 August 1769; HHStA, Staatskanzlei: Wissenschaft und Kunst, Karton 11, Kaunitz to Klopstock, 28 August 1769. Cf. Leslie Bodi, *Tauwetter in Wien* (Frankfurt a/M, 1977), pp. 109–116.

[80] Wurzbach XI, 82; Novotny, *Staatskanzler Kaunitz*, pp. 117–118, 212.

[81] Erich Schmidt, *Lessing: Geschichte seines Lebens und seiner Schriften*, 2 Vols. (Berlin, 1909), II, 132, 154–155, 167.

[82] Schlichtegroll I, 146; Wurzbach, XI, 82; Hormayr, *Lebensbilder*, p. 31. On the importation of French household items and clothes from Paris, where Kaunitz kept a personal account, see HHStA, Sonstige Sammlungen: Grosse Korrespondenz, Fasz. 405, Starhemberg to Kaunitz, 26 March 1764.

Austerlitz, his entertainments included Czech folk music and dances.[83] His command of Latin was clearly flawless, and he had at least a smattering of English, which he studied intensely in 1733.[84] Above all, he was thoroughly grounded in German. His father had already considered German his "native language" and directed Schwanau to make sure young Wenzel Anton was well grounded in German grammar.[85] In maturity, he commanded an elegant and fluid Chancellery German whose stylistic polish, by the standards of the day, leaps immediately to the fore. So strong was Kaunitz's support of German as a language of government communication as early as 1761, that some Hungarian historians have even regarded him as the true father of Joseph II's notorious German language ordinance of the 1780s.[86] He also believed strongly in government support of "native" artists and intellectuals, and wanted to draw the great names of the German intellectual world to Vienna – which he considered the "capital" of Germany. And most of all, as the famous German philologist and philosopher, Ernst Platner, reported: "he forces all who have a German tongue to speak German."[87] Kaunitz can, therefore, not be understood in any cultural context except the broad cosmopolitan one which he embodied so well.

However, the most puzzling dimension of Kaunitz's character and the source of some of the most caustic anecdotes about his eccentricities concerned his demeanor. By some accounts, Kaunitz could be a pompous and difficult man. Peers and superiors, in particular, found his comportment cool and even offensive. He could be extremely blunt and frank, and could cut to the quick with a dry but biting sarcasm. He did not hesitate to speak his mind and lectured his aristocratic confrères sternly about laziness, opulence, superstition and incompetence. Easily offended, he could be callously offensive to others. He could exude an air of regal splendor and demand adherence to strictest etiquette, though himself notorious for his disregard of it. He was confident of his abilities, stubbornly autonomous, untouched by any false modesty, and not at all inclined to hide his light under a bushel. And as a last straw, he seemed to be vain and affected in appearance and dress. This is the Kaunitz that

---

[83] Khevenhüller-Metsch III, 253.

[84] Klingenstein, *Aufstieg des Hauses Kaunitz*, pp. 298–299.   [85] *Ibid.*, pp. 211–212.

[86] Éva H. Balázs, *Bécs és Pest-Buda a régi századvégen, 1765–1800* (Budapest, 1987), p. 73 and her "La Hongrie dans l'empire des Habsbourg au XVIIIe siècle: une société à deux visages," in Roland Mortier and Hervé Hasquin, eds., *Etudes sur le XVIIIe siècle*, Vol. XV, *Unité et diversité de l'empire des Habsbourg à la fin du XVIIIe siècle* (Brussels, 1988), p. 78.

[87] HHStA, Staatskanzlei: Wissenschaft und Kunst, Karton 1, Platner to (?), 29 May 1787. Cf. Heinrich von Srbik, "Ein Charakterbild des Staatskanzlers Kaunitz aus dem Nicolaischen Kreis", *ΕΠΙΤΥΜΒΙΟΝ: H. Swoboda dargebracht* (Reichenberg, 1927).

emerges from the reports of the society of privilege – from a king of Prussia or a Prussian ambassador, from an Austrian Court Chamberlain or a high-born minister of the crown.[88]

Yet when we look at the reports of Kaunitz's friends, his subordinates or employees, the reports of artists and intellectuals, of craftsmen and impresarios, a completely different picture emerges. A member of Kaunitz's household could recall only an attractive man of moderation, honest, sincere, conscientious and tolerant – a man who was invariably kind, gracious and affable with others and was regarded highly by the common man.[89] The gracious and congenial host of virtually nightly *assemblés* is also the subject of Karl Zinzendorf's diaries, where descriptions of Kaunitz's eccentricities are distinctly conspicuous by their complete absence.[90] Voltaire, whom Kaunitz never met personally, heard only of the latter's charm and wit in Paris during 1750–1753.[91] Mozart could report only how cordial, sympathetic and amiable Kaunitz had been to him;[92] Jean-Etienne Liotard that he could not have been better received.[93] Platner discovered an "extraordinary" man of great mental and physical energy even in old age whom narrow-minded and short-sighted people easily misunderstood. He found anecdotes of purported eccentricities to be sheer fabrications, and discerned only an indulgent, understanding and generous father and grandfather. The air of pride and condescension, Platner noted, was reserved for the aristocracy who had nothing but "their titles, orders and riches"; the pleasant, unaffected and agreeable face was reserved for "precisely a man of no rank."[94]

The key to this paradoxical behaviour becomes clear when it is supplemented with other well-known traits of Kaunitz. He tended to be aloof and had few really intimate friends. He was unpopular with his peers, but remained genuinely indifferent to this isolation. He offered his convictions with a calm certitude, even an air of infallibility. He never displayed an iota of personal greed, but he accepted gifts and honors

[88] Hinrichs, ed., *Friedrich der Grosse und Maria Theresia*, pp. 142–144; Leopold von Ranke, ed., "Maria Theresia, ihr Staat und ihr Hof im Jahre 1755. Aus den Papieren des Großkanzlers Fürst," in *Zur Geschichte von Oesterreich und Preußen zwischen den Friedens-schlüssen zu Aachen und Hubertusburg*, Vol. XXX of *Sämtliche Werke* (Leipzig, 1875), pp. 16–18; Khevenhüller-Metsch, *passim*, especially III, 70–74; IV, 11, 46, 76, 87; Wurzbach XI, 81–85; Hormayr, *Lebensbilder, passim*; N. William Wraxall, *Memoirs of the Courts of Berlin, Dresden, Warsaw and Vienna in the Years 1777, 1778 and 1779*, 2 Vols. (London, 1800), II, 465–495; Arnheim, "Urtheil," pp. 292–293; Charles Joseph, Prince de Ligne, *Fragments de l'histoire de ma vie*, ed. by Félicien Leuridant, 2 Vols. (Paris, 1927–1928), I, 144, 239–240; Platner as in fn. 87.   [89] Wurzbach XI, pp. 81–85.
[90] HHStA, Kabinettsarchiv: Zinzendorf Tagebuch, Vols. 6–25, *passim*.
[91] Besterman, ed., *Voltaire's Correspondence* XXIX, 205, No. 6187.
[92] Anderson, ed., *Letters of Mozart* II, 814–815, No. 459.
[93] Walter Koschatzky, "Jean-Etienne Liotard in Wien," in his *Maria Theresia und Ihre Zeit*, p. 315.   [94] Platner, as in fn. 87.

blithesomely.[95] What emerges here very clearly is the concept of *megalopsuchia* (self-respect) spelled out in Aristotle's *Nichomachean Ethics*. When we consider the emphasis Thomasius had placed on "Decorum" at Leipzig, and the degree to which this was defined in Aristotelian terms, these behavioral traits form a much more seamless whole with the broader eudemonist political postulates Kaunitz articulated than has heretofore been recognized. As for his putative eccentricities in dress, it might be added that Kaunitz was hardly as foppish as some reports make him out. He certainly prized being fashionable, and seemed invariably *au courant* with the latest word in sartorial elegance. But a careful study of Kaunitz iconography reveals no tendency to wild excess or affectation.[96]

If much of Kaunitz's behaviour can thus be traced to specific philosophic roots rather than arbitrary eccentricities, it nevertheless displays the kind of philosophical eclecticism which Peter Gay has identified as a central feature of the mind of the Enlightenment.[97] In that tradition, and, again, in the footsteps of Thomasius, Kaunitz also tended to denigrate metaphysics and inclined instead to a pragmatic utilitarianism. He was impressed with the sober practicality of the Dutch on his cavalier tour.[98] In Austrian Lombardy he was the driving force behind the effort to create a scientific and technical academy, and here, too, revealed a strong hostility to academic traditionalism.[99] In maturity, he was much taken with science and mechanics,[100] prided himself on being able to carry on technical conversations with experts, fêted scientists who toured through Vienna,[101] and generally had a very high respect for professionals of every kind. Indeed, despite his skepticism and hard-boiled realism in virtually all political matters, experts who presented their case with an air of professional assurance were most likely to be able to deceive him. An unscrupulous art dealer was able to pass off a forged Correggio on him and, as we shall see, numerous project mongers were not only successfully able to get his ear but also his backing, sometimes with wretched results.[102]

[95] Novotny, *Staatskanzler Kaunitz*, *passim*.

[96] See, for example, the portraits by Bernardo Belloto, Jakob Schmutzer, Johann Michael Millitz, Francesco Casanova, and Johann Nepomuk Steiner.

[97] Peter Gay, *The Enlightenment: An Interpretation*. Vol. I: *The Rise of Modern Paganism* (N.Y., 1966), pp. 160–166.

[98] Klingenstein, *Aufstieg des Hauses Kaunitz*, pp. 232–238; Arneth, "Biographie", pp. 20–22.

[99] Franco Venturi, *Settecento riformatore*. Vol. V: *L'Italia dei lumi (1764–1790)*, Part 1: *La rivoluzione di Corsica. Le grandi carestie degli anni sessanta. La Lombardia delle riforme* (Turin, 1987), pp. 769–773.

[100] MZA, Rodinný archiv Kouniců, Carton 3, various undated notes on mechanical and scientific matters.

[101] HHStA, Kabinettsarchiv: Zinzendorf Tagebuch, 3 and 7 June 1761.

[102] Schlichtegroll I, 143–144, 146–147; Wurzbach XI, pp. 82–83; Karniel, *Toleranzpolitik*, p. 285.

Where historians have most readily recognized Kaunitz as a child of the Enlightenment, however, is in the realm of religion. Typically, he has been called a "rabid anti-clerical and probable atheist"[103] – a judgement which certainly reflected the sentiment in the Vatican, where he was known as "il ministro eretico".[104] This facile judgement needs some qualification. We know that Kaunitz's father belonged to that circle of progressive politicians who recognized the economically retarding features of the Counter-Reformation and inclined in the direction of limiting the secular power of the Church. By no means impious or irreverent, the movement was an integral aspect of the so-called "Catholic Enlightenment". That young Kaunitz was nurtured in this tradition becomes evident from his university and cavalier tour reading.[105] He could chuckle at the irreverent comments about Catholic pieties of young English noblemen, and he seems to have been critical of clerical opulence whenever he encountered it.[106] Yet even as this negative position on the temporal power of the Church radicalized over the years, it never involved questioning the dogmatic premise of Catholicism. That he went out of his way to assure the pious Maria Theresia of his scrupulous observance of liturgical precepts[107] may not be very meaningful, but his dutiful adherence to the externals of the faith after her death went well beyond what might have been necessary to keep up mere appearances.[108] Kaunitz's role in the posthumous publication of the apologia for reform Catholicism by his friend and assistant, Friedrich Binder, remains unclear,[109] but the confessional commitment in the parish church at Austerlitz that Kaunitz commissioned is thoroughly unambiguous. In short, there is no evidence which allows us to conclude that Kaunitz was a freethinker or atheist. In this connection, the parallel assertion that Kaunitz was a Freemason is also difficult to confirm. Later Masonic sources which allude to a Count Kaunitz probably refer to one of Kaunitz's sons, and a police report in the 1790s explicitly affirms that he was not a Mason.[110] The one Masonic source which categorically claims

---

[103] T. C. W. Blanning, *Joseph II and Enlightened Despotism* (London, 1970), p. 23; a similar description ("Spirito volterriano e irreligioso") in Franco Valsecchi, *L'assolutismo illuminato in Austria e in Lombardia*, 2 Vols. (Bologna, 1931–1934), I, 46.

[104] Schlichtegroll I, 155.

[105] Klingenstein, *Aufstieg des Hauses Kaunitz*, pp. 94–95, 179, 242.

[106] *Ibid.*, pp. 240–242.   [107] Arneth, *Maria Theresia* IX, 138.

[108] Schlichtegroll I, 144; Wurzbach XI, 81.

[109] Friedrich Binder von Kriegelstein, *Philosophische Schriften*, 2 Vols., ed. by August Veith Schittlersberg (Vienna and Prague, 1783).

[110] Novotny, "Staatskanzler Fürst Kaunitz," p. 206; Eugen Lennhof, *Die Freimaurer* (Vienna, 1929, reprinted 1981), p. 118; Erich Kaforka, "Der Kampf zwischen Aufklärern und Obskuranten in Wien" (unpublished Ph.D. dissertation, University of Vienna, 1931), p. 22; Edith Schwarz, "Die Freimaurer in Österreich, vor allem in Wien, unter Kaiser Franz II., 1792–1809" (unpublished Ph.D. dissertation, University of Vienna, 1940), p. 86.

"Count Kaunitz" was inducted into the Order in Vienna on 7 March 1743[111] must be referring to his father, Maximilian Ulrich, since Kaunitz was on his Turin embassy during this whole period.

Similarly, while Kaunitz's intellectual debt to Western Enlightenment thinkers is relatively obvious, he seldom acknowledged specific thinkers in his memoranda, and a personal contact with specific individuals in these philosophical circles is also difficult to ascertain. During his French embassy, he sought out the salons of Mmes. Geoffrin, Blondel and Dupin, and remained full of affectionate nostalgia for the experience for decades thereafter, corresponding with these salon matrons, and lavishly entertaining Mme. Geoffrin when the latter visited Vienna in 1766.[112] There was, however, no substantive intellectual exchange with any of the famous French *philosophes*. Kaunitz was an avid collector of French books, one of the first subscribers to the *Encyclopédie* and an enthusiastic reader of Voltaire.[113] Other elements of French Enlightenment thought are also clearly recognizable in Kaunitz's arguments and policies, but specific personal links again appear to be absent. Here again, the common view that Kaunitz was an incurable francophile tends to distort our understanding of the Viennese milieu within which he operated.

Though the subject still needs scholarly investigation, there appears to have been a dramatic turn to a broad cosmopolitan literacy in Austrian aristocratic circles in the second half of the eighteenth century, and the strong French component may very well have been the result of the closer and broader contacts with France as a result of the French alliance beginning with the Seven Years War. We get a glimpse of such channels of literary transmission from the correspondence between Kaunitz's friend, Giacomo Durazzo, and the Parisian poet and dramatist, Charles Simon Favart. The latter not only forwarded theatrical materials to Vienna, but acted as Durazzo's "literary agent," keeping him advised of all Parisian publications and fulfilling book orders where requested.[114] From the diary

---

[111] Gustav Kuess and Bernhard Scheichelbauer, *200 Jahre Freimaurerei in Österreich* (Vienna, 1959), pp. 19–21.

[112] MZA, Rodinný archiv Kounicŭ, Carton 5, Mme. Blondel to Kaunitz, 1 September 1753, 18 June 1767, 24 February 1768, 20 December 1780; Carton 11, Mme. Geoffrin to Kaunitz, 24 March 1767, 27 April 1768; Carton 15, Kaunitz to Mme. Geoffrin, 9 March 1767. HHStA, Sonstige Sammlungen: Grosse Korrespondenz, Fasz. 405, Kaunitz to Mme. Blondel, 31 July 1774. HHStA, Kabinettsarchiv: Zinzendorf Tagebuch, 4 October 1766, 26 January 1767. Cf. Novotny, *Staatskanzler Kaunitz*, pp. 66–67.

[113] MZA, Rodinný archiv Kounicŭ, Carton 5, book order from Carl Wilhelm Ettinger in Gotha, 7 April 1787; Carton 15, notes copied from Voltaire's works, n.d.; Schlichtegroll I, 146; Wurzbach XI, 82.

[114] Charles Simon Favart, *Mémoires et correspondance littéraires, dramatiques et anecdotiques*, 3 Vols. (Paris, 1808, reprinted Geneva, 1970), I, II, *passim*; Favart as "agent littéraire," I, 7, Durazzo's request to be kept informed on all publications, I, 86.

of the young Count Karl Zinzendorf, who arrived in Vienna in 1761, we get a clear picture of just how *au courant* Viennese high society was with an amazingly broad spectrum of Western (and especially French) books. Voltaire and the *Encyclopédie* were apparently common currency with both men and women at social gatherings,[115] and new books appeared to be passed from hand to hand, and avidly devoured by each in turn.[116] From the sheer range of titles, from politics and philosophy, through science to erotica, it would appear that whatever censorship restrictions might have existed for the broader public, there seemed to be virtually no restrictions on the reading of the elites.[117]

Kaunitz, therefore, did not have a peculiarly francophile mind, but was only part of the cosmopolitan culture of his century with its international French face. English authors also figured prominently in this constellation. Thus, for example, we find that when the British ambassador, Sir Robert Murray Keith, presented Karl Zinzendorf with a copy of Adam Smith's *Wealth of Nations*, he was surprised to discover a week later that Kaunitz had not only already read it, but was prepared to engage in a lively debate on the value of labor in net product.[118] Similarly, tangential comments by Kaunitz make clear a wide familiarity with German cameralist thinkers ranging from Justi to Schlözer and Bielfeld, while his association with Italian *illuministi* is much clearer still. To begin with, there was his fruitful friendship with Durazzo and Calzabigi, both of whom considered themselves citizens of good standing in the republic of letters, and were as responsible as anyone for keeping Kaunitz up with latest intellectual developments. In addition, Kaunitz was not only familiar with the outpourings of the *Il Caffè* group, but often much influenced by their thought. Many of its most prominent members found service in the Austrian administration of Milan, or were granted academic engagements thanks to Kaunitz. These included the leading political economists of their day, Pietro Verri and Alfonso Longo, the historian and economist, Gianrinaldo Carli, the influential social reformer and philosopher, Cesare Beccaria, the outstanding poet, Giuseppe Parini, and above all, the

---

[115] Some typical examples: HHStA, Kabinettsarchiv: Zinzendorf Tagebuch, Vol. 6, 16 March 1761, Vol. 11, 5 October 1766, Vol. 17, 7 January 1772.

[116] Thus, for example, Zinzendorf received Arthur Young from Kaunitz's seventeen-year-old (!) daughter, and Rousseau from Princess Kinsky. *Ibid.*, Vol. 7, 10 May 1762, Vol. 8, 8 April 1763.

[117] Customs officials, Ludwig Zinzendorf advised his brother Karl, searched the bags but not the pockets of nobles. Casual mention of friends and relatives in high places would also guarantee "a more gentle treatment" when importing forbidden books. DOZA, Handschriften, Vol. 64, Ludwig Zinzendorf to Karl Zinzendorf, 8 September 1766.

[118] HHStA, Kabinettsarchiv: Zinzendorf Tagebuch, Vol. 22, 6 and 15 March 1778. On Kaunitz's efforts to get English works translated cf. DOZA, Handschriften, Vol. 65, Ludwig Zinzendorf to Karl Zinzendorf, 25 January 1769.

mathematician and encyclopedic philosophe, Paolo Frisi, whose erudition Kaunitz especially prized.[119]

Whatever his relationship with or debt to specific *philosophes*, however, the important point is that Kaunitz felt himself to be one of them. He certainly explicitly called himself a *"philosophe"* and insisted he had the right to do so because he was interested in "public enlightenment and the abolition of harmful prejudices for the sake of humanity."[120] In the pursuit of this goal, there was no dramatic dichotomy between the personality and mind of Kaunitz – between the public and private man. Philosophical eclectic, realist, skeptic and pragmatist, individualist and humanist, confident of his worth, he understood the active political life to be one of conscientious public service. The eudemonistic emphases of the cameralist tradition already found strong expression in Kaunitz as early as his cavalier tour. He bitterly admonished rulers guilty of public neglect, considered the "exploitation and desecration" of common people the root of all underdevelopment, praised those princes who did justice to their subjects by not saddling them with excessive taxes and burdens, and lavished praise and respect on individual enterprise.[121] Civic responsibility and individual dignity, in brief, were the personal motto and social prescription articulated by both the youth and the octogenarian who could look back from the perspective of 1794 and affirm it was "a matter of common knowledge" that he had always believed in the primacy of domestic policy.

[119] Adam Wandruszka, *Österreich und Italien im 18. Jahrhundert* (Vienna, 1963), pp. 59–83; Venturi, *Settecento riformatore*, V/1, 769–773.
[120] HHStA, Staatskanzlei: Wissenschaft und Kunst, Karton 1, Kaunitz to de Silva, 29 March 1769.   [121] Klingenstein, *Aufstieg des Hauses Kaunitz*, pp. 234–235.

2   Chancellor of State

The office which Kaunitz assumed in May 1753 was a relatively new one. The creation of a specific ministry, charged with the conduct of "foreign affairs and confidential dynastic matters," had occurred only in February 1742.[1] Of course, ministries in the modern sense did not exist in eighteenth-century Austria. The monarch remained the final instance of executive as well as legislative authority. Ministers were simply heads of specific departments of the central government's administrative machinery.[2] The German title, Court Chancellor (*Hofkanzler*), is therefore a much more accurate description of a minister's functions. In the Habsburg Monarchy of the eighteenth century there were numerous such Court Chancellors responsible for a variety of executive departments, all with different regional jurisdictions: Austria, Bohemia, Hungary, Transylvania or the Holy Roman Empire. The creation of a Court Chancellery (*Hofkanzlei*) in 1742 whose agenda brought together the private affairs of the dynasty, or "Haus" – in this case the House of Habsburg – with the conduct of all diplomatic relations (which in eighteenth-century German were called "Staatssachen"), thus eventually saddled the ministry with the colourful name of "House, Court and State Chancellery" (*Haus-, Hof- und Staatskanzlei*). Almost from the beginning this unwieldy title was abbreviated to Chancellery of State (*Staatskanzlei*), and the minister himself was generally referred to as Chancellor of State (*Staatskanzler*).

More explicitly ministerial forms of government emerged in the eighteenth century as part of the general trend towards professionalism and bureaucratization from the previously more conciliar forms of decision-making. Among the by-products of this development was the

---

[1] *ÖZV* I/3, 479–485; II/1/i, 77–79; see also Grete Klingenstein, "Institutionelle Aspekte der Österreichischen Aussenpolitik im 18. Jahrhundert," in Erich Zöllner, ed., *Diplomatie und Aussenpolitik Österreichs* (Vienna, 1977), pp. 82–86; and Erwin Matsch, *Der Auswärtige Dienst von Österreich(-Ungarn), 1720–1920* (Vienna, Cologne and Graz, 1986), pp. 51, 181.

[2] Otto Hintze, "Die Entstehung der modernen Staatsministerien," in *Staat und Verfassung: Gesammelte Abhandlungen zur allgemeinen Verfassungsgeschichte*, 2nd ed., Gerhard Oestreichs, ed. (Göttingen, 1962), pp. 275–320.

increasing tendency to segregate government business into discrete areas of ministerial competence. This kind of strict division into exclusive spheres of ministerial responsibility, however, was a trend that had not yet reached its full development. Older, conciliar forms and assumptions about government decision-making still overlapped with emerging ministerial specialization in the eighteenth century, and this, in turn, substantially defined the nature of ministerial competence once more modern ad-ministrative forms began to take shape. This was particularly true for the new Habsburg foreign ministry created in 1742. It inherited many of its assumptions about spheres of competence from its conciliar predecessor. What is more, conciliar foreign-policy decision-making did not cease with the establishment of a formal foreign ministry. The two forms overlapped for some years, and only after two decades could the ministry largely extinguish the competence of its conciliar rival.

However, the range of competence exercised by the new Chancellery of State owed much to the agenda deemed appropriate to its conciliar predecessor. While this involved the great issues of foreign policy first and foremost, this was certainly not exclusively so. Foreign-policy decisions required a comprehensive view of the dynasty's whole patrimony, and because no similar pan-monarchic domestic body existed in the Habsburg Monarchy, those domestic concerns which bore upon foreign-policy decisions relevant to the patrimony as a whole had by necessity to be discussed in the same body. This domestic perspective was not only inherited but refined by the Chancellery of State under Kaunitz. With the growth of other domestic ministries with the same professional ethos as the new foreign ministry, of course, this domestic perspective could easily be conceived as unwarranted interference by the foreign minister in the affairs of other ministries. Finding an appropriate structure whereby the domestic influence of the new foreign minister could be safeguarded was thus no easy matter, but, in the absence of a truly pan-monarchical domestic administration, it was imperative that such a mechanism be found to lend dynastic decision-making professional coherence and direction. Naturally, this enhanced the authority of the nominal foreign minister to such a degree that it easily aroused the jealousy of his ministerial colleagues – and, indeed, occasionally even made the monarch uneasy. It is therefore not surprising that this comprehensive view of the Chancellery of State did not survive Kaunitz. No subsequent foreign minister, including Metter-nich, wielded the kind of domestic influence that Kaunitz did. While it lasted, however, it became a central feature of Habsburg enlightened absolutism.

The evolution of the Habsburg Foreign Ministry

The conduct of foreign relations had been since medieval times the exclusive prerogative of the sovereign. In practice, naturally, few decisions were taken by the monarch without consulting trusted advisers. But in 1498 when Emperor Maximilian I, under pressure from the Estates of the Holy Roman Empire, was compelled to create a formal body for the purpose, called the Imperial Aulic Council (*Reichs-Hofrat*), its very genesis made the Emperor reluctant to lay any serious diplomatic business before it. In 1518 he formally affirmed that the "personal, confidential, great matters of the Emperor" – what was often picturesquely called the "arcana" of the dynasty – were to remain his exclusive preserve. He would continue to make decisions in this area either by himself or in confidential consultation with a few hand-picked advisors.[3] In the 1520s these consultations became institutionalized by the formation of a Privy Council (*Geheimer Rat*) to advise the monarch on "confidential great matters," and by 1541 the Privy Council enjoyed explicit precedence over the Aulic Council.[4] Its membership consisted of the Grand Master of the Household (*Obersthofmeister*), the Seneschal or Grand Court Marshall (*Obersthofmarschall*), the Vice-Chancellor of the Holy Roman Empire (*Reichsvizekanzler*) and one or two others who enjoyed the trust of the Emperor. Diplomatic correspondence and other paper work was handled through the Imperial Vice-Chancellor's office, the Imperial Chancellery (*Reichskanzlei*), and in this way he came to be regarded as the functional Habsburg foreign minister.[5]

However, as membership in the body began to grow, it became an increasingly unwieldy instrument. What is more, as the power of the Holy Roman Emperor continued to decline in the sixteenth century and the Habsburgs began to look to their own hereditary territories as the basis of their European power, the transaction of all foreign affairs through the Imperial Chancellery proved not always to serve the real interests of the dynasty.[6] Accordingly, Emperor Ferdinand II created a new chancellery in 1620 for his Austrian hereditary provinces called the Austrian Court Chancellery (*Österreichische Hofkanzlei*). The new chancellery, however, did not simply have territorial administrative responsibilities as did its

---

[3] *ÖZV* I/1, 23–29; I/2, 84–91.
[4] Eduard Rosenthal, "Die Behördeorganisation Kaiser Ferdinands I.: Das Vorbild der Verwaltungsorganisation in den deutschen Territorien," *AÖG* LXIX (1877), 55–93; 228–232.
[5] *ÖZV* I/1, 44–52; cf. Lothar Gross, *Die Geschichte der deutschen Reichshofkanzlei von 1559 bis 1806* (Vienna, 1933); Matsch, *Auswärtige Dienst*, pp. 33–37.
[6] Klaus Müller, *Das kaiserliche Gesandtschaftswesen im Jahrhundert nach dem Westfälischen Frieden (1648–1740)* (Bonn, 1976), p. 22.

sister chancelleries for the Kingdoms of Bohemia and Hungary; it was also charged with the conduct of the private affairs of the dynasty and a number of heraldic ceremonial functions.[7] This rather peculiar commission, which reflected well the ambivalence of Habsburg Emperors towards the Holy Roman Empire as a whole on the one hand and their own hereditary lands on the other, created distinctions which in early modern times were not easy to make. It is therefore not surprising that a rivalry between the Austrian Court Chancellery and the Imperial Chancellery soon grew up. The ensuing bureaucratic dispute over conduct of the diplomatic correspondence was not to be decided for a century.[8]

During this time, the Privy Council became so unwieldy – reaching a total membership of 150 by 1700 – that in 1699 Emperor Leopold I selected some key members of it and created a new limited advisory body, calling it the Privy Conference (*Geheime Konferenz*). Again the agenda of this body was potentially very broad, and it was by no means confined to foreign policy. After being briefly abolished under Joseph I, the Privy Conference was reinstated and its membership set at nine.[9] In the meantime, the struggle between the Imperial Chancellery and the Austrian Court Chancellery for control of the diplomatic correspondence came to a climax. In the course of the seventeenth century, the advantage swung from the former to the latter. Indeed, when Leopold first formed the Privy Conference, the Imperial Vice-Chancellor was conspicuous by his absence from it. Much of this decline was due to the fact that the Imperial Chancellery served not only the Emperor but also the official permanent Imperial Chancellor, the Elector of Mainz, who was not always pro-Habsburg. However, the unimpeachable loyalty of three successive Imperial Vice-Chancellors at the end of the century, Leopold Wilhelm Königsegg (1669–1694), Gottlieb Windischgraetz (1694–1695) and Dominik Andreas Kaunitz (1698–1705), managed to reverse this trend. By the end of Leopold's reign the Imperial Chancellery was more firmly in control of the administration of foreign affairs.[10]

All this changed dramatically in 1705. In that year the immensely ambitious and, from the Habsburg point of view, not always friendly Archbishop and Elector of Mainz, Lothar Franz von Schönborn, managed to secure for his nephew, Friedrich Karl, the influential post of Imperial

---

[7] *ÖZV* I/1, 150–160; Matsch, p. 37.
[8] Lothar Gross, "Der Kampf zwischen Reichskanzlei und österreichischer Hofkanzlei um die Führung der auswärtigen Geschäfte," *Historische Vierteljahrschrift* XXII (1924–1925), 279–312.
[9] Henry Frederick Schwarz, *The Imperial Privy Council in the Seventeenth Century* (Cambridge and London, 1943); *ÖZV* I/1, 53–67, I/3, 52–55; Bérenger, *Finances et absolutisme autrichien*, pp. 37–42.
[10] Gross, "Der Kampf", pp. 301–306; Gross, *Reichshofkanzlei*, pp. 58–62.

Vice-Chancellor. Shortly after his arrival in Vienna, Schönborn discovered that the Habsburgs had no intention of entrusting their diplomatic correspondence to a "foreigner", and Imperial Vice-Chancellor became an empty title.[11] The incumbent Austrian Court Chancellor, Count Philipp Ludwig Sinzendorf, was quick to seize the opportunity. In October 1706, he managed to extract an imperial order giving his Chancellery full control of all diplomatic matters with the exception of those that specifically concerned the Holy Roman Empire.[12] From this point onwards it was therefore the Austrian Court Chancellor who was regarded as the functional Habsburg foreign minister. As the volume of diplomatic paperwork grew, aides were taken on, and by 1720 the whole Chancellery had to be reorganized. Not only was a separate department created for foreign affairs, but this department so preoccupied the Chancellor that he no longer had time for the Chancellery's domestic administrative and judicial business. These tasks were therefore shunted off to a subsidiary or "second" Austrian Court Chancellor.[13]

Yet Philipp Ludwig Sinzendorf was still far from being a foreign minister in any full sense of the word because the Privy Conference, of which he was undoubtedly the most vital member, still remained the real forum of diplomatic decision-making. Even the administration of diplomatic correspondence was not the exclusive prerogative of the Austrian Court Chancellor. Affairs of the Empire, as we have seen, remained in the domain of the Imperial Vice-Chancellor. The centuries of conflict with the Ottoman Turks had led in 1610 to the transfer of diplomatic correspondence with the Porte to the War Ministry (Hofkriegsrat), and to this in time had been added all Russian transactions as well.[14] Moreover, other ministries could and did correspond with foreign diplomats or with Habsburg agents abroad in areas they felt concerned them. Men such as Prince Eugene of Savoy, head of the War Ministry, virtually conducted a secret diplomacy of their own.[15] Hence, the only person with an overview of the full spectrum of foreign affairs remained the monarch himself.

Nevertheless, the department for foreign affairs in the Austrian Court Chancellery continued to develop. In 1726, a new aide was appointed with the upgraded title of "Secretary of State" (Staatssekretär), Johann Christoph von Bartenstein. He not only took on additional clerical staff, enlarging his department, but even more significantly he became the

---

[11] Hugo Hantsch, *Reichsvizekanzler Friedrich Karl Graf von Schönborn (1674–1746)* (Augsburg, 1929).   [12] *ÖZV* I/3, 43–49.

[13] *Ibid.*, I/1, 167–169; Matsch, pp. 47–50.

[14] *Ibid.*, I/1, 169, 268; II/1/i, 78–79, 241; II/2, 421–422; Müller, *Gesandschaftswesen*, pp. 24, 30–31.

[15] Müller, *Gesandschaftswesen*, pp. 33–59; Max Braubach, *Die Geheimdiplomatie des Prinzen Eugen von Savoyen* (Cologne and Opladen, 1962).

permanent secretary of the Privy Conference.[16] It was from this position that Bartenstein gradually rose to be the commanding figure of Habsburg foreign policy until the arrival of Kaunitz in 1753. As the years wore on he not only came to dominate his corrupt, obese, ageing minister, Sinzendorf, but for that matter the other members of the Privy Conference as well. By the time Maria Theresia ascended the throne in the fall of 1740, the entire Conference presented a picture of creeping senility. Sinzendorf was only a few weeks from his sixty-ninth birthday; Count Gundacker Thomas Starhemberg, who had made his reputation in finance and treasury matters a generation earlier, was about to turn seventy-seven; Count Alois Raymund Harrach, who had a long diplomatic career filled with failures behind him, was seventy-one; and Count Lothar Joseph Königsegg, who clung to his Conference post despite having been a failure as head of the War Ministry and an even more dismal failure as a general in the recently terminated Turkish war, was sixty-seven.[17] Confronted by such an array of grizzled patriarchs, it is little wonder that the young queen was later to complain that she lacked reliable advisers upon her accession,[18] or that she leaned increasingly on Bartenstein, whose influence grew accordingly.[19]

The basic core of the Privy Conference was occasionally augmented by other ministers when discussions touched upon matters within the purview of their offices. Among these was the War Minister, Alois Harrach's dilatory younger brother, Johann Joseph Harrach, aged sixty-two. In addition, two more energetic and younger men were sometimes also asked to attend Privy Conference meetings. The first of these was the Bohemian Court Chancellor, Count Philipp Joseph Kinsky, whose willful and stubborn arrogance did not endear him to anyone. The second was the man who was destined to enjoy the most extended term in office of any Imperial Vice-Chancellor in history, Count Rudolf Colloredo.[20] After the ill-fated Schönborn's departure from Vienna in 1734, he was replaced by the suitably pro-Austrian Count Johann Adolf Metsch, but the latter was

---

[16] Klingenstein, "Institutionelle Aspekte," p. 20. On Bartenstein see Alfred Ritter von Arneth, "Johann Christoph Bartenstein und seine Zeit," *AÖG* XLVI (1871), 1–214; Max Braubach, "Johann Christoph Bartensteins Herkunft und Anfänge," *MIÖG* LXI (1953), 99–149; and Joseph Hrazky, "Johann Christoph Bartenstein, der Staatsmann und Erzieher," *MÖStA* XI (1958), 221–251.

[17] On the Privy Conference at the accession of Maria Theresia see Arneth, *Maria Theresia* I, 90–91; Eugen Guglia, *Maria Theresia, Ihr Leben und Ihre Regierung*, 2 Vols. (Munich, 1917), I, 53–56.

[18] Joseph Kallbrunner, ed., *Kaiserin Maria Theresias Politisches Testament* (Munich, 1952), pp. 26–27. Originally published by Alfred Ritter von Arneth, ed., "Zwei Denkschriften Maria Theresias," *AÖG* XLVII (1871), 267–355. I have used the Kallbrunner edition throughout.

[19] Khevenhüller-Metsch II, 163; Kallbrunner, ed., *Testament*, pp. 27–28.

[20] Khevenhüller-Metsch I, 176.

so infirm that Colloredo had to be assigned the role of "substitute" Vice-Chancellor in 1737. Colloredo was an intellectual mediocrity who probably could not have recovered the Imperial Vice-Chancellor's influence on foreign policy under the best of circumstances. As it was, the election of Charles Albert of Bavaria as Holy Roman Emperor dashed any expectation Colloredo had of becoming Imperial Vice-Chancellor upon Metsch's death. In the event he had to wait until the election of Maria Theresia's husband, Francis Stephen of Lorraine, to the imperial dignity before finally being made Imperial Vice-Chancellor.[21] By that time, however, a proper foreign ministry had already been established in Vienna, and the piper who called the tune there was Bartenstein.

The measure of Bartenstein's dominance became apparent upon the death of his nominal department head, Sinzendorf, in February 1742. The foreign affairs department was formally severed from the Austrian Court Chancellery and raised to the level of Court Chancellery on its own.[22] This was the culmination of a development that had become increasingly apparent since Bartenstein's appointment as Secretary of State, and was now in any case made virtually imperative by the termination of the long integral connection between the Holy Roman Empire and the lands of the House of Habsburg at the death of Emperor Charles VI in 1740. Bartenstein's ascendancy was further enhanced by the queen's choice for the official new post of Chancellor of State: Count Corifz Anton Ulfeld. Ulfeld had had a modest diplomatic career and was last Habsburg ambassador at Constantinople. He returned to Vienna and was made a member of the Privy Conference in August 1741. Although there were a number of aspirants for the new post of Chancellor of State, Ulfeld was fortunate to be Bartenstein's candidate for the job. Unfortunately, this reflected not so much Bartenstein's confidence in Ulfeld's ability as his conviction of Ulfeld's mediocrity and malleability, and the years were to prove the Secretary of State's assessment entirely correct.[23] In short, for the next eleven years, Bartenstein continued to be the functional foreign minister of the Monarchy.

During this time death began to claim the hoary veterans of the Privy Conference one by one. Sinzendorf was followed by Alois Harrach in November 1742 and by Gundacker Starhemberg in July 1745. Since Kinsky and Colloredo were occasionally asked to attend the Privy

---

[21] On Colloredo see *ADB* IV, 420–422; Wurzbach II, 430; *NDB* III, 329. When the Privy Conference met to discuss issues related to the Holy Roman Empire, it was called an "Imperial Conference" (*Reichsconferenz*).   [22] *ÖZV* I/3, 479–485; II/1/i, 77–79.

[23] William Coxe, *History of the House of Austria*, reprint of 3rd ed., of London 1847, 3 Vols. (N.Y., 1971), III, 344–345; Egbert Silva-Tarouca, *Der Mentor der Kaiserin* (Zürich, Leipzig and Vienna, 1960), p. 103.

Conference, but widely not considered as actual members of the body until later,[24] the Conference was reduced to the tractable Ulfeld and the well-nigh fossilized Königsegg, with, of course, the ubiquitous Bartenstein as secretary. The new members that had to be recruited to fill the gaps did little to raise the intellectual level of the Conference. On 11 September 1743, Maria Theresia appointed two men: Count Friedrich August Harrach, son of the recently deceased Alois Harrach and soon to be Bohemian Court Chancellor as well, a dyed-in-the-wool reactionary who had a reputation for snobbish mimicry and sarcasm;[25] and Count Ferdinand Leopold Herberstein, a brusque misanthrope who had been forced on Maria Theresia by her father in 1738 as Master of her Household and who had attempted every psychological ploy short of extortion to be named to the Privy Conference.[26] Perhaps fortunately for all concerned, Herberstein died unexpectedly within a year, and was replaced on 31 August 1744 by a young personal favourite of the sovereign, Count Johann Joseph Khevenhüller-Metsch. A quintessential and well-connected courtier, he had begun a diplomatic career that showed rapid progress. But in 1742, he received the ceremonial post of Grand Court Marshall, whence he was to rise to become Grand Chamberlain and finally, the highest ceremonial post at court, Grand Master of the Household. Though a man of some modest talent, in these honorific offices which were beginning to lose their political significance precisely at this time, Khevenhüller was to congeal into a model of ritualistic immutability.[27]

The limitations of its members notwithstanding, the political agenda of the Privy Conference actually expanded during the decade of the 1740s. While, as we have seen, domestic questions were never precluded in discussions of the Privy Conference or its predecessor, the Privy Council, certain issues had become the preserve of specific other forums. In 1697 Leopold I had even created a parallel council explicitly for domestic affairs (*Deputation*), which began as a temporary expedient but soon became a permanent fixture. Its membership overlapped with the Privy Conference, but as the body met with decreasing frequency by the 1730s and 1740s, its agenda gradually migrated to the Privy Conference.[28] Under Charles VI a separate Conference for Finance (*Finanzkonferenz*) was established in 1716.[29] This body was increasingly dominated by Gundacker Starhemberg, who was also a member of the Privy Conference. In the spring of 1741, one

[24] Khevenhüller-Metsch I, 176.   [25] *Ibid.*, II, 328–329, I, 176.
[26] *Ibid.*, I, 176, 226–228.   [27] On Khevenhüller in general see *Ibid.*, I, 74–98.
[28] ÖZV II/1/i, 176; H. I. Bidermann, *Geschichte der österreichischen Gesamt-Staats-Idee*, 2 Vols. (Innsbruck, 1867, 1889), I, 11, 42.
[29] ÖZV I/1, 127–129; Friedrich Mensi, *Die Finanzen Österreichs von 1701 bis 1740* (Vienna, 1890), pp. 460–466; Carl Schwabe von Waisenfreund, *Versuch einer Geschichte des österreichischen Staats-, Credits- und Schuldenwesens* (Vienna, 1866), pp. 131–133.

of Maria Theresia's first administrative adjustments was to abolish this
Conference and delegate its responsibilities into the hands of Starhemberg
alone.[30] In effect, however, Starhemberg brought the business of the
Conference for Finance into the Privy Conference. Thus, when extended
consultations were necessary in such critical questions as the financing of
the War of the Austrian Succession, it was through an ad hoc commission
of the Privy Conference that Starhemberg undertook the task.[31] On the
whole, therefore, the Privy Conference drew more and more domestic
questions into its purview until these became a substantial portion of its
agenda by the late 1740s.[32] The culmination, of course, was the famous
debate over the great reforms instigated by Haugwitz, which was held on
28 January 1748.[33]

This was the Privy Conference as Kaunitz knew it when, in November
1747, having already been selected as Habsburg delegate for the upcoming
peace conference at Aachen, he began to attend meetings. He was not, as
yet, a formal member of the Conference but rather was merely drawn into
those discussions that touched on his upcoming diplomatic mission. Upon
his return from the peace conference, however, he was formally made a full
member of the Conference to replace the recently deceased Kinsky. His
first appearance on the morning of Tuesday, 25 February 1749, set the tone
of Kaunitz's future relationship with his fellow Conference members. He
arrived affecting his usual dress and manner and immediately became the
butt of Harrach's savage mimicry. But Kaunitz, "being the first to speak,
expressed himself in such eloquent and judicious terms" that Harrach's
"astonishment and surprise was evident in his face and in his whole
manner."[34] In short, though the junior member of the Privy Conference in
age, rank and seniority, Kaunitz's intellectual domination of the body was
evident from the outset, and was, furthermore, confirmed by the famous
foreign policy discussions which ensued that spring and summer. After the
sudden death of Harrach in June of the same year, moreover, Kaunitz's
predominance was only strengthened by the appointment of a successor.
He was the rough and ready Field Marshall Count Károly Batthyány, who
after an illustrious military career had recently been made guardian and
head of the household (Ajo) of the young crown prince, Joseph.[35] Not a

---

[30] ÖZV I/1, 137; I/3, 420; II/1/i, 51–52.   [31] Ibid., II/1/i, 52.
[32] Ibid., II/1/i, 176; II/2, 159, 170.   [33] See below, p. 77.
[34] Khevenhüller-Metsch II, 191, 296–298, 303–304.
[35] Ladislaus Batthyany-Strattmann, "Karl Joseph Batthyany, Feldmarschall und Erzieher
Erzherzog Josephs," in Kulturabteilung des Amtes der Burgenländischen Landes-
regierung, ed., Maria Theresia als Königin von Ungarn (Eisenstadt, 1980), pp. 63–66. Cf.
Sidonie Binder, "Carl Joseph Batthyany" (unpublished Ph.D. dissertation, University of
Vienna, 1976).

man of great intellectual sophistication, he in any case tended to be sympathetic to Kaunitz's "new" foreign policy.[36] The triumph of Kaunitz's ideas were signaled at the end of 1749 by his promotion to the Order of the Golden Fleece and by his appointment as ambassador to Paris.[37] The implementation of the first phase of his broader diplomatic objectives there may have proved unexpectedly difficult, but by then he had already established the widespread reputation of being the most talented minister of the court of Vienna. There is reason to believe that even before his actual departure for France in the fall of 1750, Maria Theresia had already decided to make Kaunitz Chancellor of State at the first suitable opportunity.[38] When that opportunity came, Kaunitz was in Paris. On 8 December 1751, the Grand Master of the Household and senior Privy Conference member, Königsegg, died, vacating a post to which Ulfeld could be honourably removed. It was obviously a matter that had long been pre-determined and required little reflection, for a scant two days later the Empress's private secretary, Ignaz Koch, sent the formal written offer on to Kaunitz. If the subsequent appointment of Kaunitz proved not to be a simple operation, it was due primarily to difficulties caused by Kaunitz himself.

Upon penetrating the screen of all the ostensible personal reasons why Kaunitz now said he could not accept Maria Theresia's offer, it is clear that he was perfectly well prepared to take on the office for which he had been destined from childhood, but only on his own terms. These conditions included a free hand to reorganize the Chancellery of State the way he saw fit, and, above all, the removal of Bartenstein.[39] Kaunitz conceded that Bartenstein's long-range foreign policy aims did not diverge dramatically from his own, but the methods were too subjective, inefficient and unprofessional. Lacking diplomatic experience, Bartenstein had never mastered the art of political tact in his communications with foreign representatives. Despite the enormous growth of paperwork over the previous two decades, he still tended to draft minutes and memoranda

---

[36] Jacob Strieder, *Kritische Forschungen zur österreichischen Politik vom Aachener Frieden bis zum Beginne des Siebenjährigen Krieges* (Leipzig, 1906), pp. 26–27; Arneth, "Biographie," pp. 184–185; Arneth, *Maria Theresia* IV, 282–283.

[37] Kaunitz was raised to the Order of the Golden Fleece on 30 November 1749 (Khevenhüller-Metsch II, 371). He was known to be ambassador-designate as early as June 1749. Gaston von Pettenegg, ed., *Ludwig und Karl, Grafen und Herren von Zinzendorf: Ihre Selbstbiographien* (Vienna, 1879), p. 58.

[38] Arneth, *Maria Theresia* IV, 321; Beer, ed., *Aufzeichnungen des Grafen William Bentinck*, pp. 45, 71, 87, 117–119; Schlitter, ed., *Correspondance*, p. 56; Grete Klingenstein, "Kaunitz kontra Bartenstein: Zur Geschichte der Staatskanzlei in den Jahren 1749–1753," in Heinrich Fichtenau and Erich Zöllner, eds., *Beitrage zur neueren Geschichte Österreichs* (Vienna, Cologne and Graz, 1974), pp. 243–263; and her *Aufstieg des Hauses Kaunitz*, pp. 284–301. [39] Schlitter, ed., *Correspondance*, pp. 155–162.

personally. Nor, finally, did the maintenance of his personal influence stop short of highly questionable practices in his capacity as secretary of the Privy Conference which smacked of the kind of highly personal and arbitrary method of conducting business that Kaunitz wished to change.[40] The prospect that the aged Bartenstein would dutifully submit himself to the new order of things in the Chancellery of State and become the obedient executor of Kaunitz's will was virtually nil. A recalcitrant rival would be an impediment to the free hand which Kaunitz demanded. If Kaunitz were to accept the commission proffered him, one thing was certain: "two pipers in one tavern [were] intolerable!"[41]

As for the ministry itself, Kaunitz wished to make it a much smoother-running and more efficient instrument than he perceived it to be. In his view, order had to replace the chaos that governed the filing and retrieval system, since, without ready access to all relevant information, no clear overview could emerge. Secondly, the Chancellor should not permit himself to get bogged down in bureaucratic detail, and for this reason must be prepared to entrust much preliminary work to relatively independent, eminently skilled and highly ranked subordinates. Further, the ministry should serve as a sort of apprenticeship training center for future diplomats and ministry officials in order to cultivate a hitherto unknown sense of professionalism and *esprit de corps*. But above all, Kaunitz was concerned that policies emerging from the ministry should always reflect the interests of the state and not the arbitrary prejudices of the minister. All foreign-policy decision-making processes had therefore to be thoroughly co-ordinated so that the Habsburg Monarchy always spoke with one clear and consistent voice, and all officials were animated by the same spirit. Difficult though it may have been for Maria Theresia to evict Bartenstein from the Foreign Ministry, the outcome was never in doubt. The formal announcement came on Maria Theresia's thirty-sixth birthday and Kaunitz assumed the office which he was to hold longer than anyone else in the history of the Habsburg Empire.[42]

In the wake of administrative reforms which saw the amalgamation of the Austrian and Bohemian Court Chancelleries into a single Directory,[43] the personnel of the Austrian Court Chancellery were removed from their former offices to the Bohemian Court Chancellery, which, in turn, was remodeled and enlarged accordingly. The old Austrian Court Chancellery on the Ballhausplatz now became the new headquarters of the Chancellery of State. The building, originally designed by Johann Lukas von

---

[40] For Kaunitz's critique of Bartenstein see *Ibid.*, pp. 4–5, 9–10, 13–14, 158–162. Cf. Klingenstein, "Kaunitz kontra Bartenstein", pp. 248–249.
[41] Khevenhüller-Metsch III, 109–111.   [42] *Ibid.*, III, 108, 111.
[43] See below, pp. 77–78.

Hildebrandt in 1717 and first erected in 1719, was now completely remodeled according to Kaunitz's specifications by the court architect Nicolà Pacassi (1716–1790). The interior renovations took some six months to complete, and it was not until mid-November 1753 that Kaunitz was actually able to move into his new office. In the interim he worked out of his private residence, remodeling not only the building but also the structure of his ministry.[44]

The changes which Kaunitz wrought in the Chancellery of State were at once evolutionary and revolutionary. The growth of the foreign affairs department of the Austrian Court Chancellery into an autonomous ministry had carried in its train a gradual growth of personnel. Initially, the Chancellor availed himself of the one aulic councillor to help handle diplomatic dispatches. Then, in the reorganization of the Chancellery in 1720, Sinzendorf was formally assigned two aulic councillors as aides: Johann Georg von Buol and Johann Theodor Imbsen. The very next year a filing clerk with the title of *Registrator*, Anton von Schneller, was added. When Buol died in 1726 and was succeeded by Bartenstein, the latter added a formal dispatch clerk (*Expeditor*), two chancery clerks (*Kanzelist*) and two document drafters (*Konzipist*). Though Imbsen took on another post in 1734 and his position as second aulic councillor in the foreign affairs department was thereafter left vacant, subordinate personnel continued to grow.[45] By the time the foreign affairs department became the independent Chancellory of State in 1742, Maria Theresia personally approved the employment of as many as eight chancery clerks and an assistant *Registrator*.[46] But by 1749, only six of the possible eight clerks had been engaged,[47] and thereafter no personnel changes occurred until the arrival of Kaunitz. Yet, despite this very limited growth in staff, the work load of the ministry continued to expand. In 1742, diplomatic correspondence with Russia was transferred from the War Ministry; and in 1749 massive reforms of the central administration brought the Chancellery of State numerous ceremonial functions, including the issuing of patents of nobility.[48]

Kaunitz made remarkably few changes in the support staff, though there was some internal realignment and rationalization. All but three staff members were retained and five new ones were hired. The old filing clerk,

---

[44] HHStA, Staatskanzlei: Vorträge, Karton 73, Kaunitz to Maria Theresia, 1 November 1753. The exterior renovations were not completed until 1767. Cf. Hans Aurenhammer, "Der Bau und seine Geschichte," in Bundespressedienst, ed., *Schicksal eines Hauses* (Vienna, 1987), pp. 5–11.   [45] Klingenstein, "Institutionelle Aspekte," pp. 82–85.
[46] *ÖZV* I/3, 480.
[47] HHStA, Staatskanzlei: Vorträge, Karton 61, "Lista" of Staatskanzlei personnel, n.d. (June 1749).   [48] *ÖZV* I/i, 169, 268; II/2, 280–281.

Schneller, kept his title and salary but was otherwise retired. The assistant *Registrator*, Otto Reiner Kesaer, became the sole officer responsible for filing. The dispatch clerk, Johann von Wasserthal, who had served since 1730, retained his post. The new post of archivist (*Archivar*), which Kaunitz created, was given to a newcomer, Elias von Hochstättern. Two of the six chancery clerks were let go, and a third was shifted to the drafting section as a *Konzipist*. Of the now three document drafters one was let go and two new ones were hired, making a total of four *Konzipisten* and four chancery clerks. To these was added a ninth who could perform either duty according to need. Kaunitz also retained the two servants employed by the Chancellery.[49]

More radical were the changes Kaunitz made at the executive level. Since the removal of Ulfeld and Bartenstein had at one fell swoop eliminated all senior officials in the Foreign Ministry, Kaunitz could begin with a blank slate. He himself naturally replaced Ulfeld, but in the place of Bartenstein he engaged no fewer than four senior officials. His old friend and private secretary, Friedrich von Binder, Edler von Kriegelstein, became his principal aide,[50] with the official title of State Referendary (*Staatsreferendar*). In effect, he became deputy minister and chief executive officer of the Chancellery of State. Under Binder, Kaunitz placed three department heads modeled after the *Premiers Commis* of the French Foreign Ministry, with the double title of Aulic Councillors and Privy State Officials (*Hofräte und Geheime Staatsoffiziale*). The first, Adeodat Joseph Philipp du Beyne de Malechamps, who had been a secretary at the Habsburg legation in Turin, was placed in charge of Italian matters. The second, Johann Jakob von Dorn, who had been employed in the Belgian administration, took charge of affairs that concerned the Low Countries. The third, Henrich Gabriel von Collenbach, who had hitherto been in the service of the Prince of Nassau, became a generalist.[51] These men brought an air of modern professionalism to a ministry that had hitherto been the preserve of a rugged individualist, and foreign diplomats were quick to notice the change. Formal access to the Chancellor was fixed to a single day of the week, Tuesday, and his subordinates were not available at all. Nor could the diplomatic corps easily turn to individual members of the Privy Conference, since Kaunitz insisted that all business had to be funneled through his office. Above all, the old scope for easy corruption seemed to have disappeared overnight. Even the hostile Prussian envoy, Carl Joseph Maximilian Freiherr von Fürst und Kupferberg, had to admit: "not only

---

[49] The list of the staff in 1753 is published in Khevenhüller-Metsch III, 373.
[50] On Binder see *ADB* II, 648–649; Wurzbach I, 399; *NDB* II, 244.
[51] Khevenhüller-Metsch III, 110. Cf. Klingenstein, "Institutionelle Aspekte," pp. 87–90.

is Count Kaunitz himself incorruptible and much too circumspect to betray himself; even his subordinates are inaccessible. "[52]

The arrival of Kaunitz in the Chancellery of State also brought administrative changes that touched on other organs of the central government. The Foreign Ministry's spheres of competence were rationalized when the continued anomaly of having diplomatic correspondence with the Porte handled by the war ministry was finally eliminated.[53] In order to achieve maximum co-ordination, Kaunitz further instituted formal regular correspondence with ministries which up to this point had been merely ad hoc and personal.[54] Most significant of all, however, were the changes in the relationship between the foreign ministry and the Privy Conference. By 1753 the Privy Conference had once again become a forum predominantly, though not exclusively, concerned with foreign affairs. As an aftermath of the Haugwitz reforms a new Domestic Conference (*Conferenz in Internis*) had been established in 1749 under Friedrich Harrach. However, the purpose of this new instance seemed to be less the supervision of all domestic business, than the provision of an honourable way to get rid of Harrach, and a convenient technicality to strip the Privy Conference of its domestic responsibilities.[55] Harrach died within a few months, and by 1753 the *Conferenz in Internis* had largely atrophied, so that some seepage of domestic business back to the Privy Conference had occurred. But, by and large, the Privy Conference had lost most substantive input in domestic affairs permanently; its foreign policy prerogatives were to follow in short order – in no small measure thanks to Kaunitz.

The first Privy Conference that Kaunitz attended in his capacity as Chancellor of State took place on 23 May 1753. The meeting was called not in the usual manner, by the senior member's official " council announcer ", but by an impersonal memo containing time, place and agenda, circulated by Kaunitz. Bartenstein's old position of secretary to the conference was now filled by Kaunitz's trusted Referendary, Binder, and, in addition, Privy State Official du Beyne de Malechamps was also brought along as the expert on the matters under discussion. Together the three completely changed the framework of the meeting. Kaunitz himself spoke – perhaps one should even say pontificated – for over two hours, and his subsequent report to the Empress was anything if not thorough. It included the minutes of the meeting itself and, all relevant supplementary documents, as well as his personal recommendations, the full file totaling 120 pages.[56] The

[52] Ranke, ed., "Maria Theresia," pp. 16–17.   [53] *ÖZV* II/2, 421–422.
[54] HHStA, Staatskanzlei: Notenwechsel. (The entire archival holding under this heading was established by Kaunitz.)   [55] See below, pp. 77–78.
[56] HHStA, Staatskanzlei: Vorträge, Karton 72, Konferenzprotokoll, Kaunitz report and enclosures, 23 May 1753. On the manner in which the conference was called and conducted see Khevenhüller-Metsch III, 114–115.

report sufficiently impressed the Empress to make her want to see her new minister in action first hand. A little over two weeks later, she indicated she would attend a Conference personally, and for this reason the meeting place was moved from the senior member's residence to the imperial palace. Kaunitz was delayed at an ambassadorial reception, and by the time the meeting finally began the Empress had already left. But Kaunitz seized the precedent and insisted that henceforth all meetings were to be held at the palace, not at private residences.[57] Finally, although the Privy Conference continued to meet with some regularity well into the Seven Years' War, it was increasingly Kaunitz who determined precisely when these meetings would occur. Regularly scheduled meetings as such did not exist, their frequency began to decline, and other conference members soon found occasion to complain bitterly about the growing "despotism"[58] of the Chancellor of State.

The outbreak of the Seven Years' War brought about a further increment in the Chancellery of State's sphere of competence when the Court Chancellery in Vienna, which administered the Austrian Nether- lands and the Duchy of Milan, was abolished and its two departments, a so-called Netherlands Council (*Niederländischer Rat*) and an Italian– Spanish Council (*Italien-Spanischer Rat*), were absorbed by Kaunitz's ministry. The very titles of these departments bespoke the old Spanish succession claims of Charles VI, and much of the Emperor's foreign policy reflected the preeminence of this ministry in the internecine strife over policy determination with its sister Chancelleries of Austria, Bohemia and Hungary. The principal premise of the shift in foreign policy for which Kaunitz was responsible was that the interests of the Austrian– Bohemian–Hungarian heart of the Habsburg state had to take precedence over those of the peripheral lands. These areas were, in Kaunitz's view, ultimately dispensable, and therefore should under no circumstances dictate policy to or drain resources from the real nucleus of the Monarchy. The Austrian Netherlands was often the object of diplomatic barter, of which the arrangement with the French in 1757 and the Bavarian exchange projects are only the most prominent, and the Duchy of Milan was seen by Kaunitz primarily as a defensive outpost.[59] If it was thus publicly announced that the Belgian and Italian Councils had been transferred to the Chancellery of State "because of the existing connection between foreign policy and the domestic affairs of these two lands,"[60] it meant that the administration of these territories was being redefined. No longer an

[57] Khevenhüller-Metsch III, 119.   [58] *Ibid.*, IV, 123.
[59] HHStA, Italien-Spanischer Rat: Lombardei Korrespondenz, Fasz. 110, Kaunitz to Cristiani, 17 April 1758.
[60] *ÖZV* II/2, 422–423; Khevenhüller-Metsch IV, 319–321.

integral part of the domestic heart of the Monarchy, they now became lands associated *sui generis* with the integrated core of the Habsburg Monarchy.

In the wake of this creation of Belgian and Italian Departments within the Chancellery of State, finally, Kaunitz undertook further personnel changes within his ministry. Dorn and du Beyne de Malechamp were raised to referendary rank and given charge of the new departments, though the latter resigned over a personal squabble at the end of 1761, and was replaced by his former assistant, the able Venetian, Luigi Giusti.[61] This created two vacancies at the State Official level. These Kaunitz filled with Christian Augustin von Beck and the former archivist, Hochstättern. The new archivist, Joseph von Sperges, was to rise rapidly in Kaunitz's estimation, and was himself to become head of the Italian Department after 1766.[62] The ancient dispatch clerk, Wasserthal, was retired and replaced by Anton Johann von Hilleprand. The number of document drafters was reduced to three – Friedrich Knoch, Tobias Harrer and Andreas Tassara – but the number of chancery clerks raised to nine – Niclas Appel, Friedrich Wilhelm von Dorn, Franz Anton Hayden, Joseph Haydfeld, Joseph Keßler, Adam von Lebzelter, Emanuel Tassara and Adam Winckler. A third servant was also taken on.[63]

From War Cabinet to Council of State

In the summer of 1756 a new advisory body came into existence which elevated Kaunitz to the position, if not the title, of a prime minister. As the diplomatic crisis which was to lead to the outbreak of the Seven Years War intensified, and it became apparent that Frederick II of Prussia was beginning mobilization preparations, it was determined to set up a ministerial council in Vienna to co-ordinate the diplomatic, military and financial measures that might prove necessary under the circumstances. Accordingly, the Empress formally ordered Kaunitz to begin chairing a weekly meeting of *ex officio* ministers consisting of Friedrich von

---

[61] Carlo Capra, "Luigi Giusti e il dipartimento d'Italia a Vienna, 1757–1766," *Società e storia* No. 15 (1982), 63–64; Sonja Scharrer, "Il dipartimento d'Italia a Vienna, persone e istituzioni" (unpublished Ph.D. dissertation, Università Cattolica of Milan, 1991), pp. 28–225.

[62] Franz Pascher, "Joseph Freiherr von Sperges auf Palenz und Reisdorf (1725–1791)" (unpublished Ph.D. dissertation, University of Vienna, 1965). A brief summary of this thesis has been published under the same title in *ÖGL* X (1966), 539–549.

[63] HHStA, Staatskanzlei: Vorträge, Karton 85, "Status der Kays. König. Geheimen Hof und Staatskanzlei" (December 1759); HHStA, Österreichische Akten: Österreich-Staat, Fasz. 3, Hof- und Staatskanzlei personnel list, 1 August 1760.

Haugwitz, president of the Central Directory, Field Marshall Reinhard Wilhelm von Neipperg, representing the War Ministry, and Franz Ludwig von Salburg, the head of the Commissariat for Military Supply.[64] While these meetings were styled "conferences" (*Conferenzen*), they were in no way related to the meetings of the Privy Conference. The former was meant to be a co-ordinating body for the war effort – in short, a War Cabinet – the latter was the old omnibus policy advisory council.[65] Unfortunately, this has led to much confusion in the historical literature about the activities of the Privy Conference in the Seven Years War, and Kaunitz's ministerial "conference" will be described here as the "War Cabinet" for the sake of clarity.[66] In the first meeting which took place on 8 July, it was decided to meet every Sunday at the very least, and more frequently if necessary. Meetings were to be held at the Chancellery of State, with secretarial functions to be performed by Kaunitz's staff. Binder and one of the ministry's State Officials were to be present on every occasion, but since du Beyne de Malechamps, Dorn and Collenbach rotated this duty amongst themselves, all three became integrally connected with the Cabinet.[67] Because the War Cabinet was a conference of ministers to co-ordinate the war effort, it is also frequently called the "military conference" in the literature. This too leads to confusion, for there was yet a third "conference" which met occasionally during the Seven Years War, made up entirely of War Ministry officials and field commanders which was a military conference in the stricter sense of the word. This Military Conference, too, was attended and dominated by Kaunitz.[68]

The distinction between the Privy Conference and the War Cabinet was blurred all the more the subsequent spring when, following the disastrous battle of Prague, Maria Theresia ordered them to meet together on a regular basis. This became the "*Conferenz in Mixtis*," as Khevenhüller picturesquely described it,[69] and it lasted only from May until December 1757. Broadening consultation in this way tended, in the event, to retard

---

[64] HHStA, Staatskanzlei: Vorträge, Karton 78, Maria Theresia to Kaunitz, Kaunitz to Maria Theresia, 6 July 1756. The former was published in Arneth, *Maria Theresia* V, 467.

[65] See the attendance notations on the minutes of the War Cabinet, HHStA, Staatskanzlei: Vorträge, Kartons 78ff., *passim*.

[66] Schlitter confuses a Privy Conference meeting of 17 July with a War Cabinet meeting of 18 July (Khevenhüller-Metsch IV, 176), and remains ambiguous about the distinction throughout the notes in this volume. Many War Cabinet minutes are therefore printed by him (pp. 176–413), even though Khevenhüller, who was only a member of the Privy Conference, did not attend most of them.

[67] HHStA, Staatskanzlei: Vorträge, Karton 78, "Protocollum der Zusammentretung," 8 July 1756. Cf. Max Lehmann, "Urkundliche Beiträge zur Geschichte des Jahres 1756," *MIÖG* XVI (1895), 487–491.

[68] Schlitter has also published an example of minutes from these conferences. Khevenhüller-Metsch IV, 302–312.   [69] *Ibid.*, p. 91.

rather than expedite matters. Kaunitz grew increasingly impatient and irritable. Following the setback at the battle of Leuthen, he seized the opportunity to demand that Privy Conference members henceforth be banned from meetings of the War Cabinet. His official pretext was that Imperial Vice-Chancellor Colloredo, who had adopted an extremely faint-hearted approach to the war,[70] could not give unprejudiced advice on purely domestic matters such as the proper co-ordination of the war effort, and hence had to be excluded for this reason. In order not to give personal offence, however, his fellow Privy Conference members had to share this banishment. In reality, it seems clear that Kaunitz found working with the members of the Privy Conference, with most of whom he was in any case on poor personal terms, more and more burdensome. For the Privy Conference, having found most domestic matters excluded from its purview, soon discovered that important diplomatic matters were increasingly being kept from its members as well.[71] The handwriting on the wall was obvious; the Privy Conference was losing its political significance.

In the War Cabinet itself, it was not long before economic difficulties began to create problems. Within a very short period of time after the outbreak of the war, even the most pessimistic projections on the cost of conducting the conflict were being surpassed, while not even the revenues calculated for peace-time could be collected in full. This naturally led to bitter debates on the most efficacious financial expedients to be adopted. In these debates the traditional mercantilistic exponents of extraordinary taxation tended to enjoy more influence than advocates of more novel public credit schemes. Kaunitz, as a fervent supporter of the latter option, found himself outmaneuvered at virtually every turn, but he failed to be persuaded. He thus concluded that the fiscal expedients he favoured had not received an adequate hearing in any impartial forum, and that laudable and promising measures were therefore being rejected without good cause.[72]

Kaunitz's exasperation at the adoption of measures which, in his opinion, had not received due unprejudiced consideration was enhanced by the shortcomings of the War Cabinet which were becoming even more apparent. Every minister in the cabinet was so enormously preoccupied and sometimes even overwhelmed with the minutiae of his own department that he often had to absent himself from meetings. Hence, Haugwitz often sent Count Johann Chotek, the Directory's second-in-command, in his stead, and Salburg even more frequently was represented by his sub-ordinate, Count Joseph Maria Wilczek.[73] As economic problems

---

[70] Arneth, *Maria Theresia* V, 11–12.
[71] Khevenhüller-Metsch IV, 138, 143–144, V, 103.   [72] See below, pp. 118–125.
[73] HHStA, Staatskanzlei: Vorträge, Kartons 78–91, War Cabinet minutes, *passim*.

worsened, the Empress decided to add more ministers with economic portfolios to the cabinet. First came the chairman of the Vienna City Bank, Rudolf Chotek. He was soon joined by the head of the treasury (*Hofkammer*), Count Karl Ferdinand Königsegg.[74] These men in turn often insisted on bringing along Aulic Councillors from their own departments to buttress arguments they would make in meetings.[75] All this led less to the anticipated efficiency of the War Cabinet and more to interministerial strife. It was natural that ministers should seek to exonerate their own departments and to blame others when problems arose. Natural temperamental differences – Neipperg, for example, tended to be languid and Haugwitz impetuous[76] – escalated into bitter ministerial struggles. Mutual recriminations meant that some ministers – Haugwitz and Salburg, for example – were barely on speaking terms. In the desperate quest for more effective administration, departments seemed almost haphazardly to be shifted from one minister to another. In January 1757, Haugwitz wrested the Department of Mines and Minerals from Königsegg only to lose it to Rudolf Chotek in August 1758. The dispute between Haugwitz and Salburg led to the latter's resignation at the end of 1757 and the incorporation of his whole ministry into Haugwitz's Central Directory, creating even more confusion and chaos in that department.[77] On the whole, therefore, the War Cabinet did not produce the desired co-ordination and co-operation, but rather, showed the shortcomings of a conference of *ex officio* ministers.

This made Kaunitz's task of chairing the War Cabinet more difficult and essentially thankless. Yet the burdens on himself and his ministry were overwhelming. In the effort to co-ordinate the war effort, the Chancellery of State, in addition to its normal diplomatic correspondence, was also responsible for harmonizing the military movements of the allies. Kaunitz carried on detailed operational correspondences with Austrian generals such as Browne, Charles of Lorraine, Daun, and Loudon as well as Imperial, French and Russian commanders. In addition, he was responsible for correspondence with Austrian military attachés at French, Russian and Swedish army headquarters; with special envoys such as General Adolf Nikolaus Buccow, who was sent to St. Petersburg with the express purpose of co-ordinating war plans; and with numerous special agents such as Johann Georg Grechtler, an Aulic Councillor in the War Ministry, who reported on obstacles to Kaunitz's idea of appointing

---

[74] *Ibid.*; Cf. Arneth, *Maria Theresia* V, 1–2, 467.
[75] HHStA, Staatskanzlei: Vorträge, Kartons 78–91, War Cabinet minutes, *passim*.
[76] Khevenhüller-Metsch IV, 142.
[77] *Ibid.*, p. 142; *ÖZV* II/1/i, 206–248. Cf. below, pp. 79–80.

Loudon field commander of the Austrian forces.[78] Further, imperial instructions to generals in the field – the so called "Cabinet Schreiben" – all originated in the Chancellery of State. Kaunitz either outlined or dictated the dispatches, which were drafted generally by Binder. These drafts were then proofread and corrected by Kaunitz personally and, after receiving royal approval, were sent off through the foreign ministry's dispatcher.[79]

By the summer of 1758, Kaunitz had reached the point where he felt that only fundamental changes could rescue this deteriorating situation. On 6 August, he submitted a report to Maria Theresia recommending the establishment of a permanent Domestic Conference (*Conferenz in Internis*) which would differ from the War Cabinet in certain very fundamental ways. Kaunitz envisioned the new conference as an advisory body only, not as a council of *ex officio* ministers. The Privy Conference could not serve for the purpose because experience had clearly demonstrated that its members did not have sufficient acquaintance with domestic matters. The War Cabinet had shown itself to be equally bankrupt. Its members were so burdened down with work that they tended to regard attendance at Cabinet meetings as an incidental chore, "where opinions can be expressed off-hand without great preparation or a thorough analysis of the points at issue." What was more, a conference of ex-officio ministers tended to assess proposals from the perspective of interministerial rivalries rather than on their own merits with the result that excellent ideas, such as the public credit schemes proposed by Kaunitz's protégé, Zinzendorf, did not get the fair hearing they deserved. Kaunitz therefore suggested that the new Domestic Conference consist of men whose only task would be the impartial assessment of all proposals with the aim of benefitting the Monarchy as a whole. Nevertheless, there would be two exceptions to the rule of banishing ministers from the new conference, and these would

---

[78] HHStA, Sonstige Sammlungen: Kriegsakten, Fasz. 413, Kaunitz–Browne correspondence, 1756–1757; Fasz. 413, 415, Kaunitz–Charles of Lorraine correspondence, 1756–1757; Fasz. 416–417, Kaunitz–Daun correspondence, 1757–1762; Fasz. 418–419, Kaunitz–Loudon correspondence, 1759–1762; Fasz. 411, Kaunitz–Prince Zweibrucken correspondence, 1758; Fasz. 426, Kaunitz correspondence with French Generals, 1756–1763; Fasz. 430, Kaunitz correspondence with Russian Generals, 1756–1761; Fasz. 427–428, Kaunitz correspondence with General von Kettler, Austrian military attaché at French headquarters, 1757–1763; Fasz. 431–433, Kaunitz correspondence with Generals Saint-André, Rall and others, Austrian military attachés at Russian headquarters, 1756–1760; Fasz. 434, Kaunitz correspondence with General Mednyanssky, Austrian military attaché at Swedish headquarters, 1757–1762; Fasz. 432, Kaunitz–Buccow correspondence, 1756–1759; Fasz. 425, Kaunitz–Grechtler correspondence, 1757–1761.
[79] HHStA, Sonstige Sammlungen: Kriegsakten, Fasz. 411–434, *passim*, secretarial notes and drafts, 1756–1763. Cf. below, pp. 262–263.

apply to those ministries whose very nature compelled them to take the larger over-view of the interests of the state – the Ministry of War and Kaunitz's own Chancellery of State. However, Kaunitz explicitly opposed the creation of an office of Prime Minister, not only because no suitable individual for such a post was at hand, but also because the Empress herself fulfilled this task most effectively.[80]

There was little enthusiasm for this plan on the part of the Emperor and the Empress in 1758: Francis Stephen may have regarded it as a potential circumscription of his growing influence in financial matters; Maria Theresia had allowed an earlier *Conferenz in Internis* under Harrach to atrophy precisely because she regarded Haugwitz's Central Directory as the appropriate body for such tasks.[81] But as the war dragged on with no clear end in sight, as the economic problems multiplied and as the administrative chaos intensified, the idea of fundamental structural reform once more surfaced. Haugwitz's Central Directory was assailed on all sides, and began to suffer set-backs in its spheres of competence.[82] Dissatisfaction with the workings of both the Privy Conference and the War Cabinet were also growing, and a reassessment of the whole conference system was ordered.[83] By the fall of 1760, Maria Theresia had come around to Kaunitz's view, and after some coaxing the Emperor became a convert as well. On 9 December 1760, Kaunitz reiterated his proposal of August 1758, and this time it received royal assent. Not unlike those of August 1758, Kaunitz's recommendations aimed at the creation of a permanent consultative council, called Council of State (*Staatsrat*), to analyze and debate whatever reforms might be recommended before they were adopted or rejected. Again, he stressed that members of the Council should have no other governmental responsibilities to distract them and that they should be under oath to give frank and unprejudiced assessments of the issues before them. Lack of co-ordination, lack of system, lack of basic premises had created a situation in which "a large number of things had been done detrimental to the welfare of the State, and an immense number of other things left undone which could have been advantageous to it." Kaunitz, with his Enlightenment faith in the dialectics of debate, believed that the advisory Council of State would be the answer to this problem.[84] To some extent, the idea was based on the concrete example of

---

[80] HHStA, Kabinettsarchiv: Staatsrat Präsidium, Karton 1, Kaunitz to Maria Theresia, 6 August 1758. Quoted in part in *ÖZV* II/3, 1–2.   [81] *ÖZV* II/1/i, 177–178.

[82] See below, pp. 80–82.

[83] *ÖZV* II/3, 2–3; II/1/i, 266; Arneth, *Maria Theresia* VII, 1–4.

[84] HHStA, Kabinettsarchiv: Staatsrat Präsidium, Karton 1, Kaunitz to Maria Theresia, 9 December 1760 (four copies, including original). Original draft and German translation in HHStA, Staatskanzlei: Vorträge, Karton 87. Additional copy in HHStA, Österreichische Akten: Österreich-Staat, Fasz. 3. Published in part in *ÖZV* II/3, 3–10.

the French *conseil d'état*, but, even more significantly, it mirrored the political philosophy of the *philosophes* who felt they could impart "enlightenment" to an absolute monarch precisely through such an advisory body.[85]

Since the entire proposal had been discussed orally for some weeks, royal assent was a mere formality. Indeed, the very next day letters of appointment were ready for five of the proposed six-member body. Apparently, Kaunitz and Maria Theresia had been discussing suitable candidates for some time, and among those considered were Rudolf Chotek, Ludwig Zinzendorf, and the authorized minister in Brussels, Karl Philipp Cobenzl. In the event it was determined that in addition to Kaunitz himself, the body was to consist of Haugwitz, who was to be chairman (*Erster dirigierender Staatsminister*), General Leopold Daun, Count Heinrich Cajetan Blümegen, an avid disciple of Haugwitz and intendant of Moravia, and the elderly Anton Stupan von Ehrenstein, a former Aulic Councillor in the Directory with the reputation of a conscientious, liberal but skeptical bureaucrat wary of grandiose schemes. The sixth member of the Council was appointed in January 1761, in the person of Aegid Freiherr von Borié, formerly a member of the Imperial Aulic Council and an ardent, energetic, though, at times, doctrinaire apologist for absolutism. The Council of State also received an Administrative Officer, Anton König von Kronburg, as well as two secretaries and two chancery clerks.[86]

The Empress had wished Kaunitz to submit a detailed organizational plan for the new council, but he recommended that this be the first item on the agenda for the Council of State itself.[87] Kaunitz also advised the Empress on salaries and support staff, so the two court secretaries and two chancery clerks were assigned to König's supervision. Finally, on Monday, 26 January 1761, the ceremonial opening of the Council of State took place in the presence of the Empress, the Emperor and the Emperor's brother, Prince Charles of Lorraine.[88] In his final proposal, Kaunitz abandoned the idea of making the head of the war ministry an *ex officio* member of the new council, and although an exception was made when Daun became War Minister for four years (1762–1766), thereafter the only minister to sit on the Council of State *ex officio* was the Chancellor of State.[89] This confirmed a formal domestic role for Kaunitz which he had informally occupied to varying degrees since his accession to the Chancellery of State in 1753.

[85] Gerald Oppenheimer, "Nation, Société, Loi, Représentation: Political Language and the Philosophes" (unpublished Ph.D. dissertation, University of Chicago, 1976).

[86] Arneth, *Maria Theresia* VII, 10–18; Carl Freiherr von Hock and Hermann Ignaz Bidermann, *Der österreichische Staatsrath (1760–1848)* (Vienna, 1879), pp. 11–12; ÖZV II/3, 12–15; Konrad Schünemann, *Österreichs Bevölkerungspolitik unter Maria Theresia* (Berlin, n.d.), pp. 16–30.   [87] ÖZV II/3, 10–11.   [88] *Ibid.*, pp. 14–15.

[89] *Ibid.*, II/1/i, 267–281; II/3, 11–26; Hock and Bidermann, *Staatsrath*, pp. 7–13.

From this point onwards, it was to be the Council of State that was to prove his principal, though by no means exclusive, forum for the articulation of domestic policy.

Kaunitz opened the first session with a brief speech on the nature and purpose of the Council of State and then presented his lengthy proposal on agenda and procedures for the body. The Council was to consist of a maximum of eight members, of whom a certain number had always to be of the knightly estate (mostly lesser gentry or recently knighted commoners). Lords would receive the title Minister of State (*Staatsminister*) and knights, the title Councillor of State (*Staatsrat*). Meetings would be held every Monday and Friday at court, at which the administrative officer would summarize the issues at hand and the members of the Council would then proceed to give their candid views, beginning with the Junior Councillor. The specific purpose of this procedure was to prevent any potential intimidation of knights by lords. In cases of serious disagreement, the entire file of opinions was to be recirculated and supplementary views solicited. The Monarch was then to draw the appropriate conclusions and enact the necessary decision with a so-called "imperial resolution". Maria Theresia and Francis Stephen would occasionally preside personally, and the crown prince, Joseph, also attended sessions with some regularity beginning in May 1761.[90] Other ministries and departments could be called to report to the Council, but under no circumstances would they ever be informed of the details of a Council debate, which were kept in strictest secrecy. These procedures were unanimously seconded by the members of the Council and immediately received royal assent, so that the body could begin work without delay.[91] As we shall see, Kaunitz also insisted on the adoption of an ideological framework for Council action, which, in effect, institutionalized the very principle of reform.[92]

It is perhaps not surprising that some of Haugwitz's protégés might impute personal ambition rather than concern for the public good to Kaunitz's insistence on a Council of State – as did the President of the Supreme Court of Moravia, Count Franz Anton Schrattenbach.[93] But the preposterous notion that the Council of State was an innocuous and impotent body – a "phantasmagoria" – to which Kaunitz could banish political adversaries, thus emasculating their power, defies comprehension.[94] The Council of State had no executive power, but it was the funnel through which all important legislative proposals went. Further, since it

---

[90] In the period 1761–1765 there were 210 such "royal" sessions. Khevenhüller-Metsch VI, 555–582.   [91] *ÖZV* II/3, 15–26.   [92] See below, pp. 83–84.

[93] *ÖZV* II/1/i, 280–281, fn. 1.

[94] This is the thesis of Friedrich Walter (*ÖZV* II/1/i, 272–278; "Kaunitz' Eintritt in die innere Politik. Ein Beitrag zur Geschichte der österreichischen Innenpolitik in den Jahren 1760/61," *MIÖG* XLVI (1932), 37–79; see pp. 45–51).

was a forum in which all proposed measures were subject to the dialectics of debate, it could make all options clear to the Monarch and its consensus would, in a wider sense, reflect the consensus of the entire society. In this sense, it can also be argued that the Council of State was the main legislative body of the Monarchy, even though legislation for the most part originated from organs of the executive branch, and that Kaunitz's fundamental principles were its ideological spearhead. Against the proponents of the traditional feudal corporate order as modified by the Counter-Reformation, the Council of State represented the one point of departure for policies devoted to the entire state.

It has also been argued the Council of State created a "check" (*Hemmung*) whose effect was to retard, rather than accelerate the workings of government.[95] There is certainly no doubt that a controlling instance of this sort, by debating the merits of proposed legislation, would obviously hamper precipitous implementation of measures, but in some ways the Council of State also accelerated legislation. Ministers of the crown who were at once grand seigneurs of the realm had effectively sabotaged fundamental structural reform for generations. By moving questions of policy up to a new forum dominated by committed reformers, traditional ministries were deprived of some of their freedom of action, and the time-honoured propensity for provincial and ministerial particularism was indeed "checked".

What is more, in some ways the Council of State was also a check on the crown. Against the proponents of a centralized Directory such as Haugwitz, intoxicated as they were by the Prussian model, the Council of State was designed to prevent the evolution of what has been aptly called an "irresponsible central executive,"[96] by hedging absolutism about with a check which would prevent it from crossing the thin line between absolute and arbitrary government. As Otto Hintze has observed, the Council of State was the principal safeguard that made the evolution of Prussian-style autocracy impossible in Austria.[97] The weakness of the Council of State was that its consensus did not bind the Monarch. The Monarch was expected to be "reasonable" – to recognize the efficacy of any given measure because of its inherent logic. By and large, Empress Maria Theresia lived up to this lofty ideal, but when a monarch like her

---

[95] *Ibid.* As a Nazi sympathizer, and enthusiast for the *Führerprinzip*, Walter felt that critical situations like the Seven Years War demanded dictatorial efficiency. As he put it, they "cried out for leadership by one will": "Eintritt," p. 43.

[96] Rosenberg, *Bureaucracy*, p. 22.

[97] Otto Hintze, "Der österreichische und der preussische Beamtenstaat im 17. und 18. Jahrhundert: Eine vergleichende Betrachtung," in his *Staat und Verfassung*, p. 345. Cf. Schünemann, *Bevölkerungspolitik*, pp. 16–18, and his "Die Wirtschaftspolitik Josephs II. in der Zeit seiner Mitregentschaft," *MIÖG* XLVII (1933), 15–16.

son, Joseph II, refused to do so, Kaunitz regarded it as an act of stubborn and willful despotism whose dire consequences for the entire social organism could not be underestimated.[98] The premise of this conception was the typical Enlightenment faith in rational man which may seem exceedingly naive in retrospect, but which was the lodestar of the intelligentsia of the eighteenth century. It would be unreasonable criticism to suggest that Kaunitz was unable to transcend his times.

By the end of the first year of the Council's activities, Maria Theresia was certainly persuaded that it performed to her entire satisfaction. First evidence of this came in April 1762 when the Empress approved additional secretarial and clerical appointments for the Council. The sentiment was confirmed in June when she decreed that henceforth members of the Council were to have precedence over all other ministers and department heads at court. König was at this juncture promoted to full Councillor of State status as well. At the same time she began to use the device of "honorary" appointments to the Council as a marks of special distinction at the court. The first recipients of these titular appointments were Binder and Koch.[99] As for Kaunitz, while the Council of State now gave him an official channel for input on domestic policy, it also served to ease his administrative burdens considerably. Though the Council did not bring an end to either the Privy Conference or the War Cabinet, the former's decline continued as it met with decreasing frequency,[100] and the latter was much unburdened when policy debates were removed to the new council and it was restricted to technical executive functions for the duration of the war.[101] Since the Council of State had its own referendary and staff, these developments therefore substantially lightened the work load on Kaunitz's Foreign Ministry officials, and thereafter the organizational adjustments which took place in the Chancellery of State resulted in very few new external responsibilities. The political position of the Chancellor himself, moreover, remained constant for the subsequent twenty years, though from Kaunitz's own viewpoint it was hardly an unchallenged station or an office without its problems.

[98] For Kaunitz's bitter assessment of Joseph, see his famous memorandum prepared for Leopold II in 1790, in Karl Otmar Freiherr von Aretin, *Heiliges Römisches Reich, 1776–1806: Reichsverfassung und Staatssouveränitat*, 2 Vols. (Wiesbaden, 1967), II, 204–205, No. 36.   [99] *ÖZV* II/1/i, 313; II/3, 32.

[100] See Khevenhüller's bitter complaints in Khevenhüller-Metsch IV–VIII, *passim*, especially V, 103.

[101] HHStA, Staatskanzlei: Vorträge, Kartons 88–91, War Cabinet minutes, *passim*.

Co-Regency adjustments

The death of Emperor Francis I in August 1765 radically changed the political situation in the Habsburg Monarchy. Beyond the fact that Maria Theresia herself was deeply affected by the sudden and unexpected death of her husband, the introduction of her son, Joseph II, as Co-Regent on 23 September 1765 created tensions which required Kaunitz to re-define the parameters of his activities. Although there were some areas of co-operation between Joseph and Kaunitz, it was not long before the new Emperor revealed some fundamental disagreements with the old Chancellor. In 1765, it must be remembered, Joseph was by no means a political novice. Having attended Council of State meetings regularly since that body's inception, he had certainly learned more than to recognize "the faces and wigs" of its members, as he claimed.[102] He had already submitted radical reform proposals in 1761[103] and 1763,[104] and it could not have come as a complete surprise when he did so again in his new capacity of Emperor at the close of 1765.[105] Joseph's ideas were diametrically opposed to those of Kaunitz both in tone and policy, and no matter how successfully Kaunitz defended his policies, he could not fail to be disturbed by the new wind that was blowing from the young Co-Regent.[106] Kaunitz's discomfiture was soon underscored when a major military memorandum he had submitted to Joseph in December 1765 was given the cold shoulder, so that he had cause to suspect that his influence was on the wane.[107] The deaths of two leading Council of State members, Haugwitz on 30 August 1765, and Daun on 5 February 1766, and the required resulting changes of personnel only added to these suspicions.

Joseph, unlike Kaunitz, had gotten along well with Daun and had adopted Daun's candidate for heir to the presidency of the War Ministry, Field Marshall Count Franz Moritz Lacy, as his own. In the event, Kaunitz was not even consulted on the appointment. Matters were in a sense even worse with the replacement for Haugwitz. Maria Theresia fastened upon the Austrian ambassador to France, Count Georg Adam Starhemberg,[108] who had been touted by Kaunitz as his own eventual

---

[102] *MTJC* III, 336. [103] *Ibid.*, I, 1–12.
[104] Derek Beales, "Joseph II's 'Rêveries'," *MÖStA* XXXIII (1980), 142–160.
[105] *MTJC* III, 335–361.
[106] Adolf Beer, ed., "Denkschriften des Fürsten Kaunitz," *AÖG* XLVIII (1872), 98–158.
[107] HHStA, Staatskanzlei: Vorträge, Karton 96, Kaunitz to Maria Theresia, 2 December 1765.
[108] On Starhemberg see Reinhard Eichwalder, "Georg Adam Fürst Starhemberg (1724–1807): Diplomat, Staatsmann und Grundherr" (unpublished Ph.D. dissertation, University of Vienna, 1969), a précis of which was published under the same title in *ÖGL* XV (1971), 199–201.

successor in the Chancellery of State – though there are clear indications this was done more for Maria Theresa's benefit than out of any conviction. Starhemberg's designation for the Council of State therefore left the impression that he was being moved one step closer to his ultimate destination, the Foreign Ministry. Starhemberg himself suspected this, thought he had detected imperial displeasure at the running of the foreign office, and, according to some sources, may actively have been intriguing for power.[109] Suspicions could only have been reinforced when, in November 1765, Starhemberg was raised to the rank of a prince of the Holy Roman Empire[110] – a dignity which was not bestowed on Kaunitz until he had been Chancellor of State for eleven years. Kaunitz's ill humour must have been apparent in the winter of 1766, for Maria Theresa went out of her way to emphasize her continued confidence in him. In early April, she bestowed the Grand Cross of the Order of St. Stephen on him – by special dispensation set in gold with diamonds and other gems valued by the Venetian ambassador at 20,000 Gulden – and presented him with an equally stunning gem-encrusted Grand Cross of the Military Order of Maria Theresa of which he was chancellor.[111] Yet, in the perspective of other events, these honours could be regarded as the type of gesture that was meant to sweeten and encourage retirement.

It was under these circumstances that Kaunitz received the news, on 27 April 1766, that his referendary on affairs of the Austrian Netherlands, Dorn, had suddenly and unexpectedly died at the age of forty-four. Five days later the referendary for Italian affairs, Giusti, was also dead. Kaunitz had been close to both men and was severely shaken by the twin blow. In addition, Binder was ailing and unable to continue fulfilling his exacting tasks. At one blow, therefore, all three referendaries of Kaunitz's Chancellery of State were removed, requiring a complete reshuffling of the Ministry. All these events made Kaunitz, as he put it, "reconsider a lot of things."[112] He had often noted that finding suitably qualified subordinates was an extremely difficult task,[113] and he had stated at the outset when assuming his office that if he ever detected the slightest lack of confidence in him on the part of his sovereign, he would resign.[114] There is little doubt there was scant motivation to engage in extensive personnel arrangements when the position of the minister himself was in doubt. After some

[109] DOZA, Handschriften, Vol. 64, Ludwig Zinzendorf to Karl Zinzendorf, 23 January and 26 February 1766. Cf. Arneth, *Maria Theresia* VII, 287–290, 298, 540–542; Derek Beales, *Joseph II*, Vol. I: *In the Shadow of Maria Theresia, 1741–1780* (Cambridge, 1987), pp. 143, 146.   [110] Khevenhüller-Metsch VI, 153–154.

[111] Arneth, *Maria Theresia* VII, 292–294, 542.   [112] *Ibid.*, 294–295.

[113] HHStA, Belgien: Vorträge, Fasz. 7, Kaunitz to Maria Theresia, 16 April 1757; Fasz. 8, Kaunitz to Maria Theresia, 28 July 1762.

[114] Schlitter, ed., *Correspondance*, p. 162.

reflection Kaunitz therefore wrote Maria Theresia on 4 June that he felt he was no longer in a position to train new staff or otherwise reorganize his ministry; as a result, he asked to be relieved of all his offices, including the essentially honorific one of Chancellor of the Maria Theresia Order. He recommended Starhemberg as successor to all his posts.[115]

The initial action of the shocked and deeply wounded Maria Theresia was to return the resignation to Kaunitz with the remark that she never wanted to hear that sort of thing again.[116] But in a series of subsequent highly emotional discussions filled with mutual reproaches, Kaunitz remained firm and the Empress finally consented to his retirement after Starhemberg and the new Chancellery of State staff had acquired sufficient exposure to run the ministry.[117] Kaunitz insisted that this period should not exceed two years, and in the interim the ministry should be run by an executive triumvirate. He would assume the title Supreme Chancellor of State, Starhemberg would become Chancellor, and Binder's replacement, Count Joseph Anton Pergen, would become Vice-Chancellor.[118] Starhemberg himself was reluctant to accept such an appointment[119] and both Maria Theresia and Joseph II firmly rejected the notion. Both Starhemberg and Pergen were to be content with the title State and Conference Minister (*Staats- und Conferenzminister*) – that is, membership in the Council of State and the Privy Conference – and Pergen's appointment was only titular.[120] Further, Kaunitz's resignation was not to be publicized, and he was to continue to discharge his duties as before.[121] After some weeks and with apparent reluctance, Kaunitz accepted this verdict and proceeded with the re-organization of his ministry.

Although Binder had officially retired from the Chancellery of State and had been promoted to the Council of State, he was such a close friend and long-time working colleague of Kaunitz that no one believed he was

---

[115] Adolf Beer, ed., *Joseph II., Leopold II. und Kaunitz: Ihr Briefwechsel* (Vienna, 1873), pp. 489–500. Cf. Khevenhüller-Metsch VI, 196–197, 446–448.

[116] HHStA, Staatskanzlei: Vorträge, Karton 97, Maria Theresia to Kaunitz, n.d. (August 1766). Cf. Beer, ed., *Joseph II., Leopold II. und Kaunitz*, pp. 501–503; Arneth, *Maria Theresia* VII, 300–303.

[117] Beer, ed., *Joseph II., Leopold II. und Kaunitz*, pp. 503–506; Arneth, *Maria Theresia* VII, 300–303.

[118] DOZA, Handschriften, Vol. 64, Ludwig Zinzendorf to Karl Zinzendorf, 28 July 1766; Khevenhüller-Metsch VI, 450; on Pergen see Paul P. Bernard, *From the Enlightenment to the Police State: The Public Life of Johann Anton Pergen* (Urbana, Ill., and Chicago, Ill., 1991).   [119] Arneth, *Maria Theresia* VII, 308–310.

[120] DOZA, Handschriften, Vol. 64, Ludwig Zinzendorf to Karl Zinzendorf, 19 August 1766; Khevenhüller-Metsch VI, 198.

[121] The prolonged exchanges on this matter between Maria Theresia, Joseph and Kaunitz are in HHStA, Staatskanzlei, Vorträge, Karton 98. Cf. Beer, ed., *Joseph II., Leopold II. und Kaunitz*, pp. 512–516. Bernard, *From the Enlightenment to the Police State*, pp. 64–70, is unclear on Pergen's duties in the Foreign Office, and erroneously concludes that Pergen's honorary appointment to the Council of State was real.

actually leaving the ministry.[122] In fact, Kaunitz made it clear in a memo to his staff that his trusted friend's experience and expertise were not to be lost to the department, and that Binder was to be given continued full access to all Chancellery of State files. Furthermore, while Kaunitz was unable to push through Pergen's formal appointment as Vice-Chancellor, he left his subordinates in no doubt that this would be Pergen's functional post.[123] He was, in short, entrusted with Binder's old task of chief administrative officer of the ministry, and to further emphasize his dominant position, no referendaries were appointed to replace Binder, Giusti and Dorn. However, the number of department heads, with the official title of Aulic Councillor and State Official (*Hofrat und Staatsoffizial*), was now raised to five: the veteran Collenbach, formerly a generalist, now became a specialist for affairs of the Holy Roman Empire; Hochstättern became a specialist for the Levant; the former archivist, Joseph von Sperges, was promoted the head of the Italian department; August von Lederer was made head of the Belgian section; and Andreas Krufft, a former secretary, made a titular councillor and official without portfolio. This tendency towards increased specialization[124] was further enforced with the naming of four so-called Court Secretaries (*Hofsekretär*) at a higher salary than the usual clerical staff. These included the official court translator for Oriental languages, Anton Seleskovitz; a talented recent graduate of the Academy of Oriental Languages (which Kaunitz had helped to found in 1754), Franz Maria Thugut, who started as Seleskovitz's assistant and was, in time, to become Chancellor; and Anton Spielmann, who became Binder's special assistant and was also to make a considerable albeit disagreeable name for himself. Finally, the number of clerks was increased to eleven, while the number of servants was kept at three.[125]

Regarding Starhemberg, who now replaced Haugwitz as chairman of the Council of State, Kaunitz significantly made no official announcements. Apparently, the Chancellery of State's designated heir was to be trained exclusively by the Chancellor himself and not by a process of immersion in the ministry's business. Clearly Starhemberg's lack of official contact with the Foreign Ministry not only proved to be the first step in Kaunitz's indefinite retention of his office, but also in Starhemberg's exclusion from his position as heir-apparent to Kaunitz. Starhemberg's

---

[122] DOZA, Handschriften, Vol. 64, Ludwig Zinzendorf to Karl Zinzendorf, 19 August 1766.
[123] HHStA, Staatskanzlei: Vorträge, Karton 98, Kaunitz to Chancellery staff, 20 October 1766.
[124] Too narrow a specialization, on the other hand, was also discouraged, and Kaunitz's office directives of 1766 and 1770 wanted to make sure privy councillors in his ministry remained open and flexible. See Matsch, pp. 60, 192–200.
[125] Khevenhüller-Metsch VI, 450–457; Arneth, *Maria Theresia* VII, 315–318.

growing unpopularity with Joseph in any case doomed his career. After fewer than four years in the Council of State, he was sent to Brussels as authorized minister in the Austrian Netherlands. He returned to Vienna in 1783 to take up the post of Grand Master of the Household and remained without political influence until Joseph's death in 1790, when he became a member of the revived Privy Conference of Leopold II and Francis II.[126] Similarly, Pergen's promising future in the Chancellery of State was also quickly darkened when he started to lose the confidence of his chief. A talented and ambitious but devious, unprincipled, yet at times also rigid sycophant,[127] Pergen left Kaunitz increasingly disenchanted.[128] The Chancellor, therefore, took advantage of a major ministerial shuffle inspired by Joseph in 1771, which included Binder's removal from the Council of State, to bring his old friend back to the foreign ministry in an official capacity and to shunt Pergen off to the post of adjunct to the governor of the province of Lower Austria.[129] Binder now resumed his duties of chief administrative officer, and the Chancellery of State continued to be run much as it had been before 1766.[130]

Though Kaunitz had by this time obviously abandoned his idea of retiring, his relations with Joseph continued to be rocky. To begin with, the Emperor was not at all persuaded that the kind of arms-length administrative policy Kaunitz had advocated for Belgium and Milan were the most appropriate, and he tended to favour tighter control from Vienna. During a trip through Milan on his way to Rome in 1769, Joseph took the opportunity to assess Kaunitz's administration there at first hand and came away thoroughly dissatisfied with everything from taxation and administration policies to personnel.[131] Kaunitz tried to take the criticism

---

[126] On Joseph's dislike of Starhemberg see Alfred Ritter von Arneth and M. A. Geffroy, eds., *Correspondance secrète entre Marie-Thérèse et le Cte de Mercy-Argenteau avec les lettres de Marie-Thérèse et de Marie Antoinette*, 3 Vols. (Paris, 1874), II, 86–87; Eichwalder, "Starhemberg," pp. 163–164.

[127] All these characteristics come through glaringly in HHStA, Sonstige Sammlungen: Grosse Korrespondenz, Fasz. 242, Pergen–Püchler correspondence, 1763–1766. Bernard, *From the Enlightenment to the Police State*, pp. 3–63, confirms these personality traits and provides further evidence.

[128] Pergen himself sensed that his influence was on the wane and did not hesitate to give vent to his frustrations in complaints to his chief and others. HHStA, Sonstige Sammlungen: Grosse Korrespondenz, Fasz. 406, Pergen to Kaunitz, n.d. (1770–1771). Cf. Bernard, *From the Enlightenment to the Police State*, pp. 67–70.

[129] See below, pp. 107–108.

[130] HHStA, Sonstige Sammlungen: Grosse Korrespondenz, Fasz. 406, Kaunitz to Binder, 10 August [1771].

[131] ÖNB, Handschriftsammlung: Series nova, Nr. 1612, Joseph to Maria Theresia, 18 August 1769. I am indebted to Carlo Capra for pointing this source out to me. Cf. HHStA, Familienarchiv: Hofreisen, "Karton 1, Bericht des Grafen Firmian an Maria Theresia über den Aufenthalt des Kaisers Joseph II in Mailand im Sommer 1769."

with grace: "I am very sorry to learn that the government [of Milan] has failed to satisfy (or so it appears) His Majesty the Emperor," he noted, but then added diplomatically that Joseph's memorandum was "a work in which one recognizes perfectly both profundity of spirit and a true desire to ensure the happiness of people." In his own defence, however, he then immediately explained in some detail how he had been invariably fulfilling explicit imperial commands, and he defended these policies vigorously. He acknowledged that suitable personnel was difficult to choose from a distance, but asserted that he had made every effort to make the right choices.[132] Joseph's critiques were to result in a substantial restructuring of the Milanese administration during 1770–1771, but the policy continued to be executed by Kaunitz, and his position as well as his ministry's administration of the Italian province remained untouched.[133]

A similar, but much more serious conflict arose after the first partition of Poland over the administration of the newly annexed province of Galicia. In many ways the conflict had its origins in the very *raison d'être* of the partition. Kaunitz and Maria Theresia resorted to this "Prussian solution" to the diplomatic crisis engendered by the Russo-Turkish war rather reluctantly; Joseph tended to be more focused on territorial compensation for the loss of Silesia. Hence, once partition had been accepted on principle in 1771, the debates on the administration of the new province reflected these fundamentally different premises. Kaunitz early persuaded Maria Theresia that the former Polish territories ought not to be fully integrated into the core of the Monarchy, but administered *sui generis* by his Foreign Ministry "in its essentials on the same basis as the Netherlands." This effort to maintain Galicia in "merely a loose, more federal bond" with the remainder of the Monarchy was soon bitterly opposed by Joseph, who favoured a tighter integration and wished to create a separate Court Chancellery in Vienna for the province.[134]

By the time Joseph made his position clear in August 1772, Kaunitz had retired to his estates at Austerlitz in Moravia. He had suffered recurring bouts of illness all through the year,[135] and once the partition crisis had been ended, he resolved on a period of rest and recuperation. During his absence Binder handled most of the routine business of the ministry, and it was thus Binder who caught the initial brunt of Joseph's fury over the Galician administration. In the face of Joseph's determined stand Maria

---

[132] ÖNB, Handschriftsammlung: Series nova, Nr. 1612, Kaunitz to Maria Theresia, n.d. (September 1769).

[133] Carlo Capra, "Il Settecento," in Domenico Sella and Carlo Capra, *Il Ducato di Milano dal 1535 al 1796* (Turin, 1984), pp. 425–431.

[134] Horst Glassl, *Das österreichische Einrichtungswerk in Galizien (1772–1790)* (Wiesbaden, 1975), pp. 27–37, 56–57; Arneth, *Maria Theresia* VIII, 414–415; Matsch, pp. 65–67.

[135] HHStA, Staatskanzlei: Vorträge, Karton 110, Kaunitz to Binder, 14 September 1772.

Theresia became extremely depressed and hinted at abdication,[136] while Binder, who was in any case highly temperamental, sent a bitter report of Joseph's stand to his master. Kaunitz, however, retained a stoic calm:

You know, my friend, that on a hundred occasions I have always held to this principle: a good citizen must strive as long and as hard as he can to serve the state and his sovereign, often even despite him. For this reason, therefore, and because it also appears that it could not have been so maliciously intended, let us temporize for now ...[137]

In short, Kaunitz accepted that his ministry's administration of Galicia would be temporary, and that the battle had been lost in principle. On October 9, after his return to Vienna, he therefore proposed that he should be given a free hand in the new province for a limited period of two years, or be relieved of the responsibility immediately.[138] Again Joseph intervened. He had come away from the Polish partition crisis with the firm impression that Kaunitz, with his increasing age, was becoming slow and inefficient, and he did not want to see the Galician administration infected with these faults. He therefore prevailed on his mother to reject Kaunitz's proposal without necessarily accepting his immediate resignation. He wanted Galicia to receive a Chancellery on the Transylvanian model, and Pergen appointed Chancellor "in a few months", but in the meantime Kaunitz was to continue to oversee the administration of the province.[139] Kaunitz accepted the decision without comment, and dutifully drafted the appointment decrees.[140]

In the event, Kaunitz's administration of Galicia was to last well over a year, during which time the tone of the new Austrian administration was clearly set and policies were initiated which served as guidelines for the development of the province for over a generation. Pergen traveled to Galicia as interim governor to institute the new Habsburg regime, though he was hamstrung by the uncertain attitude of Joseph. The young Emperor now had second thoughts about a separate Galician Chancellery, and began to consider the idea of incorporating Galicia directly into the administrative purview of the Austro-Bohemian Chancellery. When

---

[136] *Ibid.*, Maria Theresia to Binder, 11 September 1772. Cf. Arneth, *Maria Theresia* VIII, 415–416.
[137] HHStA, Staatskanzlei: Vorträge, Karton 110, Kaunitz to Binder, 14 September 1772; Cf. Arneth, *Maria Theresia* VIII, 608.
[138] HHStA, Staatskanzlei: Vorträge, Karton 110, Kaunitz to Maria Theresia, 9 October 1772.
[139] DOZA, Handschriften, Vol. 66, Ludwig Zinzendorf to Karl Zinzendorf, 21 and 27 October 1772; Arneth, *Maria Theresia* VIII, 416–417; ÖZV II/3, 296. The account in Bernard, *From the Enlightenment to the Police State*, pp. 91–114, is faulty.
[140] HHStA, Staatskanzlei: Vorträge, Karton 110, Kaunitz to Maria Theresia, 14 October 1772.

Pergen wrote Kaunitz for clarification, the response he received showed clearly the depth of the rift between the Emperor and the Chancellor of State. Kaunitz quite explicitly told Pergen: "you know how little inclination I have to seek such information," adding that it was in any case "a matter of total indifference to me in particular." All he could advise was for Pergen to wait with patience until Joseph had made up his mind.[141]

In the meantime, Joseph, who had been visiting Transylvania, now decided to make an unscheduled inspection tour of Galicia as well. Though Maria Theresia opposed this extension of Joseph's travel schedule, Kaunitz advised she give her blessing, since the trip in any case appeared to be "almost inevitable."[142] Once in Galicia Joseph appeared both restless and relentless in his wish to transform the new province.[143] He deluged Vienna with memoranda, complaints and questions. Kaunitz himself, while on his usual August vacation at Austerlitz, abruptly received a list of 154 questions on various details concerning Galicia which the Emperor had told Pergen he wanted answered immediately.[144] While Pergen's local provincial officials were at work on their responses well into October,[145] in Vienna Kaunitz and his Galician staff laboured with particular alacrity, for a 572-page detailed response was dispatched within three weeks.[146] Since Joseph had made similar requests from the War Ministry as well, it was difficult to see how this would accelerate rather than slow down government business. As Maria Theresia observed: "When the Emperor receives your answers as well as those of Lacy and Pergen, what will he do with that huge pile of paper?"[147] But as these responses were dispatched, Joseph was already on his way back to Vienna, where he now let it be known that he had decided to set up a separate Galician Chancellery after all, though he had become so disenchanted with Pergen while on his tour, that his choice for Chancellor now fell on Count Eugen von Wrbna. As

---

[141] HHStA, Sonstige Sammlungen: Grosse Correspondenz, Fasz. 406, Kaunitz to Pergen, 12 July 1773.

[142] HHStA, Staatskanzlei: Vorträge, Karton 112, Kaunitz to Maria Theresia, 20 June 1773.

[143] HHStA, Familienarchiv: Hofreisen, Karton 4, Joseph's "Journal ... über die Reise durch Galizien," July–September 1773. Cf. Johann Polek, "Joseph's II. Reisen nach Galizien und der Bukowina und ihre Bedeutung für letztere Provinz," *Jahrbuch des Bukowiner Landes-Museums* III (1895), 26–34; Hubert Rumpel, "Die Reisen Kaiser Joseph II. nach Galizien" (unpublished Ph.D. thesis, University of Erlangen, 1946), pp. 40–45.

[144] HHStA, Familienarchiv: Hofreisen, Karton 5, Joseph to Pergen, n.d. (July 1773), including Joseph's questions, which he styled "Politische Puncta".

[145] *Ibid.*, Pergen to Joseph, 10 September 1773. The final answers by the various councillors among whom Pergen had divided the work take up an entire carton of 1,200 folio pages (*Ibid.*, Karton 6).

[146] HHStA, Staatskanzlei: Vorträge, Karton 113, Kaunitz to Joseph, 2 September 1773, appending "Beantwortung der von S. M. dem Kaiser aufgestellten 154 Fragepuncte" (including Joseph's questions).

[147] *Ibid.*, Maria Theresia to Kaunitz, 2 September 1773.

Binder was later to reveal to Maria Theresia, Kaunitz, too, had become disenchanted with Pergen, and was equally unenthusiastic about Wrbna.[148] But Kaunitz was more interested in easing the tensions between himself and the Emperor, for he accepted the Wrbna nomination without dissent.[149] Shortly thereafter, seeing that most of the areas of friction appeared to have their source in the Galician administration, Kaunitz decided to resign his post as provisional head of the Galician department. Citing the Emperor's own contention that the business of the Galician administration was overburdening the *Staatskanzlei*, he asked to be relieved of these responsibilities immediately, "completely, and forever." This time the request was granted.[150]

But if Kaunitz hoped by this resignation to ease the tensions between himself and Joseph, he soon discovered how bitterly mistaken he was. Even after the Austro-Polish Convention of 18 September 1773, which formally ceded Galicia to Austria, diplomatic conflict between the two countries continued. Vienna insisted that the eastern border of Galicia should run along the river Sbrucz, while Warsaw wished to draw the line along the river Sereth. Maria Theresia wished to be conciliatory, and Kaunitz was inclined to support her, but Joseph expressed a more unyielding stance in the most violent terms, labeling all recommendations for concessions as acts of cowardice and irresponsibility.[151] Kaunitz could not help but be wounded by the Emperor's vitriolic outpourings, and by the end of 1773 his forbearance was at an end. On 7 December, at the end of a regular memorandum on the border adjustment question, he added a request in his own hand to be relieved of all his offices as soon as possible.[152] Eventually the crisis was overcome, though not before Maria Theresia and Joseph both in turn also threatened to "retire" or "resign",[153] and while Kaunitz thus remained in office, relations with Joseph also continued to be rocky.

The problem was that the impatient and zealous Emperor's mind seethed with projects of radical reform. While Kaunitz tended to second those that touched on social issues, he tenaciously opposed the young co-regent's administrative schemes, which, among other things, would have reintroduced a cabinet of *ex officio* ministers.[154] The Emperor and the

---

[148] *Ibid.*, Binder to Maria Theresia, 16 November 1773; DOZA, Handschriften, Vol. 66, Ludwig Zinzendorf to Karl Zinzendorf, 27 August 1773.

[149] Arneth, *Maria Theresia* VIII, 419–422.

[150] HHStA, Staatskanzlei: Vorträge, Karton 113, Kaunitz to Maria Theresia, 16 November 1773, including imperial resolution.

[151] Adolf Beer, *Die Erste Theilung Polens*, 3 Vols. (Vienna, 1873–1880), III, 64–72.

[152] HHStA, Staatskanzlei: Vorträge, Karton 113, Kaunitz to Maria Theresia, 7 December 1773. Printed in part in Arneth, *Maria Theresia* VIII, 617. Cf. Arneth and Geffroy, eds., *Correspondance secrète* II, 86–89.   [153] See below, pp. 111–112.

[154] See below, pp. 99–100.

Chancellor also continued to be at loggerheads over foreign policy. During the crisis that led to the War of the Bavarian Succession, Joseph was the man of action and Kaunitz the man of restraint at the Viennese court.[155] These sorts of conflicts led Joseph to accuse Kaunitz of laxity and incompetence,[156] and led Kaunitz to return to his theme of resignation. He asked to be relieved of his post again in March 1776[157] and in May 1779.[158] Each time Maria Theresia prevailed upon her son to moderate his criticism and upon Kaunitz to remain at his post. Yet it was difficult to effect a genuine reconciliation between the two men. Though the real problem was that Kaunitz and Joseph were often at odds on the conduct of foreign policy, the fact that Maria Theresia usually tended to side with Kaunitz in these matters meant that Joseph was obliged to focus his dissatisfaction not so much on what was being done, but on how it was being done. Consequently, the Emperor continued to harp on his theme of a ministerial cabinet or a revived Privy Conference as an instrument whereby he could gain greater supervisory control over the Chancellery of State.[159]

Such ideas became superfluous after 1780 when Joseph became sole monarch, and it is significant that they were not raised again thereafter. But in the decade of the 1770s, Kaunitz's ministry seemed under constant siege by the co-regent. Kaunitz, for his part, was tenacious in his defence of the Chancellery of State. He insisted that few sovereigns in Europe could boast such a complete knowledge of the international situation as Maria Theresia and Joseph II. He noted that all reports and instructions of any importance were not forwarded to the monarchs in extract form but rather in the original. Matters of small or no consequence were delivered in précis form, but always with the original attached. No instructions left the ministry without royal approval, and all communications with other ministries, including the most mundane and routine, were entered into record books, complete with a précis, that were always available for inspection. He pointed with pride to the incorruptibility of his staff, its *esprit de corps* and professionalism, and the lack of a single complaint in

---

[155] I have discussed this point with reference to the broader literature on the War of the Bavarian Succession in "Prince Kaunitz and the Primacy of Domestic Policy: A Response," *International History Review* II (1980), 626–627.

[156] HHStA, Familienarchiv: Sammelbände, Karton 7, Joseph to Leopold, 16 January 1772; Beer, ed., *Theilung Polens* III, 64–72; Adam Wandruszka, *Leopold II*, 2 Vols. (Vienna and Munich, 1963–1965), I, 346. Even more revealing are those reports by Leopold on Joseph's attitude to Kaunitz which are not published by Wandruszka: HHStA, Familienarchiv: Sammelbände, Karton 15/Allegato di No. 3, "Impiegati Principali a Vienna e nello Stato secondo i respettivi Dipartimenti e carattere loro," n.d. (1778–1779). I am indebted to Professor Wandruszka for pointing this source out to me.

[157] *MTJC* II, 108–109.

[158] HHStA, Staatskanzlei: Vorträge, Karton 129, Kaunitz to Maria Theresia, 21 May 1779.

[159] HHStA, Staatskanzlei: Vorträge, Karton 120, Joseph to Maria Theresia, 21 April 1776; *ÖZV* II/3, 48–73; Hock and Bidermann, *Staatsrath*, pp. 28–32.

the more than twenty years for which he had had the honour of directing the Monarchy's foreign policy.[160] Much of the tension between Joseph and Kaunitz would dissipate once the Emperor was in unquestioned control after 1780, and indeed, Joseph became quite content with the Chancellor and his ministry.[161] Ironically, a simple personnel change even before then made Joseph much more tranquil. In response to Kaunitz's last offer of resignation after the Peace of Teschen in May 1779, the Empress consented to any changes in the Foreign Ministry if he would remain in office. By this time Binder, whom Joseph had never liked, had become so infirm that he was unable to continue in his duties even with the assistance of Spielmann.[162] Kaunitz therefore submitted his friend's resignation and returned to his old request of having a formal Vice-Chancellor assigned to his ministry. This seemed a "precipitous" move to Maria Theresia, who felt Kaunitz had neither aged nor diminished in his capacity one iota over the previous five years, but she was prepared to give in nonetheless.[163] Kaunitz nominated the Habsburg representative at the recent peace conference, Count Philipp von Cobenzl, for the position.[164] Kaunitz claimed that he had been impressed by Cobenzl's handling of the Teschen negotiations, and reported that he found him to have a perceptive mind, a ready practicality, and a conciliatory nature.[165] He had certainly been an enthusiastic supporter of Cobenzl's tariff reform proposals in 1769–1775.[166] Whether Cobenzl was really a man after Kaunitz's heart, however, remains open to question. His original choice for the Teschen negotiations was actually his more clear-cut favorite and protégé, Ludwig Cobenzl, son of the deceased authorized minister to Belgium and cousin of Philipp, and the appointment of the latter was due only to a last-minute illness which befell the former.[167] Late in life Kaunitz was also to make some bitter comments about Cobenzl when the latter betrayed his chief in the second Polish partition crisis,[168] but at this stage Kaunitz clearly seems to have accepted Cobenzl as a reasonably effective and efficient chief administrative officer of his ministry.

[160] HHStA, Staatskanzlei: Vorträge, Karton 114, Kaunitz to Maria Theresia, 20 February 1774.   [161] Wandruszka, *Leopold II* II, 88–89.
[162] HHStA, Familienarchiv: Sammelbände, Karton 15/Allegato di No. 3, "Impiegati Principali a Vienna" cited in footnote 156 above.
[163] Arneth and Geffroy, eds., *Correspondance secrète* III, 318–319.
[164] On Philipp Cobenzl see Wurzbach II, 391–392; *ADB* IV, 363–369; *NDB* III, 298–299.
[165] HHStA, Staatskanzlei: Vorträge, Karton 129, Kaunitz to Maria Theresia, 21 May 1779. Cf. Arneth *Maria Theresia* X, 644; Hanns Schlitter, ed., *Kaunitz, Philipp Cobenzl und Spielmann: Ihr Briefwechsel 1779–1792* (Vienna, 1899), pp. iii–iv.
[166] See below, pp. 150–153.
[167] Wurzbach II, 292; Hermann Hüffer, "Cobenzl, Ludwig," *ADB* IV, 356.
[168] HHStA, Handschriftensammlung, W 808, "Les Entretiens du Prince de Kaunitz dans les dernières semaines de sa vie, 1794, par L'Abbé [Sebastian] Comte d'Ayala, Ministre résident de la République de Raguse à Vienne."

More significantly, Cobenzl had made a very favourable impression on Joseph, whom he had accompanied on a trip to France in 1777,[169] and much of the Emperor's anger became diffused when he felt he was able to place his own man into Kaunitz's ministry. Both monarchs accordingly acceded to the request for their own reasons, and Cobenzl thus replaced Binder in the Chancellery of State with the official title of Vice-Chancellor.[170] Kaunitz, of course, had no intention of receding into the background to become an occasional gray eminence. He reminded Cobenzl that all the ministry's business, whether written or oral, had to be conducted in the Chancellor's name as long as he retained that post,[171] and he continued to discharge his duties at the same pace as usual. In short, Cobenzl's role was to relieve Kaunitz of routine work loads and to act as a conduit to the mercurial emperor; policy formulation remained the prerogative of the minister. For Joseph, who in this way could feel he had better control of the Foreign Ministry, it seemed a salutary change; for Kaunitz nothing had really changed except that he had now won the fuller confidence of the temperamental Emperor.

[169] Arneth, *Maria Theresia* X, 643–644; Arneth, ed., "Graf Philipp Cobenzl und seine Memoiren," *AÖG* LXVII (1886), 21–22, 119–124; *ADB* IV, 363–364.

[170] *ÖZV* II/1/i, 495.

[171] HHStA, Sonstige Sammlungen: Grosse Korrespondenz, Fasz. 406, Kaunitz to Cobenzl, 14 July 1779.

3 The structure of government

The modernization of the Habsburg Foreign Office under Kaunitz was only part of a larger trend towards more professional forms of government in the eighteenth century. The principal feature of this incipient professionalization was increased bureaucratization, and it was the growth of professional impersonal bureaucracies that in turn became the leading edge of confrontation with more traditional indirect forms of government. By the eighteenth century this struggle already had a venerable history, but no decisive results. Nowhere in Europe had the great early modern conflict between emerging royal absolutism and intermediate feudal social corporations resulted in a decisive victory for either side. Eighteenth-century governments remained condominiums between a crown, increasingly articulating the concept of the impersonal state under its supreme authority, and feudal corporations stubbornly clinging to the patrimonial ideals of indirect rule through autonomous local authorities.

In this extended political struggle of the seventeenth and eighteenth centuries the Habsburg Monarchy remained in a rather peculiar position. A patrimonial conglomerate whose centrifugal particularisms were enhanced by constitutional, judicial, cultural and linguistic differences, it was legally bound together only by the Pragmatic Sanction which did little to enhance the authority of the crown over its subordinate social corporations. The great seventeenth-century victories of the crown were more confessional and cultural than political, and Habsburg Monarchs in the seventeenth and early eighteenth centuries were not "absolute" by any stretch of the imagination.[1] To this was added the complication that the Habsburgs were not only rulers of various territories in the Danubian basin, but also Holy Roman Emperors. In this capacity they sought to defend the imperial mystique and prerogative against the corrosion of territorialism pursued by the princes. But as these territorial princes asserted supreme authority over their respective autonomous feudal corporations, the Emperor could only hope to check territorialism by

---

[1] Bérenger, *Finances et absolutisme autrichien*; Evans, *Making of the Habsburg Monarchy*.

posing as the protector of these intermediate local authorities. Ironically, therefore, policies of centralization in his own territories contradicted policies he was compelled to pursue as Emperor; yet the very inability to marshall the resources of his own patrimony effectively weakened his imperial position.[2]

The critical nature of the crisis of 1740–1741, and the separation for the first time in over three centuries of the crown of the Holy Roman Empire from those of the individual lands of the House of Habsburg, liberated Maria Theresia from policies that were the antiquated baggage of the imperial dignity, and gave her a somewhat freer hand at home than her predecessors had enjoyed. The Habsburgs could now belatedly embark on a programme of absolutism of the kind that in other monarchies such as France had already been established in the previous century. However, by the middle of the eighteenth century, a new wind was already blowing from the European Enlightenment, carrying with it its own distinct political ideas. The Habsburg Monarchy thus experienced not merely a great conflict between absolutism and particularism, but a tripartite struggle among the forces of the traditional feudal corporate order, the proponents of the seventeenth-century style absolutism, and the advocates of "enlightened absolutism" as defined by the intellectuals of the eighteenth century.

The Haugwitz revolution

In its initial phases, the establishment of French or Prussian style absolutism proceeded along traditional lines. It came in response to the existential crisis of the Monarchy of 1740–1741, and was inspired by a man whose ideas were the very essence of seventeenth-century absolutism, Count Friedrich Wilhelm Haugwitz. The son of a Saxon general whose estates were in Silesia, he entered Austrian service by joining the Silesian provincial government in 1725. Here he soon so distinguished himself in the provincial tax administration that in 1742 he was made head of the provincial administration of the fragments of Silesia left to Austria. His first major recommendations for wholesale reform were presented at the close of the subsequent year while he was in the capital for consultative talks. These famous proposals, or *Notata*, laid out the essentials of Haugwitz's policies, which remained substantially unaltered in the subsequent twenty years.[3] In his view, the Silesian Provincial Estates bore

---

[2] Henry E. Strakosch, *State Absolutism and the Rule of Law in Austria, 1753–1811* (Sydney, 1967) (German version: *Privatrechtskodifikation und Staatsbildung in Österreich (1753–1811)* [Munich 1976]; subsequent references are to the original English edition), pp. 17–28.

[3] On Haugwitz see Walter, *Paladine*, pp. 24–39; Wurzbach VIII, 68–69; Eberhard Haugwitz, *Die Geschichte der Familie von Haugwitz*, 2 Vols. (Leipzig, 1910), I, 117–136.

direct responsibility for the province's inability to mount any concerted resistance against the invasion of Frederick. Through financial mismanagement and corruption the Estates had saddled the province with debts and left it defenceless before an aggressor. He therefore urged that the whole tax collection and recruitment process be taken over by the crown by setting up a specific royal bureaucracy for the task. And, because Haugwitz believed that such an administrative structure designed to look after the economic interests of the crown would by itself be too weak, he insisted that it also be given full political administrative powers. Finally, to oversee the activities of this new crown bureaucracy, a special central department "for the political and financial administration of Silesia" (in the Chancellery jargon of the day "pro politicis et cameralibus") should be set up in Vienna.[4]

In developing these ideas Haugwitz had been impressed by cameralist theorists, and especially by one of the most ardent apologists for absolutism, Wilhelm von Schröder, to whose work, *Fürstliche Schatz- und Rentkammer*, he often made explicit reference.[5] Schröder's antagonism towards provincial Estates was uncompromising, and his defence of the princely prerogative most outspoken. He insisted that the only reliable recourse of a prince was to a standing army and a full treasury, administered by a loyal bureaucracy and overseen by a central directing collegium.[6] Despite the political radicalism of men such as Schröder, however, their vision of government was underlain by an innate social and economic conservatism and a narrow fiscalism which has not escaped the attention of astute analysts.[7] Haugwitz, too, reflected these aspects rather well when he insisted that "aristocratic privileges and liberties are to be held sacred, and it is precisely for this reason that abuses of them are not to be tolerated."[8] Nor is there any doubt that purely fiscal considerations dominated his thinking. The *Notata* had insisted that "a well arranged financial administration is the soul of the state,"[9] and its unification of it with the political administration meant nothing less than the subordination of the latter to the imperatives of the former.

If the ideological roots of Haugwitz's reform proposals are to be found

---

[4] *ÖZV* II/2, 130–152.
[5] Friedrich Walter, "Die ideellen Grundlagen der österreichischen Staatsreform von 1749," *Zeitschrift für öffentliches Recht* XVII (1937), 195–205; cf. *ÖZV* II/1/i, 99–111.
[6] Heinrich von Srbik, "Wilhelm von Schröder. Ein Beitrag zur Geschichte der Staatswissenschaften," *Sitzungsberichte der kaiserlichen Akademie der Wissenschaften, philosophisch-historische Klasse* CLXIV (1910), 1–161; Louise Sommer, *Die österreichischen Kameralisten in dogmengeschichtlicher Darstellung*, 2 Vols. (Vienna, 1920–1925), II, 79–123.
[7] Hubert C. Johnson, "The Concept of Bureaucracy in Cameralism," *Political Science Quarterly* LXXIX (1964), 378–402.   [8] *ÖZV* II/2, 202.   [9] *Ibid.*

in a particularly Hobbesian brand of Cameralism, he found practical confirmation of his ideas in the administrative system of Prussia as he understood it. The maximum concentration of power apparently afforded by the Prussian Directory seemed to him to guarantee the efficiency the Habsburg administration lacked. Haugwitz noted with exasperation that Frederick II seemed easily able to extract over 50% more revenue from Silesia than it had yielded under Austrian rule while paradoxically lightening the over-all burden by virtue of the simplicity and efficiency of the collection process, and accordingly recommended that, after the then still anticipated reconquest of the province, Prussian structures should be taken over unaltered.[10] This proved to be an effective argument with an Empress indignant at Frederick's ability to support his entire army for a full year on Silesian revenues, where previously they had barely been able to support two Habsburg cavalry regiments.[11] Haugwitz's proposals thus found quick acceptance, and the decree commissioning him to undertake his proposed reform was issued on 12 March 1744. The Estates of Silesia suddenly found itself deprived of all responsibilities for the financial and political administration of the province. The only remnant of real political power that it retained was the traditional monopoly over local judicial administration.[12] The resultant separation of political and economic from judicial administration was, in fact, the key development that laid the ax to the old "complex interpenetration of administrative and judicial powers" which was the essential basis of feudal corporate particularism. It freed the crown from the legal constraints to which the corporate authorities had subjected the public sphere of government, and permitted it to pursue political absolutism heretofore functionally impossible.[13] Yet there is every indication that for Haugwitz this was merely the result, not the goal of the reform, for he made no real attempt to improve the administration of justice. His concern was to strengthen the revenue-collecting mechanism of the state.[14]

Haugwitz's reforms proved so successful in Silesia that they soon became the model for other provinces, and in 1747 he was able to win the support of the Empress for a universal application of his plan in all the Austrian and Bohemian lands. Explicit constitutional commitments made it impossible to apply the reform to the Kingdom of Hungary and the province of Tyrol, and the peripheral Belgian and Italian territories were not even considered. But in the remaining territories, the Haugwitz

---

[10] *Ibid*, pp. 140–142; Friedrich Walter, "Preussen und die österreichische Erneuerung von 1749," *MIÖG* LI (1937), 415–429.   [11] Kallbrunner, ed., *Testament*, p. 77.
[12] *ÖZV* II/1/i, 115–116.   [13] Strakosch, *State Absolutism*, pp. 29–49.
[14] Joseph Kallbrunner, "Zur Neuordnung Österreichs unter Maria Theresia: F. W. Haugwitz und die Reform von 1749," *Österreich* (1918/19), pp. 115–130.

revolution struck with bewildering speed. In mid-June 1747, Haugwitz met with representatives from the Aulic War Council to determine the size of the planned new state-financed military establishment and to ascertain the funds necessary to maintain it. In the ensuing discussions, a standing army of 108,000 men was decided upon, at an estimated annual cost of 14 million Gulden. To raise this sum Haugwitz posited fourteen fundamental principles upon which the universal system had to be based. The most revolutionary of these was the regular taxation of seigniorial demesnes in peacetime. Significantly, this taxation was justified with the argument that, without an adequate force to protect the crown, "it is impossible to protect and defend the aristocratic privileges that are dependent on it." Furthermore, while "God-pleasing justice and natural equity" demanded the taxation of seigniorial land, the rate was much lower than for peasant holdings.[15]

The final decision on the adoption of the Haugwitz system for all Austrian and Bohemian lands came with a Privy Conference meeting of 29 January 1748. Kinsky and Harrach in particular did their best to sabotage the proposed reform, but the Empress remained firm. Thereafter, Haugwitz began a series of negotiations with the Estates of various provinces, and concluded a recess of different duration with each of them whereby the central government took over the collection and administration of taxes. Once this was accomplished, the Estates were also deprived of most of their political administrative duties and found themselves reduced simply to judicial administration. An entirely new, crown-directed administrative structure came into existence, which included an intendancy for each of the provinces (*Länderdeputation*, later called *Representation und Kammer*) overseeing an extensive system of crown-appointed county officials called "circle offices" (*Kreisamt*). The reform culminated in the establishment of a central ministry or Directory to head this new provincial administrative structure – the so-called *Directorium in publicis et cameralibus* – with Haugwitz as its president. The old Austrian and Bohemian Chancelleries were abolished and their former judicial functions, which was all that was left to them after the Directory had appropriated their other powers, were assembled in another new ministry, functioning both as a Ministry of Justice and Supreme Court, the Supreme Judiciary (*Oberste Justizstelle*) under the former Austrian Chancellor, Johann Friedrich Seilern. The creation of a special supervisory Domestic Conference (*Conferenz in Internis*) similar to the Privy Conference was short-lived, and the real supreme minister in domestic affairs was Haugwitz. This reality became

---

[15] *ÖZV* II/1/i, 117–126; II/2, 152–188; Adolf Beer, "Die Staatsschulden und die Ordnung des Staatshaushaltes unter Maria Theresia," *AÖG* LXXXII (1895), 88–93.

increasingly obvious in the following years, as the Directory began to eat away at the competences of the other ministries and departments of the central government.[16]

Haugwitz's cameralist conception of bureaucratic efficiency tended to favour the concentration of governmental functions in a central collegial directory, and there is little doubt Maria Theresia found herself very much drawn to a system which so enhanced her authority. The gravitational pull of Haugwitz's Directory began in 1753 when ceremonial functions previously performed by the Bohemian and Austrian Chancellors were transferred to it by the simple device restoring the official titles without a concomitant restoration of the offices. Haugwitz remained president of the Directory, but now received the additional title of Supreme Bohemian and First Austrian Chancellor.[17] This very revealing adjustment in forms was gradually followed by similar changes in substance. It has already been noted that Haugwitz's ideas on the separation of the administrative and judicial functions of government were purely practical, not ideological. His position on the transformation of heretofore public rights into private rights that this separation of powers entailed remained ambiguous, and he never clearly understood how the reduction of seigniorial rights to mere property rights was the key judicial development clearing the path to political absolutism.[18] Thus, while initially willing to concede that all so-called "*materiae mixtae*" (adjudication of entailed estates, interpretation of guild privileges, birthrights, hunting rights, and the like), which so long had both a public and private function in the feudal corporate order, fell under the agenda of the Supreme Judiciary, he wrenched back these competences to the Directory when he perceived they could affect revenue collection.[19]

Other ministries fared even worse. In 1753, the Central Directory for Commerce (*Universalcommerzdirectorium*) became a subordinate department of the Directory. By 1755, the Directory had taken over so many of the duties of the Treasury (*Hofkammer*) that Haugwitz was able to suggest the latter be abolished altogether.[20] Only the fact that the Treasury fulfilled functions in Hungary, where Haugwitz's reforms could not be applied, allowed it to survive.[21] The same could be said of the government's official appointees to the board of the private Vienna City Bank (*Ministerial-bancodeputation*), who could not be absorbed without damaging the credibility of the bank – the one financial institution able to retain public

[16] *ÖZV* II/1/i, 148–248; II/2, 195–206.   [17] *ÖZV* II/1/i, 211–212.
[18] Strakosch, p. 38.   [19] *ÖZV* II/1/i, 194–195; II/2, 294–330.
[20] *Ibid.*, II/1/i, 206–209.
[21] I. Nagy, "Die ungarische Kammer und die Wiener Zentrale Finanzverwaltung, 1686–1848," *Acta Historica Academiae Scientiarum Hungaricae* XXII (1976), 291–327.

confidence in the era.[22] With the outbreak of the Seven Years War, the pace of collegial concentration of power was intensified. The Ministry of Mines and Minerals (*Münz- und Bergkolleg*), the Commissariat for Military Supply (*Generalkriegskommissariat*) and the Department of Invalid Veterans (*Invalidenhofkommission*) all followed suit in 1757. Further, as the need for new administrative functions was perceived, they almost automatically found concrete expression as new subsidiary departments of the Directory. This was the case with both the Police Commission (*Polizeihofkommission*) formed in 1749, and the Commission in Charge of Poor Relief (*Stiftungshofkommission*) formed in 1751. In short, with the exception of the Ministries of War, Justice, and Foreign Affairs, Haugwitz's Directory ran virtually all other governmental business in Austria and Bohemia.[23]

Such concentration of governmental functions was not without its difficulties. On the one hand, stripping the Supreme Judiciary of functions that potentially interfered with revenue collection obscured the very essential separation of public and private rights to such a degree that the justification for separating the judicial and political functions of government in the first place was dubious. Under the impact of the fiscal pressures created by the Seven Years War, conservatives such as Haugwitz's own second-in-command in the Directory, the reactionary Johann Chotek, were thus was able to argue that the Supreme Judiciary was so over-staffed and underworked, that for reasons of pure economy, it could be reabsorbed by the political administration.[24] Indeed, personnel changes in the provincial government of Lower Austria which consolidated the separate political and judicial bureaucracies in April 1759 left feudal reactionaries convinced that Haugwitz's reform had suffered an irretrievable blow, and that only the ongoing war crisis prevented a complete return to a unified judicial and political administration.[25]

On the other hand, the accretion of functions quickly began to burden the Directory down. It became mired in petty detail and judicial wrangles until finally its efficiency was increasingly impaired. This was especially true after the outbreak of war. The Directory's absorption of the Commissariat for Military Supply, initially undertaken because that ministry had discharged its quartermaster functions inadequately during

[22] Hermann Ignaz Bidermann, "Die Wiener Stadt-Bank: Ihre Entstehung, Ihre Eintheilung und Wirksamkeit, Ihre Schicksale," *AÖG* XX (1859), 341–445; Mensi, *Finanzen Österreichs*, pp. 179–299, 573–637, 708–743.   [23] *ÖZV* II/1/i, 148–248.
[24] *Ibid.*
[25] Khevenhüller-Metsch V, 99; cf. Emile Karafiol, "The Reforms of the Empress Maria Theresa in the Provincial Government of Lower Austria, 1740–1765" (unpublished Ph.D. dissertation, Cornell University, 1965), pp. 197–235.

the campaign of 1757, proved no solution since inexperience at Haugwitz's ministry created even greater confusion in this vital area.[26] In the words of Khevenhüller, the only result was to go "from one disorder to another."[27] The Department of Mines and Minerals, absorbed to eradicate an enormous deficit created by poor administration, continued to run such a deficit under Haugwitz that it had to be mortgaged to Rudolf Chotek's Vienna City Bank within eighteen months.[28] In short, in his temperamental impatience, Haugwitz's political appetite surpassed his Ministry's digestive capacity. Thus, ironically, the administrative reforms motivated by an anxiety to safeguard the fiscal performance of the Directory began to impede that very performance.

Though an awareness of the potential limitations of Haugwitz's system during war-time preceded the actual outbreak of hostilities by some years, even pessimistic projections underestimated the actual costs of protracted conflict. Initially Kaunitz, too, remained relatively sanguine. "No matter how unpleasant the picture itself may be," he noted in 1754, he by no means regarded the situation as "desperate" and was convinced that appropriate remedies could be found.[29] In the event, however, these optimistic prognoses were disappointed within months. As early as the campaign of 1757, it became apparent that the Habsburg Monarchy was unable to marshall the resources sufficient to the need at hand. Thereafter, as decisive military victories eluded the Habsburg armies, a desperate search for fiscal expedients to alleviate the growing financial crisis revealed clearly the Directory's increasing inability to fulfill its primary task. It was at this stage that Kaunitz, as a partisan of public credit schemes conceived by Ludwig Zinzendorf, became convinced that unwise measures, such as extraordinary taxes, were being all too hastily adopted while other worthy ideas such as Zinzendorf's were not being given the consideration they deserved.[30] Though Kaunitz was unsuccessful at this point in his effort to introduce what would later become the Council of State, it became increasingly clear that some re-evaluation of the structure of government was imperative. The Directory's acquisition of certain judicial functions tended to lead to such chaos and delay that, apparently, even the Empress began to have doubts about Haugwitz's system.[31] Critics, who included virtually the entire executive staff of the Directory, became more boldly vocal by the day. Johann Chotek, while willing to credit the new system with having increased revenues, saw the separation of judicial and political functions of government as the source of unnecessary personnel increases,

[26] ÖZV II/1/i, 223–230; II/2, 355–356.   [27] Khevenhüller-Metsch V, 41.
[28] ÖZV II/1/i, 222–223; II/2, 92–94.
[29] HHStA, Staatskanzlei: Vorträge, Karton 75, Kaunitz to Maria Theresia, 13 November 1754.   [30] See below, pp. 118–127.   [31] Khevenhüller-Metsch V, 99.

entailing expenses which had to be cut at all costs. Directory Aulic Councillor, Anton König von Kronburg, seconded these sentiments, emphasizing the degree of administrative confusion to which the accumulation of competences had led, and pointing out that, at best, the Haugwitz system was a peace-time arrangement which had been rendered unworkable by the exigencies of war. Much of this criticism, even if motivated at times by thoroughly reactionary sentiments, was entirely justified. Directory personnel had almost quadrupled in a decade (from sixteen in 1749 to fifty-nine in 1760), and costs naturally rose concomitantly. Moreover, while Haugwitz was an imaginative innovator, he was not an equally gifted administrator. But in the final analysis, it was his inability to meet the ongoing demands of the war that proved his undoing.[32]

Because Haugwitz's system proved unable to raise the sums initially anticipated and because the costs of the war proved to be much higher than predicted, the Directory President and Supreme Chancellor was especially vulnerable to criticism from financial experts. While Kaunitz's protégé, Ludwig Zinzendorf, generally found his economic prescriptions rejected, his diagnosis of the limitations of Haugwitz's fiscal innovations were broadly shared. Above all, it was Directory Vice-President Johann Chotek's younger brother, Rudolf Chotek, who led the attack. As Chairman of the Board of the semi-official Vienna City Bank and Head of the Department of Trade and Commerce since 1749, he had negotiated the Austro-Bavarian Currency Convention of 1753, instigated the government lottery of the same year and compiled the new tariff ordinances for Bohemia, Moravia and Silesia in 1753 and Austria in 1755. Untouched by novel ideas but stubborn in the defence of the limited mercantilist notions he had acquired, Chotek had to suffer the indignity of having his Commerce Department absorbed by the Directory in 1753. But shortly after the outbreak of the war, his star began to rise. His advice was instrumental in defeating Zinzendorf's public credit schemes. In July 1758, he was able to wrest the Department of Mines and Minerals from the Directory. And on 27 December 1759, he was made President of the Treasury, the one economic portfolio which had escaped Haugwitz's concentration of ministries. While Chotek shared the view of his brother and other conservatives that the administrative and judicial functions of government ought to be reunited, he felt all financial functions ought to be exercised by a wholly independent finance ministry.[33] The key to Chotek's success was

[32] Jaroslav Prokeš, "Boj o Haugvicovo 'Directorium in publicis et cameralibus' r. 1761," *Věstník královské české společnosti nauk* (1926), Essay No. iv, pp. 17–18; *ÖZV* II/1/i, 259–261.

[33] On Chotek see A. Wolf, "Graf Rudolf Chotek, K.k. österreichischer Staats- und Conferenzminister," *Sitzungsberichte der kaiserlichen Akademie der Wissenschaften. Philosophisch-historische Klasse* IX (1852), pp. 435–437.

undoubtedly the patronage of Emperor Francis I, who, as the restorer of private Habsburg family fortunes, had a considerable reputation as a fiscal wizard, and who may have entertained ambitions to become Supreme Finance Minister himself.[34] In any case, Chotek emerged as the dominant voice in economic matters and Haugwitz's influence declined accordingly.

Though Haugwitz's position was rapidly being eroded, Maria Theresia remained fiercely loyal to him. In November 1759, she insisted that he be promoted to the Order of the Golden Fleece as a sign of her continued confidence in him. As Head of the Order, Emperor Francis was able to dampen the effect of the appointment by insisting in his turn on the simultaneous appointment of Rudolf Chotek as a precondition,[35] but the military victories of 1759 gave Haugwitz the upper hand, which only the unexpected Prussian recovery of 1760 reversed. By that point resources were strained to breaking point and the danger of imminent collapse made it necessary to reassess fundamentally all aspects of government policy. As Kaunitz came to the reluctant conclusion that victory in this war was no longer possible, the broader war aim of the destruction of Prussia was abandoned and peace initiatives were accordingly launched. Of course there was the hope that some fortunate military stroke could still debilitate Prussia permanently while these negotiations were going on, and preparations for a campaign in 1761 had to proceed apace in case they collapsed.[36] Both short-term and long-term considerations thus pointed to the necessity of dramatic action: the former required addressing the immediate needs of the next campaign; the latter required reassessing the whole financial and administrative structure of the Monarchy to strengthen its position in the post-war world.

Rudolf Chotek's moment had now come. In December 1760, he was appointed to chair a special commission whose task it would be to produce a whole new finance system to replace that of Haugwitz.[37] Furthermore, to ensure the rapid enactment of the commission's anticipated recommendations, it was necessary to re-evaluate the entire conference system, from War Cabinet to Privy Conference, and the entire administrative apparatus of the central government.[38] In the course of these discussions, attention was once more drawn to Kaunitz's critique of the War Cabinet and his recommendation for an advisory council on domestic matters of August 1758. At the time, Emperor Francis had opposed the idea but now

---

[34] Hanns Leo Mikoletzky, *Kaiser Franz I. Stephan und der Ursprung des Habsburgisch-Lothringischen Familienvermögens* (Vienna, 1961), pp. 28–29.

[35] Khevenhüller-Metsch V, 138–139.

[36] HHStA, Staatskanzlei: Vorträge, Karton 87, Kaunitz to Maria Theresia, n.d. (December 1760).   [37] On the details of this commission, see below, pp. 125–126.

[38] HHStA, Kabinettsarchiv: Staatsrat Präsidium, Karton 1, undated and unsigned notes on conference system. Cf. *ÖZV* II/3, 2–3.

both the Empress and he were gradually won around.[39] Finally, early in December 1760, Kaunitz was ordered to formally resubmit his proposals. At the same time Johann Chotek was ordered to resubmit his ideas on the reunification of administrative and judicial functions of government in a formal proposal.[40]

The Kaunitz reform

Of the three major re-evaluations now undertaken – Kaunitz on the council system; Johann Chotek on the administrative system and Rudolf Chotek on the financial system – Kaunitz was the first to submit his report on 9 December 1760. As we have seen, this led to the creation of the Council of State in relatively short order, and the Council of State, in turn, decisively influenced the response to the reports of the Chotek brothers. While the creation of the Council of State was a victory for Kaunitz, the choice of personnel revealed that he had to make some compromises in order to achieve his main objective. He was unable to place any of his protégés on the Council, while Haugwitz not only assumed the chairmanship, but could also count on the support of Daun, Blümegen, and, in most cases, Stupan. The conservatives, however, were even worse off. They could only pin their hopes on the administrative officer, König, who seemed to have seconded Johann Chotek's critiques of Haugwitz, and even he proved to be a disappointment to them. Kaunitz's position, however, was not as weak as it seemed, for he succeeded in establishing not only the institutional but also the ideological framework within which the Council was to operate.

Before beginning with the analysis of specific recommendations, Kaunitz insisted that the second meeting of the Council, on 30 January 1761, be devoted to discussing those general principles of statecraft which ought to serve as the ideological premise and policy guideline for all future Council deliberations. His memorandum positing these fundamental principles has been the object of considerable scorn by the principal historian of the reforms of 1760 and 1761, who dismissed them as nothing but self-evident platitudes. Nothing could be less justified. Kaunitz's principles posited the notion that reforms furthering the development of agriculture, industry and commerce, and enriching society as a whole, must precede and dictate the character of revenue collection. More precise information on the actual trade balance of the Monarchy ought to be garnered; taxation ought to be expressed in percentages not fixed amounts; government ought to be

---

[39] *Ibid.*, Kaunitz to Maria Theresia, Maria Theresia to Kaunitz, 2 December 1760. Arneth, *Maria Theresia* VII, 4–9, 495–496.   [40] *ÖZV* II/3, 85.

sensitive to the needs of the private sector and even be prepared to learn from it; tariffs needed to be reformed, monopolies avoided, immigration of skilled individuals encouraged.[41]

In short, while many of these "principles" clearly grew out of classic cameralist agendas, Kaunitz nevertheless posited a fundamental shift in government policies, which represented precisely the reverse premise from which Haugwitz had proceeded, from a narrow fiscal focus to a broader social one. Further, the importance Kaunitz placed on a broad acceptance of these premises as the guidelines for future policy for the entire Habsburg bureaucracy should not be underestimated. It was not enough that the Council of State endorsed these principles or that they subsequently received royal assent. On 4 February 1761, they were circulated to the fourteen most important officials in the Monarchy for comment: the Chotek brothers, Bartenstein, Vice-President of the Treasury and member of the Chotek finance commission, Peter Ferdinand Freiherr von Prandau, and all ten provincial intendants. Johann Chotek further solicited the comments of Directory Aulic Councillors Karl Joseph Cetto von Kronstorf, Karl Holler von Doblhoff and Hermann Lorenz von Kannegießer. All these officials tended to pay lip service to the long-range validity of Kaunitz's principles, but their reservations, which invariably focused on short-range fiscal need, revealed that, in fact, they did not accept them.[42] Effectively, therefore, the principles remained the ideological programme of only the Council of State, and this made the Council doubly important.

The Council of State's most immediate pressing business, after its organizational and ideological framework had been set, was to consider the respective reports of the Chotek brothers. Rudolf Chotek's finance commission had submitted a preliminary report on 14 December, and Johann Chotek, who, upon Haugwitz's promotion to the Council of State, became President of the Directory (a rather ironic instance of the cat being charged with guarding the canary), submitted his on 23 December 1760. The former focused primarily on areas of the government's fiscal profile where cuts could be made, and recommended above all organizational improvements. It could hardly come as a surprise that for Rudolf Chotek, now head of all three important economic portfolios, these improvements would amount to creating a strong, unified finance ministry for the entire Monarchy.[43] The report of the senior Chotek brother was also predictable. He reiterated sentiments already expressed earlier, calling for the abolition of the Directory and the Supreme Judiciary, the reintegration of the judicial and administrative functions of government, and, in line with his brother, the sundering of the financial administration into an independent

---

[41] Walter, "Eintritt," pp. 52, 74–79.   [42] *ÖZV* II/1/i, 282–285.
[43] *Ibid.*, II/1/i, 291–292; II/3, 164.

ministry. The recommendations did not call for a complete return to the pre-1749 separate Austrian and Bohemian Chancelleries, wishing to retain the unification achieved by the Directory and calling the new Chancellery the "German Court Chancellery" (*Deutsche Hofkanzlei*). But the reactionary cutting edge of the proposals came with what was to happen to the provincial administration of intendants once their Central Directory disappeared. Here, nothing short of restoring the old feudal corporate order seemed to be the logical conclusion for Chotek.[44]

Rudolf Chotek's preliminary report could be dealt with in short order by the Council of State. Its members agreed with Kaunitz that the question of reorganizing the financial portfolios of government was best considered in the context of the overall administrative re-organization outlined by Johann Chotek.[45] This abruptly cut short any further administrative reform proposals from this group, which was ordered to focus more clearly on strictly fiscal questions.[46] Johann Chotek's report received an even ruder reception. Even the Administrative Officer, König, took it upon himself to point out "as a matter of information" that Chotek's assumption that the issue had already been settled in principle was by no means justified, and to warn that a restored Court Chancellery would give new political life to the Provincial Estates. All the members of the Council of State agreed, with Haugwitz in particular insisting the Directory remain as it was.[47] Kaunitz remained coy. He had suggested as early as 1758 that the Directory suffered from certain essential defects, but had not been specific about what these were.[48] He now asserted that the Directory was certainly not exempt from re-assessment and careful scrutiny by the Council of State. However, Johann Chotek's proposals were thoroughly inadequate, completely lacking in the necessary detail. The central government was too important to be tampered with lightly, and before anything was done a much broader sampling of views needed to be solicited. He therefore recommended that the twenty leading officials of the Austro-Bohemian lands be required to submit written assessments of the administrative system as it existed before 1749, and of the Haugwitz system. They were also to posit recommendations on what improvements were to be made – and, in particular, how the provincial administrations

[44] HHStA, Österreichische Akten: Österreich-Staat, Fasz. 3, Johann Chotek to Maria Theresia, 23 December 1760. Published in part in *ÖZV* II/3, 85–86; cf. Prokeš, "Boj o Haugvicovo," pp. 24–25.   [45] *ÖZV* II/1/i, 292.

[46] HHStA, Kabinettsarchiv: Staatsratprotokolle, Vol. 1, No. 13 of 1761, imperial resolution, 13 February 1761.

[47] Haugwitz's undated rebuttal in HHStA, Österreichische Akten: Österreich-Staat, Fasz. 3, enclosed with the Chotek report as in fn. 44.

[48] HHStA, Kabinettsarchiv: Staatsrat Präsidium, Karton 1, Kaunitz to Maria Theresia, 6 August 1758.

were to be organized. The Empress ruled entirely in the spirit of Kaunitz, and the imperial request to the twenty officials (drafted by Kaunitz himself) was accordingly dispatched on 15 February 1761.[49]

The responses were some weeks in coming,[50] and in the meantime, attention shifted to the more immediate pressing economic problems. Rudolf Chotek's finance commission submitted its second report on 17 January 1761, but once again its concrete proposals were slim. The most important was the suggestion to resort to printing paper money. During the Council of State debates on this in March, Kaunitz gave the idea qualified support, but only as a last resort. Instead, he suggested Zinzendorf's public credit schemes be revived and circulated through the Council, where they subsequently found the acceptance that had so long eluded them when Chotek was the dominant voice in economics.[51] However, since Zinzendorf's scheme called for tapping the credit of the Provincial Estates of the Monarchy, it now became necessary to bring these bastions of feudal particularism into political play precisely when the issue of provincial administration was about to be discussed. On 22 April, the Provincial Estates were ordered to dispatch delegates to Vienna for 13 May 1761. There the delegates were assembled into a so-called "Credit Deputation", chaired by Zinzendorf, which remained in existence until well after the war.[52] Hence, throughout the discussions on administrative reform, the Estates Deputies had to be courted to gain their fiscal co-operation. The situation, in short, was hardly propitious for radical attacks on the feudal elite.

If the Estates Deputies held out hope of a *quid pro quo* with the crown, winning concessions on the administrative structure of the state in return for financial co-operation, Kaunitz was not about to disillusion them. The first session of the Credit Deputation was addressed by Kaunitz himself, and his tone was conciliatory and flattering.[53] Then, when Zinzendorf's scheme was safely launched, the responses to the questionnaire of 15 February began to come in. These were revealing indeed, for they demonstrated the extent of the official resistance to Haugwitz's innovations even among personnel of the Directory itself. Johann Chotek repeated his suggestions of December 1760. The Directory councillors Cetto, Doblhoff

[49] HHStA, Kabinettsarchiv: Staatsratprotokolle, Vol. 1, No. 12, imperial resolution, 15 February 1761. Cf. *ÖZV* II/3, 90–94; Prokeš, "Boj o Haugvicovo," pp. 26–28.

[50] HHStA, Kabinettsarchiv: Staatsratprotokolle, Vol 1, No. 45, records the responses.

[51] HHStA, Kabinettsarchiv: Staatsratprotokolle, Vol. 1, No. 767 of 1761, protocol record, 8–25 March 1761; HHStA, Kabinettsarchiv: Nachlaß Kaunitz, Karton 1, Kaunitz to Maria Theresia, n.d. (March 1761); HHStA, Kabinettsarchiv: Materialien zur Geschichte des Staatsrats von Kutschera, Part III, Section 6/A/i, "Anordnung eines Finanz-System."   [52] *ÖZV* II/3, 164–166. Discussed in detail below, p. 000.

[53] HHStA, Kabinettsarchiv: Nachlaß Kaunitz, Karton 1, "Anrede an die Ständische Deputierte," n.d. (May 1761).

and Kannegießer (the latter in particular once having been the confidant of Haugwitz) all agreed with Chotek, with Kannegießer going even one step further, suggesting the reinstitution of separate Austrian and Bohemian Chancelleries. Directory Vice-Chancellor Bartenstein, of course, had been an open critic of Haugwitz since 1753 and did not change now. Rudolf Chotek supported his brother fully, and, as expected, stressed the importance of a totally independent finance ministry. Somewhat more surprising was the response of the President of the Supreme Judiciary, Karl Adam Breuner. Haugwitz's system was the cause of all the Monarchy's present ills, he insisted. A full return to the old pre-1749 system, which, in his view, worked well, was the only solution. The provincial authorities also joined the chorus of criticism. Most focused on details of provincial administration, but invariably to the detriment of Haugwitz and full of praise for the old order. All agreed that administrative and judicial functions had to be reunited, and finance set up as a separate matter. Most were prepared to accept the unification of the Austrian and Bohemian Chancelleries, but Franz Joseph Pachta of Bohemia, Franz Anton Schrattenbach of Moravia and Franz Ludwig Kienburg of Styria were opposed even to that.[54] If the Council of State were to pay heed to the consensus of these respondents, the decision would be simple and self-evident.

Given this near-unanimous clamor for a return to the old order, and given the pressure of Estates Deputies in Vienna, it was perhaps fortunate for Council of State members that its deliberations were strictly confidential. Conservatives would have been surprised to discover that during the critical debate in November and December 1761 their concerns were virtually ignored. Instead, a debate emerged between the proponents of Haugwitz's system and what might best be described as the Enlightenment party, because it brought a fresh wave of new ideas from Western Europe into the fray. At the senior level of government, this party was spearheaded by two men: Kaunitz and Zinzendorf. During 1761, Zinzendorf had finally made his breakthrough. Rudolf Chotek's finance commission had been a bitter disappointment, chained as it was by its mercantilist preconceptions to narrow and unimaginative proposals. Zinzendorf's plan, on the other hand, once given its opportunity, scored an enormous success when the Estates Deputies underwrote a bond issue of 18 million Gulden.[55] Hence, where his unsolicited initiatives had been repeatedly rebuffed in the past, his advice was now actually sought.

Zinzendorf supported the idea of separating the financial from the political administration, but worked out a much more elaborate and

---

[54] Prokeš, "Boj o Haugvicovo," pp. 28–43.   [55] See below, pp. 126–127.

sophisticated plan on the form that financial administration should take than Chotek's super finance ministry. The principal problem he felt needed to be remedied was the lack of accurate and reliable budgetary ledgers. His plan, therefore, called for the generic sub-division of the financial administration into three ministries. The first of these would be the Treasury (*Hofkammer*), which ought to be divided into five departments – respectively overseeing administration of ordinary revenues, administration of crown estates, administration of state mine and mineral monopolies, administration of mineral retail sales, and currency. The second would be a specific Revenue Office (*General-Kasse*) created for the purpose of collecting mortgaged revenues and servicing the debt. Since credit and debt operations had for so long been the province of the reputable Vienna City Bank, the chairman of the bank's board (a crown appointee from the outset), could be placed in charge of the Office so as not to undermine the confidence of creditors. Finally, a Court of Audit (*Hofrechenkammer*), undoubtedly inspired by the French *Chambre des Comptes*, was to be established as a completely independent bookkeeping ministry, acting as the Monarch's principal organ of control and supervision.[56] These were ideas that Kaunitz and Zinzendorf had no doubt discussed for some time and may have constituted part of Kaunitz's unspecified reservations about the Directory as early as 1758. In any case, these detailed proposals now received the enthusiastic endorsement of Zinzendorf's long-time patron, and through him that of the Empress as well. Maria Theresia and Kaunitz held lengthy secret discussions on the matter during October,[57] and obviously the Empress had made up her mind in principle before the Council of State began its debates in November.

   Against the attack on his system by the twenty officials consulted, of course, Haugwitz remained firm. The fusion of the Austrian and Bohemian lands had to be maintained. Political and financial administration had to remain in the same hands so as not to emasculate the latter. Judicial matters had to be kept separate so as not to burden the Directory with needless petty detail. Over the course of the year, however, Haugwitz had made some modifications to his ideas. He was now prepared to have the Directory give up those judicial functions he had insisted on wresting from the Supreme Judiciary for efficiency's sake in 1751, and he had no objections to returning the overwhelming chores of the Commissariat for Military Supply to the War Ministry. Haugwitz's protégé, Blümegen, deviated little from his master's view, though he was prepared to see the

[56] HHStA, Kabinettsarchiv: Nachlaß Zinzendorf, II: Handschriften, Vol. 2b, "Vorschlag des Gr. Zinzendorf, die neuen Einrichtungen der Finanz-Stellen betr.," 7 October 1761.
[57] HHStA, Kabinettsarchiv: Nachlaß Kaunitz, Karton 1, "Wegen der Finanz Einrichtung geheime mündliche Äusserung gegen die Kayßerin K[önigin]," October 1761.

creation of a separate Court of Audit as suggested by Zinzendorf. Stupan was taken with Zinzendorf's tripartite financial administration, and perfectly willing to reunite judicial and administrative matters, though purely as a cost-saving measure. Borié, too, seconded the Zinzendorf ideas, but, also for merely practical reasons, he could not see how the wide-ranging agendas of political and judicial administration could be harmonized. He therefore recommended they remain separate. All agreed that the Commissariat for Military Supply could be severed from the Directory, and all wished to retain the administrative unity of Austria and Bohemia.[58]

It was Kaunitz's view, however, that was decisive. His lengthy and wide-ranging observations began with praise for Haugwitz's positive accomplishments: his courageous incursion into the chaotic system of privilege and particularism had finally set the Monarchy on the right path. But the means to that laudable end had been confused and inadequate. There was insufficient co-ordination and overview; too many functions operating at cross-purposes were united into one department while other, related functions were separated; too many reform proposals were hastily dismissed as unwarranted intrusions into the private preserve of department heads; too many appointments were the result of "prejudices, favoritism, aristocratic status, ancestral credit and other irrelevancies," instead of merit; too much money was wasted. To remedy this, general guidelines were as important as specific administrative changes. Hence, Kaunitz repeated the importance of his fundamental principles of February, above all stressing the necessity of economic portfolios escaping a narrow fiscal vision and adopting a broader social view with respect to raising the general level of economic performance. He stressed the importance of more accurate, detailed annual budgetary statistics, of clear bookkeeping and supervision, and of systematic and precise instructions to all ministries and departments of government.

Only after this elaborate preamble did Kaunitz turn to the actual issue at hand. Here, he began by reiterating the essential arguments of Zinzendorf about a tripartite financial administration, adding that mortgaged as well as unmortgaged revenues ought to be paid into a Revenue Office in order to create a single, centralized pan-monarchical authority for all credit and debt operations. He also added that inadequate bookkeeping procedures in the past made a Court of Audit virtually indispensable. The Commissariat for Military Supply could become a department of the Aulic War Council, which, of course, would necessitate re-organizing that entire ministry. With respect to the separation of the political and judicial administration Kaunitz did not, as all the others had

---

[58] Prokeš, "Boj o Haugvicovo," pp. 43–48; *ÖZV* II/1/i, 294–297; II/3, 86–101.

done, address himself merely to the practical aspects. Functionally, such a union in his view would entail little or no savings, but this was hardly the essential point. Justice was, in principle, not an executive matter and the sovereign ought to remain distant from all private litigations. As far as Kaunitz was concerned, even those notorious matters classified as *materiae mixtae* which touched on the preserves of ministries other than the Supreme Judiciary were "nevertheless primarily judicial matters concerning private rights." How much of this came from Montesquieu can never be known, but what is clear is that Kaunitz understood very well that the transformation of feudal public rights into private rights was a vital cog in the process of modernizing society. Equally deliberate in its attack on the feudal social structure was Kaunitz's view on provincial and local administration. Since provincial institutions ought to mirror central institutions, he felt specific details could not be addressed until the reform of the central administration had been completed. But as a preliminary observation, he noted that there could be only one agent of executive power in each province, and that Provincial Estates had to be as subordinate to him as all other provincial institutions. Finally, Kaunitz concluded with a plea for more professional and uniform organization of all government institutions.[59]

The decision of the Empress may have been a foregone conclusion, given the secret talks she had had with Kaunitz in October. In any case, the imperial decision followed in every detail the recommendations of Kaunitz:[60] indeed, it was he who now drafted the appropriate announcement and appointment letters.[61] These were dispatched on 23 December; the Grand Master of the Household, Uhlfeld, was formally informed on 29 December, with the ceremonial proclamations taking place the following day. The Supreme Judiciary continued to exist as before, acquiring however all *materiae mixtae* from the Directory. The Directory ceased to exist, and in its place a number of new ministries sprang up. Political administration was placed in the hands of a central Bohemian and

[59] HHStA, Staatskanzlei: Vorträge, Karton 88, "Votum des Grafen Kaunitz-Rittberg [sic] über die neue Einrichtung aller Länder-Stellen," 20 November 1761. Four additional copies in HHStA, Österreichische Akten: Österreich-Staat, Fasz. 4. Published, but with significant omissions, in *ÖZV* II/3, 101–121. Cf. Prokeš, "Boj o Haugvicovo," pp. 48–64; Arneth, *Maria Theresia* VII, 23–25; Hock-Bidermann, pp. 14–15.

[60] HHStA, Kabinettsarchiv: Staatsratprotokolle, Vol. 4, No. 3467, imperial resolution, n.d. (December 1761). At the same time Maria Theresia issued a note to all ministerial and department heads that in this instance the old habit of criticizing her reforms would be severely punished: "Wie ich dann künftighin die zur Gewohnheit wordene freche Reden und Critiquen über alles, was Ich zur Wohlfart Meiner Unterthanen verfüge, behörige zu ahnden gedencke".

[61] HHStA, Staatskanzlei: Vorträge, Karton 88, draft of appointment letters, December 1761.

Austrian Court Chancellery (*Böhmisch- und österreichische Hofkanzlei*). The financial administration was to be split into three ministries: the Treasury, a Revenue Office whose head would simultaneously be chairman of the Vienna City Bank Board as well as of the Credit Deputation of the Estates, and a Court of Audit. The Commissariat for Military Supply became an autonomous department of the Aulic War Council. Rudolf Chotek, given the choice of heading credit and debt operations or becoming Austro-Bohemian Chancellor, chose the latter, complaining bitterly that his "demotion" was the work of Kaunitz and Zinzendorf and predicting that the entire new system would collapse within two years.[62] Zinzendorf left the Credit Deputation and became the Head of the Court of Audit. Johann Chotek went to the war ministry as Head of the Commissariat for Military Supply. Thus, two senior ministerial vacancies were left to be filled. The Treasury went to the conservative and unimposing former intendant of Carniola, Johann Seifried Herberstein. The Revenue Office, which carried with it the chairmanships of the Vienna City Bank and the Credit Deputation, went to the immensely ambitious, fiscally and socially conservative but politically flexible president of the Bohemian Court of Appeal, Karl Friedrich Hatzfeld zu Gleichen, whose economic reputation rested on his prior activities in the Bohemian intendancy's trade and commerce section.[63]

These appointments, of course, did not end the debates on the administrative reforms undertaken. The new ministries still needed precise instructions on their respective competences and duties, and all subordinate personnel still needed to be appointed. In addition, the entire thorny issue of provincial administration had been left to a latter date. Clarifying all these matters was to be not a matter of weeks or even months, but years. Basically, these problems can conveniently be considered under two rubrics: those that involved political administration and those that involved the financial administration. In both cases, Kaunitz was to play the central role in finalizing the details of the great reform of 1761.

Some hints of the political problems to come surfaced almost immediately when the reactionary Rudolf Chotek was instructed to produce a draft instruction for his new Austro-Bohemian Chancellery, within the precise reform guidelines articulated by Kaunitz. His response was

---

[62] HHStA, Kabinettsarchiv: Staatsratprotokolle, Vol. 4, No. 3467, Maria Theresia to Chotek, n.d. (December 1761). Cf. Arneth, *Maria Theresia* IX, 335–336, 592.

[63] *ÖZV* II/3, 122–125, 168–170, 194–196, 201–202, 360–362, 401–402; Pettenegg, ed., *Zinzendorf*, pp. 84–89. On Hatzfeld see Wurzbach VIII, 51–52; *NDB* VIII, 63–64; Margarethe Picha, "Der Aufstieg des Grafen Karl Friedrich Hatzfeld zu Gleichen bis zu seinem misglückten Versuch ein Premier-ministerium in internis zu gründen" (unpublished Ph.D. dissertation, University of Vienna, 1940).

anything but unquestioning obedience. In a passionate memorandum of 9 February, he presented a draft instruction without much reference to new principles, and took advantage of the opportunity to protest against the imposition of centralization on Austria and Bohemia, demanding the reconstitution of the old pre-1749 Chancelleries precisely because the new system excluded Provincial Estates from power.[64] Supported by the entire Council of State, the Empress called Chotek to heel, insisting her resolve was unalterable. But Chotek was not easily dissuaded. Fighting innovation tooth and nail, Chotek dragged matters out so that the final instruction for his ministry could not be promulgated until 21 June 1762.[65] Thereafter came the problem of personnel and salaries, which involved Chotek in such lengthy disputes with other ministries about who was to inherit which members of the old Directory staff, that it was November before the issue was settled.[66]

Only at this point was it possible to turn to what was clearly the most critical issue of all: the nature of the provincial administrative structure to be introduced. Once again, the Austro-Bohemian Chancellery was to work out a detailed plan within strict guidelines originating with Kaunitz's proposals of 20 November 1761 and 9 January 1762. These included the principle that the head of each provincial administration was to have control over every aspect of the government's responsibilities (political, financial, commercial and judicial), but was to discharge these responsibilities through completely autonomous provincial departments.[67] Kaunitz had recommended that a special *ad hoc* commission be constituted to work out the full details,[68] and this body of ministers and various Aulic Councillors, chaired and dominated by Rudolf Chotek, was ordered to begin work in June 1762. Chotek submitted the commission's preliminary report on 3 October, but failed to outline a detailed implementation plan. Instead the commission report focused on personnel appointments and, in particular, recommended drawing the old feudal elite into close partnership with the crown administration.[69] This was to be done by re-instituting the

---

[64] Jaroslav Prokeš, "Instrukce vydaná r. 1762 pro českou a rakouskou dvorní kancelář," *Věstník královské české společnosti nauk* (1926), Essay No. v, pp. 9–10.

[65] The instructions are published in full in *ÖZV* II/3, 129–163, and are analyzed in detail by Prokeš, "Instrukce vydana r. 1762," pp. 24–42.

[66] HHStA, Kabinettsarchiv: Staatsratprotokolle, Vol. 8, No. 3248, imperial resolution, 25 October 1762. Staff contracts were to take effect on 1 November 1762.

[67] *ÖZV* II/1/i, 358.

[68] HHStA, Staatskanzlei: Vorträge, Karton 89, Kaunitz to Maria Theresia, 9 January 1762; Karton 88, Kaunitz to Maria Theresia, 20 November 1761.

[69] Some information on the pressure exerted by various Provincial Estates to once more play a more active political role has recently been examined in the Carinthian case by Armin A. Wallas, *Stände und Staat in Innenösterreich im 18. Jahrhundert* (Klagenfurt, n.d.), pp. 109–113.

political authority of the Lieutenancy Councils – that is, the assembly of the highest feudal offices of the provinces. This was generally referred to as the Stadtholder system (*Statthalterei*).[70] In Bohemia, for example, fourteen feudal offices from the Grand Burgrave of Prague to the Master of the Horse held the rank of Stadtholder, and these together constituted the Lieutenancy Council.[71] This last suggestion was dismissed outright by Maria Theresia, while personnel appointments were deferred until a detailed plan for the structure of local government was worked out.[72] Chotek's second report was submitted on 12 January 1763, and it was immediately forwarded to the Council of State for consideration.[73]

Consistency and stubbornness were Chotek's outstanding character-istics, and he did not fail now. The idea of a revived Lieutenancy Council remained the central feature of the commission's report. This idea cut no ice with the Council of State, and in particular with Kaunitz, who dismissed the report because "in this way, all too much power would be placed into the hands of the Estates again, and the good which was accomplished by the system of 1748 would be overturned and destroyed."[74] Though this was also the sentiment of Maria Theresia, Chotek and the commission members were able to throw up such a screen by requesting clarification on a host of details – from the title the head of the provincial administration was to have, onwards – that the entire matter forced the commission to produce a third major report on 8 April, which was then again submitted to the Council of State.[75] Kaunitz's contribution strove to stick to those details the commission ostensibly needed clarified, though he could not repress his sarcasm in noting how indifferent he was to what specific title the head of the provincial administration should have.[76] Maria Theresia's decision, which was dispatched to Chotek on 20 April, made it clear that she had no intention whatsoever of concessions to the traditional provincial elites, and that she intended to establish provincial admin-istrative structures without input from the Estates.[77]

This was not the final word for Chotek. Within a week he submitted yet another report laden with objections which forced another Council of

[70] František Roubík, "K vývoji zemské správy v Čechách v letech 1749–1790," *Sborník Archivních Praci* XIX (1969), 66–68.
[71] On the history of the Lieutenancy Council, see František Roubík, "Místodržitelství v Čechách v letech, 1577–1749," *Sborník Archivních Praci* XVII (1967), 539–601.
[72] Roubík, "K vývoji zemské správy," pp. 68–69.
[73] HHStA, Kabinettsarchiv: Staatsratprotokolle, Vol. 10, No. 1275, protocol record.
[74] HHStA, Staatskanzlei: Vorträge, Karton 91, Kaunitz Staatsrat Votum, 14 March 1763.
[75] HHStA, Kabinettsarchiv: Staatsratprotokolle, Vol. 10, Nos. 1275 and 1412, protocol record.
[76] HHStA, Staatskanzlei: Vorträge, Karton 91, Kaunitz Staatsrat Votum, 15 April 1763.
[77] HHStA, Kabinettsarchiv: Staatsratprotokolle, Vol. 10, No. 1275, Maria Theresia to Chotek, 20 April 1763. Cf. Roubík, "K vývoji zemské správy," pp. 71–72.

State debate on the subject,[78] this time specifically focusing on the Stadtholder system, whose reinstitution Bohemian notables had been demanding since 1761.[79] In his official Council contribution, Kaunitz registered his opposition in measured tones.[80] But before the Empress made her final decision, he submitted yet another report to her, this time in strict confidentiality, in which he gave vent to his true feelings:

> I, too, am Bohemian and have estates in Moravia. Therefore, if I were to consult my self-interest, I would have every ground to endorse the opinion of those who now propose to elevate the nobility and Estates above their present status, and to play the administration of supreme executive power into their hands. However, if one keeps one's oath and duties in mind, then one must think first of one's gracious sovereign and of the common good. Therefore, I cannot understand how the very servants of Your Majesty could have forgotten themselves to this extent... The greatest political coup of the system of 1748 consisted in abolishing the Stadtholder system... I am especially shocked by the attitude adopted by the [Austro-Bohemian] Court Chancellery, which has now exposed itself completely. If, as is hardly to be doubted, it blew into the same horn as the Stadtholders who are to be re-instated, then it would be, if not impossible, at least unbearably difficult to bring anything positive to fruition... Your Majesty ought to make your all-highest displeasure very clear to the Court Chancellery, and remind them that they are *homo principis* and not *statum et nobilitatis*... To absolve myself before God and Your Majesty for any responsibility in this, I must advise with deepest respect, that I regard the re-introduction of the Stadtholder system as something which at one fell swoop would destroy all reforms and all hopes, and would deal your all-highest power the deadliest of blows.[81]

The young crown prince, Archduke Joseph, was also caught up in the heat of the moment. Having attended Council of State meetings since the beginning, he rarely had much of substance to add other than that he wished things would move faster.[82] But now he bestirred himself to compose a scathing and violent confidential memorandum for his mother in which he asserted that it ought to be the future policy of the dynasty " to pull down and impoverish" the aristocracy.[83] Pleased with the unanimous backing of the Council of State, and particularly pleased that her two favourite ministers, Haugwitz and Kaunitz, would find themselves in full agreement, the Empress rejected the feudal particularist aspects of the Chotek commission report.[84] The feudal case was irretrievably lost.

[78] *Ibid.*, p. 73. Cf. HHStA, Kabinettsarchiv: Staatsratprotokolle, Vol. 10, No. 1412, protocol record.   [79] Prokeš, " Boj o Haugvicovo," p. 43.
[80] HHStA, Staatskanzlei: Vorträge, Karton 91, Kaunitz Staatsrat Votum, 1 May 1763.
[81] *Ibid.*, "Geheimer Vortrag", 1 May 1763. Cf. Arneth, *Maria Theresia* VII, 29–31; *ÖZV* II/1/i, 360–361; Hock & Bidermann, p. 18.
[82] Schünemann, *Bevölkerungspolitik*, p. 27.
[83] Beales, "Joseph II's 'Rêveries'", pp. 155–160, especially p. 155.
[84] HHStA, Kabinettsarchiv: Staatsratprotokolle, Vol. 10, No. 1412, imperial resolution, 3 May 1763.

Provincial administrations were henceforth to be called "Gubernia," but their structures and agenda were to be essentially the same as Haugwitz's intendancies. The reasonably free hand Haugwitz had left the nobility in the administration of justice, however, was now gone. Judicial administration became just another autonomous branch of the Gubernium. Finally, the crown-appointed head of the Gubernium was to be united with the office of head ("capo") of the Provincial Estate. This was not a complete innovation, nor was it implemented consistently in every province, but on the whole it did tend to enhance the crown's political power further, and continued the process of limiting the Estates' freedom of action.[85]

The debates over the financial administration were even more drawn out, and, in the event, never resolved as clearly as the political issue. The main reason for this was that in this debate the conflict was less between the reformers on the one hand and the forces of the feudal corporate order on the other. The confrontation was between the two reforming parties, the old absolutists and the new Enlightenment group. As with the Austro-Bohemian Chancellery, difficulties began to arise with the economic portfolios in the wake of the imperial order to each of the ministers to draw up detailed agendas for their respective ministries within the Kaunitz guidelines of 9 January 1762. Kaunitz had talked about the necessity of co-ordination between the three ministries, but negotiating its modality led more frequently to conflict than co-operation. Herberstein came into jurisdictional conflicts almost immediately with both Hatzfeld and Zinzendorf. Co-ordinating the activities of the Treasury with the Vienna City Bank was understood by Herberstein to give him a virtual veto over Hatzfeld's activities. Hatzfeld, on the other hand, in the best tradition of Chairmen of the Board of the Vienna City Bank, was nervous that undue government interference would corrode confidence in the bank. Most Council of State members sided with Hatzfeld, and while Kaunitz too wished to retain the structure of the bank as it was, he did feel the Treasury needed to be kept informed on the details of those mortgaged crown revenues collected by the bank. This compromise was then enacted by the Empress. Herberstein's conflict with Zinzendorf had to do with his reluctance to surrender the financial records of the Department of Mines and Minerals to the Court of Audit on the grounds that he could not

---

[85] *Ibid.*, and No. 1275, Maria Theresia to Chotek, 5 May 1763. Cf. *ÖZV* II/1/i, 358–363; Dickson, *Finance and Government* I, 272–277; Franz Ilwolf, "Der ständische Landtag des Herzogtums Steiermark unter Maria Theresia und ihren Söhnen," *AÖG* CIV (1915), 166–168; Roubík, "K vývoji zemské správy," p. 73, with full text of the instruction to the Gubernium, pp. 78–88, and personnel lists, pp. 164–165.

administer that department properly if its bookkeeping was not done by his ministry. Only Stupan supported this view in the Council of State, with Kaunitz sarcastically supporting Zinzendorf as might be expected: it, no doubt, pained "the old treasury councillors, and presumably at their behest it also very much pains the new president" that their sphere of activity had been reduced, but this was no ground to alter the explicit intent of the reform. The Empress agreed.[86]

These are but two early examples of the kinds of difficulties that continued to plague the relationship of the economic portfolios for the subsequent three years. Even the detailed delineation of jurisdiction promulgated by the Empress on 8 March 1762[87] did not solve the problem. In part, this was due to the fact, as Borié frankly pointed out, that Herberstein was in principle opposed to the drift of the reform enacted in 1761.[88] But, in part, it was also due to the fact that the separation of competences envisioned in the Zinzendorf–Kaunitz proposals was hardly as clear in practice as it had been in theory and the instruction of 8 March made numerous compromises with the original plan. Ordinary taxes (*Contributionale*) continued to be administered by the Austro-Bohemian Chancellery, and while mortgaged revenues flowed into Hatzfeld's tills, unmortgaged ones were still controlled by the Treasury. In short, the idea of centralizing receipts in a Revenue Office remained only a programme for the future, and did not reflect the reality of the early 1760s.[89] An explicit directive from the Empress for Herberstein, Hatzfeld and Zinzendorf to meet in person every Saturday to co-ordinate activities,[90] hardly helped, as this gave even more opportunity for mutual *ad hominem* recriminations.

All these difficulties were still further complicated by the fact that Zinzendorf's Court of Audit enjoyed the right of prior audit – "ab ante" as it was called. Being audited already caused sufficient resentment, and occasionally even passive resistance, but actually having planned expenditures prevented by an auditor infuriated virtually every minister affected.[91] Beyond that, there was the problem that the Commissariat for Military Supply had to co-ordinate the military budget with the finance portfolios. As a result, the Revenue Office did not receive military funds, while on the other hand the Commissariat did not relish its subordinate position and its lack of complete independence.[92] After the end of the Seven Years' War, furthermore, the personal ambitions of Emperor Francis I made them-

---

[86] *ÖZV* II/3, 170–177; II/1/i, 326–330.   [87] *Ibid.*, II/3, 177–184.

[88] *Ibid.*, 177–178, fn. 2.

[89] Adolf Beer, "Die Finanzverwaltung Österreichs, 1749–1816," *MIÖG* XV (1894), 237–366, pp. 244–246; *ÖZV* II/1/i, 331–338.

[90] Hanns Leo Mikoletzky, *Österreich: Das Grosse 18. Jahrhundert* (Vienna, 1967), p. 213.

[91] HHStA, Kabinettsarchiv: Nachlaß Zinzendorf, II: Handschriften, Vols. 4 and 11, critiques and Zinzendorf responses.   [92] *ÖZV* II/3, 395–431.

selves felt, as he took a personal hand in the State debt servicing operations. Hatzfeld was placed at the Emperor's disposition, severely restricting his freedom of action and, indeed, leaving his status ambivalent.[93] Finally, there was the problem that the demise of the Directory had left the Department of Trade and Commerce in limbo. Kaunitz had recommended that the Department either become an independent ministry or an autonomous department of the Austro-Bohemian Chancellery. But he did not wish to see commerce subordinated to the finance portfolios which "always" hindered trade with tariffs and taxes.[94] Initially set up as an independent ministry under Franz Reinhold Andler-Witten, its obligation to "co-ordinate" policies with provincial authorities soon made some sort of accommodation with the Austro-Bohemian Chancellery necessary. Within weeks the Department fell under the sway of the Chancellery, and its status as an independent ministry collapsed.[95]

By the end of 1763, it was obvious to everyone concerned that the new administrative structure, but especially the finance portfolios, still needed substantial fine tuning. This was highlighted above all, as Stupan noted,[96] by the fact that once the provincial Gubernia were in place, they were the funnel through which directives from many ministries in Vienna flowed. These now began to receive conflicting instructions from the different branches of the central government, which of course handicapped effectiveness. In the face of this dilemma, Maria Theresia turned to the Council of State for advice. Here, mostly at the behest of Haugwitz, the debate was rapidly transformed from one on what adjustments the system needed to one re-evaluating all the changes undertaken in 1761. In a lengthy memorandum of 15 March 1764, Haugwitz vigorously pressed the case that the confusions which had manifested themselves were an indictment of the logic of the entire reform. The only solution was a return to his old system.[97] Both König, who was promoted to a full member of the Council in 1762, and Blümegen supported this call. On the other hand, Stupan and Borié remained opposed – as, quite naturally, did Kaunitz. He conceded that the agendas of the finance portfolios needed to be overhauled, but refused to say how. For those sorts of details, he suggested, Hatzfeld and Zinzendorf should be consulted. Otherwise, however, while lavishing praise on Haugwitz's anti-feudal zeal, he could not endorse a

---

[93] Arneth, *Maria Theresia* VII, 156–157; Beer, "Finanzverwaltung," p. 245; Mikoletzky, *Kaiser Franz*, pp. 27–28; Dickson, *Finance and Government* II, 63–64.

[94] HHStA, Staatskanzlei: Vorträge, Karton 88, Kaunitz to Maria Theresia, 20 November 1761.   [95] *ÖZV* II/3, 343–349. Cf. below, pp. 147–148.

[96] *Ibid.*, I/1/i, 369, fn. 3.

[97] *Ibid.*, I/3, 203–207. The ensuing debates are discussed in great detail in *Ibid.*, II.1/i, 366–421; II/3, 203–259; and in Friedrich Walter, "Der letzte grosse Versuch einer Verwaltungsreform unter Maria Theresia (1764/65)," *MIÖG* XLVII (1933), 427–469.

return to the old system.[98] The stalemate could not be broken. Rebuttals and counter-rebuttals ensued, but by August 1764, the proponents had not budged from their respective positions. Finally, the Empress implemented Kaunitz's advice to consult Hatzfeld and Zinzendorf, and these two men responded with a joint report on 11 September.

The Hatzfeld–Zinzendorf report sided squarely with Kaunitz that the fundamental premise and essential drift of the reform of 1761 had been correct. It also defended the principle of tripartite financial administration, but added that this had never come to pass as originally envisioned. Continued mixed jurisdictions had necessitated a degree of co-ordination among various ministries which retarded business with an endless stream of interministerial correspondence. The two ministers, therefore, recommended that the finance portfolios (Treasury, Revenue Office, Bank and Court of Audit) remain as originally constituted, but that all but the Court of Audit be given to the charge of the same minister. Further, ordinary taxation was to be taken from the Austro-Bohemian Chancellery and given to the Treasury, and the Court of Audit's right to prior audit (*ab ante*) extended to cover the financial records of the Provincial Estates.[99] These recommendations were debated at great length, with Chotek fiercely resisting any diminution of his ministry. Haugwitz also persisted in his position, nominating, in his last effort to push through the re-establishment of a Directory, none other than Kaunitz himself as Supreme Minister. However, this carrot of personal aggrandizement failed to win over his rival, and the essential features of the Hatzfeld–Zinzendorf report carried the day. Kaunitz remained the dominant voice, being twice asked by the Empress to chair *ad hoc* committees to work out the specific details of the changes to be implemented.[100]

On 14 May 1765, the first imperial decision was announced. The Treasury, bank chairmanship and Revenue Office were to be united under a single minister, and this was to be Hatzfeld. State debt operations were to remain the province of Emperor Francis, though after his sudden death shortly thereafter, these too were returned to Hatzfeld.[101] Herberstein was rather unceremoniously pushed into retirement. The Court of Audit was to remain as it was under Zinzendorf. The Austro-Bohemian Chancellery was to surrender all fiscal business to the Treasury, but was to be compensated by confirming the incorporation into it of the heretofore independent Department of Trade and Commerce. Subsequent meetings of the Kaunitz

[98] HHStA, Staatskanzlei: Vorträge, Karton 93, Kaunitz's "Ohnmaßgebliches Darfür-halten," 18 May 1764.   [99] *ÖZV* II/3, 223–233.
[100] HHStA, Kabinettsarchiv: Nachlaß Zinzendorf, II: Handschriften, Vol. 2c, Minutes of Kaunitz Committee meetings, 18 and 20 May 1765.
[101] On 21 October 1765. See Beer, "Finanzverwaltung," p. 245.

committee on 18 and 20 May determined the finer details of the degree of co-ordination necessary with the Austro-Bohemian Chancellery when the Treasury was dealing with the provincial authorities. Finally, the plan to audit the records of the Provincial Estates was dropped, Kaunitz being convinced they would never voluntarily submit to such an audit.[102]

The ascent of Joseph II

It could hardly be expected that these reforms of 1765 would put an end to controversies concerning the administrative structure of the Habsburg government. But for the remainder of the reign of Maria Theresia, its essential features were to be left untouched, despite persistent efforts to alter them. The advocates of change, however, now were a whole new group of men, led above all by the Empress's son Joseph. The sudden death of Emperor Francis I elevated the twenty-four-year-old crown prince to the dignity of Holy Roman Emperor and, within weeks, Maria Theresia also created him "Co-Regent" of her hereditary provinces and kingdoms. Unlike his father who had the same title, Joseph was determined to turn the office into a meaningful position of power. The young Emperor's impatience, irritability, propensity to sarcasm and zeal for reform are well known. Politically he claimed to be an eclectic, and there is certainly a considerable amount of eclecticism that can be detected in his later policies. Joseph could also frequently vacillate between positions articulated by the two reforming parties at court, but on the whole his political instincts followed largely in the footsteps of Haugwitz.

This became evident almost immediately after his elevation to the Co-Regency. When, only a few days after the death of Emperor Francis, Haugwitz too succumbed to an equally sudden and unexpected fatal heart attack, Joseph took up his cause. Late in 1765, he submitted a lengthy reform proposal to his mother which, in essence, echoed Haugwitz even if it was cast in the garb of Joseph's own peculiar brand of ascetic impatience. Throughout his memorandum, Joseph revealed his penchant, which was later to grow into an obsession, for interfering in the tiniest details of people's lives in order to abolish luxury, decadence and corruption, and to force humanity to be good. The administrative changes he recommended, however, were the heart of the matter. In 1760, he admitted, he "went overboard" for the "new ideas," but later he "came to see that [he] had accepted in five minutes what, after prolonged reflection, [he] could no longer contemplate." His recommendations now were clearly those of a pupil of Haugwitz. Financial and political administration ought to be

---

[102] HHStA, Kabinettsarchiv: Nachlaß Zinzendorf, II: Handschriften, Vol. 2c, imperial resolution on Minutes of Kaunitz Committee, 18 and 20 May 1765.

united in a reconstituted Directory, though credit and debt and other fiscal operations could be performed by a separate centralized Treasury, much as the Treasury had never been entirely absorbed by Haugwitz's Directory in the 1750s. The Council of State ought to become a body of *ex officio* ministers with supervisory control over the entire machinery of state, and it ought to absorb the Court of Audit to make its surveillance more effective.[103]

Whether out of sheer bewilderment or to elicit an explicit rebuttal, Maria Theresia turned the memo over to Kaunitz for comment. The response of 18 February 1766 was couched in flattering terms about the Co-Regent's sincerity and concern for the public good and, in general, trod more carefully than Kaunitz had been accustomed to doing in the past. Yet, in essence, it rejected Joseph's ideas, with their austere air of regimented puritanism:

Despotic regimes might content themselves with intimidations and punishments. However, in a Monarchy where we are dealing with civilized nations we must also take care to reward merit, not to stifle a certain spiritual progress, with its love for prince and fatherland, and not to rob ourselves of the benefits of those achievements created by thoughts and feelings. It must never be forgotten that it is a greater joy and more worthy of a noble soul to reign over free and thinking beings, than to rule over base slaves.

Stressing pragmatism, Kaunitz began with the premise that "all prohibition is odious," and carried it to Joseph's censorious despotism point-by-point. After a vigorous defence of the reforms of 1760–1765, he concluded by describing the result as "the simplest, most reasonable and best system of government possible." He rejected all attempts to turn the Council of State into a ministerial council, insisting that the key to its utility was its total impartiality. It was for this reason that heads of various departments had been excluded from it. For the same reason, supervisory control was also rejected for the Council as incompatible with its *raison d'être*. Above all, absorbing the Court of Audit was unacceptable since this would turn an impartial advisory council into a mere "department like any other." Further, financial and political administration were "Rome and Carthage", charged with what amounted to mutually exclusive pursuits: increasing revenue and decreasing the burdens on taxpayers. Such matters had to be administered separately, with only the sovereign, advised by the Council of State, making the difficult decisions, now in favour of one, now the other.[104]

---

[103] *MTJC* III, 335–361.
[104] The bulk of the Kaunitz response is published in Beer, ed., "Denkschriften des Fürsten Kaunitz," pp. 98–158. The missing passages were subsequently published by François Fejtö, *Un Habsburg révolutionnaire, Joseph II: Portrait d'un despote éclairé* (Paris,

In the face of this rebuttal, Joseph's proposals died on the vine. But no matter how successfully Kaunitz defended the *status quo*, it could hardly be expected that the last word had been spoken on the matter. Nothing irritated the impatient young Co-Regent more than what he perceived to be needless delays in discharging government business. Despite the reforms of 1765, the grounds for this kind of discontent were still plentiful. To begin with, the Council of State shortly after its inception found itself inundated with virtually every trivial matter which arose. Well over 3,000 items had to be debated every year,[105] and the junior member of the Council who was obliged to submit his views first thus faced an enormous task. Since this was the elderly but conscientious and deliberate Stupan, Council deliberations almost invariably became a long, drawn-out process. An anonymous critique had pointed out as early as 1762 that the Council needed to be simplified and rationalized.[106] Hatzfeld and Zinzendorf had also echoed these sentiments in their joint report of September 1764.[107] Joseph's memorandum of 1765 showed that this issue, for one, was still very much alive half a decade after the Council was created.

A second matter which assumed increasing significance after 1765 was the position of the Court of Audit. Zinzendorf's modern bookkeeping methods, his constant demand for the prompt submission of financial records to his ministry and, above all, his right to audit *ab ante*, involved him in disputes with virtually every other ministry. Nor was Zinzendorf's fertile imagination, always ripe in expedients, appreciated by his more plodding colleagues. By 1766 the fundamental philosophical differences between Hatzfeld and Zinzendorf on economic policy led to a souring of their formerly cordial relationship and within a very short time the two ministers were no longer on speaking terms.[108] Thereafter, Hatzfeld began a concerted attack on the Court of Audit, insisting that its activities simply had to be circumscribed if it was not to retard, indeed cripple, administrative efficiency.[109] Finally, there was the general problem of the torpid pace of business brought about by the increased bureaucratization which had occurred in the Habsburg Monarchy under Maria Theresia, and by the accompanying growth in paperwork which impeded proceedings.

Maria Theresia came around to her son's view that some action was necessary in the face of these problems shortly after her recovery from a bout of smallpox in 1767. There obviously seemed little doubt in her mind

1953). (German translation by Ursula Rohden, *Joseph II.: Porträt eines aufgeklärten Despoten* (Munich, 1987), pp. 96–103; my citations refer to this translation).
[105] HHStA, Kabinettsarchiv: Staatsratprotokolle, Vols. 1–71, *passim*.
[106] Hock-Bidermann, p. 19; *ÖZV* II/1/i, 312–314; II/3, 32.   [107] *ÖZV* II/3, 223–233.
[108] Pettenegg, ed., *Zinzendorf*, p. 102; Beer, "Staatsschulden," p. 34.
[109] HHStA, Kabinettsarchiv: Nachlaß Zinzendorf, Part II, Vol. 3, Hatzfeld Votum, 1 May 1768; Picha, "Hatzfeld"; *ÖZV* II/1/i, 404, 482–483.

about where to begin, and that was to consult Kaunitz. Since no one had a clearer, overall perspective nor a better sense of her "way of thinking", she informed Kaunitz that he was to undertake a review of the entire apparatus of state.[110] Kaunitz was reluctant to accept the commission unless it was endorsed by Joseph as well, but once assured of that, he set to work immediately.[111] Whatever ideas Kaunitz may have had about retiring within two years in 1766 now dissipated entirely as he became engrossed by this project. On 25 January 1768, his labours were complete and he submitted an eighty-one-part memorandum in response to the Empress's call. In general, he felt the structure of government in Austria and Bohemia was not beset by any major problems or disorders, reiterating that the Council of State had been the one major cure of the ailments from which the central administration suffered. He also repeated the importance of general policy guidelines: options ought to be examined without prejudice or precipitate action; states could become wealthy only by enriching their subjects. Though these principles sounded like self-evident platitudes, Kaunitz affirmed, they were all too seldom the basis of action.[112]

Turning to specifics, Kaunitz launched a withering attack on bureaucratic red tape: reports did not have to be re-written as they passed from office to office; polite baroque formalities could be eliminated altogether; inquiries could be made orally instead of occasioning a vast correspondence; routine reports could be shortened; privy councillors ought to be assigned specific responsibilities; the number of conferences and meetings could be reduced. On the other hand, institutions were, on the whole, sound and only minor adjustments were necessary. The Council of State ought to order its agenda by priorities so that important matters would never be neglected. The task of drafting the summary and first opinion on any matter under discussion ought to be rotated amongst Council members so as not to overburden any one of them. In other areas there was even less to do. The Supreme Judiciary needed no improvements, and its judgments needed not to be debated by the Council of State or even considered by the sovereign. The more clearly independent the judiciary was from the executive and legislative power, the better. The Department of Trade and Commerce could be integrated more tightly into the Austro-Bohemian Chancellery, and its affairs could be discharged directly through Gubernial commissions. The various autonomous sections of the Treasury could achieve greater administrative unity by having its privy councillors

[110] HHStA, Familienarchiv: Sammelbände, Karton 70, Maria Theresia to Kaunitz, n.d. (1767).
[111] HHStA, Staatskanzlei: Vorträge, Karton 100, Kaunitz to Maria Theresia, 11 November 1767, including imperial resolution.
[112] *Ibid.*, Karton 101, Kaunitz to Maria Theresia, 25 January 1768.

appointed to various departments simultaneously. Finally, Kaunitz concluded with a vigorous defence of the Court of Audit and its president, Zinzendorf, seeing no need for change in that area.[113]

The usual procedure might now have been the circulation of this report among all the relevant ministers and privy councillors, followed by a debate amongst them of each of the points in turn made. Kaunitz, however, did not think this procedure suitable. In order to prevent any kind of ministerial jealousy, Kaunitz recommended that the Empress keep both the report as well as all oral communication with him a secret. She should, he suggested, regard his report merely as a starting point and solicit from other government officials independent and candid reports on what improvements they, in turn, felt should be made in the administration.[114] Maria Theresia's acceptance of this last suggestion has had the effect of completely obscuring the primary role of Kaunitz in the subsequent reforms of 1768. Identical requests to other ministers, drafted by Kaunitz, were sent out on 11 February 1768 without any reference to Kaunitz's report. Nor, for that matter, did Kaunitz choose to play a very prominent role in subsequent debates, as ideas began to flood into the Council of State over the course of the year. Yet the final results were much in line with his original suggestions. Of course, this hardly meant that men such as Rudolf Chotek had come around to Kaunitz's way of thinking. It did illustrate, however, the almost complete ascendancy Kaunitz had won over Maria Theresia by the late 1760s.

With respect to the reforms in the Council of State itself, of course, it can come as no surprise that Kaunitz's ideas surfaced again. Not only was he a member, but after the deaths of Haugwitz and Daun, the Council came to be dominated by his supporters. Haugwitz's replacement was Starhemberg, who faithfully mirrored Kaunitz's ideas on a wide range of subjects, while the Daun vacancy was filled with Friedrich Binder, Kaunitz's closest friend and associate, who had been a titular member since 1762.[115] Finally, a seventh member was added in 1768 to lighten the burdens on the others. He was to be one of the most outstanding leaders of the Enlightenment party, Tobias Philipp Freiherr von Gebler. Formerly a privy councillor in the Mines and Minerals Department and later in the Austro-Bohemian Chancellery, Gebler was a man of broad vision and sophistication. A major dramatist and sometime collaborator of Mozart, he was a true *philosophe* in the best tradition of the eighteenth century and, hence, a man after Kaunitz's heart.[116] Under the circumstances, in the course of the

---

[113] *Ibid.*   [114] *Ibid.*   [115] *ÖZV* II/1/i, 313.
[116] On Gebler see: *ADB* VIII, 484–485; *NDB* VI, 122; Wurzbach V, 118–120; Hans Schläger, "Tobias Philipp Freiherr von Gebler: Sein Leben und Wirken in Österreich" (unpublished Ph.D. thesis, University of Vienna, 1971).

debates on Council of State reforms, Kaunitz could now afford to ask to be relieved of having to participate in all discussions except those he deemed to be important. Not only was he granted this request, but the Council of State reforms which ensued on 16 December 1768 mirrored his ideas of January. The agenda of the body was to be ordered by priorities, divided into three gradations, which were to be determined by the member who was first to submit his opinion (*Votum*). This task was to be rotated among the junior members, Stupan, Borié and Gebler, every ten items. Opinions were to be kept brief and meetings were now to be held only weekly, on Thursday morning.[117]

It can also come as no surprise that the reform of 1768 left Zinzendorf's Court of Audit essentially untouched. Its activities in auditing matters only indirectly touching on finance were circumscribed, but this was a great relief for everyone concerned, including Zinzendorf's staff. One need scarcely guess why Zinzendorf alone, of all the ministers involved in the reform debates, received not merely instructions but also expressions of the Empress' "exceptional satisfaction" at his conduct of business.[118] On the other hand, it is quite surprising that Chotek and Hatzfeld fell in line with Kaunitz's original suggestions. Of course, they did not know he had made them, and their own preferences took them into completely different areas. Chotek's idea of reform still harked back to the pre-1749 days, and focused on re-acquiring judicial competences for the Austro-Bohemian Chancellery. Hatzfeld's idea for reform harked back to the pre-1761 days, and focused on restricting the activities of the Court of Audit and on the greater collegial concentration of the central administration. Neither would relent even as it was clear their prospects were dim. Both had to receive repeated instructions to address themselves to those problems pointed out by Kaunitz, and both had to be sternly restricted to very specific guidelines that in many cases repeated points from Kaunitz's memorandum verbatim. Hence, it was mostly despite Chotek and Hatzfeld, and not because of them, that Kaunitz's ideas found concrete expression in December 1768. The Department of Trade and Commerce was more tightly integrated into the Austro-Bohemian Chancellery, and several of its administrative duties were transferred to the provincial authorities. The autonomy of the Treasury's various departments was affirmed and expanded, and a detailed list of the duties of all personnel was to be submitted to see where overlap could be eliminated.[119]

Finishing touches were put on the reform of 1768 in the course of the subsequent year. Privy councillors, court secretaries and clerks had their

---

[117] *ÖZV* II/1/i, 431–432; II/3, 34–35.   [118] *Ibid.*, II/1/i, 383–404; II/3, 318–319.
[119] *Ibid.*, II/3, 277–286, 302–313.

duties very precisely defined and, once again, Kaunitz was consulted before any orders were issued.[120] But Kaunitz was pleased to note that the imperial resolutions of the past year had generally been in accordance with his proposals of January 1768, and he had nothing further to add.[121] This was certainly no exaggeration. The reforms of 1768 did not introduce wholesale changes, but merely minor modifications of the reforms of 1761 and 1765. Almost at every turn they followed closely the directions that had been first indicated by Kaunitz, and they clearly reflected his conviction that no radical disorders or problems existed in the administrative structure of the Habsburg Monarchy. The fact that debate on administrative issues did not cease after 1768 does not mean that this faith was misplaced. It was not deficiencies in the structure of government so much as the persistence and ambition of men like Hatzfeld that kept reopening the issue. Above all, however, from January 1769 Joseph II's increasing restlessness began to manifest itself ever more insistently, and to occasion continuing and heated debate over the nature of the administration.

Within a month after adjustments to the Council of State had been made, Joseph began to sense that he was the fifth wheel on the Council cart. In order to give expression to his feeling of impotence, he began to insist he would no longer sign documents except with the qualification "qua Corregens" (as Co-Regent) to underscore his signature's essentially *pro forma* character.[122] All attempts to dissuade him in this failed,[123] and for the remainder of the reign of Maria Theresia, the qualification is invariably to be found next to Joseph's name on official documents. The Emperor's main problem with the Council of State, however, was the specific individuals on it. Stupan was old, frail and slow. Binder, Gebler and to some extent Borié were all Kaunitz's men. Starhemberg, who also came to agree with Kaunitz more and more, had made a poor impression on Joseph, and Blümegen was "too timid and compliant *vis-à-vis* mother."[124] Blümegen, in particular, irritated Joseph because he had all too often taken the liberty of drafting imperial resolutions before a decision had actually been made.[125] A similar ambition to control the agenda and the secretariat of the council had cost König his position and led to the elimination of the Referendary position in August 1770.[126] As a result, the Emperor's

---

[120] HHStA, Staatskanzlei: Vorträge, Karton 104, Maria Theresia to Kaunitz, 29 September 1769.   [121] *Ibid.*, Kaunitz to Maria Theresia, 23 October 1769.
[122] *MTJC* I, 233–241.
[123] HHStA, Kabinettsarchiv: Varia der Kabinettskanzlei, Fasz. 20a, Simon Thaddäus Reischach to Maria Theresia, 28 and 31 January 1769.
[124] Khevenhüller-Metsch VII, 106.
[125] Schünemann, "Wirtschaftspolitik," pp. 37–38.
[126] *ÖZV* II/1/i, 433–434; II/3, 39–41.

response now was to suggest he personally supervise all Council of State resolutions, and he was quite pleased when his mother acceded to the wish. But it was not long before Joseph realized that this did little to increase his effective power.[127]

Precisely during these years a serious socio-economic crisis beset the Monarchy, highlighted by the great Bohemian famine of 1770–1772. After an inspection tour of that province, Joseph decided that the drastic problems he had witnessed first-hand required more than personnel changes; they required even more drastic administrative cures.[128] In the fall of 1771, Joseph proposed to his mother that she select some "honest, unselfish ... perspicacious and diligent person" and give him "absolute confidence" to oversee the entire government.[129] The Emperor undoubtedly had himself in mind, and it must have come as somewhat of a surprise to him when a candidate for this prime ministerial job appeared in the person of Hatzfeld. Hatzfeld had not been happy with the outcome of the reform of 1768, and in the subsequent months continued to express his dissatisfaction with what he claimed to be inefficient government. During this time, he gradually turned from a supporter of the essential principles of the reform of 1761 to an advocate of the concentration of ministerial power surpassing even Haugwitz. When he was finally requested to present a specific plan late in 1770, Hatzfeld submitted a series of elaborate proposals from February to August 1771, calling for the unification of the Austro-Bohemian Chancellery, the Treasury (including the Vienna City Bank chairmanship) and the Court of Audit under the authority of a single minister, who would then also be admitted to the Council of State.[130] Fate was on Hatzfeld's side for, in the previous November, Rudolf Chotek had suffered a stroke which left him unable to speak. As his condition deteriorated, Maria Theresia decided to remove him from his post in June 1771 and, without actually changing the structure of the government, gave Hatzfeld the opportunity to demonstrate the efficacy of his suggestions. Without losing his other posts, he was now made Austro-Bohemian Chancellor as well.[131]

This *de facto* accretion of power was not enough for Hatzfeld. He continued to press for the full implementation of his scheme. The reception of the idea in the Council of State was unfriendly in the extreme. Binder was full of bitter innuendos about Hatzfeld's overweening ambition. Gebler, Stupan and Blümegen remarked none too subtly that such a heavy

---

[127] *MTJC* I, 335–336; Arneth, *Maria Theresia* IX, 296–297; *ÖZV* II/1/i, 435–436.
[128] HHStA, Familienarchiv: Sammelbände, Karton 7, Joseph to Leopold of Tuscany, 19 September 1771.   [129] *ÖZV* II/3, 42–43.
[130] *Ibid.*, 315; Picha, "Hatzfeld," p. 89.
[131] Khevenhüller-Metsch VI, 81. Chotek died a few days later.

work load would be too much even for the energetic Hatzfeld. Kaunitz chose to ignore Hatzfeld's *de facto* position altogether. If the Empress saw fit to appoint the same man to two separate ministries, so be it. As far as the *de jure* restructuring of government was concerned, it was ridiculous to make changes again "after so many deliberations." Hatzfeld's Council of State ideas and Court of Audit proposals did not even deserve discussion, but should be rejected "simply and without further debate."[132] Perhaps the matter would have died there had Joseph not chosen this precise moment to press for some sort of super-minister. As it was, the Empress now put her son in the uncomfortable position of delineating his proposal more fully with the clear implication that the "honest, unselfish, perspicacious and diligent" individual chosen would be Hatzfeld not Joseph.

The Emperor beat a hasty retreat. In his response of 27 November 1771, he returned to the theme that it was the personnel, not the structure, that needed to be changed. Fortunately, there were excellent pretexts at hand. In the first place, three vacancies had occurred on the Council of State. In January 1770, the authorized minister in Brussels, Karl Cobenzl, died and it was decided to replace him with Starhemberg.[133] Shortly thereafter, Borié was appointed Austro-Burgundian ambassador to the Imperial Diet at Regensburg, and König, as has been noted above, was dismissed.[134] In the second place, Joseph now intervened in favour of the administrative *status quo*, which meant that Chotek's death created another vacancy. Hence, the Co-Regent outlined a ministerial shuffle of major proportions. Only Zinzendorf could remain in his ministry, though the Court of Audit's right to prior audit ought to be abolished. Hatzfeld was to be stripped of all his offices and given Starhemberg's position on the Council of State. The Austro-Bohemian Chancellery should go to Blümegen, who, as a consequence, would have to leave the Council of State. Binder, whom Joseph had grown to dislike intensely, was also to be removed from the Council of State to some honorary post such as Director of the Court Archive. This, of course, now left numerous vacancies, all of which Joseph proposed to fill with a whole new generation of men. The Treasury could go to Leopold Kollowrat-Krakowsky, former Vice-Chancellor in the Austro-Bohemian Court Chancellery; the chairmanship of the Vienna City Bank to Eugen Wrbna; and the Council of State vacancies to Franz Karl Freiherr von Kressel and Pál Festetics, Aulic Councillors in the Court Chancellery and Treasury, respectively.[135] What these men had in common

---

[132] HHStA, Kabinettsarchiv: Kaunitz Voten, Karton 2, No. 2745 of 1771, Council of State opinions, 31 August to 4 September 1771.
[133] Eichwalder, p. 199; Arneth, *Maria Theresia* X, 211–212.
[134] *ÖZV* II/1/i, 433–434; cf. Peter Muzik, "Egid Valentin Felix Freiherr von Borié (1719–1793): Leben und Werk eines österreichischen Staatsmannes" (Unpublished Ph.D. dissertation, University of Vienna, 1972).   [135] *MTJC* I, 352–356.

was not so much their economics or politics,[136] but that they were the personal favourites of Joseph. Clearly in this way the Emperor sought to create his own party which, in turn, would give him the kind of influence on affairs he had desired for some time. We know that Kaunitz was asked to review Joseph's recommendations,[137] but his advice to the Empress appears to have been oral, for no written response is extant. In any case, Kaunitz could have had no major complaints about the proposed shuffle, particularly since, in essence, it put an end to Hatzfeld's planned super-ministry. Interestingly enough, Hatzfeld was stripped of his offices and promoted to the Council of State within a very short period of time, with the official notification being drafted by none other than Kaunitz days before it was actually sent.[138] Meanwhile, Hatzfeld, not yet aware of Joseph's plans for him, set to work trying to convert the Emperor to his viewpoint. In a little more than a week he succeeded and Joseph now dispatched a rapid *volte-face* to his mother. Hatzfeld was right after all, he said, and he was now prepared to endorse these ideas. Of the two possible candidates for supreme minister, Hatzfeld and Blümegen, he preferred the former.[139] But now it was too late. The Empress, having consulted Kaunitz, prepared to implement what largely amounted to her son's original plan. Blümegen and Binder left the Council of State; Hatzfeld joined it. Blümegen became Austro-Bohemian Court Chancellor; Binder returned to the Foreign Ministry. Kollowrat became head of the Treasury and Chairman of the Vienna City Bank. The Court of Audit lost its right of audit *ab ante*, but Zinzendorf remained in charge. The Council of State was supplemented by Kressel, though Festetics was passed over in favour of Johann Friedrich von Löhr, a nephew of Borié and former councillor in the Supreme Judiciary. The Council of State Referendary position was definitively eliminated, and in its place a new executive officer for the council's secretariat (*Staatsrats-Kanzlei Direktor*) was appointed, Joseph Koller, who was to wield little official power but much unofficial influence in his fifteen years in this position.[140]

If Hatzfeld's ambitions were thus shattered, he nevertheless scored a final triumph over his rival Zinzendorf. Throughout 1771, he had asserted that the Treasury could perform internal audits more cheaply and quickly

---

[136] As is suggested by Schünemann, "Wirtschaftspolitik," pp. 37–38.
[137] HHStA, Staatskanzlei: Vorträge, Karton 108, "Geheimes Gutachten des Kaysers," with Kaunitz file notation, December 1771.
[138] *Ibid.*, draft of letter to Hatzfeld, 30 November 1771.   [139] *MTJC* I, 357–358.
[140] Khevenhüller-Metsch VII, 106–107, 407–408; *ÖZV* II/3, 315–316. On the rejection of Festetics, see below, p. 312. On Joseph Koller, see Hock-Bidermann, pp. 23, 103, and especially Václav Černý, "Pozemková reforma v. XVIII. století," *Časopis pro dějiny venkova* XIV (1927), 37–39, who was the first to appreciate Koller's tremendous hidden influence at court. (References to Černý, "Pozemková reforma," are to Vol. XIV of the *Časopis* unless stated otherwise.)

than any separate ministry, and he had converted Gebler, Stupan and Blümegen to that view. Zinzendorf's main defender was Binder, but after the ministerial shuffle of 1771 the complexion of the Council of State changed. With Binder out and Hatzfeld in, there was now near unanimous support for the abolition of the Court of Audit. Kaunitz, himself, was silenced, if not persuaded; while Zinzendorf, who had been seriously ill for some time, was in no physical condition to wage a protracted debate. The fate of the Court of Audit was sealed. By a decree of 20 January 1773, it lost its independence and became an arm of the Treasury.[141] While Zinzendorf was retired with every honour the court could devise, including titular membership in the Council of State,[142] it was clear that the political following of Kaunitz was in retreat and that of Joseph on the advance.

Meanwhile, Joseph's impatience and irritation were growing by the day. The Bohemian famine had reached crisis proportions by the spring of 1772, and all government remedial efforts seemed pitifully inadequate to the Emperor. At the same time, the Polish Partition crisis made him fear the Habsburg Monarchy would suffer an international setback. In the face of these problems, therefore, the Co-Regent returned to his idea that only drastic methods could rescue the Monarchy from the brink of catastrophe. Once again, on 13 June 1772, he recommended the appointment of a dictator to ride roughshod over the Empire's constitutions and customs. This man should be permitted to employ "all possible means," including the freedom to make sweeping personnel changes, to set the Monarchy straight again. He must have "unlimited power" and "the complete trust" of the Empress, for only in this way could any reform with lasting merit be undertaken.[143] At first, Maria Theresia simply waited some months. Then she attempted to sidestep her son's suggestion by focusing on specific Bohemian problems,[144] but Joseph responded that all efforts would be wasted without the "introduction of another administration."[145] Once again she turned to Kaunitz who, in turn, attempted to draw together the basic premises and principles of the internal administration he had articulated so often before. He concluded that no major overhaul of any kind was necessary. If there were problems in the Monarchy, they were not with the structure of its government.[146] The Empress, however, realizing that this was hardly enough to silence, much less persuade Joseph, wanted Kaunitz to do more. She asked him to produce an even more detailed

---

[141] ÖZV II/1/i, 487–490; II/3, 327–340.
[142] Pettenegg, ed., Zinzendorf, pp. 138–139.
[143] Schünemann, "Wirtschaftpolitik," pp. 41–43.
[144] HHStA, Familienarchiv: Sammelbände, Karton 7, Maria Theresia to Joseph, 6 October 1772.   [145] Ibid., Joseph to Maria Theresia, 6 October 1772.
[146] HHStA, Staatskanzlei: Vorträge, Karton 110, Kaunitz to Maria Theresia, n.d. (November or December 1772).

analysis which addressed itself to specific faults in the administration which could be corrected.[147]

Kaunitz now knew that his job was to win over the Emperor and he set about doing this in every way possible. He began to compose what was to be the longest memorandum of his career, quoting and flattering Joseph throughout, making every effort to come to grips with specific complaints the Emperor had made over the years. He then asked Joseph to peruse the first draft. In a second draft, Kaunitz made large-scale changes incorporating virtually every one of Joseph's suggestions, so that he had every reason to believe it would meet with the Co-Regent's approval.[148] The final draft was formally submitted to Maria Theresia on 1 May 1773. This enormous report was divided into three sections: one addressed itself to socio-economic problems, particularly inequitable taxation; a second focused on what Kaunitz called "moral defects" of the administration; and the third concerned deficiencies in the governmental structure proper. In the second of these, Kaunitz once again stressed the necessity of precise instructions to the bureaucracy, and of very clear, "well-understood" ideological premises and guidelines. Because he felt that, for the most part, problems in the Habsburg government were those of execution rather than structure, the apparently self-evident could not be repeated often enough. For similar reasons he warned against rigid and "despotic" administrative hierarchies which stressed only "slavish obedience," and urged instead that greater scope for initiative be given to lower levels of the bureaucracy.[149]

But when it came to the third portion of the memorandum, Kaunitz was hard-pressed to come up with sweeping recommendations. He was willing to admit that the Council of State still did not operate quite as smoothly and efficiently as it should, but this was mostly because it still busied itself with excessive trivia. There was no need to deal with every current issue as a matter of course. Otherwise, it was merely a matter of adhering more precisely to the operational procedures already adopted in 1768. Only one major change could be discussed, and that was to implement Joseph's suggestion of 1765 that the Council take over the functions of the Court of Audit. With the absorption of Zinzendorf's old ministry by the Treasury, Kaunitz simply could not bring himself to have "blind faith in the assertions of the financial authorities." The idea of entrusting central accounting to the Council of State suddenly became much more attractive.

---

[147] Arneth, *Maria Theresia* IX, 306.
[148] HHStA, Staatskanzlei: Vorträge, Karton 111, Joseph to Kaunitz, 20 April 1773, Kaunitz to Maria Theresia, 1 May 1773.
[149] HHStA, Staatskanzlei: Vorträge, Karton 112, Kaunitz's "Allergnädigst anbefohlenes Gutachten über die Verbesserung des Systematis in Internis," 1 May 1773.

The only other area where Kaunitz could see the need for any structural changes was at the local level with the county office (*Kreisamt*). Already in 1771, he had called the deliberate disregard of royal decrees "the main evil of the Monarchy" and had singled out the county officers as the key to combatting it.[150] The county office was the most vital cog of enlightened absolutism, since the crown relied on its local agents both for precise information on local conditions and for guaranteeing the strict enforcement of its decrees. This, Kaunitz felt, was too much for a single county officer to do, and the best solution was to subdivide counties into as many districts as were necessary for them to be handled effectively by one man. The creation of a whole new level of local bureaucracy would naturally entail expenses, but these would be well worth it. Trying to save money by using seigniorial bailiffs for the job would be counter-productive. Clearly, such seigniorial "blood-suckers and tyrants of the peasants" would serve the interests of their lords more than the crown.[151]

If Joseph led Kaunitz to believe he endorsed this huge memorandum, he revealed his true sentiments to his brother. He had "had to refute" a giant plan of Kaunitz, he wrote, made up of "theoretical ideas" impossible to execute.[152] The "refutation" took the form of his own plan, which he presented to his mother three days before Kaunitz submitted his final draft. Yet again, Joseph focused on a concentration of power, carving out a predominant role for himself. The Council of State should become a secret cabinet under himself, directing and overseeing both domestic and foreign policy. The head of the cabinet would determine priorities and assign duties to various departments. The central administration should, once again, unite the political and financial portfolios for the sake of efficiency. Provincial governments could be expanded by creating a middle-level authority between the Gubernium and the County Office. Provincial Estates could be given a bit more freedom of action, and could be allowed to elect their own head. Joseph must have been sufficiently realistic about the prospects these plans had for fulfillment, for he simultaneously sent his mother a "second project" focusing on Council of State reform alone, in case the Empress chose to reject his first scheme. The second proposal followed Kaunitz's recommendations, but added that the ordering of the agenda by priorities ought to be done by himself.[153]

Joseph's duplicity, his scarcely veiled contempt for Kaunitz, and his violent disagreement with the old Chancellor of State over the fate of the

---

[150] HHStA, Kabinettsarchiv: Kaunitz Voten zu Staatsratakten, Karton 2, No. 2140 of 1771, Kaunitz Staatsrat Votum, 6 July 1771.
[151] HHStA, Staatskanzlei: Vorträge, Karton 112, Kaunitz's "Allergnädigst anbefohlenes Gutachten über die Verbesserung des Systematis in Internis," 1 May 1773.
[152] *MTJC* II, 6–7.   [153] *ÖZV* II/3, 53–73.

newly-acquired province of Galicia, finally pushed Kaunitz to breaking point. On 7 December 1773, Kaunitz asked to be relieved of all his posts.[154] Once more, though, the Empress prevailed on him to change his mind. "Your note did not shock or surprise me," she said, "but it grieved me, grieved me greatly." He must remain to help her, otherwise they might as well both retire.[155] Thereupon she delivered what must have been a stinging verbal rebuke to her son, for Joseph now felt compelled to submit his resignation as Co-Regent as well.[156] But maternal authority prevailed. Joseph wrote a flattering letter of reconciliation to Kaunitz,[157] and a compromise between the two men on the structure of government ensued. Kaunitz was given the opportunity to refute Joseph's sweeping recommendations, but was careful to do so by emphasizing the areas of agreement between the two of them.[158] Joseph, in turn, now endorsed Kaunitz's great report with very minor qualifications. The idea of a secret cabinet and a shake-up of the central administration were dropped. Joseph was given the right to order Council of State priorities personally. An effort was also made to give the Council an audit function. The accounting system that was set up, however, did not live up to anyone's expectations and was dropped again within a few months. Otherwise, the Council remained unchanged.[159] A similar compromise was reached on county reform. Joseph dropped his idea of a new middle-level provincial bureaucracy and Kaunitz dropped the idea of district officers. Instead, county office personnel was increased to include military officials and the county officers were provided with very precise operational guidelines designed to exclude local lords from excessive influence and to guarantee the full implementation of imperial decrees.[160] These compromises may not have been enough to end all tensions between Kaunitz and Joseph – there were too many other areas of disagreement for that. They were enough, however, to end any further discussion in Maria Theresia's reign on the Monarchy's structure of government.

---

[154] HHStA, Staatskanzlei: Vorträge, Karton 113, Kaunitz to Maria Theresia, 7 December 1773.   [155] Arneth, *Maria Theresia* VIII, 617–618.
[156] Th. G. von Karajan, *Maria Theresia und Joseph II. während der Mitregentschaft* (Vienna, 1865), pp. 28–31.   [157] *MTJC* II, 22.
[158] HHStA, Staatskanzlei: Vorträge, Karton 114, Kaunitz to Maria Theresia, 20 February 1774.   [159] Hock-Bidermann, p. 41; *ÖZV* II/3, 77–84.
[160] HHStA, Staatskanzlei: Vorträge, Karton 122, Kaunitz to Maria Theresia, 22 March 1777, including imperial resolution. Cf. Ignaz Beidtel, *Geschichte der österreichischen Staatsverwaltung, 1740–1848*, 2 Vols. (Innsbruck, 1896–1898), I, 176–177.

4   The financial crises of the Monarchy

At the heart of the structural changes of the Habsburg central and local administration under Maria Theresia lay an economic, or more precisely, a fiscal imperative. Governments in the *ancien régime* often seemed in a state of permanent penury, leading a hand-to-mouth existence from one financial crisis to another. Waging costly foreign policies motivated by baroque dynastic self-images and mercantilist concepts of international rivalry, governments found that their expenditures were regularly in excess of revenues. The more dramatically dynastic pretensions surpassed the capacity of the respective societies to uphold them – as was the case in the Habsburg conglomerate under Charles VI – the more drastic these fiscal crises became. Since the full mobilization of the state's economic resources in a modern fashion was beyond dynastic governments still encumbered by various feudal contracts and obligations, their prime recourse was to taxes and loans, the raising of which was subject to its own unique difficulties. Securing adequate revenues in the face of these limitations was therefore an ever-present concern. In short, social and political conditions dictated a sort of fiscal obsession.[1]

It did not escape the attention of early modern governments and economists that these fiscal anxieties were ultimately dependent on the strength of the overall economy as much as on their ability to tap these resources. Mercantilists had developed a considerable body of economic theory designed to promote the expansion of the state's commercial and industrial base within a broader ideal of autarky. The central European variant of mercantilism, known as cameralism, produced three highly articulate spokesmen in Austria, though none of the three were native sons: the Rhinelander, Johann Joachim Becher, whose principal work, *Politischer Diskurs von den eigentlichen Ursachen des Auf- und Abnehmens der Städte, Länder und Republicken* appeared in 1668; his brother-in-law, Philipp Wilhelm von Hörnigk, who produced the famous *Österreich über alles wenn es nur will* in 1684; and the Saxon, Wilhelm von Schröder, whose

[1] C. B. A. Behrens, *The Ancien Régime* (London, 1967), pp. 140–141.

Fürstliche Schatz- und Rentkammer of 1686 was to be formative in the development of Haugwitz's reform ideas.[2]

Becher, Hörnigk and Schröder, of course, differed in many respects but all three tended to emphasize internal economic problems inherent in the relative underdevelopment of the Habsburg lands more than Western mercantilists. They retained the mercantilist premise of autarky, emphasizing a favourable balance of trade and the inflow of specie through minimizing imports and maximizing exports. By geographic necessity, however, their focus was less on overseas trade and more on increase of domestic production. Economic development was to be fostered by enhancing the economic structural unity of the Monarchy. Internal tariffs were to be reduced while external ones were to be raised; domestic industrial development was to be stimulated through the granting of subsidies and monopolies and through pointing consumer demand to domestic products; unused land and resources were to be exploited; the flow of commodities within the Monarchy was to be facilitated by the improvement of transportation systems; domestic markets were to be increased by implementing every conceivable measure to raise the population base.[3]

As the very name of "cameralist" suggests, however, the central concern of these economists was the princely "camera" or treasury. They focused, above all, on the problem of increasing state revenues, and their economic programmes were designed essentially to raise the taxable capacity of society. What is more, in exploring the means by which the state could exploit and marshall the consequent hoped-for economic prosperity, they developed what Hubert Johnson has aptly called "a distinct bureaucratic ethos" and a social conservatism that did not easily accept the destabilization inherent in economic growth. Narrow fiscalism, social conservatism and torpescent bureaucratization thus ironically retarded and obstructed the very programme of economic development of which it intended to take advantage.[4] Habsburg economic policies were therefore marked by an ambivalence between the fiscal imperative, which at times assumed ruinous proportions, and the broader economic prescriptions, which, increasingly, were advocated by a growing segment of opinion.

[2] Johann Joachim Becher, *Politischer Diskurs von den eigentlichen Ursachen des Auf- und Abnehmens der Städte, Länder und Republicken* (Frankfurt, 1668); Philipp Wilhelm von Hörnigk, *Österreich über alles wenn es nur will* (1684), in the modern edition ed. by Gustav Otruba (Vienna, 1964); Wilhelm von Schröder, *Fürstliche Schatz- und Rentkammer* (1686), in the edition of Leipzig, 1704.
[3] Sommer, *Kameralisten*; Herbert Hassinger, *Johann Joachim Becher, 1635–1682: Ein Beitrag zur Geschichte des Merkantilismus* (Vienna, 1951); Heinrich Gerstenberg, "Philipp Wilhelm von Hörnigk," *Jahrbücher für Nationalökonomie und Statistik* CXXXIII (1930), 813–867; Srbik, "Wilhelm von Schröder"
[4] Johnson, "Concept of Bureaucracy," pp. 378–402.

The Haugwitz reforms and the Seven Years War

In 1740 the fiscal focus predominated overwhelmingly. State revenues of approximately 22 million Gulden per annum were heavily charged, and disposable income may have been as low as 2–3 million Gulden. The state debt had climbed to 101 million Gulden, and the liquid assets of the crown stood at a mere 87,000 Gulden at the accession of Maria Theresia. Regular tax revenue, which was administered by the Estates of the various provinces, was commonly in arrears, and a major English loan of £320,000 Sterling dating from 1737 was due for repayment between 1743 and 1752.[5] The famous tax increase voted by the Hungarian Diet at the tempestuous session of September 1741 was in fact quite modest, and that the War of the Austrian Succession could be contested at all was due largely to an annual subsidy of £300,000 Sterling (c. 1,500,000 Gulden) voted by the British Parliament.[6] Domestic fiscal resources and even fiscal potential, in short, were totally inadequate to meet the crisis at hand.

This did not mean that no efforts had been made to ameliorate the root causes of the problem. Certainly cameralist prescriptions had not gone totally unheeded in the generation before 1740, and promising steps had been taken by the government to foster economic growth. State-sponsored factories were established, and private entrepreneurs were encouraged to found others, especially in textile manufacturing. Mining experienced an upswing, and building a veritable boom. Efforts had been made to exploit the trade potential of the Mediterranean, the Levant and the Far East by establishing trade companies, creating new trade links and improving internal and expanding external trade routes. But on the whole these policies yielded economic results that were more prodigious in their promise than their results. Even domestic trade was hamstrung by internal tariffs, provincial particularism and prejudice and ignorance about economic development. The essential problem remained the social and economic conservatism of the vested interests, particularly the landed aristocracy and the Church, which expressed itself primarily in obstinate opposition to structural changes that were a precondition for sustained economic growth.[7]

---

[5] Dickson, *Finance and Government* II, 2–6, 380, 403; Gustav Otruba, "Staatshaushalt und Staatsschuld unter Maria Theresia und Joseph II.," in Richard Georg Plaschka, Grete Klingenstein, *et al.*, eds., *Österreich im Europa der Aufklärung*, 2 Vols., (Vienna, 1985), I, 200–201, 248. There is a slight discrepancy between the figures reported by Otruba and Dickson, but the overall picture is consistent.

[6] On the British subsidies, with their slight variations from year to year, see Dickson, *Finance and Government* II, 158–172, 391–393.

[7] Heinrich Ritter von Srbik, *Der staatliche Exporthandel Österreichs von Leopold I. bis Maria Theresia* (Vienna and Leipzig, 1907, reprinted Frankfurt am Main, 1969);

The dimensions of the problem were clearly recognized even in the reign of Charles VI by such perceptive middle-level bureaucrats as Christian Julius Schierl von Schierendorff,[8] but no concerted action was taken until the advent of Haugwitz. As we have seen, Haugwitz placed the blame for revenue shortfalls directly on the Estates, financial mismanagement and corruption as well as on a taxation system whose cadastral estimates were dishonest, unreliable and unjust. Thus, substantial increases in revenue could be achieved merely by placing the responsibility of tax collection into the hands of an impartial professional bureaucracy, and substituting antiquated contributions in kind for cash payments. But in face of the manpower goals the War Ministry projected as imperative for a peace-time military establishment, the requisite 14 million Gulden in tax revenue, which would entail the virtual doubling of the war tax from the Austro-Bohemian lands, could not be raised by simple efficient fiscal management of the existing tax system. Haugwitz therefore posited the revolutionary principle of regular taxation of seigniorial lands in peacetime in the name of "God-pleasing justice and natural equity."[9] Though the "just" share of the tax burden which the nobility was thus required to assume on seigniorial lands was, in the event, calculated at a rate ranging from 30% to 50% lower than that levied on peasant land, it still aroused bitter resentment which normally expressed itself in tax evasion.[10]

Seigniorial tax evasion took many forms. Among the most prevalent was passing on the additional burden to the peasant either by exceeding the tax ceiling on peasant land, or by reviving numerous antiquated feudal dues, which amounted to the same thing. The other popular form of seigniorial tax evasion was hiding assets – and, in particular, under-reporting the actual amount of land under cultivation or the value of the gross product harvested, or both. Since the official cadastres had been compiled by voluntary seigniorial reports of their holdings, the effect was merely to sanction this abuse. For this reason complete revisions of the various provincial cadastres were undertaken between 1748 and 1756. These "Theresian Cadastres" still relied on seigniorial reports and did not undertake formal surveys. But now these reports had to be confirmed by officials who undertook at least a visual inspection. What is more, other sources of seigniorial revenue derived from manufactories and

Mikoletzky, *Österreich*, pp. 85–96, 121–124, 155–161; Wangermann, *Austrian Achievement*, pp. 21–55.

[8] Alfred Fischel, "Christian Julius v. Schierendorff. Ein Vorläufer des liberalen Zentralismus unter Joseph I. und Karl VI.," in his *Studien zur österreichischen Reichsgeschichte* (Vienna, 1906), pp. 139–305.   [9] Beer, "Staatsschulden," pp. 89–90; see pp. 74–75 above.

[10] The older literature on the subject has now been supplanted by Dickson, *Finance and Government* II, 185–271.

the like – the so-called *adminicula* – were included in the reports for the first time.[11]

Despite the limitations of the Theresian Cadastres and despite the continuation of seigniorial abuses, the total effect of the Haugwitz reform was nevertheless nothing short of spectacular. Revenues were estimated to have increased a full 50 % and in some cases well beyond that.[12] Criticism of the reform, of course, was vehement, though the Empress did not pay much heed to it as long as it was articulated by outright reactionaries. But in 1753 the more trusted Johann Christoph Bartenstein joined the ranks of the critics. Having been removed from the Chancellory of State, he was made Vice-Chancellor of Haugwitz's Central Directory. He had barely been in this position for six months when he drafted a confidential memo to the Empress expressing doubt that the Haugwitz reform could realize its objectives. The burden of his argument was that Haugwitz's taxation was too harsh, but he also pointed out that projected revenues could by no means be relied upon.[13] In this situation Maria Theresia turned to Kaunitz. Just as she had corresponded with him through her private secretary behind the backs of Uhlfeld and Bartenstein on vital foreign policy issues during 1750–1752, so too she now utilized the same channel to carry out secret discussions with him on this important domestic issue behind the back of Haugwitz and his Directory officials. It was agreed that Koch should carry out a discreet investigation of the problem. In the fall of 1754 he in turn produced a report which showed that war-time costs would indeed be almost double the peace-time ones, and that recruitment goals would probably be substantially undershot.[14] When Kaunitz examined Koch's report, he was forced to concede that the negative analyses of the Haugwitz finance system were essentially accurate, and he therefore recommended that he meet with Koch secretly on a regular basis to work out a solution.[15] In the course of these discussions it became clear that in the event of war extraordinary fiscal measures would have to supplement the Haugwitz system.

---

[11] *Ibid.* Here, too, Dickson synthesizes and corrects the older literature, including the classic study of the Bohemian cadastre, Josef Pekař, *České katastry, 1654–1789* (Prague, 1932).

[12] *ÖZV* II/1/i, 255; Dickson, *Finance and Government* II, 398–399.

[13] HHStA, Staatskanzlei: Vorträge, Karton 73, Bartenstein to Maria Theresia (original drafts), 4 and 28 November 1753; HHStA, Kabinettsarchiv: Nachlaß Zinzendorf, II: Handschriften, Vol. 2b, copies of the above as well as Bartenstein to Maria Theresia, 31 January 1756.

[14] HHStA, Staatskanzlei: Vorträge, Karton 75, Koch Memorandum, n.d. (November 1754). Cf. Franz A. J. Szabo, "Haugwitz, Kaunitz, and the Structure of Government under Maria Theresia, 1745 to 1761," *Historical Papers/Communications Historiques: Saskatoon 1979* (Ottawa, 1980), pp. 119–120.

[15] HHStA, Staatskanzlei: Vorträge, Karton 75, Kaunitz (m.p.) to Maria Theresia, 13 November 1754.

The high cost of war in the fiercely competitive world of the eighteenth century was a problem that faced all European countries, and the financial expedients to which they resorted covered a vast gamut. Effort could, of course, be made to increase direct taxes, but this ordinarily required the consent of the Estates and could usually proceed at best by meager increments. In any case this is what the Haugwitz reform had done, so that this option had already been pushed as far as it would go for the moment. To increase direct taxes in the Hungarian half of the Monarchy was also virtually impossible. Increasing and imposing new extraordinary and indirect taxes was a second option, but this could retard the very economic development whose profits it was designed to skim. In any case, as the Russian example under Peter I demonstrated, even an incredibly ingenious range of extraordinary taxes realized far lower yields than was expected.[16] Other expedients, such as inflation of the currency as was the case in Prussia, or writing off debts by declaring bankruptcy as was the case in France, were short-range solutions with serious long-term liabilities. English experience, however, pointed to yet another way: the systematic exploitation of public credit. Throughout the eighteenth century England covered on average one-third of its expenditures by public borrowing – a figure which reached as high as 40% during the American War of Independence. In the process it developed investment and credit facilities which provided the financial infrastructure of the subsequent industrial revolution, and allowed England to become the dominant great power it became despite its unpromising physical assets.[17]

Kaunitz owed his conversion to public credit ideas to a man whom he delighted in calling his "pupil"[18] and who became his principal adviser in economic matters, Count Ludwig von Zinzendorf.[19] Descended from an Austrian Protestant émigré family and a nephew of the famous Pietist of the same name, Zinzendorf re-converted to Catholicism in 1739 and entered Austrian government service with the provincial government of Lower Austria. After meeting and impressing Kaunitz in 1749, Zinzendorf was offered an attaché position in the Paris embassy. Zinzendorf intended to launch a diplomatic career, but he soon impressed his new master with his aptitude for economic problems and consequently was channeled by Kaunitz into this direction because, as Kaunitz put it, "we have a serious

---

[16] Vasili Klyuchevsky, *Peter the Great*, trans. by Liliana Archibald (London and N.Y., 1958), pp. 158–164.

[17] P. G. M. Dickson, *The Financial Revolution in England* (London and N.Y., 1967), pp. 8–12.   [18] Schlitter, ed., *Correspondance*, p. 18.

[19] On Zinzendorf see Pettenegg, ed., *Zinzendorf*; *ADB*, 353–356; Christine Lebeau, "Ludwig et Karl von Zinzendorf, administrateurs des finances: Aristocratie et pouvoir dans la Monarchie des Habsbourg, 1748–1791," 2 Vols. (unpublished Ph.D. thesis, University of Paris IV–Sorbonne, 1991), which was regrettably not available at the time of writing.

shortage of experts in this field. " Zinzendorf was accordingly instructed to make a thorough study of English and French literature on the subject. He was also permitted to travel within France as well as to England and Holland to collect information first-hand, and he soon developed a special interest and expertise in public credit and banking and in new methods of bookkeeping.[20] Upon Zinzendorf's return to Vienna in 1753, Kaunitz arranged for his protégé to receive the post of a privy councillor in the Directory's Department of Trade and Commerce, where his ideas rapidly alienated his conservative department head, Count Rudolph Chotek. When Zinzendorf had the temerity to go over Chotek's head to present his views on public credit to Emperor Francis himself, tensions grew to the point where the young privy councillor was forced to leave his department. Kaunitz came to his rescue with a special diplomatic mission to Russia in 1755. When he returned at the end of that year, Kaunitz asked him to work out a detailed plan on using public credit to supplement the crown's revenues during time of war.[21]

Zinzendorf completed his commission early in July 1756. Owing to the diplomatic crisis which was soon to result in the Seven Years War, submission of the plan was delayed for a few weeks. But on 24 July it was sent to Kaunitz and, on 11 August, Zinzendorf had a lengthy personal conference with him to explain the details of the proposal.[22] Zinzendorf's scheme was modeled on the most important and most successful short-term English government bonds, the so-called Exchequer Bills. Convinced that the bulk of liquid assets within the Monarchy lay distributed over a broad mass of middlingly prosperous citizens, Zinzendorf felt this reservoir could be tapped with short-dated paper in relatively small denominations. The issue was to take the form of endorsable bearer-bonds with detachable premium certificates (*Coupons-Obligationen*). Both matured premium certificates and bonds proper should be redeemable for cash at a specifically constituted exchange, or accepted as currency by all official revenue offices in the country. Because the voluntary loan bond issue was not likely to be swallowed up as quickly as the government needed the cash to conduct the war, an additional compulsory issue of bonds should be released to be used in salary payment virtually like paper money (*Zahlungs-Obligationen*). The total issue was to be for 15 million Gulden at 5% per annum in bills of 30, 120, 600 and 1,200 Gulden, and the requisite sinking fund was to be raised by a combination of an Estates loan and a lottery. To further boost confidence in the bonds, Zinzendorf recommended the government bind

---

[20] HHStA, Staatenabteilung: Frankreich Varia, Karton 22, Kaunitz to Koch, 11 October 1751 and 15 May 1752.   [21] Pettenegg, ed., *Zinzendorf*, pp. 46–63.

[22] *Ibid.*, pp. 67–68. The most important study of Zinzendorf's financial schemes is Johann Schasching, *Staatsbildung und Finanzentwicklung* (Innsbruck, 1954).

itself to a very precise repayment schedule, which it ought to publish in advance.[23]

When the Zinzendorf plan was first aired verbally with Haugwitz and Rudolph Chotek in August and September 1756 it met with such a cool response that Zinzendorf was convinced his career in any economic portfolio was over. He begged Kaunitz to be allowed to enter the diplomatic service instead. Kaunitz, however, persuaded him not to give up so quickly, and after a brief stint as editor of the official court circular published by the Chancellery of State, Zinzendorf was made Vice-President of the Department of Mines and Minerals in February 1757. From this position he began a publicity campaign designed to draw attention to his expertise. He wrote a history of the Vienna City Bank, followed this up with a comparative history of all European banks, and finally translated, with a commentary, the publications of John Law.[24] In the meantime, despite the negative responses of Haugwitz and Chotek, Kaunitz persuaded Maria Theresia not to reject the Zinzendorf scheme before submitting it to a special commission for closer examination. In September the bonds plan was published as *A Proposal to Relieve the Credit of the Estates*.[25]

The *ad hoc* commission which examined the proposal supported it with only minor modifications, which Kaunitz readily seconded. He was careful to point out that the Zinzendorf proposal was in no way similar to the notorious system of Law and expressed the hope that it would be adopted quickly.[26] But even an acceptance in principle by the Estates of Lower Austria to underwrite the experiment failed to move Rudolph Chotek who, in his capacity as Chairman of the Vienna City Bank, absolutely refused to accept the bonds or their premium certificates as cash at the bank's tills. He was convinced that such a plan would deplete the capital reserves of the

[23] But for minor shifts of focus, the Zinzendorf plan remained substantially unaltered in the subsequent years. It was first printed in September 1757, then re-printed with revisions in July 1759. HHStA, Kabinettsarchiv: Nachlaß Zinzendorf, II: Handschriften, Vol. 33, "Pro-Memoria an eine Ständische Deputation einen Vorschlag zu Erleichterung des Ständischen Credits betr., Im September 1757"; *Ibid.*, Vol. 18, "Projet de Finance pour la continuation de la Guerre" is the 1758 manuscript version of *Ibid.*, Vol. 35, "Finanz-Vorschläge zur Fortsetzung des gegenwärtigen Krieges...im Monat Juli 1759." The manuscript version is important because it identifies specific critics by name, which did not appear in the printed version. The German version of the manuscript is to be found in Kaunitz's papers: HHStA, Staatskanzlei: Vorträge, Karton 84. Both printed proposals are discussed by Schasching, *Staatsbildung*, pp. 10–16; the 1759 one only by Beer, "Staatsschulden," pp. 7–9.

[24] Pettenegg, *Zinzendorf*, pp. 69–72. Cf. HHStA, Kabinettsarchiv: Nachlaß Zinzendorf, II: Handschriften, Vol. 101, "Geschichte und Beschreibung des Wiener Stadt Banko" (1758); Vols. 103 and 104, "Beschreibung der vornehmsten europäischen Banken" (1758); Vol. 106 in index, but missing from files, "4 Memoiren über die Banken und über das Sistem des Law."   [25] Cf. footnote 23 above.

[26] HHStA, Staatskanzlei: Vorträge, Karton 81, Kaunitz to Maria Theresia, 14 October 1757 (includes summary of commission report).

bank to such an extent that it would collapse outright.[27] Chotek's arguments were supported by Haugwitz, Bartenstein and Directory councillors Anton Stupan von Ehrenstein and Franz Anton Saffran – a heterodox coalition (Zinzendorf later preferred to call it a "cabal"[28]) which ensured defeat for the bonds scheme. In response to this failure Zinzendorf set to work re-fashioning his proposal. In the revised version the bonds would still have to be accepted as cash, but would be issued by the Vienna City Bank directly and would not be redeemable for a period of three years after the end of the war. The preliminary loan issue would be for 6 million Gulden, but in the place of a second issue to be used in salaries, Zinzendorf now recommended an outright issue of compulsory paper currency to be destroyed as bond revenues flowed in. In addition, Zinzendorf responded specifically to thirty-two distinct objections that had either already been or were likely to be made. He tried to show that the Vienna City Bank was a more flexible institution than Chotek made out, that the inflow of paper into state tills was hardly the credit liability that Stupan and Haugwitz had suggested, that the compulsory elements of the plan were not as unacceptable as Saffran insisted, and that the general fear of paper, especially in the face of Law's experiments in France, which was expressed by Bartenstein, was unjustified. Zinzendorf also dismissed fears that the project might prove inflationary by arguing that the money supply within the Monarchy was inadequate and that the only effect would be stimulatory.[29]

Kaunitz, who, as will be seen shortly, had become increasingly dissatisfied with the various fiscal expedients that were being adopted as the Seven Years War progressed, now took it upon himself to re-introduce the Zinzendorf plan in March 1758. Urging reconsideration of Zinzendorf's "reasonable, deft and thorough" proposal, he drafted an imperial order requiring the broadest possible consultation on the Zinzendorf scheme.[30] The Empress duly adopted the suggestion, but the effect remained the same. Chotek's opposition remained adamant. He called Zinzendorf's ideas "impractical" and "harmful" and remained convinced that any such scheme would destroy the public's confidence in the Vienna City Bank, which in turn would undermine the one reliable creditor the state had during the war.[31] Broadening consultation further added few voices of support for Zinzendorf. Most opinions, such as that of Treasury

[27] Ibid., Karton 82, Chotek to Maria Theresia, 6 March 1758. Cf. Pettenegg, Zinzendorf, p. 73.   [28] HHStA, Kabinettsarchiv: Zinzendorf Tagebuch, Vol. 6, 1 May 1761.
[29] HHStA, Kabinettsarchiv: Nachlaß Zinzendorf, II: Handschriften, Vol. 18, "Projet de Finance" (1758); HHStA, Staatskanzlei: Vorträge, Karton 81, Zinzendorf plan in German draft (March, 1758).
[30] HHStA, Staatskanzlei: Vorträge, Karton 82, Kaunitz to Maria Theresia, 19 March 1758.
[31] Ibid., Chotek to Maria Theresia, 6 April 1758.

councillor, Peter Ferdinand Prandau, were more influenced by Chotek. Above all it was Chotek's trump card which seemed to have the greatest effect: recourse to innovation was dangerous, especially when traditional methods sufficed for the purpose.[32] Kaunitz made every effort to allay these fears in yet another lengthy memorandum in which all objections to the Zinzendorf plan were dismissed point by point. Kaunitz suggested that the scheme was not only eminently feasible, but, by this stage of the war, absolutely necessary.[33] But it was all to no avail. Maria Theresia remained skeptical and was clearly affected by Chotek's vision of the collapse of the whole bank.[34] Again the Zinzendorf proposals came to naught.

By this time the Seven Years War was coming to the end of its second year, and it had become very apparent that even the most liberal estimates on war expenses had fallen short of the mark. In its first meeting of 8 July 1756 the War Cabinet, chaired by Kaunitz, expected annual military expenditures to double (to 28 million Gulden) during the conflict. The Cabinet remained confident that the additional 10 to 12 million Gulden required annually could be raised through the utilization of foreign and domestic credit, and that forced loans or "other similar measures" would be unnecessary.[35] However, problems soon materialized. Haugwitz began by requesting a loan of 12 million Gulden from the various provincial Estates of the Monarchy, but the response was an unpropitious omen for the future. Carinthia, Carniola and Upper Austria refused outright to raise the 4 million requested of them. The other Estates declared that they were prepared to do their utmost to come up with the remaining 8 million, but even in their initial burst of enthusiasm, all Haugwitz could report in actual receipts was 1,340,170 Gulden.[36] As the war progressed two further unpleasant realities became manifest. The first was that the war-time military expenditure was not double but more than triple the peace-time costs, and the second was that even the revenues calculated for peace-time could not be collected in full. Of the nearly 392 million Gulden that the Seven Years War consumed, barely over 144 million came from ordinary taxes.[37] Some relief could be found in the French subsidies agreed to in the

---

[32] *Ibid.*, note of Peter Ferdinand Prandau, concurring with one by Franz Anton Saffran, n.d. (March–April, 1758). Cf. Chotek objection cited by Zinzendorf in "Projet de Finance" (Objection No. 28).

[33] HHStA, Staatskanzlei: Vorträge, Karton 82, Kaunitz to Maria Theresia, 19 March 1758.

[34] *Ibid.*, Maria Theresia's resolution on Kaunitz's confidential report of 9 March 1758.

[35] *Ibid.*, Karton 78, War Cabinet minutes of 8, 9 and 18 July 1756.

[36] *Ibid.*, minutes of 18 July and 8 August 1756. Minutes of the meeting of 18 July are published in part in Khevenhüller-Metsch IV, 176–183.

[37] Dickson, *Finance and Government* II, 124–147, 388–390, which revises substantially upward the earlier total estimate of 260 million Gulden in Beer, "Staatsschulden," pp. 116–124.

Franco-Austrian alliance, which were administered by Kaunitz through the Belgian department of his ministry, and amounted to some 25 million Gulden over the course of the war. But even at its height this came to only 7.5 million Gulden per year, and represented a relatively modest portion of escalating annual costs, which reached nearly 64 million Gulden by 1761.[38]

Before long it became clear that extraordinary fiscal measures to supplement traditional loans, taxes and subsidies were now unavoidable. While Kaunitz pressed the Zinzendorf bond plan, others thought in more traditional terms – focusing primarily on the levying of extraordinary taxes.[39] In the summer of 1757 an anonymous author recommended the imposition of a 10% collateral inheritance tax modeled on the old Roman *vicesima hereditatum*, and both Haugwitz and Chotek became immediate supporters of the idea.[40] Kaunitz advised caution. He conceded that the imposition of such a tax on certain classes of fortuitous beneficiaries might become necessary, but added that no legislation should be passed without first submitting the idea to an impartial commission for consideration. Above all, he advised the Empress, it had to be determined if such an additional burden could in fact be borne, particularly by the poorer subjects of the Monarchy, and whether the proposed tax could in any way harm industrial or agricultural productivity. The commission also needed to determine, Kaunitz added, whether it would upset the principle of retaining a "just proportion" of the tax burden among the different classes of the country.[41] Haugwitz, whose priorities were fiscal, not social, did not appreciate what he perceived to be undue interference in Directory business by Kaunitz.[42] Kaunitz, for his part, was convinced that Haugwitz was placing unrealistic expectations on French subsidies and extraordinary taxes. With barely veiled sarcasm he observed:

It does not require much reflection or any profound insight to invent all kinds of ways and means of squeezing money out of our subjects. He who wishes to do so in a manner both reasonable and beneficial to the Monarch and the state, however, must first, or at least at the same time, devote an equal measure of zeal to increasing the subjects' wealth so that they might bear this additional burden.[43]

---

[38] Dickson, *Finance and Government* II, 173–184 is the most up-to-date analysis of the French subsidies and corrects errors contained in the earlier A. O. von Loehr, "Die Finanzierung des Siebenjährigen Krieges: Ein Versuch vergleichender Geldgeschichte, " *Numismatische Zeitschrift*, new series XVIII (1925), 105–106; and Paul P. Bernard, "Kaunitz and Austria's Secret Fund, " *East European Quarterly* XVI (1982), 129–136.

[39] For a concise list of the main extraordinary taxes imposed in the Seven Years War see Dickson, *Finance and Government* II, 129.

[40] HHStA, Kabinettsarchiv: Nachlaß Zinzendorf, II: Handschriften, Vol. 35, draft decree [August 1757). Cf. Wilhelm Funk, "Erbsteuer, " *ÖStWB* I, 861; Josef Ritter von Hauer, *Beiträge zur Geschichte der österreichischen Finanzen* (Vienna, 1848), pp. 53–54.

[41] HHStA, Staatskanzlei: Vorträge, Karton 81, Kaunitz to Maria Theresia, 12 July 1757.

[42] Arneth, *Maria Theresia* V, 221–222.

[43] HHStA, Staatskanzlei: Vorträge, Karton 81, Kaunitz to Maria Theresia, 15 August 1757.

The rift between Haugwitz and Kaunitz soon deepened. The Directory reconsidered the inheritance tax scheme, but instead of circumscribing it more, it now proposed to extend it to close relatives and to gifts. Kaunitz reacted with unprecedented indignation, regarding the new proposal as an excessive infringement of the rights to private property. "Nothing is more intolerable to men," he noted, "than to be robbed of their natural freedom to do with their private property as they wish." He suggested that "wisdom demands of a legislator that human liberty be not unduly circumscribed," and that the tax was immoral as well as impractical.[44] However, the findings of the special commission on the subject did not agree. Kaunitz remained unconvinced. He suggested that while "cunning and malice" would always find a way of extorting the fruits of "the bitter sweat of others", a state, at least, ought to "avoid changes of the kind which impose heavy blows and exploitations of this sort on poor and simple subjects" – especially when such marvelous ideas as the Zinzendorf proposals had not been tried first.[45] Kaunitz found an ally in Bartenstein[46] and the two were able to throw enough sand into the machinery to hold up implementation of the tax until June 1759. Public resistance then impeded the decree further, so that a series of supplementary explanatory decrees were necessary between June 1760 and September 1761 before the tax became effective.[47]

In the meantime three more extraordinary taxes were planned. The first was a poll tax (*Klassensteuer*) on a graduated scale according to wealth which was expected to raise 6.5 million Gulden. The second was a *don gratuit* in kind consisting of over three tons of flour and 1.5 million Metzen of oats. The third was a 10% capital gains tax (*Interessensteuer*). Kaunitz again expressed his serious reservations about these taxes, and especially about the capacity of the lower levels of society to cope with all three simultaneously. Once more he recommended extensive consultation before any such measures were introduced.[48] His plea fell on deaf ears. Since the funds were required for the campaign of 1759 there seemed to be no time to waste on discussions. Haugwitz was instructed to begin with the collection of the first two taxes on 22 August,[49] and the formal capital gains decree followed on 10 October 1758 with a payment deadline of 15

---

[44] *Ibid.*, Kaunitz to Maria Theresia, 14 October 1757.
[45] *Ibid.*, Karton 82, Kaunitz to Maria Theresia, 5 March 1758.
[46] HHStA, Kabinettsarchiv: Nachlaß Zinzendorf, II: Handschriften, Vol. 35, Bartenstein's "Unschuldige Gedanken," 23 August 1757, and "Anmerkungen", 11 January 1759.
[47] *Ibid.*, final decree, 6 June 1759; supplementary explanatory decree for Niederösterreich, 26 September 1761; for other provinces see Funk, "Erbsteuer", p. 861.
[48] HHStA, Staatskanzlei: Vorträge, Karton 83, Kaunitz to Maria Theresia, 19 August 1758.
[49] HHStA, Kabinettsarchiv: Nachlaß Zinzendorf, II: Handschriften, Vol. 33, Instructions-Puncte, 22 August 1758.

December of the same year.[50] The poll tax was subsequently amended and increased in April 1759 and continued in revised form even after the war as a way of servicing the national debt.[51]

By 1759, however, more voices than Kaunitz's began to express the view that the limits of extraordinary taxation had been reached, and that other measures would now be required.[52] Kaunitz thought the time propitious to re-introduce the Zinzendorf project once more. In July Zinzendorf's plan was published with his responses to all the objections to it which had hitherto been made. A few days later, in a general discussion of war finances, Kaunitz wrote Maria Theresia that in view of the projected revenue shortfalls and the exhaustion of all other expedients, nothing remained but to resort to the Zinzendorf suggestions.[53] The finance experts, however, disagreed. Rudolf Chotek, a favourite of the Emperor Francis, was, as we have seen, rising to the peak of his influence precisely at this time. The argument made by Chotek and other reactionaries was that substantial savings could be realized by systematically dismantling the Haugwitz administrative structure and re-uniting political and judicial administration in the pre-1748 fashion.[54] The 1759 experiment along these lines with the provincial government of Lower Austria entailed fewer savings than Chotek suggested, but his position remained strong enough to defeat any attempts to introduce the Zinzendorf plan.[55]

As a result, different albeit short-range options had to be exercised. In December 1758 the crown's tobacco monopoly in Upper, Lower and Inner Austria was farmed out to the respective Provincial Estates, and in August 1759 the same was done in the remaining "hereditary provinces," for a total revenue of 1.2 million Gulden a year.[56] In January 1760 army reductions, particularly in the officer corps, were undertaken,[57] and in the meantime the entire structure of government was re-assessed. In financial matters it was again Chotek whose voice was the most influential. In October 1760 he reached the peak of his success when he was appointed to chair a special commission consisting of Treasury and Directory officials to look into all matters pertaining to finance, credit and debt operations. The preliminary report of Chotek's commission, submitted on 14 December

---

[50] *Ibid.*, imperial decree, 10 October 1758. Cf. Arneth, *Maria Theresia* VI, 254.
[51] Hauer, *Beiträge*, pp. 54–56.   [52] Arneth, *Maria Theresia* VI, 225.
[53] HHStA, Staatskanzlei: Vorträge, Karton 84, Kaunitz to Maria Theresia, 24 July 1759. The published version of Zinzendorf's plan in HHStA, Kabinettsarchiv: Nachlaß Zinzendorf, II: Handschriften, Vol. 35, "Finanz-Vorschläge zu Fortsetzung des gegenwärtigen Krieges" (July, 1759).   [54] See above, pp. 80–82.
[55] Karafiol, "The Reforms of the Empress Maria Theresa," pp. 197–235.
[56] Hauer, *Beiträge*, pp. 68–69; Dickson, *Finance and Government* I, 397. Details and figures differ slightly.   [57] Arneth, *Maria Theresia* VI, 95–97. Cf. below, p. 272.

1760, echoed the favourite theme of the reactionaries that money ought to be saved by re-uniting the administration of the political and judicial spheres of government. In addition it recommended the consolidation of all economic portfolios into a single "Finance Conference".[58]

This time, however, Chotek was completely outmaneuvered by Kaunitz. By successfully introducing the advisory Council of State early in December 1760 he now created precisely the kind of impartial consultative agency he had been advocating for years, which would carefully assess proposals before they were adopted. The Council of State was made up entirely of reformers, and in this kind of forum Chotek's reactionary ideas stood little chance of success. The commission's report was considered by the Council in January and February 1761 and received a rude rebuff: it was ordered to worry less about administrative changes and more about raising revenues and curtailing expenses.[59] The commission's second report followed within ten days and was also not given a very hospitable reception. Its main recommendation urged the printing of paper money to cover war expenses, but the calculations on revenues and expenditures that it had been ordered to make first were disorganized and incomplete. In the Council of State Kaunitz argued that while recourse to paper money might become necessary, it would be better to consider other ideas first. Again he urged the Zinzendorf plan be examined, and this time he succeeded.[60]

As Kaunitz piloted it through the Council of State further alterations were made.[61] Instead of being issued by the Vienna City Bank, the bonds were to be released under the joint guarantee of all the provincial Estates of the hereditary provinces. The administrative vehicle would be a specially constituted deputation of Estates delegates presided over by a government minister and his staff. The size of the initial issue was raised to 12 million Gulden and the sinking fund was to be raised by an additional compulsory issue of 6 million to be assumed by the Estates. In return the Estates'

[58] ÖZV II/1/i, 291–292; Pettenegg, *Zinzendorf*, p. 83; Prokeš, "Boj o Haugvicovo," pp. 24–25; Kurt Janetschek, "Die Finanzierung des Siebenjährigen Krieges (ein Beitrag zur Finanzgeschichte des 18. Jahrhunderts)" (unpublished Ph.D. dissertation, University of Vienna, 1959), p. 104; Dickson, *Finance and Government* II, 36, 82.

[59] HHStA, Kabinettsarchiv: Staatsratprotokolle, Vol. 1, No. 13 of 1761, imperial resolution, 13 February 1761; Kutschera Materialien, Part III, Section 6, § A/i.

[60] *Ibid.*, Staatsratprotokolle, Vol. 1, Nos. 197 and 264 of 1761, protocoll record, 8–25 March 1761. (Chotek was sternly warned [No. 197] not to attempt to discredit the Zinzendorf plan.) HHStA, Staatskanzlei: Vorträge, Karton 88, Kaunitz Staatsrat Votum, 13 March 1761; cf. HHStA, Kabinettsarchiv: Nachlaß Kaunitz, Karton 1, Kaunitz to Maria Theresia, n.d. (February–March, 1761).

[61] The most detailed analysis of the implementation remains Hans Gross, "Die Ständische Kredit-Deputation und der Plan eines erbländischen Nationalkredits (ein Beitrag zur Finanzpolitik unter Maria Theresia" (unpublished Ph.D. dissertation, University of Vienna, 1935), which is followed closely by Dickson, *Finance and Government* II, 133–138. Cf. Schasching, pp. 18–22.

obligations to the crown could be discharged in premium certificates or "coupons", and the interest rate was raised to 6% per annum.[62] Once the plan had received royal assent, Zinzendorf himself was named head of the "Estates Credit Deputation" (*Ständische Kredit Deputation*),[63] and the Estates were ordered to dispatch delegates to Vienna for 13 May 1761,[64] where they were formally received by Kaunitz.[65] Zinzendorf reached an agreement with the delegates in relatively short order after their arrival, and on 30 June the bond issue was formally proclaimed. The bonds were released simultaneously in Vienna, Prague and Trieste in denominations of 25, 100, 250, 500 and 1,000 Gulden. The two lower denominations were to be Payment Bonds, while the rest were to be Loan Bonds.[66] Once the bonds were launched by the Patent of 1 August 1761, Zinzendorf pressed for the establishment of an official exchange where the bonds could be traded and cashed. Though the exchange was officially proclaimed by decree on 14 August 1761 it seems not to have survived beyond 1762 and was established on a permanent basis only in 1771.[67]

The bonds proved moderately successful but failed to bring anywhere near the revenues of English exchequer bills. After five years of war and an array of unpleasant government fiscal extortions, the public was naturally much more suspicious of the bond issue than it might have been at the beginning of the war. Consequently, after an initial rush, demand began to drop for bonds in the lesser denominations of 25 and 100 Gulden, and after a few weeks they were already trading as much as 14% below face value.[68] Demand for bonds in higher denominations remained very weak from the start. Major creditors with large cash reserves found it much more profitable to speculate in the standard loan notes the government had taken out since 1756. These were trading as much as 30% below face value so that adventurous speculators could potentially realize profits far in excess of the mere 6% offered by the Estates bonds. All in all, waiting five

[62] HKA, Kredit und Staatsschuldenakten: Ständische Kredit Deputation, Rote No. 2, imperial resolution, 2 April 1761.
[63] *Ibid.*, Maria Theresia to Zinzendorf, 15 April 1761; *Ibid.*, Rote Nr. 4, Kaunitz to Zinzendorf, 23 May 1761.
[64] *Ibid.*, Rote No. 4, "Rescript an alle Länder Repraesentations-Praesidenten, und respectivè Capi deren Ständen," 22 April 1761.
[65] HHStA, Kabinettsarchiv, Zinzendorf Tagebuch, Vol. 6, 24 May 1761.
[66] HKA, Kredit und Staatsschuldenakten: Ständische Kredit Deputation, Rote No. 4, Zinzendorf to Maria Theresia, 27 June 1761; Ständische Kredit Deputation Patent, 30 June 1761.
[67] *Ibid.*, Rote No. 6, Zinzendorf to Maria Theresia and Maria Theresia to Zinzendorf, 2 July, 18 July, 4 August and 13 August 1761; Börse Patent, 14 August 1761. Cf. Gross, "Die Ständische Kredit-Deputation," pp. 34–41, 49–53; Franz Baltzarek, *Die Geschichte der Wiener Börse* (Vienna, 1973), pp. 19–28; Arnold Hilberg, *Das erste Jahrhundert der Wiener Börse* (Vienna, 1871), pp. 5–7.
[68] HHStA, Kabinettsarchiv: Zinzendorf Tagebuch, Vol. 6, 20 September 1761.

years to institute systematic public borrowing in this form in the event crippled the scheme, and cost the government dearly both in the short and long run.

Under these circumstances the prospects for continuing the war into 1762 seemed grim indeed. In October 1761 Kaunitz estimated that a deficit of 15 million Gulden could be expected for the upcoming year, and any hope that such an amount could be raised by another credit operation or other expedients was "totally futile." Hence, Kaunitz concluded, all that remained was major cuts in the military establishment.[69] But even the implementation of the cuts Kaunitz had urged made only a modest dent in the projected deficit. In January 1762 it was still estimated that 12 to 13 million Gulden would have to be raised somehow for the upcoming campaign. Owing to the great administrative reform implemented at the end of 1761, however, there had been important personnel changes in the economic portfolios and these dramatically affected the discussions on financial expedients. Rudolph Chotek had departed to the Austro-Bohemian Chancellery. The third report of his commission had once again failed to fulfill its task, and Chotek's economic reputation was now in decline.[70] Zinzendorf left the Estates Credit Deputation to become head of the Court of Audit. A new Revenue Ministry came into being, and its head chaired both the Vienna City Bank and the Estates Credit Deputation: this was the enormously energetic and ambitious Hatzfeld.[71]

When Hatzfeld assumed his portfolio he was generally regarded as an ally of Zinzendorf, and by uniting Chotek's and Zinzendorf's old posts in his person the conflict between the Vienna City Bank and the Estates Credit Deputation was brought to an abrupt end. Hatzfeld also moved quickly to face the prospective deficit for 1762 by producing a plan which drew on both Chotek and Zinzendorf. This involved transferring 3 million Gulden of the Estates Credit Deputation bond subscription from voluntary Loan Bonds to compulsory Payment Bonds, and issuing paper money in the form of Vienna City Bank notes (*Banco-Zettel*). The latter were to be similar to Zinzendorf's compulsory bonds in that they were to be accepted at state tills as well as being used in a portion of salary payments. Indeed, not only were half of all moneys outstanding to the state to be payable in notes, one third were required to be paid in them. On the other hand the notes did not bear interest and were similar to paper money in all respects except that they were not compulsory in the private sector and were not

[69] HHStA, Staatskanzlei: Vorträge, Karton 88, Kaunitz Votum, 17 October 1761.
[70] HHStA, Kabinettsarchiv: Staatsratprotokolle, Vol. 2, No. 1415 of 1761. Cf. Maria Theresia to Chotek, 2 August 1761, cited in Beer, "Staatsschulden," pp. 121–122.
[71] See above, p. 91.

officially proclaimed currency of the realm. The notes could also be exchanged for 5% interest-bearing compulsory bonds.[72]

A commission chaired by Kaunitz in February 1762 decided to accept and implement the first suggestion.[73] With skepticism on all sides, the second proposal also followed suit. Since the 1758 and 1759 versions of Zinzendorf's bond scheme had recommended virtually the identical kind of bank note, it is not surprising that he now endorsed Hatzfeld's proposal fully even while expressing some pessimism about how effectively bank notes would solve the problem at hand.[74] Kaunitz, too, supported the idea. Fearing the Monarchy was on the verge of "a general bankruptcy," he could see few other options. Suspicious of paper money, he feared a cash shortage if too large a portion of state revenues were collected in notes. He also feared the circulation of these notes would result in a decline of the value of compulsory bonds. Because of these fears Kaunitz advised proceeding cautiously, issuing only 2 million Gulden of notes at a time and determining the size of the total issue by public reaction.[75] But need overwhelmed caution. An issue of 12 million in bank notes were printed in denominations of 5, 10, 25, 50 and 100 Gulden, and issued by decree simultaneously on 15 June 1762.[76]

The pessimism of Zinzendorf and fears of Kaunitz proved justified. The bank notes flooded the state tills, compulsory bonds fell in value and the cash shortage became ever more acute. By September Hatzfeld himself admitted that bank notes in their current form had failed to meet their objective fully. If the war continued into 1763, he saw no option but to declare the bank notes compulsory currency of the realm.[77] But whether the war could actually be continued remained doubtful. Field-Marshall Daun reported that militarily it was absolutely impossible, and that the army would be lucky to make it through the winter.[78] While peace negotiations were begun, however, their outcome remained uncertain and hence, despite everything, plans had to be made for financing a campaign

---

[72] Beer, "Staatsschulden," p. 16; Schasching, pp. 22–23; Gross, "Die Ständische Kredit-Deputation," pp. 68–77; Dickson, *Finance and Government* II, 136–141; Gustav Otruba, *Die Wirtschaftspolitik Maria Theresias* (Vienna, 1963), p. 25; Franz Mensi-Klarbach, "Papiergeld (bis zum Beginne der Valutarregulierung)," *ÖStWB* II, 271–272.

[73] HHStA, Kabinettsarchiv: Nachlaß Zinzendorf, II: Handschriften, Vol. 36, Commission protocoll, 10 February 1762. Cf. Gross, "Die Ständische Kredit-Deputation," pp. 54–70; Schasching, p. 21; Arneth, *Maria Theresia* VI, 256.

[74] HHStA, Kabinettsarchiv: Nachlaß Zinzendorf, II: Handschriften, Vol. 36, Zinzendorf to Maria Theresia, 17 March 1762.

[75] HHStA, Staatskanzlei: Vorträge, Karton 89, Kaunitz to Maria Theresia, 8 February 1762.

[76] HHStA, Kabinettsarchiv: Nachlaß Zinzendorf, II: Handschriften, Vol. 36, Banco-Zettel Decree, 15 June 1762.   [77] Schasching, p. 23.

[78] HHStA, Staatskanzlei: Vorträge, Karton 90, Binder to Maria Theresia (including report from Daun), 22 October 1762.

in the upcoming year. In November 1762 Kaunitz was appointed to chair another commission which looked into the problem. Hatzfeld felt that a new issue of 10 million Gulden in bank notes should be printed, but this time as compulsory currency. Zinzendorf felt the bonds scheme should be tried again, this time issuing only compulsory bonds in the amount of 21.9 million Gulden at 5% interest.[79]

Kaunitz was pessimistic about both options, but creating a compulsory paper currency during war time seemed to him the greater evil. Accordingly he recommended resorting to the compulsory bonds again, but that preparations should begin for introducing paper money if peace were not restored within two or three months.[80] Whether these expedients would yield enough actual cash to wage a campaign Kaunitz remained skeptical as 1762 drew to a close.[81] On 1 February 1763 an 11 million Gulden compulsory bond issue was proclaimed, with an additional 10.9 million planned for 1 July. Fortunately by then the Seven Years War had ended. Instead of the 10.9 million Gulden compulsory bond issue, only 5,940,00 Gulden at 4% interest were released. Bankruptcy was avoided at the eleventh hour; only peace, Zinzendorf noted, had prevented a complete collapse.[82]

New priorities and post-war recovery

In the January 1761 opening session of the newly-founded Council of State, Kaunitz had urged the adoption of an ideological premise for future policy which represented a fundamental shift in economic attitude. Above all, he reiterated his favourite theme that the narrow fiscal focus which had characterized so much of the Monarchy's official thinking had to give way to a broader economic vision. Only after sufficient attention had been paid to fostering economic growth in general, could one begin to think of revenue collection. Governments, he had further urged, should try to avoid deficits, and in order to do that needed a clear picture of revenues and expenditures.[83] This is precisely what Chotek's finance commission of 1760–1761 had been ordered to do repeatedly, but by the time it finally produced the figures demanded on 17 January 1762, it was overtaken by events and more accurate accounting from Zinzendorf's new Court of Audit. The commission was accordingly dissolved on 8 March 1762.[84]

---

[79] HHStA, Kabinettsarchiv: Nachlaß Zinzendorf, II: Handschriften, Vol. 36, Commission Protocoll, 15 November 1762.
[80] HHStA, Staatskanzlei: Vorträge, Karton 90, Kaunitz Votum, 16 November 1762.
[81] *Ibid.*, Kaunitz to Maria Theresia, 29 December 1762.   [82] Schasching, p. 24.
[83] Walter, "Eintritt," pp. 74–79.   [84] Dickson, *Finance and Government* II, 82–83.

Though the structural changes of the central administration, and especially of the economic portfolios at the end of 1761, established a new decision-making framework, short-range fiscal problems still overwhelmed the respective ministers throughout 1762. The economic exigencies of the war effort seemed to interfere at every turn with the implementation of a new economic attitude, and only the termination of the conflict brought a real change.

When the war ended early in 1763 there was a broad consensus in Habsburg government circles that a fundamental re-evaluation of the state's "financial system" had to be undertaken, but little consensus on how this should be done. On the one hand was the cameralist tradition of Haugwitz now energetically spearheaded by Hatzfeld; on the other hand was the Western Enlightenment movement whose chief economic spokesman was Zinzendorf, the protégé of Kaunitz. The respective positions of these two men provided the parameters within which the principal economic debates of the subsequent decade took place. The driving ambition of Hatzfeld and the dogmatic convictions of Zinzendorf left little room for compromise, and, as we have already seen, a bitter personal enmity soon developed between the two men.[85] In these conflicts Kaunitz invariably sided with Zinzendorf, but even this influential support proved inadequate in the long run. Hatzfeld eventually emerged victorious, though not before a substantial portion of Zinzendorf's proposals had been implemented – thanks largely to Kaunitz.

In 1763 Zinzendorf clearly had the upper hand. In the immediate post-war atmosphere, filled as it was with projects and plans for the Monarchy's economic future, Maria Theresia continued to rely on Kaunitz, who stressed that before any new projects were undertaken, it was necessary to have an accurate accounting of revenues and expenditures. The statistics, in turn, could pinpoint specific policy requirements, even if, in general terms, there was little doubt what the post-war priorities had to be. The first was to decrease the national debt and the second was to do the utmost to encourage industrial, agricultural and commercial growth. Indeed there was an integral connection between the two since sustained economic growth would make servicing the national debt easier, and decreasing the national debt would help stimulate economic growth. In any case, details could be worked out by economic experts, and the man to whom it was best to turn first was Zinzendorf.[86]

---

[85] See above, p. 101.

[86] HHStA, Staatskanzlei: Vorträge, Karton 91, Kaunitz to Maria Theresia, 22 March 1763. This report shows that Kaunitz intentionally stepped aside when, in accordance with his advice, the Empress subsequently ordered extensive and regular consultation among the economic experts in the various government departments concerned. There was no

Accordingly Zinzendorf was saddled with two major tasks in 1763. The first of these, of course, was the specific duty of his new ministry, the Court of Audit: a comprehensive statistical "inventory" of state revenues and expenditures. Zinzendorf appointed Johann Matthias Puechberg as Head Bookkeeper (*Hauptbuchhalter*), and in the subsequent months he, in turn, produced the massive nine-volume "Staats Inventarium" which was the first thorough pan-monarchical overview of the Monarchy's finances ever undertaken, and revealed clearly the economic devastation the Seven Years War had wrought. The national debt, which had been 101 million Gulden in 1740 and 118 million in 1756, had skyrocketed to almost 285 million by 1763. Furthermore, the annual deficit, which had been estimated at 12 million during the war year of 1761, could not be eliminated with the return of peace. It remained at a staggering 7.5 million because so many crown revenues had been mortgaged during the war that annual receipts were substantially reduced. What is more, a substantial portion of these (which amounted to 41% of net revenue) had to be expended on interest payments on the national debt.[87] This dismal financial picture led directly to Zinzendorf's second major task: working out a detailed economic strategy for post-war recovery.

In two major memoranda in the summer of 1763 Zinzendorf outlined his long-term economic strategy. The essential objects of his proposals were to liquidate the enormous state debt that had accumulated, and to put the crown's credit operations on a sounder footing for future exigencies. The means Zinzendorf proposed included the consolidation of credit and debt operations into a single "national credit system" and the commercialization of these operations along the lines of the English example. Though preferring to rely on voluntary credit, he acknowledged that this might not be feasible at the current stage of the Monarchy's economic development. If recourse to forced loan operations hence became virtually unavoidable, Zinzendorf wished them to inspire as much public confidence as possible, not only by the prompt and punctual payment of interest and amortization of capital, but also by placing the entire process into the hands of a disinterested "intermediary" body. For this the Estates Credit Deputation

---

deliberate exclusion of the Chancellor of State as suggested by Dickson, *Finance and Government* II, 38–39.

[87] Dickson, *Finance and Government* II, 36–39, 82–84, 378–379; Beer, "Staatsschulden," p. 21, and table following p. 135; Gustav Otruba, "Wirtschaft und Wirtschaftspolitik im Zeitalter des Aufgeklärten Absolutismus," in Erich Zöllner and Alexander Novotny, eds., *Die Wirtschaftsgeschichte Österreichs* (Vienna, 1971), pp. 206–207, 225–234; Hock-Bidermann, pp. 79–82. I have largely followed Dickson's figures, which seem the most persuasive. For Puechberg and the Staats Inventarium see Hanns L. Mikoletzky, "Johann Matthias Puechberg und die Anfänge der Hofrechenkammer," *Jahrbuch des Vereins für Geschichte der Stadt Wien* XVII–XVIII (1961–1962), 133–148.

seemed the most logical choice, since Estates credit had proved itself the most efficacious in the war. In terms of mechanics, Zinzendorf not only wanted to continue with his bond issues, but to make the bonds the single uniform method of public borrowing. To commercialize the procedure he again pressed for the creation of an appropriate permanent Exchange (the Exchange of 1761 having been extremely short-lived). In addition, to acquire more solid backing for future credit operations, Zinzendorf urged that a National Bank under the joint guarantee of all the Estates should be established, with branches in all major provincial centers.[88]

Zinzendorf was well aware of the political implications of these ideas and expected them to meet with stiff resistance. The consolidation of the credit of the different Estates into a single national credit posed a serious threat to the particularism and privileges of the Estates and would abet the centralizing tendencies already in progress. Nor could the Vienna City Bank, and its chairman Hatzfeld, be expected to accept sanguinely the loss of its special status.[89] But on the whole Zinzendorf remained optimistic, and his mentor, Kaunitz, even more so. Further, optimism seemed justified, for the first step of the strategy – reducing the national debt – was widely endorsed. Even before the war had ended, Zinzendorf had pointed to interest payments on the national debt as the first priority. Kaunitz had also echoed this sentiment in 1761, and in July 1762 he submitted a detailed calculation which showed how much money could be saved if interest payments could be reduced. He urged that this reduction be undertaken immediately upon the establishment of peace.[90] The modality was left to Zinzendorf. He, in turn, hit upon the idea of extending the already introduced capital gains tax to 20% in order to effectively tax back a substantial portion of the interest payments. Introduced in 1763, this tax was refined in 1764 not only to encourage the cashing of high interest-bearing bonds, but also immediate reinvestment in lower-interest ones.[91]

The capital gains tax, of course, was an indirect strategy. The more direct one would have been to simply call in all bonds whose interest rates were above 4%, but Zinzendorf feared this was not possible owing to lack of capital for an orderly redemption on even a limited scale.[92] The disappointing results of the capital gains taxes of 1763 and 1764, however, made Kaunitz much bolder in calling for a redemption of all bonds bearing

---

[88] Schasching, pp. 32–39; Dickson, *Finance and Government* II, 45–46. The bank proposal had been floated by Zinzendorf in 1761, but failed despite Kaunitz's support. See Friedrich Walter, "Die Wiener Stadtbank und das Bankprojekt des Grafen Kaunitz aus dem Jahre 1761," *Zeitschrift für Nationalökonomie* VIII (1937), 444–460.
[89] Schasching, p. 39. [90] Beer, "Staatsschulden," p. 124.
[91] Franz Mensi-Klarbach, "Finanzgeschichte," *ÖStWB* II, 55; Hauer, *Beiträge*, p. 52; Pettenegg, pp. 90–91; Dickson, *Finance and Government* II, 41–42.
[92] Schasching, p. 40.

more than 4% interest, and encouraging re-investment at 4%. Expecting most investors to take advantage of the reinvestment opportunity, Kaunitz estimated that a sinking fund of around 8 million Gulden would be sufficient for the purpose. He felt confident that the operation would result in an annual 1.5 to 2 million Gulden increase in state revenue.[93] A special commission under the chairmanship of Kaunitz, consisting of Hatzfeld, Zinzendorf and the members of the Council of State, endorsed the idea in two meetings in May 1765.[94] But while Zinzendorf hastened to support his protector, Hatzfeld had his reservations.[95] There was the traditional fear that his Vienna City Bank's cash reserves would be depleted by such an operation, and this was fueled by a calculation that far more than 8 million Gulden would be required in the sinking fund. Hatzfeld persuaded the commission that a minimum figure of 18 million Gulden would be a more accurate estimate, but Kaunitz responded with the surprisingly optimistic position that raising even this sum was "not only possible but also certain."[96]

What made Kaunitz so confident was the fact that after the death of Emperor Francis, Maria Theresia and Joseph II agreed to contribute a substantial portion of the inheritance to the state. In a last will and testament drawn up in 1751 Francis made some modest provisions for his friends and family, but he surprised many by declaring his oldest son sole heir for the bulk of his estate, valued at some 32 million Gulden. This caused immediate problems, because the original intention of having Joseph succeed Francis in Tuscany had been amended in favour of a Tuscan secundogenitur under Joseph's brother, Leopold. Many doubted Joseph had any rights to the family funds from Tuscany, and Maria Theresia feared that the testament was "not executable."[97] Kaunitz disagreed. Chairing yet another special commission in October 1765, he pushed through a report which not only declared the will valid, but asserted that while Joseph was entitled to Tuscan family funds, he was not

[93] HHStA, Kabinettsarchiv: Zinzendorf Nachlaß, II: Handschriften, Vol. 87, Kaunitz to Maria Theresia, 28 March 1765.
[94] Ibid., Vol. 2c, Commission Protocolle, 18 and 20 May 1765.
[95] The essential documents on this debate are preserved in Vol. 87 of the Zinzendorf Nachlaß, as above. They include: Zinzendorf Votum, 5 June 1765; Commission Protocoll, 14 October 1765; Votum Separatum of Hatzfeld, 14 October 1765; Kaunitz to Maria Theresia, 22 October 1765; Kaunitz to Hatzfeld, 26 October 1765; Zinzendorf Votum, 28 October 1765; Kaunitz to Maria Theresia, 28/29 October 1765; Blümegen pro memoria, n.d. (October 1765), Zinzendorf Anmerkung, 29 October 1765; Hatzfeld Anmerkung, n.d.; Zinzendorf Anmerkung, n.d.
[96] HHStA, Staatskanzlei: Vorträge, Karton 96, Kaunitz to Maria Theresia, 29 October 1765. Cf. Kabinettsarchiv: Nachlaß Kaunitz, drafts of commission protocol, 28 October 1765.
[97] HHStA, Familienarchiv: Sammelbände, Fasz. 70, Maria Theresia to Kaunitz, n.d. (September, 1765); Joseph to Kaunitz, 9 September 1765.

liable for any Tuscan debts.[98] Despite Leopold's bitter resistance, Joseph, fully supported by Kaunitz, successfully pushed through a transfer which amounted to over 2 million Gulden from Tuscany.[99]

The sum that Joseph was accordingly able to transfer to the state treasury exceeded 19 million Gulden, and became the core of the cash reserves required to carry out the redemption plan. Kaunitz defeated Hatzfeld's proposal to carry out the operation in stages, by arguing that it would undermine the effort to make 4% the normal interest rate in the entire state, and by showing that a phased redemption would be more advantageous to large investors than to small ones. Accordingly 5% and 6% bonds were called in for 1 November 1766, with investors being given the option to re-invest in bonds bearing 4% interest. Such reinvestments were not as frequent as expected, and recent estimates suggest that the total cost of the operation was nearly 20 million Gulden. It did, however, have the desired effect. The capital of the state debt was reduced to 256 million Gulden, and the annual interest payments fell from over 13.5 million to around 10.5 million, where they remained until 1779 when the War of the Bavarian Succession caused a dramatic increase. Thus an annual increase of over 3 million Gulden in revenues was realized – a figure which well exceeded even the optimistic projections Kaunitz had made in March 1765. In addition, as Zinzendorf had already pointed out in 1763, lower interest rates had a salutary effect on the economy as a whole. They stimulated private enterprise and individual initiative, energized the real estate market and encouraged more industrial and commercial investment.[100]

That the reduction of interest payments on the state debt was regarded in official circles as the beginning of a new era in the economic life of the Monarchy becomes evident from the fact that within two weeks after the interest payment operation was ordered, a now rare Privy Conference was assembled to discuss the guidelines to be adopted for future economic policy. This conference, held on 17 April 1766, was the first assembly of all major government notables since the death of Emperor Francis, and was chaired by the young co-regent himself. The discussions were oral, and Kaunitz was reported to have spoken for an hour and a half. A good

---

[98] HHStA, Staatskanzlei: Vorträge, Karton 96, Kaunitz to Joseph, 9 October 1765 (including imperial resolution, report of meeting, Vota of Hagen, Stettner, Colloredo and Batthyány); also Familienarchiv: Sammelbände, Fasz. 70, Kaunitz to Joseph, n.d. [9 October 1765); Joseph to Kaunitz, 9 October 1765.

[99] *MTJC* I, 139–174; Arneth, *Maria Theresia* VII, 172–178; Wandruszka, *Leopold II* I, 136–155. For Kaunitz's support of Joseph see HHStA, Familienarchiv: Sammelbände, Fasz. 70, Joseph to Kaunitz, 3 and 6 November 1765.

[100] Beer, "Staatsschulden," pp. 18–32, 136, statistical table; Hock-Bidermann, p. 80; Schasching, pp. 40–44; Dickson, *Finance and Government* II, 51–57.

portion of the meeting addressed itself to the future of credit and debt operations, and the stabilization of a new "financial system", but Kaunitz again preferred to look beyond the fiscal difficulties to the broader economic problems that faced the Monarchy. He focused on two topics of prime concern to him: excessive taxation and excessive tariff regulation. While it is an exaggeration to characterize Kaunitz's contribution as the sole voice of the new physiocratic ideas in the face of determined mercantilism,[101] he nevertheless clearly reflected elements of economic liberalism still alien to the Austria of that time.

Having been loath to resort to extraordinary taxation even during war time, Kaunitz now lamented with even more vigour the excessive strain that was being put on the national economy through heavy taxation. He pleaded for reductions, especially in those instances where taxation tended to enfeeble commerce, and he suggested that the key to a healthy economy was not an obsessive concern with purely fiscal matters and an impatient urge to build up large cash reserves. What was needed much more, Kaunitz said, was a consensus on policies designed to maximize agricultural, industrial and commercial productivity. He did not doubt that the current system of heavy taxation produced great revenues, but he insisted that people could be taxed only in proportion to their capacity to pay. Under those circumstances, the existing system, a child of war-time imperatives, would be self-defeating in the end, leading to the ruination of trade and industry and the total impoverishment of the peasants. Kaunitz also criticized overabundant tariff regulations. Internal tariffs were clearly severe impediments to the development of a national economy, but Kaunitz opposed the heavy duties placed on the importation of foreign industrial products as well. Experience taught, he suggested, that such prohibitions only encouraged circumvention by smuggling, and the subsequent sale of such products at double the price. In the final analysis, Kaunitz noted, it was again the consumer who suffered.[102]

As a result of this conference of April 1766, the crown moved to deal with a number of economic problems simultaneously. The two finance ministers, Hatzfeld and Zinzendorf, were ordered to work out a detailed plan for a definitive "peace-time financial system." The Austro-Bohemian Chancellery was ordered to launch extensive local investigations with the intent of uncovering any measures which might be inhibiting economic growth. And Kaunitz himself was asked to submit a detailed written report on the whole question of excessive taxation. Hatzfeld coyly delayed his report, but Zinzendorf rushed to refine the ideas he had already submitted

---

[101] Paul von Mitrofanov, *Joseph II: Seine politische und kulturelle Tätigkeit*, 2 Vols., trans. from Russian by V. von Demelic (Vienna, 1910), I, 400.
[102] Arneth, *Maria Theresia* VII, 210–211, 449–450.

in 1763. Again he called for the creation of a new stock exchange, a new national deposit bank, and a trading company. The stock exchange was to be given a monopoly, in that all trade in bonds was to be declared illegal if not transacted through the brokers of the exchange. While Estates Credit Deputation bonds were to be the uniform means of public borrowing, the bonds themselves would cease to be usable in lieu of cash at government tills. Instead of bonds, the new national deposit bank, guaranteed by the Estates, would issue bank notes as in 1762 – required in up to half of payments due to the state, but not a compulsory currency in the private sector. In addition, it would be the task of the new bank to maintain public and private interest rates at 4 %.[103]

During the spring and summer of 1767 the Zinzendorf proposals were debated at eleven different meetings of a special commission consisting of the two finance ministers, several privy councillors from the finance portfolios and the members of the Council of State, excluding Kaunitz. An open split in the commission soon appeared. Hatzfeld, supported by Stupan and Borié, bitterly attacked the Zinzendorf plans as too complicated and expensive, while chairman Stahremberg and Binder supported Zinzendorf. At the end of July, however, the matter was brought before the Council of State alone, this time with Kaunitz present. In the presence of both Maria Theresia and Joseph II, Kaunitz came out strongly in favour of Zinzendorf. The purpose of the stock exchange, he said, was to establish an open marketplace in which competition would ultimately lead to improvements of the products dealt in. Competition among potential buyers would also raise the value of Estates Credit Deputation bonds, and at the same time increase the cash fund of the exchange. Kaunitz also endorsed the coercive clauses of the Zinzendorf plan, because he felt that the original exchange established in 1761 failed precisely because it lacked such powers. The bank proposal received Kaunitz's enthusiastic support as well. As long as investors found a lending market which would return an interest rate exceeding 4 %, all attempts to maintain the country's normal interest rate (as well as the state's borrowing rate) at that level would be in vain. The Zinzendorf bank would close this avenue. Finally, Kaunitz supported the idea of a trade company, because he felt it would stimulate domestic industry.[104]

The Kaunitz intervention seemed to prove decisive. At a specially

[103] DOZA, Handschriften, Vol. 64, Ludwig Zinzendorf to Karl Zinzendorf, 19 August, 24 September and 7 December 1766; Schasching, pp. 56–60; Beer, "Staatsschulden," pp. 38–44; Hock-Bidermann, pp. 82–85; Arneth, *Maria Theresia* IX, 431–433; Dickson, *Finance and Government* II, 66–67.
[104] DOZA, Handschriften, Vol. 64, Ludwig Zinzendorf to Karl Zinzendorf, 10 March 1767; Beer, "Staatsschulden," pp. 45–46; Eichwalder, p. 132.

summoned meeting of the Privy Conference at which Kaunitz spoke for three hours, the Empress accepted part of the Zinzendorf proposals immediately. A bank in accordance with his recommendations was to be set up, and Zinzendorf himself was to become its president. The Austro-Bohemian Chancellery was ordered to forward a request to all provincial Estates to guarantee the new bank. In addition, both the new stock exchange and trade company proposals were accepted in principle, though further deliberation was ordered on the details of implementation.[105] Kaunitz was full of optimism. He thought the greatest obstacles to a reform of the state's economy were on the verge of being overcome, and his own "dearest wishes nearing fulfillment." Indeed, he was so confident that he was ready to begin formulating the next step in the Monarchy's economic transformation: a systematic and sweeping agrarian reform.[106] Within a few short weeks, however, a complete *volte-face* took place. On 20 August 1767 Zinzendorf submitted his recommendations for the locations and personnel of the bank and the stock exchange. The recommendations went uneventfully through the Council of State, Kaunitz again supporting all of Zinzendorf's suggestions warmly.[107] But instead of gaining the fully-anticipated royal assent, instructions were suddenly received to table the matter for the moment.[108]

The key to this turn-around was the political emergence of the Co-Regent, Joseph II. In the summer of 1767 Maria Theresia fell ill with smallpox, and the Emperor assumed control of decision-making. After the Empress's recovery Joseph retained the initiative, so that no important decisions were made without his consent.[109] The idea of underwriting a new national bank met with stiff resistance from the Provincial Estates,[110] and Hatzfeld swiftly exploited the opportunity to argue that the whole bank proposal was unfeasible. Hostile to Zinzendorf and his main political allies, Kaunitz, Starhemberg and Binder, Joseph was easily persuaded by Hatzfeld and the heterodox coalition supporting him: Borié, Stupan, Blümegen and the Empress's secretary, Cornelius Nenny.[111] On 21 October the Starhemberg commission was formally informed of the official reversal of policy, and Zinzendorf, to his "great vexation," was powerless as the

[105] DOZA, Handschriften, Vol. 64, Ludwig Zinzendorf to Karl Zinzendorf, 10 March, 8 April and 6 October 1767; Beer, "Staatsschulden," pp. 46–47.

[106] HHStA, Österreichische Akten: Österreich-Staat, Fasz. 5, Kaunitz to Maria Theresia, 21 April 1767. Cf. below, p. 163.

[107] HHStA, Kabinettsarchiv: Kaunitz Voten, Karton 1, No. 1996 of 1767, Kaunitz Staatsrat Votum, 16 September 1767.

[108] *Ibid.*, Staatsratprotokolle, Vol. 25, No. 1996, secretarial note, 18 September 1767.

[109] DOZA, Handschriften, Vol. 64, Ludwig Zinzendorf to Karl Zinzendorf, 28 June and 18 September 1767 and 18 December 1768.   [110] Schasching, pp. 77–79.

[111] DOZA, Handschriften, Vol. 64, Ludwig Zinzendorf to Karl Zinzendorf, 18 December 1768.

decisive advantage now shifted to Hatzfeld.[112] On 11 November the latter was ordered to modify the Zinzendorf plans and to submit recommendations not only for a peace-time, but also for a war-time financial system. In the context of the great administrative reform proposals of 1768, Kaunitz commented bitterly on this turn of events. He noted how Zinzendorf's ideas had already been approved by all relevant authorities, including the Empress herself, and was now being reversed in anticipation of Hatzfeld's finance system. Though this had still not been submitted. Kaunitz felt that, from conversations with Hatzfeld, it could be predicted "almost with certainty" that "not only can nothing better be expected from him, but also nothing that can match the quality of Count Zinzendorf's proposals." Kaunitz therefore held any further delay in the implementation of the Zinzendorf plan to be a waste of time, for far broader economic priorities were pressing and required attention.[113]

Hatzfeld finally submitted his proposal on 6 June 1768. Far less concerned with developing and commercializing the infrastructure of public borrowing, Hatzfeld was obsessed with the narrower problem of servicing the state debt. He opposed structural innovations on the grounds that they would shake the confidence of traditional creditors and adversely affect the credit rating of the state. In case of war Hatzfeld estimated an annual deficit of 17 million Gulden, which he was confident could be raised by foreign loans and voluntary domestic credit. Expenses could in the meantime be covered by the extensive issue of bank notes as in 1762.[114] Zinzendorf's telling rebuttal argued that Hatzfeld was far too optimistic in his assessment of foreign credit – noting that it would have to be four times as great as in the previous war – and far too sanguine about the effectiveness of bank notes, especially over a period of several years.[115] The debate that ensued was bitter in the extreme. In the Council of State, Kaunitz's trusted right-hand man, Binder, led the attack on Hatzfeld with the result that the peace- and war-time systems were separated and considered on their individual merits. Hatzfeld was put on the defensive and forced to submit repeated clarifications. Having been critical of Zinzendorf's bonds, he was especially vulnerable on the efficacy of using bank notes on a large scale in war time. Accordingly, he amended his proposal and now advocated the immediate introduction of bank notes in order to get the public sufficiently accustomed to them that their

---

[112] Hock-Bidermann, pp. 84–87; Pettenegg, ed., *Zinzendorf*, p. 113.

[113] HHStA, Staatskanzlei: Vorträge, Karton 101, Kaunitz to Maria Theresia, 25 January 1768, section 69.

[114] Hock-Bidermann, pp. 86–88; Arneth, *Maria Theresia* IX, 436–438; Beer, "Staatsschulden," pp. 49–57; Schasching, pp. 80–81; Dickson, *Finance and Government* II, 68–71.   [115] Schasching, pp. 81–83.

introduction in war time would not come as such a shock.[116] In the decisive Council of State session on Hatzfeld's peace-time system in February 1770, Kaunitz swung his full weight against Hatzfeld. The peace-time system of Hatzfeld had evoked so much bitter disagreement that one could not "dare to recommend" its adoption. Further, Hatzfeld was still so unclear that even the *status quo* was preferable to any "precipitous step" of this sort.[117]

Hatzfeld emerged from this confrontation at least a partial victor. Decision on the Hatzfeld modifications of the Zinzendorf exchange, on the immediate introduction of bank notes and on Hatzfeld's whole war-time system was postponed until further discussions could take place. But the essentially negative features of his peace-time system were adopted. The diverse credit system remained intact, and at least an effort toward making all government papers redeemable on demand was ordered.[118] Zinzendorf's entire scheme to centralize and commercialize all public borrowing thereby suffered an irretrievable reverse. Yet Hatzfeld, too, soon failed with his supplementary war-time system. After much debate, in which Kaunitz made little effort to hide his disenchantment with developments so far, Hatzfeld's war-time system was rejected in January 1771.[119] What remained from the ruins of both men's projects were Zinzendorf's exchange and Hatzfeld's scheme to issue bank notes in peace time.

The exchange, of course, could hardly fulfill the role Zinzendorf had originally envisioned for it, though its re-establishment in 1771 now proved permanent. It gradually evolved into a stable and vital institution, and contributed substantially to the modernization of economic activity within the Habsburg Monarchy.[120] Kaunitz gave only a lukewarm endorsement to Hatzfeld's bank notes,[121] but the experiment was deemed worthwhile. A decree of 1 August 1771 provided for 12 million Gulden in bank notes to be issued in denominations from 5 to 1,000 Gulden. The notes were compulsory in half of all payments due to the Vienna City bank, but were otherwise redeemable for specie. Gradually, more and more notes were retained by the public, and the amounts in circulation increased every year. After 1780 the temptation to issue more and more bank notes grew with the national debt. In 1797 the notes were finally made fully compulsory and

[116] Beer, "Staatsschulden," pp. 57–58; Schasching, p. 112.
[117] HHStA, Kabinettsarchiv: Kaunitz Voten, Karton 1, Nos. 3570 and 3657 of 1769, Kaunitz Staatsrat Votum, 24 February 1770.
[118] *Ibid.*, Staatsratprotokolle, Vol. 33, Nos. 3570 and 3657 of 1769, imperial resolutions, 6 July 1770.
[119] *Ibid.*, Vol. 37, No. 3951 of 1770, imperial resolution, 4 January 1771.
[120] Baltzarek, *Wiener Börse*, pp. 25–156 and his "Die Wiener Börse – eine Gründung Maria Theresias," in Koschatzky, ed., *Maria Theresia und Ihre Zeit*, pp. 237–238; Dickson, *Finance and Government* II, 75–76.
[121] HHStA, Kabinettsarchiv: Kaunitz Voten, Karton 1, No. 3951 of 1770, Kaunitz Staatsrat Votum, 23 November 1770.

new printings followed. By 1811 there were 1,060,798,753 Gulden in circulation in bank notes, the national debt was over 700 million Gulden, and the state was forced to declare bankruptcy.[122]

During the final stages of the debates over the rival finance systems a tone of dejected fatalism entered Kaunitz's memoranda. This was due not only to the personal defeat he suffered with the collapse of Zinzendorf's public credit and bank schemes, but also to his own failure to effect any serious circumscription of extraordinary taxation. When ordered to produce a detailed report on the problem after the Privy Conference of April 1766, he had still been optimistic. But by the autumn of that year it already became clear that the demands of the military establishment (which on some estimates consumed 50% of net revenues)[123] would make tax reduction difficult. Kaunitz regarded wars essentially as socio-economic endurance contests, and therefore opposed the maintenance of a military establishment of such dimensions that its costs would hinder economic development. He regarded finances as "the mainspring of all policies", and healthy finances, in turn, depended on a well-developed credit system and a booming economy. Economic prosperity, however, could result only if the state did not overburden its subjects, particularly its peasants.[124] He returned to this same theme in his formal report on extraordinary taxation which he submitted on 28 July 1767.

Kaunitz began his report with the premise that the common people of the Monarchy were "oppressed by such heavy and manifold tax burdens" that there was no doubt further impositions would lead to a "complete weakening and ruination, especially of peasants." In a well-balanced economic system the determination of general levels of taxation depended, in his view, on four factors: 1) that the taxes be proportionate to the real wealth of the state and the capacity of its subjects to pay them, 2) that they be justly equal, 3) that they not adversely affect the general standard of living, and 4) that they be collected at the lowest possible cost. Most of the extraordinary taxes imposed in the last war out of "pressing necessity" overstepped these bounds and would best be abolished, even if only cautiously and gradually. While this would, of course, affect revenues, Kaunitz asserted that extraordinary taxes so overburdened people that they produced "no *real increase* in revenues proportionate to this burden" and hence were counter-productive. Kaunitz was also convinced that tax

---

[122] Arneth, *Maria Theresia* IX, 440–441; Beer, "Staatsschulden," pp. 69–70; Mikoletzky, *Österreich*, pp. 215–216; Dickson, *Finance and Government* II, 74–75, 375.

[123] Dickson, *Finance and Government* II, 37.

[124] HHStA, Staatskanzlei: Vorträge, Karton 99, Kaunitz to Maria Theresia, 24 January 1767.

collection and administration procedures were inefficient, and that substantial savings could be realized if various taxes were consolidated and the entire tax structure simplified. He concluded by recommending a full investigation by the Austro-Bohemian Chancellery to determine how this policy could be implemented.[125]

Fiscal shortsightedness, however, continued to characterize most of the responsible finance officials of the Monarchy even in the relatively improved conditions of the post-war era. So cool was the response to the idea of tax cuts, that even the very investigation that Kaunitz had suggested was left by the wayside. This did not deter Kaunitz from emphasizing the point over and over again. Indeed, in his great reform proposal of 1773 he singled out excessive and inequitable taxation as one of the three primary defects of the Monarchy, though to little avail.[126] Other than drastic military cutbacks there was, as Dickson has recently shown, "only limited scope for retrenchment of expenditure,"[127] and as long as Joseph II was the dominant voice in this regard, lavish military spending was not open to challenge. The serious consequences of this rejection of Kaunitz's recommendations cannot be underestimated. As Wangermann has pointed out, the maintenance in peace time of the special taxes imposed during the Seven Years War "undermined the effectiveness of the government's entire programme of reforms, and helped to bring about economic catastrophe in Bohemia in the early 1770s and a near collapse of the entire economy during the War of the Bavarian Succession."[128] Thus, by the end of Maria Theresia's reign, "Austria was clearly suffering from long-term tax exhaustion, despite the growth of wealth and population."[129]

Foundations for economic development

The reverses in the spheres of public credit and extraordinary tax made Kaunitz focus with ever more determination on other, broader policies to stimulate economic growth. In the seminal domestic reform proposal of 25 January 1768 he urged that servicing the national debt should not overshadow all other policies. In a pointed remark directed at Hatzfeld's central obsession, he expressed the conviction that the economic health of the Monarchy was not dependent on "the payment of several millions more or less of debt." Care simply had to be taken not to let expenditures

---

[125] *Ibid.*, Karton 100, Kaunitz to Maria Theresia, 28 July 1767, italics in original.
[126] *Ibid.*, Karton 112, "Kaunitz Gutachten über die Verbesserung des Systematis in Internis," 1 May 1773.   [127] Dickson, *Finance and Government* II, 39.
[128] Wangermann, *Austrian Achievement*, p. 90.
[129] Dickson, *Finance and Government* II, 2.

get out of hand, particularly in the military establishment. This could be done simply by setting up a specific budget for each government department, audited by the independent Court of Audit, and strictly enforced. Cash surpluses should then be used to foster other economic improvements. Of these broad concerns Kaunitz singled out three in particular which he felt deserved special attention. First and foremost was the improvement of agriculture, which he held to be one of the most important tasks of any state. Secondly he pressed for the creation of a trade company to stimulate domestic industry, with state support taking the form of share purchases in an otherwise public institution. Thirdly, Kaunitz lamented the state of tariff regulations in the Habsburg Monarchy, calling for a more efficient and rational approach to the whole problem. He suggested a beginning be made by creating a central excise office for the entire Monarchy.[130]

Government policies fostering agricultural prosperity will be discussed in detail below.[131] The stimulation of domestic industrial production by promoting commercial opportunities was the second point in Kaunitz's programme of economic development. Generally opposed to the direct industrial subsidies or the granting of monopolies which had characterized the early reign of Maria Theresia, Kaunitz preferred more indirect encouragement of industry.[132] To begin with, Kaunitz advocated direct government action in improving the communications infrastructure in the Monarchy.[133] The implementation of this policy led to major improvements in the road, canal and river networks of the Habsburg Monarchy, whose economic benefits need hardly be belabored at length.[134] Zinzendorf's idea of a trading company, which Kaunitz endorsed so warmly, fared less well. Official government policy, with which Kaunitz fully agreed, was prepared to be of assistance in smoothing the path to the establishment of such a company, but tended to shy away from direct state action. Investors in the private sector, for their part, were too fearful of the risks with the result that a trading company remained a mere desideratum for many years. Kaunitz had had a history of supporting trading company projects: in 1760 he had endorsed an elaborate plan by his friend Raniero Calzabigi, and in 1763 he seemed to be engrossed in an even more all-

---

[130] HHStA, Staatskanzlei: Vorträge, Karton 101, Kaunitz to Maria Theresia, 25 January 1768, sections 48–50, 58–60, 63–79.   [131] See below, pp. 158–180.

[132] HHStA, Kabinettsarchiv: Kaunitz-Voten, Karton 1, No. 1332 of 1767, Nos. 858 and 960 of 1768, No. 3461 of 1769, Kaunitz Staatsrat Voten, 24 June 1767, 24 and 30 April 1768, 15 October 1769.

[133] Ibid., No. 1283 of 1767 and No. 476 of 1772, Kaunitz Staatsrat Voten, 1 July 1767 and (?) March 1772.

[134] Otruba, Wirtschaftspolitik, pp 159–164; Franz Ilwolf, "Fluszregulierung und Wasserbauten, 1772–1774," AÖG 97/II (1909), 1–18.

encompassing scheme devised by Lieutenant-Colonel Hermann Caratto, but he was not able to get either idea much past the conceptual stage.[135]

In the autumn of 1774, however, the Austrian ambassador to London reported to Kaunitz that a Dutch-born German named Wilhelm Bolts (Bolz) had approached him with a proposal to undertake East Indian trade under Austrian colours. The assets from Bolts's prospering Indian ventures had been seized during Lord Robert Clive's energetic restructuring of Indian trade after the Seven Years War, and Bolts now sought to re-establish himself in this enterprise with Austrian backing. In approaching Vienna through the Habsburg ambassador in London, he asked for a line of credit from the Austrian treasury amounting to about 350,000 Gulden to finance the project. Kaunitz was captivated with the idea and quickly became the driving force behind the proposal within official circles in Vienna. Others were more skeptical. Joseph, under the influence of his brother Leopold who had also met Bolts, soon took an active dislike to the man and the project. He was prepared to supply Bolts with a garrison of twenty-five soldiers and to underwrite the wares to be sold in Asia, but not to finance a ship, crew or equipment. For this kind of financing Kaunitz placed Bolts into contact with the Belgian businessman Charles Melchior André Proli – one of the most ambitious and energetic capitalists of the Habsburg Monarchy. Proli and a group of partners undertook to finance Bolts, who thereupon purchased a 680-ton English vessel, *The Earl of Lincoln*, renamed it *Joseph und Theresia*, hoisted Austrian colours, picked up his wares in Leghorn and sailed to India in September 1776.[136]

Soon thereafter Proli discovered that Bolts had been forced to declare

---

[135] Dickson, *Finance and Government* I, 134; II, 45–46, 65. On the Caratto plan, see HHStA, Staatskanzlei: Vorträge, Karton 92, Kaunitz to Maria Theresia, n.d. (December 1763), including the Caratto plan. Zinzendorf assessed the Caratto plan as being based "on sound principles, but impractible in its gigantic application." DOZA, Handschriften, Vol. 64, Ludwig Zinzendorf to Karl Zinzendorf, 17 January 1767.

[136] On the entire project see Franz von Pollack-Parnau, *Eine österreichische-ostindische Handelscompagnie, 1775–1785*, Beiheft zur *VSWG*, No. 12 (Stuttgart, 1927). Some of Pollack-Parnau's conclusions have been criticized and revised by Karl Otmar Freiherr von Aretin, "Fürst Kaunitz und die österreichisch-ostindische Handelskompagnie von 1775: Ein Beitrag zur Geschichte des österreichischen Staatsbewußtseins unter Kaiser Joseph II.," *VSWG* XLVI (1959), 361–377; further new information is provided in Walter Markov, "Die koloniale Versuchung: Österreichs zweite Ostindienkompanie: Supplementa zu F. von Pollack-Parnau," in Plaschka and Klingenstein, eds., *Österreich im Europa der Aufklärung* I, 593–603. See also Arneth, *Maria Theresia* IX, 469–485; Adolf Beer, "Die österreichische Handelspolitik unter Maria Theresia und Joseph II.," *AÖG* LXXXVI (1898), 103–110; Otruba, *Wirtschaftspolitik*, pp. 129–131; Otruba, "Verwaltung, Finanzen, Manufakturen, Gewerbe, Handel und Verkehr, technisch-gewerbliche Bildung und Bevölkerungsentwicklung," in Erich Zöllner and Hermann Möcker, eds., *Österreich im Zeitalter des aufgeklärten Absolutismus* (Vienna, 1983), pp. 131–133; Mikoletzky, *Österreich*, pp. 235–237; Dickson, *Finance and Government* I, 191–204. The following paragraphs are largely based on these sources.

bankruptcy in England shortly before his departure, and he now quickly proposed to lessen his personal risks by founding a joint-stock East Indian Trading Company. Kaunitz was forced to rue his enthusiasm for Bolts, but not for the idea of a trading company, placing hope in the capacity of Proli to rescue the situation. Proli began on a poor footing by asking for too many monopoly and tariff concessions from an Austrian government grown suspicious of such measures, and his initial request for a license was rejected. With the consistent backing of Kaunitz, however, Proli remained persistent. In 1779 he arranged for an even heavier ship, suitably named *Fürst Kaunitz*, to be sent to China, and began working on a new proposal for the government in Vienna. Joseph, though he had returned from his 1777 trip to France filled with enthusiasm about maritime trade and even talked about building new harbours,[137] remained equally adamant that, while private entrepreneurs could conduct all the trade they wished with Asia, he was opposed to state involvement of any kind. In the meantime, Bolts had also purchased another ship in Surat, and, ignorant of Proli's dispatch of a second ship, appropriately named it *Fürst Kaunitz* as well. Bolts's *Fürst Kaunitz* arrived in Leghorn in the fall of 1779, where its wares were sold at a satisfactory profit. This quickly revived enthusiasm for East Indian trade, and smoothed the path for Proli's second proposal for an East Indian Trading Company, which Kaunitz introduced to the Empress with all the powers of persuasion at his command. By April 1780 he seemed to have succeeded when the Empress finally approved a licence in principle, and gave her permission for the foundation of a company. However, Joseph once more scuttled the plan, leading to such a spirited rebuttal by Kaunitz that a special commission was set up to draft terms of a licence that might be acceptable to the Emperor. Though the commission's draft received the full support of the Council of State, Joseph remained opposed and ordered no further action until the return of Bolts. He warmed slightly to Kaunitz's ideas in 1781 when Proli's *Fürst Kaunitz* discharged at Trieste with considerable profit, but the Bolts–Proli venture soon proved a financial disaster. In part this was due to the fact that the enterprise was significantly undercapitalized; in part due to the collapse of the favourable conjuncture for neutral shipping with the termination of the Anglo-French naval war in 1783. By 1785 Proli was forced to declare bankruptcy.

It would be a mistake to ascribe Kaunitz's persistent backing of Proli to the rumored possibility that Proli's nephew, Balthasar, was an illegitimate son of the Chancellor of State, and that Proli's firm therefore had a "hot line" to the Ballhausplatz.[138] However, there is little doubt that Kaunitz's enthusiasm was so great that he hastened to lend his support with an

---

[137] Mitrofanov, *Joseph II* I, 94.
[138] As suggested by Markov, "Die kolonialische Versuchung," p. 597.

alacrity that bordered on rashness and a determination totally out of proportion to the significance of the enterprise. His equally strong support for the creation of the ill-fated Austrian navy, which will be discussed below,[139] his doomed plans for the development of the port of Goro,[140] his efforts to revitalize Ostend–Leghorn–Trieste trade routes,[141] and his support for young Karl Zinzendorf's "commercial journeys" throughout Europe,[142] all show a devotion to the stimulation of commerce – and particularly maritime commerce – which reveals the centrality of commercial activity to economic development in Kaunitz's thought. It was this concern, above all, that motivated the third major economic proposal in his great memorandum of 1768: the complete reform of the tariff policies of the Habsburg Monarchy.

The legislation governing trade and commerce Maria Theresia had inherited from her father had been strictly mercantilist, characterized by restrictive prohibitions both externally and between provinces. Indeed, all of Charles VI's tariff ordinances were issued province by province, based on narrow provincial interests, and with no co-ordination by the crown in the interests of the Monarchy as a whole. Whether or not Maria Theresia recognized the degree to which such economic particularism retarded the industrial and commercial development of her Monarchy, she certainly articulated early in her reign a clear determination to foster this sector of the economy. It also seems clear that her sense of the need for inter-provincial co-ordination lay behind the creation of a pan-monarchical Central Directory for Commerce (*Universalcommerziendirectorium*) in 1746, and that the Empress envisioned a liberalization of the domestic tariff schedule as a result of such co-ordination. The first head of this new body, Philipp Kinsky, had barely acquainted himself with the scope of the problem when he died in January 1749. His successor was the inflexible mercantilist, Rudolph Chotek, who, while prepared to adjust inter-provincial tariff schedules, seemed never to question the fundamental centrifugal premises governing them. These unimaginative policies elicited vigorous criticism from the business community, which in this way

---

[139] See below, p. 295–302.

[140] G. Bigatti, "Politica delle acque ed assetti territoriali nella Lombardia delle riforme" (unpublished Ph.D. thesis, University of Milan, 1990). I am indebted to Carlo Capra for this reference.

[141] DOZA, Handschriften, Vol. 64, Ludwig Zinzendorf to Karl Zinzendorf, 13 September 1766.

[142] *Ibid.*, Vols. 51–55, 63–66, *passim*. Cf. Hans J. Teuteberg, "Österreich und das 'Engelländische Commercium' im Zeitalter des Merkantilismus," in Herwig Ebner, Walter Höflechner, Helmut J. Mezler-Andelberg, Paul W. Roth and Hermann Wiesflecker, eds., *Festschrift: Othmar Pickl zum 60. Geburtstag* (Graz and Vienna, 1987), pp. 649–676.

constituted an ongoing lobby for the liberalization of domestic commerce. External tariffs and prohibitions, on the other hand, enjoyed a broader consensus, and were regarded as a vital instrument of industrial development. In the early years of Maria Theresia's reign, infant industry was fostered by direct government subsidies, tax exemptions, readily granted monopolies, and protection from competition by strict import prohibitions. These, however, were received with retaliatory measures by other states, which deprived many industries of their natural markets and led to fierce trade wars and thriving smuggling activities. Hence, old ideals of autarky increasingly tended to be amended by eighteenth-century cameralists such as Justi and Sonnenfels, whose more pragmatic flexibility in turn opened the door to the liberal economic ideas of the physiocrats and of the Scottish Enlightenment.[143]

It would be a mistake to regard Kaunitz as the leading voice in mercantile and industrial development in the Habsburg Monarchy, though it is clear that his influence contributed substantially to the growing economic liberalism which characterized the later years of Maria Theresia's reign. In many ways, the ideological statement which Kaunitz insisted the Council of State adopt as a policy guideline served as a summary of his views and as a starting point for the further evolution of government policies on economic development. Kaunitz not only believed that government should be sensitive to the needs of businessmen, but also that bureaucrats should make an effort to learn from the private sector. His own reading of it was clear-cut: "commerce inherently tolerates no coercion." As a consequence he favoured as much freedom as possible for commercial and industrial entrepreneurs, and advocated a retreat from the earlier policy of subsidies and monopolies. Central to the animation of domestic commerce and industry, however, was tariff reform, guided by the principle "that everything which inhibits domestic agriculture, industry and flourishing commerce is to be considered highly harmful and abominable, and is to be reformed."[144]

The administrative reform of 1761 aimed at creating an independent ministry of Trade and Commerce (*Hofcommerzienrat*) as a successor to the Commerce Directory of 1746, but its president, Franz Reinhold von Andler-Witten, a conservative mediocrity, soon fell under the sway of Rudolph Chotek with whom he was compelled to co-ordinate provincial and local policy. Within weeks of the establishment of the ministry, Andler-Witten and Chotek submitted a joint proposal which subordinated

---

[143] Adolf Beer, "Die Zollpolitik und die Schaffung eines einheitlichen Zollgebietes unter Maria Theresia," *MIÖG* XIV (1893), 237–240; *ÖZV* I/3, 522–524; Otruba, *Wirtschaftspolitik*, pp. 142–151 and his "Verwaltung, Finanzen," pp. 110–121.
[144] Walter, "Eintritt," pp. 77–78.

the ministry to the Austro-Bohemian Chancellery, as an autonomous Department of Trade and Commerce. Kaunitz endorsed the amalgamation as a way of lessening interministerial friction, but the net result was that Rudolph Chotek's inflexible mercantilist voice continued to set the tone of this body. As a result, even an explicit instruction by the Empress to consider an abolition of all domestic tariff barriers met with predictable resistance, based on the argument that such an action would lead to a loss of revenues.[145] The prospects of relaxing import prohibitions and lightening external tariffs was also resisted. To make matters worse, the young Joseph also revealed strong protectionist leanings, in his great reform proposal of 1765, and Kaunitz's critique of them did not alter the Emperor's view. Kaunitz's arguments at the State Conference of 17 April 1766, opposing the protectionist system and emphasizing the necessity of stimulating trade and commerce, therefore also met with little success. In fact, only two days after the meeting, Joseph himself, after "ripe reflection", expressly confirmed all prohibitive measures passed, and ordered this confirmation circulated to all provincial authorities.[146]

However, he also ordered an investigation into anything which might be inhibiting the economy, and requested extensive local reports. These investigations led to what has been called the first offensive of free trade, led by the head of the local commerce agency (*Commerzconsessus*) of Lower Austria, Count Philipp Sinzendorf. Sinzendorf's enthusiastic support of free trade made sufficient impact for the question to be studied by a special commission headed by the Emperor personally, but not enough to cause a change of policy. In 1767 these first impulses towards free trade were rejected.[147]

In 1767 another impetus towards freer trade came from the seigniorial lobby. The harvest had been good, and the large landowners easily persuaded the Austro-Bohemian Chancellery to press their case for a relaxation of export prohibitions on grain. In the subsequent Council of State debates, Kaunitz, supported by Starhemberg, largely adopted a pragmatic middle ground. He felt that no definitive policies could be adopted without clearer statistical evidence, but he was suspicious about reports of grain surpluses when at the same time bread prices seemed to be undergoing spiraling inflation. On the whole he favoured following the English example which to his mind had the most advanced agricultural economy in Europe. He noted that the English strove to keep balanced

[145] Beer, "Zollpolitik," pp. 243–250; *ÖZV* II/1/i, 338–341; II/3, 345–346; Helen P. Liebel-Weckowicz, "Free Trade and Protectionism under Maria Theresa and Joseph II," *Canadian Journal of History* XIV (1979), 357.
[146] Arneth, *Maria Theresia* IX, 608–609.
[147] Schünemann, "Wirtschaftspolitik," p. 20.

grain prices by regulating export and import according to need, though, he repeated, such regulation was also not possible without reliable statistics.[148] Joseph, initially persuaded to endorse a relaxation of grain embargoes, soon drew back in the wake of the great famine that struck most of Germany and to a lesser extent England and France in the autumn of 1770. The immediate response to the crisis was to free the grain trade between provinces and to abolish import duties on grain from abroad for a year. When the harvest of 1771 also proved catastrophic, these measures were extended for another year. Joseph, convinced that the crisis was the direct result of the export relaxations of 1767, now favoured draconian prohibitive measures. In October 1771 he decreed that all exportations of grain were to be punished with the death penalty (although a subsidiary secret instruction ordered the commutation of the penalty in every instance).[149]

In that same year a special commission, chaired by the Austro-Bohemian Aulic Councillor Franz Karl von Kressel, was set up to introduce and supervise emergency relief measures, but debates on the broader remedial policies to be adopted were even more heated than before.[150] In September 1770 the younger half-brother of Ludwig Zinzendorf, Karl, returned from an extended European commercial tour, on which he became a convert to physiocratic ideas,[151] and immediately began a vigorous campaign against prohibitions. In the midst of the famine crisis Karl Zinzendorf argued that prohibitions against grain exports had caused a decline in foreign markets and a subsequent lower level of domestic production. The profits in good years such as 1767 were therefore insufficient to enable the purchase of high-priced grains sold in bad years. Zinzendorf's ideas fell on the receptive ears of Binder and also made a convert of Kressel, so that the free trade lobby began to gather momentum.[152] Kaunitz still shared Joseph's view that current shortages were at least the partial result of previous excessive exports, but in his analysis of the long-range causes he adopted the more liberal view. Heavy taxation and "the multifarious hindrances on

[148] HHStA, Kabinettsarchiv: Kaunitz-Voten, Karton 1, Nos. 1987, 2285 and 2336 of 1767, Kaunitz Staatsrat Voten, 8 September, 23 and 30 October 1767; Eichwalder, pp. 138–140.
[149] Joseph Kumpfmüller, "Die Hungersnot von 1770 bis 1772 in Österreich," (unpublished Ph.D. dissertation, University of Vienna, 1969), p. 37.
[150] Fritz Blaich, "Die wirtschaftspolitische Tätigkeit der Kommission zur Bekämpfung der Hungersnot in Böhmen und Mähren (1771–1772)," VSWG LVI (1969), 299–331; Erika Weinzierl-Fischer, "Die Bekämpfung der Hungersnot in Böhmen 1770–1772 durch Maria Theresia und Joseph II.," MÖStA VII (1954), 478–514.
[151] DOZA, Handschriften, Vol. 54, Karl Zinzendorf to Ludwig Zinzendorf, 9 and 13 May 1770.
[152] Liebel-Weckowicz, "Free Trade and Protectionism," 359–365 and her "Modernisierungsmotive in der Freihandelspolitik Maria Theresias," in Koschatzky, ed., Maria Theresia und Ihre Zeit, pp. 156–157.

industries" were really to blame for the crisis, and he insisted that the key to its resolution was the abolition of all duties and taxes detrimental to economic growth. These "hindrances" had to be "cleared out of the way", and more energetic measures taken to foster a vigorous economic life.[153]

These comments were not vague generalizations, but specific allusions to the ongoing debate on tariffs which continued to rage since the setback Maria Theresia suffered in 1762. The problem was subjected to repeated investigations in the subsequent years, and numerous adjustment to the tariff schedule had been made. But there was no real breakthrough. By the time Kaunitz repeated the demand for a more rational approach to tariff policies and the creation of a central excise office for the Monarchy in January 1768, however, his case was strengthened by the arrival of a new ally. In December 1767 Kaunitz had succeeded in placing Philipp Cobenzl, the nephew of his Authorized Minister in Belgium, Karl Cobenzl, into a privy councillor vacancy in Hatzfeld's treasury. Within a year Cobenzl was appointed head of the customs department within the ministry, and it was he who was now charged by Maria Theresia to work out a detailed plan on tariff reform, as suggested in its general outlines by Kaunitz's memorandum. Cobenzl presented his tentative proposals in December 1769. These focused on the abolition of internal customs barriers, the outright elimination of prohibitions, and the simplification of external tariffs by the creation of a simple single duty on imports, exports and goods in transit.[154]

The Council of State was deeply divided, with Blümegen an entrenched protectionist and Binder an equally outspoken free trader.[155] Kaunitz, arguing that this ideological battle would be reflected in other departments as well, accordingly advised that no decision be taken on specific details until a decision had been reached on the fundamental principles involved.[156] The Empress concurred and set up a special commission under the chairmanship of the uncommitted Starhemberg, consisting of Chotek, Hatzfeld, Ludwig Zinzendorf, Cobenzl, and members of the Council of State to study the question.[157] In the confrontation that ensued, Hatzfeld catalogued revenue losses which would result from such a proposal, and Chotek dismissed Cobenzl as a "novateur", arguing coolly that his only interest was establishing sound ground rules for effective tariffs. Since the

[153] HHStA, Kabinettsarchiv: Kaunitz Voten, Karton 2, No. 256 of 1772, Kaunitz Staatsrat Votum, n.d. (February 1772).
[154] Beer, "Zollpolitik," pp. 258–261, 306–308. Cobenzl passed over this part of his life rather fleetingly in his memoirs. See Arneth, ed., "Cobenzl," pp. 107–108.
[155] Schünemann, "Wirtschaftspolitik," p. 39.
[156] HHStA, Kabinettsarchiv: Kaunitz Voten, Karton 1, No. 233 of 1770, Kaunitz Staatsrat Votum, n.d. (between 7 and 14 February 1770).
[157] Ibid., Staatsratprotokolle, Vol. 34, No. 233, imperial resolution, 15 February 1770.

commission was split evenly between protagonists and opponents of freer trade, their irreconcilable differences ensured a long and indecisive debate, despite pressure from the Empress. The death of Chotek in July 1771, and the ensuing ministerial shuffles, resulted in a redistribution of political power that promised to resolve the deadlock. On 20 August 1773 the Empress appointed a new commission, consisting of representatives of the Austro-Bohemian Chancellery, the Department of Trade and Commerce, the Treasury and the Court of Audit which once more resulted in stalemate. But when the problem was then forwarded to the Council of State, the free trade lobby had the upper hand. Gebler still expressed fears that the lifting of prohibitions could lead to the outflow of specie and massive unemployment. However, Löhr took the opposite point of view, laying the blame for the decline of industry since the war squarely on the coercive and prohibitive measures adopted since then. Kressel agreed. In his view the prohibitive system merely encouraged smuggling and reprisals on the part of other countries which an agricultural state such as Austria could ill afford. Even Hatzfeld moderated his former conservative stance, defending prohibitions but being prepared to confine them to "proper limits."[158]

The slight balance in favour of the reformers was tipped decisively by Kaunitz. In his delayed submission of 20 January 1774, he argued that the essence of the economic life of a state consisted of initiative, activity, exchange, struggle, and competition. "All this," he continued, "is destroyed by coercion and prohibition." Seconding the arguments of Löhr and Kressel, he suggested that if the purpose of prohibitions was to keep money in the country, that end was not being achieved. Domestic wealth did not depend on the number of enterprises, but on their value, so that ten factories keeping half a million Gulden a year in the country were not as important as one which exported for a million. Given the enormous export potential of agriculture, one could regard the entire agrarian sector as a "factory" which drew money into the country. The logical conclusion one therefore had to draw, Kaunitz stated, was that all customs measures adopted had to take "freedom as the rule [and] prohibitions as the exception." And in his view there ought to be "very few cases" in which such exception should be considered "necessary or advisable."[159]

Before Maria Theresia could make her final decision, however, Joseph intervened. In a major memorandum, dated 11 February, he outlined his entire economic programme, which continued to adhere to the mercantilist

---

[158] Beer, "Zollpolitik," pp. 265–274; Liebel-Weckowicz, "Free Trade and Protectionism," p. 362; Schünemann, "Wirtschaftspolitik," p. 45–46.

[159] HHStA, Kabinettsarchiv: Kaunitz Voten, Karton 2, No. 1939 of 1773, Kaunitz Staatsrat Votum, 20 January 1774.

ideal of autarky. While in favour of abolishing all internal tariffs and tolls, the Emperor insisted on the exclusion of all foreign products which could be manufactured domestically. Even if people suffered as a result of prohibitions, Joseph avowed, "the Monarchy has always to be regarded as a society of 13 million people" in which, "even if 2 or 3 million people are subjected to some burdens, 10 million nevertheless profit." He felt the destitution of "a few mountain regions in Bohemia, [and] 100 industrialists in Vienna" could be borne with equanimity if, as a result, the whole Monarchy "stood as one man in protecting itself." He frankly admitted that Austrian enterprises were not likely to be very competitive internationally because it was necessary to subject them to higher tax levels to support the military establishment, and since he regarded Austria's neighbors as being self-sufficient he also dismissed prospects for grain exports as limited.[160]

The Emperor's intervention forced a recirculation of the whole matter through the Council of State. Gebler supported the Emperor enthusiastically, but Löhr, Kressel and Hatzfeld all dissented – Löhr suggesting that if the outflux of capital were stopped, the influx would stop as well, killing foreign trade altogether; Kressel insisting that nations which "completely lock themselves up" grow ever poorer and weaker.[161] Kaunitz, already aware of Maria Theresia's final decision, rested his case on his previous submission. The Empress's resolution ensued on 27 April. Basing itself primarily on the opinion of Kaunitz, it posited as "the fundamental rule and unyielding guiding principle" the Kaunitzian formula that freedom in trade was to be the rule and prohibition the exception.[162] Kaunitz clearly did not expect this victory, for when Maria Theresia submitted her final order to the Austro-Bohemian Chancellery to implement Cobenzl's tariff ordinance to him for comment, he replied that because he had not expected this success, his joy at it had been all the greater.[163] The final decree continued to encounter obstacles, as the Treasury President, Kollowrat, protested the implementation would raise

[160] HHStA, Staatskanzlei: Vorträge, Karton 114, Joseph Nota, 11 February 1774. Cf. Adolf Beer, "Studien zur Geschichte der österreichischen Volkswirtschaft unter Maria Theresia: I. Die österreichische Industriepolitik," *AÖG* LXXXI (1895), 95–97; Schünemann, "Wirtschaftspolitik," pp. 47–50.
[161] Schünemann, "Wirtschaftspolitik," pp. 50–51.
[162] HHStA, Kabinettsarchiv: Staatsratprotokolle, Vol. 48, No. 1939, imperial resolution, 27 April 1774. Schünemann, working from the original *Staatsratakten* in which the Vota are undated, sees Kaunitz's Votum of 20 January as a reply to Joseph's Nota of 11 February. The protocol record makes clear that the original debate was terminated and re-opened only as a result of Joseph's intervention.
[163] HHStA, Staatskanzlei: Vorträge, Karton 114, Kaunitz to Maria Theresia, 30 March 1774, including imperial resolution and draft resolution for Austro-Bohemian Chancellery.

administrative costs and result in an annual revenue loss of 3 million Gulden. But these objections merely delayed the official proclamation, which followed on 15 July 1775.[164]

[164] Hock-Bidermann, pp. 93–94; Beer, "Zollpolitik," pp. 274–278.

5   The transformation of society

Cameralists had been aware that at the heart of the economic problems of the Habsburg Monarchy lay an archaic social structure whose stubborn defence by the privileged orders of society constituted the principal impediment to the success of the reforms they envisioned. By and large, however, they were a conservative lot in questions of social policy, and their prescriptions tended to be overlaid with a heavy cloak of paternalism.[1] Modern historians have argued that early modern elites sought to rationalize social structures by the imposition of a "social discipline" on inchoate traditionalist populations, with the intent of increasing both control and productivity.[2] If the long-range agenda of this effort was an endeavor "to foster and give full scope to the creative energies of the individual members of society by means of the state's direction,"[3] the key to its success was the internalization of the new rigorous social norms. Yet this could be achieved only by the transformation of mere "subjects" into more autonomous "citizens," and herein lies the central historiographical problem of enlightened absolutism.

If the more traditional interpretations which emphasize the reactionary, retarding features of enlightened absolutism are correct, then what transformation of society occurred was insignificant, indirect and unwanted. In short, it would be justified to regard eighteenth-century developments as mere conservative holding-actions intent on preserving traditional hierarchical structures. If, on the other hand, powerful members of the traditional elite foresaw and welcomed a fundamental reshaping of society, then not only the effect but also the intent of enlightened absolutism was the liberation of individuals from the bonds that tied their ancestors. That the latter was the case in the Habsburg Monarchy of the

---

[1] Johnson, "Concept of Bureaucracy," pp. 378–402; Raeff, *Well-Ordered Police State,* *passim.*

[2] Gerhard Oestreich, *Neostoicism and the early modern state* (Cambridge, 1982), pp. 258–272; Christoph Sachße and Florian Tennstedt, eds., *Soziale Sicherheit und Soziale Disziplinierung* (Frankfurt a/M, 1986); Winfried Schulze, "Gerhard Oestreichs Begriff 'Sozialdisziplinierung in der Frühen Neuzeit'," *Zeitschrift für Historische Forschung* XIV (1987), 265–302.   [3] Raeff, *Well-Ordered Police State,* p. 257.

154

eighteenth century becomes clear when we examine the central question of the evolution of the legal status of Habsburg peasants under enlightened absolutism. Here the intent was comprehensive enough, even if the success in changing the whole pattern of landholding was only partial. Yet the effort to transform bonded serf into self-sufficient and enterprising yeoman was only symptomatic of a larger effort to revolutionize the whole value system of society. Judicial, educational and cultural changes were intended to metamorphose tightly-controlled subjects into dynamic autonomous citizens which, in time, were to render the very existence of the regulatory state problematic. More than anything else, this constituted the heart of the "enlightenment" of "enlightened absolutism" in the Habsburg Monarchy.

The agrarian sector

Despite the undeniable progress made in industry and commerce in the eighteenth century, the Habsburg Monarchy remained an overwhelmingly rural society throughout the period. Since the economy was predominantly agricultural, it should not be surprising that agrarian problems were among the most important issues that preoccupied the governing circles of the Monarchy. These problems were very complex indeed, because conditions varied so greatly from one crown land to the other. Seigniorial involvement with agricultural production and conditions of peasant land tenure were extremely heterodox, not only from region to region but within provinces themselves. There was a broad range of peasant status and peasant obligations, whether these were discharged in cash, in kind, in labour obligations, or in a combination of the three. As a consequence agrarian legislation tended to be regional rather than pan-monarchical in its focus, though certain common underlying trends clearly emerge if the agrarian policy of Habsburg enlightened absolutism is examined as a whole.

The seventeenth-century Habsburg Counter-Reformation state had witnessed a profound transformation of the rural economy, and, indeed, to some extent was the product of these changing relationships in the countryside. In an effort to take advantage of the commercial opportunities which emerged from the so-called price revolution from about the 1570s on, the seigniorial elite of the Monarchy began to make entrepreneurial adjustments, developed new techniques of estate management, and strove to consolidate their latifundia. As inflation diminished the value of feudal rents, the relationship between lord and peasant also underwent a tremendous change, and there is little doubt that the material, legal and social position of the peasants deteriorated in the course of the seventeenth century. Entrepreneurial estate farming tended to be more prevalent in Bohemia and Hungary than in the Austrian provinces, where nobles rented out their arable land and preferred to specialize in forestry and other activities. But demands on peasants became more burdensome everywhere.[4]

Peasants frequently responded to seigniorial subjection and exploitation with open revolt or flight from the manor, as well as with dilatory and indifferent discharging of contractual obligations to the lord. In response, crown intervention at the manorial level gradually emerged. After serious peasant disturbances in Bohemia in 1679–1680, Leopold I issued the first regulatory decree on peasant obligations, focusing above all on labour services, which were known by their Czech name, robot, throughout the Monarchy. The legislation was extended to Moravia in 1713, and reiterated in new robot patents for both provinces in 1717.[5] Provisions against undue oppression of peasants were also inserted into resolutions of the Royal Hungarian Diet in 1715. In subsequent Diets in 1723 and 1729 further articles were promulgated preventing nobles from making demands upon their peasants which exceeded the feudal contracts (Urbare).[6] In the wake of serious peasant revolts in the Slavonian counties of the Croatian Kingdom, Charles VI proceeded to impose compulsory uniform urbarial contracts on all three counties in 1737.[7] At the same time he revamped the Bohemian Robot patent and issued a revised decree on 27 January 1738.[8]

The common feature of this spate of agrarian legislation was that it

[4] Evans, Making of the Habsburg Monarchy, pp. 85–91; Karl Richter, "Die böhmischen Länder von 1471–1740," in Karl Bosl, ed., Handbuch der Geschichte der böhmischen Länder, Vol. II (Stuttgart, 1974), pp. 208–223; Helmuth Feigl, Die Niederösterreichische Grundherrschaft vom ausgehenden Mittelalter bis zu den theresianisch-josephinischen Reformen (Vienna, 1964), pp. 13–50; Ernst Bruckmüller, "Die Grundherrschaft," in Alfred Hoffmann, ed., Bauernland Oberösterreich: Entwicklungsgeschichte seiner Land- und Forstwirtschaft (Linz, 1974), pp. 28–62; Bohuslav Rieger, "Grundherrschaft," ÖStWB I, 34–43; Alfred Hoffmann, "Die Grundherrschaft als Unternehmen," Zeitschrift für Agrargeschichte und Agrarsoziologie VI (1958), 123–131.

[5] Karl Grünberg, Die Bauernbefreiung und die Auflösung des gutsherrlich-bäuerlichen Verhältnisses in Böhmen, Mähren und Schlesien, 2 Vols. (Leipzig, 1894), I, 127–135; Kamil Krofta, Dějiny selského stavu (Prague, 1949), pp. 226–282.

[6] Johann Seedoch, "Die Urbarialregulierung Maria Theresias," in Gerda Mraz and Gerald Schlag, eds., Maria Theresia als Königin von Ungarn (Eisenstadt, 1980), pp. 84–85; Seedoch, "Die Auswirkungen der Theresianisch-Josephinischen Reformen im Gebiet des Heutigen Burgenlandes," in Helmut Feigl, ed., Die Auswirkung der Theresianisch-Josephinischen Reformen auf die Landwirtschaft und die ländliche Sozialstruktur Niederös- terreichs (Vienna, 1982), pp. 45–46.

[7] Ibid.; cf. Stanko Gludescu, The Croatian–Slavonian Kingdom, 1526–1792 (The Hague and Paris, 1970), pp. 189–190.

[8] Grünberg, Bauernbefreiung I, 135–141; II, 30–42; Krofta, Dějiny selského stavu, pp. 243–249; Josef Kalousek, ed., "Řády selské a instrukce hospodářské 1698–1780," Archiv Česky XXIV (1908), 177–197.

essentially sought to regulate and stabilize rather than transform the rural *status quo*. While a certain paternalistic cameralist eudemonism was not absent, the decrees were for the most part motivated by a fear that peasant unrest would spread to other areas of the Monarchy, and, above all, by a desire to protect the peasant's capacity to pay state taxes. Plots recorded in the land registry as peasant lands (*rustikal*) were taxable, while noble lands (*dominikal*) were not, so that seigniorial encroachments on *rustikal* holdings in effect reduced the crown's tax base. What was more, peasants overburdened by manorial dues and labour obligations were too impoverished to yield revenues on the scale expected by the government. Unfortunately, even when apparently firm provisions for enforcement appeared to be included in these decrees, as for example with the Bohemian patent of 1738, the net effects were largely nugatory. Enforcement depended too much on the lords themselves, or on local officials in seigniorial pay. Interpretations of the often complex clauses detailing exceptions to the rule were rendered by manorial courts, and sheer ignorance and outright disobedience were rife.[9]

These burning agrarian problems in the final years of Charles VI continued to remain to the fore at the accession of Maria Theresia. The first agrarian regulations of her reign were promulgated for Transylvania in 1747, followed by *urbarial* decrees for Croatia in 1755 and for Slavonia in 1756.[10] In the Austrian and Bohemian lands substantive new incursions by the crown into serf–seignior relations came as a concomitant of the Haugwitz reforms of 1748. In the 1750s enforcement provisions already included in the Bohemian *robot* patent of 1738 were given new teeth, and in the remaining provinces an agency of peasant protection specifically mandated to discharge this new duty without regard to seigniorial sensibilities ("sine respectu personarum") was established.[11] By 1761, as the *urbarial* regulation focus shifted to Hungary, the primary forum for discussions had become the Council of State, and in this body entirely new considerations were raised which were to add a whole new philosophical dimension to agrarian reform in the next two decades. The most prominent proponents of the new ideas were Borié and Kaunitz. Both men stressed

---

[9] *Ibid.*; Krofta, pp. 287–294; Jaroslav Prokop, "Robotní patent z roku 1738 v Čechách," *Sborník Archivních Praci* XVIII (1968), 377–411.

[10] P. Prodan, "Die Aufhebung der Leibeigenschaft in Siebenbürgen," *Südostforschungen* XXIX (1970), 3; Ivan Erceg, "Die Theresianischen Reformen in Kroatien," in Heinz Haushofer and Willi A. Boelcke, eds., *Wege und Forschungen der Agrargeschichte: Festschrift zum 65. Geburtstag von Günther Franz* (Frankfurt a/M, 1967), pp. 146–147; Gludescu, *Croatian–Slavonian Kingdom*, pp. 191–196.

[11] Grünberg, *Bauernbefreiung*, I, 146–160; II, 55–64; Kalousek, ed., "Řády selské," pp. 296–300, 314–318; Krofta, pp. 307–310; Helen Liebel-Weckowicz and Franz A. J. Szabo, "Modernization Forces in Maria Theresa's Peasant Policies, 1740–1780," *Social History – Histoire sociale* XV (1982), 304.

not only the economic but also the political advantage to be derived from preventing seigniorial oppression of peasants, and from winning the common man to the cause of the crown.[12] The perspective that was gradually emerging increasingly viewed the peasantry as an active political constituency rather than mere revenue-generating subjects of cameralist paternalism. By 1763, the new political emphasis on the peasantry found even stronger expression as Kaunitz asserted: "Other sovereigns increasingly seek to curb the nobility, because the true strength of the state consists of the greatest number of its people, namely the common man. It is he who deserves priority consideration."[13] By the Hungarian Diet of 1764 Kaunitz's thought already explicitly began to reflect Enlightenment natural rights ideas. Peasant protection now ceased to be a matter of mere economic or even political utility, and had become an agenda "which conscience absolutely demands."[14] In a sense, therefore, the debates on the implementation of the Hungarian *urbarium* revealed that a critical turning point in political attitudes to the peasant question had already been reached.

The most vital catalyst in this shift of agrarian perspectives, however, lay in the crisis of agricultural supply. The poor productivity of forced peasant labour, combined with relatively static demand in agricultural products and poor yields resulting from inefficient tilling methods, created a stagnant rural economy by the later seventeenth and early eighteenth centuries. Famine was an ever-present threat and seemed to strike with cyclical regularity, while harvest shortfalls could be expected up to 50% of the time. Systematic peasant impoverishment led to an increase in vagrancy, and large numbers of beggars proliferated throughout the Monarchy. Even in relatively prosperous Upper Austria alone, for example, it was estimated in 1727 that out of a total population of 300,000, some 26,000 people were beggars.[15] Cameralist reformers, tending to focus much more on industry and commerce, generally held very conservative views on agriculture. They failed to address social problems, advocated few structural changes, and sought to remedy the problem of agricultural supply with prohibitive measures such as export bans, price controls and the like, which were largely ineffective and often merely aggravated the

---

[12] Győző Ember, "Der Österreichische Staatsrat und die Ungarische Verfassung, 1761–1768," *Acta Historica Academiae Scientarum Hungaricae* IV (1959), 130–137.
[13] HHStA, Staatskanzlei: Vorträge, Karton 91, Kaunitz to Maria Theresia, 1 May 1763.
[14] *Ibid.*, Karton 94, Kaunitz to Maria Theresia, 1 December 1764. Cf. below, pp. 325–326.
[15] Josef Kočí, "Die Reformen der Untertänigkeitsverhältnisse in den böhmischen Ländern unter Maria Theresia und Joseph II.," in Plaschka and Klingenstein, eds., *Österreich im Europa der Aufklärung* I, 128–129; Roman Sandgruber, "Agrarpolitik zwischen Krisen und Konjunkturen," in Hoffmann, ed., *Bauernland Oberösterreich*, pp. 99–100.

problem.[16] One can therefore speak of a genuine crisis of agricultural production which became increasingly apparent as population figures began to rise from the mid-eighteenth century onwards – a crisis highlighted in particular by the pressing necessity of military food-supply requirements during the Seven Years War.[17]

Growing awareness of this problem of agricultural supply increasingly permeated cameralist thought as the century wore on. Earlier mercantilists had focused on rural population growth because it would lead to increased consumption and demand, would generate greater tax revenues, and would bolster the military potential of the state. Planting of flax, hemp, mulberry trees and the like was encouraged because of their value as raw materials in industrial production. By the early eighteenth century, however, officials such as Schierendorff recognized the retarding features of entrepreneurial estate farming. By the mid-eighteenth century the lessons of the English agricultural revolution, and news of experiments in serf labour service reforms in such places as Denmark, were beginning to make inroads in Central Europe, and cameralists such as Justi already showed much more awareness of the urgency of food supply, and revealed a greater sensitivity to the growing crisis in agrarian production.[18] These views were occasionally reflected in bureaucratic thought during the 1750s, but they were brought into sharp focus in the 1760s in large part because of the views expressed in the newly-formed Council of State. Here the novel perspectives of the French physiocrats found an increasingly sympathetic hearing, and though one can hardly speak of outright converts, the growing influence of these theories is unmistakable.[19]

This tendency is also evident in the developing thought of Kaunitz. His ideological "programme" for the Council of State early in 1761 still

[16] Edith Murr Link, *The Emancipation of the Austrian Peasant, 1740–1798* (N.Y., 1949), pp. 23–30; Roman Sandgruber, "Marktökonomie und Agrarrevolution: Anfänge und Gegenkräfte der Kommerzialisierung der österreichischen Landwirtschaft," in Anna M. Drabek, Richard G. Plaschka and Adam Wandruszka, eds., *Ungarn und Österreich unter Maria Theresia und Joseph II.* (Vienna, 1982), p. 131.

[17] Helmuth Feigl, "Landwirtschaft und Grundherrschaft unter dem Einfluß des Physiokratismus," in Zöllner and Mocker, eds., *Österreich*, pp. 86–87; Ernst Bruckmüller, "Die Anfänge der Landwirtschaftsgesellschaften und die Wirkungen Ihrer Tätigkeit," in Feigl, ed., *Auswirkungen der Theresianisch-Josephinischen Reformen*, pp. 45–46; B. H. Slicher van Bath, *The Agrarian History of Western Europe, A.D. 500–1850* (London, 1963), pp. 221–239; John Komlos, *Nutrition and Economic Development in the Eighteenth-Century Habsburg Monarchy* (Princeton, N.J., 1989), pp. 23–118.

[18] Fischel, "Schierendorff," pp. 216–221; Černý, "Pozemková reforma," pp. 18–25; Sigmund von Frauendorfer, *Ideengeschichte der Agrarwirtschaft und Agrarpolitik im deutschen Sprachgebiet* (Munich, 1963), I, 139.

[19] Feigl, "Landwirtschaft und Grundherrschaft," pp. 84–102, esp. p. 87; and his "Die Auswirkungen der Theresianisch-Josephinischen Reformgesetzgebung auf die Ländliche Sozialstruktur Österreichs," in Plaschka and Klingenstein, eds., *Österreich im Europa der Aufklärung* I, 53–57.

revealed his strong indebtedness to the cameralist tradition of the Habsburg Monarchy. The explicit fiscal association of rural prosperity with tax revenue potential is still quite clear, and agricultural supply tended to be seen in the context of a requirement for industrial expansion. But the assertion that all impediments to increased agricultural productivity had to be eliminated, "even if they entailed a considerable revenue advantage," already exhibited new directions.[20] By the time of the momentous Privy Conference meeting of 17 April 1766 on economic priorities, increased agricultural output had become one of the pillars of Kaunitz's economic prescriptions.[21] Instrumental in this crystallization of Kaunitz's agrarian focus were the various agricultural societies which were created in the various provinces of the Monarchy.

Originating in Scotland in 1723, agricultural societies began to proliferate in Western Europe during the 1750s and to make inroads in Germany in the early 1760s. They reflected not only the growing interest in the theory and practice of agriculture, but also the heightened awareness of the agrarian production crisis and the emerging influence of physiocratic doctrines. Most of these societies conceived themselves as spearheads of the agricultural revolution, experimenting with crop diversification, animal husbandry, tilling innovations, and the like, and propagating their findings through specialized publications.[22] Unlike many Western European groups, Habsburg agricultural societies were introduced virtually by royal fiat, beginning in Carinthia in 1764 and spreading quickly to other provinces, and tended to be viewed as local instruments of government policy.[23] Kaunitz, who had a strong personal interest in horticulture and prided himself on his specialized knowledge in that field,[24] certainly was inclined to view them as the best vehicles for the effective and widespread implementation of salutary agricultural innovations, particularly crop diversification. He strongly advocated government experimentation with the cultivation of non-indigenous plants in every province of the Monarchy, and where positive results were achieved, agricultural societies

[20] Walter, "Eintritt," pp. 76–77.   [21] Arneth, *Maria Theresia* VII, 210–211, 449–450.
[22] Jerome Blum, *The End of the Old Order in Rural Europe* (Princeton, N.J., 1978), pp. 287–292; Bruckmüller, "Anfänge der Landwirtschaftsgesellschaften," pp. 38–53; Rudolf Rübberdt, *Die Ökonomischen Sozietäten* (Würzburg, 1934).
[23] Karl Dinklage, "Gründung und Aufbau der theresianischen Ackerbaugesellschaften," *Zeitschrift für Agrargeschichte und Agrarsoziologie* XIII (1965), pp. 200–211; Dinklage, *Geschichte der Kärnter Landwirtschaft* (Klagenfurt, 1966), pp. 151–166; Karl Pömer, "Die Ackerbau- und Landwirtschaftsgesellschaften," in Hoffmann, ed., *Bauernland Oberösterreich*, pp. 628–640; Bruckmüller, "Anfänge der Landwirtschaftsgesellschaften," pp. 51–68.
[24] HHStA, Sonstige Sammlungen: Grosse Korrespondenz, Fasz. 405, Starhemberg to Kaunitz, 26 March 1764; MZA, Rodinný archiv Kouniců, Karton 11, Instructions on arboretum at Austerlitz; Karton 15, Instructions for estate gardener.

were to be charged with informing and encouraging private cultivators to follow suit.[25] Above all, Kaunitz was a fervent advocate of the potato, urging that its cultivation be energetically fostered in the face of widespread resistance to this crop. He noted its excellent performance in relatively poor soil, and saw it as an ideal dietary supplement – especially since cereal harvest shortfalls loomed large in the later 1760s. Agricultural societies were accordingly ordered to propagate the virtues of this root-crop,[26] but even government-sponsored mass plantings and propaganda met with skepticism.[27] Kaunitz sometimes inclined to stern measures, and in 1768 he urged that the Austro-Bohemian Chancellery and its Department of Trade and Commerce be made to focus much more on agricultural productivity – indeed, he even proposed to make landowners accountable for the introduction of agricultural improvements.[28] But in the event it was only famine and growing population pressures that encouraged an increase in potato production and consumption as the century neared its end, and it was not until the nineteenth century that the potato became a staple of the Central European diet.[29]

The same preoccupation with the crisis in agricultural production that animated agrarian innovations also led to fundamental structural changes in the rural social order. Forward-looking agronomists and state officials increasingly began to recognize that agricultural productivity was impeded as much by the inefficiencies of the feudal seigniorial social structure as by technical backwardness. Entrepreneurial estate farming was gradually seen to be inefficient, and its structural underpinnings – serfdom, dues in kind, labour services – to be counter-productive.[30] But if the technical aspects of the agricultural revolution were difficult to implement, structural changes were harder still. Often bitter seigniorial resistance makes it clear that structural change to the rural social order was the real crux of the confrontation between the crown and the privileged elite of the Mon-

[25] HHStA, Kabinettsarchiv: Kaunitz Voten, Karton 1, Nos. 377 and 595 of 1767, Kaunitz Staatsrat Voten, 13 March and 8 April 1767.

[26] HHStA, Kabinettsarchiv: Kaunitz Voten, Karton 1, No. 1029 of 1767, Kaunitz Staatsrat Votum, 10 May 1767; Staatsratprotokolle, Vol. 25, no. 1029, imperial resolution, n.d. (May 1767).

[27] Roman Sandgruber, "Produktions- und Produktivitätsfortschritte der Niederösterreichischen Landwirtschaft im 18. und frühen 19. Jahrhundert," in Feigl, ed., *Auswirkungen der Theresianisch-Josephinischen Reformen*, pp. 113–116; Kalousek, ed., "Řády selské," pp. 429, 444.

[28] HHStA, Staatskanzlei: Vorträge, Karton 101, Kaunitz to Maria Theresia, 25 January 1768, § 49.

[29] Blum, *Old Order in Rural Europe*, p. 273; Roman Sandgruber, *Österreichische Agrarstatistik, 1750–1918*, Part 2 of Alfred Hoffmann and Herbert Matis, eds., *Wirtschafts- und Sozialstatistik Österreich-Ungarns* (Munich, 1978), p. 58.

[30] Sandgruber, "Produktions- und Produktivitätsfortschritte," pp. 95–138; Feigl, "Landwirtschaft und Grundherrschaft," pp. 90, 93–94.

archy.[31] Latent opposition to the political and fiscal incursions of the crown here threatened to become open revolt – as was indeed to be the case with Joseph II's land and tax reform of 1789. Reformers thus faced two distinct though interlinked problems: one of policy as such; one of the means of implementing it effectively. Concern with the latter often accounts for the apparent conservatism of the former. The intent, however, was not the preservation or stabilization, but the transformation of the social order.

The impetus for these reforms came either from members of agricultural societies, or from the same stratum of individuals as those who generally made up these societies: academics, bureaucrats, progressive landlords, innovative estate stewards, or bourgeois professionals who recognized that the feudal social structure retarded economic development. Many of the principal features of the agrarian legislation of the 1770s and 1780s already found expression in their proposals as early as the mid-1760s. All found a sympathetic ear in Kaunitz. These included the suggestion of a Dutch textile entrepreneur in Carinthia, Jan (Johann) van Thys, that large estates should be split up into smaller freeholds and ownership transferred to the peasants in return for a quitrent. At Kaunitz's urging the reform was not only introduced on an experimental basis on the royal estate of Bamberg in Carinthia,[32] but Thys himself soon joined the inner circle of the Chancellor's closest economic advisers.[33] Similarly, the Hither Austrian provincial councillor, Wilhelm Ernst von Felsenberg, developed a proposal in the fall of 1766 based on physiocratic experiments implemented in Baden-Durlach by the margravial Privy Councillor, Johann Jakob Reinhard, and one of the foremost German physiocrats, Johann August Schlettwein.[34] Ernst envisioned the establishment of a whole network of so-called "economic inspectors" charged not only with fostering agricultural productivity but with regulating the entire complex social web of the rural economy. Kaunitz was so enthusiastic about the sober pragmatism of Ernst that he urged a universal application of the proposals to all the hereditary provinces, in concert with such experts as Thys and

---

[31] Koči, "Reformen der Untertänigkeitsverhältnisse," pp. 130–132; Feigl, "Ländliche Sozialstruktur," pp. 53–55; Sergij Vilfan, "Die Agrarsozialpolitik von Maria Theresia bis Kudlich," in Heinz Ischreyt, ed., *Der Bauer Mittel- und Osteuropas im Sozio-Ökonomischen Wandel des 18. und 19. Jahrhunderts* (Cologne and Vienna, 1973), p. 5; Gutkas, "Probleme der Landwirtschaft zur Zeit Maria Theresias und Josephs II.," in Feigl, ed., *Auswirkung*, pp. 1–35.

[32] HHStA, Staatskanzlei: Vorträge, Karton 98, Kaunitz to Maria Theresia, 3 November 1766; Karton 100, Kaunitz to Maria Theresia, 1 September 1767.

[33] DOZA, Handschriften, Vol. 64, Ludwig Zinzendorf to Karl Zinzendorf, 8 September 1766.

[34] Helen P. Liebel, *Enlightened Bureaucracy versus Enlightened Despotism in Baden, 1750–1792* (Philadelphia, 1965), pp. 40–69.

Sonnenfels, but above all in close co-ordination with agricultural societies.[35] Finally, Kaunitz became an enthusiastic disciple of the proposals of the Lower Austrian provincial commerce councillor and tariff reformer, Philipp Joseph Sinzendorf, which urged the abolition of common pasture lands, and the establishment of small farmsteads or tilled strips in their stead.[36] This, too, led to experimental implementation on crown lands under a junior treasury official and former estate steward for Count Harrach, Anton Koczian,[37] and in due course to a series of decrees pressing common pasture division in Bohemia and Moravia,[38] which, while a failure in the short run, slowly and gradually were crowned with success in the long run.[39]

The cumulative effect of the various agrarian reform proposals which Kaunitz supported in these years was to help him crystallize his own overall agrarian reform programme. In April 1767, when it appeared that Ludwig Zinzendorf's sweeping national credit and economic development proposals were about to be adopted, Kaunitz felt the time ripe to step forward with "useful new reform proposals" to accelerate the Monarchy's economic development. These consisted of a six-point programme: 1) the abolition of serfdom, 2) the commutation of compulsory labour services into cash payments, 3) the parceling of large estates (*Meierhöfe*) into smaller peasant freeholds, 4) the abolition of common pasture lands, 5) reform of the lay tithe, and 6) the gathering and tabulation of precise economic statistics with the objective of formulating clearer policies of economic development. Kaunitz was well aware that such policies would not be easy to implement and that seigniorial resistance would be difficult to overcome, "but we should not shrink from the undertaking," he urged, "for with caution and firmness even the apparently impossible can in time be made possible."[40] By the fall the political climate had altered considerably. The Zinzendorf economic reform programme had been rejected, and Kaunitz's "useful new reform proposals" lay in limbo. The

---

[35] HHStA, Kabinettsarchiv: Kaunitz Voten, Karton 1, No. 3286 of 1766, Kaunitz Staatsrat Votum, 15 January 1767.

[36] *Ibid.*, Kaunitz-Voten, Karton 1, No. 42 of 1767, Kaunitz Staatsrat Votum, 3 February 1767; Staatsratprotokolle, Vol. 24, No. 42, Maria Theresia to Rudolph Chotek, 10 February 1767; Vol. 26, No. 2085, imperial resolution, 1 October 1767.

[37] DOZA, Handschriften, Vol. 65, Ludwig Zinzendorf to Karl Zinzendorf, 7 January 1769.

[38] HHStA, Kabinettsarchiv: Kaunitz Voten, Karton 1, No. 2085 of 1767, Kaunitz Staatsrat Votum, 24 September 1767; Decrees of 5 November 1768, 24 March and 23 August 1770. Hock-Bidermann, p. 70; Link, *Emancipation*, pp. 66–67; Václav Černý, "Dělení pastvin v zemích českých v l. 1768–1848," *Časopis pro dějiny venkova* XI (1924), 213–217.

[39] Černý, "Dělení pastvin," XI (1924), 217–227, XII (1925), 25–46, 287–325; Kalousek, ed., "Řády selské," pp. 396–399; 433.

[40] HHStA, Österreichische Akten: Österreich-Staat, Fasz. 5, Kaunitz to Maria Theresia, 21 April 1767.

new assertiveness of Joseph here made itself felt for the first time, for he dismissed Kaunitz's proposal with the comment that it threatened "to affect the most essential, indeed one may say the palladium of seigniorial rights" and was therefore unworkable.[41] This did not deter the Chancellor of State. As he worked on his comprehensive reform proposals which were to result in the major government overhaul of 1768,[42] he repeated his agrarian agenda in concise terms: agricultural improvements should be one of the crown's principal concerns. The introduction of agricultural innovations should be a highest priority, though major structural changes should be implemented on crown estates first in order to demonstrate their necessity for agricultural modernization and their benefits to all parties. These changes should include the abolition of common pasture lands, the commutation of compulsory labour services into cash payments, the parceling of large estates into smaller peasant freeholds, and the transfer of legal hereditary ownership to these peasants.[43]

In this sweeping agrarian reform programme of Kaunitz one can speak of distinct physiocratic features, but not of a consistent physiocratic programme. The typical Enlightenment emphasis on voluntary contractual arrangements between lords and peasants was entirely consistent with physiocratic notions, while the transformation of the enserfed manorial subject into a citizen whose freedom from personal bondage and whose property rights were now guaranteed by the state echoed physiocratic-inspired land-reform programmes all over Europe.[44] Yet, despite the obvious effort to promote elements of capitalist agriculture, the central physiocratic tax reform propositions, particularly the famous *impôt unique*, were entirely absent in these reform proposals. These emphases establish clearly the degree to which agrarian reform was motivated more by the concern with agricultural productivity than with taxation policy. When we also consider that the entire agrarian reform programme of enlightened absolutism was thus in the main posited before the Silesian peasant uprisings, which many historians are wont to regard as its source, the agrarian productivity motive becomes even more evident.

In advocating this agenda, Kaunitz was joined by a growing chorus of voices in the ensuing years, including academics, publicists and bureaucrats,[45] which led to a second experiment at *robot* commutation on crown

[41] *Ibid.*, Joseph Votum, 27 April 1767.   [42] See above, pp. 102–105.
[43] HHStA, Staatskanzlei: Vorträge, Karton 101, Kaunitz to Maria Theresia, 25 January 1768, § 49, § 67.
[44] Otto Stolz, "Die Bauernbefreiung in Süddeutschland im Zusammenhang der Geschichte," *VSWG* XXXIII (1940), 1–4; Liebel, *Enlightened Bureaucracy*, p. 43.
[45] Grünberg, *Bauernbefreiung* I, 190–192; II, 161–170 and his *Franz Anton von Blanc* (Munich and Leipzig, 1921), p. 26; Černý, "Pozemková reforma," pp. 25–27; Václav Novák, "Raabův systém a provádění jeho na některých panstvích v Čechách," *Časopis*

estates in Bohemia and Styria.[46] But plans worked out by Koczian and his superior, Count Franz Khevenhüller, the President of the Cameral Estates Administration, apparently did not produce any clear picture on the profitability of such enterprises, and the matter was once again tabled.[47] In the meantime, a new round of *urbarial* legislation in the Austrian and Bohemian lands was sparked by an open revolt against labour services in 137 peasant communities in Silesia in 1767.[48] A preliminary investigation revealed extensive seigniorial abuses of feudal contracts, and this resulted in the establishment of an *urbarial* commission which was soon overshadowed by its most radical member, an invalid veteran from Freiburg im Breisgau, Franz Anton von Blanc.[49] Steeped in natural rights philosophy, his memorandum urged the proclamation of a sweeping new regulatory decree, providing for weekly and yearly labour service maxima, in which traditional seigniorial rights should be respected only insofar as they were compatible with peasant rights to enjoy a minimum standard of living.[50] When the memoranda of Blanc and the other commission members, which suggested that the Silesian peasantry had been reduced to virtual slavery, reached the Council of State, where Hungarian reports from 1765–1766 were still fresh in everyone's mind, the reactions there readily echoed the sentiments of Blanc. All supported a comprehensive *robot* patent for Silesia. Gebler read the reports "with shock, nay, with true revulsion" and proclaimed to be deeply moved by the sufferings of the peasants. Borié declared: "This is worse than in Hungary!" Kaunitz recorded that he was in full agreement.[51]

Under the influence of Blanc and with the full support of the Council of State, the growing natural rights perspectives of the 1760s now became the dominant tone of the new legislation. Of course, traditional concerns with averting rural unrest and maintaining peasants in a "taxable condition" were not displaced. Rather a new moral tone pervaded the discussions, which certainly transformed traditional outlooks.[52] Maria Theresia was

---

pro dějiny venkova VIII (1921), 139; Jan Procházka, *Parcelování velkostatků (Raabisace) za Marie Terezie v Čechách* (Prague, 1925), p. 7.
[46] HHStA, Kabinettsarchiv: Kaunitz Voten, Karton 1, No. 2474 of 1770, Kaunitz Staatsrat Votum, 4 August 1770; Grünberg, *Bauernbefreiung* I, 202–203.
[47] DOZA, Handschriften, Vol. 65, Ludwig Zinzendorf to Karl Zinzendorf, 25 April 1770.
[48] Grünberg, *Bauernbefreiung* I, 160–188; Krofta, pp. 310–311.
[49] For the background of Blanc, see Grünberg, *Blanc*, pp. 5–12; *NDB* II, 283–284.
[50] Grünberg, *Bauernbefreiung* II, 102–109 and his *Blanc*, pp. 21–25.
[51] HHStA, Kabinettsarchiv: Kaunitz Voten, Karton 1, No. 2270 of 1769, Kaunitz Staatsrat Votum, 19 July 1769; Hock-Bidermann, p. 68; Grünberg, *Bauernbefreiung* I, 168–171.
[52] The image of the lazy, shiftless peasant virtually disappeared from bureaucratic descriptions, and a certain romanticized idealization of rural life gradually began to set in. Feigl, "Landwirtschaft und Grundherrschaft," p. 88 and his "Ländliche Sozialstruktur," pp. 58–59; Vilfan, "Agrarsozialpolitik," pp. 29–30.

very clear on this, hurrying the debates along with the words: "This is pressing and very important. The welfare of so many oppressed people is at stake, and it could also serve to set a new standard."⁵³ Endorsing the Council of State recommendations and ordering the drafting of a comprehensive Silesian patent, she wrote, fully in the spirit of Blanc, that "self-evidently, neither an *urbarium* nor a contract, and least of all a custom, of no matter what antiquity," would be allowed to interfere with the higher priority of sustaining the peasants.⁵⁴ Estate protests were accordingly brushed aside, and Blanc was commissioned to draft the Silesian patent.⁵⁵ After another Council of State discussion, in which Kaunitz successfully pressed for a clarification of some clauses to the benefit of the peasants,⁵⁶ the Silesian *Robot* Patent was proclaimed on 6 July 1771.⁵⁷

The Hungarian and Silesian investigations and debates sensitized the whole bureaucracy to the agrarian problem. Reports of bleak conditions elsewhere in the Monarchy began to filter in, and the necessity of *urbarial* legislation was increasingly recognized in other provinces. There were sporadic uprisings on some estates, and a flood of peasant complaints to local officials.⁵⁸ The most notorious revelations came from the Bohemian estates of Prince Heinrich Mansfeld at Dobřis, where every kind of seigniorial abuse seemed to be practised. In the Council of State there was unanimous assent that Mansfeld and his estate officials be dealt with severely, though there was some disagreement on whether this ought to entail compensation payments to his serfs. Kaunitz took the firm line that compensation be "expressly commanded, since it is a matter of natural fairness." He agreed with his colleagues that Mansfeld should also be fined 3,000 Dukats (13,500 Gulden), "though he certainly deserved a harsher penalty."⁵⁹ In accordance with the advice of the Council of State, Maria Theresia made a stern example of Mansfeld. Some of his estate officials were arrested and his estate steward jailed. The administration of his

⁵³ HHStA, Kabinettsarchiv: Staatsratprotokolle, Vol. 36, No. 2270, Protocol record of a resolution by Maria Theresia of June 1770.
⁵⁴ *Ibid.*, imperial resolution, 26 July 1770; cf. Grünberg, *Bauernbefreiung* II, 118–121; Hock-Bidermann, pp. 68–69.   ⁵⁵ Grünberg, *Bauernbefreiung* I, 174–175.
⁵⁶ HHStA, Kabinettsarchiv: Kaunitz Voten, Karton 2, No. 1674 of 1771, Kaunitz Staatsrat Votum, 16 May 1771; Staatsratprotokolle, Vol. 39, No. 1674, imperial resolution, 25 May 1771.   ⁵⁷ Grünberg, *Bauernbefreiung* II, 135–146.
⁵⁸ *Ibid.*, I, 190–192; II, 155–161; Arneth, *Maria Theresia* IX, 342–343, 593; Liebel-Weckowicz and Szabo, "Modernization Forces," pp. 314–315; Jiří Svoboda, *Protifeudální a sociální hnutí v Čechách na konci doby temna (1740–1774)* (Prague, 1967), pp. 22–31; Anton Mell, *Die Anfänge der Bauernbefreiung in Steiermark unter Maria Theresia und Joseph II* (Graz, 1901), p. 87.
⁵⁹ HHStA, Kabinettsarchiv: Kaunitz Voten, Karton 1, No. 671 of 1770, Kaunitz Staatsrat Votum, 3 May 1770. Cf. Hock-Bidermann, p. 69; Arneth, *Maria Theresia* IX, 342–343.

estates was taken away from him "for several years," and he was directed to pay full financial compensation to his wronged serfs – an amount precisely calculated at 18,579 Gulden, 20 Kreuzer. Though the Empress chose to fine Mansfeld only 2,000 Dukats, she ordered that he also pay the full costs of the government investigation. Altogether Mansfeld therefore faced a total liability in excess of 30,000 Gulden (or, about five times the average annual salary of a university professor and ten times that of a high school teacher). Any appeal by the prince was explicitly forbidden. The judgment was publicized throughout the province, and the Austro-Bohemian Chancellery was instructed to make sure all victims had benefited from the full judicial recourse to which they were entitled.[60]

The Dobřis scandal galvanized the government into further action. On 12 July 1770, Maria Theresia informed Chotek that the Dobřis revelations clearly raised "justified concerns" that similar problems existed elsewhere in Bohemia. She therefore commanded him to launch a detailed investigation in every circle, demanding a report within two months.[61] Independently, the Aulic War Council was reaching similar conclusions. As preparations were being made to implement conscription, an army brief of July 1771 reported the poor physical condition of prospective conscripts and diagnosed the *robot* and seigniorial abuses as the main problem. It, too, recommended restrictions on labour services, as well as the division of large estates into small peasant holdings.[62] From these reports, as well as investigations undertaken in the Austrian provinces, it gradually became apparent that existing legislation was inadequate in the context of the new perspectives which now increasingly animated government circles. In Hither Austria, Tyrol and Upper Austria, where serfdom was less onerous and labour services uncommon, older legislation from the fifteenth and sixteenth centuries appeared to contain adequate provisions to circumscribe abuses.[63] In Lower and Inner Austria (Styria, Carinthia and Carniola), on the other hand, well-founded peasant grievances were revealed, which led to the determination to introduce *robot* patents there. A decree for Lower Austria was promulgated with comparatively few

[60] HHStA, Kabinettsarchiv: Staatsratprotokolle, Vol. 34, No. 671, imperial resolution, and Maria Theresia to Hatzfeld, 10 May 1770. Cf. Grünberg, *Bauernbefreiung* I, 199–200, where different amounts are indicated; and Kalousek, "Řády selské," pp. 405–423.
[61] HHStA, Kabinettsarchiv: Staatsratprotokolle, Vol. 34, No. 671, Maria Theresia to Chotek, 12 July 1770; Arneth, *Maria Theresia* IX, 345; Grünberg, *Bauernbefreiung* II, 187–188.
[62] Josef Kalousek, ed., "Dodavek k řádům selským a instrukcím hospodářským 1388–1779," *Archiv Český* XXIX (1913),491–530. Cf. Komlos, *Nutrition*, pp. 55–118.
[63] B. Rieger, "Unterthans- und Urbarialverhältnisse," *ÖStWB* I, 43–47; Bruckmüller, "Die Grundherrschaft," pp. 39–54; Georg Grüll, *Die Robot in Oberösterreich* (Linz, 1952), p. 175.

difficulties on 6 June 1772,[64] but the first government overtures to the Styrian Estates showed that Inner Austria was to be a much more difficult matter.[65]

At the same time, the recent acquisition of the province of Galicia confronted Habsburg officials with agrarian conditions that were even more dismal than any encountered thus far in the Monarchy. When Kaunitz assumed responsibility for the civil administration of Galicia in September 1772, he reported to the Empress that preliminary reports were agreed that the peasants in the newly-acquired province lived in conditions of functional slavery, where lords could even kill serfs "for the most part with impunity." Before Pergen was dispatched as new governor, therefore, among the principles Kaunitz posited as fundamental guidelines for the new provincial administration were the restriction of noble "liberties", the establishment of a just relationship between peasant and lord, the gradual abolition of serfdom, and the rapid abolition of excessive *robot*.[66] Such a dramatic crown incursion on the manor was no simple matter. Kaunitz understood that if *urbarial* legislation were to be effective, it required the establishment of a reliable administrative infrastructure to enforce it, the compilation of a systematic cadastral survey on which to base it, and an overhaul of the judicial system to eliminate the arbitrary power of seigniorial courts.

Of these, Kaunitz focused first and foremost on the extension of the Austro-Bohemian *Kreis* administration to Galicia, which, despite his repeated urgings,[67] took some months to implement.[68] The compilation of a cadastre was accomplished more quickly. Kaunitz endorsed a provisional patent released by Pergen on 22 December 1772, ordering all land-owners to submit reports on real estate holdings, harvest yields, revenues and peasant labour services enjoyed by them. All land was declared taxable with no rate differentiation, in contrast with other parts of the Monarchy, between seigniorial and peasant lands. Kaunitz felt this alone would already take the pressure off noble encroachments on peasant land and provide an incentive to lease portions of the demesne. If all land was equally taxed, but lords, under the new Austrian rules, could only extract limited labour services only in strict proportion to the size of the peasant

---

[64] Rieger, "Unterthans- und Urbarialverhältnisse," p. 49; Link, *Emancipation*, pp. 48–52; Feigl, *Niederösterreichische Grundherrschaft*, pp. 325–326; Karl Gutkas, *Geschichte des Landes Niederösterreich* (St. Pölten, 1973), p. 342; Liebel-Weckowicz and Szabo, "Modernization Forces," pp. 318–319.   [65] Mell, *Bauernbefreiung*, pp. 88–94.

[66] Roman Rozdolski [Rosdolsky], *Stosunki poddańcze w dawnej Galicji*, 2 Vols., (Warsaw, 1962), II, 11–14.

[67] HHStA, Staatskanzlei: Vorträge, Karton 110, Kaunitz to Maria Theresia, 11 November, 2 December 1772; Karton 111, Kaunitz to Maria Theresia, 12 February 1773.

[68] AVA, Hofkanzlei, Karton 229, Staatsratprotokoll, 21 March 1773; HHStA, Staatskanzlei: Vorträge, Karton 112, Kaunitz to Joseph, 20 June 1773.

holdings, the economic inefficiencies of pre-partition manorial relationships would be obvious. Some of Kaunitz's severest critiques, however,
were reserved for patrimonial courts:

> The patrimonial [legal] jurisdiction of the nobles over their farmers and other
> subjects is the main reason for the tyranny hitherto exercised by seigneurs over their
> serfs, and for the slavish oppression of the later. If the peasant is therefore to be
> elevated from his current wretched condition and restored to the rights of
> humanity, he must be removed from the hands and influence of the officials and
> stewards of the nobility. The best *urbarial* legislation, and the strictest prohibition
> of all abuses, will have no substantial and certain effect, so long as the peasant must
> seek law and justice directly from his lord.

Manorial judicial officials could be kept in place, he suggested, but only if
they passed qualification exams, and only under the strict supervision of
the crown. Every local court was therefore to employ three officials to
defend the interests of the peasants, with the first instance of appeal being
the local circle office.[69]

Kaunitz also made it clear from the outset that, of all the options
available for dealing with the extensive Polish royal estates now inherited
by the Habsburgs in the new province, the one that would "undoubtedly"
contribute most to "the common good", would be the transformation of
these demesnes into peasant freeholds.[70] He was persuaded that even if the
implementation process would be relatively slow, conditions were generally
favourable because many of the technical innovations for improved
agricultural output were by no means unknown to local peasants.[71] Here
again Kaunitz kept stressing productivity over taxability. The fundamental
aim, he suggested, was to achieve "the highest yields on crown estates, and
indeed on all private estates, of which these are capable." Accordingly,
Kaunitz recommended to Maria Theresia that a Bamberg-like experiment
be undertaken immediately on the royal estate of Jaworow near Lemberg,
as a way of showing the Polish nobility the advantages of the novel
"economic principles." He proposed that the trusted Koczian be given a
completely free hand on this estate to begin a systematic programme of
"abolishing abuses and oppressions ... commuting *robot*, partitioning the
demesne among peasants," and instituting whatever other technical
changes he felt necessary to improve the agrarian economy without
interference from any quarter, even if initial agricultural yields or revenues
might reveal temporary shortfalls. Gradually, Kaunitz asserted, the
benefits that would emerge would be too obvious for anyone to ignore.[72]

---

[69] Rozdolski, *Stosunki poddańcze* II, 15, 27–28, 33.
[70] HHStA, Staatskanzlei: Vorträge, Karton 110, Kaunitz to Maria Theresia, 11 November
1772.   [71] *Ibid.*, Karton 111, Kaunitz to Maria Theresia, 21 January 1772.
[72] Rozdolski, *Stosunki poddańcze* II, 62–63.

Before any of these measures bore fruit, Kaunitz's festering dispute with
Joseph on the manner in which Galicia ought to be administered came to
a head. After the Emperor's personal inspection tour of the province in the
summer of 1773, his dissatisfaction was mirrored in the 154 detailed
questions which he demanded Kaunitz answer summarily.[73] The responses
of the resulting voluminous document at every turn focused on the many
defects of agriculture, "all occasioned by the all too excessive slavery of the
peasant," and emphasized the need for a comprehensive *urbarial* regulation as soon as possible. Kaunitz was even inclined to blame large-scale
peasant flight, which became one of the central obsessions of subsequent
Habsburg administrators, "solely and exclusively on the oppressions
that the poor peasant has to suffer at the hands of his seigneur" (even
though Austrian military conscription laws were probably as significant
a cause).[74] These discussions continued long after Kaunitz resigned his
Galician responsibilities in November 1773. Some of the most glaring
seigniorial abuses were rapidly reformed, but formal promulgation of a
robot patent was to be some years in coming. Discussions leading up to
the Galician decree, as also with those for Inner Austria, were very protracted. Resistance was fierce and implementation difficult. The Styrian
and Carinthian patents were not passed until 1778; the Galician one not
until 1781; that of Carniola not until 1782.[75] However, Kaunitz did not
participate in these discussions, because by then the fundamental premises
of regulatory legislation had already been established.

The *locus classicus* of the debates remained Bohemia, and it was here
that the issues of principle were fought out in detail. Chancellor Chotek
had consistently maintained that no new legislation was necessary, and
that if peasants were overburdened, it was with state taxes not with noble
demands. The Council of State, led by Gebler and Kaunitz, on the other
hand, favoured legislative action.[76] The investigations of the summer of
1770 heightened awareness of the need for action, but it took a natural

[73] AVA, Hofkanzlei, Karton 229, Joseph's questions, 5 August 1773; Kaunitz's "Beant-
wortungen", 2 September 1773; HHStA, Staatskanzlei: Vorträge, Karton 112, Kaunitz to
Maria Theresia, 2 September 1773 (including Joseph's questions and their answers).
HHStA, Familienarchiv: Hofreisen, Karton 4 and 5, Joseph's journal of his trip through
Galicia and ancillary documents, July–September 1773. Substantial excerpts published in
Rozdolski, *Stosunki poddańcze* II, 14–43.
[74] Joséf Buszko, "Theresianisch-Josephinische Agrar- und Bauernpolitik in Galizien und
ihre Folgen," in Plaschka and Klingenstein, eds., *Österreich im Europa der Aufklärung* I,
67–86, especially 72–73.
[75] Mell, *Bauernbefreiung*, pp. 94–150; Link, *Emancipation*, pp. 52–61; Ludwig von Mises,
Die Entwicklung des gutsherrlich-bäuerlichen Verhältnisses in Galizien (1772–1848)
(Vienna and Leipzig, 1902). pp. 40–41; Rozdolski, *Stosunki poddańcze* I, 69–104.
[76] Arneth, *Maria Theresia* IX, 343–344; Grünberg, *Bauernbefreiung* II, 169–171.

disaster to make it obvious. The harvest failures and ensuing catastrophic famine of 1771–1772, accompanied by rebellions on about seventy-two estates which began in February 1771, underscored the plight of the Bohemian peasants. Joseph II personally traveled to Bohemia to assess the situation and to co-ordinate famine relief measures in October 1771. The immediate offshoot was an administrative shake-up which brought men with known progressive views on agrarian reform to the fore. Bohemia received a new governor, the energetic Karl Egon von Fürstenberg, while a special *urbarial* commission was established under Count Franz Khevenhüller, which included Blanc, to set guidelines within which the entire *robot* problem could be regulated.[77] Though Fürstenberg soon bombarded Vienna with extensive reports and recommendations for agrarian reform,[78] and the Khevenhüller commission was driven along by the passionate commitment of Blanc, a combination of Estates resistance to any royal incursions in manorial affairs and disagreement among reformers themselves tended to bog matters down. A party led by Blanc wanted robot regulated within a maximum labour obligation of three days per week, according to the size of the peasant holding. Borié, basing his argument on the ideas of the agrarian councillor of the Austro-Bohemian Chancellery, Johann Paul von Hoyer, insisted that labour services had to be tied more precisely to property rights of the lords even if the resulting *robot* exceeded three days. A third point of view, represented most energetically by Kressel, remained totally opposed to any comprehensive regulation on the grounds that conditions varied too much from estate to estate.[79]

Gebler and Kaunitz supported Blanc. They criticized the Borié–Hoyer position as being based on the completely unwarranted assumption that the cash evaluations of the yields of peasant holdings could be viewed merely as net income, for which lords had to be compensated accordingly. By this logic peasants would be pushed to their physical limit in seigniorial demands, and this simply could not be allowed because an Austrian peasant was "not a slave in the Roman or Turkish sense." All fears of relieving peasant burdens too much were completely unfounded. The

[77] Arneth, *Maria Theresia* IX, 347 (for a complete list of the commission members); František Roubík, "Relace císaře Josefa II. o jeho cestě do Čech, Moravy a Slezska r. 1771," *Časopis pro dějiny venkova* XIII (1926), 102–119; Svoboda, *Protifeudální*, pp. 41–50; Schünemann, "Wirtschaftspolitik," pp. 39–40; Liebel-Weckowicz and Szabo, "Modernization Forces," p. 317; Weinzierl-Fischer, "Bekämpfung der Hungersnot," pp. 478–514.

[78] HHStA, Kabinettsarchiv: Kaiser Franz Akten, Karton 63, "Vorträge des böhmischen Oberstburggrafen Karl Egon von Fürstenberg über den Verfall des Königreichs Böhmen und über dessen Abhilfe," 1771–1773.

[79] Grünberg, *Bauernbefreiung* I, 206–207; II, 210–211; Hock-Bidermann, pp. 71–73; Arneth, *Maria Theresia* IX, 347–349.

Blanc option would certainly give the peasantry more free time, but what he did with that time was his own business.[80] At the same time Kaunitz also submitted his mammoth reform proposals of 1 May 1773 urging *robot* reform, and labeling labour services one of the three fundamental ills of the Monarchy.[81] Yet, in the face of so much disagreement, Maria Theresia remained reluctant to make a final decision. Instead she proposed to issue an interim provisional *urbarial* decree until the debate was resolved.[82] This was firmly opposed by Kaunitz, who stood resolutely by his position that a definitive patent was needed.[83] At the last moment decisive support arrived from an unexpected quarter: Hatzfeld, now "directing minister" of the Council of State. Hatzfeld had recently been sent to persuade the Bohemian Estates of the necessity of *robot* reform but had received such a rude rebuff that he now joined the Kaunitz–Blanc–Gebler faction in pressing for a regulatory decree.[84] The Empress gave way. Kaunitz and Blanc were ordered to meet and draft the official guidelines within which the *robot* was to be regulated,[85] and these were the formally issued in September 1773.

The effect of this action on the Bohemian Estates was to make them redouble their efforts to prevent state interference on the manor, and, failing that, to deprive that intervention of effectiveness.[86] The Estate objections were dismissed by Blanc, and a draft of the robot patent was submitted on 24 January 1774. The entire matter was on the verge of conclusion when Emperor Joseph II stepped in. Though he had consulted with Kaunitz at length, Joseph did not share his minister's conclusions. In what amounted to a decisive veto, he deferred to the protests of the Bohemian Estates. He declared that no comprehensive legislation was feasible, and that abuses could be abolished only on a case by case basis. Instead of a decree, he proposed to issue an instruction directing serfs and seigneurs to come to voluntary *urbarial* agreements along Borié–Hoyer lines within six months, or risk having these drawn up estate by estate by the local circle captains.[87] The Empress gave in to her son, and the appropriate instruction was issued on 7 April 1774. It set the framework of

[80] *Ibid.*
[81] HHStA, Staatskanzlei: Vorträge, Karton 112, Kaunitz to Maria Theresia, 1 May 1773. Cf. above, pp. 110–111, 142.
[82] Arneth, *Maria Theresia* IX, 351; Grünberg, *Bauernbefreiung* II, 213.
[83] HHStA, Staatskanzlei: Vorträge, Karton 112, Kaunitz to Maria Theresia, 18 June 1773.
[84] DOZA, Handschriften, Vol. 66, Ludwig Zinzendorf to Karl Zinzendorf, 14 and 28 July 1773; Grünberg, *Blanc*, p. 39.
[85] HHStA, Staatskanzlei: Vorträge, Karton 112, Maria Theresia to Kaunitz, n.d. (resolution on report of 18 June 1773).   [86] Grünberg, *Bauernbefreiung* II, 219–220, 222–226.
[87] HHStA, Familienarchiv: Sammelbände, Karton 7, and Staatskanzlei: Vorträge, Karton 114, Joseph's Gutachten, 23 February 1774; Arneth, *Maria Theresia* IX, 353–355; Hock-Bidermann, p. 73.

a three-day maximum per week for *robot*, but when the lords asked for a public notice confirming that "voluntary" agreements could exceed three days, they were granted it. Under the circumstances it is hardly surprising that the scheme proved an utter failure, and that nothing had been accomplished when the six-month deadline expired in November.[88]

At this point Maria Theresa again seized the initiative and ordered renewed work on a regulatory patent "without the slightest delay," though, in deference to her son, she now leaned to the Borié–Hoyer option.[89] By the time she approved the ensuing *urbarial* commission report in February 1775, however, events had overtaken the legislators. Driven to extremes, the peasants of northern and eastern Bohemia rose in open revolt in January 1775. The unrest spread rapidly, and a major military action was required to quell the uprising in April.[90] Kaunitz did not like giving the impression that a *robot* patent was released in response to an uprising, and advised a delay in formal proclamation so that it could later be made with "all majesty and solemnity possible."[91] But Joseph, badly shaken, was at this point fairly chafing at the bit to get on with matters.[92] He still believed that regulatory legislation was unwise, but, forced to choose, he now preferred the Blanc formula over the Borié–Hoyer one because the latter's more precise calculations would make taxation too complex.[93] A delighted Blanc, who had continued to criticize his rivals' plans,[94] was accordingly dispatched to Kaunitz's new summer residence at Laxenburg, where the two men now produced the final drafts of the legislation.[95] The *robot* patents were thus promulgated on 13 August for Bohemia and 7 September for Moravia.[96]

[88] HHStA, Kabinettsarchiv: Staatsratprotokolle, Vol. 49, No. 263, imperial resolution, 26 February 1774; DOZA, Handschriften, Vol. 66, Ludwig Zinzendorf to Karl Zinzendorf, 3 September 1774; Khevenhüller-Metsch VIII, 9–10, 199–200; Arneth, *Maria Theresia* IX, 355–358; Grünberg, *Bauernbefreiung* II, 228–234. An apologia for Joseph in Beales, *Joseph II* I, 349–350.

[89] Grünberg, *Bauernbefreiung* II, 237, 252; Khevenhüller-Metsch VIII, 243–244.

[90] HHStA, Familienarchiv: Sammelbände, Karton 7, Joseph to Leopold, 3 April 1775. Cf. Krofta, pp. 321–322. For a brief summary of the uprising and a guide to the extensive Czech literature on the subject, see Gerhard Hanke, "Das Zeitalter des Zentralismus (1740–1848)," in Bosl, ed., *Handbuch*, pp. 489, 496–497; less reliable: Victor-L. Tapié, *L'Europe de Marie Thérèse: du baroque aux lumières* (Paris, 1973), pp. 288–295, 374.

[91] HHStA, Staatskanzlei: Vorträge, Karton 119, Kaunitz to Joseph, 7 August 1775; Arneth, *Maria Theresia* IX, 367.

[92] HHStA, Familienarchiv: Sammelbände, Karton 7, Joseph to Leopold, 3 August 1775; additional similar letters published in *MTJC* II, 71, 81.

[93] HHStA, Staatskanzlei: Vorträge, Karton 119, Joseph Vortrag, 6 August 1775. Cf. Hock-Bidermann, pp. 77–78; Arneth, *Maria Theresia* IX, 364–368.

[94] Grünberg, *Bauernbefreiung* II, 250–251.

[95] HHStA, Staatskanzlei: Vorträge, Karton 119, Blanc to Kaunitz, 28 June 1775; Khevenhüller-Metsch VIII, 96, 248–249.

[96] Krofta, pp. 323–330. Full texts of the patents in Grünberg, *Bauernbefreiung* II, 257–270; Kalousek, ed., "Řády selské," pp. 488–508.

Of course, a precise regulation of peasant labour services to curb seigniorial abuses thereof was hoped to be a mere necessary interim measure until such time as a broad consensus would develop among landowners, favouring the abolition of serfdom, land division into peasant freeholds, and the commutation of *robot* into cash payments. The patents of 1775 urged precisely such a course of action, and royal example set the precedent with renewed vigor. Certainly, private initiatives had been few and far between since earlier discussions were tabled in 1770. Kaunitz was full of enthusiastic praise for isolated incidents of such reform, and Maria Theresia went so far as to assert that "the abolition of serfdom is the only thing that still keeps me at the helm of state."[97] But renewed government discussions in December 1772 on the subject resulted only in another cautious experimental abolition programme under Hoyer on some more crown estates during the next two years.[98] In order to accelerate the process, Kaunitz decided to grasp the nettle personally. In the summer of 1773 he began a massive implementation of land division and *robot* commutation on all his own estates on the models of Thys and Koczian, and persuaded his protégé, Ludwig Zinzendorf, to give serious consideration to a similar action.[99] But even the example of the Chancellor of State himself fell on barren soil; the real break-through came only in 1775.

While Hoyer had sub-divided crown estates into smaller peasant holdings, he inclined towards short-term leases; not to hereditary ownership. Manorial buildings, equipment and livestock were not divided among the peasants, and many legal elements of serfdom remained intact. In stark contrast, a more radical plan along the lines of the Thys reform of Bamberg, which Kaunitz used on his estates, was developed by a commercial councillor, recently promoted to the central Department of Commerce in Vienna after twenty-three years' experience at the local level in Trieste, Baron Franz Anton von Raab. As a native Carinthian, Raab was probably familiar with Thys's views, and he certainly showed himself an ardent apostle of the agricultural revolution, clearly sensitive to the Monarchy's crisis in agrarian production. By 1775 he had developed and submitted his own plan for *robot* abolition. In return for rents based on the size of the holding, all vestiges of serfdom were to be explicitly abrogated, legal ownership of the land was to be transferred to the peasant, and manorial buildings, equipment and livestock were to be sold off. The Raab proposal was approved by Maria Theresia, and in June he was sent to two former Jesuit estates in Bohemia to assess the viability of implementing his

---

[97] Arneth, *Maria Theresia* IX, 349–350; Černý, "Pozemková reforma," p. 29.
[98] Grünberg, *Bauernbefreiung* II, 237; Hanke, "Zeitalter des Zentralismus," pp. 490–491.
[99] DOZA, Handschriften, Vol. 66, Ludwig Zinzendorf to Karl Zinzendorf, 13 June 1773.

scheme there. After submitting a detailed report he was instructed to go ahead with his plan. By the spring of 1776 the programme was expanded, and by April 1777 twenty-three estates were being reformed.[100] Whether this royal example would be followed by private landowners remained an open question. Certainly the *robot* patents of the summer of 1775 pleased no one. Lords continued to regard them as an unwarranted intrusion into manorial rights. In many places they did not even let their serfs know about the patent, and where it was known, often it was not enforced.[101] At the same time, the expectation of the peasants to be released from the formal bonds of serfdom, and to have the *robot* abolished entirely, were also not satisfied. There were renewed outbreaks of rebellion in the summer of 1775, and reports of ongoing restlessness continued to reach Vienna throughout 1776. Enforcement of the decree by specially-commissioned military authorities, under General Oliver Wallis for Bohemia and General Richard d'Alton for Moravia, left both lord and peasant feeling implicitly threatened.[102] Above all there was a dramatic increase in clandestine emigration of serfs, which caused great anxieties in populationist-minded court circles.[103] In this atmosphere, Maria Theresia held out little hope that the gradual voluntary implementation of the Raab system on private estates could salvage the situation. She confided to Court Councillor, Franz von Greiner: "Nothing can be done with the Estates; they have no head and no will; one must proceed prescriptively."[104]

Joseph II rather facilely concluded that the *Robot* Patent "did not have the effect one expected of it because it was written in an incredibly bungling and nearly unintelligible manner."[105] The Empress, however, realized that the problems were far more serious than that. Swayed by Blanc who argued that there could never be peace in the countryside so long as serfdom, "that despised bond of humanity", and labour services were the basis of the rural social structure,[106] she unequivocally blamed the nobles for the ongoing difficulties. She felt that peasants were driven "to despair

---

[100] On the implementation of the Raab system: Novák, "Raabův systém," VIII (1921), 137–163, 203–212, IX (1922), 42–57; Josef Kazimour, *K dějinám dělení velkostatků v. 18. století* (Prague, 1921); Procházka, *Parcelování*, pp. 12–53; Černý, "Pozemková reforma," pp. 39–48, on Hoyer, pp. 286–309; Krofta, pp. 331–332; William E. Wright, *Serf, Seigneur, and Sovereign: Agrarian Reform in Eighteenth-Century Bohemia* (Minneapolis, 1966), pp. 59–70. On Raab see Wurzbach XXIV, 155–156; Černý, "Pozemková reforma," pp. 27–39.

[101] Ernst Denis, *La Bohême depuis la Montagne-Blanche*, 2 Vols. (Paris, 1903), II, 561.

[102] Kalousek, ed., "Řády selské," pp. 513–516.

[103] Arneth, *Maria Theresia* IX, 377–378; Liebel-Weckowicz and Szabo, "Modernization Forces," pp. 323–325.

[104] Alfred Ritter von Arneth, "Maria Theresia und der Hofrat von Greiner," *Sitzungsberichte der kaiserlichen Akademie der Wissenschaften. Philosophisch-Historische Klasse* XXX, No. 3 (Vienna, 1859), p. 341.   [105] *MTJC* II, 87, No. 225.

[106] Grünberg, *Bauernbefreiung* II, 294–295.

by the excesses of the lords.'' Seigniorial "tyranny" was well known and well established, and only stern legislation could change matters.[107] On 16 January 1777 Joseph reported in exasperation to his brother that Maria Theresia was contemplating nothing short of an agrarian revolution:

The Empress wanted to upset the whole labour services patent which was published a year ago. With all possible solemnities, she wanted to abolish serfdom, and regulate arbitrarily contracts and rents which peasants, to whom one has leased the land, have paid to their lords for centuries. She wanted to change the whole rural economy and system of ownership. Finally, she wanted to alleviate the debts and obligations of the serfs without having the slightest regard for the lords.[108]

To his mother he emphasized his fear that such actions could lead to the total economic collapse of the Kingdom of Bohemia, and insisted that only a strict observance of the patents of 1775 could be decreed at the moment. Furthermore, only when the peasants had become "more pliant in their refractoriness" (an expression often used in the training of horses) could the admittedly "harsh and inconvenient" aspects of serfdom be taken under advisement.[109] In this dramatic difference of opinion, both mother and son turned to Kaunitz.

Kaunitz reported to Joseph that he agreed with the Emperor in practice, if not in principle. In his view the two highest priorities had to be the establishment of peace and tranquility in the countryside without the use of force, and ensuring the success of the abolition of labour services and serfdom. He agreed the latter could not be implemented effectively at one fell swoop by royal fiat. Instead he continued to put faith in the efficacy of good example. Kaunitz accordingly produced a draft of a patent along the lines suggested by Joseph. Peasant unrest should be generously ascribed to ignorance rather than ingratitude or ill will, but now it must be made clear that no radical legislation was forthcoming, and that further alleviations of burdens were entirely contingent on the reestablishment of peace and order. At the same time the nobles were to be sternly warned that abuses would incur royal disgrace. They should also be urged with all possible cogency to follow the royal example currently being carried out by Raab.[110] Joseph wanted a terser decree, and Kaunitz accordingly produced

[107] Alfred Ritter von Arneth, ed., *Briefe der Kaiserin Maria Theresia an ihre Kinder und Freunde*, 4 Vols. (Vienna, 1881), II, 66–67.
[108] HHStA, Familienarchiv: Sammelbände, Karton 7, Joseph to Leopold, 16 January 1777. Quoted in part in Fejtö, *Joseph II*, pp. 157–158; and Beales, *Joseph II* I, 355.
[109] HHStA, Familienarchiv: Sammelbände, Karton 5, Joseph to Maria Theresia, 18 January 1777.
[110] HHStA, Staatskanzlei: Vorträge, Karton 122, Kaunitz to Joseph, 31 January 1777 (including draft patent).

increasingly concise and less benevolent sounding drafts until they met with the Emperor's approval.[111]

On 5 February 1777 Kaunitz forwarded his final patent draft to the Empress, and reiterated at length his arguments why her proposed legislation was not feasible, and why he endorsed Joseph's note of 18 January. He saw the Bohemian economy on the verge of collapse, and precipitous action could not only bring economic ruin but could very well tempt Frederick II of Prussia to take advantage of the situation. One could count with far greater certainty on the Raab example being followed if it was done out of conviction rather than mere obedience. As far as policing seigniorial abuses were concerned, everything depended on the crown officials on the spot, the county captains. These should therefore receive a whole new set of instructions and guidelines, in order to make the royal will felt on the manorial level. The next day he supplemented this report with the suggestion that all theoretical objections that had been raised to *robot* abolition over the past decade should be collated and forwarded to Raab, with the instruction to rebut them in detail.[112]

Kaunitz's and Joseph's anxieties about economic collapse were not entirely unjustified. In the aftermath of the harvest failures and famine earlier in the decade, the money supply in Bohemia diminished dramatically and private credit began to dry up. Lesser nobles in particular naturally felt that the *robot* patents would curtail their revenues and lead to complete bankruptcy. The question of relief measures had been debated at some length during the last weeks of 1775 but led nowhere.[113] Kaunitz had recommended a 4 million Gulden subsidy from Belgian funds for Bohemia, with cash advances explicitly offered "*only to those nobles who benefit their serfs by introducing the innovations Your Majesty is initiating through Court Councillor Raab.*"[114] These proposals, too, were rejected, and the fear of many landowners that they were teetering on the brink of bankruptcy was widespread indeed by the winter of 1777.[115] Maria Theresia was not persuaded easily. For a month she continued to press her case. Blanc made every effort to win over Kaunitz.[116] But on 28 February

[111] *Ibid.*, Kaunitz to Joseph, 1 and 4 February 1777 (including further drafts).
[112] *Ibid.*, Kaunitz to Maria Theresia, 5 and 6 February 1777.
[113] *Ibid.*, Karton 119, Maria Theresia to Kaunitz, 30 December 1775 (including copies of conference protocols and correspondence with Joseph – a bundle that the Empress labeled the "tristes debris" of the discussions); HHStA, Kabinettsarchiv: Staatsratprotokolle, Vol. 55, No. 2255, protocol record; *MTJC* II, 94–102.
[114] HHStA, Staatskanzlei: Voträge, Karton 120, Kaunitz to Maria Theresia, and additional "Geheimer Vortrag", both of 12 January 1776, including imperial resolution; italics in the original.   [115] Arneth, *Maria Theresia* IX, 597–598.
[116] HHStA, Familienarchiv: Sammelbände, Karton 7, Joseph to Leopold, 6 and 13 February 1777.

the latter repeated that he supported Joseph,[117] and the Empress finally gave way.[118] On 1 March 1777 Kaunitz's draft patent was formally proclaimed.[119] An effort by Maria Theresia to issue a supplementary decree to readjust the labour obligations of the lowest classes of peasants, cottagers (*Häusler*), was discouraged by Kaunitz on the grounds that it would give the impression of discord at the top, and the matter was accordingly tabled.[120] On the other hand, the advice to commission Raab to write a defence of his *robot* abolition system was followed. His eighty-seven page manuscript was presented to Kaunitz, who made suitable editorial changes. Shortly thereafter it was published under the title *Unterricht über die Verwandlung der k.k. böhmischen Domänen in Bauern-güter.*[121]

All now depended on the local county officials and hence, very clearly, much hinged on the instructions given to these officials. Of course, enforcing the "precise execution" of royal decrees, and reporting back on local conditions in detail, were their main functions. In Kaunitz's view, however, county officials had to be instructed to pay particularly close attention to the agrarian sector. This meant, above all, inculcating in local administrators the three principles which Kaunitz held to be the fundamental priorities of the government: 1) all impediments to agricultural productivity, whether structural or technical, had to be discovered, reported and remedied; 2) the trust of the common people of the Monarchy had to be won, the conviction spread that the crown had only their best interests at heart, and "every expedient measure proposed, which would lead to [the peasant's] enlightenment, relief and tranquility"; 3) the Raab *robot* abolition system had to be strongly encouraged, clearly explained, and all assistance rendered to promote its widespread implementation.[122] These principles summarized neatly Kaunitz's policies for the trans-

---

[117] HHStA, Staatskanzlei: Vorträge, Karton 122, Kaunitz to Maria Theresia, 28 February 1777.

[118] HHStA, Familienarchiv: Sammelbände, Karton 70, Maria Theresia to Kaunitz, 28 February 1777; Karton 7, Joseph to Leopold, 13 March 1777. At Joseph's and Hatzfeld's insistence, Blanc was shunted off to his native Hither Austria. Subsequent efforts by Kaunitz to rehabilitate Blanc by having him appointed "accredited agent" and ambassador-in-waiting to the newly established United States of America failed in the face of Joseph's ongoing antipathy to him. Cf. HHStA, Staatskanzlei: Vorträge, Karton 137, Kaunitz to Joseph, 19 March 1783.

[119] Kalousek, ed., "Rády selské," pp. 523–526.

[120] HHStA, Staatskanzlei: Vorträge, Karton 122, Kaunitz to Maria Theresia, 22 March 1777; Kabinettsarchiv: Kaunitz Voten, Karton 3, No. 665 of 1777, Kaunitz Staatsrat Votum, 7 April 1777; Kabinettsarchiv: Staatsratprotokolle, Vol. 61, No. 665, imperial resolution, 8 April 1777.

[121] The draft MS with editorial changes in *Ibid.*, Kaunitz Voten, Karton 3, under the title "Die Verwandlung der k.k. Böhmischen Domainen in Bauerngüter, Vienna," 1777.

[122] *Ibid.*, Kaunitz to Maria Theresia, 22 March 1777.

formation of rural society in the Monarchy, and became the leitmotif of government action in the last years of Maria Theresa's reign. In October instructions were issued to all county officials raising the investigation of thirty-four specific areas of potential peasant grievance to the *ex officio* duty of these local administrators.[123]

Gradually, the desired effect was achieved. Among the first landlords to follow the royal example were Chancellor Blümegen himself and Count Johann Baptist Mittrowsky.[124] A real corner was turned when one of the bitterest opponents of *robot* abolition, Prince Ferdinand Lobkowitz, changed his mind, and commissioned Hoyer to implement an abolition programme on several of his estates. Kaunitz still preferred Raab's system over Hoyer's – calling it one of "indisputably greater perfection", primarily because it abolished all elements of serfdom – but the precedent set "by a man who previously had been so notoriously set against it", deserved commendation and encouragement.[125] To accelerate the implementation of the Raab system, Kaunitz's third point in particular was adopted. The magistrates of the city of Budweis (České Budějovice) were advised in August 1778 that costs associated with implementation would be underwritten by state credits. The next year two copies of Raab's *Unterricht*, along with model contracts, were sent to every circle office, and repeated circular letters to *Kreis* officials urged them to expedite the process in every manner possible.[126]

In the following years steady progress was made on other private estates, and within a decade very dramatic breakthroughs had occurred. Substantial parceling of *dominikal* land could be reported in Bohemia, more in Galicia and Moravia, and a greater proportion still in the Austrian provinces.[127] In Carinthia and Carniola, for example, 208 of the 275 *dominikal* estates existing in those provinces were subdivided and leased. While peasants in such areas as Bohemia and Galicia tended to be cautious about contracting agreements because of bitter past experiences, momentum was clearly building, and voluntary *robot* abolition manifestly seemed to be working as reformers such as Kaunitz had expected. Joseph II's sweeping land and tax reform of 1789, which seemed to render such

---

[123] Kalousek, ed., "Rády selské," pp. 523–533.
[124] Wright, *Serf, Seigneur, and Sovereign*, p. 67.
[125] HHStA, Staatskanzlei: Vorträge, Karton 124, Kaunitz to Maria Theresia, 9 December 1777, including appendix: "Vergleich der Operationen auf den k.k. kameral Herrschaften und des Hh. Hofrat v. Hoyer." Cf. Černý, "Pozemková reforma," pp. 286–288.
[126] Procházka, *Parcelování*, pp. 15–16; Kalousek, ed., "Rády selské," pp. 537–544.
[127] Statistics for Bohemia, Moravia and Silesia in Černý, "Pozemková reforma," XV (1928), 287–312. Statistics for Galicia and the Austrian provinces in Friedrich Lütge, "Die Robot-Abolition unter Kaiser Joseph II.," in Haushofer and Boelcke, eds., *Wege und Forschungen der Agrargeschichte*, pp. 162–168.

agreements superfluous, tended to slow down and even arrest the process.[128] The experience of the French Revolution and Napoleon then led to outright sclerosis, despite efforts to revive the momentum by a decree in 1798, and retarded full emancipation until 1848.[129]

From subject to citizen

The dynamic which saw the benevolent paternalism of peasant protection evolve into peasant emancipation designed to produce autonomous and productive farmers also affected other areas of social development. Dramatic shifts occurred in judicial and educational policies in which the influence of the Enlightenment is perhaps more transparently evident than in many other reforms, and certainly Enlightenment rhetoric flourished in the debates surrounding their implementation. But as Raeff has recently shown, such reforms too had their antecedents in cameralist ordinances of the smaller German states during the previous two centuries.[130] This was also true for the Habsburg Monarchy, though the evolution took place in a much shorter period of time. Both judicial and educational reform began modestly, within traditional cameralist and Catholic frameworks, until internal momentums and external pressures by committed reformers took these policies well beyond initial bounds.

Judicial reform in the Habsburg Monarchy was a direct product of Haugwitz's administrative reforms of 1749 in which a complete separation of the administrative and judicial functions of government was undertaken.[131] Thereafter, in the interests of efficiency, it soon became apparent that the extreme judicial particularism that had characterized the legal system of the various provinces of the Monarchy would have to be streamlined. In his ideological statement for the Council of State in 1761, Kaunitz posited as "self-evident" that legal uniformity was a critical prerequisite to economic development.[132] At the same time, the creation of more unitary laws within the Monarchy was imperative to guarantee the success of the other reforms undertaken. Uniform laws implied uniform application, which was a further blow to local and regional particularism because such codification processes disciplined social relations in increasingly general and abstract terms, and as such were an instrument of power

---

[128] Lütge, "Robot-Abolition," pp. 159–160, 165–168.
[129] Jerome Blum, *Noble Landowners and Agriculture in Austria*, 1815–1848 (Baltimore, Md., 1948), pp. 56–90. A slightly less bleak picture is emerging from recent research, but no new exhaustive studies have yet been done. Cf. Lütge, "Robot-Abolition," pp. 168–170; Vilfan, "Agrarsozialpolitik," pp. 31–39; John Komlos, *The Habsburg Monarchy as a Customs Union* (Princeton, N.J., 1983), pp. 45–51.
[130] Raeff, *Well-ordered Police State*, pp. 135–146.   [131] See above, pp. 76–78.
[132] Walter, "Eintritt," p. 77.

in developing absolutism.[133] Under these circumstances, both the codification of civil law and the rationalization of penal law became objectives Maria Theresia felt required to pursue.[134]

The codification of civil law was ordered in 1753, and, after extensive debate involving a complex dialectic between rival compilation committees, resulted in the presentation of a draft of a new civil code – the so-called *Codex Theresianus* – to the Empress in 1766.[135] When this draft came to the Council of State in December 1766, it was clear that its members hardly had the time to analyze the contents in detail in light of the volume of material with which they already had to concern themselves. It also became obvious that the draft had not addressed the issue of judicial procedure, which the compilation commission intended to tackle only after the formal publication of the *Codex*. With respect to the first problem there was unanimous assent that an independent legal authority should produce a precis and assessment of the draft *Codex*, and here the choice fell on the reform-minded Moravian jurist, Heinrich Xaver Hayek von Waldstätten.[136] On the second problem only Borié dissented from the majority which fully endorsed the position of Kaunitz: if the many conflicting civil laws of the different provinces of the Monarchy were rationalized, then a rationalization and simplification of the courts and of judicial procedure had to be an integral part of the process, and consequently such reform had to constitute "an essential part of the new code" if the whole enterprise was not to be left incomplete.[137]

Accordingly, the more systematic approach suggested by Kaunitz was ordered by the Empress. A rationalization of the courts was specifically

[133] Gianfranco Poggi, *The Development of the Modern State* (London, 1978), pp. 73–74.

[134] The literature on the codification of the civil law in the Habsburg Monarchy is enormous, though much of it is legal rather than historical analysis. The best synthesis is Wilhelm Brauneder, "Das Allgemeine Bürgerliche Gesetzbuch für die gesamten Deutschen Erbländer der österreichischen Monarchie von 1811," *Gutenberg Jahrbuch* LXII (1987), pp. 205–254, which lists the full literature. The standard English-language analysis, Strakosch, *State Absolutism and the Rule of Law*, is marked by such a cavalier treatment of detail that it cannot be used without the older Philipp Harras Ritter von Harrasowsky, *Geschichte der Codification des österreichischen Civilrechts* (Vienna, 1868); and Wiener Juristische Gesellschaft, ed., *Festschrift zur Jahrhundertfeier des Allgemeinen Bürgerlichen Gesetzbuches*, 2 Vols. (Vienna, 1911) (henceforth cited as *ABGB Festschrift*).

[135] Harrasowsky, *Geschichte*, pp. 38–125; Friedrich Korkisch, "Die Entstehung des österreichischen Allgemeinen Bürgerlichen Gesetzbuches," *Zeitschrift für ausländisches und internationales Privatrecht* XVIII (1953), 264–274; Brauneder, "Das Allgemeine Bürgerliche Gesetzbuch," pp. 208–209. Full text of Codex in Philipp Harras Ritter von Harrasowsky, ed., *Der Codex Theresianus und seine Umarbeitungen*, 5 Vols. (Vienna, 1883–1886).

[136] Hans von Voltelini, "Der Codex Theresianus im österreichischen Staatsrat," in *ABGB Festschrift*, pp. 38–40.

[137] HHStA, Kabinettsarchiv: Kaunitz Voten, Karton 1, No. 3260 of 1766, Kaunitz Staatsrat Votum, 23 April 1767.

demanded, and at the same time, the Lower Austrian representative on the original commission drawing up the *Codex*, Joseph Ferdinand Holger, was instructed to begin the drafting of a new code of judicial procedure, with explicit directives to attempt to introduce greater uniformity into the various provincial procedures. While this was being completed Waldstätten was charged with a careful examination and assessment of the work already completed.[138] Waldstätten's critical appraisal of the draft *Codex*, which focused on its prolix complexity, was repudiated by the compilation commission, but found strong support with all members of the Council of State except the conservative Blümegen. Binder was particularly emphatic on the principle of universality of application, a terse simplicity of style, and, in the spirit of Thomasius, an excision of the extensive recourse to Roman law which the draft still contained. In order to demonstrate what he had in mind, he had his own *Konzipist*, Johann Bernhard Horten, rework a portion of the draft in this spirit, and presented it to the Council as a model for the whole.[139] Kaunitz fully supported Binder and again attacked the draft as an inadequate document. As he saw it, the fundamental objective behind drawing up a comprehensive code was "to abrogate the Roman Law and all the previous confused, partly obscure, partly mutually contradictory laws, and to introduce in their stead a general and uniform law" which accorded more with "the genius of our century." This aim, Kaunitz insisted, had not been achieved by the draft *Codex*. Indeed, in depending on concepts and definitions derived from a Roman Law that was daily growing more obsolete, the document was dooming itself to unintelligibility by future jurists. In addition, the draft *Codex* contained so many definitions and explanations that it combined the functions of a law code with a legal text book – two functions which should be kept strictly separate. Finally, since the commission's draft did not rescind all existing provincial laws but merely those in which a direct conflict existed, Austrian jurisprudence largely retained "the prolix, unconnected and self-contradictory chaos" of the existing legal system, which itself was already "a load for many camels." Under the circumstances Kaunitz recommended the drafting of a "systematic plan" for the revision of the entire work along the lines of Horten.[140]

A desperate rear-guard action by Blümegen failed to make an im-

---

[138] HHStA, Kabinettsarchiv: Staatsratprotokolle, Vol. 23, No. 3260, Imperial resolution, 1 May 1767. Cf. Voltelini, "Codex," p. 39.

[139] M. Friedrich von Maasburg, *Gutächtliche Aeußerung des österreichischen Staatsrathes über den von der Compilationscommission im Entwurfe vorgelegten Codex Theresianus civilis* (Vienna, 1881), pp. 4–9; Voltelini, pp. 40–41.

[140] HHStA, Kabinettsarchiv: Kaunitz Voten, Karton 1, No. 2021 of 1770, Kaunitz Staatsrat Votum, 14 October 1770. Cf. Maasburg, *Gutächtliche Aeußerung*, pp. 10–13; Voltelini, p. 42.

pression, and the brief of Kaunitz proved decisive. The draft *Codex* was deemed inadequate, and Horten was commissioned to produce a full revision of it in the spirit of Binder and Kaunitz. This was to be no simple matter. The completed portion of Horten's revision was subject to much criticism by members of the compilation commission, which defended both Roman law and lengthy textbook-style legal definitions. As Horten proceeded with his task both Gebler and Binder remained ardent supporters, but shortly thereafter the retirement of Binder and the appointment of Hatzfeld to the Council of State added new strength to the conservative critics.[141] Hatzfeld's opposition to Horten and his revised code was so strong that Kaunitz sidestepped the usual Council of State channels and successfully appealed to the Empress personally to order the Council to speed up its deliberations.[142] But Hatzfeld was able to enlist the support of Joseph II by raising doubts on the issue of property inheritance rights, and the intervention of the Emperor on behalf of the growing tide of conservative resistance to the codification programme insured that the whole process virtually ground to a halt by late 1773.[143] Thereafter the focus of the compilation commission was largely concentrated on the issue of judicial procedure. By 1780 the Supreme Judiciary, the vanguard of judicial conservatism, even felt the time right to request that the whole idea of a civil code be abandoned. It deprecated the tendency towards "universal laws," and energetically supported the old practice of issuing decrees province by province. Though this request was rejected by the Empress shortly before she died, a reformed civil code might have died on the vine had Joseph not performed an abrupt *volte-face*, and put new energy into the process in the 1780s.[144] The reformers and the conservatives thus arrived at a stalemate during the reign of Maria Theresia on the introduction of a unitary civil code, and by 1780 Kaunitz, at best, achieved only a negative success.

This was decidedly not to be the case with the draft penal code – the so-called *Nemesis Theresiana* – which had also been completed by 1766 and subjected to the same kind of assessment Waldstätten had conducted for the civil code by the far less critical president of the Prague Appeals Court, Franz Xaver Wirschnick. The completed draft and assessment, which were presented to the Empress on 16 February 1769, represented a judicial

[141] Harrasowsky, *Geschichte*, pp. 125–142; Voltelini, pp. 42–82; Korkisch, "Entstehung des österreichischen Allgemeinen Bürgerlichen Gesetzbuches," pp. 276–278; Brauneder, " Das Allgemeine Bürgerliche Gesetzbuch," pp. 213–214.
[142] HHStA, Staatskanzlei: Vorträge, Karton 111, Kaunitz to Maria Theresia, 23 and 26 February 1773, including draft note to Hatzfeld and imperial resolution.
[143] Voltelini, p. 49; Korkisch, "Entstehung des österreichischen Allgemeinen Bürgerlichen Gesetzbuches," pp. 278–279.
[144] Harrasowsky, *Geschichte*, pp. 142–167; Strakosch, pp. 98–215.

compromise. The draft penal code was considerably more progressive than the old code of Charles VI, but it retained provisions for such cruel forms of capital punishment as being burned alive or drawn and quartered, and it sanctioned the judicial torture of suspects in capital crimes. In practice the *Nemesis* was not as brutal as in theory, as judges were instructed to exercise mercy, and as the Empress personally reviewed all capital cases to see if clemency was in order.[145] But for a man like Kaunitz the very existence of such legal provisions as were posited in *Nemesis* was a medieval anachronism. In this case Kaunitz followed quite consciously in the footsteps of the main Enlightenment spokesman demanding mitigation of the cruelties of criminal procedure, Cesare Beccaria, Marchese di Bonesana.

Beccaria's spectacularly successful *Essay on Crimes and Punishment* of 1764, which insisted that the punishment must fit the crime and that torture had to be abolished, had made a great impression upon Kaunitz. Shortly after its appearance he was already writing Cobenzl, his authorized minister in Belgium, that "humanity" cried out against judicial torture, and that its existence showed "how little legislators have appreciated the value of men.[146] When Beccaria, who was a native of the Duchy of Milan, was invited by Empress Catherine II of Russia to come to St. Petersburg to assist in the legal reforms she was then undertaking, Kaunitz made every effort to keep him in Milan. In April 1767 he wrote to his governor, Firmian, that on the strength of the *Essay*, it would be disastrous to lose such an educated, perspicacious and independent thinker.[147] He strongly endorsed Firmian's suggestion that Beccaria be offered a chair of law in Milan. When the *Essay* was condemned by the Church, Kaunitz continued to lend it and Beccaria personally his fullest support, winning, incidentally, Voltaire's lavish praise.[148] In 1769 Beccaria officially received a chair of political economy, and when the Court Education Commission (*Studien-hofkommission*) recommended an annual salary of 2,000 Lire, Kaunitz used his influence with the Empress to have the sum raised to 3,000.[149]

It was in the spirit of Beccaria's *Essay* that Kaunitz submitted a memorandum to Maria Theresia on 20 February 1769, only two days after the *Nemesis* had been accepted. In his view not only did the new penal code lack precision and clarity, it prescribed cruel and unusual punishments that

[145] Hock-Bidermann, p. 42; Arneth, *Maria Theresia* IX, 198–199.
[146] De Boom, *Les Ministres Plénipotentiaires*, pp. 239–240.
[147] Angelo Mauri, "La cattedra di Cesare Beccaria," *Archivio storico italiano* Series 7, XX (1933), 207–209; Venturi, *Settecento riformatore*, V/1, 449–450.
[148] Voltaire to Kaunitz, 3 July 1766, in *The Complete Works of Voltaire*, Vol. CXIV (Banbury, 1973), pp. 295–296.
[149] Arneth, *Maria Theresia* X, 176–180; Mauri, "Cesare Beccaria," pp. 199–262; Wandruszka, *Österreich und Italien*, pp. 69–71.

sullied the name of the Empress. Kaunitz noted that the draft code still made references to witchcraft and other superstitions, which he considered "laughable" in these "enlightened times," and he totally opposed the retention of judicial torture, being particularly offended by the graphic illustrations of torture methods in the code.[150] Others, such as the professors of law and political economy at the University of Vienna, Karl Anton Martini and Joseph von Sonnenfels, echoed this sentiment equally vociferously, and this led the Empress to order an investigation into the problem of whether torture should be restricted or eliminated altogether. The retentionists, who included Stupan and Hatzfeld in the Council of State as well as almost the entire Supreme Judiciary, proved to be no feeble force. But in August 1775 the debate was given decisive direction by the intervention of Joseph, who expressed the conviction that the abolition of torture would not only be "a just and harmless measure, but a necessary one" as well.[151] Kaunitz endorsed this position energetically, and with this Maria Theresia joined the abolitionist camp.[152] The official decree abolishing torture in Austria, Bohemia, Galicia and the Banat was issued on 2 January 1776. On the same day Kaunitz was instructed to undertake negotiations with the provincial administrations of the Austrian Netherlands and the Duchy of Milan for the extension of the reform to those provinces.[153] Though Kaunitz implemented these instructions immediately, local conservative resistance was to delay a successful extension of the legislation to these areas until after the death of Maria Theresia.[154]

If uniform and just laws could respect the dignity and enforce the rights of the autonomous citizen, autonomy itself was as much an internal as an external quality. If the state sought to implant what Melton has aptly called "moral autonomy"[155] as well as productive initiative in its populations, this was something which could be achieved only through education, and education in turn could only become an instrument counteracting the perceived underdevelopment of the Monarchy if the general intellectual horizons of the baroque Counter-Reformation edifice were broadened. One of the distinguishing features of the Theresian reform period in the Habsburg Monarchy was that great oaks grew from little acorns, in the sense that a small change highlighted the need for changes

[150] Hock & Bidermann, pp. 42–43.
[151] Ibid., pp. 44–47; Arneth, Maria Theresia IX, 200–213.
[152] HHStA, Staatskanzlei: Vorträge, Karton 119, Kaunitz to Maria Theresia, 31 December 1775.   [153] Ibid., Maria Theresia to Kaunitz, 2 January 1776.
[154] On Lombardy, Capra, "Il settecento," pp. 524–533; on Belgium, W. W. Davies, Joseph II: An Imperial Reformer for the Austrian Netherlands (The Hague, 1974), pp. 57–58.
[155] James Van Horn Melton, Absolutism and the Eighteenth-Century Origins of Compulsory Schooling in Prussia and Austria (Cambridge, 1988), p. xxii.

elsewhere in ever-widening circles and with accelerated momentum. The Empress's physician-in-ordinary, for instance, began his public career in Vienna with an attempt to reform the University's medical faculty. This soon underscored the need for university reform in general, and that in turn led to a head-on collision with the Jesuit controlled State Censorship Commission. The battle to wrest control of the censorship board from the hands of the Jesuits in favour of a more secular and statist committee was won by Gerard van Swieten in 1759, and during the 1760s and 1770s the state's control of censorship functions was firmly established.[156] As we have observed earlier, the diary of Count Karl Zinzendorf leaves the distinct impression that, for the elite at least, these two decades were an era in which censorship was virtually non-existent. Certainly Joseph noted it sarcastically in 1765, and others also observed that almost any published work, no matter how objectionable, could be found in select Viennese salons.[157] However, for the majority of the population censorship remained a very real determinant even after the reform of 1759, and a liberal or conservative exercise of the censorship functions remained the subject of ongoing debate. Indeed, during the 1760s van Swieten found himself under considerable pressure from conservatives such as Archbishop Migazzi with the result that the State Censorship board appeared headed on a more restrictive course.[158] However, after the creation of the Council of State, the most difficult cases would often find their way to that forum for arbitration, and, in his capacity as a member of the Council, Kaunitz was thus able to use his influence to lend direction to the tone of state censorship.

The direction that Kaunitz laid down was uncompromisingly liberal. He insisted that "an excessive censorship of books would lead us back into the old barbarism" of previous times, and he expressed his particular concern at the censorship of books addressed primarily to professionals.[159] In a case in which a legal study of the validity of sworn statements was attacked by the Austro-Bohemian Chancellery as undermining morality, Kaunitz again emphasized that harsh censorship was an over-reaction. He could not endorse the principle whereby a whole valuable book was rejected merely because some of its passages had been deemed offensive, and he

---

[156] Grete Klingenstein, *Staatsverwaltung und kirchliche Authorität im 18. Jahrhundert* (Vienna, 1970), pp. 158–202. On van Swieten's university reform: Erna Lesky, "Gerard van Swieten: Auftrag und Erfüllung," in Erna Lesky and Adam Wandruszka, eds., *Gerard van Swieten und seine Zeit* (Vienna, Cologne and Graz, 1973), pp. 11–62; and Frank T. Brechka, *Gerard van Swieten and his World, 1700–1772* (The Hague, 1970), pp. 132–142.   [157] *MTJC* III, 352; Klingenstein, *Staatsverwaltung*, pp. 201–202.
[158] Grete Klingenstein, "Van Swieten und die Zensur," in Lesky and Wandruszka. eds., *Gerard van Swieten*, pp. 93–106.
[159] HHStA, Kabinettsarchiv: Kaunitz Voten, Karton 1, No. 2191 of 1767, Kaunitz Staatsrat Votum, 7 October 1767.

warned that this sort of approach to censorship could have seriously detrimental effects on the development of knowledge in general.[160] Above all he remained firmly opposed to any suggestion that the clergy should have any hand in the censorship process. When the Bishop of Olomouc complained in the summer of 1767 that superstition and free-thinking were rife in the land and suggested a reintroduction of ecclesiastical censorship to combat the trend, Kaunitz violently opposed the idea, and affirmed the existing policy of keeping censorship "out of the hands of the clergy as much as possible."[161] Kaunitz also was opposed to any attempts to stifle criticism in the arts. When Maria Theresia wished to exile the poet Raniero Calzabigi on the pretext that he had meddled in the affairs of the theater in Vienna, Kaunitz came to the poet's defence with the argument that every theater patron had the right "to express what he thinks of [the work performed] either orally or in writing." A man of letters, Kaunitz insisted, in fact rendered "an essential service to society in communicating to it the fruits of his meditations." Indeed, in his view, it was only by permitting such debates to go on that the minds of the most enlightened nations in Europe were formed. The right of the man of letters to call into question policies affecting the arts was therefore not to be tampered with.[162]

But perhaps the best example of Kaunitz's influence in lending a liberal direction to censorship came in his defence of the writings of Joseph von Sonnenfels during 1767. Sonnenfels, who had been professor of political economy at the University of Vienna since 1763, rapidly developed a reputation as one of the most vociferous and influential spokesmen of new reform ideas in Austria.[163] His lectures, books, and weekly journal begun in 1765, *Der Mann Ohne Vorurteil* (*The Man Without Prejudice*), soon made him the focus of conservative criticism. The attempt to silence Sonnenfels began as early as 1767 when Archbishop Migazzi launched an attack on the publications of Sonnenfels for undermining the authority of the Church.[164] Kaunitz and van Swieten were effectively able to block any reprimand[165] but it was not long before Sonnenfels was again the object of attack by Austro-Bohemian Chancellor Chotek when a Viennese doctoral

---

[160] *Ibid.*, No. 1748 of 1767, Kaunitz Staatsrat Votum, 6 August 1767.
[161] *Ibid.*, No. 1543 of 1767, Kaunitz Staatsrat Votum, 25 July 1767.
[162] HHStA, Staatskanzlei: Vorträge, Karton 114, Kaunitz to Maria Theresia, 9 March 1774.
[163] The extensive literature on Sonnenfels may best be approached through Karl-Heinz Osterloh, *Joseph von Sonnenfels und die österreichische Reformbewegung im Zeitalter des aufgeklärten Absolutismus* (Lübek and Hamburg, 1970) and Helmut Reinalter, ed., *Joseph von Sonnenfels* (Vienna, 1988).
[164] Joseph Feil, *Sonenfels und Maria Theresia* (Vienna, 1859), p. 11.
[165] HHStA, Kabinettsarchiv: Kaunitz Voten, Karton 1, No. 45 of 1767, Kaunitz Staatsrat Votum, 20 January 1767; August Fournier, "Gerhard van Swieten als Censor," *Sitzungsberichte der phil.-hist. Classe der k.k. Akademie der Wissenschaften* LXXXIV (1876), 428.

disputation defended such principles of Sonnenfelsian political economy as the abolition of torture and the death penalty. Chotek warned that Sonnenfels could become dangerous if he were permitted to continue to talk about and publish ideas which challenged existing legislation and institutions.[166] Again Kaunitz rushed to the defence, insisting that Sonnenfels's ideas did not deserve the "critical and harsh rebukes of the Court Chancellery." The whole point of Sonnenfels's academic post, Kaunitz argued, was to air ideas to improve the laws and constitution of the Monarchy, and what was being done was not an open attack on the state but the positing of political theses for dispute. Under the circumstances Kaunitz expressed the suspicion that Chotek's attack on Sonnenfels was, at best, a personal vendetta against Sonnenfels, and perhaps even an attack "against his very chair." Kaunitz therewith won over the Empress, and Sonnenfels was explicitly permitted to continue to write and teach according to his principles, as this was deemed to be part of his job as professor of political economy.[167] But this decision did not silence the critics, and only in a third debate in the Council of State in November, where Kaunitz argued that Sonnenfels must "be granted the necessary freedom in writing, for otherwise one would fail completely in achieving the objective of combating ignorance and abounding prejudice," were the full liberal parameters of the censorship of Sonnenfels delineated.[168]

If Kaunitz's main argument against excessive censorship was thus that it retarded the progress of knowledge, it was an argument that proceeded from the premise that education was a vital concern of a modern society. Perceptive observers had long been aware of a virtual educational crisis in the Habsburg Monarchy. The root cause of the frequently diagnosed underdevelopment of the Monarchy in relation with other European states was seen to be the inadequacy of the educational system at every level, primary, secondary and post-secondary.[169] Reform initiatives tended to

[166] Osterloh, *Sonnenfels*, pp. 126–128.
[167] HHStA, Kabinettsarchiv: Staatsratakten, Karton 1 (the only carton that survives), No. 1420, Stupan, Blümegen, Starhemberg and Kaunitz Staatsrat Vota, 20 June–July 1767; Recirculation (4 July); Stupan, Blümegen and Starhemberg Staatsrat Vota; Imperial resolution, 20 July 1767. Cf. Hock-Bidermann, p. 61.
[168] HHStA, Kabinettsarchiv: Kaunitz Voten, Karton 1, No. 2531 of 1767, Kaunitz Staatsrat Votum, 15 November 1767; Staatsratprotokolle, Vol. 26, No. 2531, Maria Theresia to Chotek and Hatzfeld, 17 November 1767.
[169] Gustav Strakosch-Graßmann, *Geschichte des Österreichischen Unterrichtswesens* (Vienna, 1905), pp. 83–138, still remains a reliable introduction to the reform of education at all levels under enlightened absolutism. A recent synthesis is Helmut Engelbrecht, *Geschichte des österreichischen Bildungswesens*, Vol. III: *Von der frühen Aufklärung bis zum Vormärz* (Vienna, 1984).

come first at the higher levels, for here a preponderantly noble clientele, aware of the progress achieved in Protestant Germany, perceived its own material interests to lie in change.[170] Kaunitz's own father devised an educational plan for his son, which showed a clear awareness of the shortcomings of indigenous Habsburg higher institutions.[171] Many of his peers shared these concerns, and tentative initiatives were already beginning to be taken in the reign of Charles VI to address the problem, by attempting to found more "modern" institutions for nobles.[172] Under Maria Theresia these reform initiatives gained momentum with van Swieten's dramatic incursions into the medical faculty of the University of Vienna, and the subsequent reform of other faculties, where the key to success was the co-operation of a reform-minded episcopate resolved to break the Jesuit dominance of higher education which had been the main impediment to change.[173] From there, with Protestant German precedents ever before the eyes of reformers, other institutions in the Monarchy from universities to gymnasia were gradually transformed in the subsequent decades.[174]

Klingenstein has observed that it was one of the marked peculiarities of enlightened absolutism in the Habsburg Monarchy that the integral connection between upper and lower levels of education came to be recognized quite clearly, and that the desire for educational systematization gradually produced the need to build from the bottom up.[175] The impetus for the reform of primary education came from many directions. Cameralist theories and cameralist ordinances had focused on the necessity of producing self-disciplined, productive citizens, while religious reform movements such as Pietism and reform Catholicism sought to cultivate more inward forms of popular devotion through education.[176] The survival

---

[170] On the whole problem of the reform of higher education see Grete Klingenstein, "Bildungskrise: Gymnasien und Universitäten im Spannungsfeld theresianischer Aufklärung," in Koschatzky, ed., *Maria Theresia und Ihre Zeit*, pp. 213–223; Gerald Grimm, *Die Schulreform Maria Theresias* (Frankfurt a/M, Bern, N.Y., Paris, 1987); Strakosch-Graßmann, *Unterrichtswesen*, pp. 145–158.

[171] Klingenstein, *Aufstieg des Hauses Kaunitz*, pp. 112–157.

[172] Grete Klingenstein, "Vorstufen der theresianischen Unterrichtsreform in der Regierungszeit Karls VI," *MIÖG* LXXVI (1968), 327–377; Grimm, *Schulreform*, pp. 257–268.

[173] Viktor Kreuzinger, *Gerard van Swieten und die Reform der Wiener Universität unter Maria Theresia bis zur Errichtung der Studienhofkommission* (Vienna, 1924); Lesky, "Gerard van Swieten," pp. 11–62; Brechka, *Gerard van Swieten*, pp. 132–142; on the role of reform Catholicism, see below, pp. 211, 217–218.

[174] Klingenstein, "Bildungskrise," pp. 218–221; Engelbrecht, *Aufklärung*, pp. 180–203; Grimm, *Schulreform*, pp. 287–432.   [175] Klingenstein, "Bildungskrise," p. 219.

[176] The most important work on this subject is Melton, *Absolutism*. On the religious and economic roots of the reforms, see pp. 3–168. Cf. Strakosch-Graßmann, *Unterrichtswesen*, pp. 158–172; Engelbrecht, pp. 7–20; Raeff, *Well-Ordered Police State*, pp. 137–142.

of so-called "crypto-Protestantism" in the face of the most sweeping measures of Counter-Reformation highlighted the bankruptcy of the sensual baroque culture of images in its most fundamental mission, and inclined Catholic reformers to look with new interest at reconstituting the basis of the culture along more Protestant literary lines.[177] Pedagogy stressing inwardness and self-discipline as developed by the Pietist, August Hermann Francke, in Halle during the seventeenth century served as the model. In the eighteenth century it was adapted to Catholicism by the Silesian abbot of Sagan, Johann Ignaz Felbiger, and from there soon began to penetrate Habsburg lands.[178] Through the 1740s and 1750s numerous initiatives along these lines were evident all over the Monarchy, though they petered out with the onset of the Seven Years War.[179]

Even if these initiatives tended to have only modest results, awareness of the problem remained keen. In 1765 Joseph II grasped the nettle. In his famous memorandum of that year he complained bitterly of the neglect of education in the Habsburg Monarchy. Part of his grievance focused on the excessive confessional dimension of education to the detriment of more pragmatic subjects, but the remainder was imbued with an austere air of regimented puritanism which was typical of Joseph. The weaknesses and corruptions of the Monarchy's educational institutions were due to their location in urban centers, he asserted, where overpaid teachers and spoiled students thought less of the task in hand than of "dissipation" and entertainment.[180] In his careful assessment of this memorandum for Maria Theresia, Kaunitz singled out these references to education for special attention. Since society needed minds as much as bodies, he noted, nothing was more important in their development than education. He praised the Emperor for his attention to the subject, and agreed that the function of education was to produce "virtuous citizens." But he could hardly agree that the decadence of urban centers was the heart of the problem. Cities bred "politeness and urbanity" which were fundamental qualities of an educated person, and without which men became "if not odious, then at least socially disagreeable." Manners and knowledge were not incompatible by any means, and moving educational institutions to isolated rural

---

177 James Van Horn Melton, "From Image to Word: Cultural Reform and the Rise of Literate Culture in Eighteenth-Century Austria," *Journal of Modern History* LVIII (1986), 95–124; his "Von Versinnlichung zur Verinnerlichung: Bemerkungen zur Dialektik repräsentativer und plebejischer Öffentlichkeit," in Plaschka and Klingenstein, eds., *Österreich im Europa der Aufklärung* II, 919–941; and his *Absolutism*, pp. 60–90.

178 Melton, *Absolutism*, pp. 23–59, 91–105. Cf. Franz Volkmer, *Johann Ignaz Felbiger und seine Schulreform* (Habelschwerdt, 1890); Ulrich Kromer, *Johann Ignaz Felbiger* (Freiburg im Breisgau, 1966); Josef Stanzel, *Die Schulaufsicht im Reformwerk J. I. Felbiger (1724–1788)* (Paderborn, 1976).   179 Engelbrecht, pp. 91–98.

180 *MTJC* III, 335–361; cf. above, pp. 99–100.

areas would thus be counter-productive – as well as an absurd expense. If there were problems with the educational system, they were structural, and therefore the reform of public education was "the most essential" task of legislation.[181]

Not content with these remarks, Kaunitz proceeded to outline his proposals for a complete overhaul of public education in the Habsburg Monarchy. He saw society divided into three categories, or "orders of citizens": the broad masses of peasants and workers, the bourgeoisie, and the upper classes. He argued that each required its own educational track. It would be a mistake to regard this classification as a mere reflection of the traditional feudal hierarchy, for Kaunitz made clear that under the last category he understood not merely the upper and lower nobility, but also all army officers, office holders, and *rentiers*. In view of his frequent emphasis on merit and on professionalism, his professed hatred of privilege, and his stress on the need for nobles to obey their superiors no matter how common their background,[182] it is evident that Kaunitz was not speaking of a restrictive hierarchy of birth so much as he was arguing for a multiple-track educational stream. The first of these tracks, Kaunitz argued, required the most attention because it would affect the largest number of people. Pedagogical principles and content had to be "fixed and uniform" in all schools of the Monarchy, and to this end it would be necessary to produce a standard set of guidelines. These should include a clear precis of religious beliefs designed to curb abuses now extant; a "moral" section designed to instill a "horror of theft, mendacity, drunkenness, ingratitude and other vices not punished by law," and to cultivate patriotism in their stead; and, finally, a third section focusing on the "enlightened and skillful" development of the rural economy. The second track addressed merchants and craftsmen, and here Kaunitz emphasized the need for well-supported specialized vocational schools, and the establishment of professional standards in the various trades. The best and most skillful teachers had to be employed for the purpose, and scrimping on salaries here would be a false economy indeed. For the third track, Kaunitz wished to see higher studies generally shortened and reoriented to more practical subjects. Less time was to be spent on dead languages like Latin and Greek and on "speculative" subjects such as theology and philosophy, more on public law, history, geography, mathematics, fine arts, modern languages and gymnastics. Educational reform had been in the wind for a generation in Europe, he concluded; it

---

[181] Beer, ed., "Denkschriften des Fürsten Kaunitz," pp. 100–102.
[182] Some examples: HHStA, Staatskanzlei: Vorträge, Karton 125, Kaunitz to Maria Theresia, n.d. (January 1778); HHStA, Kabinettsarchiv: Kaunitz Voten, Karton 2, No. 2633 of 1773, Kaunitz Staatsrat Votum, 4 December 1773.

was high time the Monarchy addressed this agenda as well.[183] Bearing striking resemblance to French education proposals of the same time, particularly those of Louis-René Caradeuc de La Chatolais and the Abbé Nicolas Baudeau, Kaunitz's proposals clearly show the same concern for government action and pedagogical uniformity at a national level. Above all, Kaunitz shared what R. R. Palmer has aptly called a concern for education "combined with a kind of manpower planning."[184]

However, neither Joseph's original memo, nor Kaunitz's response to it, led to any concerted government action. There is little doubt that the arguments Kaunitz made were helpful in his successful support of the establishment of a copper-engraving academy in 1766 and of a crafts academy in 1767,[185] but the education system as a whole, and especially elementary education, was not systematically addressed until 1769. In the event it was Maria Theresia's confessional concerns that proved to be the trigger for reform, for early in that year she received a memorandum from the prince-bishop of Passau, Leopold Ernst Firmian, which clearly touched a raw nerve. Firmian, fully in the spirit of reform Catholicism, warned that heresy was still widespread in Upper and Lower Austria, and that only a systematic school reform with the help of the state could "root out the hidden weeds."[186] The Empress took immediate action. On 30 May she forwarded Firmian's memorandum to the Austro-Bohemian Chancellery, with instructions for Chotek to transmit it to the Gubernia of Upper and Lower Austria and to produce a suitable report with recommendations. The Chancellery Privy Councillor whom Chotek sent to work on this task, Florian Perdacher von Pergenstein, was, like his chief, of a conservative mold, and it was therefore not surprising that the Chancellery report which followed was cautious and negative, emphasizing the difficulties and impediments to such reform.[187]

The Council of State, however, was another matter. The debate was dominated by Gebler, who was the most outspoken on a subject that was clearly close to his heart. Already familiar with Felbiger, he was strengthened in his resolve by another Felbiger disciple, the rector of St. Stephen's school in Vienna, Joseph Messmer, who had prepared an elaborate proposal calling for the establishment of a normal school in Vienna informed by the pedagogical methods in use in Sagan, and for the

---

[183] Beer, ed., "Denkschriften des Fürsten Kaunitz," pp. 102–106.
[184] R. R. Palmer, *The Improvement of Humanity* (Princeton, N.J., 1985), p. 57. Cf. Harvey Chisick, *The Limits of Reform in the Enlightenment* (Princeton, N.J., 1981), p. 89–104.
[185] See below, pp. 200–202.
[186] Joseph Alexander Freiherr von Helfert, *Die Gründung der österreichischen Volksschule durch Maria Theresia* (Prague, 1860), pp. 121–122, full text on p. 617; also reproduced in Engelbrecht, pp. 489–490.
[187] Helfert, *Gründung der österreichischen Volksschule*, pp. 123–127.

creation of a Court Education Commission to look into the whole problem of education reform in Upper and Lower Austria. Gebler's contempt for the Chancellery report was quite transparent: doubts about whether the common man should be taught to read and write might have been excusable in Russia prior to the reign of Peter I; to hear them in Vienna from a government office in these times was incomprehensible. Not platitudes, but the methodical implementation of reform was called for in this situation. Messmer's proposal was put forward as a practical alternative. The qualifications of other Council of State members were swept aside by Kaunitz's wholehearted approval of Gebler's "well-founded suggestions," and as a consequence Messmer's plan for a normal school in Vienna was approved and implemented. At the same time a Lower Austrian Gubernial Commission was established with the brief of overseeing school reform in that province. By October 1770 the Empress decreed that education reform was high on her agenda, and that consequently a Court School Commission encompassing the other hereditary provinces would be established.[188]

In the meantime a new log was added to the fire by none other than Kaunitz's second-in-command in the Foreign Ministry, Anton Pergen. In 1769 Pergen had been given the job of overseeing the ministry's foreign language school, the so-called "Oriental Academy", which had been founded by Kaunitz in 1754 as a language training facility for the diplomatic corps. From its foundation the academy was headed by a Jesuit named Joseph Franz. Franz lacked administrative capacities, and under him the academy soon fell into such debt that part of its property had to be sold and the school resettled in the hostel of St. Barbara. In 1769 Franz was dismissed. The Vice-Director, Father Johann de Deo Negrep, took his place and Pergen was given supervisory control from the Foreign Ministry. Pergen was a man of great ambition. He had been charged by the Empress to submit a quarterly report on the progress of the academy under Negrep, and being dissatisfied with what he found, he soon parlayed this commission into a general plan for the reform of the entire educational system of the Monarchy.[189]

The Pergen memorandum of 26 August 1770 was one of the most far-ranging and systematic plans for education reform ever to be submitted to Maria Theresia. The echoes of Kaunitz's proposals of 1766 were unmistakable, and the debt to La Chatolais and Baudeau, though unacknowledged, seemed even more transparent. The memo insisted that

[188] *Ibid.*, pp. 128–149; Melton, *Absolutism*, pp. 200–204; Engelbrecht, pp. 98–100.
[189] Helfert, pp. 190–195; Arneth, *Maria Theresia* IX, 227–228; Bernard, *From the Enlightenment to the Police State*, pp. 70–71. On the Oriental Academy, see Matsch, *Auswärtige Dienst*, pp. 76–78.

all supervision and control of the entire school system had to be assumed by the state through a central Education Directory, and demanded the complete exclusion of all religious orders from the educational process. Much in line with Kaunitz's proposals, Pergen recommended the abandonment of Latin in all disciplines but medicine, and stressed the need to cultivate patriotism and "uniformity in the general way of thinking," with standardized curricula and texts. Also along the lines of Kaunitz's earlier proposal, Pergen posited the establishment of three tiers of education: universal primary schooling (*Allgemeine Trivialschulen*), professional or vocational schools (*Realschulen*) for the bourgeoisie, and Gymnasia (*lateinische Schulen*) for nobles, commoners of means, and "poor but exceptionally talented" pupils. The qualification in this last category is particularly reminiscent of Kaunitz, and sets these Austrian proposals apart from the French precedents on which they appear to be based. In a supplementary memo of 16 July, Pergen included the education of women in his purview, whose essential role in "human and civil society" demanded inclusion in the universal education programme of the state. He recommended girls be taught religion and morality, reading and writing, some science, mathematics and drawing, and, of course, home economics and handicrafts.[190]

These proposals were brought before the Council of State on 18 January 1771. Not surprisingly, Kaunitz waxed enthusiastically that the memo did Pergen "exceptional honour" and earned him "special marks of all-highest satisfaction." The sentiment was echoed by Binder, Gebler and Stupan, though all assumed that the proposal would have to be introduced gradually, and they stressed that obviously the supply of trained secular teachers was inadequate. All three agreed that in his attack on religious orders Pergen had perhaps gone too far, and the great defender of the orders on the Council, Blümegen, following in the footsteps of Cardinal Migazzi, felt that this part of the plan was totally unrealistic. Kaunitz seconded the objections of his colleagues on the practical impossibility of excluding the religious orders from education, though he did still think it a worth-while long-term objective, and he recommended Pergen be given an opportunity to respond to the critique.[191] When Joseph also expressed

[190] Helfert, pp. 196–206; Melton, *Absolutism*, pp. 204–206.
[191] HHStA, Staatskanzlei: Interiora, Fasz. 67b, Gebler Staatsrat Votum, n.d. (January 1771); AVA, Nachlaß Pergen, Karton 1, Stupan Staatsrat Votum, 23 January 1771, Binder Staatsrat Votum, 30 January 1771, Blümegen Staatsrat Votum, 1 February 1771; HHStA, Kabinettsarchiv: Kaunitz Voten, Karton 1, No. 239 of 1771, Kaunitz Staatsrat Votum, 21 March 1771. Cf. Hock & Bidermann, p. 63; Helfert, pp. 209–212. The Migazzi critique discussed in Cölestin Wolfsgruber, *Christoph Anton Kardinal Migazzi: Fürstbischof von Wien* (Saulgau, 1890), pp. 296–298.

his support,[192] the Empress decided to commission Pergen to submit a shorter plan on practical implementation, and ordered him to respond to the critique of Blümegen in particular.[193]

Three months later Pergen submitted his reply. He did not regard financing a serious problem, but admitted there were not a sufficient number of qualified lay teachers to fill the needs of the Monarchy. Precisely for this reason, however, he recommended the establishment of the teachers' colleges he had originally suggested as quickly as possible. On the issue of the religious orders he remained totally inflexible, regarding the whole issue as a simple either/or proposition.[194] The Council of State unanimously endorsed the principle of the Pergen plan, though the issue of the religious orders remained an unresolved thorn in the debate. For the moment Kaunitz recommended making a start by creating the suggested State Education Directory (*Schulen Ober-Directorium*), and asking Pergen to nominate a Director, which recommendations the Empress endorsed on 6 September.[195] Though Pergen proposed a number of candidates, in the Council of State the unanimous choice fell on Pergen himself, Kaunitz insisting that "no better choice could be made for the purpose." Kaunitz also approved of Pergen's plan to bring in foreign educational experts, even if these were Protestant, though this notion met with considerable resistance from Stupan, Binder, and, of course, Blümegen.[196] The Empress compromised. She would permit the recruiting of a Protestant so long as he came merely as an adviser, not a teacher or supervisor. The presidency of the Education Directory was offered to Pergen, though his suggestion on clerical exclusion was ordered to be tabled for the moment.[197]

This Pergen could not accept. For him the whole plan was contingent on the exclusion of all religious orders from education, and in his reply to the Empress on 22 November he therefore rejected the presidency of the proposed Education Directory.[198] For Kaunitz this was the beginning of his disenchantment with Pergen. He analyzed Pergen's rigidity with

[192] AVA, Nachlaß Pergen, Karton 1, Joseph Gutachten, 15 April 1771.
[193] HHStA, Kabinettsarchiv: Staatsratprotokolle, Vol. 38, No. 239, imperial resolution, 16 April 1771.
[194] AVA, Nachlaß Pergen, Karton 1, Pergen to Maria Theresia, 16 July 1771.
[195] HHStA, Kabinettsarchiv: Kaunitz Voten, Karton 2, No. 2809 of 1771, Kaunitz Staatsrat Votum, 4 September 1771; Staatsratprotokolle, Vol. 40, No. 2809, Imperial resolution, 6 September 1771.
[196] HHStA, Kabinettsarchiv: Kaunitz Voten, Karton 2, No. 3530 of 1771, Kaunitz Staatsrat Votum, 3 November 1771. Cf. Helfert, pp. 231–232; Bernard, *From the Enlightenment to the Police State*, pp. 80–81.
[197] HHStA, Kabinettsarchiv: Staatsratprotokolle, Vol. 41, No. 3530, imperial resolution, 8 November 1771.
[198] Helfert, p. 233; Bernard, *From the Enlightenment to the Police State*, pp. 82–83.

nothing short of exasperation. Pergen admitted there were not enough lay teachers in the Monarchy to replace all monastic orders, Kaunitz noted, therefore it was "impossible for him to insist on the dismissal of the present ecclesiastical teachers."[199] It was the kind of stubborn mentality that Kaunitz could not appreciate. In the great ministerial shuffle that followed within a week, Pergen was not only removed from any educational posts, but from Kaunitz's Chancellery of State as well.

After the ministerial shuffle of December 1771, the strongest voice for education reform in the Council of State was Kressel. Despite Pergen's bitter opposition, Kressel preferred a piecemeal approach, and this soon set the dominant tone of the Council.[200] With Kaunitz no longer lending his support, and with Kressel dominating the debates on the issue, Pergen gradually faded from the picture. Kressel's influence in turn grew. Having impressed both Maria Theresia and Joseph with his work on the commission created to implement relief measures during the Bohemian famine crisis of 1771–1772, Kressel became head of the Jesuit Commission in 1773. The abolition of the Jesuit order, which controlled so much of Austria's education, led directly to more debates on education reform. But the acquisition by the state of all Jesuit property also suddenly made resources available which made the implementation of education reform fiscally feasible.[201] In the Jesuit Commission a new reform plan was accordingly drafted by Martini, one of its members, which proposed using former Jesuit property to finance a system of universal compulsory schooling. The proposal had many of the same emphases on standardization and uniformity that Pergen had brought forward, and outlined a similar three-tracked education system, but it adopted a more flexible approach to implementation and to clerical orders.[202] Kaunitz gave his enthusiastic support, though he cautioned that education reform was not merely a matter of implementation, but of ongoing administration, and for this reason proper direction was indispensable. He therefore supported the dismissal of Archbishop Migazzi from the Court Education Commission (Studienhofkommission) and the appointment of Kressel as its head. On 12 February 1774 this suggestion was implemented, and the long-awaited education reform was begun.[203] Felbiger himself was brought from Sagan to supervise the primary education network, and to draft Maria Theresia's famous General School

[199] HHStA, Kabinettsarchiv: Kaunitz Voten, Karton 2, No. 4021 of 1771, Kaunitz Staatsrat Votum, 9 December 1771.
[200] Helfert, p. 239–243; Bernard, From the Enlightenment to the Police State, pp. 85–86.
[201] See below, pp. 241–247.   [202] Melton, Absolutism, pp. 210–211.
[203] HHStA, Kabinettsarchiv: Kaunitz Voten, Karton 2, No. 2805 of 1773, Kaunitz Staatsrat Votum, 27 December 1773; Staatsratprotokolle, Vol. 48, No. 2805, Imperial resolution, 4 January 1774. Cf. Hock & Bidermann, p. 65.

Ordinance (*Allgemeine Schulordnung*) which was decreed on 6 December 1774.[204]

The cultural dimension

In August 1782 Wolfgang Amadeus Mozart, then seeking to establish himself in Vienna, wrote to his father:

Count Thun, Count Zichy, the Baron Swieten, even Prince Kaunitz, are all very much displeased with the Emperor, because he does not value men of talent more, and allows them to leave his dominions. Kaunitz said the other day to Archduke Maximilian, when the conversation turned on myself, that "such people only come into the world once in a hundred years and must not be driven out of Germany, particularly when we are fortunate enough to have them in the capital."[205]

The voice was not only that of Kaunitz the sophisticated connoisseur of the arts, but also that of Kaunitz the reformer intimately involved with the question of the role of culture in a modern society. We have seen that Kaunitz was a cultivated and enthusiastic patron of the arts,[206] but a mere personal devotion to the arts by itself has relatively limited significance. Indeed, the archetype of this kind of narrow cultural focus was at hand in the person of King Frederick II of Prussia, whom Voltaire acidly but accurately accused of having brought Athens only to his study, while maintaining Sparta as the real model for his country.[207] The use of art as a political instrument to affirm and legitimate particular social values, social structures or individual positions, is, of course, as old as patronage itself. Allegorical display as a concrete instrument of power was a particularly central feature of the Baroque and was one of the most effective tools of the Counter-Reformation in the Habsburg Monarchy. Secular elites from traditional manorial lords to kings also sought to harness the affective power of the arts for these purposes – Louis XIV of France perhaps representing the apex of this development, with his cultivation of the cultural despotism of a Lully, a Molière, or a LeBrun as a deliberate instrument of royal absolutism.[208] Kaunitz, however, went well beyond such concepts of patronage and articulated a public cultural policy which prefigured the cultivation of the autonomous artist as an indispensable element in development of society.

During the discussions which were to lead to the restructuring of the Academy of Fine Arts in Vienna, Kaunitz asserted that the "support of the

---

[204] Engelbrecht, pp. 102–106, 491–501.
[205] Anderson, ed., *Letters of Mozart*, II, 814–815.   [206] See above, pp. 23–29.
[207] Peter Gay, *Voltaire's Politics* (N.Y., 1965), p. 171.
[208] A good discussion of this in Robert Isherwood, *Music in the Service of the King* (Ithaca, N.Y., 1973) and in John B. Wolf, *Louis XIV* (New York, 1968), pp. 357–378.

fine arts in a state is an important part of the concern of a wise ruler." The value of art was not only aesthetic but also economic. Support of artists would enhance tourism, lead to foreigners commissioning works, benefit and enrich craftsmen, stimulate industry, and keep money spent abroad on luxury items at home. "France provides a convincing example of this," Kaunitz suggested:

Louis XIV may have enlarged his kingdom and built his reputation on his grand military operations and conquests, but his memory today would be held, if not in abomination, then in hatred and sadness by the nation which purchased his victories with such heavy sacrifices of money, men and resources that it still feels the after-effects to this day, if this king had not at the same time, even during wars, encouraged and improved the arts ... Certainly the great masters Poussin, LeBrun, Girardin, Mansard and many others have contributed more to the welfare of the nation by improving the taste in cultural artifacts and training good students, than have Condé, Turenne, Luxembourg, Vauban, Villars and other generals. The latter would have completely impoverished France with unmanageable debt, despite her territorial expansion, if the former had not raised her up again in their own sphere.

A good deal of Italy would be impoverished too, Kaunitz added, if it were not for the tourist trade, which it owes not only to its antiquities but to its many contemporary artists. By contrast German art was more imitative than original because the preconditions to cultural creativity were lacking. Government policy, therefore, should be to create these conditions, initially at least in major urban centers, "from which good taste will then gradually spread to the provinces."[209]

The most important of these urban centers in all of Central Europe, of course, was the imperial capital, Vienna. As we saw from Mozart's letter to his father, as well as from Kaunitz's efforts to bring Lessing to Vienna,[210] Kaunitz wished Vienna to become a magnet for all of the most talented individuals in Germany and the Habsburg Monarchy. Above all, he believed that it was in the interest of the imperial dignity that the Monarchy become a well-known patron of the arts and humanities, and he was instrumental in bringing important collections to the imperial library.[211] Kaunitz also favoured the imperial acceptance of book dedications and honorary patronage posts from abroad. In the former case Kaunitz would even advise acceptance of a dedication where his personal

[209] AABK, Ve·waltungsakten, Fasz. 1, Kaunitz to Maria Theresia, 25 May 1770. Cf. Carl von Lützow, *Geschichte der kaiserlichen königlichen Akademie der Bildenden Künste* (Vienna, 1877), p. 52; Walter Wagner, *Die Geschichte der Akademie der Bildenden Künste in Wien* (Vienna, 1967), pp. 37–40; Ernst Wangermann, "Maria Theresa: A Reforming Monarchy," in A. G. Dickens, ed., *The Courts of Europe* (London, 1977), pp. 302–303.
[210] See above, p. 28.
[211] HHStA, Staatskanzlei: Vorträge, Karton 101, Kaunitz to Maria Theresia, 20 April 1768, Van Swieten to Maria Theresia, 25 April 1768, Kaunitz to Maria Theresia, and Maria Theresia to Kaunitz, 30 April 1768.

enthusiasm for the work in question was slim or non-existent. Thus, he recommended the Empress accept a dedication from the Lyon book publisher, Bruys Ponthur, for a life of St. Theresa despite his own coolness towards confessional mysticism,[212] and he suggested Joseph accept the dedication to Klopstock's *Hermanns Schlacht*, though he personally was not enthusiastic about the poet or the entire *Sturm und Drang* movement.[213] In the latter case, for example, Kaunitz persuaded both Joseph and Maria Theresia to accept the title of honorary Patron of the Art Academy of Santa Luca in Rome in 1773,[214] and almost succeeded in prevailing upon the Empress to become an Honorary Protector of the British Academy of Sciences in 1770, but for her objection that this entailed too many religious "inconveniences."[215] For the same reason he pressed for the vigorous propagation of the products of Austrian ingenuity, as is well illustrated by his attempt to spread the fame of Anton Mesmer's magnetic discoveries.[216]

Kaunitz also had a strong conviction that native artists should be patronized and encouraged. His personal patronage, which focused on Moravians, Viennese and Lombards, showed this tendency, even when Kaunitz recognized that these were not always artists of the first rank.[217] In imperial commissions that come closest to what we may consider public commissions which Kaunitz was asked to supervise, we also see this trend very clearly. In the renovation of the Schönbrunn palace grounds which Kaunitz was asked to supervise,[218] the commission for the thirty-two garden sculptures went to Johann Christian Wilhelm Beyer, whose workshop contained no fewer than six young Viennese sculptors – at least three of whom, Johann Hagenauer, Leonhard Posch and Franz Zauner, were in time to be more famous than their master. Beyer also agreed to work only with domestic marble, and after the discovery of a new quarry in Tyrol, he went so far as to recommend an import prohibition on foreign marble altogether. The allegorical programme drawn up for this commission by Kaunitz is also an interesting study of the aspirations of enlightened absolutism. Instead of glorious echoes from imperial Rome,

---

[212] *Ibid.*, Karton 115, Kaunitz to Maria Theresia, 15 September 1774.

[213] *Ibid.*, Karton 104, Kaunitz to Joseph, 16 August 169, Kaunitz to Maria Theresia, 17 August 1769; HHStA, Staatskanzlei: Wissenschaft und Kunst, Karton 11, Kaunitz to Klopstock, 28 August 1769. Cf. Bodi, *Tauwetter*, pp. 94–95.

[214] AABK, Verwaltungsakten, Karton 2, Kaunitz to Joseph and Maria Theresia, 18 January 1773.

[215] HHStA, Staatskanzlei: Vorträge, Karton 106, Kaunitz to Maria Theresia, including imperial resolution, 14 November 1770.

[216] HHStA, Staatskanzlei: Wissenschaft und Kunst, Karton 6, Kaunitz to Mercy-Argenteau, 1 April 1775.

[217] Burg, *Zauner*, pp. 19–23; Kroupa, "Václav Antonín Kaunitz-Rietberg a vytvarná umení," pp. 75–78.

[218] HHStA, Familienarchiv: Sammelbände, Karton 70, Maria Theresia to Kaunitz, n.d.

virtuous republican heroes from Plutarch dominate. Nymphs from the entourage of Bacchus and Flora represent the protectors of agriculture; while Hygeia and Sibyl of Cumea represent care for the physical and spiritual health of the citizens. As Wangermann has pointed out, this "brings us close to the ideas of the French Revolution even at the residence of the Habsburg dynasty."[219]

The promotion of public cultural institutions in the capital, however, was to be Kaunitz's most visible role in the cultural politics of the Habsburg Monarchy. Foremost amongst these was to be Vienna's Academy of Fine Arts. The establishment of an art academy in Vienna dated back to 1688, when the Tyrolese painter, Peter Strudel, founded a school for artists that was soon drawn under official government protection. The academy collapsed with Strudel's death in 1714, but it was reopened on firmer footing as an official institution in 1726, and it was raised to the status of a higher educational institution in 1751. From 1759 until his death in 1770 the academy was dominated by its rector, the stylistically rather stiff and mannered court painter, Martin van Meytens. Most contemporary cultural observers in the neo-classical vanguard were agreed that the tenure of Meytens marked an era of decline and decay, and certainly the newer aesthetic ideals found little reflection in the academy during these years.[220]

The leading edge of the neo-classical movement in the visual arts was to be a new institution, founded in November 1766, the Copper Engraving Academy (*k. k. Kupferstecher-Academie*). Engraving was an extremely important art in the eighteenth century, fulfilling all the functions that photography fills today. Its economic significance was patent, as all technical illustrations in professional books originated from engraved plates, but it also fulfilled the function of making reproductions of famous art works widely available, much as photographic coffee-table books do today. The lack of skilled engravers in Vienna led the government to subsidize two artists, Jakob Mathias Schmutzer and Johann Gottfried Haid, to study the art in London and Paris, and upon their return Schmutzer proposed the establishment of an academy for drawing and engraving. Kaunitz, as we have seen, was an avid collector of engravings, and, given his reputation as a connoisseur, it is not surprising that he was named "Protector" of the new academy, probably at his own request.[221]

[219] Wangermann, "Maria Theresa," p. 311; Dernjac, *Schönbrunn*, pp. 22–81.
[220] The standard history of the academy is Wagner, *Geschichte der Akademie* (for this early period see pp. 13–28), which supplants the earlier Lützow, *Geschichte*.
[221] Wagner, *Geschichte der Akademie*, pp. 28–31; Kroupa, "Václav Antonín Kaunitz-Rietberg a výtvarná umění," pp. 72–73.

Schmutzer was delighted that "such an enlightened" minister, who was so respected in the artistic community, had been appointed Protector,[222] and with good reason. From the very beginning Kaunitz became an active agent, pressing the interests of the academy with the Empress. In July 1767 he supported the lifting of an import duty for engravings from abroad.[223] In November 1769 he solicited a crown subsidy so that students could take trips into the countryside in order to draw landscapes, and at the same time secured an exemption from the usual duty for passing the city gates after 9:00 p.m. for academy students.[224] In August 1769 he attained permission for the students of the academy to copy the paintings of the imperial gallery, and succeeded in having the academy quarters enlarged.[225] A year later he issued "passports" to students, signed by him personally, so that they could move freely about the countryside and not be arrested as spies while drawing landscapes from nature.[226] Above all, Kaunitz was instrumental in securing the consent of the monarchs to expand the personnel of the academy. He was able to take on Joseph von Sonnenfels as permanent academic secretary in 1768,[227] and shortly after that was successful in securing a number of staff appointments. To meet enrollment pressures, Kaunitz proposed that the engraver Johann Friedrich Bause, a member of the Leipzig Academy of Art, be lured to Vienna by offering him twice his current salary.[228] Soon four more junior engravers were brought from the Paris workshop of the famous Johann Georg Wille, with whom Schmutzer had studied, and with whom Kaunitz had been in contact for some time.[229] At the same time, other artists, such as Franz Anton Maulbertsch, Josef Roos, and Johann Christian Brand, frustrated by the sterility of the Art Academy, became associated with the Copper Engraving Academy, until the latter became a serious rival for the former.[230] Enrollments also continued to rise, reaching 219 by 1770. It was small wonder, therefore, that the engraver Anton Domanök, who at Schmutzer's suggestion had been appointed to head up a new Crafts Academy (*Possier-*,

[222] AABK, Verwaltungsakten, Fasz. 1, Schmutzer to Maria Theresia, n.d. (1766).
[223] HHStA, Kabinettsarchiv: Staatsratakten, Karton 1, No. 1320, Kaunitz Staatsrat Votum, and imperial resolution, 8 July 1767.
[224] HHStA, Staatskanzlei: Vorträge, Karton 102, Kaunitz to Maria Theresia, 16 November 1769.
[225] AABK, Verwaltungsakten, Fasz. 1, Kaunitz to Maria Theresia, including imperial resolution, 18 August 1769. The copy of this Vortrag in the Foreign Ministry is dated 21 August. HHStA, Staatskanzlei: Vorträge, Karton 104.
[226] AABK, Verwaltungsakten, Fasz. 1, "Passport", 18 August 1770.
[227] HHStA, Staatskanzlei: Vorträge, Karton 102, Kaunitz to Maria Theresia, 16 November 1768.
[228] *Ibid.*, Karton 106, Kaunitz to Maria Theresia, 2 August 1770; AABK, Verwaltungsakten, Fasz. 1, Kaunitz to Maria Theresia, 15 August 1770.
[229] Georges Duplessis, ed., *Mémoires et Journal de J.-G. Wille*, 2 Vols. (Paris, 1857).
[230] Kroupa, "Václav Antonín Kaunitz-Rietberg a výtvarná umění," pp. 72–73.

Verschneid und Graveurakademie) in 1767, specifically requested in 1770 that Kaunitz be appointed "Protector" of his academy as well.[231]

The personal union, as it were, of these two academies under one head, and the almost simultaneous death of Meytens, led to the logical conclusion that efficiency dictated the unification of all three academies, not only under one "Protector", but into an integrated new Academy of Fine Arts. This is precisely what was proposed in May 1770 by the Abbé Johann Marcy, canon of Leitmeritz (Litomerice), and an honorary member of the Copper Engraving Academy. Marcy suggested his plan would convince the world that "the fine arts [were] on the throne" in Vienna, and added that "certainly no one is in a better condition to undertake and establish such a fine institute for our lands ... than Prince Kaunitz."[232] The assessment that Kaunitz was commanded to make of this proposal led to his comments on the value of art already quoted above. He went on to add that native genius needed properly guided study to be refined fully, and that it was now time to bring to their fruition all the promising starts in this sphere since the days of Leopold I. Kaunitz noted that the two academies under his protectorate were well-attended and vigorous, while the Art Academy had become "stale and feeble." Marcy's plan, he concluded, would help all three institutions, for the three academies often worked at cross-purposes, and unification would definitely be in the interests of efficiency. He therefore gave the plan his full support.

Kaunitz, however, did not stop there. He went on to suggest that the whole issue involved more than merely an improved constitution for the art academies. Marcy, Kaunitz said, had dealt only with the structure of the academies, not with the equally important question of "the extension and improvement of their curricula and good taste." He pointed out that there was an integral connection between the arts and the humanities, and that refinement of the former required cultivation of the latter. At a time when a systematic aesthetics was only beginning to be formulated by philosophers, Kaunitz already insisted that the teaching of art history, aesthetics and related humanities had to be an integral part of any art academy, and that there should be reciprocal co-operation between artists and scholars. To this end it was necessary to attract scholars, philosophers and art historians to the academy in Vienna, and to sponsor a journal through the academy so that works of Austrian artists could become known to the world. Kaunitz wanted to recruit famous men for this task, and suggested that someone like Winckelmann, who was by then already

---

[231] Wagner, *Geschichte der Akademie*, pp. 32–33. Otruba, *Wirtschaftspolitik*, p. 191.

[232] AABK, Verwaltungsakten, Fasz. 1, Marcy's original Entwurf, n.d. (probably April or May 1770) and subsequent "Réflexions sur le plan de Réunion des beaux arts," 26 June 1770. Cf. Wagner, *Geschichte der Akademie*, p. 37.

dead, would have been perfect.[233] The ideal for which Kaunitz aimed with this proposal was that of what Sonnenfels called "the urbane artist." This typically neo-classical Enlightenment ideal stressed the intellectual and moral autonomy of artists, their emancipation from traditional patrons, and their elevation to a whole new social status.[234]

In the subsequent months, Kaunitz had to reiterate this recommendation several times before the unification plan was accepted in principle. Even then, though Kaunitz was commissioned to draw up the statutes for the new academy, he was informed that for financial reasons actual implementation would have to wait for a "future better time."[235] By the end of 1771 Kaunitz was galvanized into further action when the former curator of the Liechtenstein art collection, Vincenz Fanti, submitted his own unification plan, proposing himself as head. Kaunitz would brook no rival, and in a report of 20 March he dismissed Fanti's proposals, reiterated his own and Marcy's, and asked for the resignation in his favour of the current "Protector" of the Art Academy, Count Adam Losy von Losymthal.[236] An additional opinion sought from the Austrian painter, Anton Maron, who was then in Rome, seconded Kaunitz's proposal,[237] and Kaunitz finally received his approval to begin the merger as well as his appointment as "Protector" of the Art Academy.[238] Kaunitz was officially proclaimed "Protector" of the Art Academy on 18 October, but long before then he displayed considerable impatience to get on with the task of uniting all three academies. On 23 May, for example, he cautioned the Empress that the longer she delayed the unification, the more complicated and costly it would be. Maria Theresia, however, had in the meantime called Maron to Vienna, and resolved not to do anything until he arrived, so that final approval was delayed until October 1772, almost two-and-a-half years after Kaunitz's first proposal. Finally, on 1 November he was able to issue a formal "Protectorate Decree" announcing the creation of the United Academy of Fine Arts. Early in the new year he instructed the academy members to elect an academic governing council, and on 19 December 1773 he promulgated the official statutes of the academy.[239]

[233] As fn. 209 above.
[234] Kroupa, "Václav Antonín Kaunitz-Rietberg a výtvarná umění," p. 74.
[235] AABK, Verwaltungsakten, Fasz. 1, Kaunitz to Maria Theresia, 15 August 1770, 24 March 1771 and 15 May 1771, including imperial resolution.
[236] *Ibid.*, Fanti to Maria Theresia, 15 February 1772; Kaunitz to Maria Theresia, 20 March 1772.
[237] AVA, Studienhofkommission: Wien, Akademie der Bildenden Künste, Fasz. 61, Maron to Maria Theresia, n.d. (1772).
[238] Maria Theresia to Kaunitz on report of 20 March (see fn. 236 above).
[239] AABK, Verwaltungsakten, Fasz. 2, Kaunitz to Maria Theresia, including imperial resolutions, 23 May 1772 and 27 October 1772; Protektorats-Decree, 1 November 1772 and 16 January 1773; AABK, Sitzungsprotokolle des akademischen Rates, Fasz. 1/B,

As with the Copper Engraving Academy, Kaunitz always took his role of "Protector" of the new united academy seriously, and never regarded it as a mere honorary post. He took an active interest in the hiring of academy personnel, closely supervised academic competitions and the distribution of prizes, used his influence to guarantee adequate funding for the institution as a whole as well as for various individual artists, carefully followed and commented perceptively on the internal administration of the academy – in short, demonstrated at all times an uncommonly enthusiastic support for the arts that, as Wagner has pointed out, went well beyond the economic motives many historians are wont to stress.[240] The leitmotif of this support continued to be the emancipation of the artist which his memorandum of 1770 had foreshadowed. At the suggestion of Sonnenfels, for example, Kaunitz undertook to help artists rid themselves of comparisons with artisans by recommending the abolition of the guild regulations to which they were still subject. Using the example of the Austrian Netherlands, where the pursuit of art was free from such regulation, Kaunitz convinced Joseph to enact similar legislation for the heartlands of the Monarchy.[241] He demonstrated considerable faith in native artists, and enthusiastically supported a plan to discover talented young artists by having drawings done at provincial intermediate schools submitted to the Academy twice a year.[242] He intervened decisively when the philistine hands of moralizing censors attempted to stifle free artistic expression.[243] He encouraged aspiring artists to refine their technique with exposure to the great masters and to the treasures of antiquity by initiating the imperial endowment of a number of scholarships of 600 Gulden each for study in Rome.[244] In a similar vein, lastly, he supervised the transfer and systematic rearrangement of the imperial art collection to the Belvedere palace where both students of the Academy and the general public were admitted free of charge.[245]

Kaunitz to academic council, 19 December 1773. The statutes were not actually published until 1800. Cf. Wagner, *Geschichte der Akademie*, pp. 40–45.

[240] AABK, Verwaltungsakten, Fasz. 2 and 3, *passim*, Kaunitz to Maria Theresia and Joseph, 1773–1780. For Kaunitz's activities in the internal business of the academy, see AABK, Sitzungsprotokolle des akademischen Rates, Fasz. 1/A–H, *passim*. Cf. Wagner, *Geschichte der Akademie*, pp. 44–54; and Burg, *Zauner*, pp. 18–23.

[241] Wagner, *Geschichte der Akademie*, pp. 48–49.

[242] AVA, Studienhofkommission: Wien, Akademie der Bildenden Künste, Fasz. 61, Kaunitz to Kollowrat, 14 December 1783.   [243] Burg, *Zauner*, pp. 18–19.

[244] Walter Wagner, "Die Rompensionäre der Wiener Akademie der bildenden Künste, 1772–1848: Nach den Quellen im Archiv der Akademie," *Römische Historische Mitteilungen* XIV (1972); Kroupa, "Václav Antonín Kaunitz-Rietberg a výtvarná umění," p. 73.

[245] HHStA, Familienarchiv: Sammelbände, Karton 70, Joseph to Kaunitz, 22 November 1780. Cf. Wangermann, "Maria Theresa," p. 303; Alfons Lhotsky, *Festschrift des Kunsthistorischen Museums zur Feier des Fünfzigjährigen Bestandes*, Section II: *Die*

Despite Kaunitz's most earnest wishes, his generally successful associations with the institutions devoted to the visual arts were not to be duplicated with the theater. In the 1740s Vienna had two main theaters: a court theater, still very much baroque and Italian in its tone and specializing in lavish ballets and *opera seria*, and a municipal theater specializing in popular comedies, farces and burlesques in the popular Viennese idiom. The former had originally been housed in the palace complex itself, while the latter was located near one of the main gates of the city wall, the Kärntnertor. By the 1740s the court theatre's productions were already outmoded, and in 1744 it was shut down and turned into a ballroom. Instead a house adjoining the palace was leased to an impresario who remodelled it into the new Court Theater (*Theater bei der Hofburg*), and shortly thereafter assumed the lease of the municipal theater as well. This gradually led to the blurring of the distinction and certainly of the audience segregation of the two. Both theaters were subject to bold theatrical reforms in the 1750s. The *Theater beim Kärntnertor* tried to move toward more serious German drama along the lines urged by Johann Christoph Gottsched, while the *Theater bei der Hofburg* moved from the world of the Italian baroque to classical French drama. French drama was all the rage with the younger generation to which Kaunitz belonged, and even before productions were officially mounted by the Court Theater, amateur performances in private palaces had been widespread. When the court assumed direct control of the theaters and appointed Giacomo Durazzo director of the Court Theater, French drama came into its own in Vienna, by all accounts flourishing at a very high standard. In 1754 Durazzo engaged the composer Christoph Willibald Gluck to write the musical numbers for many of the productions mounted, and by 1761, with the arrival of the librettist Raniero Calzabigi in Vienna, the great Gluck opera reform emerged, establishing a new pinnacle in the history of Western culture.[246]

These were all developments Kaunitz followed closely and patronized avidly. There is evidence that he personally secured numerous French plays for Vienna through his French ambassador. There is also evidence that he played an active role in engaging theater troupes and individual

Geschichte der Sammlungen, Part 2: *Von Maria Theresia bis zum Ende der Monarchie* (Vienna, 1941–1945), pp. 445–446.
[246] The literature on all these developments is enormous, but the standard histories are Zechmeister, *Die Wiener Theater* and Oscar Teuber, *Die Theater Wiens*, Vol. II, Part 1: *Das K. K. Hofburgtheater seit seiner Begründung* (Vienna, 1895). For the Gluck literature see Gerhard Croll and Winton Dean's article on Gluck in Stanley Sadie, ed., *The New Grove Dictionary of Music and Musicians*, 20 Vols. (London, Washington D.C. and Hong Kong, 1980), VII, 455–475. See also Chapter 1, fnn. 72–75.

actors and dancers. But despite his close friendship with Durazzo and Calzabigi, and despite his willingness to intervene as a protector on their behalf, as well as on behalf of other theatrical figures he valued, there is not sufficient evidence to substantiate the recent claim that Kaunitz was actually the unnamed overall supervisor of theater (*Directorial Praesident*) vaguely alluded to in some documents.[247] Theater was his life-blood, but he seemed to play no official role in its development. All this changed when both theaters closed for a period of official mourning after the death of Emperor Francis I. The *Theater beim Kärntnertor* opened after eight months, but on lease rather than under direct court administration. The Court Theater remained closed, and post-war fiscal constraints made the prospects of its reopening in the near future dim indeed. This was a great disappointment to its former patrons, so that pressure for the return of French theater began to mount. Kaunitz was in the vanguard of this lobby. He pleaded with the Empress and the emperor not only to re-open the *Theater bei der Hofburg*, but also to lend imperial patronage and generous subsidies to the various productions, in order, as he put it, to restore German and French drama and Italian *opera buffa* to a level "worthy of the court ... and of a public as distinguished as the one of this city."[248] These appeals led nowhere. It was only when the adventurer and impresario, Giuseppe d'Afflisio, took over the lease of the *Kärntnertor* theater, and offered to take over the direction of the Court Theater as well, that French drama returned to Vienna in 1768. There are indications that Kaunitz wished at this stage to assume some official role, and that he broached the subject with the Empress. Maria Theresia, however, was so suspicious of the putative immorality of the theater that she would hear nothing of it. Kaunitz made every effort to paint Afflisio in as respectable a garb as he could,[249] but while the Empress would consent to the re-opening of the Court Theater under Afflisio's control, she would not permit Kaunitz to assume any official post in these theatrical activities.[250]

Of course this did not stop Kaunitz from throwing himself into the theatrical mêlée in order to preserve the French stage in Vienna. He drafted the subscription notice himself,[251] personally contacted members of the high aristocracy in Vienna in an attempt to solicit subscriptions,[252] and

[247] For the argument that Kaunitz was the heretofore unidentified *Directorial Praesident* of the court theaters, see Zechmeister, *Die Wiener Theater*, pp. 36–37, 397.

[248] Teuber, *Die Theater Wiens*, p. 136; HHStA, Staatskanzlei: Interiora, Fasz. 108, Kaunitz to Joseph, 6 November 1767.

[249] *Ibid.*, Kaunitz to Maria Theresia, 8 August 1768.

[250] Arneth, *Maria Theresia* IX, 271–272; Teuber, pp. 137–149; Julia Witzenetz, *Le Théâtre Français de Vienne (1752–1772)* (Szeged, 1932), pp. 29–31.

[251] HHStA, Staatskanzlei: Interiora, Fasz. 108, Kaunitz draft, 8 August 1768.

[252] *Ibid.*, Kaunitz to Saxe-Hildburghausen, Kaunitz to Liechtenstein, 11 August 1768.

played a central role in securing first-rate actors and actresses.[253] Despite Kaunitz's best efforts, however, Afflisio was soon in financial difficulty and had to surrender his lease to the enthusiastic Hungarian magnate, János Koháry. At these signs of trouble Kaunitz only intensified his efforts to retain a suitably splendid French stage. He made a public appeal for a lottery designed specifically to rescue the theater,[254] and redoubled his efforts to find sufficient subscribers.[255] He supervised contracts Koháry signed with particular actors, and even helped actresses caught in compromising positions to avoid detection by the authorities.[256] In short, Kaunitz acted as the "Protector" of the Court Theater in all but name.[257] Finally, in July 1770, Kaunitz made one more attempt to transform his unofficial influence into an official position. He presented Koháry with a letter the impresario was to give to the Empress, requesting the formal appointment of Kaunitz as "Protector" of the two theaters in Vienna. Once again the plan foundered on Maria Theresia's sense of morality.[258]

Not long thereafter, Kaunitz's theatrical ambitions suffered a final setback. With the development of Austrian bourgeois culture, new theatrical directions were emerging. Above all, there was growing support, led by Joseph von Sonnenfels, for the new wave of reformed German drama. In August 1770 Sonnenfels published his famous "Report on New Directions in the Theater" in the name of Koháry, emphasizing the value of German bourgeois drama at the expense of classical French. Kaunitz was incensed, both at Koháry and at Sonnenfels. He charged Sonnenfels with attempting "maliciously to incite the public against foreign drama," and called the Report "a tissue of useless, malicious, and prejudiced things." He severely reprimanded Koháry for having taken this step without first consulting him, and threatened to withdraw his support completely.[259] But Sonnenfels represented the wave of the future in this dispute. Over the subsequent year the attendance at French plays continued to decline, and on 29 February 1772, the curtain fell for the last time on classical French drama in Vienna.[260] Kaunitz did not give up

---

[253] *Ibid.*, Kaunitz to Afflisio, 23 August 1768; Kaunitz to Mercy-Argenteau, 6 January 1769; Kaunitz to Orsini-Rosenberg, 6 February 1769; Kaunitz to various actors, Autumn 1769.

[254] *Ibid.*, Kaunitz, "Adresse au Public", n.d. (1769).

[255] *Ibid.*, Kaunitz subscription project, 10 October 1769. Cf. Witzenetz, pp. 37, 121–125.

[256] HHStA, Staatskanzlei: Interiora, Fasz. 108, Kaunitz to Koháry, 13, 16 and 17 July 1770.

[257] On these activities, cf. Teuber, pp. 151–164, and Anhang (Appendix), pp. viii–xviii; Zechmeister, *Die Wiener Theater*, pp. 71–84.

[258] HHStA, Staatskanzlei: Interiora, Fasz. 108, Koháry to Maria Theresia, letter dictated and edited by Kaunitz, 20 July 1770. Cf. Teuber, p. 161.

[259] *Ibid.*, Kaunitz to Koháry, 29 August 1770.

[260] Arneth, *Maria Theresia* IX, 274–275; Teuber, pp. 166–171; Witzenetz, *Le Théâtre Français*, pp. 39–47; Hilde Haider-Pregler, "Die Schaubühne als 'Sittenschule' der Nation: Joseph von Sonnenfels und das Theater," in Reinalter, ed., *Sonnenfels*, pp. 191–244.

without a struggle. He attempted to solicit the support of Maria Theresia and Joseph to lend their influence to a revival of French plays, and as late as 1775 he was still drafting projects designed to generate public support for such a revival.[261] He even went so far as to personally draft new theater designs in the hopes that this might attract patrons.[262] But it was all in vain. Joseph had thrown his support energetically behind Sonnenfels and the new wave. When Koháry, too, went bankrupt, Joseph transformed the Court Theater into the German National Theater (*Deutsches National-theater*), making it the center of reformed German drama. The court took over direction of the new theater, and the supreme management and direction went not to some eminent "Protector", but were assumed by Joseph himself.[263]

[261] HHStA, Staatskanzlei: Interiora, Fasz. 108, Kaunitz memoire, 10 February 1775.
[262] MZA, Rodinný archiv Kouniců, Carton 3, Kaunitz's "Dessein de lampions pour les Coulisses des Théâtres" and his "Dénombrement du nombre des places que peut donner la Salle de Spectacles, inventée par Mr. le Prince de Kaunitz-Rietberg en 1784."
[263] Arneth, *Maria Theresia* IX, 275–276; Teuber, pp. 172–202; Zechmeister, *Die Wiener Theater*, pp. 93–101. On Joseph's activities in this position see Rudolf Payer von Thurn, ed., *Joseph II, als Theaterdirektor* (Vienna, 1920).

6   Church and state

The implementation of the Counter-Reformation had decisively shaped the Habsburg Monarchy in the seventeenth century. Trentine Catholicism became in many ways the integrating ideology of the highly pluralistic patrimony of the Habsburgs, and this involved not merely a set of confessional dogmas, but broader patterns of thought and culture inextricably intertwined with a social and political infrastructure which had grown out of the economic and social upheavals of the late sixteenth and early seventeenth centuries. If there is some dispute on whether we may apply the term "confessional state" to this polity, there is little doubt that confessional issues set the predominant tone of the culture and of society, and that the Catholic Church emerged as an institution of enormous power and influence. It is therefore not surprising that when this polity proved unequal to its tasks in the highly competitive world of proto-national states in the first half of the eighteenth century, confessional issues and the role of the Catholic Church would be in many ways central problems for the Habsburgs. In the ensuing reforms the relations between Church and State were fundamentally altered. Because of the degree of integration between political and confessional issues in the Counter-Reformation state, however, these reforms were not effected in discrete confessional spheres, but had broad social, economic and political consequences.

This ecclesiastical reform momentum was to reach its high-point in the reign of Joseph II during the 1780s, and early analysts of the changes saw Joseph as the key figure in the process. As a result nineteenth-century historians coined the term "Josephinism" to describe the attack on the social, economic, political and cultural position of the Catholic Church in the Monarchy. Though we have now come to appreciate that the roots of the reform momentum go back to the early eighteenth century, and that the reign of Maria Theresia was the critical era during which reform ideas crystallized, the term "Josephinism" has continued to be applied. The precise meaning of the term has been the object of savage controversy – indeed, few debates in Central European historiography have been so protracted and so bitter as the ones over "Josephinism". The level of

rancor with which these debates have been conducted, however, does highlight the significance of the problems addressed: it points to the centricity of this phenomenon not only to an understanding of Habsburg enlightened absolutism, but to the entire evolution of Central European culture in the broadest sense of the word. If Carl Schorske can speak of the conflict and symbiosis of the "culture of grace" with the "culture of law" as both the leitmotif of *fin-de-siècle* Austria and the springboard of modernism in Western civilization,[1] we must recognize the genesis of this dialectic in the birth of "Josephinism".

Kaunitz and the rise of "Josephinism"

Many of the practical drawbacks of the time-honoured Counter-Reformation mentality had already been diagnosed at the height of the movement in the late seventeenth century, by the well-known trio of Austrian cameralists, Philipp Wilhelm von Hörnigk, Johann Joachim Becher and Wilhelm von Schröder. Hörnigk stressed that religious intolerance drove economically productive people out of the country, and hence retarded the development of industry. Becher focused on the divisive effects on society of a theologically combative priestly class, and pointed to the Church's possessions in mortmain, almsgiving, and excessive holy days, as "pernicious" to economic growth. Schröder posited the authority of the prince over the clergy and complained that the Church siphoned off too much of the country's wealth through stipends, pledges and other offerings, and then either exported or misused this capital.[2] These themes were taken up with increasing force by eighteenth-century cameralists such as Johann Heinrich Gottlob von Justi and Joseph von Sonnenfels, reaching their most focused culmination in the anonymous booklet which appeared in 1773 under the pseudonym Christian Friedrich Menschenfreund, *Untersuchung der Frage: Warum ist der Wohlstand der protestantischen Länder so gar viel grösser als der catholischen* (Examination of the Question: Why is the Prosperity of Protestant Countries so much Greater than that of Catholic Ones), which indicted the whole socio-economic, political, and theological position of the Counter-Reformation Church.[3]

---

[1] Carl E. Schorske, *Fin-de-siècle Vienna: Politics and Culture* (N.Y., 1980).

[2] Hörnigk, *Österreich über alles*, p. 103; Becher, *Politischer Diskurs*, pp. 326–423; Schröder, *Fürstliche Schatz- und Rentkammer*, pp. 122–191; Sommer, *Kameralisten* II, 490–498.

[3] Johann Heinrich Gottlob von Justi, *Grundsätze der Policey-Wissenschaft in einem vernünftigen, auf den Endzweck der Policey gegründeten Zusammenhange* (Göttingen, 1759), pp. 206–210; his *Natur und Wesen der Staaten als die Quelle aller Regierungswissenschaften und Gesetze* (Berlin, Stettin and Leipzig, 1760), pp. 458–460; Joseph von Sonnenfels, *Grundsätze der Policey-, Handlung- und Finanzwissenschaft*, Vol. I (Vienna,

This cameralist conviction that confessional policies were responsible
for the relative economic underdevelopment of the Habsburg lands did not
take long to make its way into the governing circles of the Monarchy. It
was reflected in the reform agendas of such well-known bureaucrats as the
secretary of the Central Treasury in Vienna, Christian Julius Schierl von
Schierendorff,[4] and found a ready ear in many forward-looking seigneurs
such as Kaunitz's father.[5] Such views were given momentum by a parallel,
and to some extent associated, development within the theological and
pastoral sphere of the Church itself. This was the general reaction against
ostentatious baroque display and piety, coupled with a retreat from some
of the theological positions and pastoral practices of the Counter-
Reformation. Sometimes called "Reform Catholicism" or the "Catholic
Enlightenment", it took many different forms on the European continent,
of which Jansenism and Gallicanism were the most prominent. Perhaps the
most influential of these ideas was the balanced and pragmatic reform
Catholicism of the famous Modenese provost, Lodovico Antonio Muratori, whose apologias for imperial claims in the War of the Spanish
Succession strengthened his rising popularity in Austria, while contributing
to the growth of anti-curial sentiment at the court.[6] As a consequence, the
Habsburg episcopate adopted what Hersche has called increasingly "philo-
Jansenist" views,[7] while Gallican, Jansenist and other Reform Catholic
ideas began to penetrate many religious orders. These reformers were
averse to most ritualized forms of baroque piety; explicitly rejected both
Molinism and Probabilism; had a strong distaste for Scholasticism and
neo-Scholasticism; and were generally suspicious of ultramontane policies,
usually disparagingly dismissed as the "curialism" of the "court of
Rome."[8]

1770), pp. 116–122; Christian Friedrich Menschenfreund, *Untersuchung der Frage:
Warum ist der Wohlstand der protestantischen Länder so gar viel grösser als der catholischen*
(Frankfurt and Leipzig, 1773).   [4] Fischel, "Schierendorff," pp. 211–293.
[5] Klingenstein, *Aufstieg des Hauses Kaunitz*, pp. 92–96.
[6] The extensive literature is best synthesized by Eleonore Zlabinger, *Lodovico Antonio
Muratori und Österreich* (Innsbruck, 1970); and Elisabeth Garms-Cornides, "Lodovico
Antonio Muratori und Österreich," *Römische Historische Mitteilungen* XIII (1971),
333–351.
[7] Peter Hersche, *Der Spätjansenismus in Österreich* (Vienna, 1977), pp. 50–64; Klingenstein,
Staatsverwaltung, pp. 85–87, 111–121.
[8] Ludwig von Pastor, *The History of the Popes of Rome from the Close of the Middle Ages*,
40 Vols. (London, 1923–1953), E. F. Peeler, trans., Vol. XXXV, pp. 369–391; Elisabeth
Kovács, *Ultramontanismus und Staatskirchentum im theresianisch-josephinischen Staat*
(Vienna, 1975), pp. 13–18, 33–37; Heinrich Benedikt, "Der Josephinismus vor Joseph II,"
in *Österreich und Europa: Festgabe für Hugo Hantsch zum 70. Geburtstag* (Graz, Vienna
and Cologne, 1965), pp. 183–201; Hans Wagner, "Der Einfluss von Gallikanismus und
Jansenismus auf die Kirche und Staat der Aufklärung in Österreich," *ÖGL* XI (1967),
521–523; Eduard Winter, *Der Josephinismus*, 1st ed. (Brno and Vienna, 1943), 2nd ed.
(Berlin, 1962); *idem.*, "Der Jansenismus in Böhmen und Mähren und seine Bedeutung

What brought the social, political and economic agenda of the cameralists and the diverse religious strands of reform Catholicism together was the dynasty. In their capacities as *defensor et advocatus ecclesiae*, the Habsburgs took their religious responsibilities as seriously as they did the preservation of their patrimony,[9] and, indeed, tended to see the two as obverse sides of the same coin. Of course, many lay reform-minded government officials felt drawn to the new religious ethos and many clerics were quick to endorse and support secular intrusions into religious preserves, but only for the dynasty did the two elements of reform have equal priority. Just as internal weakness and underdevelopment were graphically highlighted by crises in foreign affairs, culminating in the loss of Silesia, so the growing awareness of the limitations and inadequacies of baroque Counter-Reformation religiosity was highlighted early in the reign of Maria Theresia by a crisis that was equally shattering to the devout young queen – the discovery of substantial communities of "crypto-Protestants" in the Hereditary Provinces (especially Styria and Upper Austria). Despite the most sweeping and draconian powers given the Counter-Reformation establishment, it had manifestly failed in its primary task of eradicating heresy from these lands.[10] In Klingenstein's perceptive phrase, they "demonstrated a failure of the traditional social, political and religious controls at the local level."[11] In the face of this failure the crown initiated a policy of active intervention in the spheres which had so patently revealed their inadequacies: military organization, revenue collection and religious renewal.

It has not been customary to regard the remedial action undertaken in the military, political and economic spheres, in the form of the great Haugwitz reforms, as having a religious dimension. Certainly less attention has been lavished on the response to the religious crisis,[12] and the link

---

für die geistige Entwicklung Österreich-Ungarns," *Südostforschungen* VII (1942), 440–455.

[9] Elisabeth Kovács, "Beziehungen von Staat und Kirche im 18. Jahrhundert," in Zöllner and Möcker, eds., *Österreich*, pp. 29–30; Adam Wandruszka, "Maria Theresia und der österreichische Staatsgedanke," *MIÖG* LXXVI (1969), 174–188.

[10] On the Protestants of eighteenth-century Austria see W. R. Ward, "'An Awakened Christianity.' The Austrian Protestants and their Neighbours in the Eighteenth Century," *Journal of Ecclesiastical History* XL (1989), 53–73.

[11] Grete Klingenstein, "Skizze zur Geschichte der erbländischen Stände im aufgeklärten Absolutismus der Habsburger (etwa 1740 bis 1790)," in Peter Baumgart, ed., *Ständetum und Staatsbildung in Brandenburg-Preussen* (Berlin, 1983), p. 377.

[12] Rudolf Reinhardt, "Zur Kirchenreform in Österreich unter Maria Theresia," *Zeitschrift für Kirchengeschichte* LXXVII (1966), 105–119; Adam Wandruszka, "Geheimprotestantismus, Josephinismus und Volksliturgie in Österreich," *Zeitschrift für Kirchengeschichte* LXXVIII (1967), 94–101; Ferdinand Maass, *Der Frühjosephinismus* (Vienna and Munich, 1969); Klingenstein, *Staatsverwaltung*, pp. 164–184; Kovács, *Ultramontanismus*, pp. 13–18.

between the two has been virtually ignored.[13] For Haugwitz himself, who converted from Lutheranism to Catholicism in his early twenties, change of religion was not merely a matter of convenience and career opportunity, and it is hardly surprising that in his famous *Notata*, in which he first detailed his reform proposals, he would cite as one of his major premises the religious responsibilities of the sovereign.[14] In negotiating with Provincial Estates, he had a wide mandate to investigate problems within the Austro-Bohemian Church,[15] and in the reform of 1749 the supervision of religious matters and the regulation of clerical endowments was early made an integral part of the agenda of his Directory. That this consumed an enormous amount of time and energy – too much, indeed, for the already overburdened Directory – was conceded by Haugwitz himself in 1764,[16] and in all likelihood contributed to the creation in 1753 of the Directory's Court Commission on Religious Matters (*Hofkommission in Religionssachen*), chaired by Directory Vice-President, Bartenstein.[17] Before this unburdening of Haugwitz, however, his ministry had been in the very forefront of radical ecclesiastical reform.

The first signs of this escalation of the ecclesiastical reform pace came in 1750. Since 1716 the Habsburgs had been granted the right to levy a special tax on the Monarchy's clergy to help finance the upkeep of fortifications in Hungary. This privilege was granted by the pope for five-year terms, with the most recent "quinquennial" agreement coming into effect on 1 January 1748. Though the agreement was not scheduled to expire until the end of 1752, an effort to re-negotiate the terms for a "recess" of fifteen years was begun in 1750 and successfully concluded by March 1751.[18] At the same time a Directory brief of 26 May 1750 recommended undertaking negotiations with Rome to reduce the number of holy days in the ecclesiastical calendar, which was one of the standard desiderata of the cameralists. Here, too, the papacy proved co-operative, which resulted in the reduction of twenty-four holy days to half holy days by papal decree of 1 September 1751.[19] The Directory's next three proposals of 1751 went

---

[13] I first drew attention to this integral connection in "Intorno alle origini del giuseppinismo."   [14] *ÖZV* II/2, 130–152.   [15] Beer, "Staatsschulden," pp. 95–96.
[16] *ÖZV* II/1/i, 196, 201, 370.   [17] Reinhardt, "Kirchenreform," pp. 105–106.
[18] Mensi, Finanzen Österreichs, pp. 535, 657, 662; Maass, *Frühjosephinismus*, pp. 90–94; Dickson, *Finance and Government* II, 265–266.
[19] Arneth, *Maria Theresia* IV, 56–60; Guglia, *Maria Theresia*, II, 70–71. (Guglia, incidentally, refers to "massive" archival files from Haugwitz's Directory. Though most of these were lost in the *Justitzpalast* fire of 1927, a sense of the urgency with which Haugwitz pursued this goal can be gleaned from one of the few surviving Directory reports on the matter in HHStA, Österreichische Akten: Österreich-Staat, Fasz. 3, Haugwitz and Johann Chotek to Maria Theresia, 9 October 1753.) Ernst Tomek, *Kirchengeschichte Österreichs*, 3 Vols. (Innsbruck, Vienna and Munich, 1959) III, 224–225. On the problem of the reduction of holy days in general see Peter Hersche, "Wider 'Müssiggang' und 'Ausschweifung': Feiertage und ihre Reduktion im katholischen Europa, namentlich im

further still. Haugwitz had acknowledged an explicit intellectual debt to Schröder in his great administrative reforms of 1749, and it was Schröder's detestation of clerical (especially monastic) greed and wealth that his pupil now emulated. The first proposal was to limit the funds prospective monastic entrants could bring to an order to 1,500 Gulden or half the candidate's fortune, whichever was smaller. The second was a proposed decree to prevent all monasteries from receiving gifts, inheritances, or the like, without explicit state consent. The third proposed to raise the age at which a novice could take final monastic vows to twenty.[20] Before these three proposals could be forwarded to Rome, they ran into the determined opposition of Bartenstein. His initial critique of the Directory's proposals was that they risked "a public breach" with Rome, and that the general principles behind them revealed a dependence on "the teachings of non-Catholic legal theorists." While he acknowledged the crown's right to control clerical wealth, Bartenstein insisted that the Habsburg clergy already paid more than its just burden, and should therefore be left untouched.[21] A few weeks later he also addressed the issue of raising the age of final vows with similar arguments: the Council of Trent had already dealt with the problem exhaustively, he insisted, and opening that closed book would again only lead to an impossible conflict with Rome.[22]

Bartenstein's critique had the effect of slowing the momentum, but not of arresting it. On the issue of monastic acquisitions he was given the opportunity of drafting a more moderate proposal in which he proposed to limit the funds entrants could bring to their monasteries to 3,000 Gulden, while remaining conspicuously silent on other acquisitions.[23] Haugwitz and his Directory Vice-President, Johann Chotek, retorted with a savage rebuttal. The whole point of the plan had been to prevent the conversion of secular fortunes into mortmain ecclesiastical holdings. Since most monastic candidates came from families of middling or small fortunes, a ceiling of 3,000 Gulden in many cases subsumed their entire worldly goods. In short, the whole purpose of the reform would be defeated if Bartenstein's limit were accepted. After sarcastically pointing to Bartenstein's silence on the second issue of monastic acquisitions, the brief reiterated the arguments of 1751. Only firm action could "root the evil out of the ground." The clergy was very adept in circumventing vague legislation, and in achieving

---

deutschsprachigen Raum zwischen 1750 und 1800," *Innsbrucker Historische Studien* XII/XIII (1990), 97–122. "Half holy days" meant that attendance at mass was still obligatory, but that work was permitted on the second half of the day as on any other day.
[20] The original briefs have been lost, and their content must be inferred from records of the ensuing debates.
[21] HHStA, Staatskanzlei: Vorträge, Karton 73, Bartenstein to Maria Theresia, 11 December 1751.   [22] *Ibid.*, Bartenstein to Maria Theresia, 1 February 1752.
[23] *Ibid.*, Bartenstein draft patent, n.d. (October, 1753).

its "ultimate wishes through fraud ... or through all kinds of persuasion and intimidation," and any legislation limiting clerical wealth, no matter how modest, would invariably meet with an indignant outcry. "We therefore consider it better and more advisable," the report continued, "to arouse the outcry ... and achieve our whole objective, than to pass less effective legislation, which will in any case provoke the same complaints." Conscious of the potential complications, in short, Haugwitz's Directory nevertheless recommended a policy of overt confrontation with the Church.[24]

Neither position satisfied Maria Theresia, and she turned to another quarter for advice. By this time Uhlfeld and Bartenstein had both been removed from the Chancellery of State, where the new master since May 1753 was Kaunitz, to whom the entire file was now forwarded. Kaunitz had his protégé, Zinzendorf, prepare an elaborate study of French precedents in this matter, and in the meantime received yet another legislative proposal from the Directory. This time Haugwitz proposed to take action to eliminate abuses in "Titulature" – that is, the holding of benefices without corresponding functions or obligations. Kaunitz now recommended that all these issues be considered together at a special meeting of the Privy Conference.[25] This critical conference, held on 12 November 1753, was to determine the shape and direction of Habsburg ecclesiastical policies for more than a decade, and also marked the emergence of Kaunitz as the major voice in the process. As a result of these deliberations both Haugwitz and Bartenstein suffered setbacks to their policies.

Bartenstein's foreign policy anxieties set the tone of the meeting. The early years of the pontificate of Benedict XIV, which coincided with the War of the Austrian Succession, saw the papacy abandon its stance of strict neutrality in German affairs, and, in subtly backing Bavaria, caused the Habsburgs considerable difficulties.[26] The lessons learned from this experience seemed not to be lost on any member of the Conference. It was unanimously agreed that alienating the pope could do more harm than good, and that a confrontational policy should not be initiated. If this spelled defeat for Haugwitz, Bartenstein was to be no less disappointed. The Conference not only endorsed the premise of the Directory's original proposals, saying that these had "indisputably demonstrated" the crown

---

[24] *Ibid.*, Haugwitz and Chotek to Maria Theresia, 29 October 1753. Cf. Szabo, "Intorno alle origini del giuseppinismo," where I have quoted this report at greater length.

[25] HHStA, Staatskanzlei: Vorträge, Karton 73, Kaunitz to Maria Theresia, 2 November 1753.

[26] Rudolf Reinhardt, "Zur Reichskirchenpolitik Papst Benedikts XIV," *Römische Quartalschrift* LX (1965), 259–268; Tomek, *Kirchengeschichte* III, 221; Arneth, *Maria Theresia* IV, 51–55.

had a right to limit clerical acquisitions, but, thanks to Kaunitz and especially Zinzendorf, could now support the argument with precedents and examples from other countries as well. It therefore rejected Bartenstein's draft patent as ineffectual, and under the circumstances concluded it was imprudent to proceed at all in this direction for the moment. Finally, the conference recommended that all the other issues – specific clerical abuses, age of final monastic vows, and so on – be negotiated with Rome, nominating yet another Kaunitz protégé, Karl von Firmian, for the task.[27] These recommendations were enshrined as official policy guidelines with the now famous resolution of Maria Theresia: " *Placet*. The matter is to be tabled for now, but not forever."[28]

The *spiritus rector* of the new middle course was Kaunitz. The reform impetus was to continue, but only in co-operation with Rome and the Monarchy's reform-minded clergy. Haugwitz had been too assertive with his typical unrestrained passion; Bartenstein too timid and solicitous of the clerical establishment despite his Jansenist sympathies. The result was that Haugwitz was unburdened of most direct responsibilities for ecclesiastical affairs by the creation of an autonomous Court Commission for Religious Matters to be chaired by Bartenstein. But this commission, too, was often kept in the dark about vital negotiations with Rome, with a full overview shared only by the Empress and Kaunitz.[29] The new policy had both a diplomatic and domestic front, and both a statist and Reform Catholic face. Of these, the diplomatic offensive proved to be the less fruitful course, in part because of Kaunitz's continued moderation and caution, especially after the outbreak of the Seven Years War, in part because Benedict XIV was caught in a bitter curial crossfire in Rome. This latter problem became immediately apparent with the Firmian mission. Little progress was made on the issues under discussion. Though Benedict was generally sympathetic to Catholic reform, he confessed with astonishing candor to Firmian how his difficult position between reformers and conservatives in the Vatican virtually paralyzed him, and how even the debate about the reduction of holy days debate two years earlier had been a debilitating strain.[30] Before Firmian could report back, even more comprehensive reform

---

[27] HHStA, Staatskanzlei: Vorträge, Karton 73, Protocollum Conferentia, 12 November 1753.

[28] *Ibid.* imperial resolution, n.d. (November, 1753); cf. Maass, *Frühjosephinismus*, p. 25; Szabo, "Intorno alle origini del giuseppinismo," p. 167.

[29] Reinhardt, "Kirchenreform," pp. 105–106.

[30] Elisabeth Garms-Cornides, "Überlegung zu einer Karriere im Dienst Maria Theresias: Karl Graf Firmian (1716–1782)," in Plaschka and Klingenstein, eds., *Österreich im Europa der Aufklärung* I, 552–553. Cf. Enrico Dammig, *Il movimento giansenista a Roma nella seconda metà del secolo XVIII* (Vatican City, 1945); Fridolin Dörrer, "Römische Stimmen zum Frühjosephinismus," *MIÖG* LXIII (1955), 460–483.

proposals were being drafted in Vienna for presentation to Rome. These focused on the ongoing problem of "crypto-Protestantism", and the failure of traditional draconian Counter-Reformation methods to solve it. The new emphasis was on improved pastoral care, which was to be achieved by creating new parishes all over the Monarchy. To finance this ambitious project the government proposed a levy on the secular clergy, and the establishment of a central religious fund with this revenue. Once discreet feelers revealed that at least some quarters in Rome were receptive to the idea, Kaunitz selected the Provincial of the Austrian Barnabites, Pius Manzador, to undertake the detailed negotiations in the summer of 1756. The Manzador mission also proved fruitless, and was in any case overtaken by other events with the outbreak of the Seven Years War.[31] This was the last effort to undertake church reform with the amenable and responsive Benedict, who died within two years. His successor, Clement XIII, was an entirely different kettle of fish, and was soon to cause a dramatic intensification of Habsburg ecclesiastical reform which would resurrect the confrontational attitude advocated by Haugwitz.

In the meantime the domestic dimension of the reform process continued to gather momentum all through the 1750s, with cameralist statist ideas and reform Catholicism still working comfortably hand-in-glove. While Pope Benedict XIV could be relied upon to accept changes with benevolent passivity, no papal initiative could be expected. Under the circumstances the reform-minded episcopate of Austria looked to the state to carry its programme out, accepting even overt regalian intrusions into traditional clerical monopolies as both necessary and beneficial.[32] Hence such major reforms as the restructuring of higher education and the secularization of censorship, guided above all by the Empress's physician-in-ordinary, Gerard van Swieten, met with surprisingly little resistance; indeed, even with clerical support, led at this stage by Archbishop Migazzi himself. In the stricter religious sphere the clerical reformers could be counted on not only for support, but for determined initiatives of their own. This entailed a broad spectrum of change. It included the reorientation of the theological faculties of Habsburg universities and seminaries from Molinism, Probabilism and Scholasticism to Jansenist and other reform Catholic positions. At the popular level it embraced a whole range of measures, from purging peasant calendars of time-honoured superstitions, to a concerted attack on what were now called the "little devotional stupidities" (*Andächteleien*) of

[31] Reinhardt, "Kirchenreform," pp. 105–119; Maass, *Frühjosephinismus*, pp. 36–50; Franz A. J. Szabo, "Staatskanzler Fürst Kaunitz und die Anfänge des Josephinismus," in Plaschka and Klingenstein, eds., *Österreich im Europa der Aufklärung* I, 529–530.

[32] Karl Otmar von Aretin, "Der Josephinismus und das Problem des katholischen aufgeklärten Absolutismus," in Plaschka and Klingenstein, eds., *Österreich im Europa der Aufklärung* I, 513–514.

the baroque, a particularly favourite target being the Sacred Heart of Jesus devotions so dear to the Jesuits.[33]

The dramatic turn to an unbending conservative position that occurred in Rome with the death of Benedict XIV in the spring of 1758, and the accession of the Venetian Cardinal Carlo Rezzonico as Celement XIII, however, proved to be a major turning point. At first the new pope seemed to show some sensitivity to Habsburg needs,[34] but with the subsequent appointment of Cardinal Luigi Torrigiani to the sensitive papal Secretariat of State, things began to change. Pro-Jesuit and resolved to put an end to the Jansenist and Reform Catholic drift in Roman policy, he had little sympathy with the assertions of the modern secular state. What is more, with a physically feeble and intellectually pliable pope such as Clement, Torrigiani soon became the dominant personality of the entire pontificate.[35] It did not take long for Habsburg officials to feel the new wind emanating from Rome, and to experience first-hand the new inflexibility on even relatively minor matters.

Early in 1746 Maria Theresia had solicited an agreement from Benedict XIV to remove the province of Goricia from the jurisdiction of the Venetian episcopate of Aquileia, and to set up a new metropolitan there.[36] The new Bishop of Goricia, Karl Michael Attems, was an active reformer, and it was probably he who recommended, shortly after the outbreak of the Seven Years War, that his little bishopric be united with the larger and then vacant neighbouring one, Laibach (Ljubljana). Haugwitz's Directory supported Attems's idea, buttressing the administrative logic of such a unification with the economic argument that the combined incomes of the two bishoprics would yield surpluses which could be put to other practical uses. Maria Theresia approved the project and early in 1758 the Directory informed the Foreign Ministry, asking Kaunitz to initiate appropriate negotiations with Rome.[37] However, diplomatic feelers held out such little promise of success for the venture that Kaunitz, in accordance with his

[33] Arneth, *Maria Theresia* IX, 156–183; Guglia, *Maria Theresia* II, 74–91; Tomek, *Kirchengeschichte* III, 213–250; Klingenstein, *Staatsverwaltung*, pp. 158–202; Hersche, *Spätjansenismus*, pp. 50–70; Hersche, ed., *Der aufgeklärte Reformkatholizismus in Österreich: Hirtenbriefe 1752–1782* (Bern, 1976); Hersche, "Erzbischof Migazzi und die Anfänge der jansenistischen Bewegung in Wien," *MÖStA* XXIV (1971), Franz Wehrl, "Der 'Neue Geist'. Eine Untersuchung der Geistesrichtung des Klerus in Wien von 1750–1790," *MÖStA* XX (1967), 36–114; Kovács, *Ultramontanismus*, pp. 26–44; Hans Hollerweger, *Die Reform des Gottesdienstes zur Zeit des Josephinismus in Österreich* (Regensburg, 1976), pp. 49–66.

[34] Arneth, *Maria Theresia* X, 8–10; Pastor, *Popes* XXXV, 143–158, 194–195.

[35] Pastor, *Popes* XXXVI, 162–170; Wilhelm Baum, "Luigi Maria Torrigiani (1697–1777), Kardinalsekretär Papst Klemens XIII," *Zeitschrift für katholische Theologie* XCIV (1972), 46–78.   [36] Pastor, *Popes* XXXVI, 98–107.

[37] HHStA, Staatskanzlei: Notenwechsel, Karton 81, Directorium to Staatskanzlei, 14 January and 20 February 1758.

own guidelines of restraint in effect since 1753, recommended that the matter be dropped. But Haugwitz had lost none of his fire, and now showed that he had never been convinced entirely about Kaunitz's middle course in the first place. He persuaded the Empress to persist, and produced a draft missive to Rome that was so stinging that Kaunitz felt compelled to remind Maria Theresia of the agreed-upon policy of moderation. He, in turn, produced a milder counter-draft of his own, which requested only the temporary union of Goricia and Laibach for the duration of the war.[38] This limited request was granted by the pope[39] but it was totally unacceptable to the Directory. It protested at not having been consulted before such a step was taken, castigated Kaunitz for failing to achieve the essential government objective, and insisted that "stronger confrontations with the Roman court" were desirable.[40] Indeed, so inadequate was the Kaunitz compromise in the Directory's eyes, that Haugwitz persuaded the Empress to drop the whole matter without consulting Kaunitz further rather than to settle for paltry half-measures.[41]

This may reveal an unrepentant Haugwitz more than an inflexible papacy, but evidence of the latter trend soon accumulated. In the years between 1763 and 1764 disputes arose between Vienna and Rome over the issues of the negotiation of a concordat for the Grisons and episcopal appointments in Lombardy, in which Kaunitz's reaction at papal intransigence evolved from initial surprise to increasing exasperation and finally to outright indignation.[42] During these years, of course, papal relations with the Bourbon courts and with Portugal deteriorated even more rapidly,[43] and in Germany a strong episcopalian undercurrent simmering since the previous century burst dramatically to the surface with the publication, under the pseudonym of Justinus Febronius, of the strident *De statu ecclesiae et legitima potestate Romani Pontificis*. Written by the auxiliary bishop of Trier, Nikolaus von Hontheim, it urged the creation of a German national church under episcopal supervision, largely independent from Rome.[44] These developments outside Austria height-

---

[38] *Ibid.*, Vorträge, Karton 85, Kaunitz to Maria Theresia, 16 October 1759.
[39] *Ibid.*, Notenwechsel, Karton 4, Kaunitz to the Directorium, 3 January 1760.
[40] *Ibid.*, Karton 83, Directorium to Kaunitz, 14 January 1760.
[41] *Ibid.*, Directorium to Kaunitz, 9 February, 8 March and 29 March 1760. For fuller details on this whole episode, see Szabo, "Kaunitz und die Anfänge des Josephinismus," pp. 531–534.
[42] Ferdinand Maass, ed., *Der Josephinismus: Quellen zur Seiner Geschichte in Österreich*, 5 Vols. (Vienna, 1951–1961), I, 25–39, 109–222; Maass, ed., "Vorbereitung und Anfänge des Josephinismus," *MÖStA* I (1949), 321–378.
[43] Pastor, *Popes* XXXVI, 294–504; XXXVII, 1–361; Franco Venturi, *Settecento riformatore*, Vol. II: *La chiesa a la repubblica dentro i loro limiti* (Turin, 1976).
[44] Fritz Vigener, *Gallikanismus und episkopalistische Strömungen im deutschen Katholizismus zwischen Tridentium und Vaticanum* (Munich, 1913), pp. 27–35; Heribert Raab, "Der Reichskirchliche Episkopalismus von der Mitte des 17. bis zum Ende des 18. Jahr-

ened the tone of impatience within the Monarchy, and thereby accelerated the pace of change. At the same time the termination of the Seven Years War led to a renewed focus on domestic issues. The imperatives of economic recovery from that war further brought statist fiscal demands, which had been postponed for a decade for diplomatic reasons, to the surface again. So just as the papacy was beginning to take a harder line for ideological reasons, the state found itself required to make greater demands on the Church for socio-economic reasons. Under the circumstances, the conflict was bound to become sharper in these post-war years.

Even before the war was over, there were signs everywhere that the interim policy guidelines adopted after the momentous Privy Conference meeting of November 1753 would be re-assessed once it was over. As a result of the massive administrative reforms of 1760–1761 responsibility for ecclesiastical affairs was transferred to the new United Austro-Bohemian Chancellery. Detailed instructions drafted for this instance in 1761 explicitly envisioned expanded powers in this sphere over what had previously been exercised by the Directory. In particular they focused on the Chancellery's new duty "to secure princely rights and regalia" in this context.[45] What this entailed became obvious when the Directory, in the last year of its existence, returned to the question of the fifteen-year recess reached with Rome on the clerical fortification tax in 1751. The Directory had discovered that a papal bull dating from 1452 apparently gave the Habsburgs the right to collect such taxes without the prior agreement of Rome. On 7 August 1761 Maria Theresia commanded Johann Chotek to look into this, and also to investigate whether the tax rate could be raised as well. When these closer inspections could find no grounds for either unilateral action or a rate increase, the Empress, "having consulted numerous clerical and lay experts," concluded that appropriate archival evidence must exist and that it was merely a matter of finding it. Accordingly, the director of the Court Archives, Theodor Anton Rosenthal, was ordered to begin a systematic search of Viennese documents, while the Habsburg imperial ambassador at Mainz, Johann Anton Pergen, was asked to do the same in the archives of the Holy Roman Empire. By March 1762 both had produced thoroughly satisfactory reports. Numerous agreements with the papacy in the first half of the fifteenth century confirmed that the Habsburgs had the right to impose ordinary and extraordinary taxes on its clergy without requiring any kind of prior papal

hunderts," in Hubert Jedin, ed., *Handbuch der Kirchengeschichte*, Vol. V: *Die Kirche im Zeitalter des Absolutismus und der Aufklärung* (Freiburg, 1970), pp. 477–507; V. Pitzer, *Justinus Febronius* (Göttingen, 1976).   [45] *ÖZV* II/1/i, 319.

consent.[46] Within this political, administrative and legal framework post-war ecclesiastical reform became very predictable indeed. As the Empress concluded: "The clergy is without any question as responsible as the lay sector to bear the burdens of the war, and ... in one way or another to assume its proportionate onus."[47]

Accordingly, a number of interesting trends began to emerge in the period from 1763 to 1768. As fiscal pressures mounted, an increasing number of bureaucrats began to regard the Church as the goose whose infinite supply of golden eggs was the panacea for the economic ills of the state.[48] As conservative positions hardened in Rome the ensuing theological polarization had two effects in the Habsburg Monarchy. On the one hand a number of reform-minded bishops, led by Migazzi of Vienna, took fright and returned to more orthodox views. On the other hand the different strains of moderate Reform Catholicism were being increasingly subsumed and absorbed by a growingly strident Jansenism, which reached its high point during this decade.[49] The cameralist and Jansenist reform impulses therefore both quickened at the same time. These tendencies were all reflected within the dynasty itself. In 1765 Emperor Francis Stephen died, and in her grief his widow gave herself ever more to world-renouncing Jansenist pieties. Jesuit confessors gave way to Jansenist ones in the imperial household, and church ceremonials were reduced from their former baroque splendor to an ascetic minimum.[50] At the same time the young and impatient new emperor and co-regent, Joseph II, produced a major reform memorandum which reiterated in the strongest terms the anti-monastic legislation demanded by the also recently deceased Haugwitz in 1751–1753.[51]

It appeared as if the time had come to abandon the relative forbearance in ecclesiastical matters which had been in effect since November 1753. At the end of 1764 Maria Theresia inquired anxiously of Kaunitz if it was yet "proper and timely" to begin making further demands on Rome.[52] But Kaunitz, in turn, gave no indication that he was ready to abandon the moderate middle course he had been steering for over a decade. He took the optimistic view that the curia would be clever enough to make a virtue

---

[46] Maass, *Frühjosephinismus*, pp. 51–75; Bernard, *From the Enlightenment to the Police State*, pp. 66–67.   [47] Maass, *Frühjosephinismus*, pp. 89–90.

[48] Szabo, "Intorno alle origini del giuseppinismo," pp. 167–168.

[49] Kovács, "Beziehungen von Staat und Kirche," pp. 47–48; Hersche, *Spätjansenismus*, pp. 379–380.

[50] Peter Hersche, "War Maria Theresia eine Jansenistin?" *ÖGL* XV (1971), 14–25; Hersche, *Spätjansenismus*, pp. 148–162; Elisabeth Kovács, "Kirchliches Zeremoniell am Wiener Hof des 18. Jahrhunderts im Wandel von Mentalität und Gesellschaft," *MÖStA* XXXII (1979), 131–137.   [51] *MTJC* III, 348–352.

[52] HHStA, Staatskanzlei: Vorträge, Karton 94, Maria Theresia to Kaunitz, 4 December 1764.

out of necessity, and to endorse what it could not change anyway in order
to retain its political influence. He therefore remained confident that results
could be achieved through co-operation, and he remained convinced that
a moderate tone would reap the best rewards.[53] Kaunitz continued to
advise restraint on Vienna's part despite growing signs of papal intransigence. He responded to Joseph's demand for draconian anti-
monastic legislation with precautionary advice not to proceed with plans
to reduce monastic orders or raise the age limit for final vows.[54] In
February 1767 Kaunitz opposed the imposition of an inheritance tax on
clerical establishments, regarding it as unwise.[55] Shortly thereafter diplomatic feelers indicated that at the expiry of the fifteen-year recess on the
clerical tax for Hungarian fortifications which had been concluded in 1751,
a new fifteen-year agreement would meet with stiff resistance in Rome.[56]
Accordingly Kaunitz advised dropping the whole matter.[57] When Stupan
took a strident position against monastic orders, religious processions and
pilgrimages in the Council of State, Kaunitz again cautioned that "to
attack such matters directly would cause more harm than good, and make
for unpleasant appearances."[58] Indeed, so restrained was Kaunitz's tone
and policy, that when he advised against pressing statist assertions in a
dispute with the Court of Appeal of the Papal Nuncio in Lucerne, whose
jurisdiction included Hither Austria, he earned a bitter rebuke from the
Austro-Bohemian Chancellery. Its councillor for ecclesiastical matters
asserted that papal claims were based on the notorious medieval forgery,
the Isidorean Decretals, and therefore did not bind the state. He concluded
by sternly reminding Kaunitz: "To give way in the very least in this matter
would be as good as declaring that *the clergy are not subjects* [of the
Monarchy], a fundamentally erroneous and dangerous notion which can
never be conceded without upsetting the entire structure of the state."[59]

If Kaunitz expected such forbearance to yield results in the court of
Clement XIII, he was to be sorely disappointed. In the Duchy of Milan,
which was directly administered by the Foreign Ministry, Kaunitz began a
systematic overhaul of the ecclesiastical *status quo* which largely followed
in the footsteps of prior policies and assumptions manifest in Austria
proper for over a decade. In February 1766 all Church lands in Milan
acquired since 1716 were subjected to the same taxes as lay properties. On
3 August 1767 a special government department to supervise ecclesiastical

[53] Maass, ed., "Vorbereitung," p. 380.
[54] Beer, ed., "Denkschriften des Fürsten Kaunitz," pp. 107–109.
[55] HHStA, Kabinettsarchiv: Kaunitz Voten, Karton 1, Kaunitz Staatsrat Votum, 20
February 1767.   [56] Maass, *Frühjosephinismus*, pp. 101–104.
[57] HHStA, Kabinettsarchiv: Kaunitz Voten, Karton 1, Kaunitz Staatsrat Votum, 29 May
1767.   [58] *Ibid.*, Kaunitz Staatsrat Votum, 31 August 1767.
[59] Maass, ed., *Josephinismus* I, 58–63, 230–235, 248–252; original italics.

affairs – the so-called *Giunta economale* (Stewardship Council) – was set up, and a series of reforms ensued which included statist incursions into ecclesiastical mortmain laws, the subjection of papal bulls and other ecclesiastical communications to a state imprimatur, and the substitution of a secular censorship board for the old ecclesiastical one. None of these measures were as radical or innovative as clerical critics have suggested, but all met with bitter resistance from Rome. This papal reaction, in turn, contributed to the radicalization not only of Kaunitz but of the whole Habsburg government.[60]

By January 1768 Kaunitz had reached the point where he was prepared to recommend abandoning the policy of co-operation with the papacy and implementing ecclesiastical reform unilaterally. As yet, the precise proposals remained moderate, stressing mainly the improvement of ecclesiastical discipline, the further limitation of holy days, and the conversion of fasting obligations into other, more productive forms of good works. The initial draft of this report had toyed with more radical thoughts, such as making common cause with the Bourbon courts of Europe in the Jesuit question and demanding the complete abolition of the Order, as well as cynically diverting clerical revenues to high-profile, worthy secular causes in order "to make a good impression". But the final report dropped these ideas in the interest of maintaining a consistently moderate tone. In the event, the most significant feature of Kaunitz's proposal was the suggestion that an appropriate administrative mechanism be set up so that unilateral reform could be effected systematically. He suggested that a specially constituted commission made up of "honest bishops or prelates" and some suitable laymen should be formed to work out detailed reform proposals, and that these, in turn, should then be submitted to the Council of State for debate.[61] The discussions on the implementation of this structural mechanism became an integral part of the larger debates on the administrative reforms of 1768,[62] and, as such, was not implemented until 1769, but the decision in principle to proceed unilaterally now came with unexpected speed.

The event which crystallized the evolution of Josephinism in Habsburg government circles was the excommunication of Maria Theresia's prospective son-in-law, Duke Ferdinand of Parma, on 30 January 1768.[63]

---

[60] For the critical view, Maass, ed., "Vorbereitung," pp. 368–416; Anton Ellemunter, *Antonio Eugenio Visconti und die Anfänge des Josephinismus* (Graz and Cologne, 1963), pp. 41–60. For a more balanced modern analysis, Capra, "Il settecento," pp. 380–391.
[61] HHStA, Staatskanzlei: Vorträge, Karton 101, Kaunitz to Maria Theresia, 25 January 1768. Cf., Maass, *Josephinismus* I, 256–257.   [62] See above, pp. 101–105.
[63] Pastor, *Popes* XXXVIII, 230–236; Arneth, *Maria Theresia* IX, 19–23; Maass, *Josephinismus* I, 74–80, 267–285; Venturi, *Settecento riformatore* II, 214–236; Giovanni Gonzi,

Torrigiani's logic, undoubtedly, was to confront the tide of anti-clerical legislation, highlighted by the expulsion of the Jesuits from the various Bourbon courts, by making an example of the least powerful of them. However, the stratagem backfired. Not only did the Bourbon courts adopt a common front in defiance, the excommunication also persuaded Austrian statesmen that the papal action, in the words of Uhlfeld, neatly summarized all outstanding problems in a nutshell, and articulated principles "which cannot be permitted by any Catholic prince." Kaunitz, too, was caught up in the momentum. He now advocated making common cause with the Bourbon courts. He lambasted the secular power of the papacy, asserting that once the Church had been put into a position of political power by Constantine, it merely pursued self-serving ends until it thus caused the Reformation and tore Christianity asunder. Although some popes had since been more sensible, Torrigiani's "exorbitant presumptions" threatened to revive the worst abuses of the Middle Ages, and lead to the practice of excommunicating all monarchs who issued legislation similar to that of the Duke of Parma. "The court of Rome must be convinced once and for all that, except for matters of faith, this is no longer the time for it to dictate laws to temporal princes."[64] But the Bourbon courts did not wait for Austria, and proceeded with such radical steps – France seized Avignon and Naples Benvenuto – that Kaunitz advised backing off again.[65] The crisis came to an end when the Bourbon princes gave way in the reign of the next pope, Ferdinand of Parma ironically becoming one of the greatest apologists for the Jesuits by the 1790s.[66]

Just how much these events changed attitudes in Vienna becomes evident from other confrontations with Rome that came to a head at the same time as the Parma excommunication crisis. In 1630 Emperor Ferdinand II, in return for papal renunciation of Church estates alienated in the previous two centuries, had granted the Congregation of the *Propaganda Fide* an excise from salt monopoly revenues (*cassa salis*) to use for ecclesiastical purposes in the Kingdom of Bohemia.[67] The collection and distribution of these funds proceeded without incident until the early 1760s when the Austro-Bohemian Chancellery, under war-time economic pressures, began to demand the right to prescribe how the *cassa salis* funds ought to be spent. By 1766 the Chancellery persuaded the Empress to suspend payment of the excise to the *Propaganda Fide* in an attempt to channel it into areas determined by the Austrian government. In February

"L'espulsione dei gesuite dai ducati parmensi," *Aurea Parma* LV (1966), 154–194, LVI (1967), 3–62.   [64] Maass, *Josephinismus* I, 267–277.
[65] HHStA, Familienarchiv: Sammelbände, Karton 70, Joseph to Kaunitz, 11 July 1768.
[66] Pastor, *Popes* XXXVIII, *passim*; XXXIX, 156, 319–321.
[67] Hynek Kollmann, "O vlivu Propagandy na vznik tak řečené pokladny solní (cassa salis)," *Časopis Muzea Království Českého* LXXII (1898), 139–157.

and March 1768 the matter was debated in the Council of State. Kaunitz advised that the papal case be conceded in principle but not in practice. The rights conferred by Ferdinand II should be recognized, but the worthy religious causes on which the money was to be spent had to be chosen from a list submitted by the Habsburg court. Distributing funds to chapters and monasteries that did not meet with imperial approval would compel Vienna to tax these very ecclesiastical institutions: in the first year the exact amount doled out to them, in the second year double that amount, in the third triple, and so forth.[68] This plan, which amounted to virtual extortion, was adopted and eventually had the desired effect,[69] though it is worth noting that even Kaunitz's face-saving device of granting Rome's case in theory met with such strong objections from the Austro-Bohemian Chancellery that a second Council of State debate became necessary in April of that same year.[70] Similarly, Maria Theresia, who had originally accepted Kaunitz's advice not to press for a fifteen-year recess on the Hungarian fortifications tax,[71] reversed her position at the behest of the Treasury, which also had succeeded in breaking down Kaunitz's resistance. The "court of Rome" was to be given more time to accede to her demands, the Empress ordered. But if it did not, no further negotiations were to be initiated. "I am resolved," she wrote, "to avail myself of my due rights, and to proceed on my own authority in this case."[72] Summing up these developments in a letter to his brother in March 1768, Joseph II asserted that the present pope and his "violent" Secretary of State threatened to revive the worst kind of papal abuses, and had revealed "a nearly insupportable spirit of chicanery and stubbornness." It had all been borne with patience, Joseph wrote, but not without learning the lesson that the time for negotiations was past, and that the only way to deal with the court of Rome was to present it with *faits accomplis*.[73]

The determination to proceed unilaterally in the realm of ecclesiastical reform and the determined opposition of Rome to the general drift of Habsburg reform policy entailed the formulation of new strategies. Most significant among these, as Wangermann has pointed out, was the development of a systematic *thèse royale*, which would provide the theoretical justification for this new path.[74] Rosenthal and Pergen had

[68] HHStA, Kabinettsarchiv: Kaunitz Voten, Karton 1, Kaunitz Staatsrat Votum, 25 March 1768.
[69] *Ibid.*, Staatsratprotokolle, Vol. 27, No. 126, imperial resolution, 2 April 1768. Cf. Arneth, *Maria Theresia* IX, 79–80, 561–563; Maass, *Josephinismus* I, 81–84.
[70] HHStA, Kabinettsarchiv: Staatsratprotokolle, Vol. 27, No. 953, Staatsrat Protokoll, 21 April 1768.   [71] *Ibid.*, Vol. 25, No. 1002, imperial resolution, 3 June 1767.
[72] Maass, *Josephinismus* I, 264–266.   [73] Arneth, *Maria Theresia* IX, 550–551.
[74] Ernst Wangermann, "Josephinismus und katholischer Glaube," in Elisabeth Kovács, ed., *Katholische Aufklärung und Josephinismus* (Vienna, 1979), pp. 334–335.

already laid the groundwork with their archival researches, and the Court Librarian, Adám Kollár, showed the way when, just prior to a meeting of the Hungarian Diet, he published on his own initiative a polemical defence of the royal prerogative in ecclesiastical matters, focusing on the sovereign's right of presentation, taxation, and the like in the Kingdom of Hungary.[75] At approximately the same time the renowned professor of canon law at the University of Vienna, Paul Joseph Riegger, was commissioned to begin his massive treatise, *Institutiones iurisprudentiae ecclesiasticae*, the first part of which appeared in 1765.[76] Similarly, on 10 May 1768, on the advice of Gerard van Swieten, Franz Joseph von Heinke, the Austro-Bohemian Chancellery's new expert on ecclesiastical matters, was formally commissioned to work out "a fundamental system" clarifying the respective spheres of competence of Church and state which could serve as a guideline for unilateral action.[77]

Kaunitz, too, set to work drafting a detailed policy guideline for the Milanese *Giunta economale*. In this document he delineated what he considered the legitimate rights of the Church and the state. These were quite unequivocal: "Everything which was not divinely instituted as a specific competence of the clergy, is subject to the supreme legislative and executive power of the sovereign." Only that was recognized as divinely instituted which "Christ himself transmitted to his apostles," namely, preaching, dogma, divine service, administration of the sacraments, and the maintenance of church discipline. Beyond this the clergy enjoyed no rights without the consent of the sovereign, and therefore it remained the prerogative of that sovereign to alter or recall any privileges or rights that may at one time have been granted. The same held true for the decisions of all councils and canons that did not concern themselves with purely spiritual matters.[78] These premises justified unilateral action by the state in a variety of spheres, and the Empress therefore resolved to make them a universal proscription. After receiving royal endorsement on 15 June 1768, Kaunitz was instructed to distribute French copies of the document to all ministries and governmental departments in the Monarchy as "Principles established by Her Majesty the Empress and Apostolic Queen to serve as a guide to all Her tribunals and magistrates in ecclesiastical matters."[79] In

---

[75] Kollár was widely assumed to have been "inspired" by court circles in his research, and his work strikingly complemented that of Rosenthal and Pergen. At the suggestion of R. J. W. Evans I searched for evidence for such a connection, but was unable to find any. That Kaunitz was caught off guard by Kollár's book, finding its sentiments laudable but its publication timing inopportune, would weigh against any thesis for official inspiration. Cf. below, p. 321.

[76] Eckhart Seifert, *Paul Joseph Riegger (1705–1775)* (Berlin, 1973), pp. 126–221; for a full analysis of the *Institutiones*, pp. 231–350.

[77] Maass, *Josephinismus* III, 10, and *passim*. Cf. Wolfsgruber, *Migazzi*, pp. 269–282.

[78] Maass, *Josephinismus* I, 288–290.   [79] *Ibid.*, 322–323.

the meantime Kaunitz had instructed his Italian councillor, Joseph von Sperges, to prepare a suitable explanation for the pope of the principles which underlay Habsburg ecclesiastical policies, which was dispatched on 25 June, only days after Maria Theresia had sanctioned the abolition of ecclesiastical censorship in Milan.[80]

Further signs of the determination to proceed unilaterally also came to a head at the same time. The Greek Orthodox Ukrainian clergy in the sub-Carpathian region of north-eastern Hungary had been lured to union with Rome in the mid-seventeenth century, but the Uniate diocese of Munkacz (Munkachiv, Munkachevo) established at that time remained subordinate to the Catholic Archbishop of Esztergom (Gran). After many years of energetic lobbying by the Ukrainian bishop, Mykhailo Ol'shavskyi, to win greater autonomy for his episcopate, his conservative ultramontane superior, Bishop Károly Esterházy of Esztergom, went in the opposite direction. In May 1763 he issued a pastoral letter demoting Ol'shavskyi to a mere vicar-general for the Uniate faithful of his diocese. The aged Ol'shavskyi left the struggle to his assistant, Ivan Bradach, who carried it on with a direct appeal to the crown. This appeal won the support of the Hungarian Chancellery which feared the twin dangers of possible schism and large-scale Ukrainian emigration, and which accordingly proposed complete independence for the Greek Catholic eparchy centered on Munkacz. Esterházy won the papal nuncio and the curia to his side with a flood of memoranda, but Bradach convinced Maria Theresia, who now proposed to raise him to auxiliary bishop of Munkacz. Despite clear negative signals from Rome, which was prepared to accord Bradach only the title of Apostolic Vicar for the Greek Catholic faithful of the area, the Hungarian Chancellery persisted.[81] It asserted that, under the Hungarian constitution, it was the clear-cut right of the Apostolic King of Hungary to create new bishoprics, with the papacy retaining no rights but those of confirmation. Papal protests were transmitted to the Chancellery without comment by Kaunitz, and it, in turn, remained so deaf to all objections that initial organization was undertaken without permission from Rome. Accordingly, on 3 June 1768, Kaunitz had a rebuttal of the papal objections prepared for the nuncio, reaffirming the Hungarian Chancellery's arguments, but very clearly only to justify a *fait accompli* rather than to initiate a negotiation. "I agree completely," Maria Theresia replied, and

[80] *Ibid.*, 299–302, 306–309.
[81] Basilius Pekar, *De Erectione Canonica Eparchiae Munkacoviensis* (Rome, 1965), pp. 57–97; Eduard Winter, "Die Kämpfe der Ukrainer Oberungarns um eine nationale Hierarchie im theresianischen Zeitalter," *Kyrios* IV (1939–1940), 129–141; Basil Boysak, *The Fate of the Holy Union in Carpatho-Ukraine* (Toronto and N.Y., 1963), pp. 74–76; Boysak, *Ecumenism and Manuel Michael Olshavsky, Bishop of Munkachevo (1743–1767)* (Montreal, 1967), pp. 2–10.

asked Kaunitz to have the appropriate Latin notes prepared.[82] In submitting these four days later, Kaunitz recommended that the Empress accede to the recommendations of the Hungarian Chancellery with a clear resolution endorsing its unilateral action, which was also accepted without further ado.[83]

With this flood of statist assertions, the papacy geared itself for the counter-attack. In June the nuncio, Visconti, began by lodging a formal protest with Kaunitz about the way papal objections to the jurisdictional quarrel in Hither Austria had been dismissed. When Kaunitz rejected this protest with an air of finality, emphasizing the new principles that were governing Habsburg ecclesiastical policies,[84] it became clear to the Vatican that any hope of recovering lost ground could come only by successfully undermining these new principles and not by a piecemeal attack on specific problems. Clement XIII took the momentous step on 22 August 1768. In a personal appeal to the piety of Maria Theresia, he urged her not to accept false statist premises, asked her to protect her lands from the new principles of which Kaunitz had informed Rome, and begged her to consult her conscience and not her political advisers in this serious matter.[85]

If Kaunitz had been the only obstacle in the pope's way, the appeal might have succeeded, but this was not the case. By the summer of 1768 the decision to proceed unilaterally enjoyed a wide consensus in Habsburg governing circles. Heinke had already submitted his preliminary report on behalf of the Austro-Bohemian Chancellery, and the conviction, once expressed by Königsegg, that the only way to deal with Rome was "with bribes or bludgeons" (con denari o con bastoni),[86] was now widespread. The pope's personal appeal to Maria Theresia was therefore passed straight on to Kaunitz for comment. He noted that the papal rejection of the principles the Empress had expressly underscored made it appear as if she had not given the matter proper thought, and had allowed herself to be swayed excessively by her minister. This notion had to be rejected emphatically. He therefore undertook to draft a point-by-point rebuttal, promising to send this to her as soon as possible. The Empress agreed to delay the audience with Visconti until then, and in the event respond in the way Kaunitz would suggest.[87] Clearly the irrevocable decision had been made; only its implementation remained.

[82] HHStA, Staatskanzlei: Vorträge, Karton 101, Kaunitz to Maria Theresia, Maria Theresia to Kaunitz, 3 June 1768.
[83] Ibid., Kaunitz to Maria Theresia, Maria Theresia to Kaunitz, 7 June 1768.
[84] Maass, Josephinismus I, 313–316.   [85] Ibid., 319–322.
[86] Maass, Frühjosephinismus, p. 94.   [87] Maass, Josephinismus I, 323–324.

Dismantling the confessional state

Drawing up the theoretical framework of unilateral action was in the first instance the task of Heinke, the Austro-Bohemian Chancellery's specialist on ecclesiastical matters. Following his formal commission in May, Heinke was ready with a preliminary report early in June, which was immediately circulated in the Council of State beginning with Binder on the twelfth. Heinke's argument for the separation of Church and state leaned heavily on Jansenist writings which stressed the exemplary purity of the patristic Church, and which argued that religious purity reached its optimum when uncorrupted by worldly matters and worldly concerns. If the papacy did not understand the full implications of this, Heinke argued, the duty devolved on the sovereign "to come to the aid of the declining condition of the holy religion" by specifically prescribing the legitimate spheres of Church and state.[88] There was little novel in this argument, as Binder pointed out, and most Council of State members, including Kaunitz, urged that Heinke proceed to the final report with all due alacrity.[89] But just how satisfied Kaunitz actually was with this preliminary report remains open to question. While Heinke compiled his voluminous and scholarly final report during the fall of 1768, Kaunitz also set to work on what was probably intended to be an anonymous publication, entitled *Concerning the Sovereign Power of Roman Catholic Princes with regard to the Religion and the Clergy* (*Von der oberherrlichen Gewalt der römisch-katholischen Fürsten in Bezug auf die Religion und die Clerisey*). Both were completed early in 1769.

Of the two, Heinke's final report, "On the reorganization of the relationship of Church and State in Austria", was the more scholarly in form and theological in content. He expanded on the argument made in his preliminary report with extensive quotations from scripture and canon law, elaborate and intricate citations of historical precedents, and widespread references to leading authorities such as Samuel Puffendorf and Hugo Grotius. The Jansenist strain was even more strongly articulated than in the preliminary report, with many of the principal ideas being modelled quite explicitly on the Jansenist Church of Utrecht.[90] Hersche has suggested that much of Heinke's theological argumentation was mere rationalization, and that his principal concern was to establish the theoretical framework for political action,[91] but even the recourse to mere Jansenist rationalizations was not to be without its significance. In this way the reform Catholic momentum was to be engaged in this new phase of Josephinism, and its alliance with the cameralist-inspired secular reformers

---

[88] *Ibid.*, III, 141–154.   [89] *Ibid.*, I, 310–313.   [90] *Ibid.*, III, 154–207, and *passim*.
[91] Hersche, *Spätjansenismus*, pp. 224–225.

maintained. That this was to be no simple matter becomes clear when we turn to Kaunitz's essay.

Kaunitz explicitly set out to write a popular pamphlet which could "be read by everyone", and he was determined not to be prolix or to have recourse to "loathsome quotations". He refused to engage in the theological exercise of citing canon laws or patristic authorities, and sought to make a purely secular argument focused on a clear definition of the sovereign power of the state. The state was not only entitled to but was responsible for the supervision of everyone who held any office in that state. Since the clergy's execution of its apostolic office determined to a large degree the fundamental attitudes of the citizens of the state, the state's supervisory power extended to that "profession" as well. It therefore followed that the notion of an autonomous clergy within the state was a myth, and that any claims on the part of the Church which conflicted with the imperatives of the state were invalid. In practice this entailed the exclusive right on the part of the state of conferring benefices and of preventing pluralism. It forbade episcopal recourse to courts of appeal outside the state, and rendered the Church's right to grant asylum invalid. It meant that ecclesiastical participation in book censorship was exercised solely at the pleasure of the state. It meant that separate schools for the clergy were incongruous with uniform education for all citizens, which was essential to any well-ordered state. An excessive number of holy days and fast days were socially and economically counterproductive and therefore had to be restricted. The great proliferation of contemplative orders was particularly harmful not only because it deprived the state of many thousands of potentially useful citizens, but also because of "the irreparable harm to future generations" caused by the vow of celibacy. Above all, Kaunitz concluded, in the exercise of its office the clergy could not be permitted any kind of interference in the agenda of any other office of the state.[92]

This essay marks the culmination of Kaunitz's gradual radicalization and can be regarded as the final crystallization of his attitude towards the relationship between Church and state. The several dozen drafts on various aspects of the problem that can be found in Kaunitz's papers clearly show the influence of Diderot's *Encyclopédie*, especially the article on ecclesiastical discipline. The completely secular focus, for all its emphasis on moral values and on the virtues of the early Church, also suggests that this document is a world removed from the pietistic neo-Jansenist Catholic reform impulse that provided the backbone to Heinke's report. Certainly Kaunitz looked to religion as a convenient and effective

---

[92] Maass, *Josephinismus* I, 368–384.

teacher of civic virtues, and in this context repeatedly emphasized the necessity of religion for the masses. So, for example, he recommended waiving the printing costs for a Franciscan publication of the life of their docile founding saint,[93] judged some Jansenist literature in a positive light and endorsed popular catechisms.[94] But there was no room for the austerity and asceticism of the powerful neo-Jansenist circle of Vienna in Kaunitz's view of the matter. In January 1754, for instance, the papal prohibition on the use of timpani and trumpets in church services was proclaimed in the Habsburg Monarchy. The ban obviously had little impact, as the Jansenist-oriented Court Chancellor, Chotek, found occasion to complain about the continued use of these instruments in June 1767. In the Council of State Chotek found no sympathetic ear whatsoever. Kaunitz claimed he had never heard of the prohibition in the first place, and, in any case, since trumpets and timpani served to enliven people, their use could "cause no one any reasonable scruple." It is hard to imagine the glory of the Church music of Haydn, Mozart and Beethoven, had Kaunitz's recommendation to ignore the ban not received imperial assent, as it subsequently did.[95] The position of Kaunitz, in short, was as sternly anti-Jansenist as it was anti-ultramontane, and herein lay the crux of the debate in the following decade.

Though the decision to proceed unilaterally had been made in the summer of 1768, creating the necessary institutional structure to carry the reforms out was enmeshed in the broader administrative reforms of 1768–1769. As a result it was not until May 1769 that the recommendation made by Kaunitz in January 1768 was implemented. This amounted to a revival of the Directory's Court Commission in Religious Matters of 1753–1756. The new commission, subordinated to the Austro-Bohemian Chancellery and chaired by the Chancellor himself, already implied a programme in its very title: Consessus in publico-ecclesiasticis – in the Chancellery jargon of that day it meant that ecclesiastical matters were now identified as an unambiguous "Publicum", or state affair. The commission's function was to investigate problems systematically and to prepare appropriate recommendations and draft legislation. These briefs were then passed on to the Council of State for debate and to the Monarch for final approval. In addition to Chancellor Chotek, the commission included the Chancellery Privy Councillor Franz Karl Kressel von Qualtenberg, the privy councillor and professor of natural law at the University of Vienna, Karl Anton von Martini, the two reformist canons,

[93] HHStA, Staatskanzlei: Vorträge, Karton 101, Kaunitz to Maria Theresia, 28 June 1768.
[94] Klingenstein, Staatsverwaltung, p. 217; Hersche, Spätjansenismus, pp. 223–224.
[95] HHStA, Kabinettsarchiv: Staatsratakten, Karton 1, No. 1335, Staatsrat Voten and imperial resolution, 10–12 June 1767.

Simon Ambros von Stock, dean of the university's faculty of theology, and
Johann Peter Simen, dean of the faculty of philosophy, and, of course, the
all-important Heinke. The youngest chancellery court secretary, who had
married one of Maria Theresia's personal servants, Franz Greiner, was
made secretary of the commission.[96] The commission was marked by
reasonable harmony, for all six of its members were either firm Jansenists
or philo-Jansenists. If unilateral state action still involved serious disagreements, it was because outside the *Consessus*, and especially in the Council
of State, influential individuals were increasingly affected by the ideas of
the Enlightenment, and many a relatively conservative cameralist position
had begun to evolve to far more uncompromising secularism. The most
consistent, articulate and powerful spokesman of this group was none
other than Kaunitz. What is more, though he had his conflicts with Joseph
II in a number of other areas, he found an enthusiastic disciple in the young
co-regent in the sphere of ecclesiastical reform. Between the two of them
they occupied such commanding positions that change often went far
beyond what was envisioned by moderate reformers. As a consequence,
the creation of the *Consessus in publico-ecclesisticis* marked the high-point
of co-operation between the cameralist and Jansenist traditions in the
Monarchy, and the really decisive debates shifted from those between
Vienna and Rome to those conducted within the governing circles of the
Monarchy itself.

While Vienna was thus geared for battle with Clement XIII, the new
tone was unequivocal. As Kaunitz put it to Leopold of Tuscany's
chamberlain and political adviser, Franz Xaver Orsini-Rosenberg, when
assessing proposed ecclesiastical legislation for that principality:

Most of the articles in question are things inherent in the rights of sovereign power.
As far as I am concerned, my dear friend, one should never embark on the useless
course of asking for them, but implement them entirely without saying anything by
seizing suitable opportunities for the purpose. The more anyone enters into
negotiations with these gentlemen, the priests, the more one can count in advance
on having lost his case.[97]

But Vienna was to be spared the anticipated confrontation, for in February
1769 Kaunitz received word that the pope had died.[98] Though Vienna
expressed clear preference for a more flexible pope,[99] the conclave itself was
dominated by the anti-Jesuit pressures brought to bear by the Bourbon
Courts, and it was largely thanks to them that the Franciscan Cardinal

[96] Arneth, *Maria Theresia* IX, 57; Szabo, "Kaunitz und die Anfänge des Josephinismus,"
pp. 543–545.   [97] Maass, *Josephinismus* I, 384–385.
[98] HHStA, Staatskanzlei: Vorträge, Karton 103, Kaunitz to Maria Theresia, 12 February
1769.
[99] Augustin Theiner, *Histoire du pontificat de Clement XIV*, Paul de Geslin, trans., 2 Vols.
(Paris, 1852), I, 186–187, 204–205.

Lorenzo Gaganelli was finally elected after three months as Clement XIV. How co-operative this new pope might prove to be remained uncertain,[100] but as the newly-created *Consessus* proceeded with its work, it was obvious that no one intended to wait and find out.

Clement XIV, for his part, was quick with conciliatory overtures to Vienna. In the summer of 1769 he issued a dispensation for the daughter of the Empress, Maria Amalia, to marry the still excommunicated Ferdinand of Parma, and in September he sent her a letter of indulgence for the court chapel which Maria Theresia had requested. Kaunitz remained uncertain whether the pope was herewith manifesting "a genuinely positive disposition," or whether these were acts of political opportunism,[101] but the net effect was the same. The pope's actions had opened a door, and this "suitable opportunity" had now to be exploited to win further concessions.[102] That Clement XIV did not propose to be chary of these as well became clear when unfinished business from the reign of his predecessor was addressed. To expedite the *cassa salis* funds negotiations Kaunitz recommended a one-month ultimatum to which the pope acceded, leading to a formal agreement in which the state carried its point by the end of August 1770.[103] Similarly, Kaunitz, now confident that Clement had a reasonable attitude, felt that the issue of the establishment of a fully independent Greek Catholic bishopric and the appointment of a new Uniate bishop of Munkacz could be pushed to a successful conclusion.[104] Here, too, Clement acceded to Vienna's wishes, and in January 1771 agreed that a new, more independent Greek Catholic bishop at Munkacz was to be appointed – though it was to be some months before Vienna's candidate, Ivan Bradach, was actually consecrated.[105] Though Clement thus signaled a reversal of papal policies, it was to little avail. Having resolved to proceed unilaterally, all that such actions did at this stage was to persuade men like Kaunitz that "it is likely, given the disposition of the present pope, that something more can be had just as easily as something less."[106]

Consequently, the old agenda of Haugwitz was now not only revived but also extended. The first problem to which the *Consessus* addressed itself

[100] Arneth, *Maria Theresia* IX, 42.
[101] HHStA, Staatskanzlei: Vorträge, Karton 104, Kaunitz to Maria Theresia, 9 October 1769.   [102] *Ibid.*, Kaunitz to Maria Theresia, 7 November 1769.
[103] Maass, *Josephinismus* II, 129–148.
[104] HHStA, Staatskanzlei: Vorträge, Karton 105, Kaunitz to Maria Theresia, 12 May 1770.
[105] Arneth, *Maria Theresia* IX, 85–88; Pekar, *Eparchiae Munkacoviensis*, pp. 102–124; Winter, "Die Kämpfe der Ukrainer Oberungarns," p. 137.
[106] HHStA, Kabinettsarchiv: Kaunitz Voten, Karton 1, No. 954 of 1770, Kaunitz Staatsrat Votum, 27 May 1770.

was to broaden one of the few reforms which had been implemented successfully in 1751 – the abolition of holy days. The papal concession whereby twenty-four holy days were declared half holy days, however, proved unworkable.[107] As early as 1753 pressure began to mount to abolish these half holy days outright, and by the 1760s the idea enjoyed a wide consensus. Probably through the offices of Martini, a major memorandum on the subject by Paul Joseph Riegger was adopted by the *Consessus*. It not only recommended the abolition of all half holy days, but a sizeable reduction in the number of remaining full holy days as well.[108] Most Council members seemed to be content with the abolition of half holy days, and felt that additional demands ought to be dropped, but Kaunitz insisted that the necessity of a further reduction was "beyond doubt." What was more, he now added the idea (first floated by Gebler) of a "complete abolition of all fast days" or, at the very least, their transference to the Saturdays of Advent.[109] Though Maria Theresia endorsed the more moderate position,[110] Kaunitz persisted. He argued that if the broader demand was presented to the papacy properly, there was little doubt that Rome would accede to it.[111] The Chancellor of State carried his point on all fronts, and though negotiations were not as smooth and rapid as expected, he was able to report the conclusion of a fully satisfactory final agreement on 6 August 1771.[112]

It is interesting to note in the implementation of the decree how thoroughly statist the premises of the Habsburg government had become. There were a number of parishes in the border areas of the Monarchy that were centered outside the Habsburg domains, and others which centered in Austria but extended beyond the borders. In these circumstances, Kaunitz recommended, the line of the applicability of the new holy days law was to be the Habsburg border. All areas within it, whether parts of foreign parishes or not, were to be subject to the new law; all parts outside of it could do as they wished. These guidelines were adopted, and Kaunitz himself was commissioned to draft the appropriate order.[113] Within two years this concept had become such a firm principle that a complete

[107] Hersche, "Wider ''Müssiggang' und 'Ausschweifung'," pp. 105–106.
[108] Arneth, *Maria Theresia* IX, 58–62.
[109] HHStA, Kabinettsarchiv: Kaunitz Voten, Karton 1, No. 954 of 1770, Kaunitz Staatsrat Votum, 27 May 1770 (including rejected first draft).
[110] *Ibid.*, Staatsratprotokolle, Vol. 35, No. 954, imperial resolution; Maria Theresia to Kaunitz, 1 June 1770.
[111] HHStA, Staatskanzlei: Vorträge, Karton 105, Kaunitz to Maria Theresia 14 July 1770.
[112] *Ibid.*, Karton 106, Kaunitz to Maria Theresia, 21 August, 17 October, 26 November and 5 December 1770, including imperial resolutions; Karton 107, Kaunitz to Maria Theresia, 9 January 1771; Karton 108, Kaunitz to Maria Theresia, 6 August 1771.
[113] *Ibid.*, Karton 109, Kaunitz to Maria Theresia, 16 February 1772 (including imperial resolution and draft order).

separation of all domestic dioceses from the jurisdiction of foreign bishops was undertaken. Maria Theresia herself had come to recognize this as "a very important defect in our domestic governmental structure," and charged Kaunitz with initiating the appropriate negotiations with Rome.[114]

These steps indicate a thorough acceptance of the principle, so strongly asserted by Kaunitz, that it was the right of the state to mold and shape ecclesiastical administration to suit its own needs. Thus, for, example, when the imperatives of Hungarian politics demanded the severing of the two Transylvanian deaneries of Hermannstadt (Sibiu) and Kronstadt (Braşov) from the jurisdictional control of the Hungarian archbishop of Esztergom (Gran), it was affirmed that while the pope could be allowed input in the purely spiritual side of the matter, the fundamental objective was not to be questioned.[115] When the monastic orders of Bohemia complained about lay collection and administration of intercalary revenues from clerical benefices, Kaunitz assured Maria Theresia that she was "certainly entitled to hire lay administrators," and that she should have no doubts whatsoever about regularizing the practice by royal decree.[116] The Empress's order unhesitatingly affirmed this assertion.[117]

The attempt by the state to create ecclesiastical jurisdictional boundaries that coincided with the political ones encountered further obstacles with the annexation of Galicia. The Greek Catholic bishop of Lemberg (Lviv, Lvov, Lwow), Lev Sheptyts'kyi, was coadjutor of the exiled metropolitan of Kiev, but with the partition of Poland the bishop feared the loss of his position. To salvage it he urged Vienna to come to an agreement with Warsaw, making Lemberg the new permanent seat of the metropolitan, with future candidates chosen alternately from Polish and Austrian nominees. Kaunitz was little inclined toward the kind of Polish–Austrian co-operation envisioned by Sheptyts'kyi. He much preferred a more far-reaching, unilateral, made-in-Vienna policy of cultivating the Ukrainian Catholic clergy of newly annexed Galicia, designed to foster their loyalty not only to the Habsburg dynasty but also to the reformist ideals of Josephinism. This plan focused on the revival of the long extinct metropoly of Halycz, and its complete severance from the metropoly of Kiev. Gradually all Greek Catholic bishoprics of the Monarchy were to be subordinated to this new see. Kaunitz was obviously not blind to the "various important benefits in political considerations" which such a

[114] *Ibid.*, Karton 114, Maria Theresia to Kaunitz, 13 May 1774.
[115] *Ibid.*, Karton 104, Maria Theresia to Kaunitz, 22 June 1769; Kaunitz to Maria Theresia, 7 and 12 December 1769; Maria Theresia to Kaunitz, 6 December 1774.
[116] HHStA, Kabinettsarchiv: Kaunitz Voten, Karton 1, No. 280 of 1771, Kaunitz Staatsrat Votum, 30 January 1771.
[117] *Ibid.*, Staatsratprotokolle, Vol. 38, No. 280, imperial resolution, 7 February 1771.

rationalization of the ecclesiastical administration entailed. Initial reports indicated that a good two-thirds of the population of Galicia was Greek Catholic, he pointed out, and it was clearly in the interest of the Monarchy to do whatever was necessary to cultivate the "loyalty and attachment of the whole ... nation". In the short run Kaunitz suggested that Vienna court Sheptyts'kyi, since he was in a position to impede or facilitate ecclesiastical reform in Galicia (his brother, Athanasius, was Greek Catholic bishop of Przemysl), by sending him an assuring, if evasive, answer on the jurisdictional matter, while at the same time promising him compensation for revenues lost from those dioceses formerly under his control but now in Poland. Above all he was to be reassured that Vienna "would not fail to promote what the best interests of the Union [i.e. Uniates] required."[118]

Kaunitz's policy of fostering and encouraging the Greek Catholic clergy of the Monarchy was endorsed and saw quick results as early as 1774. The pejorative term "Uniate", commonly used in pre-partition Poland to underscore the inferiority of the Greek to the Roman Catholic Church, was banned that summer, and the Empress explicitly ordered that no effort be spared to make Greek Catholics feel equal to their Roman Catholic brethren. At the same time, a Greek Catholic seminary was established in Vienna at the Church of St. Barbara (generally called the "Barbareum"). Greek Catholic suspicions were further laid to rest the following February when Sheptyts'kyi's personal envoy, Ivan Gutz, canon of the cathedral in Lemberg, was granted a very assuring audience with the Empress in which she made clear that Habsburg policy would henceforth foster the full emancipation of the Greek Catholic Church of the Monarchy. This policy was to reach its culmination in April 1807 when the Halych metropoly was restored with two eparchies, Lemberg and Przemysl.[119] The political benefits predicted by Kaunitz were also to accrue: the Greek Catholic Church of the Habsburg Monarchy was not only to demonstrate "a loyalty to the Austrian state that went well beyond a formal compliance with legitimate authority," but was to prove to be a staunch disciple of the Josephinist ideology of the dynasty.[120]

[118] HHStA, Staatskanzlei: Vorträge, Karton 114, Kaunitz to Maria Theresia (including imperial resolution), 12 January 1774.

[119] Julian Pelesz, Geschichte der Union der ruthenischen Kirche mit Rom, Vol. II: Von der Wiederherstellung der Union der ruthenischen Kirche mit Rom von 1595 bis auf die Gegenwart (Würzburg and Vienna, 1880), pp. 596–671; Michael von Malinowski, Die Kirchen- und Staats-Satzungen bezüglich des griechisch-katholischen Ritus der Ruthenen in Galizien (Lemberg, 1861), pp. 297–384; Anton Korczok, Die griechisch-katholische Kirche in Galizien (Leipzig and Berlin, 1921), pp. 24–79; Willibald M. Plöchl, St. Barbara zu Wien, 2 Vols. (Vienna, 1975), I, 40–41; II, 211–212; Myron Stasiw, Metropolia Haliciensis (Rome, 1960), pp. 101–168.

[120] John-Paul Himka, "The Greek Catholic Church and Nation-Building in Galicia, 1772–1918," Harvard Ukrainian Studies VIII (1984), 428–433.

For much the same reason that Kaunitz advocated the reduction of holy days, he was also opposed to religious pilgrimages and processions. In 1767 he had been cautious when a drastic reduction had been recommended by Stupan, and he had recommended a *Hofkanzlei* investigation. In accordance with the Empress's order this had taken place. By the time the Chancellery report fully endorsing Stupan was ready in March 1769, Kaunitz threw his former caution to the wind. He now characterized excessive pilgrimages and processions as "very harmful" and recommended that pilgrimages to foreign countries be forbidden altogether, that processions be abolished on most holy days, and that others, such as the famous Corpus Christi procession, be transferred to Sundays.[121] This position, however, did not move the Empress, despite the broad support it enjoyed, and after months of discussion, the most she would concede was some limitations on excessive pilgrimages to a particular shrine, Mariazell.[122] This underscores an important point. Kaunitz was certainly not always successful in pushing his point of view through, and, while in some cases he would persist, in others he would not. He was less motivated by anti-clericalism on principle than by the political imperatives of the state as he understood them. These were clearly ordered by priorities. Matters such as the reduction of pilgrimages and processions clearly took second place to more vital issues. Many enlightened reformers were often unable to distinguish between the essential and unessential, and more times than not were required to abandon the substance for the shadow. Not so Kaunitz. Fundamentals were pursued with determination; secondary considerations were put off for more suitable occasions.

One objective that he did consider fundamental concerned monastic and other ecclesiastical orders. By the end of the 1760s Kaunitz's former restrained and moderate tone had given way to passionate hostility. In his memorandum of February 1769 he denounced monastic orders as the cause of the corruption of the patristic church, and, in an unashamed appeal to Maria Theresia's prejudices, had squarely laid at their door the responsibility for the Reformation.[123] Often quick to believe the worst rumors about monasteries,[124] it came as no surprise that when the second sitting of the *Consessus* revived the anti-monastic agenda of Haugwitz, Kaunitz was quick to lend it his support. In the initial debate on the

---

[121] HHStA, Kabinettsarchiv: Kaunitz Voten, Karton 1, No. 1272 of 1769, Kaunitz Staatsrat Votum, 19 May 1769.

[122] *Ibid.*, Staatsratprotokolle, Vol. 31, No. 1272, imperial resolution, 4 December 1769; Vol. 36, No. 2459, imperial resolution, 23 August 1770. Cf. Hollerweger, *Reform des Gottesdienstes*, pp. 78–94.   [123] Maass, *Josephinismus* I, 368–384.

[124] HHStA, Staatskanzlei: Vorträge, Karton 108, Kaunitz to Maria Theresia, 6 and 29 November 1771.

principle of the reduction of monastic clergy most Council of State members doubted that their number in the Habsburg Monarchy was excessive. Kaunitz alone felt otherwise. Beginning with the populationist premise that the vow of celibacy was a serious threat to "the propagation of the human race", he argued that monasteries represented a brain-drain, in which talented people removed themselves from useful social functions. He then reiterated the classic cameralist attack on the social and economic privileges of monastic orders, focusing in particular on their possessions in mortmain. He considered the very existence of monastic orders "highly detrimental" to the state, and asserted that "the supreme law of public welfare demands the reduction and limitation of this class of citizen as much as possible." He dismissed fears that such reductions would undermine the cause of religion by emphasizing the exemplary purity of the early Church when no monastic orders existed. Consequently he recommended that, as a first step, the state force all monasteries to adhere strictly to their original charters, most of which, particularly with reference to numbers, had long been transgressed.[125]

In the subsequent weeks Kaunitz found himself forced to defend his propositions point by point in great detail to his skeptical colleagues,[126] but the argument was difficult to sustain when the bishops of the Monarchy were surveyed on the issue. By mid-July the papal nuncio in Vienna, Antonio Visconti, was able to report with great satisfaction that not only had most bishops agreed that the number of monastic clergy was not excessive, but that Hungarian bishops had reported that the numbers were wholly inadequate to meet the spiritual needs of the people. Visconti was certain that reduction of monastic orders was a dead letter.[127] Kaunitz, no doubt sensing his isolation, sought to rescue the process by turning to the co-regent, who had argued for precisely such a reduction since at least 1765. Kaunitz pointed out to Joseph how much resistance such policies were likely to encounter, but emphasized the urgency of this "important and delicate matter." Under such circumstances the emperor's "strongest support" was imperative, though it was best if the imperial influence was exercised secretly.[128]

Though the frontal attack in principle had largely failed, Joseph's hidden support became obvious as the long-term objective was gradually met with indirect measures. To prevent people from becoming monks and nuns before being fully aware of the ramifications of such a step, the *Consessus* recommended that the age for permitting entry into a monastery or convent be set at twenty-one, and the age at which final vows were to be

[125] Maass, *Josephinismus* II, 139–142.
[126] *Ibid.*, pp. 142–144.
[127] Ellemunter, *Visconti*, pp. 61–62.
[128] Maass, ed., *Josephinismus* II, p. 139.

permitted at twenty-two. Young girls who had been reared in convents were to be required to live in the world at large for at least a year before being permitted to make such a commitment. This proposal generally found much greater favour in the Council of State, but, again, Kaunitz's voice was the most radical. He insisted that the state should unilaterally legislate to set the age of entry into a monastery or convent at twenty-four and the age of final vows at thirty – a suggestion which, if adopted, would probably have led to the atrophy of monasticism within a generation.[129] Joseph, at this point, clearly did not fail Kaunitz, for the imperial resolution of 18 August not only accepted the age of entry recommended by the *Consessus*, but met Kaunitz's radicalism half way by extending the age of final vows to twenty-four.[130] Despite Maria Theresia's desire to consult the pope, the appropriate decree was unilaterally proclaimed on 17 October 1770,[131] though the attempt to make it retroactively effective failed despite Kaunitz's best efforts.[132]

If matters were moving a bit too fast for Maria Theresia, it can easily be imagined how this decree affected the Vatican. Clement XIV decided to abandon the usual diplomatic channels, and in two letters – one to the Empress and one to Kaunitz – appeal directly to Vienna, arguing that the legislation would deal a heavy blow to pastoral care for subjects of the Monarchy. In his report on these to the Empress, Kaunitz noted that a papal protest was to be expected, but dismissed its substance as invalid. Maria Theresia was not so certain, and indicated a willingness to open negotiations with Rome.[133] Kaunitz now knew that the decree was in danger of severe modification and perhaps even complete repeal. In the Council of State he firmly asserted that the matter was of no concern to the Vatican.[134] Though he won the support of his colleagues,[135] the Empress remained ambivalent, refusing to authorize the recommended declaration to the nuncio.[136] Having failed to move the Empress through the Council

---

[129] Hock-Bidermann, pp. 53–54; Maass, *Josephinismus* II, 144–147. Cf. Arneth, *Maria Theresia* IX, 70–78; Ferdinand Maass, "Die Stellungnahme des Fürsten Kaunitz zur staatlichen Festsetzung der Altersgrenze für die Ablegung der Ordensgelübde in Österreich im Jahre 1770/71," *MIÖG* LVIII (1950), 656–667; Ellemunter, *Visconti*, pp. 62–84.

[130] HHStA, Kabinettsarchiv: Staatsratprotokolle, Vol. 35, No. 1936, imperial resolution, 18 August 1770. Cf. Hock-Bidermann, p. 55.

[131] Arneth, *Maria Theresia* IX, 72–73.

[132] HHStA, Kabinettsarchiv: Kaunitz Voten, Karton 1, No. 4246 of 1770, Kaunitz Staatsrat Votum, 23 December 1770; Staatsratprotokolle, Vol. 37, No. 4246, secretarial note, n.d. (December 1770); Vol. 38, No. 229, imperial resolution, n.d. (January 1771).

[133] Arneth, *Maria Theresia* IX, 73, 560; Maass, *Josephinismus* II, 148–152.

[134] HHStA, Kabinettsarchiv: Kaunitz Voten, Karton 2, No. 938 of 1771, Kaunitz Staatsrat Votum, 20 March 1771.   [135] Hock-Bidermann, p. 55.

[136] HHStA, Kabinettsarchiv: Staatsratprotokolle, Vol. 39, No. 938, secretarial record, n.d. (March 1771).

of State, Kaunitz now proceeded to draft the formal replies to the pope. Clinging tenaciously to his previous position, he dismissed the fears that the decree portended a dearth of clergy, emphasized that for several centuries there had been no monastic orders at all, and insisted that the age limit was not negotiable. Though the Empress accepted the substance of the argument, she strongly objected to the assertive and strident tone in which Kaunitz had couched the reply. "This is a polite letter, not a manifesto," she noted in the margin, and ordered a new draft prepared. Stung by the reproach, Kaunitz included a lengthy defence of his first draft along with the second, giving full vent to his offended dignity and making it clear that he had been hurt by the Empress's apparent lack of confidence in him. Maria Theresia replied in kind, but, apparently under pressure from Joseph, she conceded that she should not have doubted him and accepted a non-negotiable reply to the pope. The decree was thus left untouched.[137]

As excessive numbers of monastic clergy were combatted by setting a minimum age for monastic vows, so monastic possessions in mortmain were combatted by severely restricting acquisition rights. In its seventh sitting the *Consessus* revived this aspect of Haugwitz's 1751 proposal, and in its report of 16 November 1770 now reaffirmed the suggestion that all monastic candidates be limited to 1,500 Gulden in what they could bring to any prospective order. Kaunitz, as usual by now, was far less generous. In his opinion, "monks and monasteries must be completely debarred from all future acquisitions."[138] While the imperial resolution rejected Kaunitz's radical solution and accepted the 1,500 Gulden ceiling,[139] the matter did not end there. Within the *Consessus* itself, Martini also disagreed with the 1,500 Gulden maximum that was accepted and he therefore submitted a minority report in which he advocated the establishment of a poverty-relief fund into which all prospective gifts to monasteries had to be deposited. Such a plan would severely limit monastic cash reserves, and make future mortmain acquisitions much more difficult.[140] While the proposal failed despite the strong support given it by Joseph,[141] it certainly set the tone for the more radical decade of the Emperor's sole rule. Thus, by 1773, when a new and dramatic ecclesiastical problem presented itself, the state's victory over the monastic houses had already been won.

---

[137] Maass, *Josephinismus* II, 153–159.
[138] HHStA, Kabinettsarchiv: Kaunitz Voten, Karton 1, No. 4060 of 1770, Kaunitz Staatsrat Votum, 23 December 1770.
[139] *Ibid.*, Staatsratprotokolle, Vol. 37, No. 4060, imperial resolution, 16 January 1771.
[140] Hock-Bidermann, p. 56.
[141] HHStA, Staatskanzlei: Vorträge, Karton 107, Joseph memorandum, 24 April 1771.

The ecclesiastical issue which was to overshadow all others in the year 1773 was the suppression of the Society of Jesus. It was not an unexpected event, and had attracted the attention of European cabinets for at least twenty years. The eighteenth-century reaction against baroque Catholicism found its clearest expression in the theological, political and social attack on the Jesuit Order, and in many ways it was the one thing that held all the various strains of reform Catholicism together. The Order's political power, and its often questionable manner of exploiting this power, led to confrontations with political authorities as well, particularly in Portugal and the Bourbon courts of Spain, France and Italy, which was to lead to the expulsion of the Jesuits from these countries during the 1750s and 1760s.[142] This anti-Jesuit sentiment, shared by so many reformers in the Habsburg Monarchy, largely left Kaunitz cold. During his French embassy he still regarded "these good fathers" as being potentially very useful,[143] and once Kaunitz became Chancellor of State many foreign observers had the clear impression that he was anti-Jansenist and patently pro-Jesuit.[144]

By and large, while no friend to religious orders of any kind, Kaunitz tried to remain as fair and even-handed as possible, and did not allow himself to be swept up by the anti-Jesuit hysteria. In 1759, for example, during the height of the Jesuit expulsion crisis in Portugal, a Jesuit apologia was submitted for approval to the Censorship Board in Vienna – a board which itself had only recently been wrested from Jesuit control. When the publication of this brochure was officially permitted, the Portuguese ambassador became so incensed that he demanded permission to publish a bitter and vitriolic refutation. The head of the Censorship Board, Gerard van Swieten, remained uncertain on how to react, and, as a result, Kaunitz's opinion was solicited.[145] Kaunitz responded that while one did not wish to offend a friendly court unduly, the Portuguese pamphlet was couched in such unmeasured tones that permitting its publication would leave the impression that Vienna endorsed Lisbon's stance. One side or the other was bound to be offended no matter what Vienna did, and under the circumstances Kaunitz recommended it be Portugal.[146] Because of the potential implications of this decision Kaunitz also sought the support of the Privy Conference. This body seconded the Foreign Minister's position, but Uhlfeld and Colloredo recommended that, in future, Vienna forbid all

---

[142] Though the literature is extensive, the most detailed analysis remains Pastor, *Popes* XXXVI, 1–23, 294–504; XXXVII, 1–361.
[143] Schlitter, ed., *Correspondance*, p. 162.
[144] Pastor, *Popes* XXXVII, 319; Winter, *Josephinismus* (2nd ed.), p. 20.
[145] HHStA, Staatskanzlei: Vorträge, Karton 85, van Swieten to Bartenstein, 20 October 1759. On this whole episode in fuller detail see my "Kaunitz und die Anfänge des Josephinismus," pp. 535–537.
[146] *Ibid.*, Kaunitz to Maria Theresia, 2 November 1759.

publications either for or against the Jesuits, and Batthyány went so far as to recommend the retroactive banning of the original Jesuit apologia.[147] Kaunitz refused to back Batthyány's harsher position, but found the Uhlfed–Colloredo formula a convenient way to avoid future entanglements in the Jesuit controversies of the day.[148] Strict neutrality in these matters thus became official Habsburg policy in the years that followed.

As the anti-Jesuit momentum built in the 1760s, Kaunitz adhered strictly to this position. Efforts to recruit Austria into a Bourbon common front against the Jesuits were bound to fail, reported the Spanish ambassador to Vienna, because of the positive attitude Kaunitz had towards the Order.[149] In the Council of State debates of 1765 which addressed the Jesuit problem, Kaunitz remained silent, anti-Jesuit sentiment being spearheaded by Haugwitz.[150] Even as his own position gradually hardened, Kaunitz remained reluctant to join the anti-Jesuit crusade, and expressed deep skepticism about published Portuguese allegations of Jesuit criminality.[151] When initially drafting his famous reform proposals of January 1768, he toyed with but then abandoned the idea of making common cause with the Bourbon courts in demanding the abolition of the Jesuit Order, and advised against the actual expulsion of "so many innocent and useful subjects" even if the Order were abolished.[152] Austria, as Joseph reported to his brother, Leopold, in a memorandum proofread by Kaunitz, simply did not have "sufficient reason to wish for [the Jesuit Order's] destruction." Joseph could be swayed in this matter only by reasons of state.[153]

One reason of state that could impel Austria to make common cause with the Bourbon courts in demanding the abolition of the Society of Jesus, was to reinforce her alliance with them. Both the Habsburgs and the Bourbons were aware of this, and Bourbon pressure for the Habsburgs to join the anti-Jesuit front increased, especially after the election of Clement XIV. The occasion of the marriage negotiations between the Dauphin and Marie Antoinette proved a particularly apt lever for the Bourbon courts. The French Foreign Minister, Choiseul, appealed directly to Joseph, and Charles III of Spain directly to Maria Theresia. But these appeals were to go for naught. Joseph's putative promising reply is often quoted:

With respect to the Jesuits, and your plan for their suppression, you have my perfect approbation. You must not reckon much on my mother... However, Kaunitz is your friend; he can effect everything with the Empress. With regard to

[147] *Ibid.*, Uhlfeld Nota, 3 November 1759; Colloredo Nota, 5 November 1759; Khevenhüller Nota, 6 November 1759; Batthyány Nota, 7 November 1759.
[148] *Ibid.*, Kaunitz to Maria Theresia, 8 November 1759.
[149] Pastor, *Popes* XXXVII, 328.   [150] Hock-Bidermann, p. 48.
[151] DOZA, Handschriften, Vol. 65, Ludwig Zinzendorf to Karl Zinzendorf, 26 July 1769.
[152] Maass, *Josephinismus* I, 73–74, 256–257.
[153] Arneth *Maria Theresia* IX, 550–551.

their suppression, he is of your and the Marquis of Pombal's party; and he is a man who leaves nothing half done.[154]

However, this letter has now been proved to be spurious,[155] and the only reliable statement of the emperor's policy we possess is Joseph's report to his brother. Furthermore, just how much Kaunitz was prepared to "effect" with the Empress becomes clear from her reply to Charles III: she would be more than pleased to endorse abolition if the pope wished it, but she would not take the initiative herself.[156] Even a personal appeal by Choiseul to Kaunitz misfired. The latter simply reiterated that Vienna could not make common cause with the Bourbon courts on the matter.[157] Indeed, the fable that Kaunitz persistently hounded the Jesuits with repeated reports of their corruption and duplicity to Maria Theresia has been dismissed even by Jesuit apologists.[158]

Since Vienna clearly rejected any role for itself in demanding the abolition of the Society of Jesus, and since the pope repeatedly insisted that he could not take the initiative unless there was a consensus to do so among all the Catholic powers, the situation had all the makings of a stalemate. It was only the energetic persistence of Charles III of Spain, who was the soul of the abolitionist movement, that broke the impasse and resulted in a draft papal bull ordering the abolition of the Society.[159] In response to this draft Kaunitz noted that nothing had happened since 1770 "which would require us to change our opinions on the matter." Just as Vienna would do nothing to undermine the order, so it would not stand in the way of abolition. Kaunitz's main concern was an article in the draft bull which gave the papacy some rights to the property of the Jesuits, and foresaw its transfer to local bishops. This Kaunitz could never accept. He insisted that if the order were abolished, all its property had to revert to the state. In submitting a draft reply for Charles III to the Empress, Kaunitz urged her not to yield one iota on this point, and requested she make no "change or addition" whatsoever to the response he had submitted. Maria Theresia agreed and signed the formal reply that evening.[160] From that moment on

[154] Saul K. Padover, *The Revolutionary Emperor: Joseph II of Austria*, 2nd ed. (London, 1967), p. 41; Maass, *Josephinismus* I, 97; Pastor, *Popes* XXXVIII, 257.
[155] Derek Beales, "The False Joseph II," *Historical Journal* XVIII (1975), 467–495 and his *Joseph II* I, 460–461.
[156] Bernhard Duhr, "Die Kaiserin Maria Theresia und die Aufhebung der Gesellschaft Jesu," *Stimmen der Zeit* CX (1925/1926), 209.
[157] HHStA, Kabinettsarchiv: Kaiser Franz Akten, Karton 73, Kaunitz to Choiseul, n.d. (1770).   [158] Bernhard Duhr, *Jesuiten-Fabeln* (Freiburg, 1899), pp. 34–37.
[159] Arneth, *Maria Theresia* IX, 564–565; Duhr, "Aufhebung," p. 210; Pastor, *Popes* XXXVIII, 135–292.
[160] HHStA, Staatskanzlei: Vorträge, Karton 111, Kaunitz to Maria Theresia, 3 April 1773, including imperial resolution. Cf. Maass, *Josephinismus* II, 171–172.

the abolition itself was regarded as a *fait accompli*, and all subsequent discussions concerned themselves with ex-Jesuits and their property.

Joseph, above all, wasted no time. On 3 April 1773 he outlined his position that after the abolition of the Society, Jesuits could continue to fulfill their teaching functions as individuals until the entire educational system was reviewed, but the order's property was to be strictly controlled. Concerned that members of the order might attempt to smuggle funds out of the country, he recommended the creation of a commission to control and supervise the transfer of property and funds to the state. He also felt that the state should have a detailed plan on what to do with Jesuit funds, and that the whole prospect of abolition should be kept secret until the government was ready with this plan.[161] Kaunitz by and large endorsed Joseph's recommendations, though he felt that drawing up a specific plan on what to do with Jesuit property could be left to a commission constituted to handle the matter. His main point was to underscore Joseph's and his own earlier assertion of the state's right over the property of the clergy, and to this end enclosed his theoretical observations on the subject which he had drafted in 1769.[162] Both Joseph's and Kaunitz's reflections were then referred to Kressel, a member of the *Consessus in publico-ecclesiasticis*. He, in turn, so effectively endorsed and expanded on the Joseph–Kaunitz position,[163] that Kaunitz concurred even with those parts of the memorandum which modified his own.[164] This was a flattering recommendation, and it can therefore be no surprise that when the Empress set up a special commission to deal with all the problems resulting from the imminent abolition of the Jesuit Order, Kressel was made its chairman.

Kressel's Jesuit Commission (*Jesuitenaufhebungskommission*), which included Martini and Greiner from the *Consessus*, as well as the Empress's confessor, Father Ignaz Müller,[165] consisted of men who not only enjoyed Maria Theresia's particular trust, but who were also in the mainstream of the Jansenist reform movement.[166] The commission was instructed to address itself to several questions: whether the Jesuits could still be employed as teachers after abolition; how other teachers could be procured to replace them; but, above all, how to acquire accurate information on Jesuit property, and, subsequently, how to collect, administer and utilize

[161] HHStA, Kabinettsarchiv: Kaiser Franz Akten, Karton 73, Joseph to Maria Theresia, 3 April 1773. Cf. Khevenhüller-Metsch VII, 453–456.
[162] Maass, *Josephinismus* II, 172–177.
[163] HHStA, Kabinettsarchiv: Kaiser Franz Akten, Karton 73, Kressel to Maria Theresia, n.d. (April 1773).   [164] *Ibid.*, Kaunitz to Maria Theresia, 29 April 1773.
[165] *Ibid.*, Karton 72, commission membership list.
[166] Arneth, *Maria Theresia* IX, 104; Duhr, "Aufhebung," p. 220; Winter, *Josephinismus*, 2nd ed., p. 74; Hersche, *Spätjansenismus*, p. 156.

it.[167] Despite Joseph's incessant complaints that matters were not moving fast enough, and that one would end up being served "the mustard after the dinner,"[168] his fears were misplaced. By the time Clement XIV officially signed the bull *Dominus ac Redemptor*, which abolished the Society of Jesus on 21 July 1773, and then, after a brief misunderstanding, personally assured Maria Theresia that ex-Jesuit property rightfully fell to the state,[169] the Jesuit Commission had already submitted several reports which, in accordance with its instructions, had taken this principle for granted.[170]

From the very beginning the neo-Jansenist orientation of the Jesuit Commission revealed itself in its reports, and, as a result, Kaunitz quickly found himself in disagreement with it. The commission protocol of 9 June, which concentrated mainly on the consequences that abolition would have on the educational system, proved to be the flashpoint.[171] With the recommendation that ex-Jesuits be excluded from the teaching of all theology and ecclesiastical history, Kaunitz was in full agreement, insisting in his lengthy assessment of 21 June 1773 that all history had to be taught "purely from genuine sources and without ideological prejudice." He also agreed that if any teaching post fell vacant, it should be opened to all applicants by means of a competitive examination. Finally, he agreed that other monastic orders could be re-located in ex-Jesuit houses if necessary, but added that under such circumstances the other monastic house had to be surrendered to the state "because otherwise one would have two instead of one monkish cloister in a very short time."[172]

But agreement stopped when the commission recommended that chairs of theology, ethics and metaphysics vacated by Jesuits could be filled by other monastic orders. Here Kaunitz made no effort to hide his bitter dislike of monasticism. Replacing one order with another which shared the corruption but not the learning of the former, he wrote, "would truly be a contradiction." In his view monks, no matter how educated, how perspicacious, or how convinced of the "genuine principles" of statism, neither could nor would ever oppose the fundamental *esprit* of their orders, and only secular priests could really be trusted in this respect. Kressel met Kaunitz's contention head-on. He insisted that there were just not enough qualified secular priests to do the required job, but that there were plenty of monks, particularly Augustinians, who did not share the "slippery

---

[167] HHStA, Kabinettsarchiv: Kaiser Franz Akten, Karton 72, Maria Theresia to Kressel, 17 May 1773.   [168] *MTJC* II, 6–7.   [169] Arneth, *Maria Theresia* IX, 566–567.
[170] The instructions to Kressel of 17 May affirmed that "the property of this order indisputably reverts to the control of the sovereign." For the transfer of Jesuit property to the state, see Arneth, *Maria Theresia* IX, 96–124; Maass, *Josephinismus* II, 25–31; Mikoletzky, *Österreich*, pp. 245–251.
[171] HHStA, Kabinettsarchiv: Kaiser Franz Akten, Karton 74, Jesuit Commission protocol, 9 June 1773.   [172] Maass, *Josephinismus* II, 183–185.

morality" of the Jesuits. He concluded that the use of monastic orders in these posts was absolutely imperative, at least until appropriate secular priests could be trained.[173] This did not silence Kaunitz; rather it incited him to even harsher anti-monastic remarks.

Kaunitz conceded that in principle, monks could be used exceptionally, though "only in cases of most extreme need," as long as the employment of secular priests was the rule. But he still would not concede that such a need existed. Thus, for the eight posts for the faculty of theology, ex-Jesuits could be employed in the three positions for Latin, Greek and Hebrew languages, since these did not contain theological subject matter. As one suitable Augustinian had already been hired, it was only a question of finding four more qualified candidates in the entire Monarchy. And when it came to qualified candidates, Kaunitz reiterated, monasteries were the last place to look. Too many of their members had never even attended university, and even the more qualified ones were still dominated by "the muddled old scholastic system." Nor would Kaunitz accept Kressel's contention that there was nothing to fear from monkish *esprit de corps*. The "experience of several centuries" proved the contrary, he insisted, and, if a specific monk was free of it, it was "a very rare exception" which did not alter the rule. The passionate conclusion deserves to be quoted at length:

Most gracious Madam! I would and could never regret it enough, if under Your Majesty's glorious reign such an important and unexpected event as the abolition of the Jesuit Order were not utilized for the true benefit of the religion and the state in every possible way, and if, without the slightest need, the establishment of the contradiction of having removed what was perhaps the best of the clerical orders from teaching posts only to set worse ones in their place, were allowed ... If one permits monks to occupy teaching posts from the very beginning and without urgent need, they will in a very short time find a way to install themselves so that they will be very difficult, if not impossible, to remove.

After this salvo Kressel and the Jesuit Commission agreed to recommend the use of monks only in cases of dire need, and under those circumstances Kaunitz finally endorsed the report. With this the Empress approved the official enactment of the recommendation.[174]

The decree officially turning over all ex-Jesuit property to the state was published on 9 October 1773. Kaunitz, for his part, took little part in subsequent deliberations except when he was asked, in his capacity as Foreign Minister, to send instructions or information to Rome. Implementation was basically left in the hands of the Jesuit Commission and the Empress, and, under those circumstances, the prospects for ex-Jesuits were not very bright. The commission's protocols over the subsequent

[173] *Ibid.*, pp. 183–187.   [174] *Ibid.*, pp. 187–192.

months reveal a very militant and harsh anti-Jesuit tone. Fears constantly surfaced that the order was attempting to rob the state of its just rights to the Society's property. An ongoing fear of plots to ferret large sums of money out of the country characterized the reports of the commission, and its recommendations usually called for draconian measures.[175] Maria Theresia moderated the rabid anti-Jesuit sentiments of the commission somewhat when it came to individual cases, but the order as such received little consideration from her. As she frankly confessed:

I have not been too predisposed towards the Society for many years. I removed myself and my children [from the Jesuits] as much in matters of education as in the confessional. After the abolition of the Society, no one strove more vigorously than I to remove them from all theological chairs; and where posts were impossible to fill, I insisted it was better to leave them vacant for a year rather than to allow them to [the Jesuits].[176]

Indeed, she even ordered the destruction of all Jesuit papers and manuals, because she considered them obsolete and potentially dangerous if they fell into the wrong hands.[177] That Maria Theresia would thus go "further than even State Chancellor Kaunitz,"[178] comes as no surprise. Given the strong neo-Jansenist tendencies prevalent among ecclesiastical reformers in the Habsburg Monarchy, which were shared by the Empress,[179] the hostility was predictable. Kaunitz's attitude towards the Jesuits was much more surgical and dispassionate: he continued to promote and protect individual ex-Jesuits after the abolition,[180] and showed far less hostility than most to the order as such. In short, he shared an attitude common to many *philosophes* of the Enlightenment, which, by saying that the Society of Jesus represented the best of a bad lot, thus uttered its final word on clerical orders.

The issue of toleration

By the later 1770s all these dramatic developments caused some considerable *arrière-pensée* in reform Catholic and Jansenist ranks, as gradually the community of interest between secular and religious concerns started to come apart. One need look no further for evidence of this than to Maria Theresia herself. Goaded by the now increasingly reactionary Migazzi, she clearly had severe pangs of conscience about many of the measures being adopted in the avalanche of ecclesiastical reform. Wangermann has analyzed this retreat from the firmer, more confident pace of

---

[175] HHStA, Kabinettsarchiv: Kaiser Franz Akten, Karton 74, Jesuit Commission protocols, 1773–1774.   [176] Arneth, *Maria Theresia* IX, 118–119.   [177] *Ibid.*, p.108.
[178] Maass, *Josephinismus* II, 30, expressed considerable shock and surprise at this.
[179] Hersche, "War Maria Theresia eine Jansenistin?" pp. 14–25.
[180] Novotny, *Staatskanzler Kaunitz*, pp. 147–149.

earlier years, and has detailed the fear which seized many Enlightenment thinkers that all the signs of progress had been a mere false dawn.[181] Nowhere was this more evident than in the touchy issue of religious toleration which clouded Maria Theresia's last years. The discovery by popular missions in Moravia of some 10,000 "crypto-Protestants" in and around the town of Wisowitz (Vizovice) deeply shocked and disturbed the Empress and led to a bitter confrontation with proponents of a policy of confessional toleration – foremost among whom were her son, Joseph, and Kaunitz.

While the crisis of 1777 brought the confrontation to the surface, however, there was nothing novel about the positions taken by the Empress, Joseph and Kaunitz. Maria Theresia's lack of religious tolerance was no secret. She held fast to her strong Counter-Reformation convictions, and while her pragmatic but conservative temperament could frequently give rise to some surprisingly radical political positions, these outbursts were usually lent impetus by a kind of moral indignation. Paradoxically her very piety enhanced her sense of moral responsibility to the point of inflexible stubbornness, which in turn could result in the kind of dramatic initiatives we have seen in the agrarian question. Even her confrontations with the papacy on church–state relations were motivated by what she perceived to be the interests of the faith – whether any given pope or bishop understood this or not. But whatever progressive legislation such sentiments could lead to, they could not affect the basic Counter-Reformation intolerance that lay at their heart. Maria Theresia's piety was thus the source of both her strength and her weakness, and remained to the end the Achilles heel of her enlightened absolutism.

Joseph II was a different matter entirely. Certainly Maria Theresia strove to educate him as a devoted son of the Church, but one informed by reform Catholic perspectives. Thus, his most important teacher, Christian August Beck, the professor of natural law at the noble academy (the *Theresianum*), stressed the need to foster the true faith, but emphasized that this could not be done through coercion but only through kindness and persuasion.[182] Further, while his mother's views were unbending, those of his father were much more flexible.[183] We do not know what reading Joseph did independently, but by the time of his famous memorandum of 1765, as has been pointed out, Joseph's God was a cameralist God.[184] A sovereign, he asserted, has to look after the common

---

[181] Ernst Wangermann, "Matte Morgenröte: Verzug und Widerruf im späten Reformwerk Maria Theresias," in Koschatzky, ed., *Maria Theresia und Ihre Zeit*, pp. 67–71.

[182] Hermann Conrad, *et al.*, eds., *Recht und Verfassung des Reiches in der Zeit Maria Theresias* (Cologne & Opladen, 1964), pp. 276–279.

[183] Adam Wandruszka, "Die Religiosität Franz Stephans von Lothringen," *MÖStA* XII (1959), 162–173.   [184] Wangermann, *Austrian Achievement*, p. 96.

The issue of toleration   249

good, not after individual consciences, and forcible conversion would in any case do little to change inner convictions. The priorities expressed here were certainly wholly secular: "The service of God is inseparable from that of the state, and God wants us to utilize those whom he has endowed with talents and capacity for things, leaving the reward of good and the punishment of evil to his divine mercy."[185] In subsequent years this pragmatic utilitarian approach was enhanced by Joseph's many trips within and without the Monarchy, voyages which gradually crystallized a strong conviction that confessional toleration was not only a policy with patent economic benefits, but one that had foreign policy advantages as well, blunting the appeal of non-Catholic powers such as Prussia and Russia for Habsburg subjects.[186]

The cameralist roots of Kaunitz were even stronger. Already on his cavalier tour he contrasted the United Netherlands, where the toleration of all religions enhanced commerce, with the dirty and poor intolerant Austrian Netherlands,[187] and by the early 1760s French Enlightenment views on toleration had swept through Vienna. In the circle of Kaunitz's nightly *assemblées* Voltaire's *Traité sur la tolérance* (1763) was making the rounds early in 1764,[188] and apparently shortly thereafter Kaunitz made his first serious attempt to press for a policy of greater confessional toleration on political grounds. Lack of support from others and the outright opposition of Maria Theresia, however, made him decide not to "force the issue."[189] This did not mean that Kaunitz, cautious as he was in the matter, remained silent. Throughout the subsequent years he continued to chip away at the edifice of intolerance, though he was clearly very careful to take Maria Theresia's sensibilities into account.

What very limited success Kaunitz had in this regard tended to come in Hungary, where constitutional guarantees made the toleration of Protestants in some areas necessary. Thus, for example, he was able to prevent the cancellation of freedom of worship earlier granted the small Greek Orthodox community of Keskemeth in southern Hungary on the grounds that it would be uncharitable.[190] On another occasion he was able to push

---

[185] *MTJC* III, 352.   [186] Karniel, *Toleranzpolitik*, pp. 127–189.
[187] Klingenstein, *Aufstieg des Hauses Kaunitz*, pp. 233, 238–241.
[188] HHStA, Kabinettsarchiv: Zinzendorf Tagebuch, Vol. 9, 21, 23 and 27 February 1764.
[189] This was, in any case, how Kaunitz recalled it in 1768. I was unable to locate the original memo to which he alluded. See: HHStA, Familienarchiv: Hofreisen, Karton 3, Kaunitz's "Ohnmaßgebige Anmerkungen über ein Votum des Frh. von Borié. Die Bannatische und Sclavonische Reiß-Relation Ihr. Kays. Mayt. betreffend," n.d. (1768). The discussion on toleration in university and government circles between 1764 and 1767 is also discussed briefly in Wolfsgruber, *Migazzi*, pp. 415–417.
[190] HHStA, Kabinettsarchiv: Kaunitz Voten, Karton 1, No. 375 of 1767, Kaunitz Staatsrat Votum, 13 March 1767; Staatsratprotokolle, Vol. 24, No. 375, imperial resolution, and Maria Theresia to Esterházy, 22 April 1767.

through a Hungarian Treasury recommendation that skilled Protestant craftsmen be permitted to immigrate to certain parts of Hungary with the argument that, given the variety of religion in Hungary, "a few thousand non-Catholics more or less" could hardly pose a threat to the dominance of Catholicism.[191] In Austria and Bohemia Kaunitz confronted a thicker wall of frustration. He was able to counter a draconian decree project against blasphemy only by arguing that sufficient provisions already existed in criminal law to deal with any overt interference with religious services. But his maxim that, "though harsh punishments are the easiest, they are not the most productive and most Christian means to check disbelief," found little sympathy from the Empress.[192] Indeed, Maria Theresia was highly sensitive even to the religious activities of ambassadors of foreign powers. When she discovered that the Russian ambassador, Prince Dimitri Galitzin, had set up a private chapel outside the embassy, Kaunitz was unable to effect even tacit toleration of it despite enumerating the possible repercussions any action against Galitzin would have on the Austrian embassy in St. Petersburg and on the Franciscan missions in Russia.[193]

Such examples only underscored the degree to which Maria Theresia regarded betrayal of the religion a greater crime than treason to her person.[194] Kaunitz showed that he was well aware of this, and always took care not to overstep his bounds in this very sensitive issue. He held up uniformity of religion as a desirable ideal, and met the Empress half way by suggesting there had to be good and important reasons to make exceptions (though he also argued that fostering industry and commerce was such a reason).[195] He knew perfectly well, as he put it, that "in this city one does not tolerate anything which has even the appearance of being against good morals,"[196] and told his good friend Raniero Calzabigi: "One can't force events, as you know, my dear Calzabigi. All that one can do is to guide them if one can, and to seize the occasions when they present themselves. That is certainly what I do and will continue to do."[197] To indulge Maria Theresia's sensibilities he was scrupulous in his own observance of the sacraments, and even went so far as to have his attendance of confession

[191] *Ibid.*, Kaunitz Voten, Karton 1, No. 962 of 1767, Kaunitz Staatsrat Votum, 30 May 1767; Kabinettsarchiv, Staatsratprotokolle, Vol. 25, No. 962, imperial resolution, 3 June 1767.
[192] *Ibid.*, Kaunitz Voten, Karton 1, No. 451 of 1767, Kaunitz Staatsrat Votum, 25 March 1767; Staatsratprotokolle, Vol. 24, No. 451, imperial resolution, 20 April 1767.
[193] HHStA, Staatskanzlei: Vorträge, Karton 106, Kaunitz to Maria Theresia, including imperial resolution, 18 October 1770.   [194] Arneth, *Maria Theresia* X, 60.
[195] HHStA, Familienarchiv: Hofreisen, Karton 3, Kaunitz's "Ohnmaßgebige Anmerkungen."
[196] HHStA, Staatskanzlei: Interiora, Fasz. 108, Kaunitz to Koháry, 17 July 1770.
[197] HHStA, Sonstige Sammlungen: Grosse Korrespondenz, Fasz. 405, Kaunitz to Calzabigi, 18 September 1775.

certified by a priest so he could send this "confessional receipt" to her when he was unable to attend Holy Week religious services at court as was customary.[198]

Joseph and Kaunitz, of course, represented only the spearhead of a broader movement towards religious toleration during the 1760s and 1770s. Prominent in this movement were most of the leading academic figures we have already encountered: Sonnenfels, Riegger, Martini, and their successor Joseph Valentin Eybel. The sentiments were also articulated by the growing Masonic movement, which included numerous government officials such as Gebler and Greiner, and most of the major literary and journalistic figures of the period such as Michael Denis, Aloys Blumauer and Johann Baptiste Alxinger. There were also strong tendencies towards a more tolerant confessional approach amongst the various stripes of reform Catholics, though neo-Jansenists in particular were by no means united on this subject. In short, the momentum for confessional toleration had been building for some years before the Moravian crypto-Protestant crisis of 1777 brought the question to the forefront.[199]

Joseph II was not in Vienna when the crisis broke, having left on his famous trip to France on April 1.[200] Once reports from Moravia reached Vienna, Maria Theresia began by seeking the advice of Kaunitz. In his response of May 23, he tried above all to calm the agitated Empress. He argued that heresy in Moravia was nothing new, and that the popular missionaries had merely touched on a long extant undercurrent. He also considered it beyond doubt that the root cause of this state of affairs was the "careless conduct" of the clergy. Finally he asserted that it was impossible to eliminate by force heretical sentiments which had survived for centuries – indeed, force would do little but "strengthen the fanaticism" of the individuals concerned. From these premises Kaunitz concluded that a return to the calm which existed prior to the missionaries' activities should be the first priority, and insisted that this could be done only by permitting secret or private Protestant worship. There were no quick cures. The only remedial action Kaunitz felt would be at all efficacious was pastoral "patience, gentleness and clear instruction" of the kind that the philo-Jansenist deacon, Johann Leopold Hay, had implemented so successfully in his episcopal district.[201] The other voice of moderation came from Kressel, who had been appointed to head an

---

[198] Arneth, *Maria Theresia* IX, 138.
[199] Charles Herold O'Brien, *Ideas of Religious Toleration in the Time of Joseph II* (Philadelphia, Pa., 1969).
[200] Hans Wagner, "Die Reise Josephs II. nach Frankreich 1777 und die Reformen in Österreich," in *Österreich und Europa: Festgabe für Hugo Hantsch*, pp. 221–246; Beales, *Joseph II* I, pp. 367–385.   [201] Maass, *Josephinismus* II, 217–219.

investigatory commission to look into the matter. Kaunitz supported the idea of such a commission, though he stressed that it was important any such body focus more on the restoration of tranquility rather than on inquisitional confrontation.[202] Kressel was certainly the right man for this approach, and his investigations quickly revealed the degree to which the unrest had been the result of provocation and other devious strategies employed by the popular missions in the first place. He advised recalling the missions and engaging the talents of a Hay instead.[203] Hay was accordingly appointed to Kressel's commission and soon agreed that clerical neglect and incompetence were the real root of the problem. The other members of the commission were the equally reform-minded provosts, Ferdinand Kinderman von Schulstein and Marx Anton Wittola, both of whom preferred education over coercion.[204]

These counsels of moderation were quickly drowned out by the stormier voices of the clerical conservatives, led by the papal nuncio, Archbishop Migazzi, and Austro-Bohemian Chancellor Blümegen, who wanted dramatic, draconian and quick action, including the deportation to Transylvania of the worst offenders. Joseph was also informed, and this led to the by now very famous and frequently cited exchange of letters on the issue of toleration in which Joseph argued, first cautiously then more insistently, that religious diversity was not necessarily a political problem, decried the use of force in matters of conscience and openly urged a policy of toleration. The no less passionate responses of his mother focused on the necessity of an official religion, and urged her son not to be seduced by "false arguments" and "evil books". When Joseph returned and visited Moravia himself in August the confrontation escalated, with Joseph threatening to resign his position as Co-Regent if draconian measures were implemented, and though maternal reproaches made him moderate his tone somewhat in the course of this correspondence, he held firmly to his position. His obstinacy was not without effect, for at the very least he was able to push through the principle of fuller consultation before any precipitous action was undertaken.[205]

Kaunitz was the first to be consulted. In view of Joseph's inability to change the Empress's mind, Kaunitz knew he would have to go about positing a position of toleration very carefully. He had learned a lot from

---

[202] HHStA, Staatskanzlei: Vorträge, Karton 123, Kaunitz to Maria Theresia, 8 June 1777.

[203] HHStA, Kabinettsarchiv: Nachlaß Kressel, Fasz. 1, Kressel to Maria Theresia, 17 June 1777, and "Allerunterthänigste Bericht," 18 June 1777.

[204] Georg Loesche, "Maria Theresias letzte Maßnahmen gegen die Ketzer," *Zeitschrift des deutschen Vereins für die Geschichte Mährens und Schlesiens* XX (1916), 419–421; Reinhold Joseph Wolny, *Die josephinische Toleranz unter besonderer Berücksichtigung ihres geistlichen Wegbereiters Johann Leopold Hay* (Munich, 1973), pp. 41–67.

[205] *MTJC* II, 140–167; Arneth, *Maria Theresia* X, 63–65.

his own failures in the area over the previous decade, and he saw to it that the report would be as carefully phrased as possible. It was reworked several times and finally submitted to the Empress on 18 October 1777.[206] Kaunitz began by noting that heresy had existed in the lands of the Bohemian crown since pre-Reformation times, and even patents of 1726 and 1754 which had made it a capital crime had not been able to eradicate it. The question of what to do about it was therefore complex. In answer Kaunitz posited the premise that nothing ought to be done which conflicted "with the essence and spirit of true Christianity and with the welfare of the state." Force, to his mind, was not concomitant with true Christianity. Faith was a gift of God and the result of the operation of divine grace. Religious coercion was therefore un-Christian, and not a legitimate right of a sovereign. Monarchs did have the right to restrict entry into their kingdoms, or to exile heretics, but such actions would only serve to depopulate the state and undermine its socio-economic welfare. Deportation to Protestant areas of Hungary would also be counterproductive, since so long as Protestants lived in a Catholic environment, there was still hope for their souls. In a Protestant environment, not only they but their descendants would be lost to the faith. Under these circumstances, Kaunitz concluded, the only feasible option was to grant a certain degree of confessional toleration, and hope for effective results from the "apostolic zeal of the clergy" to reverse the heretical tide with "Christian love." Concretely he recommended that the Moravian provincial authorities be issued a secret instruction, drafted according to the following principles: 1) a distinction had to be made between peaceful, law-abiding heretics and overt trouble makers; 2) the latter should be dealt with by ordinary process of law; 3) the former had to be left to the mercy of God and the care of the clergy; 4) heretics were to be permitted private worship in their homes; 5) only those heretics were to be liable for punishment who openly slandered Roman Catholicism; 6) since forced partaking of the sacraments led to sacrilege, only "Christian patience" could be applied; 7) though heretics should not formally be excused from attending religious instruction, local authorities should look the other way, proceeding "with all possible forbearance, restraint and prudence"; and, finally, 8) minors were to be obliged to attend religious instruction.[207]

These comments were passed on to Kressel and Blümegen, while Kaunitz in turn received documentation on arrested heretics whose punishments he was asked to assess in light of his eight points. He declined

---

[206] HHStA, Staatskanzlei: Vorträge, Karton 124. An initial draft, dated 13 October, was published by Beer, ed., "Denkschriften des Fürsten Kaunitz," pp. 158–162, the report of 18 October by Maass, *Josephinismus* II, 219–223. Kaunitz's various pencil notes were not published by either.   [207] Maass, *Josephinismus* II, 219–223.

to comment on those on whom sentence had already been passed, but in the fifteen remaining cases recommended the dismissal of five and the substantial reduction of the sentences of the remainder.[208] Blümegen and Kressel accepted these suggested sentences, though Kressel made a point of underscoring the necessity of making an example of anyone who had resisted the military or openly incited others. But Kressel completely accepted Kaunitz's eight recommendations, and Kaunitz in turn accepted Kressel's insistence on firmness.[209] Blümegen was another matter. He thought that if heretics were allowed to worship in private in their homes, it would be no different from the legislation of toleration as such. He insisted on very careful investigation to prevent heretics from spreading their creed. Kaunitz objected to the excessively inquisitorial tone of Blümegen's comments. If the gathering of three or four friends in a private home took place, this was no concern for the authorities. No one should be prevented from visiting his friends, and if Protestants doing so were arrested on the suspicion that they were holding a religious service, it could have nothing but detrimental consequences. "The sovereign," he concluded, "must seek to ignore as much as possible, and therefore inquire into as little as is possible."[210]

At about the same time the original Blümegen report, having now made the rounds of the Council of State, reached Kaunitz in his capacity as a member of that body. He took advantage of the opportunity to press the case with renewed vigor. Since all the other Council of State members had opposed draconian measures, he now endorsed their stand. Because he expected his eight recommendations to meet with royal approval, he suggested that all cases of arrested heretics now be re-examined in that more generous light, and he firmly opposed deportation to remote regions of Hungary for all but the most extreme cases.[211] Kaunitz could well be pleased, as his pencil notes clearly indicate, for not only had the Council of State completely endorsed his eight recommendations, Hatzfeld even drew up a report in which the unanimous support of Kaunitz was reinforced. Kressel's commission also supported him; even Blümegen changed his mind and endorsed the recommendations in a report of 7 November; and, of course, there was the emperor himself, who continued to remain firm in his position. Kaunitz did not fail to point out this unanimity to a reluctant Maria Theresia, expressing the hope that it would ease her mind and reassure her conscience enough to move her to a resolution in accordance

[208] HHStA, Staatskanzlei: Vorträge, Karton 124, Kaunitz to Maria Theresia, 21 October 1777.   [209] Ibid., Kaunitz to Maria Theresia, 28 October 1777.
[210] Maass, Josephinismus II, 224–228.
[211] HHStA, Staatskanzlei: Vorträge, Karton, Karton 124, copy of Kaunitz Staatsrat Votum, n.d. (late October 1777).

with his original recommendations.[212] This time Kaunitz succeeded. Two days later the Empress issued the official instruction to the Moravian authorities which not only contained Kaunitz's recommendations, but, indeed, in most places his very words.[213] Joseph agreed that this was probably the most that could be had from the Empress and supported the instruction, though he could not resist the carping comment that it was still inadequate.[214]

The success was not without its setbacks, however. Within weeks Blümegen was again recommending deportation for a number of individuals still in custody, and while Kaunitz reiterated his sentiments about such dislocations in the Council of State, the Empress followed his advice in only a few cases, choosing to endorse the harsher Austro-Bohemian Chancellery suggestion in most.[215] Furthermore, despite the release of the official instructions, some local officials continued to show more inquisitorial zeal than Kaunitz would have liked. Houses were searched for heretical books, military force was often used, and further arrests took place. In the Council of State, Kaunitz was incensed: "To ransack the houses of these poor people in order to discover forbidden books there, or worse yet, to incite the army to do so by offering rewards, is diametrically opposed to the guidelines established by Her Majesty." He noted bitterly that the spirit of the instruction was not being followed, and urged a stern reminder be issued to ensure that it was. Here, too, the appropriate order went out using in large part the very words of Kaunitz.[216]

What followed this order was, at best, an uneasy peace. Maria Theresia had considerable expectations that the policy of tacit toleration combined with the pastoral innovations of Kressel, Hay and the others, would lead to the return of many heretics to the true fold. Many Protestants in Moravia saw it as the first step towards full legal toleration. Local officials continued to renege, if not on the letter, then at least on the spirit of the instruction. This last problem caught Kaunitz's particular ire, since he saw it as the very heart of the problems of the Monarchy:

All will be for naught ... if the execution of the all-highest commands remains in the hands of such people, who, because of their own blind and insurmountable prejudices, neither can nor want to understand them, and who continue to retain

---

[212] *Ibid.*, Kaunitz to Maria Theresia, 12 November 1777.

[213] HHStA, Familienarchiv: Sammelbände, Karton 7, Maria Theresia to Blümegen, 14 November 1777. Cf. Arneth, *Maria Theresia* X, 71–72.

[214] HHStA, Familienarchiv: Sammelbände, Karton 7, Joseph to Leopold, 20 November 1777.

[215] HHStA, Kabinettsarchiv: Kaunitz Voten, Karton 3, No. 2202 of 1777, Kaunitz Staatsrat Votum, [early] December 1777; Staatsratprotokolle, Vol. 62, No. 2202, imperial resolution, 12 December 1777.

[216] *Ibid.*, Kaunitz Voten, Karton 3, No. 160 of 1778, Kaunitz Staatsrat Votum, 2 February 1778; Staatsratprotokolle, Vol. 63, No. 160, imperial resolution, 9 February 1778.

the firm conviction that that which can only be regarded the result of God's mercy, human gentleness and persuasion, can and must be extorted with arrests, canings, hard labour and other criminal punishments.

He wanted to see all such officials relieved of their positions, and the entire matter entrusted only to Kressel's pastoral commission.[217]

This commission soon took matters one step further. Hay, who was its leading light, came to the conclusion that the only way to avoid further confusion and problems was to release a formal patent clearly stating the rights and limitations of the Protestants of Moravia. Kaunitz concurred with this completely. He therefore edited and then seconded Hay's draft patent enthusiastically in a report of 9 February 1780. Kaunitz was confident that the Empress was ready to accept the patent, but Blümegen objected strenuously that it would hinder future conversions, while Joseph objected that it did not go far enough. Again Kaunitz's opinion was sought. Now he was more unequivocal. In two separate memoranda he first turned on Blümegen, and affirmed that the premise of the patent was indeed one of legal toleration, whose objective was to abolish confessional coercion. The fact had to be faced that these were unconvertible Protestants, Kaunitz noted, but this did not mean they could not remain good subjects. He then turned to Joseph's insistence on an even more liberal text, and amended the patent accordingly. Joseph then agreed that if Kaunitz's amendments were left untouched, and the law enforced scrupulously and extended to every other province of the Monarchy, he would support the decree. Certain that the decree was on the verge of being passed, Kaunitz agreed with Joseph that extension was "founded in the nature of the matter, and the necessary consequence" of the resolution adopted.[218]

These expectations were now to be shattered. For a week the Empress, goaded by Migazzi,[219] fought with her conscience, and in this "cruel predicament" came to the conclusion: "the more I consider [Joseph's conditions] the less I can accept them." In two separate notes Kaunitz gave vent to his frustrations. He was "very aggrieved and highly astonished" that the Empress would want to abandon the decree at a moment of such unanimity among all her advisers. He asserted that he could not understand her objections, and gave his full support to Joseph's sentiments.[220] Events now deteriorated rapidly. On 13 May 1780 some four thousand Protestants gathered near Wisowitz and openly celebrated Maria Theresia's birthday

---

[217] *Ibid.*, Kaunitz Voten, Karton 3, No. 1893 of 1779, Kaunitz Staatsrat Votum, 7 January 1780.

[218] Maass, *Josephinismus* II, 40–61, 240–252; Wolny, *Die josephinische Toleranz*, pp. 65–66; Loesche, "Maria Theresias letzte Maßnahmen," pp. 412–440.

[219] Wolfsgruber, *Migazzi*, pp. 422–424.   [220] Maass, *Josephinismus* II, 251–253.

with a Protestant religious service. Military force was used to disperse the crowds and numerous arrests were made.[221] Though the presiding preacher was among those arrested, the Council of State advised his release. Kaunitz seconded this advice, and added wryly that the whole incident had been the result of the failure to follow his earlier advice. He fully expected "still more serious consequences and incidents than the present one [to] arise sooner or later" elsewhere.[222] It was hardly a comment devoid of bitterness, and to underscore this mood Kaunitz refused to take any further part in the discussion. All documents that came to his ministry on the subject from that date on were simply given to Binder, and all reports to the Empress on the matter were drafted and signed by the latter,[223] despite the Empress's best efforts to re-engage Kaunitz in the debate and to bring him around to her point of view.[224]

Maria Theresia, in any case, remained firm in her hard line. She confirmed her willingness to resort to draconian measures, and in September she sentenced forty-three Moravian Protestants to deportation to Hungary.[225] It was certainly a bitter irony indeed that only days before her death Maria Theresia seemed prepared to return to the draconian Counter-Reformation policy whose failure in the earlier part of the century had been largely responsible for the ecclesiastical reform impulse of her reign in the first place. But in the event these dark clouds did not presage a false dawn as some feared. The reform dynamic had a momentum of its own. The redirection of ecclesiastical policy in the 1770s by Joseph and Kaunitz from its stern Jansenist track to a more humane secularism insured a sunrise after all.

[221] Arneth, *Maria Theresia* X, 74–75.
[222] HHStA, Staatskanzlei: Vorträge, Karton 131, Kaunitz to Maria Theresia, 27 May 1780.
[223] *Ibid.*, Kartons 131 and 132, Binder to Maria Theresia, 27 May, 22 June, 30 September, 24 October and 30 October 1780.
[224] When Kaunitz forwarded a dispatch from his ambassador in Britain reporting serious popular anti-Catholic riots in London, the Empress could not restrain the sardonic remark: "One sees from this how elsewhere heretics commit excesses against the true faith while constantly preaching nothing but tolerance. I also do not learn much about freedom from this so highly praised form of government, which permits such excesses that one would enjoy more security among Turks. And despite this, all everyone wants to do is to follow English precedents and ideas." *Ibid.*, Karton 132, Maria Theresia to Kaunitz, imperial resolution on Kaunitz report of 19 June 1780.
[225] Arneth, *Maria Theresia* X, 75.

7   The military albatross

The Habsburg military establishment lay at the very center of the reform impetus and the debates surrounding it throughout the reign of Maria Theresia. Military defeats were the most obvious symptoms of the Habsburg commonwealth's relative weakness and backwardness in the three decades from the early 1730s to the early 1760s, and there is little doubt that the major impulse for political as well as military change came from a determination to redress this perceived inferiority. The political, social and particularly fiscal ramifications of creating a military establishment equal to the difficult international challenges which confronted the Monarchy were the key issues over which bitter differences of opinion prevailed. These differences, in turn, were based on differing diagnoses of the military failures of the two major wars in the Empress's reign. The military reforms of Maria Theresia thus fall into two very distinct periods. The first period covers the reforms undertaken in response to the failures of the War of the Austrian Succession, and includes the test of the mettle of the reformed army in the Seven Years War. The failure to achieve victory in this war, for which the diplomatic framework established by Kaunitz seemed to hold out so much promise, led to the second period of army reform. The premises of this reform period then dominated Habsburg military thinking well into the era of the French Revolution. In broad terms one can characterize the two phases as the era of the army as state enterprise, and the era of the army as national enterprise.

Standing armies had been one of the chief factors contributing to the rise of absolutism after the Thirty Years' War, serving both to affirm the sovereignty of a prince's domain in relationship with others and as one of his principal instruments in the domestic struggle with aristocratic particularism. The integral relationship of the two functions was underscored early in the reign of Maria Theresia. The maintenance of the integrity of her inheritance depended on military might, and the need for a certain level of military power in turn became the lever by which provincial Estates were deprived of much of their political power. Survival

258

in the predatory world of international relations and the successful implementation of absolutism at home depended on the creation of a new professional army, freed from the pluralistic chaos created by the regimental proprietorship of ambitious "military entrepreneurs" and the vicissitudes of Estates funding and control. Herein lay the essential framework of the debates surrounding the first reform period of the Habsburg army under Maria Theresia.[1]

While the new professional army acquitted itself creditably in the Seven Years' War, the Habsburg Monarchy failed to achieve its major political objective. Hence the army remained the focus of debate. Had failure been due to inadequate troop strength, to inadequate financing, to inadequate organization, to inadequate training, or to inadequate leadership? This debate was decisively influenced by Joseph II who tended to accept the views of most military men that, whatever lay at the heart of the reverses of the war, it was not a failure of leadership. Men such as these, accordingly, emulated eagerly the model of Prussian militarism which seemed to have won Frederick II so much success: a disproportionately large, well organized and well drilled standing army underwritten by massive military spending, leading inexorably to a greater integration of military and civilian life, and the subordination of the priorities of the latter to the former. In direct conflict with this lobby was a party which considered the ordering of Austrian finances as the first priority of government, and which regarded burgeoning military spending as one of the chief impediments to increased prosperity. It saw the chief failures of the war to have been in leadership and vigorously opposed the transformation of the Habsburg Athens into a Hohenzollern Sparta.

The Seven Years War

In the 1730s it seemed as if the army of Emperor Charles VI, in the words of a leading military historian, "had literally fallen asleep on the laurels of Prince Eugene."[2] A disappointing military performance in the War of the Polish Succession was followed by even more ignominious setbacks in the short Turkish War of 1737–1739. Then, with the accession of Maria

---

[1] Johann Christoph Allmayer-Beck, "Wandlung im Heereswesen zur Zeit Maria Theresias," and Hans Bleckwenn, "Die Regimenter der Kaiserin," both in Direktion des Militärwissenschaftliches Instituts, Vienna, ed., *Maria Theresia: Beiträge zur Geschichte des Heerwesens ihrer Zeit* (Graz, Vienna and Cologne, 1967), pp. 7–30; Barker, *Army, Aristocracy, Monarchy.*

[2] Johann Christoph Allmayer-Beck, "Die Armee Maria Theresias und Josephs II.," in Zöllner and Möcker, eds., *Österreich*, p. 72.

Theresia in 1740, so feeble was the military response to the Prussian rape of Silesia that the members of the predatory Alliance of Nymphemburg could conclude confidently that a complete collapse of the Habsburg Monarchy was imminent. Though the battlefield performance of the Habsburg forces in campaigns other than against Prussia was respectable, and though the Monarchy survived the onslaught with only one major loss (that of the province of Silesia), the young Queen and subsequent Empress was under no illusions about her patrimony's state of military preparedness. She waxed bitter over the condition of her armed forces and clearly saw the need for a fundamental transformation of the Habsburg military establishment.[3]

The reforms undertaken in response to this crisis proceeded on many fronts at once. The recruiting system was overhauled and troop strengths were augmented to create a standing army of 108,000 men.[4] The administrative apparatus of the War Ministry, the so-called Aulic War Council (*Hofkriegsrat*), was rationalized and brought under closer monarchical supervision. The Commissariat for Military Supply (*Generalkriegskommissariat*) was given ministerial status in an effort to reduce friction within the War Ministry and to improve military economy.[5] With the state assuming all responsibility for the military establishment, the age of the regimental proprietors came to an end and standardization in equipment and training became the rule. Everything from weapons to flags and uniforms were subjected to normative specifications, and in many cases, particularly in the artillery branch, to substantial technical innovations.[6] Particularly significant was the introduction of a new Field Service Regulation, drafted by General Leopold von Daun, which acted as a service and drill manual, as well as a handbook of elementary tactics, and which enhanced discipline, coherence and uniformity in the ranks.[7] Finally, the social status and professional training of officers were upgraded with the object of attracting talented individuals and developing a gifted and

[3] Arneth, *Maria Theresia* IV, 87; Kallbrunner, ed., *Testament*, pp. 35, 71–72.
[4] Alphons Freiherr von Wrede and Anton Semek, *Geschichte der k. und k. Wehrmacht*, 5 Vols. (Vienna, 1898–1905), I, 98–99; Jürg Zimmermann, *Militärverwaltung und Heeresaufbringung in Österreich bis 1806*, Vol. III of Gerhard Papke, ed., *Handbuch zur deutschen Militärgeschichte. 1648–1939* (Frankfurt a/M, 1965), pp. 103–104.
[5] *ÖZV* II/1/i, 18–35; Oskar Regele, *Der Österreichische Hofkriegrat, 1556–1848* (Vienna, 1949), p. 23; Zimmerman, *Militärverwaltung*, pp. 69–71.
[6] Christopher Duffy, *The Army of Maria Theresia: The Armed Forces of Imperial Austria, 1740–1780* (North Pomfret, Vermont, Vancouver and London, 1977; Bleckwenn, "Die Regimenter der Kaiserin," pp 25–53.
[7] Georg Ortenburg, ed., *Regulament und Ordnung des gesammten Kaiserlich-Königlichen Fuß-Volcks von 1749: Faksimiledruck der Originalausgbe*, 2 Vols., (Osnabrück, 1969); Alexander Balisch, "Die Entstehung des Exerzierreglements von 1749," *MÖStA* XXVII (1974), 170–194.

ambitious officer corps.[8] That all these measures began to bear fruit within a short period of time became evident from the army maneuvers in the mid-1750s,[9] but the real test would come only with the outbreak of the Seven Years War in 1756.

The fundamental question which poses itself with this war, of course, is to account for the "miracle of the House of Brandenburg" – that is, the survival of Prussia in the face of Kaunitz's grand alliance, and the failure of the Habsburg Monarchy to recover the plundered province of Silesia. Though military analysts from Napoleon on, as well as Prussophile German nationalist and Nazi historians, were inclined to credit the "military genius" of Frederick II with Prussia's survival, Frederick himself attributed his "heaven-sent" redemption to a combination of fortuitous accident and the strategic and tactical errors, "the divine stupidity", of his enemies.[10] Modern analysts have been more sensitive to the inherent limitations of eighteenth-century warfare. Difficulties in recruitment, finance and supply made armies precious commodities not to be squandered in precipitous combat. This made commanders reluctant to give battle, inclining them instead to strategies of outmaneuvering the enemy and wearing him down in an endless game of positioning. Freedom of movement was much hindered by the battle order, and especially by the linear tactics of the eighteenth century, and this gave a decided advantage to the defensive in general, and to the forces commanding interior lines in particular. Generals who had to answer to monarchs for every move they made tended to wear the mantle of accountability uneasily, and this only added to the disinclination to take risks.[11]

In all these respects Frederick II had a decided advantage. Prussia's conscription, or "canton" system, its disproportionate ratio of military to civilian population, and the military priorities of its fiscal policies, allowed it to raise requisite-sized armies with fewer difficulties than its foes. After the surprise attack on Saxony, the systematic plundering of its assets and the bodily incorporation of its army into the Prussian, Frederick not only enjoyed a resource and manpower windfall, but thenceforth operated with the enormous advantage of interior lines. As both king and commander-in-

[8] Prussia, Großer Generalstab, Kriegsgeschichtliche Abteilung II, ed., *Die Kriege Friedrichs des Großen*, Part 3: *Der Siebenjährige Krieg, 1756–1763*, 12 Vols. (Berlin, 1901–1913), I, 130–151; Guglia, *Maria Theresia* II, 19–23.

[9] Duffy, *Army of Maria Theresia*, pp. 166–167.

[10] Frederick II of Prussia, *Politische Correspondenz Friedrich's des Grossen*, 46 Vols., (Berlin, 1879–1939), XVIII, 516, No. 11403; XXI, 462, No. 13710. The phrase "the miracle of the House of Brandenburg" was first used by Frederick to describe the failure of the Austro-Russian forces to follow up effectively their victory at Kunersdorf in 1759, *Ibid.*, XVIII, 510–511, No. 11393.

[11] Problems and the relevant literature are summarized in Johannes Kunisch, *Das Mirakel des Hauses Brandenburg* (Munich and Vienna, 1978), pp. 60–89.

chief, Frederick could also afford to take the kind of military risks which even he would not have permitted his own generals, with the result that he enjoyed an advantage in both flexibility and response time.[12] Finally, Frederick was free from the need to co-ordinate his military plans with those of his allies, while Kaunitz's grand alliance, imposing though it appeared on paper, was severely hampered by problems of coalition warfare: conflicting diplomatic goals, mutual suspicion and recrimination, and poor co-ordination brought about by misunderstandings and by personality conflicts.[13] In this context the "miracle of the House of Brandenburg" does not appear to be such a miracle after all, and is largely explainable by structural problems inherent in government, military organization and warfare of the *ancien régime*.

However, as even the most forceful proponent of this thesis has conceded, the failures of individual generals contributed "to a crucial degree" to the collapse of Habsburg war aims,[14] and the central question of what proved to be the decisive liability remains open. At the time military men naturally were inclined to argue that the maximum effect was being achieved with the tools at hand; if these failed to win the political objectives of the court, then the tools were inadequate. In direct opposition to this view stood Kaunitz. Though he had had no direct political involvement with any of the Habsburg military reforms of the inter-war period, and in subsequent decades he was to claim repeatedly that he was no military expert, he was nevertheless involved with strategic deliberations in considerable detail during the war. As chairman of the War Cabinet, he was placed in the forefront of co-ordinating the war effort. He was, as we have seen, also in personal correspondence with all significant field commanders, Austrian military attachés with allied army corps, and a host of special envoys; he received all details of troop movements and supply conditions, as well as reports from line commanders through the Aulic War Council;[15] and was shown all letters from field commanders to the

---

[12] Gordon Craig, *The Politics of the Prussian Army, 1640–1945* (London, Oxford and N.Y., 1955), pp. 12–20; Otto Büsch, *Militärsystem und Sozialleben im Alten Preußen, 1713–1087*, 2nd ed. (Berlin, 1981); Peter Bachmann and Kurt Zeisler, *Der deutsche Militarismus vom 17. Jahrhundert bis 1917*, 2nd ed. (Cologne, 1986), pp. 88–93.

[13] Ernst von Frisch, *Zur Geschichte der russischen Feldzüge im siebenjährigen Kriege* (Heidelberg, 1919); Dieter Ernst Bangert, *Die russisch-österreichische militärische Zusammenarbeit im Siebenjährigen Kriege in den Jahren 1758–1759* (Boppard am Rhein, 1971); Johannes Kunisch, "Die große Allianz der Gegner Preußens im Siebenjährigen Krieg," in Bernhard R. Kroener, ed., *Europa im Zeitalter Friedrichs des Großen* (Munich, 1989), pp. 79–97.   [14] Kunisch, *Mirakel*, p. 53.

[15] KA, Protokolle in Publicis, records some typical examples: Vol. 906, No. 63, 14 January 1757; Vol. 907 (i), No. 831, 18 May 1757; Vol. 907 (ii), No. 1609, 30 August 1757; Vol. 913, No. 690, 25 March 1758, and No. 694, 26 March 1758; Vol. 924, No. 1689, 29 November 1759; Vol. 931, No. 1133, 27 June 1760; Vol. 938, No. 1298, 8 August 1761.

Empress, so that he was clearly the one minister who was as fully informed on every facet of the military situation as the Empress herself. Most importantly, however, Kaunitz was the man who actually formulated the operational directives (*Cabinet Schreiben*) which Maria Theresia dispatched to the front through the Chancellery of State.[16] Kaunitz was thus not unaware of the severe structural limitations within which the Habsburg military machine had to operate, but he still had confidence in it, and he remained persuaded that more audacity and initiative on the part of field commanders could produce the desired effect.

As signs became clear during June 1756 that Frederick II of Prussia was mobilizing his forces in order to offset his diplomatic setbacks with some bold military stroke, Vienna began to take appropriate counter-measures. The War Cabinet was set up and initiated mobilization in response to the Prussian military build-up, with the objective of concentrating 90,000 men in three phases by the end of December.[17] Habsburg counter-mobilization, however, precipitated a Prussian ultimatum whose rejection Kaunitz felt would likely lead to war. Despite these expectations, Frederick's unprovoked assault on Saxony with overwhelming manpower superiority at the end of August came as a shock and surprise to all of Europe. Within two weeks the entire electorate was occupied, and on 13 September, Frederick formally declared war on the Habsburg Monarchy and began an invasion of Bohemia. The first major engagement with the Habsburg Bohemian army under Field Marshall Maximilian Ulysses von Browne at Lobositz (Lovosice), however, came as a shock to the king.[18] In the first instance, as he noted with grudging respect, "these [were] no longer the old Austrians." The inter-war reforms had clearly transformed the Habsburg army into a fighting force that could stand on equal terms with the Prussian. A bold and imaginative commander such as Browne had achieved all his military objectives as well as inflicting higher casualties on the Prussians than he himself suffered, and was denied complete success only by the failings of his officer corps.[19] As Christopher Duffy has

---

[16] HHStA, Staatskanzlei: Vorträge, Karton 83, Kaunitz to Maria Theresia, 8 July 1758; Karton 85, Kaunitz to Maria Theresia, 12 and 19 September 1759; Karton 86, Kaunitz to Maria Theresia, 25 February and 23 April 1760.   [17] Khevenhüller-Metsch V, 179.

[18] *Ibid.*, pp. 207, 209; Christopher Duffy, *The Wild Goose and the Eagle: A Life of Marshall von Browne, 1705–1757* (London, 1964), pp. 200–203.

[19] Arneth, *Maria Theresia* V, 15–20; Alfons Dopsch, *Das Treffen bei Lobositz* (Graz, 1892); Franz Quandt, *Die Schlacht bei Lobositz* (Charlottenburg, 1909); Prussia, Großer Generalstab, ed., *Kriege Friedrichs* 3/I, 170–330; Curt Jany, *Geschichte der Preussischen Armee*, 4 Vols. (Berlin, 1928–1933), II, 362–375; Richard Waddington, *La Guerre de sept ans*, 5 Vols. (Paris, 1899–1915), I, 22–44; Duffy, *Wild Goose*, pp. 203–233; Duffy *Army of Maria Theresia*, pp. 171–173; Duffy, *The Army of Frederick the Great* (Newton Abbot, London and Vancouver, 1974), pp. 167–169.

observed, it was ironic that Browne, who "had done all that an individual commander could...was let down in a critical moment by his subordinates," while Frederick fled the field but was saved by the bold action of his Field Marshall Jakob Keith.[20] Whatever the structural limitations within which Habsburg forces operated, neither recruitment, nor supply, nor troop efficiency failed the initial test; officer quality remained the principal shortcoming.

With his marked preference for bold and aggressive officers, Kaunitz became an enthusiastic backer of Browne. He spared no effort to rebut publicly Frederick's claim of Prussian victory at Lobositz,[21] and confided that as long as the crusty Irish field marshall was in charge he could "sleep quietly."[22] Command appointments, however, were hardly up to the Chancellor of State. Indeed, even Maria Theresia acknowledged that this was an area which Emperor Francis "reserved for himself." Even if he did not have complete control of command appointments, Maria Theresia was inclined to defer to her husband, and certainly no significant changes could be made without his knowledge and consent. The Emperor, however, was plainly less favourably inclined towards Browne, and it is hardly surprising that supreme command for the campaign of 1757 was assigned to the Emperor's brother, Prince Charles Alexander of Lorraine.[23]

Despite the enormous advantages Frederick had secured himself by the seizure of Saxony, Kaunitz remained convinced that Austrian prospects after the Lobositz campaign remained excellent. At the end of October 1756 he felt no further initiatives were necessary, and that military strength should be husbanded for a more effective strike at the beginning of the next campaign.[24] However, once again it was the Prussians who struck first with a two-pronged invasion of Bohemia on 18 April 1757. Within ten days these forces had advanced on Prague, where the hesitancy and timidity of Charles of Lorraine soon led to defeat on the field, with the remnants of the Habsburg army besieged in the city. Again, Habsburg forces had fought obstinately and effectively, and again the Prussians suffered the higher casualties. Once more failure lay at the command level.[25] Kaunitz had originally intended to travel to Prague himself to bring focus and direction to the military councils, but news of the disaster reached him *en route*. After

[20] Duffy, *Wild Goose*, p. 221.   [21] Khevenhüller-Metsch IV, 45.
[22] HHStA, Sonstige Sammlungen: Kriegsakten, Fasz. 413, Kaunitz to Browne, 23 October 1756.   [23] Khevenhüller-Metsch IV, 141, 206.
[24] HHStA, Sonstige Sammlungen: Kriegsakten, Faszikel 413, Kaunitz to Browne, 23 October 1756.
[25] Arneth, *Maria Theresia* V, 169–182; Khevenhüller-Metsch IV, 82–86; *Kriege Friedrichs* 3/II, 69–163; Jany, *Geschichte der Preussischen Armee* II, 391–407; Waddington; *Guerre de sept ans* I, 278–305; Duffy, *Wild Goose*, pp. 239–259; Duffy, *Army of Maria Theresia*, pp. 173–175; Duffy, *Army of Frederick*, pp. 169–171.

assessing the situation with Field Marshall Daun, who was bringing up a second Habsburg army from south-eastern Bohemia, he returned to Vienna where a series of meetings of the *Conferenz in mixtis* awaited him. Here Kaunitz noted how the very fate of the Monarchy had been placed at risk by sluggish troop movement in the fall of 1756, and by the lax concentration of forces in April 1757. He now recommended all haste in reinforcing the second Habsburg army under Daun,[26] and pressing it to attack without undue hesitation.[27] Daun began his advance on the very day on which Frederick had decided it was time to eliminate Daun's corps before it received any further reinforcements. This led to the famous battle of Kolin on 18 June, in which a steady Daun repulsed the Prussian attacks skillfully, resulting in a crushing Prussian defeat and Frederick's withdrawal from Bohemia.[28]

The battle of Kolin brought to fruition a plan originally conceived by Daun as early as 1749, but which had been blocked by Emperor Francis – the creation of a military order of valour to enhance the social status of the officer corps, and to nationalize, as it were, the concept of honour. The Empress tabled but did not abandon the idea, and with the outbreak of the war, she turned to it anew. During the winter she discussed the idea with Kaunitz, and in April the latter was commissioned to put together a formal proposal. Kaunitz dismissed earlier ideas of a military order named in honour of a saint and asserted it must have a secular, non-denominational character, with a design which focused on the state, and which symbolized the unity and indivisibility of the Habsburg Monarchy. He proposed the colours of the House of Austria, the simple red–white–red horizontal bars, which were to distinguish the ribbon as well as the center-piece of the order's cross. Otherwise Kaunitz recommended a dignified simplicity, with the grand cross and knights' cross adorned only with the device "Fortitudini" (Valour). The order was simply to be called the "Military Maria Theresia Order." The Emperor was won around by naming him grand master, but to emphasize that this was essentially the Empress's institution, the chancellor of the order (its executive and administrative officer) was to be her man: none other than Kaunitz himself! The creation of the Maria Theresia Order was originally scheduled to be proclaimed on

[26] Khevenhüller-Metsch IV, 91–94, 329–359; Franz-Lorenz von Thadden, *Feldmarschall Daun* (Vienna and Munich, 1967), pp. 227–230.

[27] HHStA, Staatskanzlei: Vorträge, Karton 80, Kaunitz to Maria Theresia, 8 June 1756, including draft letter to Daun. Cf. Thadden, *Feldmarschall Daun*, p. 255.

[28] Arneth, *Maria Theresia* V, 195–198; Maximilian Hoen, *Die Schlacht bei Kolin* (Vienna, 1911); *Kriege Friedrichs* 3/III, 1–93; Jany II, 407–421; Waddington I, 331–346; Duffy, *Army of Maria Theresia*, pp. 175–181; Duffy, *Army of Frederick*, pp. 171–172; Thadden, pp. 256–288; Peter Broucek, *Der Geburtstag der Monarchie: Die Schlacht bei Kolin 1757* (Vienna, 1982).

13 May 1757, but the recent defeat at Prague made that thoroughly inappropriate. Once the news of Kolin reached Vienna, however, Maria Theresia seized on 18 June, which she enthusiastically described as "the birthday of the Monarchy," as the most suitable date for its formal foundation. Daun, of course, was envisioned as the first recipient of the grand cross for the victory of Kolin, but it is symptomatic of all that was wrong with the Habsburg army that when the formal presentation ceremony was finally held on 7 March 1758, the first recipient of the grand cross was the emperor's brother.[29]

By the time Charles was awarded the Maria Theresia Order, it can already be considered to have been more a consolation than a reward for merit. Shortly after the battle of Prague Browne died, and Charles resumed overall command. The campaign he waged from late June to December 1757 was certainly a disaster and must be regarded as one of the most significant turning points in the Monarchy's failure to recoup Silesia. Whether the campaign ran aground on the structural limitations of eighteenth-century warfare or on Charles's own "divine stupidity" became very clear in these six months. Kaunitz persistently argued that in order to benefit from the recent victory two things were necessary. The first was to follow it up "without the slightest delay." The second was not to underestimate the still powerful enemy.[30] In the subsequent campaign Charles was to be guilty of failures in both, paving the way for disaster. He failed to press home his occasional manpower advantages, and pursued Frederick with such a sluggish and timid strategy that discontent in Vienna was brought to the boiling point.[31] Kaunitz's efforts to animate the campaign were supported not only by strategic arguments but also by moral ones. His personal philippics against the "monster and tyrant of the North"[32] grew during the course of the war into an argument that the Prussian military state represented a radical new intrusion into the political life of Western civilization.[33] He was persuaded that Prussian power was based solely on military might, and hence that only the destruction of that military force could lead to the collapse of Prussian power. If, as Kaunitz was convinced, Prussian militarism was "incompatible with the happiness

---

[29] Jaromir Hirtenfeld, *Der Militär-Maria-Theresien-Orden und seine Mitglieder*, 4 Vols. (Vienna, 1857–1890), I, 1–36; Khevenhüller-Metsch V, 13–15; Erwin Auer, "Der Maria-Theresiaen-Orden: Von der Ordensgemeinschaft zum Verdienstorden," *Numismatische Zeitschrift* LXXIV (1951), 106–112; Mikoletzky, *Österreich*, pp. 228–229; Thadden, pp. 299–303.   [30] Khevenhüller-Metsch IV, 377–379.

[31] Arneth, *aria Theresia* V, 205–206, 504; *Kriege Friedrichs* 3/III, 160–203; Waddington I, 346–364; Jany II, 421–423.

[32] MZA, Rodinný archiv Kounicŭ, Carton 1, Kaunitz's "Vers contre le Roi du Prusse" of 1756.

[33] On the centricity of this argument in the Habsburg propaganda campaign against Prussia during the Seven Years' War, see Kunisch, *Mirakel*, pp. 17–43.

of humanity," the destruction of its basis had to be the primary military objective.[34]

In a critical Privy Conference on August 17, Kaunitz therefore pushed through his view that it was absolutely vital to avoid having to retreat to Bohemia for winter quarters, and to risk a battle by undertaking a major thrust into Silesia.[35] Though Kaunitz lost all confidence that Charles was the man who could undertake this task effectively, no change in command was made. The Emperor made it clear that he would regard such a change "a personal dishonor," and thus Charles remained at his post.[36] Even when Frederick split his forces, marching the bulk of them to the west to ward off an advancing French army, Charles's pursuit of the remaining Prussian corps lacked all urgency. Once Frederick had crushed the French and imperial armies at Roßbach, he marched back to Silesia to relieve his beleaguered forces there. Despite Charles's agonizing dilatoriness, he came too late. Breslau fell to Habsburg troops on November 22 and the bulk of Silesia was in Austrian hands.[37] Frederick understood quite clearly, as Haugwitz had pointed out in August, and as Kaunitz repeated with emphasis in November,[38] that in the framework of eighteenth-century warfare the essence of success lay in establishing quarters in enemy territory. It eased supply problems from home, while at the same time depriving the opponent of substantial resources. This is why Frederick seized Saxony and tried to establish winter quarters in Bohemia in 1756. Since Habsburg forces now held the key positions of Breslau and Schweidnitz, they had achieved their strategic objective. It remained only to hold on to the prize against an advancing Frederick, who was now clearly set to risk the kind of attack on a numerically superior foe which had cost him Kolin. There was no longer any necessity to attack Frederick, only to ward him off with as many casualties as possible. This was Daun's forte. He occupied a formidable defensive position along the banks of the river Weistritz, and stood in a good position to repeat the victory at Kolin no matter how Frederick chose to attack. But Charles had other ideas, and asserted his command prerogative to push through maneuvers that have been aptly described as "brainless."[39] At the subsequent battle of Leuthen, Charles's "divine stupidity" handed Frederick the most complete victory he was ever to enjoy over Habsburg forces in this war, lost Austria

[34] Arneth, *Maria Theresia* V, 218–219, 508.   [35] Khevenhüller-Metsch IV, 387–393.
[36] Waddington I, 559.
[37] Arneth, *Maria Theresia* V, 226–256; *Kriege Friedrichs* 3/IV, 116–163; Jany II, 445–448; Waddington I, 561–572, 686–696; Thadden, pp. 304–319; Duffy, *Army of Maria Theresia*, pp. 181–184.
[38] HHStA, Staatskanzlei: Vorträge, Karton 81, Kaunitz to Maria Theresia, 21 November 1757; Arneth, *Maria Theresia* V, 221–222.
[39] Dorn, *Competition for Empire*, p. 325.

possession of Silesia over the winter, and undid all the gains made since July.[40]

Charles's campaign from Kolin to Leuthen was a classic example of the limitations of eighteenth-century warfare. Troop movements were hampered by poor roads and difficult terrain, substantial supply problems were beginning to emerge in full force by the autumn, strategies of maneuver and counter-maneuver took their toll, aggressive action was avoided to keep the army intact, and Charles operated under a constant cloud of doubt with lack of confidence in him being so publicly expressed in Vienna's governing circles. Yet, despite all these limitations, the strategic objective of winter quarters in Silesia had been achieved and could easily have been held. Many officers had shown initiative and imagination in the lesser engagements, nor had the quality of the troops of the line been wanting. All turned on the battle of Leuthen, and Leuthen was lost only because of tactical incompetence. The only positive consequence was that efforts by Haugwitz and Kaunitz to have Charles removed from command and replaced with the more professionally competent Daun were finally successful.[41]

Kaunitz was pleased with this success, but he wanted to be certain Daun understood the underlying implications of this change of command. In a meeting with the Field Marshall before the latter's departure to take up his post, Kaunitz assailed him with ideas on "means to be employed by the imperial army, to give it advantages over those of the enemy." On the one hand he tried to impress upon Daun the need for more alacrity and willingness to take risk. Kaunitz had a clear appreciation of Frederick II's military talents: the flexibility of his tactics, his strategic daring, and his bold and tough resolve. He urged Daun to learn from his foe's strategy and tactics, particularly from his rapid marches, his logistical practices, and his mobile battlefield maneuvers. On the other hand, however, Kaunitz did not propose imitating Prussian militarism; here he stressed the necessity of emphasizing the difference between "the military constitutions" of the two states. The "tone" and "spirit" that made the Habsburg army so different from the Prussian were qualities to be cultivated, not discouraged.[42] Despite these injunctions, Frederick once again seized the initiative in

[40] Arneth, *Maria Theresia* V, 260–266; *Kriege Friedrichs* 3/VI, 1–74; Jany II, 448–459; Waddington I, 696–719; Joseph Kutzen, *Friedrich der Grosse und sein Heer in den Tag der Schlacht bei von Leuthen* (Breslau, 1851); Paul Gerber, *Die Schlacht bei Leuthen* (Berlin, 1901); Thadden, pp. 320–330; Duffy, *Army of Maria Theresia*, pp. 184–187; Duffy, *Army of Frederick*, pp. 176–179.
[41] Arneth, *Maria Theresia* V, 348–352, 526–528; Khevenhüller-Metsch V, 3–4, 169–170.
[42] MZA, Rodinný archiv Kounicü, Carton 6, Kaunitz "Note pour Mr. le Mll. Daun," n.d. (February–March, 1758).

1758. Late in April he began an invasion in force of Moravia, reaching the strongly fortified city of Olomouc on 3 May. In the Privy Conference the only question on the table was whether Daun's Bohemian army, now marching in relief of Olmütz, should risk a major battle. This time the voices were unanimously in the affirmative,[43] so that Kaunitz could draft the appropriate instruction to Daun which was dispatched the following day.[44] Since Daun was given a free hand to choose his time and place, it was a virtual certainty that battle would not be offered precipitously. However, after breaking the Prussian supply line, he established himself in such a strong position that Frederick now realized he could not take Olomouc without a major battle, but could fight it only on Daun's terms. The king, for one, had no faith in another Leuthen miracle and he decided discretion was the better part of valour. The siege was abandoned and Frederick's forces retreated through north-eastern Bohemia back to Silesia.[45]

The relatively bloodless victory earned Daun laudatory approval as the German Fabius Maximus, but in the summer campaign that was to follow Fabian tactics soon became the object of derision rather than praise. Kaunitz again tried to persuade Daun to press the Prussians with all possible force and "to risk more than in the past." He sought to lend urgency to the argument by explaining the geopolitical realities he felt made such action imperative. France was already urging peace, and Russia would not launch any more military initiatives without some major action on Austria's part. Even a lost battle would therefore be better than diplomatically disastrous inaction.[46] Daun repeatedly argued that in the pursuit of the retreating Frederick, no suitable opportunity for a decisive blow presented itself, but at Hochkirch he finally allowed himself to be talked into an attack on a Prussian position in which the surprise and the victory was complete. Its exploitation, however, was a disappointment. Daun rejected the advice of his subordinates to launch a new attack on the remnants of Frederick's army the next day, with the result that the king was able to rally his shaken forces to continue the struggle for the possession of Saxony.[47] In a rare personal appeal to Daun, Kaunitz urged

[43] Arneth, *Maria Theresia* V, 363–366; Khevenhüller-Metsch V, 35–36.
[44] HHStA, Sonstige Sammlungen: Kriegsakten, Faszikel 416, Cabinet Schreiben to Daun, 15 May 1758.
[45] E. von Sonderstern, *Der Feldzug in Mähren oder die Belagerung und der Entsatz von Olmütz* (Frankfurt a/M, 1858); Arneth, *Maria Theresia* V, 367–376; *Kriege Friedrichs* 3/VII, 66–131; Jany II, 479–484; Waddington II, 222–247; Thadden, pp. 343–349; Duffy, *Army of Maria Theresia*, pp. 187–189.
[46] HHStA, Sonstige Sammlungen: Kriegsakten, Faszikel 416, Cabinet Schreiben to Daun, 29 July, 27 September, 5 and 13 October 1758. Cf. Arneth, *Maria Theresia* V, 398–401.
[47] Arneth, *Maria Theresia* V, 417–425; Norbert Robitschek, *Hochkirch: Eine Studie* (Vienna, 1905); *Kriege Friedrichs* 3/VIII, 248–341; Waddington II, 296–332; Jany II, 495–509;

him to prosecute the campaign for the possession of Saxony with all vigor, otherwise the benefits of his victory at Hochkirch would be lost.[48] But Daun was not equal to Frederick's rapid and decisive counter-thrusts, with the result that the Habsburg army failed to hold Saxony and was forced to retreat to Bohemia for winter quarters.

By 1759 Frederick was sufficiently weakened that he could not even begin to contemplate the kind of offensive initiative he had undertaken in previous years. He could only anticipate an allied effort, which he expected would be directed at Silesia. Early in May the main Austrian army slowly began to move north; shortly thereafter Russian divisions began to concentrate at Poznań for a western offensive. The two armies intended to meet at the Oder river north-west of Glogau by mid-July, thus cutting off Silesia. Though their progress was much delayed by extreme caution and mutual suspicion, on 3 August an Austrian corps detached from Daun's main army effected a junction with the Russian army on the outskirts of Frankfurt an der Oder. The allied campaign in the summer of 1759 was to mark the optimal co-operation between the Habsburg and Russian armies, but co-ordinating their war effort was still an extremely difficult task.[49] In consequence the Cabinet Schreiben of June and July pressed Daun to take more offensive action than his characteristic caution preferred. Kaunitz explained how unlikely it was that the extremely favourable diplomatic constellation of the current war could ever recur in the future, and tried to clarify how precarious ongoing French participation in the war was. Moreover, the strain on the domestic economy could not be sustained too much longer, so that time was of the essence. In order to stress the necessity of destroying as much of the Prussian army as possible, Kaunitz was now even more explicit than he had been in 1758. "The true objective of the current war is not simply the reconquest of Silesia," rather it was inspired by attempting to avoid the nightmare of

... remaining armed beyond our means and burdening [our] loyal subjects with still more taxes instead of granting them relief from their burdens, which is to say, being compelled to introduce a militarist form of government in the Prussian manner. Such an event would force the other powers to do likewise, until finally the whole of Europe would be subjected to this unbearable burden.

This, and other evil consequences, can be prevented only by weakening the king of Prussia.

What was at stake here were not only the geopolitical interests of

---

Thadden, pp. 350–371; Duffy, *Army of Maria Theresia*, pp. 190–192; Duffy, *Army of Frederick*, pp. 184–186.
[48] HHStA, Sonstige Sammlungen: Kriegsakten, Faszikel 417, Kaunitz to Daun, 8 November 1758.   [49] Bangert, *Zusammenarbeit*, pp. 185–236.

the Habsburg Monarchy, but the very "happiness of the human species."[50]

These injunctions notwithstanding, Frederick slipped past Daun in his effort to meet the Russian threat directly. Assaulting the Austro-Russian force just east of Frankfurt at the village of Kunersdorf on 12 August, all the legendary firmness and tactical finesse of the Prussian army proved for naught in the face of the determined allies. The slaughter was so complete that the despairing Frederick hoped to find death in the mêlée. The decisive battle of annihilation seemed to have occurred; it remained only to deliver the *coup de grâce*.[51] It was to Daun's credit that he recognized the necessity of exploiting the victory with a follow-through offensive, but his caution and his hesitation proved his undoing. He vacillated between following Frederick to Berlin, or turning decisively on the remaining Prussian corps still in Silesia. Though outnumbering both, Daun dared not attack either.[52] In Vienna, all these movements were followed with growing restlessness. For Kaunitz Frederick was always the key to the Prussian war effort. He therefore urged that Daun be ordered to pursue Frederick relentlessly, "praying only that Marshall Daun puts as much vigour as he puts prudence into his expedition."[53] Daun's dilatory movements made this a somewhat vain hope, and Kaunitz's anxiety and depression reached new heights. So great was the stress that he suffered renewed attacks of his illness; so deep his pessimism that he "could not imagine" what Daun was up to.[54] Daun, however, now thought only of Saxon winter quarters, not of the destruction of Frederick's forces, and the tone of resignation that characterized the Cabinet Schreiben responses to this latest news from the front fairly reflected the deep disappointment this military passivity elicited.[55] The golden opportunity to end the war successfully, which seemed so tangible in August, was lost. In 1759 the material effort of the Monarchy had reached its peak: all fiscal measures had been stretched to the limit but yielded the required revenues, total troop strength had reached 136,000 men and supply suffered fewer interruptions than in the

---

[50] Kunisch, *Mirakel*, pp. 95–100, reprints the fair copy from the Kriegsarchiv. The original Binder draft with Kaunitz corrections in HHStA, Sonstige Sammlungen: Kriegsakten, Faszikel 417, Cabinet Schreiben to Daun, 24 July 1759.

[51] Arneth, *Maria Theresia* VI, 19–39; Manfred Laubert, *Die Schlacht bei Kunersdorf am 12. August 1759* (Berlin, 1900); *Kriege Friedrichs* 3/X; Jany II, 509–537; Waddington III, 110–180; Bangert, *Zusammenarbeit*, pp. 236–241; Duffy, *Army of Maria Theresia*, pp. 194–195; Duffy, *Russia's Military Way to the West* (London, Boston and Henley, 1981), pp. 108–112.

[52] Arneth, *Maria Theresia* VI, 40–50; Thadden, pp. 394–402; Bangert, *Zusammenarbeit*, pp. 242–271.

[53] HHStA, Staatskanzlei: Vorträge, Karton 85, Kaunitz to Maria Theresia, 12 September 1759.   [54] *Ibid.*, Kaunitz to Maria Theresia, 11 October 1759.

[55] Arneth, *Maria Theresia* VI, 54–55, 434.

previous two years, the morale and battle-field effectiveness of the troops were extremely high, commanders were given *carte blanche* to take risks and were even urged not to avoid them. In fact, only the tactical and strategic timidity of Habsburg commanders was responsible for the failure to deliver the death-blow for which Frederick was preparing suicide.

Thereafter signs of domestic strain were becoming patent in Vienna. Military expenditure suffered drastic cuts. Mule transports were reduced severely, and field commanders were to be asked to introduce economies wherever possible.[56] In this ominous atmosphere of declining prospects it was not surprising that Kaunitz was persuaded that 1760 would probably be the last campaign of the war, or at any rate, the last one which still held out any hope of victory. For this reason the operational plan to be agreed upon for the upcoming campaign was of decisive importance – too important, indeed, to be left to the generals. Early in January Kaunitz began to jot down his own ideas for the campaign of 1760, and before discussing these with the Empress he sought a professional assessment from the one officer who had emerged from the war clearly out of sympathy with the defensive-minded strategy of the majority, Ernst Gideon Loudon, Austrian corps commander at Kunersdorf. Kaunitz now took the taciturn general under his wing, and, having come to the conclusion that dramatic offensive measures were necessary in 1760 to end the war, asked Loudon's frank advice.[57] Loudon did not mince words. Only the Habsburg army's "temporizing and defensive" operations of the previous year had robbed it of the fruits of victory. It therefore followed that offensive operations had to be launched as quickly as possible in 1760, without waiting for the Russians to arrive. A main army of 75,000 men could be assembled in Saxony to keep Frederick in check, but a mobile force of 40,000 should in the meantime begin an immediate offensive in Silesia, hopefully with eventual Russian support, but without it if necessary. As soon as Frederick reacted to this invasion by dividing his forces, he should be attacked by the main army. Above all, a major battle with the foe was absolutely necessary to give any hope of a favourable peace at the end of what appeared to be the last campaign possible in this war.[58]

Once this bold plan was approved, supporters of Loudon had little difficulty in persuading Maria Theresia to entrust command of the Silesian

---

[56] HHStA, Staatskanzlei: Vorträge, Karton 86, Protocollum Conferentia, 21 January 1760, and subsequent imperial resolutions dispatched by the Staatskanzlei to other affected ministries.

[57] HHStA, Sonstige Sammlungen: Kriegsakten, Faszikel 419, Kaunitz to Loudon, 18 October 1759 and 15 January 1760.

[58] *Ibid.*, Faszikel 418, Loudon to Kaunitz, 23 January 1760.

corps to him, and to give him a free hand to proceed as he saw fit.[59] Their confidence proved not to be misplaced, as Loudon's successes at Landeshut and his capture of Glatz raised hopes for further successes.[60] Kaunitz had followed Loudon's progress with mounting excitement. Full of his praise for Loudon in Vienna, he held him up as the Monarchy's Joshua. He encouraged his newest hero with flattering letters, and regarded these successes as a vindication of the aggressive tactics he had been advocating all along.[61] But Kaunitz also did not fail to remind Loudon that this was to be regarded as the last campaign of the war, and as a consequence it had to be pursued unrelentingly. As Frederick turned to march towards Silesia in response, Kaunitz wrote Loudon that it would not take much more "to compel the desperate foe to attack us when we have the advantage, or to permit us to attack him with superior forces." On 10 August Kaunitz reiterated with even more urgency the need to risk a battle even at equal strength, for "what does not happen in this campaign will never happen." He confided to Loudon that Daun had been ordered to give battle, and urged him to press the Field Marshall with similar injunctions.[62]

These exhortations finally bore fruit in mid-August, as an elaborate plan was developed to surround and attack Frederick near Liegnitz in the early morning hours of the fifteenth. Loudon was to march his corps of 24,000 men around the rear of the Prussian position, while Daun's main army would launch a frontal assault on the vastly outnumbered enemy in the hope of effecting the war-ending battle of annihilation. However, on the evening of 14 August Frederick decided on a retreat from his position overnight, and thus ran into Loudon's corps at 3:30 a.m. with his main force. Loudon assumed the original plan was still in operation, and threw himself frantically at the Prussians. Daun's main army, which found Frederick's original position evacuated, never arrived on the scene. Loudon was badly mauled, though he withdrew in good order, much to the astonishment of Frederick. The plan to end the war had turned into a completely unforeseeable defeat. Though Loudon's initial reaction to Kaunitz was to complain bitterly that he had been left in the lurch by Daun, and though Daun's reaction at finding an empty Prussian camp had indeed been sluggish, Frederick's victory was due to fortuitous coincidence

[59] Ibid., Faszikel 419, Kaunitz to Loudon, 20 February 1760; Faszikel 418, Loudon to Kaunitz, 23 February 1760; HHStA, Staatskanzlei: Vorträge, Karton 86, Kaunitz to Maria Theresia, 25 February 1760. Cf. Arneth, Maria Theresia VI, 101–103.
[60] Wilhelm Edlen von Janko, Laudon's Leben Vienna, 1869), pp. 154–174; Arneth, Maria Theresia VI, 110–129; Kriege Friedrichs 3/XII, 69–121; Jany II, 556–561; Franz Pesendorfer, Feldmarschall Loudon (Vienna, 1989), pp. 144–146.
[61] Arneth, Maria Theresia VI, 120–125.
[62] HHStA, Sonstige Sammlungen: Kriegsakten, Faszikel 419, Kaunitz to Loudon, 4 and 29 June, and 10 August 1760.

more than to his brilliance or Daun's incompetence. Kaunitz hastened to reassure Loudon that the disaster had been the result of an unfortunate accident, but there could be fewer reassuring words for why the numerically still superior Daun did not hasten to pursue Frederick with more alacrity.[63]

With the news of Liegnitz, despondency reigned supreme in Vienna. Kaunitz confessed that in the aftermath of the defeat he was filled with grief, and now entertained little hope for "a happy end to the campaign and to the whole war." He accepted that, realistically, little more could be expected from Austria's allies, and that equally little could be done from Vienna.

In my view it is impossible to develop a sound [military] plan from here. The only way to give the situation a happier turn is if our generals exploit conditions which they encounter on the spot with hearty and vigorous resolve, and act without further questions and without the slightest delay – in other words, in the same manner in which the foe has been acting, and in which it is imperative to act.

In any case, Kaunitz was persuaded, without the occurrence of a victorious battle, all other measures were in vain.[64] Indeed, the war of maneuver which now ensued between Frederick and Daun in Silesia and Saxony even had detrimental consequences: the campaign season approached its end, resources were depleted, troops were exhausted, and battle-readiness was blunted. In the face of these realities the emotionally gratifying occupation of Berlin by Habsburg and Russian forces in October, and the return of war trophies Frederick had captured in previous battles, was of little consolation. Frederick could afford to fight for a draw; the Habsburg Monarchy needed a crushing victory to regain Silesia.

The campaign season was almost at an end when Frederick himself offered Daun the battle that was Kaunitz's last hope. On 3 November 1760 he attacked a well-positioned Daun just west of Torgau in Saxony. Despite a severe leg wound, Daun stayed on the field until the Prussian assault appeared to be broken and the battle virtually won. Leaving Generals Franz Moritz Lacy and Carl O'Donell in command, he allowed himself to be brought to a dressing station in Torgau. There he had already composed his report of the victory when the stunning news reached him that his subordinates had allowed the Prussian commanders to turn Frederick's defeat into victory. An incredulous Daun could well invoke the baroque piety that only God's manifest will could explain the tragedy; modern

[63] Joseph Kutzen, Der Tag von Liegnitz (Breslau, 1860); Arneth, Maria Theresia VI, 130–148; Kriege Friedrichs 3/XII, 167–226; Troeger, Die Schlacht bei Liegnitz (Liegnitz, 1906); Hermann Franke, Die Schlacht bei Liegnitz von 15. VIII. 1760 (Liegnitz, 1910); Jany II, 564–569; Thadden, pp. 412–425; Duffy, Army of Frederick, pp. 191–194.

[64] HHStA, Sonstige Sammlungen: Kriegsakten, Faszikel 419, Kaunitz to Loudon, 3 September 1760.

analysts have found fewer difficulties in seeing the "divine stupidity" of Lacy as the explanation. Daun acknowledged that "the entire army blames Lacy," even if he was loath to criticize anyone.[65] For Kaunitz this was the end of the great hope. In a major reassessment of the situation in December 1760, he conceded that the diplomatic constellation was not likely ever to be as favourable again as it was at the present, but concluded that "the exhaustion of our finances deserves priority consideration." Kaunitz therefore recommended peace negotiations be initiated where, in the final analysis, the Habsburg Monarchy would be prepared to settle for the restoration of Saxony and the Prussian cession of the County of Glatz.[66]

What was worse, the crisis of confidence created by Torgau could not be resolved. Despite the fact that the Habsburg Monarchy, as Duffy has pointed out, "pursued the most egalitarian policies of officer recruitment and promotion" in Europe,[67] consciousness of seniority and social status among higher officers still set serious structural limitations to making command appointments. The number of individuals who possessed sufficient personal and social authority to command unquestioned obedience while at the same time possessing the requisite professional competence in the event reduced themselves to one: Daun. Shaken by criticism and frustrated by the military disappointments of the previous campaigns, however, he was reluctant to accept command again, and apparently did so only under the condition that no offensive operations were demanded of him.[68] This was hardly a propitious omen, for it revealed the extent of the strategic objective envisioned for 1761 to be merely clinging to the parts of Silesia and Saxony already occupied to negotiate a peace on the basis of *uti possidetis*. Kaunitz succeeded in getting Loudon some freedom of maneuver with a reinforced corps in Silesia, which everyone in polite society called "the army of Kaunitz,"[69] and a glimmer of hope remained that the offensive-minded Loudon might yet achieve at least some of the larger war objective.[70] But Kaunitz was soon to be disabused of this hope

[65] Arneth, *Maria Theresia* VI, 156–182, 453–456; Jany II, 579–595; Eberhard Kessel, *Militärgeschichte und Kriegstheorie in neuerer Zeit: Ausgewählte Aufsätze*, ed. by Johannes Kunisch (Berlin, 1987), pp. 191–221; Thadden, pp. 426–436; Duffy, *Army of Maria Theresa*, pp. 199–202; Duffy, *Army of Frederick*, pp. 194–196.

[66] HHStA, Staatskanzlei, Vorträge, Karton 87, "Kurz-zusammengefaßtes Ohnmaßgeblichstes Darfürhalten des Hof- und Staats Canzlern über 10 Deliberations-Punkten," n.d. (December 1760); a later copy of the same report is dated 30 December 1760. Cf. Arnold Schäfer, *Geschichte des siebenjährigen Krieges*, 3 Vols. (Berlin, 1867–1874), III, 186–188; Arneth, *Maria Theresia* VI, 207–214.

[67] Christopher Duffy, *The Military Experience in the Age of Reason* (London and N.Y., 1987); p. 43.

[68] Schäfer, *Geschichte des siebenjährigen Krieges* III, 225; Arneth, *Maria Theresia* VI, 226–228; Thadden, pp. 440–441.

[69] HHStA, Kabinettsarchiv: Zinzendorf Tagebuch, Vol. 6, 28 August 1761.

[70] Arneth, *Maria Theresia* VI, 229–235; Kessel, *Militärgeschichte*, pp. 222–239.

when it became clear that military operations were hampered by the limited personal authority Loudon was able to exercise.

Though nominally under Daun's command, Loudon had been given an explicit free hand for his Silesian operations. The co-operation he received from fellow senior officers, however, was dismal. From Daun's headquarters Lacy poured forth a running stream of criticism. Lieutenant-generals Philip Levin Beck and Joseph d'Ayasasa refused outright to serve under Loudon, while General O'Donell, despatched with reinforcements from Daun to Loudon, refused to do so personally because he, too, would thus be subject to a younger parvenu's authority. When Loudon, the great advocate of quick offensive action, further failed to assault Frederick on his own and preferred to work out a joint plan with the Russians, accusations of incompetence were quick to surface. Certainly, there was no small degree of *Schadenfreude* among enemies of Loudon and Kaunitz that the Chancellor of State's protégé could produce no spectacular turn for the better in the fortunes of war.[71]

This led Kaunitz to the extraordinary measure of dispatching a personal agent to Loudon's camp in the person of the military supply commissar, Johann Georg Grechtler, with the secret mission of investigating whether Loudon's military capacities measured up to the task entrusted him, and whether he had adequate support personnel at his disposal to carry it out. If the answer to the latter question was negative, Grechtler was to advise how the problem might be remedied.[72] Grechtler's response was unequivocally positive about Loudon's abilities, but brutally frank that competent subordinate generals were rare in the Habsburg service, and those that did exist, such as O'Donell, Macquire, Lacy or Beck, would fail to serve in good faith under Loudon even if the latter were promoted to Field Marshall. Loudon simply lacked "a certain grand prestige" which only people of higher birth could carry off.[73] Loudon's case, in short, was a classic example of the structural limitations that the social order of the *ancien régime* placed on the exercise of military action, and it certainly tended to extinguish the faint hope that still flickered in 1761 that the war might yet turn out well for the Monarchy.[74]

Kaunitz's exasperation shone through dramatically in an assessment of the campaign which he submitted on 20 September. He acknowledged that the quality of the allied troops were uneven, but with an overall manpower advantage of approximately two to one which the allies could bring to bear

[71] Arneth, *Maria Theresia* VI, 235–242, 397.
[72] HHStA, Sonstige Sammlungen, Kriegsakten, Faszikel 425, Kaunitz to Grechtler, 5 August 1761.   [73] *Ibid.*, Grechtler to Kaunitz, 8 August 1761.
[74] Kessel, *Militärgeschichte*, pp. 240–252; Johannes Kunisch, *Der kleine Krieg* (Wiesbaden, 1973), pp. 50–78.

against Prussia, he could not persuade himself that a purely defensive posture was the only feasible option. "Our disappointed hopes must not make us lose heart," he urged, insisting that some offensive operations could still be undertaken.[75] It would be a mistake to regard this memorandum as evidence of a conviction that the war could still be won after all;[76] rather, Kaunitz sought to win some strategic advantage which could reanimate the now floundering peace talks. Loudon delivered the advantage within a matter of days by capturing the key fortress of Schweidnitz on 1 October.[77] Kaunitz felt his confidence in Loudon was vindicated, and he lost no opportunity publicly to sing the praises of his favourite general.[78] Some weeks later the Russians captured Kolberg, and the combination of the two events had the desired effect. Frederick's strategic position was so weakened that he instructed his cabinet secretary to begin preparations for peace negotiations.[79] But only hours before this order went out, Empress Elizabeth of Russia died in St. Petersburg, to be succeeded by the Prussophile heir, now Czar Peter III. This event was to change the diplomatic framework for the military operations of 1762 completely, and put the Habsburg Monarchy at a serious disadvantage.

For Kaunitz there were reasons other than diplomatic and military to end the war. After a month of discussions on budgeting in the late summer of 1761, it became clear that the Monarchy simply could not afford to maintain a military establishment of the size it had previously supported. Little economies could no longer even begin to address the larger fiscal crisis. Kaunitz reported a prospective shortfall of 28 million Gulden, and saw no fiscal measures of any kind that could help meet the deficit. As a result, the only option that remained was the painful one of reducing the armed forces by some 12% or 20,000 men.[80] Even that proposal was made in the full knowledge that resources were "no longer sufficient to meet the incredibly heavy demands of the war," and that the Habsburg Monarchy had to strive for "if not an entirely satisfactory, then at least a bearable peace."[81] Early in December 1761, at the behest of Kaunitz, each regiment

---

[75] HHStA, Staatskanzlei: Vorträge, Karton 88, Kaunitz to Maria Theresia, 20 September 1761, including enclosed memorandum, "Ohnmaßgebliche Gedancken und Anmerkungen über den gegenwärtigen Stand der Kriegs-Operationen."

[76] As suggested by Max Immich, Geschichte des europäischen Staatensystems, 1660–1789 (Munich and Berlin, 1905), p. 370, and repeated by Klueting, Die Lehre von der Macht der Staaten, pp. 179–180.

[77] Arneth, Maria Theresia VI, 237–253; Jany II, 605–613; Kessel, Militärgeschichte pp. 285–302; Duffy, Army of Maria Theresia, pp. 202–203; Duffy, Russia's Military Way, pp. 116–118.

[78] HHStA, Kabinettsarchiv: Zinzendorf Tagebuch, Vol. 6, 3 October 1761.

[79] Politische Correspondenz, Frederick to Finkenstein, 6 January 1762.

[80] HHStA, Staatskanzlei: Vorträge, Karton 88, Kaunitz to Maria Theresia, 17 October 1761; Kaunitz to Joseph, 19 October 1761.   [81] Arneth, Maria Theresia VI, 275.

in the army was reduced by two companies, so that the military establishment which faced the enemy in 1762 was, at best, capable of only a holding action. In the event the dramatic diplomatic reversals of Austria's erstwhile ally, Russia, made even such a modest military goal difficult. The setback at Burkersdorf in July and the fall of Schweidnitz in October only confirmed a verdict which Kaunitz had been prepared to accept for some time.[82] By the end of October 1762 Binder dutifully reported Kaunitz's military assessment to the Empress: continuation of the war was absolutely impossible, indeed, the army would be fortunate merely to survive the winter.[83] As was the case for the overextended finances, so too for the army: the Peace of Hubertusburg which formally ended the conflict on 15 February 1763 came not a moment too soon.

The conscription crisis

The main outlines of the post-war debate on the military establishment of the Habsburg Monarchy were already evident before the war ended. Differences of opinion turned on what military lessons were to be learned from the experience of the war, and what the implications of these lessons were for the post-war peace-time army. Military men tended to argue that the failures of the army were structural, and that, accordingly, the inter-war reform process had to be continued. In particular the size of the peace-time standing army had to be augmented substantially so that the military establishment could respond more effectively to any prospective attack on the Monarchy. In direct opposition to these assessments were the voices which tended to regard the failures of the war to have been primarily due to strategic and tactical errors made at the field command level, and who therefore saw no need to increase the peace-time standing army, or in any way to alter its recruitment policies. In the forefront of this latter camp, Kaunitz's voice was uppermost.

Central to this entire debate was the problem of conscription. In the winter following the campaign of 1760, it became increasingly apparent that traditional recruiting methods were resulting in shortfalls of the military quotas, and that losses in the ranks were becoming increasingly difficult to fill. In February 1761 the Commissariat for Military Supply accordingly argued that some forcible measures might need to be introduced. While the heart of the proposal was aimed at the possible recruitment of Prussian prisoners of war, the prospect of conscription in

---

[82] *Ibid.*, pp. 278–348.
[83] HHStA, Staatskanzlei: Vorträge, Karton 90, Binder to Maria Theresia, 22 October 1762.

any form of natives of the Monarchy elicited an immediate negative response from the Directory, which regarded such military service as an impediment to the maximal growth of an economically productive population. Kaunitz agreed that the general population, and especially the peasant population, had to be "conserved" and military demands kept to an absolute minimum, and little came of the suggestion.[84] In October the idea of conscription was taken up again by Council of State minister Blümegen, who looked to the Prussian *canton* system as a means of effecting substantial savings in recruitment costs. Kaunitz did not deny that Prussian methods were effective or even economical, but he could not recommend they be copied. The conscription policies tended to imbue the whole Prussian state with "the military spirit," and it was precisely this and the military's power to exploit the rural population "which is the greatest slavery and atrocity, and makes the Prussian regime so repulsive." Above all, however, he questioned the very premise on which such proposals were based by arguing that large armies were to be regarded not as positive things in themselves, but, at best, as "a necessary evil which robs the countryside of fit young men, cripples the strength of the state by hindering population growth, draws workers away from agriculture and industry, and causes excessive taxation."[85]

Once the war had been formally terminated, the debate on the lessons of that war began in earnest. Already on 17 February 1763 the War Ministry prepared a detailed proposal on increases in the prospective peace-time standing army in comparison with the pre-1756 establishment based on the argument that post-war diplomatic dangers continued to be great and that only an augmented force could prevent a successful preemptive strike by the enemy. Kaunitz responded to this proposal by agreeing there was little doubt that the dangers painted by the War Ministry existed, and that self-preservation demanded remaining armed even in peace-time. But, he asserted, "this nevertheless has its limits." Military expenditures had to be tailored to revenues, which, in turn, could not be determined with any precision until Zinzendorf had completed a full budgetary balance sheet. On the whole, however, it seemed clear to him that post-war fiscal

---

[84] Schünemann, *Bevölkerungspolitik*, pp. 124–127.
[85] H. Bleckwenn, ed., "Graf Kaunitz Votum über das Militäre 1762," *Zeitgenössische Studien über die altpreußische Armee* (Osnabrück, 1974), pp. 27–45. Bleckwenn, working from an undated copy of the memorandum in the Kriegsarchiv, was unable to date the document with any precision. In fact, the Votum is part of a Council of State debate in October 1761. Cf. Posaner, "Die Rolle des Staatskanzlers Fürsten Kaunitz," pp. 51–59, and HHStA, Kabinettsarchiv: Staatsratprotokolle, Vol. 3, No. 2714 1/2, protocol record, October 1761. There are also excerpts from this document dated 1761 in HHStA, Österreichische Akten: Österreich-Staat, Fasz. 4, "Kaunitz Votum über das Militär Systema."

constraints would require trimming the military budget below even pre-war spending levels with the result that the size of the peacetime standing army had "to be reduced considerably." Above all, Kaunitz stressed, military expenditures had to be seen in the context of the whole fiscal and credit picture of the Monarchy and could not be allowed to undermine its economic foundations.[86]

These patent tensions between fiscal constraint in the face of post-war economic difficulties, and putative military preparedness in the face of a possible enemy assault, became the opposite poles of the political debate for the next decade. In this debate proponents of fiscal restraint fought a constant rearguard action, and Kaunitz's argument in favour of actual manpower reductions fell by the wayside rather rapidly. A post-war military commission which investigated the state of preparedness within the army against any renewed Prussian attack concluded that security requirements demanded an increase in the permanent military establishment to 140,000 men, at an estimated cost increase in the region of 2 million Gulden. The proposals also raised the issue of recruitment, for the War Ministry had grave doubts that the recruitment practices in effect since 1748 could meet the regimental quotas of such an enlarged standing army. On 19 July 1764 General Lacy presented a devastating critique of the domestic recruitment system,[87] which brought the War Ministry back to the already vetted idea of creating a "reserve militia" through conscription which could be used to fill regional quotas where shortfalls emerged. Kaunitz met both proposals head-on. He conceded that the territorial greed and militaristic caprice of Frederick of Prussia made a sizeable Habsburg military establishment unavoidable, but improvements in that establishment had to be undertaken in such a way as not to crush taxpayers and destroy the very sources of all revenues. He recommended a redistribution of various garrisons, but he opposed the proposed budget increases on the grounds that armies were there to protect countries not to drain their resources. This same consideration applied to conscription. The military might find the process convenient, but the draftees would hardly share that sentiment. Conscription would have "the most dangerous consequences," for it would give military authorities far too much opportunity for "unending oppression and extortion after the Prussian example" over the civilian sector, and such military intrusions into civilian life had simply to be avoided at all costs. However, having lost his case for manpower cuts, Kaunitz was now compelled to address the recruitment problem, and here his main emphasis lay with the "veritable treasure"

---

[86] HHStA, Staatskanzlei: Vorträge, Karton 91, Kaunitz Votum, 3 March 1763.
[87] Edith Kotasek, *Feldmarschall Graf Lacy* (Horn, 1956), pp. 78–79.

envied by all other powers of Europe, the redoubtable border guards (*Grenzer*) of the Military Frontier.[88]

The Military Frontier was a territorial cordon administered by the War Ministry and inhabited by soldier-colonists along the entire southern frontier of the Habsburg Monarchy. It had evolved from the days of Emperor Ferdinand I as the first line of defence against the Ottoman Empire. Initially encompassing a territory from the Drava River to the Adriatic coast, it had been expanded gradually eastward through Slavonia and the Banat with the reconquest of the old Kingdom of Hungary during the seventeenth and eighteenth centuries, and was finally extended to Transylvania between 1762 and 1765. Beginning as mercenaries and "freebooting auxiliaries," the Border Guards gradually stabilized into a community of peasant-soldiers who enjoyed land tenure and confessional rights in return for their military service. Organized into conventional regiments of irregulars in the Habsburg army during the Silesian Wars, the Border Guards were prominent in most major campaigns, achieving a reputation for ferocity and brutality, but also for effectiveness and particular proficiency in irregular engagements, and providing more than 80,000 troops in the Seven Years War alone.[89] From the beginning of the war Kaunitz was an enthusiastic proponent of the Border Guards. He took strong exception to the prejudice expressed by many military professionals against these troops and lauded their courage, aggressiveness and effectiveness in irregular operations. He admitted that the Border Guards needed better officers and training, but recommended all measures be taken to "rectify" their reputation among regulars and the public at large.[90] Their subsequent contributions to such battles as Lobositz, Kolin and Kunersdorf were central and often even decisive, and by the end of the war Kaunitz had begun to develop the idea that enlarging Border Guard troop strengths might be the one economical way to maintain a sizeable peace-time army.[91] Now, in 1765, the idea had crystallized into a firm conviction that this avenue represented "the easiest, most productive and least expensive" means to augment the size of the army as a whole. He waxed lyrical at these hardy and courageous "born soldiers", and

---

[88] HHStA, Staatskanzlei: Vorträge, Karton 96, Kaunitz Votum, 23 June 1765.
[89] The literature on the Military Frontier is extensive and has been conveniently collated by Kurt Wessely and Georg Zivkovic, "Bibliographie zur Geschichte der k.k. Militärgrenze," in Direktion des Militärwissenschaftliches Instituts, Vienna, ed., *Die k.k. Militärgrenze: Beiträge zu ihrer Geschichte* (Vienna, 1973), pp. 292–324. The best English-language analyses remain Gunther E. Rothenberg, *The Austrian Military Border in Croatia, 1522–1747* (Urbana, Ill., 1960), and his *The Military Border in Croatia, 1740–1881* (Chicago, Ill. and London, 1966), which, as the titles indicate, deal only with the Croatian segment of the Frontier.   [90] Khevenhüller-Metsch IV, 251.
[91] HHStA, Staatskanzlei: Vorträge, Karton 91, Kaunitz Votum, 3 March 1763.

projected that their infantry strength could be readily increased from 50,000 to 70,000. Some could garrison Hungarian fortresses, while others could be rotated for one-year stints in Bohemia and other strategically important areas.[92]

In the War Ministry the task of dealing with Kaunitz's critique fell on General Lacy, whose main argument was concentrated on showing how misplaced was Kaunitz's optimism about Border Guards. The economy of the Military Border had suffered severely from manpower drain caused by the war, and postwar conditions in the Frontier region were hardly propitious for increasing the size of the military establishment. The War Ministry ordered reports from local commanding generals, but in the interim was able to dismiss Kaunitz's idea as unrealistic.[93] The fundamental question of whether to meet security requirements in Bohemia with a redistribution of available forces or with manpower increases, however, remained unresolved. In September the War Ministry renewed its case for increases, and though it quietly dropped all mention of conscription, it also refused to address Kaunitz's larger concerns. After expressing some irritation at this cavalier treatment of his ideas, Kaunitz concluded that it simply came down to a hard choice which the Empress had to make between providing for Bohemian security by transfers from other parts of the Monarchy or by real increases in the size of the permanent military establishment. Once more he repeated his economic arguments that the army had to be tailored to available revenues, not the other way around, and that it could never be allowed to grow disproportionately large in relation to the population as a whole. He insisted that nothing was more ruinous for a state than to strain its fiscal resources on military expenditures, which only weakened the economic infrastructure in the long run and actually made a country less prepared to face war if it occurred. Kaunitz calculated that the maximum ratio of military to civilian population that any country could tolerate without skewing its economy was 1:100 (the Prussian ratio was 1:30; that of the mercenary-supply state of Hesse-Cassel 1:15),[94] and by that standard the Habsburg military establishment was already too big and needed to be reduced rather than increased. He also repeated his argument that the Military Frontier should constitute the army's main source of new manpower. He conceded that for the moment socio-economic conditions were so bleak in the Frontier as to demand decreases not increases, but he insisted that energetic reforms

[92] *Ibid.*, Karton 96, Kaunitz Votum, 23 June 1765.
[93] HHStA, Kabinettsarchiv: Nachlaß Lacy, Karton 4, Lacy's summary and critique of the Kaunitz Votum, 25 June 1765, and Hofkriegsrat to Maria Theresia, [?] July 1765. On post-war conditions in the Military Frontier, cf. Rothenberg, *The Military Border*, pp. 42–43.
[94] Charles W. Ingrao, *The Hessian Mercenary State* (Cambridge, 1987), p. 132.

could reverse that situation. If living conditions were improved and locals had "no reason to complain about any oppressions," the Monarchy could expect to draw a flood of new settlers from the Ottoman side of the frontier which could enhance the population base dramatically.[95]

By this juncture, however, the framework of the debate was completely altered by the death of Emperor Francis and the accession of Joseph II. Joseph had aligned himself quite early with the advocates of increased military spending. His very first memorandum on political reform, dated 3 April 1761, had sternly opposed any reduction in military strength, and even went so far as to recommend doubling the standing army once peace was restored.[96] In 1763 he again urged increased military spending rather than cutbacks.[97] In 1765 Joseph's hand was strengthened when, as a result of the death of his father, titular supervision of military matters was conferred on him – a responsibility he accepted with great enthusiasm.[98] No sooner did he enter his new office than he immediately adopted the Prussian custom of appearing in uniform at all formal occasions.[99] In consultation with Daun he began preparations and planning for major maneuvers in Bohemia and Moravia for the fall of the following year.[100] In the intervening time he appointed three military inspectors to see to the maintenance of the battle-readiness of the troops then quartered in various parts of the Monarchy.[101] Finally, at the end of 1765, he returned to his theme of increasing military strength in his famous memorandum on domestic reform. He now suggested the adoption of a Prussian-style canton system, a tightening of military discipline, and the introduction of a three-year military service prerequisite for any young aristocrat wishing to join government service. A host of other recommendations included ideas designed to integrate the army further into civilian life. Soldiers were to be stationed throughout the provinces, given permission to marry, and employed in various civilian activities, including policing functions.[102]

Kaunitz's assessment of these recommendations was brief and diplomatic. He claimed not to be a military expert, and gladly left technical details to the Emperor, seconding any reforms he might wish to introduce into the War Ministry. But he could not resist making two broader points, which really represented the core of his views on military reform, and went to the very heart of debates on the subject. First, Kaunitz felt it important

---

[95] HHStA, Staatskanzlei: Vorträge, Karton 96, "Kaunitz Gutachten wie sich gegen einen feindlichen Überfall am besten sicher gestellet werden können," 2 December 1765.
[96] *MTJC* I, 1–12.   [97] Beales, "Joseph II's 'Rêveries,'" p. 159.
[98] Th. G. von Karajan, *Maria Theresia und Graf Sylva Tarouca* (Vienna, 1859), p. 69.
[99] Arneth, *Maria Theresia* VII, 185.   [100] Thadden, p. 453.
[101] Arneth, *Maria Theresia* VII, 185–186.   [102] *MTJC* III, 335–361.

to resist any attempt to integrate military and civilian administration in a society. In his view the two were animated by completely different premises: one by blind obedience to superiors, the other by respect for the law. Military precision and compliance might make a "seductive" impression on the parade ground, but one could not run a country that way. To introduce "the mechanical discipline of the military" into the civilian administration was impossible because "in the former the concern is for nothing but obedience, while in the latter it is necessary to think before acting, and the principles of the former are [therefore] exactly opposed to the latter." Secondly, he could not agree that military success was simply a matter of discipline and superior numbers. It was rather the strategic and tactical skill of commanding officers "which decides the outcome of battles and campaigns... and not only always insures victory with an army of equal size, but frequently even with a numerically inferior army." Officer training in strategy and tactics was therefore probably the most important reform that the Habsburg army could undertake.[103] These comments show very clearly the conclusions Kaunitz drew from the Seven Years War. He continued to regard Prussian militarism as a thoroughly undesirable model for Habsburg society, but he respected Frederick II's military talents, and wished Habsburg officers to emulate the latter not the former.[104]

That these were not sentiments shared in the army, or by Joseph personally for that matter, became evident when Daun died on 5 February 1766. The one senior officer most in the mold of Frederick, Loudon, also had the least chance of succeeding the deceased War Ministry president. Observers doubted Loudon would ever hold any important command if Kaunitz retired,[105] and Kaunitz's lack of influence on this appointment was clearly demonstrated by Joseph's enthusiastic endorsement of Daun's candidate for the job, Lacy. Kaunitz did not think highly of Lacy. He regarded him as politically naive, and militarily untalented – fit only for pedantic bureaucratic implementation of details.[106] Lacy, on the other hand, shared Daun's envy and dislike of Loudon, but had the full confidence of both Joseph and Maria Theresia, with whom he was on increasingly intimate personal terms.[107] Since it had been Lacy's 1764 criticism of the old recruiting system that had moved Joseph to recommend the adoption of the Prussian canton system in 1765,[108] it is perhaps not

[103] Beer, ed., "Denkschriften des Fürsten Kaunitz," pp. 109–111, 144.
[104] HHStA, Kabinettsarchiv: Zinzendorf Tagebuch, Vol. 8, 3 March 1763.
[105] Eduard Wertheimer, ed., "Zwei Schilderungen des Wiener Hofs im XVIII. Jahrhundert," *AÖG* LXII (1881), 232.
[106] Mitrofanov, *Joseph II* I, 368–369; Kotasek, *Lacy, p.* 226.
[107] Arneth, *Maria Theresia* IX, 502–511; Edith Kotasek, "Die Privatkorrespondenz des Feldmarschalls Grafen Lacy mit Maria Theresia und Joseph II.," *MÖStA* IV (1951), 167–183.   [108] Kotasek, *Lacy*, pp. 78–79.

surprising that one of Joseph's first acts after Lacy became war minister was to send him a confidential copy of Kaunitz's critique of the 1765 memorandum for refutation.[109] Not long thereafter Lacy turned again to plans for military increases. Here he was in his element, and his calculations were nothing if not precise, urging an increase in the military establishment of 64,022 men at an annual cost of exactly 16,352,055 Gulden and 25·5 Kreutzer.[110] With all the statistical information to hand, Joseph now gave the proposal all the support he could muster in one of the most forceful and characteristic memoranda of his reign, which he submitted to his mother on 28 December 1766.

Joseph began his brief with the famous Roman adage, *Si vis pacem, para bellum*. And war, in his opinion, was something for which the Habsburg Monarchy was not prepared. The last war had demonstrated that even without allocating any manpower resources to Belgium, Italy and Hungary, the military strength of the Monarchy was still not enough to meet the requirements. Increases were therefore imperative, and the creation of a Prussian-style canton system was "the only true, efficacious and inexpensive way" to secure them. Such a system, Joseph noted, would make every citizen a soldier and every soldier a citizen, which, in turn, would lead to a more efficient society and the "assurance that all orders will be carried out militarily, that is to say to the letter." The system would further facilitate training, so that the armies of the Monarchy would henceforth contain more than "mere peasants masqueraded as soldiers." Even men of a stature unfit for the infantry could be conscripted into such branches of the service as artillery. In addition Joseph recommended more work on a fortifications programme, and an intensification of cavalry training. He wanted an inventory of horses, stock-piling of arms, equipment and grain supplies, and an increase in the officer corps. Specifically, the current military strength had to be augmented (rounding up Lacy's figures) by 65,000 men, 14,000 cavalry horses, 3,000 supply wagons, 1,900 pack horses or mules, 14,000 artillery horses, 3,000 pontoon horses, 100,000 new firearms and other equipment. Joseph made no mention of costs. He did, however, go beyond specific recommendations positing, by way of conclusion, three "incontestable axioms." The first was that another war was inevitable before long, and the Monarchy had to be prepared for it. The second was that the first campaign of such a conflict would be so decisive that preparations for it could not be delayed until its

---

[109] HHStA, Kabinettsarchiv: Nachlaß Lacy, Karton 5, Joseph to Lacy, 7 March 1766.
[110] HHStA, Staatskanzlei: Vorträge, Karton 98, Lacy to Joseph and Maria Theresia, 29 December 1766. This is a judicious post-dating, and both the Emperor and the Empress had, in fact, seen the report a month earlier. Cf. Arneth, *Maria Theresia* VII, 222–225, 530.

outbreak. Finally, he insisted on the incontestability of the proposition that "nothing is more desirable for a state ... than to have a good and large army." If such a policy turned the state into an armed camp, Joseph did not mind. "The duties of citizen and soldier," he wrote, "have never appeared and still do not appear to me to be incompatible."[111]

It is difficult to avoid the conclusion, so bitterly reached by Leopold in 1778,[112] that Joseph's attitude, strident and despotic in tone, all too enthusiastically modeled itself on Prussian militarism. It also fore-shadowed an age when military priorities were to dominate society and to permeate every aspect of life. This was not a prospect Kaunitz welcomed at all. In his evaluation of the proposal, he diametrically opposed not only the recommendations made but also the very premises on which they were based. Above all, he could not subscribe to the view that the defeats of the previous war were the result of inadequate troop strength. It was the superior strategy of Frederick and his generals that was, in Kaunitz's view, the key to Prussian success. Kaunitz agreed that a strong and mobile military force was a political necessity, but he argued that two fundamental points could not be ignored. First of all, no matter how numerous the army was, it could never outnumber the combination of all potential adversaries. Secondly, there had to be an integral relationship between the military and economic strength of a state. There was no question that armies were the principal shield of a state, Kaunitz noted, but the purpose of such a shield was to provide security, not to crush those whom it was meant to protect by its weight. On this basis he therefore opposed both manpower increases and the introduction of a conscription system. He argued that the outcome of a war depended less on the readiness for the decisive first campaign than on the ability to endure for an extended period of time. This was hopeless if the economic fiber of a state was not maintained and fostered. By way of example, Kaunitz maintained that Louis XIV had laid the groundwork for French weakness in the War of the Spanish Succession precisely by attempting to maintain an unrealistically huge and expensive military establishment during his reign. As far as conscription was concerned, Kaunitz conceded that this was probably the most efficient way to raise troop strength, but he felt the social repercussions far outweighed any benefits it could possibly produce. He preferred the old recruiting system of 1748 precisely because it provided for a complete separation of the military and civilian segments of society. He predicted large-scale resistance to conscription at the local and provincial level, and suggested that the imposition of this burden, "on the peasant who is already all too oppressed," would make his lot inferior even to those chafing under

---

[111] HHStA, Staatskanzlei: Vorträge, Karton 98, Joseph Denkschrift, 28 December 1766. Cf. Khevenhüller-Metsch VI, 458–467.   [112] Wandruszka, *Leopold II* I, 343, 365.

Prussian despotism. The Habsburg Monarchy must keep its priorities straight, Kaunitz concluded: "In the case of a conflict between the maintenance of the peasantry and favouring the military, the former, as the basis for everything else, must be preferred over the latter."[113]

The arguments did not fail to have their effect on Maria Theresia. On 4 February 1767 she sent Joseph Kaunitz's critique with the comment that these objections could not be ignored, and asking him to consult Starhemberg and the Council of State and to have Lacy respond to the critique in detail.[114] In the meantime she sent on the original Lacy proposal to Zinzendorf's Court of Audit to scrutinize the budget estimates. Zinzendorf dutifully submitted his report on 19 March, cautiously skeptical of Lacy's estimates, and Kaunitz, along with the rest of the Council of State, endorsed this view.[115] Joseph would not be put off. He resolved to at least experiment with four or five regiments to test cost estimates,[116] and set up a special military commission to reexamine the issue in the light of the critiques received. Not surprisingly the commission came to the conclusion that military increases were absolutely indispensable, and endorsed Joseph's and Lacy's conscription plans. Again Kaunitz responded with a lengthy brief which repeated many of his previous arguments. Absolute security was an illusion, and no army could ever be big enough to guarantee it. Security depended on diplomacy as much as on a large military establishment, otherwise the smaller countries of Europe would have long been swallowed up by the great powers. An army had to be tailored to a state's revenues, and revenues in turn could only be extracted in proportion to the overall performance of the economy. An excessive tax burden to support a disproportionately large standing army would cripple economic development, and make credit even more difficult to get in any future conflict. He again recalled the painful fiscal realities of the last war, drew attention to the deficit, and pointed out that the key to Prussian success in the last war was less the size of its military establishment than Frederick's aggressive tactics, the windfall of Saxon revenues, and the English subsidy. In a supplementary report the very next day he followed this up with a more philosophical argument: Wealth and power required economic development, but economic development re-

---

[113] HHStA, Staatskanzlei: Vorträge, Karton 99, Kaunitz to Maria Theresia, 24 January 1767. Additional copy in HHStA, Österreichische Akten: Österreich-Staat, Fasz. 5. Cf. Khevenhüller-Metsch VI, 468–475.

[114] HHStA, Familienarchiv: Sammelbände, Karton 4, Maria Theresia to Joseph, 4 February 1767.

[115] HHStA, Kabinettsarchiv: Kaunitz Voten, Karton 1, No. 674 of 1767, Kaunitz Staatsrat Votum, 13 April 1767.

[116] HHStA, Kabinettsarchiv: Staatsratprotokolle, Vol. 24, No. 674, Joseph resolution, 16 April 1767.

quired freedom which in turn inspired patriotism, as English and Holland proved; the introduction of the Prussian conscription system could only create the kind of slavish mentality which would suffocate such sentiments. The Habsburg Monarchy should rather think of economic reform, and especially of sweeping agrarian reform, as the path to power and greatness.[117]

Maria Theresia forwarded these reports to Joseph in an almost apologetic tone, asserting that Kaunitz was only examining the military reform proposals in the context of the larger economic and political picture at her express command.[118] But this came as no consolation to Joseph, particularly as Starhemberg, whom he had also been told to consult, opposed military increases and conscription for similar reasons and with similar passion.[119] The Emperor was neither silenced nor persuaded. In bitter tones he dismissed Kaunitz's argument as being based on entirely false premises. An economically flourishing country would be only a lure to its neighbors' aggression if it did not have an army proportionate to the threat that faced it. Security was the paramount consideration, and all else was secondary. In any case, Joseph asserted, cost increases as a result of the recommended reform would be minimal: economies would be introduced and the military budget would be restructured. Nor would conscription be carried out in the cruel Prussian manner, but in a more humane manner which would lead to happy conciliation between the peasant and the military. Kaunitz's agrarian reform proposals were unrealistic, and if one was concerned about budget deficits, there was plenty of scope for saving elsewhere. For example, could policies not be implemented without so much time wasted on discussion? Could they not be implemented at less expense, employing fewer individuals and less paper work? Were not whole departments and even ministries superfluous and needless drains on the budget? Did the state really have to pay people to think, to talk, to write, to read and to reason, instead of merely to act in a simple utilitarian manner? Perhaps, Joseph conceded, this was "an all too stoic political philosophy", but in his view it was one that "the common good" dictated.[120]

This remarkably revealing memorandum, which at this early date already exposed the core of the Emperor's life-long political agenda, was naturally once again forwarded to Kaunitz by an anxious Maria Theresia. Kaunitz was hesitant to reply, admitting that it was particularly difficult for him to obey her order to do so. Yet his position remained largely

[117] HHStA, Österreichische Akten: Österreich-Staat, Fasz. 5, Kaunitz to Maria Theresia, 20 and 21 April 1767.   [118] *Ibid.*, Maria Theresia to Joseph, [22–23] April 1767.
[119] Eichwalder, "Starhemberg," pp. 141–144.
[120] HHStA, Österreichische Akten: Österreich-Staat, Fasz. 5, Joseph Votum, 27 April 1767.

unaltered.[121] Lacy's long-awaited rebuttal of his critics was equally uncompromising on the need for military increases, but he modified the original proposal by suggesting these conscripts receive six to seven weeks of military training annually and be furloughed to work their land the rest of the year.[122] The revised proposal was debated for four days by Joseph and a specially constituted military reform commission, but in the event no permanent decisions were made, and the "conscription of souls and horses" was tabled again.[123]

The debates continued over the summer, and in July Kaunitz weighed in once more with a critique of the revised Lacy proposal. He continued to insist that even in its modified form, the proposal was incompatible with the "fundamental constitution" of the Monarchy, and still represented an unacceptable burden on the rural population. Of course, there were the usual economic arguments. Even maintaining and equipping 40,000 soldiers for seven weeks was more than the debt-ridden Monarchy could afford. At the same time the man-hour loss in rural labour would be the equivalent of 80,000 *robot* days, which could hardly be inflicted on the rural economy as a whole. The size of the military establishment had to depend on what the country could afford, and security concerns had to be solved with political measures, not with larger armies. But most of all, Kaunitz stressed again the need to keep civilian and military life strictly segregated.[124] This led to an apparently stormy but fruitless confrontation between Kaunitz and Lacy on 29 July in which there were no signs of compromise on either side.[125] By September Kaunitz had committed such an outspoken criticism to paper that he himself realized that he had gone too far. Not wanting to alienate Joseph completely, he asked Maria Theresia to suppress this latest memorandum,[126] but he continued to oppose all measures which smacked of military budget increases.[127]

By the time Kaunitz prepared his great memorandum of 25 January 1768 he was becoming increasingly aware that he was fighting a rearguard action on this front. He kept his comments on the subject to a minimum, noting, not without irony: "I have insufficient knowledge of military matters, and these are in any case under His Imperial Majesty's enlightened special jurisdiction." This disclaimer notwithstanding he took the liberty

---

[121] *Ibid.*, Kaunitz to Maria Theresia, 8 May 1767.

[122] *Ibid.*, Lacy to Maria Theresia, 11 May 1767. Cf. Kotasek, *Lacy*, pp. 79–80.

[123] KA, Hofkriegsratakten 1767, 23 / June $\frac{200}{5}$, Joseph to Lacy, 30 May 1767.

[124] HHStA, Kabinettsarchiv: Nachlaß Lacy, Karton 5, Kaunitz to Maria Theresia, 27 July 1767.

[125] HHStA, Staatskanzlei: Vorträge, Karton 100, Kaunitz to Maria Theresia, Maria Theresia to Kaunitz, 28 July 1767. Additional copy in HHStA, Österreichische Akten: Österreich-Staat, Fasz. 5.   [126] Arneth, *Maria Theresia* VII, 228.

[127] HHStA, Kabinettsarchiv: Kaunitz Voten, Karton 1, No. 2474 of 1767, Kaunitz Staatsrat Votum, 7 November 1767.

to express some opinions nonetheless. He repeated his argument that wars were economic endurance contests, and that accordingly peacetime military establishments had to be kept to a minimum for economic reasons. He also could not resist the icy suggestion that what the Habsburg Monarchy needed most was "more competent generals" and better military education.[128]

For Joseph, all hopes continued to be based on the anticipated introduction of conscription, and gradually his mother was won around. While, as we have seen, the implementation of conscription was tabled in the spring of 1767, the remainder of the military reform package was gradually executed. During this time the Empress became increasingly taken with Lacy's argument that his conscript furlough system would have a minimal impact on the economy, and this proved to be the turning point in the debate.[129] Lacy attempted to diffuse financial criticism through the introduction of economizing measures within the Aulic War Council itself,[130] which even Kaunitz had to admit were more efficient than those of most other ministries.[131] He also tried to demonstrate that conscription would not mean the imposition of a new inhuman despotism by promoting measures designed to improve the socio-economic conditions of soldiers. This included, for example, care for invalids, soldiers' wives or orphans, pensions for veterans, and measures designed to facilitate military marriages.[132] These sorts of measures Kaunitz also supported fully,[133] and the change for the better in the Austrian army that Joseph reported to his brother in September 1768 was undeniable.[134] In 1769 a new General Staff Regulation (*Generalsreglement*) created a proficient modern general staff for the Habsburg army and went a long way to address the shortcomings in officers Kaunitz had always lamented.[135] Only a year later the Venetian ambassador was able to report that the state of the Austrian army was excellent and second to none in Europe.[136]

[128] HHStA, Staatskanzlei: Vorträge, Karton 101, Kaunitz to Maria Theresia, 25 January 1768, §43, 44 and 45.   [129] Kotasek, *Lacy*, pp. 79–80.
[130] Arneth, *Maria Theresia* VII, 214; Kotasek, *Lacy*, p. 90.
[131] HHStA, Kabinettsarchiv: Kaunitz Voten, Karton 1, No. 105 of 1768, Kaunitz Staatsrat Votum, 10 February 1768.   [132] Kotasek, *Lacy*, pp. 88–89.
[133] HHStA, Kabinettsarchiv: Kaunitz Voten, Karton 1, Nos. 2381 of 1767 and 912 of 1768, Kaunitz Staatsrat Voten, 14 November 1767 and 8 June 1768.
[134] HHStA, Familienarchiv: Sammelbände, Karton 7, Joseph to Leopold, 8 September 1768. Cf. Beales, *Joseph II* I, 176–191.
[135] Kurt Peball, "Das Generalsreglement der kaiserlich-königlichen österreichischen Armee vom 1. September 1769," in Direktion des Militärwissenschaftliches Instituts, ed., *Maria Theresia*, pp. 81–128; Oskar Regele, *Generalstabchefs aus vier Jahrhunderten* (Vienna & Cologne, 1966), p. 23.
[136] Alfred Ritter von Arneth, ed., *Die Relationen der Botschafter Venedigs über Österreich im achtzehnten Jahrhundert* (Vienna, 1863), pp. 314–317.

By January 1769, when Lacy was ready to begin the implementation of a conscription system, opposition to the idea had by no means abated. As Kaunitz had predicted, the conscription proposal met with determined resistance at every level. In the Council of State Borié had launched his own bitter attack on the idea in principle;[137] the Austro-Bohemian Chancellery did not like the introduction of a new military administrative structure into the provinces; the public feared that conscription would disrupt their personal lives and those of their families; and landowners foresaw drastic economic consequences if their labour force was conscripted. Lacy tried to appeal to the patriotism of the Provincial Estates, and tried to soothe fears that such legislations would turn everyone into soldiers.[138] But the seigniorial lobby, led as in 1763 by Rudolph Chotek, continued to create such a storm that Lacy was soon convinced all attacks were aimed at him personally.[139]

It was under these circumstances that the formal War Ministry proposal to introduce conscription in the Habsburg Monarchy came to the Council of State on 8 March 1769. Blümegen remained the only proponent of conscription on the Council. Binder, Borié and Starhemberg all expressed their opposition,[140] leaving, as usual, the final word to Kaunitz, who submitted his brief on 2 May. This final effort to stem the militarist flood was already permeated with fatalistic acceptance of the inevitable. He began by noting once more how similar the proposed canton system was to the Prussian one, and, in including all urban centers except Vienna, went even further. On the overall advisability of such a move, Kaunitz said, he could only refer to the views he had already expressed over the previous three years:

I had hoped to have demonstrated at that time that the introduction of this Prussian institution in its entirety is not compatible with the internal constitution of our Monarchy, with the customs and culture of our people, with the provincial administrative system existing since 1748, with royal commitments made to all Estates, with the basic policy premises in place, especially since the creation of the Council of State, and with the fulfillment of the agricultural, industrial and commercial goals that have been set.

This was the last concise cannon shot in the battle for Kaunitz. The rest of his brief conceded the principle, and addressed himself to the problem of how the War Ministry's objectives might be met, while avoiding the worst features of the "Prussian slavish military system." He had little objection

---

[137] HHStA, Kabinettsarchiv: Nachlaß Lacy, Karton 3, Lacy to Joseph, 20 December 1768.
[138] Kotasek, *Lacy*, pp. 80–81.
[139] HHStA, Kabinettsarchiv: Nachlaß Lacy, Karton 2, Lacy to Maria Theresia, 29 January 1769. Cf. Arneth, *Maria Theresia* IX, 496.
[140] Eichwalder, "Starhemberg," pp. 141–144.

to a census, which he supported for other than military reasons, but he objected to the War Ministry's proposal of collecting data on males only, and insisted that it be taken by civilian rather than military authorities. He also thought the idea of weighing and measuring potential conscripts to be a particularly inhuman and odious practice. If a canton system were in fact adopted, Kaunitz noted, officials in each canton would have sufficient indications of approximately how many able-bodies prospects were to be found in that district, without having to advertise in advance who had been "singled out as the victim for slaughter." Such people, as Binder and Starhemberg also pointed out, would probably do anything in their power to escape their fate. Finally Kaunitz wished to maximize the exemption categories, especially in urban centers.[141]

While continued Council of State objections could delay the implementation of the conscription system, they could not prevent it.[142] Maria Theresia made it perfectly clear that she now fully accepted the proposal in principle, and that she was flexible only on the way the measure was to be introduced. Lacy's triumph was virtually complete, and it was now he who, in the words of Zinzendorf, "dictated the law to the Council of State."[143] Kaunitz found himself in the unusual position of pinning his last hopes on Estates opposition to the central government, and it is ironic indeed that he was now compelled to argue that Provincial Estates had to be consulted, and that all the facts had to be laid on the table frankly before conscription was actually introduced.[144] The effect proved negligible. Consultation was indeed ordered, but only because the new system was to replace an older one which had been negotiated with the Estates. However, only the process of introduction, not the virtues and faults of the measure were to be discussed. Furthermore, in the presentation to the Estates the phrase "regimental enlistment district" was to be used rather than the pejorative word "canton." The entire system was not to be called "conscription" or "the canton system" but was to be referred to as a "recruiting regulation."[145] This language did not fool anyone, and, as expected, the Estates ignored their precise instructions and continued their opposition. But in a report of 25 November 1769 the Aulic War Council decided that sufficient "consultations" had taken place, and presented a precise proposal on the process of introducing conscription.[146]

This report was sent to the Council of State on 27 November, where

[141] HHStA, Kabinettsarchiv: Kaunitz Voten, Karton 1, No. 924 of 1769, Kaunitz Staatsrat Votum, 2 May 1769.   [142] Eichwalder, pp. 144–146.

[143] DOZA, Handschriften, Vol. 65, Ludwig Zinzendorf to Karl Zinzendorf, 23 May 1769.

[144] HHStA, Kabinettsarchiv: Kaunitz Voten, Karton 1, No. 2346 of 1769, Kaunitz Staatsrat Votum, 26 June 1769.

[145] HHStA, Kabinettsarchiv: Staatsratprotokolle, Vol. 32, No. 2346, imperial resolution, 30 June 1769.   [146] Ibid., Vol. 33, No. 4215, protocol record.

most members including Kaunitz resigned themselves to the inevitable.[147] In the event, even the most modest amendments found little reflection in the final resolution which followed on 1 February 1770. A universal census was ordered but responsible county officials were to act in co-operation with military officers. Houses were to be numbered and all animals counted as well. Parish records were to be consulted for verification, and a strict penalty of two years' hard labour was prescribed for anyone who tried to evade the count. The new conscription system was to take effect immediately in Styria, Carinthia, Carniola, Goricia, Gradisca and Silesia, and on 1 October 1770 in Bohemia, Moravia, Upper and Lower Austria. The old system would remain until the new had been introduced, and thereafter would be scrapped. Tyrol, Hither Austria, the Littorale and Hungary were not affected since constitutional oaths prevented the Monarchs from introducing the measures. As a military colony, the Military Frontier was also not affected.[148]

Final implementation proved no easy matter. Lacy was ordered to prepare a draft proclamation in conjunction with Blümegen, the one Council of State member who tended to support conscription, and concern to make the right "impression" was uppermost in their minds.[149] Despite this, resistance to conscription and the canton system persisted at all levels. Even after the formal decree, the necessary census proceeded very slowly, and it was not until March 1772 that the War Ministry was able to report that the conscription lists had been completed and regimental districts could now be established. Thirty-seven regimental conscription districts were accordingly set up, though they would not be in full operation until 1781, and their creation remained one of the most unpopular measures in the Monarchy.[150] A full Prussian military tone could never take foothold in the Habsburg Monarchy, but it was with some justice that Frederick II could now say of the Austrian army that they were "Prussians in white uniform."[151]

After conscription was decreed Kaunitz remained largely silent on military matters. In May 1774 Lacy retired for health reasons and was succeeded by Field Marshall András Hadik. The Polish partition crisis and

[147] HHStA, Kabinettsarchiv: Kaunitz Voten, Karton 1, No. 4215 of 1769, Kaunitz Staatsrat Votum, 4 January 1770.
[148] HHStA, Kabinettsarchiv: Staatsratprotokolle, Vol. 33, No. 4215, imperial resolution, 1 February 1770.
[149] HHStA, Kabinettsarchiv: Nachlaß Lacy, Karton 7, Lacy to Maria Theresia, 18 January 1770; Blümegen to Lacy, 30 January 1770.
[150] Mitrofanov, *Joseph II* I, 359–360; Beidtel, *Staatsverwaltung* I, 63; Wrede and Semek, *Wehrmacht* I, 44, 101; IV, 270–273; Kotasek, *Lacy*, pp. 82–83; Zimmermann, *Militärverwaltung*, pp. 106–114.
[151] HHStA, Staatskanzlei: Vorträge, Karton 106, Pergen to Kaunitz, reporting a conversation of Weber with Frederick II, 22 September 1770.

the recently concluded Russo-Turkish war led Hadik to the conclusion that further military increases were again necessary. He argued that the growing strength of Russia and Prussia, coupled with the feebleness of Austria's ally, France, as well as the territorial expansion of the Habsburg Monarchy all made such increases imperative.[152] Lacy, who was still acting as the Emperor's adviser, agreed with Joseph that the increases were indeed needed and suggested that instead of creating new regiments, every company in the army be strengthened by the addition of nine men.[153] Maria Theresia wanted to bring Kaunitz into the discussion,[154] but he was clearly reluctant to involve himself, and contented himself with the suggestion that rather than impose additional conscription pressures on the Austrian and Bohemian lands, further Belgian and Italian regiments could be raised and locally financed, and subsequently stationed in the Monarchy's heartland.[155] Joseph, however, stuck by his original plan and Kaunitz remained distant as ever from military questions.

Kaunitz's reluctance was clearly the result of the fundamental and apparently irreconcilable difference of views between himself and the Emperor on the place of a military establishment in society. Kaunitz obviously had been silenced but not persuaded. In his gigantic memorandum on the domestic conditions of the Monarchy which he submitted in May 1773, he continued to regard the military burden on society as one of the main millstones impeding economic progress and development,[156] and he continued to stand firm in that conviction in the years that followed. Joseph, on the other hand, clearly had other priorities. This difference of opinion came to the surface one final time during the reign of Maria Theresia at the end of the War of the Bavarian Succession. Pressing for as rapid a demobilization as possible, Kaunitz argued that war was to society what illness was to the body – "a more or less general disturbance of the natural order of things." Once the life of the patient was saved, he continued the analogy, it became necessary to restore his bodily strength in order not to expose him to further illness. Hence Kaunitz urged that as many people and horses be returned to the rural economy as possible. This meant discharging the maximum number of soldiers commensurate with minimal security. Further, horses appropriated from peasants during the war should not be sold but given back to these peasants free of charge as

---

[152] Ibid., Karton 116, Aulic War Council report, n.d. (late 1774).
[153] Ibid., Lacy Gutachten, 8 December 1774; Joseph Gutachten, n.d. (December 1774).
[154] Ibid., Karton 117, Obsrvationes Augustissimae, 3 February 1775. Quoted in part in Arneth, Maria Theresia IX, 537–542.
[155] HHStA, Staatskanzlei: Vorträge, Karton 117, Kaunitz to Maria Theresia, 14 February 1775.
[156] Ibid., Kaunitz's "Allergnädigst anbefohlenes Gutachten über die Verbesserung des Systematis in Internis," 1 May 1773.

a sort of compensation for the hardships that had been imposed on them during the course of the war.[157]

But Joseph's views, even in peace time, remained precisely the reverse. In his reply to Kaunitz the Emperor wrote:

Our provinces are impoverished and cannot afford to maintain the present military establishment... Only the improvement of our agriculture, industry, trade and finance will make possible the upkeep and expansion of our military forces to meet future eventualities.[158]

Thus, while Kaunitz felt that the army had to be tailored to society, Joseph felt society had to be tailored to the kind of army he insisted on maintaining. In the eyes of the Emperor, Kaunitz's duty was therefore not to question military expenditures so much as to find new expedients to raise more funds to cover them. Though Kaunitz discharged this duty conscientiously,[159] the philosophical gap between the Chancellor of State and the Emperor on military matters was never bridged.

Building a Habsburg navy

Fundamental differences of opinion between Joseph and Kaunitz on military matters also extended to the idea of creating a Habsburg navy,[160] though for opposite reasons. This time Kaunitz was the proponent of naval armaments, while Joseph remained an outspoken opponent, because both Joseph and Kaunitz chose to regard them less as a strictly military matter and more as a support system for commercial development. In the eighteenth century Habsburg trade routes gradually shifted from the north to the south and assumed an ever-increasing Mediterranean profile. The development of the ports of Trieste and Fiume (Rijeka) therefore became a growing priority with the government in Vienna, and the volume of trade out of these ports continued to increase, especially after the Seven Years War.[161]

These economic developments made the Habsburg Monarchy increasingly sensitive to the problem of Mediterranean piracy, with which Spain,

---

[157] *Ibid.*, Karton 128, Kaunitz to Joseph, 16 March 1779.

[158] Ernst Benedikt, *Kaiser Joseph II., 1741–1790* (Vienna, 1936), pp. 263–264.

[159] From various undated drafts of 1779 it becomes clear that Kaunitz had been ordered to work with Treasury president Kollowrat on various expedients to raise 66 million Gulden to cover military expenses. HHStA, Staatskanzlei: Vorträge, Karton 130, Kaunitz to Joseph (various drafts), n.d. (late 1779). Cf. Dickson, *Finance and Government* II, 153–155.

[160] The following section largely follows my "Unwanted Navy," which tells the story in greater detail. I have not repeated the full scholarly apparatus here.

[161] Wilhelm Kaltenstadtler, "Der österreichische Seehandel über Triest im 18. Jahrhundert," *VSWG* LV (1968), 482–576, LVI (1969), 1–104.

France and England had struggled for centuries. Indeed, by the eighteenth century privateering activities out of the so-called Barbary States of North Africa – Morocco, Algiers, Tunis and Tripoli – were already on the decline in the face of increased English and French naval strength.[162] Ironically, it was the very strength of the Western powers that increasingly compelled the pirates to confine their attacks to states with weak or no naval establishments such as the Habsburg Monarchy. Without a navy, Vienna had to cope with piracy by concluding treaties with the Barbary States that amounted to virtual extortion payments. A number of such agreements were concluded in 1748 and 1749, but violations of them occurred almost annually, and each time peace had to be purchased anew.[163]

The logical alternative of a permanent naval establishment seemed even more expensive, and for protection on the open seas the government could only urge merchantmen to arm themselves. This experiment was given its baptism by fire during the Seven Years War. In the summer of 1759 several English privateers appeared in the Mediterranean to prey on Spanish, French, Italian and Austrian shipping. Since Britain and the Habsburg Monarchy were not direct belligerents in the war, three of the English captains arranged for letters of patent to be issued them in Berlin and raided Habsburg shipping under Prussian colours. In response Kaunitz launched a vigorous diplomatic offensive designed to create a common front of all Mediterranean states against these corsairs, and even tried to persuade the Sultan to declare a holy war on them.[164] In the meantime, the Trieste merchants were warned to be on guard, and it was recommended to them that they arm their merchantmen in self-defence.

Most merchants replied that they would do so only if the government supplied them with free arms, ammunition, military personnel and provisions, but one adventurous Dalmatian entrepreneur residing in Trieste, Demetrio Voinovich, offered to arm his vessel at his own expense in return for being allowed to keep whatever booty he captured. Licensed counter-piracy was not unusual in the eighteenth century, and when the request was forwarded to Kaunitz, he reacted to the proposal with considerable enthusiasm. He was convinced such ventures did not transgress international law, and was much taken with the initiative shown by Voinovich.[165] The intrepid captain proved entirely successful in his pursuit. On the afternoon of 5 May 1760 he captured the *Lancashire Witch*

[162] Godfrey Fisher, *Barbary Legend: War Trade and Piracy in North Africa, 1415–1830* (Oxford, 1957); Salvatore Bono, *I corsari Barbareschi* (Turin, 1964).
[163] One such agreement is reproduced in Khevenhüller-Metsch V, 198–201.
[164] Ugo Cova, "Trieste e la guerra di corsa nel secolo XVIII," *MÖStA* XXIX (1976), 158–163.
[165] HKA, Kommerz: Littorale, Karton Rote No. 689, Kommerzienrat to Kaunitz, 15 December 1759; Kaunitz to Kommerzienrat, 12 January 1760.

and hanged its captain, Charles Ratcliffe, from the yardarm of his own ship for piracy. "A cruel fate," Kaunitz noted when informed of the news, "but nothing less than he deserved."[166] Voinovich was less pleased, for the booty was negligible and damage to his own ship great. When his request for government compensation was rejected, he left the glamorous life of counter-piracy and sailed for the Levant and the Far East on private business.[167]

With this unprofitable precedent before their eyes, it was small wonder that the consensus of merchants and local officials in Trieste after the Seven Years War was that armed merchantmen represented a wholly inadequate response to Mediterranean piracy. Instead a plan was developed by the future agrarian reformer, but then still local councillor with the Trieste Intendancy, Franz Anton Raab, for the creation of a naval force of eight frigates, jointly financed by Vienna and the Emperor in his capacity as Grand Duke of Tuscany, and for the development of the port of Porto Rè (Kraljevica) as a naval station.[168] This proposal was lent some urgency by the Barbary States, who broke their treaties with the Habsburgs in 1764, and became increasingly bold in their raids. While Kaunitz again tried to organize a common diplomatic front with the smaller Italian states, he saw the need for the Habsburg Monarchy to demonstrate some initiative as well. He thus gave his full backing to Raab's proposal,[169] and persuaded Maria Theresia to order implementation of the project.[170]

The preparation of the military harbor at Porto Rè and the construction of two frigates was begun in November 1764. The master ship-builder from Leghorn, Giulio Nocetti, was brought in for the construction of the vessels, while overall supervision of the project was given to Voinovich. When he had returned from his voyages in the Far East in 1764 he was surprised to discover that he had been awarded a medal for bravery by the Empress for his war-time exploit, and he was quick to put his name forward as prospective commander of the Habsburg navy. Because of his Venetian birth and Greek Orthodox faith, Maria Theresia was reluctant to appoint him, but determined intervention by Kaunitz overcame her scruples. Although not named commander of the ships themselves, he was made supervisor of the project with the title of "Ship-Armaments Director."[171]

[166] Ibid., Kaunitz to Kommerzienrat, 9 July 1760.
[167] Cova, "Trieste," pp. 164–166.
[168] KA, Commercialia, Fasz. 111, Raab Proposal, 1 July 1764; Trieste Intendancy to Hofkommerzienrat, 25 August 1764.
[169] HHStA, Staatskanzlei: Vorträge, Karton 94, Kaunitz to Maria Theresia, including imperial resolution, 11 September 1764.
[170] HHStA, Kabinettsarchiv: Staatsratprotokolle, Vol. 15, No. 2436, Maria Theresia to Hofkommerzienrat, 26 September 1764.
[171] KA, Commercialia, Fasz. 111, Voinovich to Maria Theresia, n.d. (November 1764); Hofkommerzienrat to Maria Theresia, 10 and 24 November and 20 December 1764;

By March 1766 substantial improvements to the port had been completed, and the first of the two frigates, the *Aurora*, was formally launched on 10 September. Some months later, on 29 January 1767, a second frigate, the *Stella Mattutina*, was launched and construction began on two further vessels.[172]

Two matters which had been delayed until then now became pressing: the formal appointment of a commander and the allocation of operational and armament funds for the new navy. Voinovich's candidacy for the command post was sabotaged by the governor of Trieste, Heinrich Auersperg, who took a passionate dislike to the Dalmatian, and the search for an alternate commander led Kaunitz to initiate negotiations with the Knights of Malta. The grand master of the order eventually proposed one of their number, a French naval veteran, Jean Charles de Meaussé, who was subsequently invited to come to Trieste and Vienna to negotiate the appointment. Funding proved to be a more serious problem and almost led to the abandonment of the project, until Kaunitz and the Council of State persuaded the Empress to persevere and agree to fund armaments out of cameral revenues.[173] Meaussé arrived in Trieste in January 1768, and after a thorough inspection, traveled on to Vienna in April. The initial impression Meaussé made was that of the consummate professional, and almost everyone, especially Kaunitz, was impressed.

However, in the discussions which followed, matters soon turned sour. Meaussé's aristocratic self-consciousness and his transparent penchant for empire-building soon provoked bitter animosity in Vienna. He insisted on a much larger naval establishment than had been projected, vetoed any naval station but the civilized port of Trieste, wanted complete independence in his command, and demanded that all officers under him be nobles. By August his candidacy had collapsed. Worse still was the problem of administrative jurisdiction. All departments of the central government were equally fearful that they might end up having to bear the financial burden of the navy, and so each in turn eagerly shunted off the responsibility to the other. The Department of Trade and Commerce argued that navies were after all military institutions, and therefore the frigates were best placed under the jurisdiction of the War Ministry. The Aulic War Council argued that the only function of the prospective navy was to protect commerce, and that therefore the Department of Trade and Commerce was its most suitable superior. The nominal superior of the

Kaunitz to Kommerzienrat, 18 December 1764; Maria Theresia to Kommerzienrat, 1 January 1765.

[172] Karl Gogg, *Österreichs Kriegsmarine, 1440–1848* (Salzburg, 1972), p. 57.

[173] HHStA, Kabinettsarchiv: Staatsratakten, Karton 1, No. 1372, Stupan, Blümegen, Stahremberg and Kaunitz Voten, and imperial resolution, June 1767.

Department of Trade and Commerce, Austro-Bohemian Chancellor Chotek, concluded that a navy was a luxury the Habsburg Monarchy simply could not afford.

Kaunitz's exasperation at all these debates shone through in the Council of State. Having consistently supported the establishment of a modest navy, he now saw the project in danger of complete collapse. He reacted strongly to the suggestion that the whole enterprise be liquidated. He repeated all the reasons why the navy had been established in the first place, and agreed that it was an expense that could itself not promise any profit. But, he added, all military expenditures were a necessary evil whose complete abolition would be "very desirable," if that were possible. The central point in this case was to spare no effort to help foster trade from the port of Trieste, and if the whole matter was in a shambles now, it was the result of the indecision and confusion in the Austro-Bohemian Chancellery and its Department of Trade and Commerce. If they had a better way of dealing with Mediterranean piracy, let them spell it out. After all, it was they who had recommended establishing a navy in the first place! In short, the Monarchy had to persevere; the naval project could not be abandoned now.[174]

As a result of Kaunitz's strong intervention, all suggestions to liquidate the fleet were rejected, and the search was begun for a suitable replacement for Meaussé. After more than a year an acceptable candidate had still not been found. In the interim the ships, maintained by skeleton crews, languished in the harbour of Porto Ré. One even capsized and had to be refloated at considerable expense, so that while the navy was not yet active, it was nonetheless draining resources from the treasury. This distressing state of affairs now brought Joseph into the fray. He quickly ordered the creation of an *ad hoc* commission, consisting of members of the Council of State, the Department of Trade and Commerce and the governor of Trieste, to study the problem. Closely supervised by Joseph himself, the commission came to the conclusion that the only reasonable course of action was to integrate the two Habsburg frigates into the Tuscan navy and to create a joint Austro-Tuscan fleet under the command of the Tuscan naval commander, Giovanni d'Acton, also a Knight of Malta.[175]

Tuscany, since 1765 a Habsburg secundogenitur ruled by Joseph's younger brother Leopold, had strong naval ties with Austria. Despite the severance of the Grand Duchy's personal connection with the imperial title at the death of Francis I, Leopold had been authorized as early as March 1767 to issue imperial patents and to fly imperial colours on Tuscan

---

[174] HHStA, Kabinettsarchiv: Kaunitz Voten, Karton 1, No. 1676 of 1768, Kaunitz Staatsrat Votum, 29 July 1768.
[175] HHStA, Staatskanzlei: Vorträge, Karton 105, Commission protocol, 9 February 1770.

ships.[176] For some time the subject of Mediterranean piracy had been a frequent topic for discussion in the personal correspondence between the Emperor and his brother.[177] The commercial link between Trieste and Leghorn was lucrative to both sides and needed protection. So integral was the connection, in fact, that two of the Tuscan ships had been built at the Porto Rè installation after the completion of Austrian frigates.[178] Late in 1769 Leopold agreed in principle to the creation of a common fleet and dispatched d'Acton to iron out the details. This led to an agreement in February 1770 whereby the two Austrian frigates were joined to the three Tuscan vessels to form "a common armada." It was agreed to meet maintenance costs in proportion of two to three by Vienna and Florence respectively, but supplies had to be purchased at Trieste. Tuscany assumed legal jurisdiction and commissioned all officers, but had to agree to give priority in such commissions to Habsburg subjects. It also had to guarantee to give adequate protection to the Adriatic as well as the west coast of the Italian peninsula. The practice of Tuscan ships flying imperial colors remained unchanged, but all naval co-ordination between Vienna and Florence was henceforth conducted on the diplomatic level, which now made Kaunitz the funnel through which all discussions passed.[179]

D'Acton completed the outfitting of the ships and assumed command of the joint navy on 24 July 1770. Three days later the fleet left on its first escort mission. Though the Austro-Tuscan naval agreement had been intended to last twenty years, in the event it barely lasted three. The venture ran smoothly as long as the navy was merely patrolling the waters around the Italian peninsula, but in the fall of 1771 Habsburg merchants wanted to arrange for the fleet to escort a convoy of merchantmen bound for Cadiz. When it became clear that such an expedition would entail extraordinary costs which Tuscany was not willing to meet, Joseph decided to cancel the naval agreement and to liquidate the whole venture. Kaunitz held up matters briefly by arguing that in the midst of the then raging Russo-Turkish war, the Habsburg Monarchy could not sell her interest in the joint navy without giving rise to fears in Constantinople that Vienna was reneging on its mediation efforts. But by 1774 the disengagement was complete, and the Habsburg Monarchy ceased to be even the miniscule naval power it had briefly been.

The failure of this experiment by no means put an end to Kaunitz's enthusiasm for the idea, and he persistently pressed the case for the creation of a modest naval force. When Joseph returned from his 1777 trip to France apparently quite taken with the prospective benefits of maritime

---

[176] *Ibid.*, Karton 99, Kaunitz to Maria Theresia, including imperial resolution, 2 March 1767.
[177] Wandruszka, *Leopold II* I, 196–197.   [178] Gogg, *Kriegsmarine*, p. 57.
[179] HHStA, Staatskanzlei: Vorträge, Karton 105, Commission protocol, 9 February 1770.

commerce, Kaunitz took the initiative of proposing the creation of a new navy in January 1778.[180] Although Joseph rejected the idea, Kaunitz did not give up. During the War of the Bavarian Succession, British privateers under Prussian colors terrorized the Adriatic coastline again,[181] while the Bolts–Poli East Indian trading company venture put new emphasis on the need for protection on the seas. Early in 1780 a colonel in the Habsburg army who had accompanied Joseph on his trips to Trieste and Croatia, Moritz Benjowsky, took a new initiative by submitting a plan for the creation of a navy. Benjowsky's detailed proposal included a full budget calling for an initial outlay of 500,000 Gulden and a subsequent annual budget of 170,000 Gulden, and plans for the construction of a sixty-gun battleship, two frigates of thirty-two and two of twenty-six guns respectively, and sixteen smaller vessels with an additional thirty-four cannons among them.[182]

Kaunitz immediately took a keen interest in this plan and allowed himself to be convinced by Binder that only the open and firm backing of the Chancellor of State could give the project any chance of success.[183] Kaunitz accordingly submitted a report to Joseph on 29 March 1780 backing Benjowsky's plans. Again Kaunitz stressed that Habsburg commerce needed protection from attack by Barbary Coast pirates if it were to expand. He also tried to emphasize the economic ripple-effect: "the powerful influence of maritime commerce on industry and the general wealth of the state is proven as much by the example of those states that cultivate it as those that do not." He was fully persuaded that the "energetic" Benjowsky was the right man to carry such a project out, and felt funding could be secured by persuading the pope to issue a crusading bull of the type already granted to the Kings of Portugal, Spain and Naples, which permitted the state to levy extraordinary taxes on monastic institutions for the purpose of combatting Barbary Coast piracy.[184]

Joseph remained skeptical. He expressed doubts that Benjowsky was the man to carry through such a "dangerous [and] grand enterprise", and concern that building a navy might "excite the jealousy" of other maritime powers and lead to diplomatic embarrassments. Kaunitz asked to see the Emperor personally in order to ease his doubts on the matter, and Joseph proposed to meet the very next day. This gave Kaunitz little time to prepare his case, and he asked Binder to help him plan for Joseph's anticipated objections. Binder told Kaunitz that Joseph had linked in his

[180] *Ibid.*, Karton 125, Kaunitz to Joseph, 23 January 1778, including imperial resolution.
[181] Gogg, *Kriegsmarine*, p. 82.
[182] HHStA, Staatskanzlei: Vorträge, Karton 131, Benjowsky project, n.d. (early 1780).
[183] HHStA, Familienarchiv: Sammelbände, Karton 70, Binder to Kaunitz, 29 March 1780.
[184] HHStA, Staatskanzlei: Vorträge, Karton 131, Kaunitz to Joseph, 29 March 1780.

mind plans for a navy with those calling for a government-backed East India company. Being opposed to the latter he was probably opposed to the former almost automatically. Hence the problem would be to separate the two plans in the Emperor's mind. Diplomatic fears could be defused by pointing out that a small navy would not really be a threat to any maritime power. The danger to commerce could be stressed by pointing out that some Austrian merchantmen had only recently been seized by pirates. Above all, Joseph's consent might be secured by noting how imperative a navy would become if war broke out with the Turks – an eventuality that seemed imminent.[185]

Kaunitz probably used all these arguments and more in his conversations with Joseph. Though there is no record of them, subsequent events show that all of Kaunitz's persuasiveness was to no avail. In Joseph's mind the naval project remained inseparably linked with the East India company project. After his return from Russia in late 1780 Joseph remained adamantly opposed to such a company, giving among other reasons for his opposition the contention that the state would have to create a navy to protect East Indian trade. This, he added, was out of the question since the Monarchy could hardly afford a satisfactory navy when, as the War of the Bavarian Succession had demonstrated, it still did not have a satisfactory army.[186] Six months after the death of Maria Theresia he repeated these sentiments, calling a navy a "most useless and vain" enterprise because it could not be strong enough to reflect the might of the Monarchy and to be competitive in the face of other naval powers.[187] On that rock, Kaunitz's naval projects foundered for good.

---

[185] HHStA, Familienarchiv: Sammelbände, Karton 70, Joseph to Kaunitz, Kaunitz to Joseph, and Binder to Kaunitz, 30 March 1780.
[186] Pollack-Parnau, *Handelscompagnie*, p. 64.
[187] Hugo Hantsch, *Die Geschichte Österreichs*, 2 Vols. (Graz, 1953), II, 207.

8 The problem of Hungary

Within the Habsburg Monarchy of the eighteenth century, the Kingdom of Hungary was *sui generis*. Though not all the territories which were subordinate to the ancient crown of St. Stephen (Hungary proper, the Kingdom of Croatia-Slavonia, the Grand Principality of Transylvania, the Banat of Temesvár, and the Military Frontier which stretched along the border with the Ottoman Empire from the Adriatic to Transylvania) were governed in the same fashion, all remained largely outside the purview of the reforms described in detail in the preceding chapters. The status of the Hungarian lands within the Habsburg complex remained ambiguous, with the kingdom's degrees of sovereignty and association remaining matters of debate even after the 1711 Peace of Szatmár and the 1723 acceptance of the Pragmatic Sanction by the Hungarian Diet had set the constitutional framework. By these two agreements the Kingdom of Hungary was hereditary in the male and female lines of the House of Habsburg, as well as "indivisible and inseparable" from the other Habsburg territories. Yet the indigenous political institutions and socio-economic structures, dominated by an assertive nobility, remained largely intact and continued to exercise such control as to make the assertion of the royal prerogative in a manner analogous to Bohemia and Austria virtually impossible.

The border between Hungary and the other Habsburg lands remained a very real border, and even the "Bohemian Party" of seventeenth-century cameralist reformers, who had been the strongest protagonists of sacrificing the far-flung peripheral territories of the Monarchy in favour of an integrated and strengthened core, thought primarily of Bohemia and Austria and regarded Hungary as a mere defensive glacis.[1] During the course of the eighteenth century, however, Hungary's position as a key component in the core of the Monarchy became increasingly obvious, especially when Habsburg ties with the Holy Roman Empire were temporarily severed during the Austrian succession crisis. The accession of

---

[1] Arnold Gaedecke, *Die Politik Oesterreichs in der Spanischen Erbfolgefrage*, 2 Vols. (Leipzig, 1877), II, 69–70; Klingenstein, *Aufstieg des Hauses Kaunitz*, pp. 49–52.

Maria Theresia thus not only tested the validity of the legal hypothesis of the Pragmatic Sanction, but also forced a whole new perspective on the "indivisible and inseparable" core triad of the Habsburg Monarchy. This was accelerated by what might be termed the "ideological shift" of the Habsburg government. The Counter-Reformation ideology which had integrated Austria and Bohemia was at best only partially accepted in Hungary, even during its high-point in the eighteenth century.[2] In the reign of Maria Theresia this confessional consensus was supplanted by a cameralist eudemonism which regarded the political problem of Hungary as being of a kind – albeit of a worse kind – with the problems of the rest of the Monarchy. This problem centered primarily on the backwardness of the Kingdom of St. Stephen, marked above all by the continued power of the feudal corporate order, which impeded both Hungary's modernization and socio-economic development as well as its integration with other parts of the Monarchy.

These problems were complex enough, but their analysis by historians has been more complex still, for the historiography of enlightened absolutism in Hungary is complicated by subsequent changes in vocabulary as well as by the skewed perspectives of latter-day nationalism and official Marxism. Enlightenment intellectuals did not shrink from using a highly polemical tone against opponents, and the debates on Hungary proved no exception. Regrettably, the key words in the polemical exchanges – "republic," "nation," "freedom," – have assumed entirely different meanings in our century. The Hungarian "nation," as defined by the notorious sixteenth-century jurist, István Werbőczi, was made up only of the "populus" (nobles, clergy and free cities) which were not necessarily ethnically Magyar. The "plebs" (serfs and others without political rights), many of whom were Magyar, were not members of the "nation."[3] Hence, the word "nation" would today be more suitably translated as "class". Similarly, "freedom" meant aristocratic freedom from the onerous burdens of other classes and would today more accurately be called "privilege." Finally, "republic" referred to the right of self-government, but self-government by the privileged classes alone. For this reason the exercise of "republican freedoms" was also known as "gentry democracy," which today would be more precisely defined as "oligarchy." Therefore, the "Hungarian nation's" defence of its "republican freedoms"

---

[2] Evans, *Making of the Habsburg Monarchy*, pp. 235–274.

[3] Endre Arató, "A magyar 'nemzeti' ideológia jellemző vonásai a 18. században," in Gy. Spira and J. Szűcs, eds., *Nemzetizég a feudalizmus korában. Tanulmányok* (Budapest, 1972), pp. 130–181; Moritz Csáky, "Die Hungarus-Konzeption: Eine 'Realpolitische' Alternative zur Magyarischen Nationalstaatsidee?" in Drabek *et al.*, eds., *Ungarn und Österreich*, pp. 73–74.

actually meant the Hungarian aristocratic oligarchy defending the privileges of its class.[4] Yet so powerful were Hungarian nationalist perspectives for some historians that even post-war official Marxism, in its reluctance to identify enlightened absolutism (and its Habsburg proponents) as a "progressive" element of the "historical dialectic," actually defended the aristocracy in its "national" mission of resisting reform to uphold the "independence" of the Kingdom.[5] Vocabulary and nationalist or ideological preconceptions, in short, thus have frequently obscured the predominantly social focus of enlightened absolutist reform in Hungary.

Kaunitz's Hungarian "system"

For nearly two centuries after the Habsburgs first lay legal claim to the crown of Hungary in 1526, the position of the dynasty in the Kingdom was precarious and uncertain. For most of the period the Habsburgs had effective control over, at most, a third of the territory of the medieval Kingdom of Hungary. The dynasty faced now declared, now undeclared war with the Ottoman Empire on a front cutting through the middle of the Hungarian plain. It was confronted with open rebellion and more frequent passive resistance by the indigenous nobility, and even its loyal political elites vacillated between "half-hearted opposition" and "lukewarm conformity" to the regime.[6] With the defeat of the Rákóczi rebellion, and the conclusion of the compromise peace of Szatmár in 1711, however, a workable *modus vivendi* between the dynasty and the Hungarian elites seemed to have been concluded. Not only was the Pragmatic Sanction accepted by the Hungarian Diet with relative ease, it also received critical material support when put to the test with the accession of Maria Theresia. The famous display of loyalty by the Hungarian nobles at the Diet of September 1741, in stark contrast to the treasonable collaboration with

---

[4] On aristocratic "freedoms" and "liberties" in early modern Europe see Roger Lockyer, *Habsburg and Bourbon Europe, 1470–1720* (London, 1974), pp. 185–192; A. R. Myers, *Parliaments and Estates in Europe of 1789* (London, 1975); D. Gerhard, "Regionalismus und Ständisches Wesen," *Historische Zeitschrift* CLXXIV (1952), 307–337.

[5] Győző Ember, "A Habsburg abszolutizmus osztály politikája Magyarországon az 1760-es években," *A Magyar Tudományos Akadémia Társadalmi-Történeti Tudományok Osztályának Közleményei* XIII-XIV (1964/65), 1–46; Ember, "Zur Klassenpolitik des Habsburgerabsolutismus in Ungarn in den sechziger Jahren des 18. Jahrhunderts," in Commission Nationale des Historiens, Hongrois, ed., *Nouvelles études historiques*, 2 Vols. (Budapest, 1965), I, 389–413, especially 391–392; Mathias Bernath, "Ständewesen und Absolutismus in Ungarn des 18. Jahrhunderts," *Südost-Forschungen* XXII (1963), 347–348. Recently Hungarian historiography (including Ember himself!) has begun to move away from this point of view.

[6] Evans, *Making of the Habsburg Monarchy*, p. 266.

invading enemy forces of some of their Austrian and Bohemian confrères, clearly revealed the new political consensus that reigned in Hungary.[7]

This delicate balance was upset by the stark realities about the condition of the Monarchy as a whole which the War of the Austrian Succession laid bare. The Monarchy's military vulnerability led not only to the Haugwitz revolution in Austria and Bohemia, which raised royal revenues considerably, but was soon followed by an attempt to extract similar increases from Hungary. A new Hungarian Diet, summoned in 1751, proved less cooperative than Maria Theresia had hoped, and left her clearly disenchanted. Although a 700,000 Gulden increase in the annual tax quota was voted by the assembly, it was 500,000 Gulden less than had been requested by the crown.[8] Yet this was not as decisive a turning point as has sometimes been suggested. The reaction of Kaunitz, at the time Habsburg ambassador to Paris, can be considered fairly typical. Having been kept apprised of developments in the Diet by the Empress's private secretary, he affirmed that he had not even dared to hope for as "passable" a result as had ensued. He therefore tended to regard the modest tax increases voted as a positive sign, and was encouraged to believe that with "wisdom, patience, firmness and equity," it was possible to embark on "a solid political system" which would introduce "the necessary remedies" to combat the political defects of Hungary.[9]

What ensued was hardly a "solid political system", but rather what many Hungarian historians long considered the "darkest stain" of the reign of Maria Theresia: the tariff ordinances of 1754.[10] Whether these tariff ordinances were a punitive retaliation for the recalcitrance of the Diet of 1751, as has been suggested,[11] however, is open to question. What is certain is that extremely conservative mercantilists, led by the reactionary Count Rudolf Chotek, drew up a series of tariff regulations which attempted, among other things, to serve the ideal of autarky by forcibly diverting outflowing Hungarian capital from Silesia and Saxony to

---

[7] Győző Ember, "Magyarország a Habsburg Birodalomban," in Győző Ember and Gustáv Heckenast, eds., Magyarország története, 1686–1790, 2 Vols. (Budapest, 1989), I, 351–390; Ember, "Az Országgyűlések," Ibid., I, 391–425.

[8] Henrik Marczali, Magyarország Története III. Károlytól a Bécsi Congressusig (1711–1815), Vol. VIII of Sándor Szilágyi, ed., A Magyar nemzet története (Budapest, 1898), pp. 280–285; Arneth, Maria Theresia IV, 180–220; Ember, "Az Országgyűlések," pp. 425–426.   [9] Schlitter, ed., Correspondance, pp. 119–120.

[10] The classic critique is Ferenc Eckhart, A bécsi udvar gazdasági politikája Magyarországon Mária Terézia korában (Budapest, 1922), who asserted that Vienna's tariff policy not only stifled the growth of the Hungarian economy, particularly the industrial sector, but was directly responsible for subsequent Hungarian backwardness and underdevelopment.

[11] For example by János Varga, "Magyarország a Habsburg abszolutizmus rendszerében," in Erik Molnár, et al., eds., Magyarország története, 2 Vols. (Budapest, 1967), I, 343–344.

domestic Habsburg markets.[12] The policy certainly had negative repercussions on import and export prices for Hungarians, though it must be
pointed out that the ideal of autarky also had the same effects on the other
parts of the Monarchy.[13] But as Anton Spiesz has now demonstrated, there
was no conscious plan to destroy Hungarian industry and, indeed, within
a few years such industry was actively encouraged.[14] Other studies have
tended to regard Hungarian underdevelopment as the result of long-range
factors rather than the specific discriminatory policies of Maria Theresia.[15]
Habsburg policies are increasingly being recognized as being divergent
rather than monolithic, and those elements which promoted Hungarian
economic development have been given their due.[16]

In fact, the real turning point in the Habsburg government's attitude
towards Hungary was less the frustrating Diet of 1751 or the tariff
ordinances of 1754, but the experience of the Seven Years War. In the
initial stages of the war, Hungarian regiments and Hungarian supplies
were naturally an integral part of the overall strategic and logistical
calculations which shaped the Habsburg war effort, but higher Hungarian
officials were conspicuous by their absence from the War Cabinet. This was
particularly noteworthy for the Hungarian Court Chancellor, since 1746
Lipót Flórián Nádasdy, whose office really represented the Monarch's
secretariat and co-ordinating instrument for relations with the Hungarian
"nation". Nádasdy, who also held the ceremonial office of Grand Master
of the Horse,[17] belonged to the traditional conservative elite in which local
loyalties outstripped loyalty to the Monarch, and could therefore not be
considered a reliable instrument of the royal will. As long as expectations

---

[12] Beer, "Zollpolitik," pp. 239–244; Liebel-Weckowicz, "Free Trade and Protectionism,"
pp. 355–358.

[13] Adolf Beer, "Studien zur Geschichte der österreichischen Volkswirtschaft unter Maria
Theresia: I. Die österreichische Industriepolitik," *AÖG* LXXXI (1895), 19.

[14] Anton Spiesz, "Die Wirtschaftspolitik des Wiener Hofes gegenüber Ungarn im 18.
Jahrhundert und im Vormärz," *Ungarn Jahrbuch* I (1969), 61–62; Spiesz, "Die Slowakei
in der Sozial- und Wirtschaftsgeschichte Mittel- und Osteuropas," *Bohemia* X (1969),
63–68; Otruba, *Wirtschaftspolitik*, pp. 42–43.

[15] Zs[igismund] P[ál] Pach, *Das Entwicklungsniveau der feudalen Agrarverhältnisse in Ungarn
in der zweiten Hälfte des 15. Jahrhunderts* (Budapest, 1960) and *Die ungarische
Agrarentwicklung im 16.-17. Jahrhundert: Abbiegung vom Westeuropäischen Entwick-
lungsgang* (Budapest, 1964); I. T. Berend, "Az iparfejlődés és az úgynevezett parasztipar
kérdéséhez," *Történelmi Szemle* VIII (1965), 175–184; L. Katus, "A kelet-európai
iparosodás és az 'önálló tőkés fejlődés'" *Ibid.* X (1967), 1–45; Domokos Kosáry, "Les
Antécédents de la Révolution Industrielle en Hongrie: hypothèses et réalités," *Acta
Historica Academiae Scientiarum Hungaricae* XXI (1975), 365–375.

[16] Gusztáv Heckenast, "A magyarországi ipar a XIII. században és a bécsi gazdaság-
politika," *Történelmi Szemle* XVII (1974), 502–506; Éva H. Balázs, "Karl von Zinzendorf
et ses relations avec la Hongrie à l'Epoque de l'absolutisme éclairé," *Etudes Historiques
Hongroises* 1975, 2 Vols. (Budapest, 1975), I, 451–453.

[17] Zoltán Fallenbüchl, *Magyarország főméltóságai* (Budapest, 1988), 82.

for a relatively brief and successful war prevailed, it did not seem pressing
to bring the Hungarian Chancellor into the War Cabinet. After the disaster
of Leuthen, however, the prospect of a longer war changed all that. In
March 1758 Nádasdy was forced to resign, and yield his office to the
former Grand Master of the Household for Hungary, Count Miklós
Pálffy, who by the standards of the Hungarian nobility passed as a
reformer.[18]

Central to these developments, of course, were problems pertaining to
war finance. The Hungarian direct war tax (*Contribution*) of approximately
4.3 million Gulden was proportionally at about the same level as the 4.1
million collected for the Austrian lands and the 5.9 million for the
Bohemian provinces,[19] and as long as these sums formed the bulk of war
finance in the early months of the war there was little cause for friction.
Maria Theresia's decision at the outset of the conflict to centralize military
revenues in Haugwitz's Directory caused some administrative difficulties.
The degree of required co-ordination with the Hungarian Chancellery was
hotly debated, with some Chancellery officials, such as Ferenc Koller,
eager to assume an active role, while others, such as Jakob Szvetics,
content to have revenues flow directly from Hungarian county treasuries to
Haugwitz's Directory. As long as the Diet's prescriptive right to vote
taxation was respected, Nádasdy was happy to avoid direct involvement in
these administrative complexities, with the result that the Hungarian
Chancellery had no real reason to be involved in the War Cabinet.[20]

As costs escalated and officials increasingly resorted to such fiscal
devices as indirect taxation, forced loans, and the like in Austria and
Bohemia, the relative proportion of Hungarian contribution to the war
effort declined. At the same time the personal profits of the seigniorial elite,
fed by the hothouse atmosphere of high demand during the war, grew
dramatically, much to the bitter consternation of such crown officials as
Council of State referendary, König.[21] Since the extraordinary fiscal
devices applied in Austria and Bohemia could not be implemented in
Hungary without the consent of the Diet, other means to raise money in
the Kingdom of St. Stephen had to be sought. This not only brought Pálffy
to the presidency of the Hungarian Chancellery, but within a very few
months also to regular attendance in the War Cabinet. Special Hungarian
wartime taxes could never be successfully implemented, and yielded only

[18] Marczali, *Magyarország története*, pp. 285–288; Domokos Kosáry, "Felvilágosult
  abszolutizmus – felvilágosult rendiség," *Történelmi Szemle* XIX (1976), 700; Balázs, *Bécs
  és Pest-Buda*, pp. 113–116. On Pálffy in general, see Henrik Marczali, *Grof Pálffy Miklós
  főkancellár emlékiratai Magyarország kormányzásáról* (Budapest, 1884).
[19] Dickson, *Finance and Government* II, 389–390.
[20] *ÖZV* II/1/i, 224–225; II/2, 355–362.
[21] Schünemann, *Bevölkerungspolitik*, p. 231.

about half a million Gulden throughout the war, but under Pálffy's Chancellorship voluntary war credits began to expand dramatically to a high of over 2.5 million Gulden in 1760 alone.[22] In the War Cabinet itself, Pálffy waxed confident that Hungarian contributions to the common cause would meet rising requirements,[23] but his ability to deliver on these promises declined precipitously. By 1762 these cash credits had declined to less than 10% of their 1760 levels.[24]

In the last months of the war, as finances became desperate, one more direct appeal to the Hungarian nobility was attempted. Leading magnates were summoned to a conference in Vienna in December 1762, where the appeal was prepared by Kaunitz himself. As he had frequently done with the generals during the war, so he now sought to appeal to the Hungarian magnates with a frank exposé of the diplomatic situation in which the Monarchy found itself. By presenting intercepted documents from Prussia, he tried to show that Prussian machinations with the Ottoman Porte could yet lead to a confrontation with the Turks, and that under such circumstances the self-interest of the Hungarians demanded a willingness to make greater military contributions by raising the war tax level. Not "charity but patent necessity" should persuade the Hungarians not to deny the crown "proportionate help." Above all, he hoped to elicit a sense of common effort with an explicit appeal to a pan-monarchical vision: "This important observation is actually intended to suggest that the common welfare [of the Monarchy] demands that all the hereditary lands [of the House of Habsburg] mutually render each other all possible assistance, and observe complete equity in this process." In the covering report to the Empress Kaunitz stressed that his brief intended to show the Hungarian nobles that assenting to major increases was in their own interest. Their "protective privileges and other objections" could no longer be permitted, since these could offer no security against the Monarchy's dangerous foes, and since, in any case, the matter at hand concerned "the welfare and preservation of the whole Monarchy."[25]

These dramatic eleventh-hour appeals, which raised the specter of complete collapse in the most graphic terms, went for naught. In the formal response to the Queen, Pálffy and the Hungarian Chancellery showed themselves as the tools of the parochial noble interests that they were.

[22] Dickson, *Finance and Government* II, 389.
[23] HHStA, Staatskanzlei: Vorträge, Karton 86, Protocollum Conferentiae, 21 January 1760. For Pálffy's attendance record see also *Ibid.*, Kartons 83–87, Konferenz Extrakte, *passim*, and Khevenhüller-Metsch V, 236–259.
[24] Dickson, *Finance and Government* II, 389.
[25] HHStA, Staatskanzlei: Vorträge, Karton 90, Kaunitz to Maria Theresia, 25 November 1762, including his "Aufsatz, umb die Hungarischen Magnaten von der Nothwendigkeit der Hülffe zu überzeugen".

Pálffy was prepared to endorse a modest tax on the Hungarian clergy of about 500,000 Gulden annually for the repair and upkeep of fortifications, and he offered a small one-time *don gratuit* from the counties, but there was no movement whatsoever on the more substantial question of increasing the war tax quota. Kaunitz's despair is evident in the response he advised Maria Theresia to make to this offer. There was no point in giving the Hungarian elite the opportunity to assert how "co-operative" it had been if it was not prepared to respond to the crown's desperate appeal in any meaningful way. If the nobles chose deliberately to evade the main point, the Empress should now respond in kind: she should simply turn down Pálffy's suggestion of a clerical tax on the grounds that the clergy were already overburdened, and say no more. When Maria Theresia accepted this suggestion, it was clear that the old politics of consensus had been broken for good.[26]

During the closing years of the war, moreover, as the old War Cabinet gave way to the Council of State, the creation of this new advisory body complicated matters further. The War Cabinet was clearly an *ad hoc* mechanism to facilitate the war effort; the Council of State equally clearly was intended to be a permanent pan-monarchical institution. That it should, as such, even discuss Hungary was a matter of great dispute. The logic that had led Kaunitz to recommend the creation of the Council, of course, implicitly demanded that at least certain Hungarian matters be discussed. But the Hungarian elite was notoriously sensitive about any institutional change that threatened to alter the political *status quo*. And since the Council of State, aptly characterized as the "braintrust" of the Monarchy,[27] included no Hungarians when it was initially founded, Kaunitz advised Maria Theresia that in the public proclamation of its creation it was best to call it "Council of State for the German Hereditary Provinces."[28] The qualifying phrase was for public consumption only. Within a matter of days after the Council of State began operations, Hungarian matters started to appear on its agenda,[29] while Borié began to study Hungarian issues carefully and soon became the Council's official expert on Hungary.[30]

---

[26] *Ibid.*, Kaunitz to Maria Theresia, 20 December 1762, including imperial resolution.

[27] Andor Csizmadia, "Adám Franz Kollár und die ungarische rechtshistorische Forschung," *Sitzungsberichte der österreichischen Akademie der Wissenschaften. Philosophisch-Historische Klasse*, Vol. CCCXCVIII (Vienna, 1982), p. 5.   [28] *ÖZV* II/3, 15–26, pt. 3.

[29] HHStA, Kabinettsarchiv: Staatsratprotokolle, Vol. 1, No. 59. Some Hungarian matters discussed in the Staatsrat during the 1760s were published by Győző Ember, ed., "Der österreichische Staatsrat und die ungarische Verfassung, 1761–1768," *Acta Historica Academiae Scientiarum Hungaricae*, part i in VI (1959), 105–153, part ii in VI (1959), 331–371, and part iii in VII (1960), 149–182.

[30] Győző Ember, "Der österreichische Staatsrat und Ungarn in den 1760er Jahren," in Drabek *et al.*, eds., *Ungarn und Österreich*, p. 47.

As reports from Hungarian ministries began to make their way into the Council of State, the reality could no longer be disguised. At the end of June 1761, Pálffy protested to Maria Theresia that the Council had no business discussing Hungarian matters since this violated the famous clause of the constitution which guaranteed Hungarian business would be handled only by Hungarians ("ut negotia hungarica per Hungaros tractentur").[31] In the Council of State meeting which discussed Pálffy's protest, Borié pointed out that the law only stipulated that Hungarian business be conducted by Hungarians but in no way prohibited the Queen from seeking the advice of non-Hungarians. Since the Council of State was formally only an advisory body with no executive or administrative authority, the Hungarian constitutional prohibition clearly did not apply. This legal technicality allowed Kaunitz to recommend evading Pálffy's main point, and sweeping the essential political stratagem under the rug. In drafting the formal response, Kaunitz would not even allude to such legal ambivalences as might give opportunity for any "national grievance". The Hungarian Chancellor's real concerns were to be sidestepped. The Queen was simply to call Pálffy to heel in indignant and "majestic" tones, informing him that she had not transgressed any constitutional clauses and that she was prepared to overlook his impertinence this one time on condition that nothing of the sort happened again.[32]

This episode set the tone of the Council of State's deliberation of Hungarian matters for the remainder of Maria Theresia's reign. The fiction that the Council of State had jurisdiction only over the "German Hereditary Provinces" was publicly maintained, though in 1765 the word "German" was quietly dropped in official state-handbook descriptions.[33] Informally, the Empress, in her capacity as Queen of Hungary, could seek advice from whomever she wanted. The fact that all controversial Hungarian issues were discussed by the Council of State as a matter of course, and that the Council in this way became a pan-monarchical institution, was to be passed over in silence. Indeed, Starhemberg was to assert quite explicitly that reforming the constitutional structure of Hungary should not only be a concern, but the *primary* concern of the body.[34] This clearly showed how the institution of the Council of State shifted the Habsburg attitude towards the Kingdom of Hungary. More so than in the famous Diet of 1741, the perception of the position of Hungary within the Monarchy was decisively transformed from a still peripheral one to one which regarded it an integral part of the central core. If it had been sufficient in the past to co-ordinate policies in Hungary with those

---

[31] *ÖZV* II/3, 26–28.
[32] *Ibid.* II/1/i, 309–312; II/3, 28–29; Schünemann, *Bevölkerungspolitik*, pp. 226–229.
[33] Arneth, *Maria Theresia* IX, p. 294.   [34] *ÖZV* II/3, 44–45, fn. 2.

pursued in Austria and Bohemia, the Council of State represented the new ideal of full integration.

Unfortunately, maintaining the public fiction that the Council's mandate excluded Hungarian matters made it impossible to appoint a trustworthy and enlightened Hungarian to it. Already, early in 1762, a councillor in the Lieutenancy Council, Baron (later Count) Ferenc Balassa, had recommended the appointment of a special "referendarius in Hungaricis" to the Council of State. The suggestion was turned down because of the discontent it would arouse among the Hungarian establishment and because, as Kaunitz put it, the idea was "constitutionally" impossible.[35] This became obvious in 1771 during the ministerial shuffle inspired by Joseph II. When filling Council of State vacancies, Joseph, in whom subtlety was not a strong point, reasoned that since Hungarian matters were discussed in the Council, a Hungarian expert needed to be appointed to it (especially after Borié's transfer to a sensitive diplomatic post in 1770). His candidate was the thoroughly loyal and enlightened treasury official, Pál Festetics.[36] But the very mention of the idea sent Pálffy's successor, Chancellor Ferenc Esterházy, into paroxysms not unlike his predecessor, and Festetics's worthy candidature was by-passed to maintain the fiction.[37]

This discrepancy between the letter and the spirit of the law set the important precedent of keeping Hungarian authorities in the dark about over-all objectives and policies. This conspiratorial dimension of Habsburg enlightened absolutism was soon to be systematized, but it first required at least some reliable Hungarian advisors and a coherent overall policy. It was one thing to recognize that the feudal corporate order was the principal impediment to modernization; it was another to formulate coherent and effective policies to achieve requisite reforms. Kaunitz had to confess that he did not know enough about Hungarian laws or even personnel to formulate detailed proposals,[38] and even Borié, who was now beginning to immerse himself in these matters, had no Hungarian expertise prior to his appointment to the Council of State.[39] However, an embryonic but disjointed group of enlightened Hungarian reformers did exist, and these now gradually began to emerge from the shadows as the Council turned to them for advice. These early Hungarian advocates of enlightened absolutism have had rough treatment at the hands of Hungarian

[35] Ember, ed., "Staatsrat," i, 331–332, No. 25.
[36] MTJC I, 352–356, No. 152. On Festetics see Josef Bölöny, "Maria Theresias vertrauter Ratgeber: Paul Festetics (1722–1782)," in Koschatzky, ed., Maria Theresia und Ihre Zeit, pp. 105–112; cf. Dezső Szabó, A herceg Festetics-család története (Budapest, 1928).
[37] Khevenhüller-Metsch VII, 107–108.   [38] Ember, ed., "Staatsrat," i, p. 125, No. 4.
[39] Ember, "Der österreichische Staatsrat und Ungarn," p. 47.

historiography. Either ignored altogether or reviled as "careerists" and "traitors", they are only recently being recognized in any positive way.[40] Perhaps part of the problem for nationalist historians was the fact that though all these men claimed to be patriotic Hungarians, they were not all ethnic Magyars. Such was the case with the first official "discovered" by Borié, a councillor in the Hungarian Chamber, Anton Cothmann.

Cothmann came to the attention of Borié and the Council of State as a result of the Hungarian Chamber's reports on the sale of lands which had reverted to the crown. It had been a long-standing ambition of Habsburg absolutism to circumvent the tax-exemption of the nobility by tying taxes to any land which was re-granted to private hands. In the summer of 1761 Cothmann was commissioned to re-examine this problem, and in typical enlightenment exuberance, produced a report which exceeded his mandate and went to the heart of the matter – wholesale social and political change in Hungary. He was forced to point out that tying tax to land had been expressly forbidden by the Diets of 1647 and 1741, but he then proceeded to outline other social and economic proposals by which the feudal corporate order could be undermined.[41] Cothmann's brief had the effect of bringing the whole issue of the Hungarian constitution to the center of the discussion, and it moved Kaunitz to elaborate at length on the coherent political system – that is, the short- and long-range strategies and objectives – which enlightened absolutism ought to implement with respect to the problem of Hungary.

In Kaunitz's view, Hungarian policies deserved the highest priority because effectively marshaling the resources of that kingdom could double the power of the dynasty. The essential constitutional problem, however, was the privileged position of the aristocracy. It guaranteed that whatever benefits might accrue to the country would profit only the nobility, not the common man. Incursions into these "harmful privileges" were possible, as Habsburg successes in Belgium demonstrated, but they required the consistent application of an overall plan. Kaunitz's preliminary strategy posited twelve points: 1) The court must apply a judicious policy of rewards and punishments to Hungarian officials to encourage zeal for the policies of the government and to guarantee their execution. 2) The Hungarian Chancellery and Chamber were the key institutions where this policy was to be applied. 3) Nobles who opposed the court had to be convinced that the crown would neither forgive nor forget, thus closing all career opportunities for them and their families. 4) The Queen should avoid summoning the Hungarian Diet. 5) The court should begin to make

[40] Domokos Kosáry, "Aufgeklärter Absolutismus – Aufgeklärte Ständepolitik: Zur Geschichte Ungarns im 18. Jahrhundert," *Südost-Forschungen* XXXIX (1980), 215.
[41] Ember, ed., "Staatsrat," i, pp. 123–125, 130–137, Nos. 1, 4 & 10.

inroads into the bastions of particularism, the county administrations. Special attention should be paid to the locally elected deputy high sheriff (*alispán*). No sweeping policy should initially be applied, but with the same carrot-and-stick device recommended for officials of the organs of central government, individual deputy sheriffs should be co-opted for the crown until a sufficient number of them had been won over to permit overt general reforms. 6) The explicit provisions of the Hungarian constitution were to be assiduously respected, and the crown must never let on that its policy was to limit the "freedom of nobility". 7) While strictly abiding by the concessions forced on the crown by the constitution, care was to be taken to grant no new privileges. Any privilege not explicitly guaranteed by law was always to be interpreted in favour of the rights of the crown. 8) Transylvania and the Military Frontier should never be re-incorporated into the Kingdom of Hungary. 9) These two territories should be regarded as experimental fields to introduce reforms later to be spread to Hungary proper. 10) Above all, the standard of living of Hungarian peasants had to be raised. The abuses of the nobility in its "oppression of the peasants" had to be abolished, and the common man won for the crown. 11) A beginning should be made in this direction on crown lands. 12) The rights of the crown over the ecclesiastical establishment and over reverted estates should provide the opening through which the entire constitution could be revised.[42]

Kaunitz's system, as can be seen, posited a pragmatic gradualist approach aimed at undermining the society of privilege of feudal Hungary. It also can be said to be conspiratorial in the sense that the intended victims were to be kept in the dark – and, indeed, led on to believe that the crown, at worst, was intent only upon adapting the feudal order to the times. This policy of secrecy, and sometimes even outright deceit, however, should not be construed as a pernicious plot of foreigners against Hungary. Hungarian reformers, too, were compelled to adopt this conspiratorial tone. Ferenc Balassa, for example, complained at the "distressed and unhappy state" that he found himself in by not being able to serve the crown "freely and openly," but being obliged by social pressures to fulfill his duties in a "secret, underhanded and deceitful" manner.[43] Kaunitz's approach was also not at all dissimilar to the one used to deal with budding feudal reaction towards the end of the Seven Years' War in the Austro-Bohemian lands which Kaunitz cynically exploited, first to oust Haugwitz's reform

---

[42] *Ibid.*, pp. 135–137, No. 10. Cf. Balázs, *Bécs és Pest-Buda*, pp. 67–70; Balázs, "A felvilágosult abszolutizmus Habsburg variánsa," in Ember and Heckenast, eds., *Magyarország története*, II, 868–870.

[43] Schünemann, *Bevölkerungspolitik*, p. 184. Similarly also HHStA, Kabinettsarchiv: Nachlaß Nenny, Karton 2, Balassa to Nenny, 26 January 1766.

program, but then to implement an even more radical reform programme in its place.[44] The Hungarian nobility was to be outmaneuvered in a similar fashion, though Kaunitz's "system" clearly recognized that this would be neither simple nor quick. The important thing was to make a start, for the old relationship between the Austro-Bohemian and Hungarian parts of the Monarchy which characterized the previous half century had ceased to meet the demands of the whole.

Only days after the Seven Years War ended, Kaunitz stressed that post-war fiscal considerations made imperative the immediate implementation of his Hungarian system. The combined pressure of having to maintain a sizeable military establishment and liquidating a massive war debt meant continuing strains on the economy, and one of the few areas not yet strained to the utmost was the Hungarian war tax, whose reform accordingly seemed a high priority to be pursued "with all possible means." But this raised the entire question of the Hungarian constitutional impediments which guaranteed noble privilege, and which many felt were an insurmountable obstacle to change. Kaunitz did not agree. He was persuaded that "the great obstacles which govern this situation" could now "finally be cleared with patience, effort and time, and the foundations of a solid system be laid in this sphere."[45] Enlightened absolutism was about to make itself felt in the tradition-bound Kingdom of Hungary.

Policies of political penetration

It is perhaps not surprising that for Kaunitz the primary dimension of the implementation of enlightened reform was the careful cultivation of suitable personnel, and the systematic creation of a modern bureaucratic infrastructure. The leitmotif of Kaunitz's reform of his own ministry, and his recommendations for the reform of other government departments, was an emphasis on more professional forms of government. In Hungary this was certainly easier said than done. To begin with, as Kaunitz recognized, suitable individuals who combined skill and proficiency with unquestioned loyalty to the crown were "rare to find" in Hungary.[46] Even the organs of the executive branch of government were largely filled by men with divided loyalties – to the Monarch, to the "nation", and to their own self-interest – and their unreliability was as obvious from the tone they adopted as from their explicit statements.[47] Until this "fundamental defect" had been corrected with a patient application of rewards and punishments, reform legislation alone would have little impact.[48] Secondly,

---

[44] See above, pp. 86–95.
[45] HHStA, Staatskanzlei: Vorträge, Karton 91, Kaunitz [Staatsrat] Votum, 3 March 1763.
[46] Ember, ed., "Staatsrat," ii, p. 332, No. 25.   [47] *Ibid.*, i, p. 139, No. 13.
[48] Schünemann, *Bevölkerungspolitik*, pp. 232–233.

the balance of political power in Hungary lay in the hands of the gentry. These tenacious bastions of the old feudal order not only completely dominated local administration from the level of county down, but in sheer quantity far outnumbered the number of royal appointees.[49] Finally, there was the notorious xenophobic parochialism, best expressed in the famous maxim *extra Hungarium non est vita, si est vita non est ita*,[50] of the Hungarian elite: a cultural and intellectual obstacle perhaps even more difficult to overcome than political ones.

Given the importance of finding suitable personnel, it is therefore not surprising that Kaunitz's "system" stressed this dimension first and foremost. Repeatedly over the years, Kaunitz urged the encouragement and promotion of specific Hungarian officials who came to his attention, even if he disagreed with these individuals on specific issues. Thus, he was full of praise for Cothmann, though he did not share his economic policy with respect to Hungary.[51] He thought Balassa's "enthusiasm" for the royal prerogative so commendable that he urged his promotion, even if Balassa had missed the point with the Council of State.[52] He lauded Balassa's "industry, zeal and skill," but, above all, Kaunitz was impressed by Balassa's willingness to get to the heart of "Hungarian flaws."[53] When a councillor in the Hungarian Chancellery, Baron Ferenc Koller, suggested the use of the royal salt monopoly as a means of taxing the nobility indirectly, Kaunitz noted that such zeal could not be encountered frequently but was indicative of a "new spirit" which had to be supported and promoted with all possible "care and prudence".[54] Finally, when the court librarian, Ádám Kollár, published his famous defence of the royal prerogative in ecclesiastical matters of Hungary at a most inopportune time, prior to a meeting of the Hungarian Diet, it was Kaunitz who rushed to his defence. Kaunitz was impressed by Kollár's "perspicacity, scholarship and great zeal to serve," and insisted the man had to be protected even if caution demanded that the truth not be so boldly and publicly stated as it had been by him.[55] Once men of this ilk had shown their colours as true disciples of enlightened absolutism, Kaunitz, and with him the entire Council of State, consulted them frequently on many important

---

[49] Julius (Gyula) Szekfű, *Der Staat Ungarn: Eine Geschichtsstudie* (Stuttgart & Berlin, 1918), p. 140. A detailed analysis of the local administration in Andor Csizmadia, *A magyar közigazgatás fejlődése a XVIII. századtól a tanácsrendszer létrejöttéig* (Budapest, 1976), pp. 37–64; Csizmadia, "Les Problèmes de l'administration provinciale en Hongrie au XVIIIe siècle," *Acta Juridica Academiae Scientiarum Hungaricae* XI (1969), pp. 355–389.

[50] "There is no life outside of Hungary, and if there is life, it is not the same."

[51] Ember, ed., "Staatsrat," i, pp. 136–137, No. 10; p. 149, No. 19.

[52] *Ibid.*, i, p. 138, No. 11; p. 332, No. 25.

[53] Schünemann, *Bevölkerungspolitik*, p. 184.

[54] Ember, ed., "Staatsrat," ii, p. 335, No. 28.

[55] Maass, *Josephinismus*, I, pp. 206–207.

Hungarian issues.[56] The full scope of their influence on Habsburg policy still needs to be studied at much greater length by Hungarian historians, but clearly without them even limited reform would have been impossible. From Ferenc Balassa's secret correspondence with Maria Theresia's private secretary, Cornelius Mac-Nenny, for example, it becomes quite obvious that much of what has heretofore passed as policy initiatives formulated by non-Hungarians to the detriment of the Kingdom's sovereignty, in fact originated with these Hungarian apostles of enlightened absolutism.[57]

This stratum of enlightened Hungarian officials always remained a minority, though it was a critical minority. The influence of the crown had to extend beyond this group if it was to be effective. Kaunitz had been ever conscious of the fact that it was one thing to enact reforms and another to see them carried out. He often called the deliberate disregard of royal decrees "the main evil of the Monarchy", and singled out local officials as the key to combatting it.[58] If this was a problem in Austria and Bohemia, it was an epidemic in Hungary. Though the county high sheriff (főispán) was a crown appointee, he was generally less effective than the real power at the county level, the deputy sheriff, who was elected by the local gentry. Ignoring orders from above had become a fine art with the deputy sheriffs who were entitled to table all measures with the quaint phrase cum respectu ad acta (filed with respect), which virtually amounted to the Hungarian equivalent of the notorious Polish liberum veto.[59] That Kaunitz would regard this stratum of local officialdom as fertile ground for co-opting the gentry into the service of the crown might seem excessively naive, but his hopes in this regard must be seen in the proper context.

First, it must be kept in mind that Kaunitz was aware that the crown had a long row to hoe, and he, therefore, suggested concentrating on individuals before a systematic overhaul of local administration was undertaken. Secondly, precedents in Bohemia gave grounds for cautious optimism. There is a clear parallel between Kaunitz's view of the Hungarian counties and his view of the Austro-Bohemian local administrative units, the so-called Kreise. These also began as seigniorial offices which were co-opted by the crown during the Haugwitz reforms. Initially it was not at all uncommon for circle captains to exhibit remnants of the feudal mentality.

[56] Ember, ed., "Staatsrat," passim.
[57] HHStA, Kabinettsarchiv: Nachlaß Nenny, Kartons 1 and 2, Balassa–Nenny correspondence, 1763–1767. Balassa was also concerned with the problem of finding reliable Hungarian personnel for implementing the programme of enlightened absolutism. His own list of recommended individuals included Ferenc Koller, Antal Brunsvick, Pál Festetics and Jakob Szvetics. Ibid., Karton 1, Balassa to Nenny, 26 September 1764.
[58] HHStA, Kabinettsarchiv: Kaunitz Voten, Karton 2, No. 2140 of 1771, Kaunitz Staatsrat Votum, 6 July 1771.   [59] Bernath, "Ständewesen und Absolutismus," pp. 352–353.

It took many years of imposing guidelines and standards, of issuing detailed instructions, and of the judicious application of personal rewards and punishments before the circle office became that iron fist of enlightened absolutism at the local level which was to give nightmares to the feudal seigniorial elite. Obviously, the process would take even longer in Hungary since the deputy sheriff was locally elected and could not be dismissed at will. But there were few alternatives. In Kaunitz's view, it was obviously important that such local officials become loyal agents of the crown, but it was equally important that they were thoroughly familiar with local conditions. The relationship between the central government and local administrators had to be reciprocal. Not only was informed input necessary from the local level; measures often also had to be adapted to local conditions if a genuine change in the social fabric were to be effected.[60] In short, the imposition of loyal and devoted outsiders on the county structure would be ineffective, even if it were possible.

It should be noted, moreover, that the approach to the county administration was not limited to the attempt to co-opt the deputy sheriff with prospects of various rewards – the Hungarian gentry luxuriated in its bucolic parochialism and was often impervious to the lure of civilization. Some measure of control was attempted by issuing the counties with extremely detailed guidelines and instructions that paralleled exactly those issued to Austro-Bohemian county captains. But in addition to the identical emphasis on the local enforcement of police and welfare measures, the Hungarian directives contained provisions which were clearly designed to shake up the local administration. First, triennial elections for county officials were ordered and, secondly, certain professional standards were imposed. This not only encouraged a frequent turnover in personnel, but also automatically weeded out certain "unqualified" individuals on a permanent basis. The name given to the Hungarian translation of these famous instructions of 1768 at once reveals both the programme and the long-range hopes of the crown: *Megújulás* (renewal or regeneration).[61]

The attempt to impose professional standards on public servants brings us to the final obstacle, the cultural or intellectual one. It is important to remember that the organs of feudal power could hardly be called a "civil service", since the key to holding office was influence and position, not professional qualification. A professional bureaucracy was, in fact, created

[60] HHStA, Staatskanzlei: Vorträge, Karton 112, "Allergnädigst anbefohlenes Gutachten über die Verbesserung des Systematis in Internis," 1 May 1773, and *Ibid.*, Karton 122, Kaunitz to Maria Theresia, 22 March 1777.
[61] Csizmadia, *A magyar közigazgatás fejlődése*, p. 70; Károly Mártonffy, ed., *A magyar közigazgatás megújulása* (Budapest, 1940), pp. 95–111; Andor Csizmadia, ed., *Bürokrácia és közigazgatási reformok magyarhonban* (Budapest, 1979), pp. 65–85.

only under Maria Theresia. It began with the dramatic increase in staff among the organs of the executive branch,[62] and it spread to the local level with the imposition of qualification exams, the demand for detailed records, the limitation of certain offices to salaried professionals, and so on.[63] Kaunitz was the strongest advocate of the professionalization of government among the inner circles of the court; he imposed it ruthlessly in his own ministry; and he wished to see it become the premise of reform for all other institutions of the Habsburg Monarchy. But, of course, the pool of qualified professionals was meager in the Monarchy in general and in Hungary in particular. Hence, for Kaunitz, the key both to the creation of an effective bureaucratic infrastructure and to changing the entire cultural and intellectual attitude of a society lay in education. Hungarians, in particular, he argued, should be encouraged to study such things as constitutional law in modern secular institutions rather than in Jesuit Colleges, and their education should be facilitated through scholarships. In addition to the inducement of scholarships, promising Hungarian youths ought to be informed of employment opportunities in the civil service, but warned that only those possessing high academic qualifications could aspire to these jobs.[64]

In short, Vienna was interested in broadening the horizons of the Hungarian nobility by both direct and indirect means. It has not escaped the attention of Hungarian historians that Hungarian nobles studying at the Theresian academy in Vienna or those who were recruited for the Hungarian royal bodyguard were exposed to the cosmopolitan influences of the Monarchy's capital, and became in this way important transmitters of more enlightened ideas – a phenomenon manifest most directly by the gradual growth of a noble Masonic movement in Hungary in the late 60s and early 70s.[65] That Kaunitz wished to encourage such trends is evident from the instructions he drafted for diplomatic couriers when this task was taken over by the Royal Hungarian Noble Bodyguard in March 1780. Hungarian guards were not only to safeguard and deliver dispatches, they were to use the opportunity that their various trips afforded them to get as

[62] Győző Ember, *A magyar királyi helytartótanács ügyintézésének története, 1724–1848* (Budapest, 1940), pp. 193–194; István Nagy, *A magyar kamara, 1686–1848* (Budapest, 1971), pp. 366–367.
[63] Csizmadia, *A magyar közigazgatás fejlődése*, pp. 65–78; Zoltán Fallenbüchl, "Das Beamtentum in Ungarn zur Zeit Maria Theresias," in Mraz and Schlag, eds., *Maria Theresia als Königin von Ungarn* (Eisenstadt, 1980), pp. 67–74.
[64] Ember, ed., "Staatsrat," iii, pp. 164, 168, Nos. 80 & 86.
[65] Éva H. Balázs, "Contribution à l'étude de l'ère des lumières et du Joséphisme en Hongrie," *East European Quarterly* VI (1972), 27–43; Balázs, "Freimaurer, Reformpolitiker, Girondisten," in Éva H. Balázs, Ludwig Hammermayer, Hans Wagner and Jerzy Wojtowicz, eds., *Beförderer der Aufklärung in Mittel- und Osteuropa: Freimaurer, Gesellschaften, Clubs* (Berlin, 1979), pp. 127–140.

much education out of the process as time permitted. To maximize their observations abroad, they were explicitly given a detailed reading list for advance study, and instructed to make regular reports on what they had learned to the Chancellery of State itself.[66] In these ways, it was hoped that a fresh wind would enter even the closed universe of the Hungarian counties. Of course, the effects of such policies would be felt only slowly over time, but by the later eighteenth century is was clear that the parochial cohesiveness of the rural gentry was indeed beginning to break up and more enlightened attitudes were in fact beginning to penetrate.[67]

The hope that any serious political penetration could occur at the apex of the hierarchy, the Hungarian Diet, seemed much less realistic to Kaunitz. That the Hungarian nobility used the meetings of the Diet to obstruct rather than to expedite government business was obvious with the Diet of 1751. Maria Theresia, who at that stage could certainly still be characterized as a Hungarophile, was met with some rude surprises. The effort to increase the number of royal free towns with voting rights in the Diet failed; the increase of the military tax voted by the Diet was far less than anticipated; and, finally, the increase that was voted was immediately passed on to an already overburdened peasantry.[68] The prospects that a new Diet would be more co-operative, especially in light of the experiences of the Seven Years War, were therefore bleak indeed.

Nevertheless, it was precisely certain realities which the war highlighted that appeared to make summoning the Diet imperative. First of all, the old feudal noble levy (insurrectio) had proved militarily so antiquated in the war as to require fundamental change.[69] Secondly, because the extraordinary fiscal contribution to the war effort by Hungary had been paltry and the necessity of maintaining a large standing army even after the war was unavoidable, the issue of the military contribution had to be addressed yet again. Finally, the experience of 1751 taught that the Hungarian nobility was likely to pass any increase voted on to their peasants. To

[66] HHStA, Staatskanzlei: Vorträge, Karton 131, Kaunitz to Joseph, 23 March 1780, and Kaunitz's "Instruction Wornach sich die Herren Officiers der Königl. Hungarischen Adeligen Leibgarde zu betragen haben, welche zu Verrichtung der Kais: Königl: Hof und Kabinets Couriers-Dienste bestimmet sind," 26 March 1780. I am indebted to Éva H. Balázs for urging me to reexamine the document in this light. Cf. also Balázs, Kaunitz és Magyarország, p. 2.
[67] Károly Vörös, "A társadalmi fejlődés fő vonalai," in Ember and Heckenast, eds., Magyarország története I, 687.
[68] Marczali, Magyarország története, pp. 280–285; Arneth, Maria Theresia IV, 180–220; Ember, "Az Országgyűlések," pp. 425–426.
[69] Horst Haselsteiner, "Wehrverfassung und Personelle Heeresergänzung in Ungarn zwischen Herrscherrecht und ständische Konstitutionalismus: Zur Rekrutierungsfrage unter Maria Theresia und Joseph II.," in Drabek et al., Ungarn und Österreich, pp. 102–105.

prevent this, specific legislation to limit seigniorial demands on serfs (a so-called *Urbarium*) needed to be promulgated. Since the Queen had formally committed herself during her coronation in 1741 not to raise war taxes without calling a Diet, even the most pessimistic prognosis could not prevent her calling the body again in 1764.[70] In any case, despite the discouraging precedents, which had inspired Kaunitz's advice never to call the Diet again, Maria Theresia still remained optimistic. Though she had closed the Diet of 1751 on a sour note by telling the assembled dignitaries that they had lost her benevolence through their actions,[71] her enthusiasm for Hungary was by no means extinguished. She continued to expect that her love of Hungary would be reciprocated by the Hungarian nobility, and that this font of good will alone would suffice for a productive Diet.[72] Accordingly, a new summons was issued in the spring of 1764.

The famous Diet of 1764–1765, however, confirmed the worst fears of the bleakest pessimist. Shortly after the royal agenda, worked out with the help of Balassa,[73] had been laid on the table at the opening sessions of the Diet in June, the Hungarian nobility quickly revealed its intention to be completely unco-operative on every issue. Indeed, the Diet became the focal point of a massive aristocratic reaction, not merely clinging blindly to the *status quo* of privilege, but actively pursuing the *status quo ante*. In response to the crown's desiderata, the Diet presented a list of nearly 250 grievances (*gravamina*), including forceful complaints about the putative debilitating effects of the 1754 tariff ordinances, and a demand for the reduction of the war tax base agreed to in 1751, ostensibly because the impoverished peasants of Hungary were fiscally exhausted and could bear no further burdens.[74] Adám Kollár's recently published defence of the crown's rights of taxation and presentation in the Hungarian Church was also greeted with outraged demands that both the book and the author be burned,[75] while the aristocratic literary outpourings, led by György

---

[70] On the Diet of 1764/65 see Mihály Horváth, "Az 1764-i országgyűlés története," *Kisebb történelmi munkái* (1868), 377–422; Arneth, *Maria Theresia* VII, pp. 105–137; Benedek Konrád Stefancsik, *Az 1764–65-i pozsonyi országgyűlés* (Kassa, 1942); Ember, "Az Országgyűlések," pp. 426–429.   [71] Marczali, *Magyarország története*, p. 284.

[72] Waldemar Lippert, ed., *Kaiserin Maria Theresia und Kurfürstin Maria Antonia von Sachsen: Briefwechsel, 1747–1772* (Leipzig, 1908), p. 220.

[73] HHStA, Kabinettsarchiv: Nachlaß Nenny, Karton 1, Balassa to Nenny, 7, 14 and 24 March 1764, and "Propositionen des Baron Balassa für den Ungarischen Landtag des J. 1764," n.d. (March 1764).

[74] Fairly typical was the frank assertion by one anonymous Hungarian magnate, described as "an upright patriot," that if the crown won its point on the noble levy, "all our noble liberties are lost." He drew the conclusion that "it would therefore be very bad and dangerous to deviate even in the slightest from our holy laws and rights." HHStA, Kabinettsarchiv: Nachlaß Nenny, Karton 1, "Außerungen eines Ungarischen Magnaten über die königliche Propositionen," 1764.

[75] Csizmadia, "Adám Franz Kollár," pp. 21–25.

Richwaldszky's *Vexatio dat intellectum*, boldly aspired to nothing less than the "ideal" of Polish gentry democracy.[76]

In accordance with the principle asserted in 1761 the Empress was determined from the very outset to lay all these critical Hungarian issues before the Council of State.[77] In the initial preparations for the Diet Kaunitz appears to have played a secondary role, though he clearly hoped that the Hungarian Estates would be moved by arguments about the Monarchy's precarious international position.[78] Once the response of the nobility to the royal agenda was received, however, Maria Theresia asked Kaunitz to become more closely involved, and to prepare an assessment on how to respond to the obstreperous Diet. Once again it was Cothmann who became Kaunitz's closest adviser on the problem, and after discussing the issues with him Kaunitz reined in his initial instinct simply to prorogue the Diet with visible signs of royal displeasure. Certainly he regarded the noble response to the crown as both "captious" and "obscurantist", and pessimistically predicted that "nothing more can be expected from the nobility in Hungary at this time." Care had only to be taken that the royal response did not prejudice the crown's prerogatives in any way, and that the way was left open to deal with the worst problems of the Kingdom by royal fiat. Here, Kaunitz felt, the priorities were very clear-cut. Increased revenues from Hungary were desirable, but under no circumstances could this happen at the expense of the peasantry:

The subjects can only bear [an increase in taxation] if the oppression of the lords is effectively abolished. Rational politics and even conscience absolutely demand this. More than a million people need to be freed from injustices that cry to the heavens. If our subjects, who alone carry the burden of taxation, are not protected from the nobility, which contributes nothing to the common good, all encouragement of Hungarian agriculture and industry will not profit but harm the crown, since the nobility will become correspondingly wealthier and more oppressive. Without this [reform] all else is mere patch-work, and we will never be able to institute anything beneficial in Hungary.

On the whole, however, Kaunitz favoured persevering with the assembly. There was no point in putting anything off to the next Diet, for there would not and probably should not be another for quite some time.[79]

[76] Kosáry, "Aufgeklärter Absolutismus," p. 217.
[77] The full range of the topics addressed by the Council during the Hungarian Diet of 1764–1765 can still be reconstructed from HHStA, Kabinettsarchiv: Staatsratprotokolle, Vols. 15–18, *passim*, but most of the records have been lost. We are fortunate to have the salient documents preserved in Ember, ed., "Staatsrat," ii, pp. 350–371, and iii, pp. 149–159. The more important contributions of Kaunitz to the debates survive in copies preserved in other places as indicated in the footnotes below.
[78] Ember, "Staatsrat," ii, p. 361, No. 52.
[79] HHStA, Kabinettsarchiv: Nachlaß Kaunitz, Karton 1, "Kaunitz Votum den Ungarischen Landtag betr.," n.d. (June–July 1764).

The Council of State's principal Hungarian specialist, Borié, argued that there was little point in continuing with the Diet, but all of his colleagues as well as Maria Theresia disagreed.[80] The Empress continued a feverish round of social activity designed to win around influential magnates, and in the meantime the Hungarian Chancellery was instructed to prepare a series of royal rescripts to be laid before the Diet. Though Kaunitz advised an attempt to bring the Diet to a successful conclusion, he proposed to do so with a very firm hand. In September he carefully worked on a long memorandum which posited a "solid" and "systematic" plan designed to yield some positive results from a difficult situation. The premise of the proposal was brutally frank in its realism. The crown had to face the fact, he argued, that the Hungarian nobility was interested "not only in the preservation but where possible the extension and consolidation of its noble liberties." The nobles could not see the crown's point of view, and inevitably gave higher priority to their private interests than to the state's, whatever the importance of the latter might be. Under the circumstances it was sheer illusion to think of persuading the Hungarian aristocracy with reasonable arguments, no matter how compelling. Magnates, prelates and nobles without exception had only "one principle and one purpose" in mind: to obstruct change. But because their *gravamina* had been so transparently self-serving, the crown now really had moral authority on its side. The Estates were certainly correct in asserting that the peasants were so overburdened as to make further taxation impossible, but this only highlighted the "true cause of the problem" – namely, as Kaunitz had already said earlier in the summer, "the oppression of the poor peasants by the nobility and the clergy." Naturally, he noted, the nobles would attempt to pose as the protectors of the peasants against further demands by the crown, but this was something a wise ruler could easily counteract. The key was to divide the people from the nobility by asserting the "duties of kingship and God-pleasing equity," and to proceed to abolish "unjust oppressions" unilaterally by royal fiat, beginning with crown estates. Such action would lift the scales from the eyes of the peasants, deprive the nobility of the opportunity of exploiting people's fears, and place "proper limits" on nobles and prelates. This was political penetration on a massive scale, bypassing the medieval constitutional framework and co-opting the masses for the crown. Kaunitz justified such an approach with the same kind of appeal to natural rights he had earlier used in counteracting the Bohemian aristocratic resurgence in the previous year: a wise monarch focuses on "the welfare of the largest part of the nation, namely the common man."

[80] Ember, ed., "Staatsrat," ii, pp. 363–364, No. 55.

After this extraordinarily prolix and passionate preamble Kaunitz came to a proposal which he considered nothing short of "the greatest and most glorious coup d'état and the foundation for all improvements in Hungary." He advised the Empress to summon the Primate, the Palatine and the Hungarian Chancellor and to inform them that she intended to return to Vienna the very next day. She was to present them with a draft decree with which she would prorogue the Diet if the assembly did not endorse it within ten days. The decree would state that since the *gravamina* of the Estates were so numerous, it was impossible to deal with them at a Diet. Consequently it was to be "agreed" that the assembly was superfluous, and that the satisfaction of the grievances would be left to the evenhanded mercy of the Queen. Above all, the Queen accepted the noble argument that the peasants were already overburdened and certainly welcomed proposals on how "the true and actual cause of this misery" could be eliminated. Since much discussion on the issue had not led to any concrete results, however, this too was to be left to unilateral investigation and reform by the crown. In return for this the original demands for an increase in the war tax and for a reform of the feudal levy would be tabled for future consideration. In the face of such an ultimatum, Kaunitz argued, noble opposition would probably collapse, but even if it did not, the threatened decree could still be promulgated as the first step in the war for the hearts of the Hungarian people.[81]

This dramatic action was clearly too precipitous for Maria Theresia, and the abandonment of the demand for increased war taxes seemed unacceptable to her. Instead of an ultimatum, she preferred to persevere with negotiations, and these now dragged on with agonizing bitterness throughout the fall of 1764 and the winter of 1765. All these issues continued to be debated by the Council of State, with Kaunitz's contribution lending the tone to the royal strategy. He recommended that the Kollár issue be defused by subjecting his book to ecclesiastical censorship by tolerant neo-Jansenists, and by urging Kollár himself to write an apologia, while all along encouraging and protecting the author and, in fact, accepting his essential thesis.[82] With respect to the feudal levy, it was evident that no significant change was possible, but Kaunitz felt it was equally obvious that the nobility sought to evade even obligations to which previous Diet agreements had committed them, and the crown should be clear and explicit in not ceding one iota here. With respect to the *Urbarium*, there could emphatically be no compromise. Concern for

---

[81] HHStA, Kabinettsarchiv: Nachlaß Kaunitz, Karton 1, Kaunitz to Maria Theresia, (?) September 1764. Draft extensively edited in Kaunitz's own hand.
[82] Maass, *Josephinismus* I, 206–208.

peasant welfare was not merely a matter which utility dictated; it was a matter which "conscience absolutely demands."[83]

By February 1765 the debates began to wind down and discussion centered on the specific items of legislation (or so-called "articles") whose promulgation would formally close the Diet. Once more the Empress turned to Kaunitz who worked closely with Cothmann to produce the draft royal proposal. Throughout these discussions Kaunitz insisted on the strictest secrecy, indicating that he could not be completely frank in the presence of even the Hungarian Chancellor or Vice-Chancellor. Since the prolonged negotiations had resulted in some movement on the war tax question after all, and the Diet was prepared to vote an increase of 600,000 Gulden,[84] the two most important issues remained the feudal levy and the proposed *urbarium*. With respect to the former Kaunitz was content with a solemn reaffirmation of the relevant articles of the Diets of 1715 and 1723; with respect to the latter he deemed it preferable not to mention the matter at all, as this would facilitate clear-cut unilateral action by the crown.[85] The debate over points of lesser significance continued for another month, but by March Kaunitz advised that it was futile to continue wrangling, and advised cutting losses by promulgating only the 47 articles for which agreement had been found, and reserving the rest to the justice of the crown.[86] In all cases, Kaunitz's proposals were adopted and once the tumultuous Diet adjourned, his master-strategy was put into effect. For the remainder of the reign of Maria Theresia – and, indeed, until 1790 – the Hungarian Diet was not summoned again.

The failure of the Diet gave the crown the opportunity to implement the most sweeping political penetration of all by pursuing the social, economic and political emancipation of the peasants which Kaunitz so strongly advocated. As we have seen, this had been described by his "system" of 1761 as one of the highest priorities of the crown, and had been advocated by him as a matter of conscience as much as necessity during the Diet of 1764–1765. Indeed, that a prosperous peasantry was the key to a prosperous state was a position Kaunitz reiterated in the context of almost all the reforms he supported. Kaunitz had stressed that a complete commitment to thoroughgoing agrarian reform had to be an ideological

---

[83] HHStA, Staatskanzlei: Vorträge, Karton 94, copy of a Kaunitz Staatsrat Votum, 1 December 1764, briefly summarized in Ember, ed., "Staatsrat," ii, p. 370, No. 62.
[84] Dickson, *Finance and Government* II, 194.
[85] HHStA, Staatskanzlei: Vorträge, Karton 95, Kaunitz to Maria Theresia, 5 February 1765, with enclosures and marginal notes by Maria Theresia.
[86] HHStA, Kabinettsarchiv: Nachlaß Kaunitz, Karton 1, Kaunitz to Maria Theresia, 6 March 1765.

premise for the Council of State,[87] and became one of its leading proponents in Austria and Bohemia. However, in Hungary Kaunitz acknowledged this was a multi-faceted problem and, given the expected resistance to change by the seigniorial elite, an even more "delicate" and critical one.[88] On the one hand, it entailed state sponsorship of the modernization of agriculture, including fostering new crops such as potatoes and rape seed, which tended to be regarded with suspicious reservation. It included careful assessments of markets and guiding Hungarian agriculture to the most profitable ones.[89] But most of all, it entailed rooting out seigniorial abuses and raising the socio-economic level of the peasantry. Kaunitz was an early opponent of serfdom, regarding the feudal obligations to which the peasants were variously subjected as detrimental to an efficient agricultural economy.[90] And, though it is fashionable to stress that agrarian legislation was motivated primarily by the anxiety to safeguard the solvency of the serfs in order to guarantee their ongoing and increased taxability,[91] it is interesting to note that Kaunitz consistently advocated a decrease in state taxes on peasants.[92]

The conviction that the emancipation of the peasants from cumbersome feudal obligations and, in particular, the commutation of labour services to cash payments, was in the patent self-interest of everyone concerned (monarch, seigneur and serf) was widespread among advocates of agrarian reform. Kaunitz, too, shared the view that much noble resistance to change was primarily due to ignorance and placed considerable faith in the efficacy of good example. That is why he pressed for the implementation of peasant reforms on crown estates even if that entailed the loss of revenue, because "the far more important beneficial consequences" would be worth the price.[93] But in the final analysis, nobles seemed oblivious to good example, not only in Hungary but in Austria and Bohemia as well and it became necessary for the crown to adopt more forceful means to implement reform. Immediately after the Diet of 1764–1765 Maria Theresia com-

[87] Walter, "Eintritt," pp. 75–76. On the Council of State's role in the agrarian reform of Hungary see Győző Ember, "Mária Terézia úrbérrendezése és az államtanács," A Bécsi Magyar Történteti Intézet Évkönyve V (1935), 103–149.

[88] Dezső Szabó, A magyarországi úrbérrendezés története Mária Terézia korában (Budapest, 1933), p. 588.

[89] HHStA, Kabinettsarchiv: Kaunitz Voten, Karton 1, No. 1029 of 1767, Kaunitz Staatsrat Votum, 10 May 1767; No. 1593 of 1768, Kaunitz Staatsrat Votum, 24 July 1768.

[90] HHStA, Staatskanzlei: Vorträge, Karton 98, Kaunitz to Maria Theresia, 3 December 1766; Ibid., Karton 100, Kaunitz to Maria Theresia, 1 September 1767.

[91] Ferenc Eckhard, "A bécsi udvar jobbágypolitikája 1761-tő 1790-ig," Századok XC (1956), 69–125; Gyula Szekfű, Magyar történet a tizennyolcadik század, Vol. VI of Bálint Hóman and Gyula Szekfű, Magyar történet (Budapest, n.d. [1935]), p. 291; Varga, "Magyarország," pp. 375–377.

[92] HHStA, Staatskanzlei: Vorträge, Karton 100, Kaunitz to Maria Theresia, 28 July 1767.

[93] Szabó, A magyarországi úrbérrendezés története, p. 668.

missioned Pál Festetics to prepare a memorandum on the best way to implement an Hungarian *Urbarium* unilaterally. His recommendations were pragmatic but ultimately ineffectual, since he suggested being so adaptable to local conditions and so flexible from county to county that virtually no coherent common legislative denominator remained.[94] At the same time as Festetics's rather eclectic procedure was being attempted in the spring and summer of 1765, sporadic peasant unrest in seven southwestern counties clearly showed that the matter was pressing indeed.[95] The investigation of these problems by the Hungarian Court Councillor, Antal Brunsvick, then accelerated matters considerably.[96] Brunsvick's report painted a bleak picture and deeply shocked many officials in Vienna, especially the Empress, who was shattered to discover that the ever-loyal Batthyánys were amongst the worst offenders.[97] For the sake of a few magnates, she avowed solemnly, she did not intend to endanger her immortal soul,[98] and an *urbarium* accordingly followed for the affected counties in December 1766.[99] Within a month, on 23 January 1767, a formal decree was promulgated for the whole of Hungary limiting labour services to one day a week. It included detailed instructions for local officials on its execution and demanded strict compliance. Indeed, it was agreed that if necessary military force would be employed to push through the reform.[100]

Compliance was not readily forthcoming. Extensive delaying tactics and efforts by the lords to turn even the peasants against the legislation hampered rapid and uniform implementation of the reform.[101] Esterházy and the Hungarian Chancellery dredged up innumerable impediments, until it became necessary to proceed county by county. Kaunitz, for one, was prepared to follow this route: what mattered in such an important and fundamental reform as this was that it be implemented well and thoroughly rather than hurriedly.[102] This turned out to be a lengthy process. The

---

[94] *Ibid.*, pp. 353–360.
[95] Károly Vörös, "Az 1765–66-i dunántúli parasztmozgalom és az úrbérrendezés," in György Spira, ed., *Tanulmányok a parasztság történetéhez Magyarországon, 1711–1790* (Budapest, 1952), pp. 299–383.
[96] Szabó, *A magyarországi úrbérrendezés története*, pp. 748–750.
[97] Arneth, *Maria Theresia* VII, 535.   [98] Marczali, *Magyarország története*, p. 300.
[99] Ibolya Felhő, ed., *Az úrbéres birtoksiszonyok Magyarországon Mária Terézia korában*, Vol. I: *Dunántúl* (Budapest, 1970), p. 11.
[100] Eckhart, "A bécsi udvar jobbágypolitikája," pp. 80–81; Seedoch, "Die Urbarial-regulierung Maria Theresias," pp. 85–88; Károly Vörös, "Az úrbérrendezés," in Ember and Heckenast, ed., *Magyarország története* II, 928–929.
[101] Dezső Szabó, *A megyék ellenállása Mária Terézia úrbéri rendeletével szemben* (Budapest, 1934).
[102] HHStA, Kabinettsarchiv: Kaunitz Voten, Karton 1, No. 4587 of 1769, Kaunitz Staatsrat Votum, 7 January 1770. Cf. Éva H. Balázs, "A nyolcvanas esztendők drámája," in Ember and Heckenast, eds., *Magyarország története* II, 1029.

Urbarium was introduced in some counties, such as Somogy and Tolna, as early as October 1767, but in others, such as Bereg, the process dragged on until November 1775.[103] Nor were the provisions of the decree implemented quite as well and thoroughly as Kaunitz had hoped.[104] In the final analysis, enforcing the decrees proved to be as difficult as passing them. Kaunitz had been well aware as early as 1765 that the county administrative apparatus would not be a willing instrument of enlightened absolutism and would require close supervision.[105] But this task could be performed effectively only by an extensive loyal professional crown bureaucracy capable of dealing with the many local problems the crown wished to see addressed. In these critical years such an instrument had not yet been forged.[106]

Yet, despite its shortcomings, the decree certainly had an important impact. Hungarian historians have not hesitated to call the agrarian legislation of 1767 "the most significant reform of enlightened absolutism" in Hungary,[107] and the political penetration sought by this policy was clearly initiated at this time. The crown's circumvention of the nobility and the establishment of a direct relationship with the serfs of Hungary was instrumental in establishing them as subjects of the ruler rather than of the seigneur.[108] It was also directly responsible for the font of peasant good will the court was to enjoy,[109] which, as Roman Rosdolsky has shown, was in turn to be so critical in the development of popular monarchism among the broad masses of central Europe in the nineteenth and twentieth centuries.[110] Finally, these measures also encouraged a much more positive attitude to agricultural productivity and helped break down traditional modes of production to which most landowners clung so tenaciously.[111]

Policies of political containment

If the dimensions of Kaunitz's "system" outlined above could best be described as policies of political penetration, they were supplemented by

---

103 For full list of implementation dates see Eckhart, "A bécsi udvar jobbágypolitikája," p. 97.
104 The implementation rate from county to county can be seen at a glance on map 12 in Imre Wellmann, "A mezőgazdaság a felvilágosult abszolutizmus korában," in Ember and Heckenast, eds., *Magyarország története* II, between pp. 936 and 937.
105 Szabó, *A magyarországi úrbérrendezés története*, pp. 506–507, 588–589.
106 Imre Wellmann, "Kontinuität und Zäsur in Ungarns Bauernleben zur Zeit Maria Theresias und Josephs II," in Plaschka and Klingenstein, eds., *Österreich im Europa der Aufklärung* I, 118.   107 *Ibid.*, p. 114.
108 Wellmann, "A mezőgazdaság a felvilágosult abszolutizmus korában," pp. 933–949.
109 Balázs, "A nyolcvanas esztendők drámája," p. 1028.
110 Roman Rosdolsky, *Die Bauernabgeordneten im konstituierenden österreichischen Reichstag, 1848–1849* (Vienna, 1976), pp. 12, 209–210.
111 Wellmann, "A mezőgazdaság a felvilágosult abszolutizmus korában," pp. 949, 984.

the much more notorious policies of political containment which he articulated. Though upon examination these policies, too, had primarily a social focus, they have been less easily recognized as such, and have engendered much bitterness among Hungarian historians. They included, as will be recalled, avoiding calling the Hungarian Diet, asserting the royal prerogative wherever possible, and narrowly circumscribing the geographic scope of the problem by asserting the separate status of Transylvania and the Military Frontier. The first of these recommendations, as we have seen, became a consistent crown policy for twenty-five years after 1765, though Maria Theresia considered calling a Diet in 1778 during the War of the Bavarian Succession.[112] In any case, in the final analysis, the Hungarian Diet was more a symptom of the problems facing the agenda for reform than a disease. It was a convenient forum, giving the aristocratic resurgence a public face, but the essential locus of seigniorial power and privilege was more broadly based.[113] The political superstructure was without doubt the feudal corporate order's first line of defence, and not summoning the Diet again opened the way for the Enlightenment to enter Hungary.[114] But the crown's initiative had to be systematically driven home by a purposeful assertion of the royal prerogative at every turn if the aristocratic resurgence was to be contained.

As we have seen, Kaunitz's mistrust of Hungarian public institutions carried over even to the organs of the executive branch, where he singled out the Hungarian Chancellery and the Hungarian Chamber in particular. In the case of the former, Kaunitz initially placed some hope in a simple change of personnel, but that this proved to be an illusion was evident when Kaunitz's ideological guidelines for the newly-founded Council of State were transmitted to all political bodies in the Monarchy with the instruction to work out specific systematic reform proposals. The response from the Hungarian Chancellor, Miklós Pálffy, was similar to that of his reactionary Austro-Bohemian colleague, Rudolf Chotek: outright disobedience and evasion – time-honoured tactics whose effectiveness was beyond question.[115] By October 1761 Kaunitz already made no attempt to hide his disenchantment with conspicuously public complaints about Hungarian leaders.[116] But the straw that broke the camel's back was the peasant question. On 20 March 1762 the Hungarian Chancellery was explicitly commanded to launch an investigation into peasant grievances at the county level. Pálffy's response was to argue that although the

---

[112] Dickson, *Finance and Government* II, 151.
[113] Ember, "Zur Klassenpolitik," p. 394.
[114] Kosáry, "Felvilágosult abszolutizmus," pp. 703–704.
[115] Ember, "Zur Klassenpolitik," p. 395.
[116] HHStA, Kabinettsarchiv: Zinzendorf Tagebuch, Vol. 6, 6 October 1761.

Chancellery had always been concerned to abolish unjust oppression of peasants, such oppression was simply not extant at present. Peasant complaints were ungrounded and malicious attempts to evade their obligations, and an investigation would be thoroughly inadvisable, for it would lend some plausibility to the peasant complaints and cause the loyal and devoted seigneurs untold distress. Whether Pálffy actually believed this, or was intimidated by his peers, is unclear, but the result was unequivocal. With the strong support of the whole Council of State, Pálffy was dismissed and replaced with as putatively reliable a Hungarian magnate as could be found, Ferenc Esterházy (he rejoiced in the pet-name "Quinquin" in the inner circles of the court).[117] Esterházy proved only marginally more co-operative than his predecessor, and from this point on Kaunitz increasingly tended to recommend keeping the Hungarian Chancellery in the dark about all essential policies, long-range intentions of the court, short-range strategies and overall motives.[118]

No effort was even made to replace the head of the Hungarian Chamber, Antal Grassalkovich. Though the regalia had increased substantially under Grassalkovich's direction, he remained a stubborn defender of the Hungarian "nation".[119] Having lost his faith in personnel changes, by 1768 Kaunitz was ready for even more drastic moves. The Hungarian Chamber was functionally subordinate to the Austro-Bohemian Chamber in Vienna (Hofkammer), of which it was essentially an autonomous department. Now Kaunitz recommended that this autonomy be abolished, the Hungarian Chamber completely absorbed into a single pan-monarchical one, Grassalkovich "promoted" to some honorific post, and the entire administration of regalia much more sharply supervised and audited by technical experts than heretofore.[120] While these suggestions did not gain royal assent, they demonstrated once more Kaunitz's desire to break the stranglehold of the feudal hierarchy of birth on the highest offices of the Monarchy. What is more, this suspicious mistrust was shared by most members of the Council of State, and was carried over to virtually all the higher offices of the Kingdom of St. Stephen. On the whole, however, these policies were directed less at the Hungarian offices mentioned than at the holders of these offices, and they were directed at them primarily because the loyalty of these officials to the material interests and privileges of their class surpassed their devotion to their governmental duties. These were but

---

[117] Schünemann, Bevölkerungspolitik, pp. 202–206; Khevenhüller-Metsch, VII, 157; Arneth, Maria Theresia VII, 107, 511.

[118] HHStA, Kabinettsarchiv: Kaunitz Voten, Karton 1, No. 1694 of 1767, Kaunitz Staatsrat Votum, 9 August 1767; No. 2487 of 1769, Kaunitz Staatsrat Votum, 23 July 1769.

[119] Nagy, A magyar kamara.

[120] HHStA, Staatskanzlei: Vorträge, Karton 101, Kaunitz to Maria Theresia, 25 January 1768.

the spearheads of the Habsburg offensive against the Hungarian nobility, which was the heart of Kaunitz's strategy of asserting the royal prerogative. Certainly Kaunitz, his Council of State colleagues, and the stratum of enlightened Hungarian officialdom were one in their support of a series of policies whose objective was to contain the Hungarian nobility. These included an attempt to restrict the number of nobles, to claim escheated fiefs for the crown, to re-grant estates only under stringent restrictions and guarantees for resident serfs, and to tie taxes to land. None of these policies enjoyed any great success, but they highlight very well the central key to the broader strategy of political containment posited by Kaunitz.[121]

Another area in which the royal prerogative could be profitably asserted was in the relationship between Church and state. The militant Counter-Reformation came late to Hungary and was in its full baroque bloom only in the eighteenth century when it was on the wane elsewhere. In this cultural and social milieu the Church, with all its vast holdings in mortmain, was the greatest seigniorial lord of all.[122] The community of interest between the nobility and the Church was cemented by the fact that high clerical office remained an aristocratic preserve. The feudal elite recognized very clearly that abrogating the privileges of the ecclesiastical establishment would set a very dangerous precedent which directly threatened their own position.[123] Hence, the neo-Jansenist rebellion against the baroque ostentation of the Church, which played so well into the hands of the statist assertions of the crown, and which was so prevalent in other parts of the Monarchy, made much less headway in Hungary. This largely explains the furor over Kollár's book on the rights of the crown over the Hungarian Church as well as the general ultramontane sympathies of the Hungarian ecclesiastical hierarchy. That is also why, for Kaunitz, the combative Kollár was so important. His book was used in the Council of State as a reference work, and Kaunitz advocated his employment as a consultant particularly in ecclesiastical matters.[124] In this way, Kaunitz wrote with satisfaction in 1768, documents confirming royal rights particularly with respect to taxation and presentation were brought to light which "otherwise probably would never have come to the attention of the

---

[121] Ember, "Zur Klassenpolitik," pp. 395–400.

[122] On his trip through Hungary Joseph II recorded a total of 9,042 clerics (including 746 seminarians) whose properties yielded revenues of 5,092,104 Gulden annually. HHStA, Familienarchiv: Hofreisen, Karton 2, "Geistliche Personal und Vermögensstand d. K. Hungarns."

[123] Marczali, *Magyarország története*, p. 288; R. J. W. Evans, "Maria Theresia and Hungary," in H. M. Scott, ed., *Enlightened Absolutism* (London, 1991), p. 196.

[124] Ember, ed., "Staatsrat," iii, p. 166, No. 84, p. 175, No. 96.

court."[125] Though he recognized that it might not always be practicable to assert these rights in the short run,[126] they were the key to success in the long run.

Of course, fiscal and political control were only part of the picture. The Hungarian Church's resistance to reform was motivated as much by antiquated attitudes and intolerance as by economic and political self-interest. In fact, in one dispute with the bishop of Pécs over the alienation of church property, Kaunitz went so far as to remark, condescendingly, that the bishop could not be blamed for his stubbornness. The whole ecclesiastical education system was so bad that nothing else could be expected.[127] Kaunitz advocated re-education for clerics,[128] and was one of the most steadfast proponents of religious diversity. Toleration of non-Catholics, as is well known, was not one of Maria Theresia's strong points and, in fact, was probably the area of bitterest disagreement between the Empress and her Chancellor of State. As we have seen, his rare interventions on behalf of a policy of greater confessional toleration in Hungary tended to die on the vine.[129]

In many ways, however, one of the most resented forms of political containment advised by Kaunitz and implemented by Maria Theresia was geographic. If the Hungarian feudal order was so firmly entrenched that only a patient gradualist approach could hope for measurable success, it was obviously preferable to confine the problem to as limited an area as possible. There were a number of factors which made this possible: Croatia had always had a special status within the Kingdom of Hungary; Transylvania became an autonomous principality during the years of Turkish overlordship; the Banat was re-conquered two decades later than the rest of Hungary and could, therefore, be dealt with as a distinct entity; and, finally, the ongoing Turkish menace required the establishment of a permanent military cordon along the southern perimeter of the kingdom. Though Kaunitz mentioned only Transylvania and the Military Frontier in his master-plan, subsequent statements demonstrate that the policy of geographic containment of the "Hungarian problem" included encouraging more autonomy for so-called "civilian Croatia",[130] and maintaining the separate status of the Banat as well.

Though the socio-political structure of Transylvania was in its essential features the same as that of royal Hungary, there were certain key

---

[125] HHStA, Kabinettsarchiv: Kaunitz Voten, Karton 1, No. 1644 of 1768, Kaunitz Staatsrat Votum, 24 July 1768.
[126] *Ibid.*, Karton 1, No. 1694 of 1767, Kaunitz Staatsrat Votum, 4 August 1767.
[127] *Ibid.*, Karton 2, No. 371 of 1776, Kaunitz Staatsrat Votum, 19 February 1776.
[128] Ember, ed., "Staatsrat," iii, p. 164, No. 80.   [129] See above, pp. 249–250.
[130] A substantial portion of the Kingdom of Croatia was taken up by the Military Frontier.

differences which gave the crown a freer hand there. The Transylvanian constitution recognized three "nations" (Hungarians, Szeklers and Saxons), and these could be played off against each other to blunt the power of the feudal estates. This was a reality Kaunitz recognized and a strategy he frankly recommended.[131] Transylvanian Diets, though in Kaunitz's view also afflicted by a "republican spirit",[132] tended to be more pliant and, on the whole, voted more satisfactory tax increases.[133] Finally, the strategic position of the principality required stationing a sizeable army there, which allowed the commanding general to exercise considerable political power.[134]

The fact that Transylvania had its own Court Chancellery in the capital gave it a status of technical parity not only with Hungary but even with the Austro-Bohemian complex. Kaunitz favoured anything that could be done to enhance this parity, and in 1765 abetted the strategy of raising it to the status of a Grand Principality. As "House" Chancellor (i.e., Chancellor in charge of dynastic claims, heraldic depiction and the like), Kaunitz had every reason to be involved. Indeed, he even used this largely ceremonial post to promulgate policies with a sharp political edge. In an age when symbolism still had a potent reality, Kaunitz felt that even the design of the Transylvanian coat of arms was important. Hungarian demands that it somehow reflect Hungarian overlordship – perhaps by the inclusion of Hungary's double cross – were to be rejected. In fact, the promulgation of the edict was to be done with special solemnity by issuing a golden bull rather than a normal one.[135] This rankled Hungarian officials for years, and in 1769 they finally found a means to counteract Transylvania's new status. The Hungarian Chancellery requested a complete re-design of the grand arms of Hungary which, of course, included the Grand Principality of Transylvania in a prominent position. Kaunitz's advice once again reflected two basic tactics: eschewing confrontation and employing conspiratorial deception. In order to silence the chorus of protests, the

---

[131] Ember, ed., "Staatsrat," i, p. 145, No. 18.
[132] HHStA, Kabinettsarchiv: Kaunitz Voten, Karton 1, No. 7 of 1769, Kaunitz Staatsrat Votum, 24 January 1769.
[133] Rolf Kutschera, *Landtag und Gubernium in Siebenbürgen, 1688–1869* (Cologne and Vienna, 1985), pp. 12–140; and Ember, "Az országgyülések," pp. 429–433. The relevant chapter by Zsolt Trócsányi, "Új etnikai kép, új uralmi rendszer (1711–1770)," of the recent László Makkai and Zoltán Szász, eds., *Erdély története: 1606-tól 1830-ig*, Vol. II of Béla Köpeczi, et al., eds., *Erdély története* (Budapest, 1986), pp. 972–1038, lacks detail on these matters.
[134] Mathias Bernath, "Die Errichtung der Siebenbürgischen Militärgrenze und die Wiener Rumänenpolitik in der frühjosephinischen Zeit," *Südost-Forschungen* XIX (1960), 171–173; Kutschera, *Landtag und Gubernium*, pp. 155–158, 227–243.
[135] HHStA, Staatskanzlei: Vorträge, Karton 96, Kaunitz to Maria Theresia, 8 November and 1 December 1765. Cf. Khevenhüller-Metsch VI, 420–428.

crown should be flexible on the Hungarian request, and should "seek to achieve its objects ... in a way which does not directly reveal the intentions of the court."[136]

Kaunitz seemed less inclined to passionate commitment in the bitter debates which raged over the reform and increase of ordinary tax levies in Transylvania. On the whole, most Council members tended to be more favourable to formulas developed by Saxon councillors such as Martin Wanckhel von Seeberg and Samuel von Bruckenthal than those developed by the Magyar Chancellor of the province, Gábor Bethlen. But Kaunitz liked the firm way in which Bethlen handled the Transylvanian Diet, and generally took a more neutral position on the rival tax reform plans.[137] Saxon support for the army's effort to extend the Military Frontier into Transylvania also earned them the backing of the local commanding general, Adolf Buccow, with the result that the two issues became intertwined. After Buccow's death in May 1764, a three-man commission was set up to investigate and administer Transylvanian border and tax questions. The body soon became dominated by Bruckenthal, whose reports and recommendations found increasing favour in Vienna.[138] In January 1767, Bruckenthal recommended a further assertion of Transylvania's separate status by severing the administration of the Transylvanian salt monopoly from the Hungarian Chamber. This was one idea Kaunitz supported completely: "though Count Grassalkovich may not like the change", there was no reason why Hungary should be permitted to "swagger" with Transylvanian revenues.[139] The main objective of all these policies was clear enough. It was part of the system of rewards and punishments to serve as an example to the Hungarian elite both of what could be obtained with a co-operative attitude and of what could be suffered with an unco-operative one.[140]

This policy extended beyond Transylvania to the other peripheral parts of the Kingdom of St. Stephen. Above all, Kaunitz was one of the strongest champions of the Military Frontier, repeatedly promoting improvements in social conditions there and advising a high degree of pragmatism and flexibility in enforcing tariff and other ordinances if these stood in the

---

[136] HHStA, Kabinettsarchiv: Kaunitz Voten, Karton 1, No. 2487 of 1769, Kaunitz Staatsrat Votum, 23 July 1769.

[137] Ember, ed., "Staatsrat," i, p. 140, No. 14, and p. 142, No. 15. Cf. Schünemann, *Bevölkerungspolitik*, p. 146.

[138] Georg Adolf Schuller, *Samuel von Bruckenthal*, 2 Vols. (Munich, 1967–1969), I, 63–187; Kutschera, *Landtag und Gubernium*, pp. 251–272; Bernath, "Die Errichtung der Siebenbürgischen Militärgrenze," pp. 173–175.

[139] HHStA, Kabinettsarchiv: Kaunitz Voten, Karton 1, No. 370 of 1767, Kaunitz Staatsrat Votum, 26 April 1767; Staatsratprotokolle, Vol. 24, No. 370, imperial resolution endorsing the change.   [140] Ember, ed., "Staatsrat," i, p. 140, No. 14.

way.[141] Confessional and national sensibilities were also to be taken into account, both in the civilian and Military Frontier portions. In the former, Kaunitz advised a largely conciliatory approach to the Greek Orthodox "Illyrian National Congress" of 1769, avoiding all measures which might lead to the alienation of the Serbs.[142] In the Military Frontier portion, he revealed a similar sensitivity. When the inspector-general of the Military Frontier died in 1768, Kaunitz objected strongly to his replacement with a Hungarian "with whose national principles this command would be in conflict." He felt such a move would weaken "that special trust" Vienna had to cultivate in the Military Frontier, and would endanger the essence of the command.[143] The extension of the Military Frontier into Transylvania further illustrates the essential political and social rather than military nature of this policy. Since the Military Frontier was subject to the command of the Aulic War Council (Hofkriegsrat), it was easy to introduce reforms of a kind which would be impossible where privilege was constitutionally protected. The more extensive the Military Frontier, the more limited the area controlled by the feudal corporate order would be.[144]

One final illustration of this point can be made with the Banat of Temesvár. After its conquest by Habsburg armies in 1718, the Banat remained under the direct control of the Emperor despite repeated Hungarian demands that it be re-incorporated into Hungary. It was one of the major triumphs of the Estates at the Diet of 1741 to extract Maria Theresia's promise that such a re-incorporation would eventually occur. However, resistance by the local population, inspired by anxieties over the deterioration in social conditions that Hungarianization would entail, permitted delaying the plan. In 1745, the Banat was subordinated to the jurisdiction of a special court commission and its ultimate fate was tabled. In the meantime Kaunitz advised making the Banat a showplace of Habsburg benevolence, particularly in the treatment of peasants and border guards. Ironically, this was one of the few instances where Kaunitz actually advised against implementing a policy of open religious toleration of Protestants. Yet the same memo eventually also posits a relatively generous treatment of Greek Orthodox minorities, who, in Maria Theresia's Weltanschauung, were every bit as heretical as Protestants. The

[141] HHStA, Kabinettsarchiv: Kaunitz Voten, Karton 1, No. 1072 and 1091 of 1767, Kaunitz Staatsrat Voten, 23 and 29 May 1767; Nos. 105 and 2334 of 1768, Kaunitz Staatsrat Voten, 10 February and 18 October 1768.
[142] Ibid., No. 2493 of 1769, Kaunitz Staatsrat Votum, 12 July 1769.
[143] Ibid., No. 825 of 1768, Kaunitz Staatsrat Votum, 24 April 1768; Staatsratprotokolle, Vol. 27, No. 825, imperial resolution, 26 April 1768.
[144] Mathias Bernath, Habsburg und die Anfänge der Rumänischen Nationsbildung (Leiden, 1972), pp. 147–165; and his "Die Errichtung der Siebenbürgischen Militärgrenze," pp. 164–192.

argument Kaunitz gives is instructive: the religious fanaticism of Hungarian Protestants can easily lead to rebellion and had revealed clear Prussophile tendencies in the last war. He was, of course, not referring to Protestants *per se*, but Hungarian Protestant nobility. The intention was to attract population to the Banat, and Kaunitz clearly had little difficulty accommodating Serbian or Romanian "schismatics." It therefore appears clear that this is yet another case where the hidden agenda of circumscribing the Hungarian nobility and preventing them from extending their "liberties" to the Banat is the key to the paradox.[145]

Kaunitz really had no inherent objections to Hungarian territorial claims as such, and under the right circumstances proved quite flexible on the issue. In 1775, the suggestion was made to elevate the Banat to the status of a principality, which raised a storm of indignant protest from Ferenc Esterházy. Though there were even some Hungarians, such a Ferenc Koller, who took a hard line opposing Esterházy,[146] Kaunitz counseled moderation, preferring no change in the *status quo* "until time and circumstances permit."[147] In accordance with this advice the matter was postponed again. Two years later, Esterházy took the initiative, requesting immediate re-incorporation. Once again, Kaunitz's recommendation, which subsequently became the official policy guideline, showed the essential social nature of his concerns. He had no objection to the incorporation on principle and was even prepared to accede to the Hungarian request, on the important condition that the "designs of the court" could be pushed through. These consisted of two main points: Hungarian tax-exemption privileges were not to be extended to the Banat, and a special royal commission was to see to it that no deterioration in the status of the peasants would ensue as a result.[148] Under these conditions the Banat was integrated into Hungary on 6 June 1778.

By the time this occurred substantial progress had been made on another issue that has not always sat well with nationalist sensibilities: the settlement of the Banat and other depopulated areas of southern Hungary with German, Romanian, Serbian and other non-Magyar colonists. One

---

[145] HHStA, Familienarchiv: Hofreisen, Karton 3, Kaunitz's "Ohnmaßgebige Anmerkungen über ein Votum des Frh. v. Boirié. Die Bannatische und Sclavonische Reiß-Relation Ihro Kays. Mayt. betreffend," n.d. (1768). This memorandum has been discussed by Balázs, "A felvilágosult abszolutizmus Habsburg variánsa," in Ember and Heckenast, eds., *Magyarország története* II, 870–872, and Karniel, *Toleranzpolitik*, pp. 137–141, who have drawn diametrically opposite conclusions from it. Mine is yet a third interpretation.

[146] Marczali, *Magyarország története*, pp. 310–311.

[147] HHStA, Staatskanzlei: Vorträge, Karton 119, Kaunitz to Maria Theresia, 28 October 1775.

[148] HHStA, Kabinettsarchiv: Kaunitz Voten, Karton 3, No. 8 of 1778, Kaunitz Staatsrat Votum, 30 January 1778.

of the most fundamental tenets of mercantilism, and particularly of its central European form, cameralism, was the notion that people are the basic asset of the state, and that therefore an increase in population means an increase in power, security, wealth and cultural progress. This so-called "populationist theory", articulated by all influential cameralists from Becher, Hörnigk and Schröder to Justi and Sonnenfels, was fully accepted by Kaunitz. In his assessment of Joseph II's great memorandum of 1765, he insisted that nothing the Emperor had said was more important than his emphasis on finding ways and means to enlarge the population of the Monarchy. In Kaunitz's view the population of the Habsburg Monarchy was insufficient, and it was not merely important to prevent depopulation but also to "augment as much as possible the one that exists."[149]

By 1766 this was not a new idea. After the liberation of the Banat in 1718, the first military governor of the region, General Claudius Florimund Mercy, received a free hand to begin resettling an area that had been virtually denuded of its population, and implemented a systematic plan to bring German and other colonists to the new Habsburg province. Mercy and his successor, Johann Andreas Hamilton, carried out this work with considerable success, but the unfortunate Turkish war of 1737–39 brought an abrupt end to these activities.[150] Maria Theresia reactivated the process in 1744, and attempted to get a colonization programme started in earnest after the War of the Austrian Succession. These efforts were conducted in a rather haphazard fashion and enjoyed only limited success, the bulk of the "settlers" being criminals or Protestants who had been forcibly deported, a policy of which Kaunitz generally disapproved. In the Seven Years War a more systematic process of recruiting war-invalided veterans and Prussian prisoners of war for settlements in southern Hungary and the Banat was begun. Kaunitz supported the effort enthusiastically, but he was skeptical that difficult settlement conditions would yield all that many volunteer colonists.[151]

After the Seven Years War these efforts were intensified with two decrees in February and April 1763 providing for the establishment of seven new settlements and the enlargement of seven others in the Banat for discharged veterans. The importance the Empress placed on this programme cannot be more graphically illustrated than by the fact that even Protestants were encouraged to settle in these areas by receiving a guarantee of the free exercise of their religion.[152] The impetus for these actions came as early as

[149] Beer, ed., "Denkschriften des Fürsten Kaunitz," pp. 106–107.
[150] Josef Kallbrunner, *Das kaiserliche Banat* (Munich, 1958), pp. 1–75; Mikoletzky, *Österreich*, pp. 117–121.
[151] Schünemann, *Bevölkerungspolitik*, pp. 75–153; Mikoletzky, *Österreich*, pp. 237–239.
[152] Anton Tafferner, ed., *Quellenbuch zur donauschwäbischen Geschichte* (Munich, 1974), pp. 203–209, Nos. 123–125.

1761 when the newly-founded Council of State began to consider the question, and agreed that more focused populationist policies were mandatory to make up for losses from the war. Kaunitz felt this was as true for the Austrian lands as it was for the Banat and the southern fringes of Hungary, and the settlement of such areas as the Wiener Neustadt basin are the direct outcome of these proposals.[153]

Hungarian reformers such as Cothmann and Balassa were also fervent proponents of populationist policies, but they soon found themselves running into difficulties which made it clear that the Hungarian nobility as a whole was much less enthusiastic. Part of the political confrontation which led to Pálffy's dismissal as Chancellor had been his opposition to such settlement plans – another clear instance of his essential solidarity with the Hungarian corporate order. Although the principal grievance of later-day Magyar nationalists was that the Habsburg settlement policy introduced German, South-Slav and other "alien" elements into former Magyar territory, thus diluting and weakening the national integrity of the Kingdom of St. Stephen, the actual complaints of the Hungarian nobility in the eighteenth century had a different focus. While some nobles clearly saw the advantages of the crown's populationist policies, the majority tended to be opposed to it. In the first instance there was the almost spontaneous visceral mistrust of and resistance to any policy which came from the central authority. Secondly, settlement projects required capital investments, and Hungarian seigneurs were not only reluctant to invest funds in such projects privately, but were indignant that the Hungarian public purse should be used for the purpose. Some also feared expenses incurred in this way could be used as a pretext by the crown to raise ordinary taxes, or to push through other tax reforms. Finally, and most importantly of all, the nobility was dubious about the policy because of its integral connection with the peasant question. Settlers were enticed to colonize these inhospitable regions of southern Hungary with a variety of inducements, including freedom from most of the most odious burdens of serfdom. For the Hungarian nobility this created a bad precedent indeed, loosening the corrosive virus of insubordination in Hungary and possibly infecting their own obedient peasants.[154]

As with the question of the commutation of peasant labour services, Kaunitz was initially inclined to believe that seigniorial resistance was due more to ignorance than to ill will, and that it could be overcome by good example on cameral estates. Hungarian reformers such as Balassa had a more skeptical view, and within short order Kaunitz, too, came to see the need for stronger crown initiatives.[155] In 1761 he recommended following

---

[153] Schünemann, *Bevölkerungspolitik*, p. 154; Otruba, *Wirtschaftspolitik*, pp. 168–169.
[154] Schünemann, *Bevölkerungspolitik*, pp. 181–233.   [155] *Ibid.*, pp. 157, 186, 201.

the Prussian example and appointing a "colonial director" (*Kolonie-direktor*) for the Monarchy to co-ordinate recruiting and settlement policies. The Prussian Privy Councillor, Johann Friedrich Pfeiffer, who had previously headed a project settling 4,000 foreign families in Brandenburg, was just then visiting Sopron and immediately offered his services. The Council of State was little inclined to support this candidacy, but Kaunitz was so impressed with Pfeiffer's earlier success that he recommended employing him to supervise the systematic settlement of the so-called Carolingian Road, built by Charles VI to connect the Military Frontier center of Karlovac with the port of Rijeka, and to develop the desolate mountainous area between them.[156] The proposal of appointing a special colonial director, however, foundered on the predictable rocks of the Hungarian constitutional shoal.

These failures persuaded Kaunitz that any attempt to work through existing bureaucratic channels would probably doom projects from the start, and in 1766 he proposed that any systematic pursuit of populationist policies in the Habsburg Monarchy required the establishment of a specific authority charged with this task. The many details associated with the settlement of new colonists – the issuing of passports, the subsidization of travel costs, the mapping out of travel routes, the preparation of settlement areas, and so on – all had to be handled by one authority if it were to be done efficiently. This proposal quickly received royal endorsement, and in accordance with personnel recommendations made by Borié the Population Settlement Commission (*Impopulationskommission*) was established in the summer of 1766 under the chairmanship of Franz Anton von Lamberg, and including Privy Councillors Festetics and Kempfen.[157] With this the systematic colonization of the Banat and other depopulated parts of southern Hungary began to flourish, and by 1772 some 52,000 immigrants had been settled there.[158]

Kaunitz was characteristically immodest about the Population Settlement Commission. He asserted that its establishment was "the best thing that has happened in the colonization business,"[159] and he proved a strong supporter of its recommendations in the Council of State. When, for example, the commission recommended in a protocol of 15 January 1767 that all immigrants be offered both a free draft and milking animal, Kaunitz thought the idea highly praiseworthy. He added, also quite characteristically, that since the Hungarian Chamber was likely to balk at

---

[156] *Ibid.*, pp. 208, 239–243; Hermann Widerhofer, "Die Impopulation und die wirtschaftliche Bedeutung der Karolinerstraße im 18. Jahrhundert" (unpublished Ph.D. dissertation, University of Vienna, 1938), pp. 18–80.

[157] Schünemann, *Bevölkerungspolitik*, pp. 329–333.   [158] *Ibid.*, pp. 372–379.

[159] HHStA, Kabinettsarchiv: Kaunitz Voten, Karton 1, No. 474 of 1767, Kaunitz Staatsrat Votum, 1 April 1767.

the measure, regular inspections to guarantee that the animals had been delivered to the colonists should be ordered.[160] The Empress accepted both suggestions.[161]

But as foreign minister Kaunitz also advised caution. Most mid-eighteenth century rulers and their advisers shared the populationist premises of the Habsburg court and were as keen to entice immigration as Vienna. Russian recruiters were particularly aggressive in the Holy Roman Empire, and Prussian recruiters had had considerable success as well. Even Spain advertised for immigrants in Germany with enticements which sometimes verged on social revolutionary appeals. As a result many German courts enacted emigration prohibitions, and the tensions which resulted created a virtual populationist cold war among many European states.[162] For this reason Kaunitz felt that colonization should not be overdone, and that the Habsburg Monarchy should be content if 1,000 German families a year were settled in depopulated areas of the Monarchy.[163] He was concerned to avoid causing any "great sensation," particularly in the face of retaliatory measures adopted by some smaller German princes such as forbidding emigration under pain of confiscation of all the emigrant's property.[164] In his view "open emigration inducements" publicized in neighbouring states "invariably [had] an odious character." He therefore recommended that such recruitments be undertaken with all possible care and circumspection,[165] and decisively vetoed the elaborate newspaper advertisement which Borié and other members of the Council of State had worked out for insertion in German papers.[166] The Empress recognized this necessity and adopted the policy laid out by Kaunitz.[167] In this, as in other Hungarian policies, Kaunitz saw cautious gradualism as the surest road to ultimate and real success.

All these policies notwithstanding, the burden of Hungarian historiography's case against enlightened absolutism has always been the economic dimension, crystallized by the Eckhart thesis.[168] Yet the debate with the Austro-German school has led to a polarization which the most recent impartial outside analysis has rendered largely irrelevant. On the issue of

---

[160] Ibid., No. 164 of 1767, Kaunitz Staatsrat Votum, 20 February 1767.
[161] HHStA, Kabinettsarchiv: Staatsratprotokolle, Vol. 24, No. 164, Maria Theresia to Hatzfeld, 24 March 1767.   [162] Schünemann, Bevölkerungspolitik, pp. 234–243.
[163] HHStA, Kabinettsarchiv: Kaunitz Voten, Karton 1, No. 474 of 1767, Kaunitz Staatsrat Votum, 1 April 1767.
[164] Ibid., No.1667 of 1767, Kaunitz Staatsrat Votum, 4 August 1767.
[165] HHStA, Staatskanzlei: Vorträge, Karton 102, Kaunitz to Maria Theresia, 20 July 1768.
[166] Schünemann, Bevölkerungspolitik, pp. 275–286.
[167] HHStA, Staatskanzlei: Vorträge, Karton 102, Maria Theresia resolution on Kaunitz report of 20 July 1768, and Maria Theresia to Lacy, n.d. (July, 1768).
[168] See footnote 10 above.

whether greater Hungary contributed a proportionately fair share to the burdens of the Monarchy as a whole, both sides have substantially overstated the case. Total Hungarian contributions, taking into account regalia and other revenues, certainly accounted for much more of the overall Habsburg budget than critics are willing to admit. On the other hand, the per-capita revenue ratio of Hungary declined by about 30 % in the course of the reign of Maria Theresia. Careful archival investigation reveals that Eckhart's figures were inflated. Gross pan-monarchical revenues from mining and metallurgy, for example, were calculated as purely Hungarian income. Revenues from the Banat were tabulated twice – both as Banat revenues and as regalia. And because of high overheads, the net income from mining and metallurgy was substantially less than the gross revenues cited by Eckhart. Essentially, the Hungarian portion of pan-monarchical revenues remained relatively steady at around 25 % for the entire period.[169]

Aspects of Habsburg economic policy towards Hungary were unquestionably discriminatory and at least somewhat debilitating to the economic growth there, but it is important to point out that this policy was always conditional and partial in its application. The main point for the advocates of enlightened absolutism, and especially for Kaunitz, was never really the question of whether or not Hungary bore its fair share of the Monarchy's burden. The question was whether or not the Hungarian feudal elite paid its fair share, and here the answer is quite unequivocally negative. Because constitutional guarantees made unilateral royal incursions into the bastions of privilege impossible (incursions of the kind that had occurred in Austria and Bohemia in 1749), it was necessary to adopt indirect measures. These incidentally, though not intentionally, sometimes affected the non-privileged sector as well. For example, Kaunitz praised Ferenc Koller's suggestion to raise the price of salt because it was "a legal means to tax the nobility indirectly", though this meant the common man had to suffer too.[170] But, despite these kinds of negative repercussions, Kaunitz always asserted that "the most essential goal" of economic policy in Hungary was to foster every conceivable benefit which did not undermine the interests of the Monarchy as a whole.[171]

The main sticking point in this regard was industrial development. Kaunitz certainly was one of the main voices in court circles calling for the

---

[169] Dickson, in *Finance and Government* II, has revolutionized work on this subject. His findings with respect to Hungary are succinctly summarized on p. 384, and in his "Staatsfinanzen in Ungarn unter Maria Theresia," in Mraz and Schlag, eds., *Maria Theresia als Königin von Ungarn*, pp. 90–95.

[170] Ember, ed., "Staatsrat," i, pp. 142–143, No. 16; ii, p. 335, No. 42.

[171] HHStA, Kabinettsarchiv: Kaunitz Voten, Karton 3, No. 669 of 1780, Kaunitz Staatsrat Votum, 17 May 1780.

restriction of proto-industrialization in Hungary, but it is highly illuminating to note the context and the qualifications. It was a simple conclusion generally drawn in Habsburg government circles that because of the loss of Silesia, the economically most advanced province of the Monarchy, a concerted effort was required to develop the proto-industrial base in other areas. This initially included generous granting of subsidies, monopolies, and the like. But when results did not live up to expectations by the late 1750s, the government began to move away from these forms of assistance. In Hungary, the tariff reform of 1754 did not actually prohibit industrial activity, but it slowed down economic activity by not supporting it. However, with the foundation of the Council of State the policy was gradually reversed. Cothmann and other Hungarian advisers argued in favour of Hungarian industrial development, and found a sympathetic ear in Borié. Gradually, the position of the court swung around to assisting that industrial development which did not compete with extant establishments elsewhere in the Monarchy. The pace of government aid was much more modest than it had been in Austria and Bohemia a decade earlier, but the main motive behind this tended to be disenchantment with subsidization in general rather than specific anti-Hungarian discrimination.[172]

Kaunitz, however, had reservations from the start. Even in his twelve-point "system", he asserted that the "current constitution" of Hungary made vibrant industrial development inadvisable.[173] The connection between the economy and the social order to which he alluded here was the fact that the Habsburg entrepreneurial sector – and especially the Hungarian one – was largely aristocratic. It was part of the virtually extortionist attempt to break privilege that led to the advice to restrict that economic activity which benefitted the nobility. This "in no way" meant, Kaunitz noted carefully, "the complete prohibition of industry in Hungary," only its *selective* fostering. Under normal circumstances "equity" and "wisdom" demanded that "every sort of industry should be promoted with the same force in Hungary as in other lands," but as long as "the Hungarian aristocracy did not contribute to the general burden," a discriminatory policy was "a necessary evil."[174] That Maria Theresia had absorbed this gospel, focused essentially on a class, becomes clear from such marginal comments as the one she placed on a noble request to alleviate tariffs on wine exports: "No further privileges for the wealthy ones, who would only

[172] Beer, "Die österreichische Handelspolitik," pp. 1–204; Otruba, *Wirtschaftspolitik*; Herman Freudenberger, "State Intervention as an Obstacle to Economic Growth in the Habsburg Monarchy," *Journal of Economic History* XXVII (1967), 493–509; Spiesz, "Die Wirtschaftspolitik des Wiener Hofes," pp. 60–73.
[173] Ember, ed., "Staatsrat," i, pp. 136–137, No. 10.
[174] HHStA, Kabinettsarchiv: Kaunitz Voten, Karton 1, No. 1100 of 1768, Kaunitz Staatsrat Votum, 11 June 1768.

enjoy the benefits themselves, and who do not deserve it!"[175] Sentiments of this kind accounted for the sharpening of the crown's discriminatory policies against Hungarian industry after 1770. Noble entrepreneurs, particularly in the textile sector, mushroomed in Hungary during the 1760s to such an extent that the Viennese department of Trade and Commerce became alarmed.[176] A special commission chaired by Chotek advised that Hungarian nobles, by applying their constitutional freedom from taxation to their industrial enterprises were, in effect, being subsidized, enjoying an enormous competitive advantage over the normally taxed ones in other parts of the Monarchy.[177] Chotek's motive for insisting that Hungarian industry be further curtailed, of course, was hardly social. But Kaunitz had already articulated the same sentiment some years earlier in a different way: the equal dispensation of favours to people who bore the common burden unequally was "a patent injustice."[178]

The reverse of this policy can be seen most graphically in the socio-economic support enlightened absolutism lent to the free cities of Hungary. Free cities were under the direct jurisdiction of the crown and could be administered and taxed much like crown estates. The reform of the corporate organs of municipal administration and the introduction of standards of professionalism show clearly the intent of the reforms of enlightened absolutism when it had a free hand.[179] What is more, the court went to considerable lengths to encourage the economic activity of these urban centers, including sponsoring the establishment of industrial enterprises. Even the policy of harnessing the gentry against the magnates found its parallel in the cities, where the crown was able to use the lesser burgesses to overcome the resistance of the leading patricians.[180] All these policies had the enthusiastic support of Kaunitz. He judged Hungarian free cities to be of extraordinary significance, both politically and economically, and advised that the crown must do everything possible to guarantee that the cities would prosper and flourish. In addition, Kaunitz, in conjunction with the whole Council of State, supported the effort to increase the number of free cities in Hungary by attempting to emancipate

---

[175] Varga, "Magyarország," p. 375.
[176] Gustáv Heckenast, "Bányászat és ipar manufaktúra-korszakunk első szakaszában," in Ember and Heckenast, eds., *Magyarország története* II, 1005–1010.
[177] Beer, "Geschichte der österreichischen Volkswirtschaft: I," pp. 32–34; Szekfű, *Magyar történet*, p. 319.
[178] HHStA, Kabinettsarchiv: Kaunitz Voten, Karton 1, No. 3057 of 1766, Kaunitz Staatsrat Votum, 12 January 1767.
[179] István Kállay, "Reformen der Städteverwaltung in den österreichischen Erbländern und in Ungarn zur Zeit Maria Theresias," *Acta Historica Academiae Scientiarum Hungaricae* XX (1974), 1–21.
[180] István Kállay, "A bécsi udvar várospolitikájának néhány kérdése Mária Terézia korában," *Századok* XCVII (1963), pp. 1055–1071.

those under seigniorial tutelage (whether secular or ecclesiastical).[181] Though the policy enjoyed only very limited success, Kaunitz nevertheless gave it a high priority. For example, of the forty-four cities under ecclesiastical jurisdiction, only two, Pécs and Győr, could acquire royal charters of freedom in the eighteenth century.[182] The Pécs case in particular was so contentious, and its bishop so resolute, that the entire matter might have been dropped. Kaunitz, however, would not give in, finally going over the bishop's head to bludgeon the pope directly to achieve the goal.[183]

It has been argued that policies of this kind were deliberate attempts by enlightened absolutism to foster and rely on the bourgeoisie to counterbalance the aristocracy.[184] In later years Kaunitz was certainly to be quite explicit about bringing commoners into positions of political power, because they provided "a useful counterweight to the arbitrariness of the mighty."[185] But during the 1760s and 1770s Kaunitz's arguments reflected less constitutional concerns and were more focused on social and economic development. Borié's argument that Hungarian free cities had provided the crown with three times as much credit during the Seven Years War as the nobility and clergy certainly underlined the immediate benefits that prosperous municipalities could afford, and found strong resonance in Kaunitz. He drew a parallel with the Belgian precedent, where, in his view, a judicious carrot and stick policy had resulted in higher than expected fiscal returns and surprisingly ample public credit in the Seven Years War.[186] At the same time Habsburg policy to increase the number and size of free cities, for which Kaunitz was so enthusiastic that he wished to see subsidized construction material provided, might even lead to the strengthening of town representation at the Diet.[187] This too was part of the larger strategy of containment of the power and influence of the nobility, which was the heart of Kaunitz's Hungarian policy.

The difficulty with a strategy such as Kaunitz's twelve-point "system" was that it took time, patience and persistence. In 1780, Maria Theresia died and her son, Joseph II, became sole ruler. Patience was not one of his virtues. The results of his *coups de main* against the Hungarian feudal order

---

[181] Ember, "Zur Klassenpolitik," pp. 400–403.

[182] Andor Csizmadia, *Az egyházi mezővárosok jogi helyzete és küzdelmük a felszabadulásért a XVIII. században* (Budapest, 1962).

[183] HHStA, Kabinettsarchiv: Kaunitz Voten, Karton 2, Nos. 371 and 2149 of 1776, Kaunitz Staatsrat Voten, 19 February and 23 September 1776.

[184] Ember, "Zur Klassenpolitik," p. 400. Cf. László Makkai, "Az abszolutizmus társadalmi bázisának kialakulása az osztrák Habsburgok országaiban," *Történelmi Szemle* III (1960), 193.

[185] HHStA, Kabinettsarchiv: Kaunitz Voten, Karton 4, No. 5987 of 1792, Kaunitz Staatsrat Votum, 26 January 1793; and Karton 6, No. 418 of 1791, Kaunitz Staatsrat Votum, n.d. (11–15 February 1791).   [186] Schünemann, *Bevölkerungspolitik*, pp. 232–233.

[187] Ember, "Zur Klassenpolitik," pp. 400–404.

are well known. Whether the continuation of Kaunitz's gradualist social revolutionary conspiracy could have reaped more benefits for Hungarian society than Joseph's impetuosity therefore remained an unanswered question. But Kaunitz understood one thing well: unless the constituent lands of the Habsburg Monarchy were prepared to subordinate themselves to what he called "the supreme law" of the common good,[188] they would suffer together to their common regret. Melancholy Central Europeans seem to have preferred the latter course.

[188] HHStA, Kabinettsarchiv: Kaunitz Voten, Karton 5, No. 2434 of 1790, Kaunitz Staatsrat Votum, 15 August 1790.

9   Conclusion

Ever since the term "enlightened absolutism" was coined by Wilhelm Roscher over a century ago, historians have disagreed bitterly on the validity of this concept as a meaningful description of that critical transition phase when the traditional corporate society of medieval and early modern Europe was being displaced by the emerging modern unitary state. Disagreements have ranged from the internal contradiction implicit in the very label of "enlightened absolutism" or even more, "enlightened despotism," through questioning the motives of the monarchs and governments purportedly engaged in such an enterprise, to wondering what kind of truth the very idea had for those eighteenth-century thinkers who accorded it any truth at all.[1] These disagreements notwithstanding, there is broad agreement that a larger dynamic of reform and change characterized many states of Europe in the second half of the eighteenth century, particularly in those which perceived their relative underdevelopment as the principal impediment to international competitiveness. Indeed, some historians have even argued that the perception of backwardness was the very precondition of the emergence of reforming regimes we have come to call enlightened absolutist.[2]

Inevitably, such debates tend to focus on individual monarchs, for even when detailed research invariably reveals that most of them were hardly as absolute as one might think from the use of the term, they were certainly the fulcrum of the policy decision-making process. There is little doubt that any assessment of enlightened absolutism must attempt to disengage the complex web of motivations that animated rulers to undertake reform initiatives – whether this was true on a very limited or on a very bold and ambitious scale. This involves an analysis of both intention and action,

---

[1] The best introduction to the historiography is the concise but penetrating essay by Charles Ingrao, "The Problem of 'Enlightened Absolutism' and the German States," *Journal of Modern History* LVIII Supplement (1986), 161–180; on the idea of enlightened absolutism for eighteenth-century thinkers, Leonard Krieger, *An Essay on the Theory of Enlightened Despotism* (Chicago, Ill., 1975).

[2] Karl Otmar Freiherr von Aretin, ed., *Der aufgeklärte Absolutismus* (Cologne, 1974), pp. 22–27.

which did not always coincide often for very practical reasons, as well as an analysis of the effects of the actions, many of which were quite unforeseen and unexpected. But excessive focus on kings and queens tends not only to overstate the actual power commanded by these monarchs, but also to trivialize the larger dynamic of change. The monarch was not *deus ex machina* implementer of policy, but merely the apex of a larger decision-making process. One should perhaps speak, more accurately, of enlightened absolutist regimes, which, in turn, as has been pointed out, not only requires "more archival research about government activity at the top" but also much more careful analysis of the perceptions and endeavors of ministers and other government officials.[3]

This is particularly true of the Habsburg Monarchy. If the underlying patterns of policy are not always clear, or, indeed, often even appear to be quite contradictory, this is due less to the shortcomings of the individual rulers (though these are frequently quite apparent) or to what has been diagnosed as "a neurosis at the center of affairs,"[4] than to the simple fact that the regime was hardly monolithic. Eighteenth-century Habsburg monarchs were not exempt from the fate of all political leaders, past and present, of having to steer a difficult course among diverse interest groups and among desirable but frequently mutually exclusive policy options. I have suggested throughout this study that in the case of the Habsburg Monarchy, these interest groups can be roughly divided into three distinct parties – not in the narrow political sense, but in the broader sense of a body of persons sharing certain premises and overall approaches. The first of these were the generally conservative interest groups and individuals who tended to wish to preserve traditional values and socio-economic and political structures. I have called the second group "cameralist reformers." These were individuals who not only tended to act in the spirit of the writings of famous cameralist theorists such as Becher, Hörnigk and Schröder, but who also looked for inspiration to the successfully implemented cameralist ordinances of what Marc Raeff has dubbed "the well-ordered police state" in Protestant Germany over the previous two centuries. The third group has been described throughout as the "Enlightenment party," not without some sense of the dangers inherent in such a label.

The Enlightenment party in the Habsburg Monarchy grew out of the cameralist reform tradition, but as a result of often bitter experience came to see the limitations and problems of the well-ordered police state. Frequently, though not invariably informed by ideas of the Western

---

[3] Eberhard Weis, "Enlightenment and Absolutism in the Holy Roman Empire: Thoughts on Enlightened Absolutism in Germany," *Journal of Modern History* LVIII Supplement (1986), 192. [4] Dickson, *Finance and Government* I, 329.

Enlightenment, this group tended to welcome the accelerating internal momentum to change inherent in the reform process and tended to be animated by a singular faith in progress. Many of these individuals explicitly thought of themselves as *Aufklärer* or *philosophes*, and openly claimed membership in "the party of humanity," though their opinions were often at variance with each other. Because the Enlightenment party grew out of the cameralist reform party, because the two shared much common ground, and because many of the latter eventually jumped on the bandwagon of the former, the distinctions between the two have not always been clear. Generally, however, cameralists began with more pessimistic assumptions about man and society, tended to focus more narrowly on fiscal concerns, and largely had more conservative social views.[5] Of course the three parties were hardly hermetically sealed: there was much disagreement within each group and frequent cross-over on specific policy matters. The important point about the reform dynamic of the Habsburg regime, however, was that policy debates were not bipolar but tripartite, with the result that the process of change was subject to a much more complex dialectic than would appear on the surface.[6]

The most influential, though certainly not the most radical voice in the Enlightenment party was that of Kaunitz. As we have seen, he was clearly the single most important and powerful minister in Maria Theresia's reign, and the animating soul of enlightened absolutism in the Habsburg Monarchy. No other minister's political activity was as far-reaching as that of Kaunitz, nor made such a decisive difference on such a broad range of policies affecting the Monarchy as a whole. Yet it is easy to overstate Kaunitz's power and influence. He did not dominate the decision-making process in the manner of a Richelieu: he could neither eliminate nor effectively silence dissent from his views. He could lend decisive direction to the reform dynamic in certain respects, but in other areas his failure to do so is equally conspicuous. We have had numerous opportunities to observe how the timely intervention of Kaunitz could make a dramatic difference to policy directions, and others how his best efforts were frustrated. But even when Kaunitz's personal recommendations were not accepted and even when he failed to lend policy the direction which he wished, his views were practically impossible to ignore. They thus provided one of the most significant elements of the framework within which the policy dialectic took place.

---

[5] These distinctions have been most lucidly set forth by Ingrao in "The Problem of 'Enlightened Absolutism'," pp. 175–177, and in *Hessian Mercenary State*, pp. 46–53.

[6] A similar tripartite struggle among conservatives, reform Catholics and proponents of radical secularism characterized the sphere of religious reform. These frequently, but by no means invariably, coincided with the conservative, cameralist and Enlightenment camps.

To understand the role of Kaunitz in the development of enlightened absolutism in the Habsburg Monarchy, we must begin with what was his first responsibility, that of being foreign minister of one of the great powers of Europe in the very ruthless and competitive eighteenth century. The twin concern of the foreign minister was the preservation of the status and the security of the Monarchy. Kaunitz conceived appropriate foreign policy development to be dependent on an assessment of the relative power of the Habsburg Monarchy in the constellation of major, middle and minor powers of Europe. A recent analysis of the concept of state power in the eighteenth century, which has given special prominence to Kaunitz's views on the subject, has shown the degree to which such analyses were based not only on quantitative military factors but also on a broad range of qualitative and contextual factors which affected the relative power of any given state. It has argued that what was traditionally seen as Kaunitz's entry into domestic politics was really Kaunitz's integration of ever-broadening domestic dimensions into his concept of state power.[7]

Up to a point this is an entirely valid conclusion. It offers us a valuable new insight into Kaunitz's foreign policy, and permits us to see the development of his view of the balance of power in a whole new light. Certainly the Diplomatic Revolution and the Seven Years War were geared towards the elimination of Prussia as a great power and the restitution of the world-system of four great European powers which emerged after the War of the Spanish Succession and the Great Northern War. Failure to achieve this objective led Kaunitz to reorient his foreign policy to one that was essentially pacifist, and focused on the development of the domestic power potential of the Habsburg Monarchy.[8] He now explicitly rejected the pursuit of "territorial compensation" in the name of maintaining the balance of power of Europe,[9] for he was persuaded that any equitable division of territorial spoils would strengthen other powers relatively more than the Habsburg Monarchy. Kaunitz's view that the existing territorial distribution would be favourable to the Monarchy if only it exploited its full domestic potential was thus a re-statement of Hörnigk's famous book title *Austria above all if it but will*.

Such a political position entailed less a policy reversal for Kaunitz than a crystallization of a long-standing premise. In his famous position paper of March 1749, which was to lead to a reversal of Habsburg foreign policy, Kaunitz had already clearly recognized that "the domestic condition of a Monarchy is ... the first and most important consideration which must be

[7] Klueting, *Lehre von der Macht der Staaten*, pp. 167–184.
[8] On this see my "Wenzel Anton Kaunitz-Rietberg (1711–1794)," pp. 270–272.
[9] For Kaunitz's memorandum on this subject see my "Prince Kaunitz and the Balance of Power," pp. 406–408.

introduced and assessed in all diplomatic policy deliberations."[10] In his first three years in office he focused relatively little on that dimension, but in 1756 underwent a baptism by fire when he became chairman of the War Cabinet. Within two years the inadequacy of the reforms undertaken since the end of the last war were dramatically highlighted not just by the military failures of 1757 and 1758, but by the weakness of the economic foundation of the war effort and by the confusion and paralysis to which cameralist conciliar forms of government were reducing the central administration. Certainly Kaunitz's awareness of these problems was given particularly poignant force by the sense that domestic weaknesses were frustrating and undermining his brilliantly conceived and executed diplomatic strategy to recover Silesia and destroy Prussia, but it is to put the cart before the horse to suggest that his diplomatic failures led Kaunitz to seek domestic scapegoats in Haugwitz's cameralist-inspired reforms.[11]

What had been an important component of Kaunitz's foreign policy all along became the most important component when the hope of ultimate victory in the war was dashed by the battle of Torgau in 1760. The restructuring of government which now swept over the Monarchy at the behest of Kaunitz was not so much a vain attempt to solve complex problems with the simplistic band-aid of new bureaucratic bodies, but a reorientation of the structures of government to meet the new objective of broader social and economic development. This change of priorities was enshrined by Kaunitz's famous ideological principles for the Council of State of 1761, and thereafter domestic reform became the preeminent consideration in Kaunitz's overall assessments of the Monarchy's position in the world. In his first great statement of principles that were to guide the Monarchy after the Seven Years' War, Kaunitz posited the "fundamental rule" of the maintenance of "general peace and good understanding with all other powers, including even the king in Prussia," and urged that the "greatest concern [be] the increase of the inner strength of the land by improvements in agriculture, industry, commerce, and financial matters."[12] A dozen years later Kaunitz told Joseph that a statesman without principles was like an architect without blueprints. His included the following:

Causing a war is a pernicious undertaking and can be justified only when survival makes it necessary ... Under the circumstances the most beneficial and reliable course for a state is to seek its strength and power in itself by promoting the standard of living.[13]

[10] Pommerin and Schilling, ed., "Denkschrift des Grafen Kaunitz," p. 206.
[11] As argued by Walter, "Eintritt," pp. 37–41.
[12] Beer, ed., "Denkschriften des Fürsten Kaunitz," pp. 63–74, especially p. 67.
[13] Ibid., pp. 74–98, especially pp. 75, 77.

Finally, as we have seen, only days before his death he summed up his long-standing philosophy that "wise domestic reforms" rendered all territorial conquests "superfluous."[14]

While calculations of the qualitative and quantitative domestic dimensions of state power thus provide valuable insights into Kaunitz's policy assumptions, however, they do not tell the whole story. Unless one is prepared to dismiss all his repeated appeals to "conscience" and "humanity" as mere cynical and hypocritical incantations before the obligatory icons of his age, and to dismiss his insistence that he was a *philosophe* as mere literary window dressing in the style of Frederick II of Prussia, the problem of the development of enlightened reform is certainly more complex than a mere sophisticated calculation and appreciation of the filaments of naked state power. As Ingrao has well emphasized, not only did enlightened reform extend well beyond issues associated with national power and security, but a concern for the latter hardly precludes an equally sincere concern for popular welfare.[15] In the case of Kaunitz the evidence is simply too overwhelming not to take the humanitarian impulses of his commitment to reform seriously.

Kaunitz's conceptions began with cameralist eudemonism, but soon outpaced traditional cameralist prescriptions. Animated by a sense of underdevelopment, his policies sought to modernize the institutional and normative framework of central European society. Such sentiments initially followed well in the footsteps of those cameralist ordinances of "the well-ordered police states" of Protestant Germany, which, in the words of Marc Raeff, sought to internalize "the values and norms of the modern, production oriented, dynamic political culture" in its populations.[16] However, Kaunitz was also patently affected by the novel ideas of the Western Enlightenment with its stress on secularism, cultural and intellectual growth, individual merit, human dignity and the liberation of individuals from traditional bonds – ideas, in short, which recognized that social change came in the wake of economic change. He summarized this point well in 1767:

The national economy deserves the greatest attention, and in this respect petty economies can frequently even be harmful, in that they hinder the driving force of economic development. Nothing animates this driving force or cultivates patriotism better than a certain freedom of the people. Where this freedom is present industry and prosperity tend to reach their highest development. England and Holland serve as examples; and for my part, I could wish nothing more for the

---

[14] Szabo, "Prince Kaunitz and the Balance of Power," pp. 400–401. Cf above, pp. 1–2.
[15] Ingrao, "The Problem of 'Enlightened Absolutism'," p. 167. Cf. Blanning, *Joseph II*, p. 72.   [16] Raeff, *Well-ordered Police State*, p. 256.

benefit of the state than that the servile mentality be banned from our lands, and that a freedom-loving industriousness be implanted instead.[17]

Many of Kaunitz's policies thus had roots in the commitment to broader economic development, but to reduce them to that single motivation would be a serious distortion. Furthermore, they were clearly animated by an optimistic confidence in progress (which incidentally also mitigated many of the specific policy setbacks he suffered). Here Kaunitz shared the faith, articulated so well by Kant, that while the age might not be an enlightened one, it was nevertheless one of enlightenment. In 1768 he put it this way:

The greatest difficulties have already been overcome: reform proposals are no longer regarded with immediate suspicion or dismissed as wrong, and the prejudices against innovation are declining day by day. Above all we no longer live in deep ignorance of everything that goes on abroad; rather such examples stimulate our own eagerness to make useful foreign discoveries and innovations our own.[18]

What we can also read between these lines, however, is the perception of the necessary role the absolute state had to play in the progress of enlightenment. Kaunitz was not only an advocate of enlightenment, but also of absolutism.

Historians have not failed to observe that the chain-reaction which began with efforts to create more competitive societies in the traditional mold was soon to lead to quite unforeseen consequences. As the regulatory state increasingly came to recognize the need to liberate individual energies in the interest of greater productivity, traditional seventeenth-century cameralist ideals received an increasingly humanitarian, autonomist and radical articulation, until the conflict between the liberty implicit in enlightenment and the authority implicit in absolutism became explicit. Such a conflict between enlightenment and absolutism did not present Kaunitz with any insoluble dilemmas. He saw the two objectives to be entirely compatible; indeed, he perceived the former to be dependent on the latter. Even historians are apt to forget that humanity walks into the future backwards: it can see only what is behind, and can surmise what is ahead only by extrapolating from the past. As a passionate apostle of reform, Kaunitz clearly saw resistance to change as the most formidable obstacle which an enlightened regime faced. Under such circumstances the utilitarian value of absolutism was patent – a pragmatic conclusion, incidentally, which was shared by most eighteenth-century Enlightenment intellectuals.

[17] HHStA, Österreichische Akten, Österreich-Staat, Fasz. 5, Kaunitz to Maria Theresia, 21 April 1767.   [18] Schünemann, Bevölkerungspolitik, p. 38.

The faith in the state as the repository of all sovereign power in society was based on the assumption that it alone could provide guidelines for social and economic development that were wholly disinterested. This assumption proceeded from the classic Enlightenment premise that the "science of man" could determine with mathematical certainty the needs of a society. The naivety of this assumption was not totally lost on Kaunitz. If all sovereign power were invested in the state, and the state recognized no independent spheres of dominion besides itself, the line between absolute and arbitrary government was a thin one. Because the argument that the state was not above the law was obviated to some extent by the fact that it remained the only authority with the right to interpret the common weal, and because in a regime which attempted to exercise absolute authority in the name of a monarch, the personality of the monarch remained an unpredictable variable, Kaunitz also understood the paradoxical need to introduce certain checks and balances on executive authority. The problem was how to introduce such checks without giving those resistant to change instruments to impede the reform process.

The solution which Kaunitz conceived for this dilemma was to insist that the public face of the regulatory state be absolute, but that this absolutism be internally mitigated by checks that prevented any slide into arbitrary despotism. Kaunitz recognized that government was not a seamless monolith, but a series of difficult choices among numerous mutually exclusive options. Hence the heart of his administrative reform of 1761–1763 was the development of autonomous ministries or departments, each developing and recommending policy based on the logic inherent in the ministry, but leaving the difficult choices "between Rome and Carthage" to the executive authority. At this level, too, there was the internal mitigation of the Council of State – the guide and conscience of the absolute monarch. Proceeding from the premise of commitment to reform, the dialectics of its debates were to disentangle the "rationality" of the difficult choices facing the monarch, thus lending consistency and direction to the reform process.

For the regime to claim absolute authority, while internally mitigating that authority to maximize its scope for enlightenment, was still far removed from actually exercising authority successfully. Thus, effective implementation of reform was one of Kaunitz's deepest concerns. It was all very well that the regime was solidly on the path to a fundamental transformation of society; it was another matter entirely to penetrate the natural forces of tradition, inertia and resistance to change at the base of the social pyramid. As we have seen repeatedly, Kaunitz had no illusions about this. Because even the most evidently beneficial and well-intentioned measure could be thwarted at the local level, Kaunitz placed great emphasis on the assiduous cultivation of the crown's local authority. But the ideal was hardly to elicit "slavish obedience" from bureaucratic subordinates; the leitmotifs were rather pragmatism, flexibility and adaptability. At the same time Kaunitz repeatedly displayed a typical enlightenment confidence in the power of persuasion to assure the ultimate triumph of the reasonable and productive social order. None of these prescriptions could guarantee rapid results, nor did Kaunitz expect them. In contrast to Joseph II, he was a gradualist, who saw that the path to enlightenment was a long and rocky one. Some historians have been tempted to overly cynical evaluations of such strategies, and have seen only the reluctance of the *ancien régime* to undertake any really substantive change. This may very well have been true elsewhere, especially in Prussia. Whatever the motives of the individual monarchs, it was certainly not true of the regime of enlightened absolutism in the Habsburg Monarchy. And if, as Franco Venturi assures us, it was in this Monarchy where enlightened absolutism struck roots whose shoots were to produce the most lasting fruits on European soil,[19] those roots were struck in the reign of Maria Theresia and owed much of their vitality to Kaunitz.

[19] Franco Venturi, *Italy and the Enlightenment* (London, 1972), p. 20.

Bibliography

ARCHIVAL SOURCES

I. BRNO, MORAVSKÍ ZEMSKI ARCHIV (MZA) (Formerly Státní oblastní archiv, Brno)

G 436: Rodinný archiv Kouniců, Václav Antonín Korrespondence and miscellanea: 20 uncatalogued cartons

II. VIENNA, ÖSTERREICHISCHES STAATSARCHIV

1. *Haus-, Hof- und Staatsarchiv* (HHStA)

(a) Staatskanzlei:
   (i) Vorträge, Kartons 61–132 (1749–1780)
   (ii) Notenwechsel:
      An die Hofkanzlei, new Kartons 2–10 (1753–1780)
      Von der Hofkanzlei, new Kartons 74–102 (1753–1780)
      Von und an der Studienhofkommission, 1 Fasz.
      An den Hofkriegsrat, Fasz. 3–7
      Von dem Hofkriegsrat, Fasz. 10–24
      Ad Hofkriegsrat, Fasz. 3/4
      An die Hofkammer, Fasz. 2–4
      Von der Hofkammer, Fasz. 3–8
      Ad Hofkammer: Finanzwesen im allgemeinen, Fasz. 5–6
      Handel und Verkehr, Fasz. 15, 21–22
      Hofkammerakten, Fasz. 26–31
      An die Hofkammer in Münz und Bergwesen, Fasz. 1
      Von der Hofkammer in Münz und Bergwesen, Fasz. 3–4
      An die Komerzhofkommission, Fasz. 1–2
      Von der Komerzhofkommission, Fasz. 6–8
      An die Bancodirektion, Fasz. 1
      Von der Bancodirektion, Fasz. 3
      An das Generalrechnungsdirectorium, Fasz. 1
      Von dem Generalrechnungsdirectorium, Fasz. 2–3
      Notae Varia, Fasz. 2
      An die Oberste Justizstelle, Fasz. 1–2
      Von der Obersten Justizstelle, Fasz. 3–5

An die Ungarische Hofkanzlei, Fasz. 1–2
Von der Ungarischen Hofkanzlei, Fasz. 3–4
An die Siebenbürgische Hofkanzlei, 1 Fasz.
Von der Siebenbürgischen Hofkanzlei, 1 Fasz.
An und von der Galizischen Hofkanzlei, Fasz. 1–2
(iii) Provinzen:
Böhmen, Fasz. 8
Galizien, Fasz. 3, 5
Illyrien, Fasz. 1
Küstenland, Fasz. 1, 3
Mähren, Fasz. 1
Militärgrenze, Fasz. 1
Niederösterreich, Fasz. 1–2
(iv) Interiora:
Fasz. 1–2, Organisierung
Fasz. 67a–67b, Orientalische Akademie
Fasz. 108, Hoftheater
(v) Wissenschaft und Kunst, Kartons 1–15
(vi) Preussen Correspondenz (Gottfried van Swieten), Kartons 54–59
(b)   Staatenabteilung:
(i) Frankreich Berichte, 1750–1753, Kartons 77, 84, 89
(ii) Frankreich Varia, 1750–1752, Karton 22
(c)   Kabinettsarchiv:
(i) Staatsratakten, 1 Karton
(ii) Staatsratprotokolle, Volumes 1–71 (1760–1780)
(iii) Staatsrat Präsidium, Karton 1 (1760–1781)
(iv) Voten des Fürsten Kaunitz zu Staatsratakten, Kartons 1–3, 6
(v) Nachlaß Kaunitz, 1 Karton
(vi) Nachlaß Kressel, 1 Fasz.
(vii) Nachlaß Lacy, Kartons 2–7
(viii) Nachlaß Nenny, Kartons 1–2
(ix) Nachlaß Zinzendorf, Part II: Handschriften:
Vols. 2b–6: Organisation der Zentralstellen
Vols. 10–12: Hofrechenkammer
Vols. 18–22: Finanz- und Kreditvorschläge
Vol. 23: Vielschreiberei Reform (1768)
Vols. 33, 35–36: Kriegserfordernisse (1756–1763)
Vols. 81, 83–88, 89a–b, 111: Finanzvorschläge
Vol. 101: Geschichte und Beschreibung des Wiener Stadt Banko (1758)
Vols. 103, 104: Beschreibung der vornehmsten europäischen Banken (1758)
Vol. 106 in index, but missing from files, 4 Memoiren über die Banken und über das Sistem des Law.
Vol. 139b: Münzwesen
Vol. 187: Miscellanea (1769–1774)
(x) Nachlaß Zinzendorf, Part III: Tagebücher des Grafen Karl Zinzendorf:

Vols. 1–25 (1747–1780)
(xi) Kaiser Franz Akten:
    Kartons 63–64: Verfall Böhmens (1771–1773)
    Kartons 72–74: Jesuitenaufhebungsakten
(xii) Direktionsakten der Kabinettskanzlei:
    Fasz. 27: Denkschrift Josephs II. (1773)
(xiii) Varia der Kabinettskanzlei:
    Fasz. 20a: Denkschriften Josephs II. and related materials
(xiv) Materialien zur Geschichte des Staatsrats von Kutschera:
    1 Karton

(d) Familienarchiv:
    (i) Sammelbände:
        Kartons 4–7, 10, 15: Maria Theresia, Joseph II, Leopold, Correspondenz und Denkschriften
        Karton 70: Kaunitz Nachlaß
        Karton 73: Colloredo Tagebuch
        Kartons 87–88: Joseph II–Kaunitz Correspondenz
    (ii) Hofreisen: Kartons 1–10 (1768–1779)

(e) Sonstige Sammlungen:
    (i) Grosse Korrespondenz:
        Fasz. 242: Koch, Püchler & Spangenberg Korrespondenz (1759–1767)
        Fasz. 247: Maria Theresia, Francis Stephen and Charles of Lorraine (1742–1763)
        Fasz. 400: Bartenstein Korrespondenz
        Fasz. 401: Korrespondenz verschiedener
        Fasz. 405–406: Kaunitz Korrespondenz
    (ii) Kriegsakten (Weisungen und Berichte):
        Fasz. 411: Prince Zweibrücken
        Fasz. 413: FM Browne and Charles of Lorraine
        Fasz. 415: Charles of Lorraine
        Fasz. 416–417: FM Daun
        Fasz. 418–419: Gen. Loudon
        Fasz. 425: Freih. v. Grechtler, et al.
        Fasz. 426: French Generals
        Fasz. 427–428: Kettler (envoy at French HQ)
        Fasz. 430: Russian Generals
        Fasz. 431: St. André (envoy at Russian HQ)
        Fasz. 432–433: various envoys to Russian HQ
        Fasz. 434: Mednyanssky (envoy at Swedish HQ)

(f) Italien-Spanischer Rat:
    (i) Vorträge, Kartons 201–204 (1757–1780)
    (ii) Lombardei Korrespondenz, Fasz. 105, 106a, 108–110, 154b–c, 155–171 (1754–1780)

(g) Belgien:
    (i) Vorträge, Fasz. 5–11 (1753–1780)

(h) Österreichische Akten:
    Österreich-Staat, Fasz. 2–6

(i)   Handschriftensammlung:
        Convolut W 808

2. Hofkammerarchiv (HKA)

(a)   Kredit und Staatsschuldenakten:
        (i) Ständische Kredit Deputation, Rote Nos. 1–4, 6, 13, 23–27.
        (ii) Staatsschuldenakten, Rote Nos. 35, 50
(b)   Kredit (A. A.-) Akten: Interessensteuerreduktion, Rote No. 10
(c)   Kommerz: Littorale, Karton Rote Nos. 625, 584, 645, 686, 689

3. Kriegsarchiv (KA)

(a)   Indeces, Vols. 877, 884, 891, 898, 905, 912, 921, 928a, 928b, 936a, 936b,
        943, 951, 961, 971, 979, 986, 992, 1001, 1025, 1050, 1070, 1091, 1103, 1115,
        1127, 1139, 1236, 1357, 1477 (1753–1780)
(b)   Protokolle in Publicis, Vols. 879, 886–887, 892–894, 899–901, 906–908,
        913–915, 917, 922, 924, 929, 931–932, 937–939, 945–946, 952–953, 955,
        962–964, 973, 980–981, 987–988, 993–995 (1753–1780)
(c)   Commercialia, Fasz. 111

4. Allgemeines Verwaltungsarchiv (AVA)

(a)   Nachläße: Pergen, 1 Karton
(b)   Studienhofkommission: Wien, Akademie der Bildenden Künste, Fasz. 61
        (Schriften des Staatskanzlers Kaunitz)
(c)   Hofkanzlei, Karton 229

III. VIENNA, ÖSTERREICHISCHE NATIONALBIBLIOTHEK (ÖNB)

Handschriftensammlung

(a)   Autographe (in form *Kästchen/Nr.*): 8/2–2; 9/49; 13/97; 144/76;
        174/84; 195/21; 289/7; 296/7–20, 21, 22; 446/21–4; 454/4–1
(b)   Series Nova: Nr. 1612, 1621, 1637, 4696

IV. VIENNA, ARCHIV DER AKADEMIE DER BILDENDEN KÜNSTE (AABK)

(a)   Verwaltungsakten, Fasz. 1–3
(b)   Sitzungsprotokolle des akademischen Rates, Fasz. 1

V. VIENNA, DEUTSCHER ORDEN ZENTRALARCHIV (DOZA)

(a)   Handschriften, Vols. 51–55, 63–68, 377–378, 381 (Zinzendorf Nachlaß)

PUBLISHED PRIMARY SOURCES

Anderson, Emily, ed. and trans., *The Letters of Mozart and his Family*, 2nd ed., 2
Vols., (London, 1966).

Arneth, Alfred Ritter von, ed., *Briefe der Kaiserin Maria Theresia an Ihre Kinder und Freunde*, 4 Vols. (Vienna, 1881).

Die Relationen der Botschafter Venedigs über Österreich im achtzehnten Jahrhundert, Fontes Rerum Austriacarum II/22 (Vienna, 1863).

"Graf Philipp Cobenzl und seine Memoiren," *AÖG* LXVII (1886), 1–181.

Maria Theresia und Joseph II.: Ihre Correspondenz samt Briefen Joseph's an seinen Bruder Leopold, 3 Vols. (Vienna, 1867–1868).

"Zwei Denkschriften der Kaiserin Maria Theresia," *AÖG* XLVII (1891), 267–355. (New edition by Joseph Kallbrunner. See below.)

Arneth, Alfred Ritter von, and Flammermont, M. J., eds., *Correspondance secrète du Comte de Mercy-Argenteau avec L'Empéreur Joseph II et le Prince de Kaunitz*, 2 Vols. (Paris, 1889–1891).

Arneth, Alfred Ritter von, and Geffroy, M. A., eds., *Correspondance secrète entre Marie-Thérèse et le Cte. de Mercy-Argenteau avec les lettres de Marie-Thérèse et de Marie-Antoinette*, 3 Vols. (Paris, 1874).

Arnheim, Fritz, "Das Urtheil eines schwedischen Diplomaten über den Wiener Hof im Jahre 1756. Aus dem schwedischen Reichsarchiv in Stockholm," *MIÖG* X (1889), 287–294.

Asow, Hedwig and E. H. Mueller von, eds., *The Collected Corrrespondence and Papers of Christoph Willibald Gluck*, Stewart Thomson, trans. (N.Y., 1962).

Beales, Derek, "Joseph II's 'Rêveries,'" *MÖStA* XXXIII (1980), 142–160.

Beer, Adolf, ed., *Aufzeichnungen des Grafen William Bentinck über Maria Theresia* (Vienna, 1871).

"Denkschriften des Fürsten Kaunitz," *AÖG* XLVIII (1872), 1–162.

Die Erste Theilung Polens, Vol. 3: Dokumente (Vienna, 1880).

Joseph II., Leopold II. und Kaunitz: Ihr Briefwechsel (Vienna, 1873).

Besterman, Theodore, ed., *Voltaire's Correspondence*, 75 Vols. (Geneva, 1953–1965).

Binder von Kriegelstein, Johann Friedrich, *Philosophische Schriften*, herausgegeben von August Veith von Schittlersberg, 2 Vols. (Vienna & Prague, 1783).

Bleckwenn, H[ans], ed., *Zeitgenössische Studien über die altpreußische Armee* (Osnabrück, 1974).

Brunner, Sebastian, ed., *Correspondances intimes de l'Empéreur Joseph II avec son ami le Comte de Cobenzl et son Premier Ministre le Prince de Kaunitz* (Paris, 1871).

Der Humor in der Diplomatie und Regierungskunde des 18. Jahrhunderts, 2 vols. (Vienna, 1872).

Casanova, Jacques, *Histoire de ma vie*, 12 Vols. (Wiesbaden, 1962).

Conrad, Hermann, *et al.*, eds., *Recht und Verfassung des Reiches in der Zeit Maria Theresias: Die Vorträge zum Unterricht des Erzherzogs Joseph in Natur- und Völkerrecht sowie im deutschen Staats- und Lehnenrecht* (Cologne, 1964).

Conze, Werner, ed., *Quellen zur Geschichte der deutschen Bauernbefreiung*. Vol. XII of Wilhelm Treue, ed., *Quellensammlung zur Kulturgeschichte* (Göttingen, 1957).

Csizmadia, Andor, ed., *Bürokrácia és közigazgatási reformok magyarhonban* (Budapest, 1979).

Deutsch, Otto Erich ed., *Mozart: A Documentary Biography*, Eric Blom, Peter Branscome and Jeremy Noble, trans. (Stanford, Calif., 1966).

Dörrer, Fridolin, ed., "Der Schriftverkehr zwischen dem päpstlichen Staats-sekretariat und der Apostolischen Nuntiatur Wien in der zweiten Hälfte des 18. Jahrhunderts: Erschließungsplan, Kanzlei- und aktenkundliche Beobach-tungen," *Römische Historische Mitteilungen* IV (1960–1961), 63–246.

Duplessis, Georges, ed., *Mémoires et Journal de J.-G. Wille, Graveur du Roi*, 2 Vols. (Paris, 1957).

Ember, Győző, ed., "Der österreichische Staatsrat und die ungarische Verfassung, 1761–1768," *Acta Historica Academiae Scientiarum Hungaricae* VI (1959), 105–153, 331–371; VII (1960), 149–182.

Favart, Charles Simon, *Mémoires et correspondance littéraires, dramatiques et anecdotiques*, 3 Vols., (Paris, 1808, reprinted Geneva, 1970).

Fischer, Heinz, and Silvestri, Gerhard, eds., *Texte zur österreichischen Verfas-sungsgeschichte. Von der Pragmatischen Sanktion zur Bundesverfassung (1713–1966)*. (Vienna, 1970).

Franz, Günther, ed., *Quellen zur Geschichte des Deutschen Bauernstandes in der Neuzeit*, (Vienna & Munich, 1963).

Frass, Otto, ed., *Quellenbuch zur österreichischen Geschichte*, 3 Vols. (Vienna, 1959).

Girard, Georges, ed., *Correspondance entre Maria-Thérèse et Marie Antoinette* (Paris, 1933).

Grossegger, Elisabeth, ed., *Theater, Feste und Feiern zur Zeit Maria Theresias, 1742–1776: Nach den Tagebucheintragungen des Fürsten Johann Joseph Khevenhüller-Metsch, Obersthofmeister der Kaiserin* (Vienna, 1987).

Grossing, Franz Rudolph, ed., *Briefe von Joseph dem Zweyten als charakteristische Beiträge zur Lebens- und Staatsgeschichte dieses unvergesslichen Selbsther-schers*, (Leipzig, 1821).

Grünberg, Karl, ed., *Die Bauernbefreiung und die Auflösung des gutsherrlich-bäuerlichen Verhältnisses in Böhmen, Mähren und Schlesien*, Vol. 2: *Akten-stücke*, (Leipzig, 1894).

Handlemann, Heinrich, ed., "Vom Wiener Hof aus der Zeit der Kaiserin Maria Theresia und Kaiser Joseph II., aus ungedruckten Depeschen des Grafen Johann Friedrich Baschoff von Echt, königlich dänischen Gesandten (von 1750 bis 1781) am kaiserlichen Hofe," *AÖG XXXVII* (1867), 457–467.

Harasiewicz, Michaele, ed., *Annales Ecclesiae Ruthenae* (Lemberg, 1862).

Hersche, Peter, ed., *Der aufgeklärte Reformkatholizismus in Österreich: Hirten-briefe 1752–1782* (Bern, 1976).

Hinrichs, Carl, ed., *Friedrich der Grosse und Maria Theresia: Diplomatische Berichte von Otto Christoph Graf von Podewils, königlicher Preussischer Gesandter am österreichischen Hofe in Wien* (Berlin, 1937).

Kallbrunner, Joseph, ed., *Kaiserin Maria Theresias Politisches Testament* (Munich, 1952). (Originally published by Alfred Arneth. See above.)

Kalousek, Josef, ed., "Řády selské a instrukce hospodářské 1698–1780," *Archiv Český* XXIV (1908), 1–564.

"Dodavek k řádům selským a instrukcím hospodářským 1388–1779," *Archiv Český* XXIX (1913), 1–558.

Khevenhüller-Metsch, Rudolf, and Schlitter, Hanns, eds., *Aus der Zeit Maria Theresias: Tagebuch des Fürsten Johann Josef Khevenhüller-Metsch, Kaiser-lichen Obersthofmeisters*, 8 Vols., (Vienna and Leipzig, 1907–1972).

Koschatzky, Walter, and Krasa, Selma, eds., *Herzog Albert von Sachsen-Teschen, 1738–1822: Reichsfeldmarschall und Kunstmäzen* (Vienna, 1982).

Krack, Otto, ed., *Briefe einer Kaiserin: Maria Theresia an ihre Kinder und Freunde* (Berlin, 1910).

Kretschmayr, Heinrich, ed., *Die Österreichische Zentralverwaltung*: Part II: *Von der Vereinigung der österreichischen und böhmischen Hofkanzlei bis zur Einrichtung der Ministerialverfassung (1749–1848)*, Vol. 2: Joseph Kallbrunner and M. Winkler, eds., *Die Zeit des Directoriums in Publicis et Cameralibus: Aktenstücke* (Vienna, 1925); Vol. 3: Friedrich Walter, ed., *Vom Sturz des Directoriums in Publicis et Cameralibus (1760/1761) bis zum Ausgang der Regierung Maria Theresias: Aktenstücke* (Vienna, 1934). (See also Friedrich Walter, *ÖZV*, in the Secondary Sources.)

Ligne, Charles Joseph, Prince de, *Fragments de l'histoire de ma vie*, ed. by Félicien Leuridant, 2 Vols. (Paris, 1927–1928).

Lippert, Waldemar, ed., *Kaiserin Maria Theresia und Kurfürstin Maria Antonia von Sachsen: Briefwechsel, 1747–1772* (Leipzig, 1908).

Maass, Ferdinand, ed., *Der Josephinismus: Quellen zur seinen Geschichte in Österreich, 1760–1790*, 5 Vols., Fontes Rerum Austriacarum II/71–75 (Vienna, 1951–1961).

"Vorbereitung und Anfänge des Josephinismus im amtlichen Schriftwechsel des Staatskanzlers Fürsten von Kaunitz-Rittberg mit seinem bevollmächtigten Minister beim Governo generale der österreichischen Lombardei, Karl Grafen von Firmian, 1763 bis 1770," *MÖStA* I (1949), 289–444.

Maccartney, C. A., ed., *The Habsburg and Hohenzollern Dynasties in the Seventeenth and Eighteenth Centuries* (N.Y., 1970).

Marcelli, Umberto, ed., "Il carteggio Carli-Kaunitz (1765–1793)," *Archivio storico italiano* CXIII (1955), 388–407, 552–581; CXIV (1956), 118–135, 770–788.

Mártonffy, Károly, ed., *A magyar közigazgatás megújulása* (Budapest, 1940).

Mraz, Gerda and Gottfried, eds., *Maria Theresia: Ihr Leben und ihre Zeit in Bildern und Dokumenten* (Munich, 1979).

Ortenburg, Georg, ed., *Regulament und Ordnung des gesammten Kaiserlich-Königlichen Fuß-Volcks von 1749* (Osnabrück, 1969).

Payer von Thurn, Rudolf, ed., *Joseph II. als Theaterdirektor: Ungedruckte Briefe und Aktenstücke aus den Kinderjahren des Burgtheaters* (Vienna, 1920).

Pettenegg, Gaston von, ed., *Ludwig und Karl, Grafen und Herren von Zinzendorf: Ihre Selbstbiographien* (Vienna, 1879).

Pommerin, Reiner, and Schilling, Lothar, eds., "Denkschrift des Grafen Kaunitz zur mächtepolitischen Konstellation nach dem Aachener Frieden von 1748," in Johannes Kunisch, ed., *Expansion und Gleichgewicht: Studien zur europäischen Mächtepolitik des ancien régime* (Berlin, 1986), pp. 165–239.

Ranke, Leopold von, ed., "Maria Theresia, ihr Staat und ihr Hof im Jahre 1755: Aus den Papieren des Großkanzlers Fürst," in *Zur Geschichte von Oesterreich und Preußen zwischen den Friedensschlüssen zu Aachen und Hubertusburg*, Vol. XXX of *Sämtliche Werke* (Leipzig, 1875), pp. 1–60.

Robbins Landon, H. C., ed., *The Collected Correspondence and London Notebooks of Joseph Haydn* (London, 1959).

Schlitter, Hanns, ed., *Correspondance secrète entre le Comte A. W. Kaunitz-*

Rietberg, Ambassadeur impérial à Paris, et le Baron Ignaz de Koch, Secrétaire de l'Impératrice Marie-Thérèse, 1750–1752 (Paris, 1899).

Kaunitz, Philipp Cobenzl und Spielmann: Ihr Briefwechsel 1779–1792 (Vienna, 1899).

Tafferner, Anton, ed., *Quellenbuch zur Donauschwäbischen Geschichte* (Munich, 1974).

Wagner, Hans, ed., *Wien von Maria Theresia bis zur Franzosenzeit: Aus den Tagebüchern des Grafen Karl Zinzendorf* (Vienna, 1972).

Walter, Friedrich, ed., *Maria Theresia: Briefe und Aktenstücke in Auswahl* (Darmstadt, 1968).

Wertheimer, Eduard, ed., "Zwei Schilderungen des Wiener Hofes im XVIII. Jahrhundert", *AÖG* LXII (1881), 201–237.

Wraxall, N. William, *Memoirs of the Courts of Berlin, Dresden, Warsaw and Vienna in the Years 1777, 1778 and 1779*, 2 Vols. (London, 1800).

Zweybrück, Franz, ed., "Briefe der Kaiserin Maria Theresia und Josephs II. und Berichte des Oberst-Hofmeisters Grafen A. Salm," *AÖG* LXXVI (1890), 109–126.

SELECT SECONDARY SOURCES

This select bibliography is largely confined to works with a strong focus on Kaunitz. Important individual articles from collected works cited as collections are also not separately listed. A fuller list of literature consulted may be found in the footnotes.

Allgemeine Deutsche Biographie, 56 Vols. (Leipzig, 1875–1912).

Aretin, Karl Otmar Freiherr von, "Fürst Kaunitz und die österreichisch-ostindische Handelskompagnie von 1775: Ein Beitrag zur Geschichte des österreichischen Staatsbewußtseins unter Kaiser Joseph II.," *VSWG* XLVI (1959), 361–377.

Heiliges Römisches Reich, 1776–1806: Reichsverfassung und Staatssouveränität, 2 Vols. (Wiesbaden, 1967).

Arneth, Alfred Ritter von, "Biographie des Fürsten Kaunitz: Ein Fragment," *AÖG* LXXXVIII (1900), 1–201.

Geschichte Maria Theresias, 10 Vols. (Vienna, 1863–1879).

Balázs, Éva H., *Bécs és Pest-Buda a régi századvégen, 1765–1800* (Budapest, 1987).

Kaunitz és Magyarország (Doktori tézises összefoglaló) (Budapest, 1990).

Bangert, Dieter Ernst, *Die russisch-österreichische militärische Zusammenarbeit im Siebenjährigen Kriege in den Jahren 1758–1759* (Boppart am Rhein, 1971).

Beales, Derek, *Joseph II*, Vol. I: *In the Shadow of Maria Theresa, 1741–1780* (Cambridge, 1987).

Beales, Derek, and Blanning, T. C. W., "Prince Kaunitz and 'The Primacy of Domestic Policy'," *International History Review* II (1980), 619–624.

Beer, Adolf, *Die Erste Theilung Polens*, 3 Vols. (Vienna, 1873–1880), Vols. I and II.

"Die Staatsschulden und die Ordnung des Staatshaushaltes unter Maria Theresia," *AÖG* LXXXII (1895), 1–136.

"Die Zollpolitik und die Schaffung eines einheitlichen Zollgebietes unter Maria Theresia," *MIÖG* XIV (1893), 237–385.

Bernard, Paul P., *From the Enlightenment to the Police State: The Public Life of Johann Anton Pergen* (Urbana, Ill., and Chicago, Ill., 1991).

"Kaunitz and Austria's Secret Fund," *East European Quarterly* XVI (1982), 129–136.

"Kaunitz and the Cost of Diplomacy," *East European Quarterly* XVII (1983), 1–14.

Boom, Ghislaine de, *Les Ministres Plénipotentiaires dans les Pays-Bas autrichiens, principalement Cobenzl* (Brussels, 1932.)

Braubach, Max, *Versailles und Wien von Ludwig XIV. bis Kaunitz: Die Vorstadien der diplomatischen Revolution im 18. Jahrhundert* (Bonn, 1952).

Burg, Hermann, *Der Bildhauer Franz Anton Zauner und seine Zeit* (Vienna, 1915).

Capra, Carlo, "Il settecento," in Domenico Sella and Carla Capra, *Il Ducato di Milano dal 1535 al 1796*, Vol. XI of Giuseppe Galasso, ed., *Storia d'Italia* (Turin, 1984), also issued as a separate volume: *La Lombardia Austriaca nell'età delle riforme (1706–1796)* (Turin, 1987).

"Luigi Giusti e il dipartimento d'Italia a Vienna, 1757–1766," *Società e storia* No. 15 (1982), 61–85.

"Riforme finanziarie e mutamento istituzionale nello Stato di Milano gli anni sessanta del secolo XVIII," *Rivista Storico Italiana* XCI (1979), 313–368.

Dickson, P. G. M., *Finance and Government under Maria Theresia, 1740–1780*, 2 Vols. (Oxford, 1987).

Dove, Alfred, "Kaunitz," in *Ausgewählte Schriften, vornehmlich historischen Inhalts* (Leipzig, 1898), pp. 94–110.

Drabek, Anna M., Plaschka, Richard G., and Wandruszka, Adam, eds., *Ungarn und Österreich unter Maria Theresia und Joseph II.* (Vienna, 1982).

Eichwalder, Reinhard, "Georg Adam Fürst Starhemberg (1724–1807): Diplomat, Staatsmann und Grundherr" (unpublished Ph.D. Dissertation, University of Vienna, 1969).

Ellemunter, Anton, *Antonio Eugenio Visconti und die Anfänge des Josephinismus: Eine Untersuchung über das theresianische Staatskirchentum unter besonderer Berücksichtigung der Nuntiarberichte, 1767–1774* (Graz and Cologne, 1963).

Ember, Győző, and Heckenast, Gustáv, eds., *Magyarorszság története, 1686–1790*, 2 Vols., Part 4 of Zsigmond Pál Pach, ed., *Magyarország története tíz kötetben* (Budapest, 1989).

Evans, R. J. W., *The Making of the Habsburg Monarchy, 1550–1700* (Oxford, 1979).

Fejtö, François, *Un Habsburg révolutionnaire, Joseph II: Portrait d'un despote éclairé* (Paris, 1953). German translation by Ursula Rohden as: *Joseph II.: Porträt eines aufgeklärten Despoten* (Munich, 1987); references are to German edition of 1987.

Fichtenau, Heinrich, and Zöllner, Erich, eds., *Beiträge zur neueren Geschichte Österreichs* (Vienna, Cologne and Graz, 1974).

Glassl, Horst, *Das österreichische Einrichtungswerk in Galizien (1772–1790)* (Wiesbaden, 1975).

Göttlicher, Silvia [Sister Maria Elisabeth, o.s.u.], "Die Stellung des Staatskanzlers Kaunitz-Rietberg zur französischen Revolution, ersichtlich aus seinen Briefen, Erlässen, Memoiren und Reflexionen" (unpublished Ph.D. dissertation, University of Vienna, 1963).

Gross, Hans, "Die Ständische Kredit-Deputation und der Plan eines erbländischen Nationalkredits (Ein Beitrag zur Finanzpolitik unter Maria Theresia)" (unpublished Ph.D. dissertation, University of Vienna, 1935).

Grünberg, Karl, *Die Bauernbefreiung und die Auflösung des gutsherrlich-bäuerlichen Verhältnisses in Böhmen, Mähren und Schlesien*, 2 Vols. (Leipzig, 1894).

Guglia, Eugen, *Maria Theresia, Ihr Leben und Ihre Regierung*, 2 Vols. (Munich, 1917).

Haugwitz, Eberhard, *Die Geschichte der Familie von Haugwitz*, 2 Vols. (Leipzig, 1910).

Helfert, Joseph Alexander Freiherr von, *Die Gründung der österreichischen Volksschule durch Maria Theresia* (Prague, 1860).

Hersche, Peter, *Der Spätjansenismus in Österreich* (Vienna, 1977).

Hock, Carl Freiherr von, and Bidermann, Hermann Ignaz, *Der österreichische Staatsrath (1760–1848)* (Vienna, 1879).

Hormayr, Joseph Freiherr von, *Österreichischer Plutarch* (Vienna, 1807), XII, 231–283. (A selection reprinted under the title *Lebensbilder großer Österreicher* [Vienna, 1947].)

Horváth, Mihály , *Magyarország történelme*, Vol. 5: *Károly trónraléptétöl II. József haláláig* (Pest, 1863).

Jäger, Gertraud, "Die Persönlichkeit des Staatskanzlers Kaunitz in der Historiographie" (unpublished dissertation, University of Vienna, 1982).

Karniel, Joseph, *Die Toleranzpolitik Kaiser Josephs II.* (Stuttgart, 1986).

"Fürst Kaunitz und die Juden," *Jahrbuch des Instituts für deutsche Geschichte* (Universität Tel-Aviv) XII (1983), 15–27.

Klingenstein, Grete, *Der Aufstieg des Hauses Kaunitz: Studien zur Herkunft und Bildung des Staatskanzlers Wenzel Anton* (Göttingen, 1975).

"Institutionelle Aspekte der österreichischen Aussenpolitik im 18. Jahrhundert," in Erich Zöllner, ed., *Diplomatie und Aussenpolitik Österreichs: Elf Beiträge zu ihrer Geschichte* (Vienna, 1977).

"Kaunitz kontra Bartenstein: Zur Geschichte der Staatskanzlei in den Jahren 1749–1753," in Heinrich Fichtenau and Erich Zöllner, eds., *Beiträge zur neueren Geschichte Österreichs* (Vienna, Cologne and Graz, 1974), pp. 243–263.

"Revisions of Enlightened Absolutism: 'The Austrian Monarchy is Like No Other'," *Historical Journal* XXXIII (1990), 155–167.

Staatsverwaltung und kirchliche Autorität im 18. Jahrhundert: Das Problem der Zensur in der theresianischen Reform (Vienna, 1970).

Klueting, Harm, *Die Lehre von der Macht der Staaten: Das außenpolitische Machtproblem in der "politischen Wissenschaft" und in der praktischen Politik im 18. Jahrhundert* (Berlin, 1986).

Kosáry, Domokos, *Művelődés a XVIII. századi Magyarországon* (Budapest, 1980; 2nd ed., 1983). Abridged English translation: *Culture and Society in Eighteenth-century Hungary* (Budapest, 1987).

Koschatzky, Walter, ed., *Maria Theresia und Ihre Zeit: Eine Darstellung der Epoche von 1740–1780 aus Anlaß der 200. Wiederkehr des Todestages der Kaiserin* (Salzburg and Vienna, 1979).

Kovács, Elisabeth, ed., *Ultramontanismus und Staatskirchentum im theresianisch-josephinischen Staat* (Vienna, 1975).

Katholische Aufklärung und Josephinismus (Vienna, 1979).

Kretschmayr, Heinrich, "Kaunitz," in Peter Richard Rohden, ed., *Menschen die Geschichte Machten: Viertausend Jahre Weltgeschichte in Zeit- und Lebensbildern*, 2nd ed. (Vienna, 1933), II, 251–256.

Kroupa, Jiří, "Václav Antonín Kaunitz-Rietberg a výtvarná umění (Kulturní politika nebo umělecký mecenát?)," *Studia Comeniana et Historica* XVIII (1988), 71–79.

Küntzel, Georg, *Fürst Kaunitz-Rittberg als Staatsmann* (Frankfurt a/M, 1923).

Liebel-Weckowicz, Helen P., "Free Trade and Protectionism under Maria Theresa and Joseph II," *Canadian Journal of History* XIV (1979), 355–373.

Liebel-Weckowicz, Helen, and Szabo, Franz A. J., "Modernization Forces in Maria Theresa's Peasant Policies, 1740–1780," *Social History/Histoire sociale* XV (1982), 301–331.

Linhart, Jan K., *Kounicové* (Brno, 1982).

Maasburg, Friedrich von, *Gutächtliche Aeußerung des österreichischen Staatsrathes über den von der Compilationscommission im Entwurfe vorgelegten Codex Theresianus civilis* (Vienna, 1881).

Maass, Ferdinand, *Der Frühjosephinismus* (Vienna, Munich, 1969).

"Die Stellungnahme des Fürsten Kaunitz zur staatlichen Festsetzung der Altersgrenze für die Ablegung der Ordensgelübde in Österreich im Jahre 1770/71," *MIÖG* LVIII (1950), 656–667.

McGill, William J., "The Political Education of Wenzel Anton von Kaunitz-Rietberg" (unpublished Ph.D. dissertation, Harvard University, 1961).

"The Roots of Policy: Kaunitz in Italy and the Netherlands, 1742–1746", *Central European History* I (1968), 131–149.

"The Roots of Policy: Kaunitz in Vienna and Versailles, 1749–1753," *Journal of Modern History* XLIII (1971), 228–244.

"Wenzel Anton von Kaunitz-Rittberg and the Conference of Aix-la-Chapelle, 1748", *Duquesne Review* XIV (1969), 154–167.

Marczali, Henrik, *Magyarország története III. Károlytól a Bécsi Congressusig (1711–1815)*, Vol. VIII of Sándor Szilágyi, ed., *A Magyar nemzet története* (Budapest, 1898).

Melton, James Van Horn, *Absolutism and the Eighteenth-century Origins of Compulsory Schooling in Prussia and Austria* (Cambridge, 1988).

Mischler, Ernst, and Ulbrich, Josef, eds., *Österreichisches Staatswörterbuch: Handbuch des gesamten österreichischen öffentlichen Rechtes*, 4 Vols. (Vienna, 1905–1909).

Mitrofanov, Paul von, *Joseph II: Seine politische und kulturelle Tätigkeit*, 2 Vols., trans from Russian by V. von Demelic (Vienna, 1910).

Mraz, Gerda, and Schlag, Gerald, eds., *Maria Theresia als Königin von Ungarn* (Catalog of the exhibition in Schloss Halbturn, Burgenland, Austria, 15 May to 26 October 1980) (Eisenstadt, 1980).

Neue Deutsche Biographie, 16 Vols. to date (Berlin, 1953–1990).

Novotny, Alexander, "Staatskanzler Fürst Kaunitz (1711–1794)," in Hugo Hantsch, ed., *Gestalter der Geschicke Österreichs* (Innsbruck, Vienna and Munich, 1962).

Staatskanzler Kaunitz als geistige Persönlichkeit: Ein österreichisches Kulturbild aus der Zeit der Aufklärung und des Josephinismus (Vienna, 1947).

Osterloh, Karl-Heinz, *Joseph von Sonnenfels und die österreichische Reformbewegung im Zeitalter des aufgeklärten Absolutismus* (Lübeck and Hamburg, 1970).

Pernes, Jiří, and Holán, Ivo, *Slavkov u Brna: Mesto a okolí* (Brno, 1987).

Plaschka, Richard Georg, Klingenstein, Grete, *et al.*, eds., *Österreich im Europa der Aufklärung: Kontinuität und Zäsur in Europe zur Zeit Maria Theresias und Josephs II.*, 2 Vols. (Vienna, 1985).

Pollack-Parnau, Franz von, *Eine österreichische-ostindische Handelscompagnie, 1775–1785: Ein Beitrag zur österreichischen Wirtschaftsgeschichte unter Maria Theresia und Joseph II.*, supplement to *VSWG*, No. 12 (Stuttgart, 1927).

Posaner, Leon, "Die Rolle des Staatskanzlers Fürsten Kaunitz in den Reformen der inneren Verwaltung Oesterreichs" (unpublished Ph.D. dissertation, University of Vienna, 1923).

Prokeš, Jaroslav, "Boj o Haugvicovo 'Directorium in publicis et cameralibus' r. 1761," *Věstník královské české společnosti nauk* (1926), Essay No. iv.

Rozdolski [Rosdolsky], Roman, *Stosunki poddańcze w dawnej Galicji*, 2 Vols. (Warsaw, 1962). German translation by Hilde Nürenberger-Mareiner as *Untertan und Staat in Galizien: Die Reformen unter Maria Theresia und Joseph II.*, ed., Ralph Melville (Mainz, 1992).

Scharrer, Sonja, "Il dipartimento d'Italia a Vienna, persone e istituzioni" (unpublished Ph.D. dissertation, Università Cattolica of Milan, 1991).

Schasching, Johann, *Staatsbildung und Finanzentwicklung: Ein Beitrag zur Geschichte des österreichischen Staatskredits in der 2. Hälfte des 18. Jahrhunderts* (Innsbruck, 1954).

Schiera, Pierangelo, ed., *La dinamica statale austriaca nel XVIII e XIX secolo: Strutture e tendenze di storia constituzionale primo e dopo Maria Teresa* (Bologna, 1981).

Schlichtegroll, Friedrich, *Nekrolog auf das Jahr 1794* (5th annual edition), 2 Vols. (Gotha, 1796).

Schünemann, Konrad, "Die Wirtschaftspolitik Josephs II. in der Zeit seiner Mitregentschaft," *MIÖG* XLVII (1933); 13–56.

Österreichs Bevölkerungspolitik unter Maria Theresia (Berlin, n.d.).

Scott, H. M., ed., *Enlightened Absolutism: Reform and Reformers in Later Eighteenth-Century Europe* (London, 1991).

Simányi, Tibor, *Kaunitz: Staatskanzler Maria Theresias* (Vienna & Munich, 1984).

Srbik, Heinrich von, "Ein Charakterbild des Staatskanzlers Kaunitz aus dem Nicolaischen Kreis," *ΕΠΙΤΥΜΒΙΟΝ: H. Swoboda dargebracht* (Reichenberg, 1927).

Szabó, Dezső, *A magyarországi úrbérrendezés története Mária Terézia korában* (Budapest, 1933).

A megyék ellenállása Mária Terézia úrbéri redeletevel szemben (Budapest, 1934).

Szabo, Franz A. J., "Haugwitz, Kaunitz, and the Structure of Government under Maria Theresia, 1745 to 1761," in The Canadian Historical Association, ed., *Historical Papers/Communications Historiques: Saskatoon 1979* (Ottawa, 1980), pp. 111–130.

"Intorno alle origini del giuseppinismo: motivi economico-sociali e aspetti ideologici," *Società e storia* No. 4 (1979), 155–174.

"Prince Kaunitz and the Balance of Power", *International History Review* I (1979), 399–408.

"Prince Kaunitz and the Primacy of Domestic Policy: A Response," *International History Review* II (1980), 625–635.

"Unwanted Navy: Habsburg Naval Armaments under Maria Theresia", *Austrian History Yearbook* XVII–XVIII (1981–1982), 29–53.

Szekfű, Gyula, *Magyar történet a tizennyolcadik század*, Vol. VI of Bálint Hóman and Gyula Szekfű, *Magyar történet* (Budapest, n.d. [1935]).

Walter, Friedrich, "Der letzte grosse Versuch einer Verwaltungsreform unter Maria Theresia (1764/65)," *MIÖG* XLVII (1933), 427–469.

Die Geschichte der österreichischen Zentralverwaltung in der Zeit Maria Theresias (1740–1780), Vol. 1, Section i of Heinrich Kretschmayr, ed., *Die Österreichische Zentralverwaltung*, Part II: *Von der Vereinigung der österreichischen und böhmischen Hofkanzlei bis zur Einrichtung der Ministerialverfassung (1749–1848)* (Vienna, 1938).

Die Paladine der Kaiserin: Ein Maria Theresien-Buch (Vienna, 1959).

"Die Religiöse Stellung Maria Theresias," *Theologisch-Praktische Quartalschrift* CV (1957), 34–47.

"Die Wiener Stadtbank und das Bankprojekt des Grafen Kaunitz aus dem Jahre 1761," *Zeitschrift für Nationalökonomie* VIII (1937), 444–460.

"Josef II.," in Carl Petersen, Paul Hermann Ruth and Hans Schwalm, eds., *Handwörterbuch des Grenz- und Auslanddeutschtums*, 3 Vols. (Breslau, 1933–1938), III, 229–234.

"Kaunitz' Eintritt in die innere Politik. Ein Beitrag zur Geschichte der österreichischen Innenpolitik in den Jahren 1760/61," *MIÖG* XLVI (1932), 37–79.

Wandruszka, Adam, *Leopold II*, 2 Vols. (Vienna and Munich, 1963–1965).

Österreich und Italien im 18. Jahrhundert (Vienna, 1963).

Wangermann, Ernst, *Aufklärung und staatsbürgerliche Erziehung: Gottfried von Swieten als Reformator des österreichischen Unterrichtswesen, 1781–1791* (Vienna, 1978).

"Maria Theresa: A Reforming Monarchy," in A. G. Dickens, ed., *The Courts of Europe: Politics, Patronage and Royalty, 1400–1800* (London, 1977), pp. 283–303.

"Reform Catholicism and Political Radicalism in the Austrian Enlightenment," in Roy Porter and Mikolas Teich, eds., *The Enlightenment in National Context* (Cambridge, 1981), pp. 127–140.

The Austrian Achievement, 1700–1800 (London, 1973).

Winter, Eduard, *Der Josephinismus*, 1st ed. (Brno and Vienna, 1943), 2nd ed. (Berlin, 1962).

Wolfsgruber, Cölestin, *Christoph Anton Kardinal Migazzi: Fürstbischof von Wien* (Saulgau, 1890).

Wolny, Reinhold Joseph, *Die josephinische Toleranz unter besonderer Berücksichtigung ihres geistlichen Wegbereiters Johann Leopold Hay* (Munich, 1973).

Wurzbach, Constant von, *Biographisches Lexikon des Kaiserthums Oesterreich*, 60 Vols., (Vienna, 1856–1891).

Zöllner, Erich, and Möcker, Hermann, eds., *Österreich im Zeitalter des aufgeklärten Absolutismus* (Vienna, 1983).

Index

Lightning Source UK Ltd.
Milton Keynes UK
UKOW04f1803161215

264869UK00001B/39/P